The Text Mining Handbook

Text mining is a new and exciting area of computer science research that tries to solve the crisis of information overload by combining techniques from data mining, machine learning, natural language processing, information retrieval, and knowledge management. Similarly, link detection – a rapidly evolving approach to the analysis of text that shares and builds on many of the key elements of text mining – also provides new tools for people to better leverage their burgeoning textual data resources. Link detection relies on a process of building up networks of interconnected objects through various relationships in order to discover patterns and trends. The main tasks of link detection are to extract, discover, and link together sparse evidence from vast amounts of data sources, to represent and evaluate the significance of the related evidence, and to learn patterns to guide the extraction, discovery, and linkage of entities.

The Text Mining Handbook presents a comprehensive discussion of the state of the art in text mining and link detection. In addition to providing an in-depth examination of core text mining and link detection algorithms and operations, the work examines advanced preprocessing techniques, knowledge representation considerations, and visualization approaches. Finally, the book explores current real-world, mission-critical applications of text mining and link detection in such varied fields as corporate finance business intelligence, genomics research, and counterterrorism activities.

Ronen Feldman is an Associate Professor and the head of the Information Systems department at the Business School of the Hebrew University in Jerusalem. Professor Feldman received his B.Sc. in Math, Physics and Computer Science (specializing in Machine Learning) from the Hebrew University and his Ph.D. in Computer Science from Cornell University in NY. He was an Adjunct Professor at NYU Stern Business School. Professor Feldman is the Chief Scientist of Digital Trowel, an Israeli company specializing in development of text mining tools and applications. A pioneer in the areas of machine learning, data mining, and unstructured data management, he has authored or co-authored more than 100 published articles and conference papers in these areas.

James Sanger is a venture capitalist, applied technologist, and recognized industry expert in the areas of commercial data solutions, Internet applications, and IT security products. He is a partner at ABS Ventures, an independent venture firm founded in 1982 and originally associated with technology banking leader Alex. Brown and Sons. Immediately before joining ABS Ventures, Mr. Sanger was a Managing Director in the New York offices of DB Capital Venture Partners, the global venture capital arm of Deutsche Bank. Mr. Sanger has been a board member of several thought-leading technology companies, including Inxight Software, Gomez Inc., and ClearForest, Inc.; he has also served as an official observer to the boards of AlphaBlox (acquired by IBM in 2004), Intralinks, and Imagine Software and as a member of the Technical Advisory Board of Qualys, Inc.

THE TEXT MINING HANDBOOK

Advanced Approaches in Analyzing Unstructured Data

Ronen Feldman
Hebrew University of Jerusalem

James Sanger
ABS Ventures, Waltham, Massachusetts

CAMBRIDGE
UNIVERSITY PRESS

32 Avenue of the Americas, New York NY 10013-2473, USA

Cambridge University Press is part of the University of Cambridge.

It furthers the University's mission by disseminating knowledge in the pursuit of education, learning and research at the highest international levels of excellence.

www.cambridge.org
Information on this title: www.cambridge.org/9780521836579

First published 2007
Reprinted 2008, 2009, 2013

A catalogue record for this publication is available from the British Library

Library of Congress Cataloging in Publication Data
Feldman, Ronen, 1962–
The text mining handbook : advanced approaches in analyzing unstructured data / Ronen Feldman, James Sanger.
p. cm.
Includes bibliographical references and index.
ISBN 0-521-83657-3 (hardback)
1. Data mining – Handbooks, manuals, etc. I. Sanger, James, 1965– II. Title.
QA76.9.D343F45 2006
005.74 – dc22 2005029330

ISBN 978-0-521-83657-9 Hardback

In loving memory of my father, Issac Feldman

Contents

Preface

The information age has made it easy to store large amounts of data. The proliferation of documents available on the Web, on corporate intranets, on news wires, and elsewhere is overwhelming. However, although the amount of data available to us is constantly increasing, our ability to absorb and process this information remains constant. Search engines only exacerbate the problem by making more and more documents available in a matter of a few key strokes.

Text mining is a new and exciting research area that tries to solve the information overload problem by using techniques from data mining, machine learning, natural language processing (NLP), information retrieval (IR), and knowledge management. Text mining involves the preprocessing of document collections (text categorization, information extraction, term extraction), the storage of the intermediate representations, the techniques to analyze these intermediate representations (such as distribution analysis, clustering, trend analysis, and association rules), and visualization of the results.

This book presents a general theory of text mining along with the main techniques behind it. We offer a generalized architecture for text mining and outline the algorithms and data structures typically used by text mining systems.

The book is aimed at the advanced undergraduate students, graduate students, academic researchers, and professional practitioners interested in complete coverage of the text mining field. We have included all the topics critical to people who plan to develop text mining systems or to use them. In particular, we have covered preprocessing techniques such as text categorization, text clustering, and information extraction and analysis techniques such as association rules and link analysis.

The book tries to blend together theory and practice; we have attempted to provide many real-life scenarios that show how the different techniques are used in practice. When writing the book we tried to make it as self-contained as possible and have compiled a comprehensive bibliography for each topic so that the reader can expand his or her knowledge accordingly.

BOOK OVERVIEW

The book starts with a gentle introduction to text mining that presents the basic definitions and prepares the reader for the next chapters. In the second chapter we describe the core text mining operations in detail while providing examples for each operation. The third chapter serves as an introduction to text mining preprocessing techniques. We provide a taxonomy of the operations and set the ground for Chapters IV through VII. Chapter IV offers a comprehensive description of the text categorization problem and outlines the major algorithms for performing text categorization.

Chapter V introduces another important text preprocessing task called text clustering, and we again provide a concrete definition of the problem and outline the major algorithms for performing text clustering. Chapter VI addresses what is probably the most important text preprocessing technique for text mining – namely, information extraction. We describe the general problem of information extraction and supply the relevant definitions. Several examples of the output of information extraction in several domains are also presented.

In Chapter VII, we discuss several state-of-the-art probabilistic models for information extraction, and Chapter VIII describes several preprocessing applications that either use the probabilistic models of Chapter VII or are based on hybrid approaches incorporating several models. The presentation layer of a typical text mining system is considered in Chapter IX. We focus mainly on aspects related to browsing large document collections and on issues related to query refinement. Chapter X surveys the common visualization techniques used either to visualize the document collection or the results obtained from the text mining operations. Chapter XI introduces the fascinating area of link analysis. We present link analysis as an analytical step based on the foundation of the text preprocessing techniques discussed in the previous chapters, most specifically information extraction. The chapter begins with basic definitions from graph theory and moves to common techniques for analyzing large networks of entities.

Finally, in Chapter XII, three real-world applications of text mining are considered. We begin by describing an application for articles posted in *BioWorld* magazine. This application identifies major biological entities such as genes and proteins and enables visualization of relationships between those entities. We then proceed to the GeneWays application, which is based on analysis of *PubMed* articles. The next application is based on analysis of U.S. patents and enables monitoring trends and visualizing relationships between inventors, assignees, and technology terms.

The appendix explains the DIAL language, which is a dedicated information extraction language. We outline the structure of the language and describe its exact syntax. We also offer several code examples that show how DIAL can be used to extract a variety of entities and relationships. A detailed bibliography concludes the book.

ACKNOWLEDGMENTS

This book would not have been possible without the help of many individuals. In addition to acknowledgments made throughout the book, we feel it important to take the time to offer special thanks to an important few. Among these we would like to mention especially Benjamin Rosenfeld, who devoted many hours to revising the categorization and clustering chapters. The people at ClearForest Corporation also provided help in obtaining screen shots of applications using ClearForest technologies – most notably in Chapter XII. In particular, we would like to mention the assistance we received from Rafi Vesserman, Yonatan Aumann, Jonathan Schler, Yair Liberzon, Felix Harmatz, and Yizhar Regev. Their support meant a great deal to us in the completion of this project.

Adding to this list, we would also like to thank Ian Bonner and Kathy Bentaieb of Inxight Software for the screen shots used in Chapter X. Also, we would like to extend our appreciation to Andrey Rzhetsky for his personal screen shots of the GeneWays application.

A book written on a subject such as text mining is inevitably a culmination of many years of work. As such, our gratitude is extended to both Haym Hirsh and Oren Etzioni, early collaborators in the field.

In addition, we would like to thank Lauren Cowles of Cambridge University Press for reading our drafts and patiently making numerous comments on how to improve the structure of the book and its readability. Appreciation is also owed to Jessica Farris for help in keeping two very busy coauthors on track.

Finally it brings us great pleasure to thank those dearest to us – our children Yael, Hadar, Yair, Neta and Frithjof – for leaving us undisturbed in our rooms while we were writing. We hope that, now that the book is finished, we will have more time to devote to you and to enjoy your growth. We are also greatly indebted to our dear wives Hedva and Lauren for bearing with our long hours on the computer, doing research, and writing the endless drafts. Without your help, confidence, and support we would never have completed this book. Thank you for everything. We love you!

I

Introduction to Text Mining

I.1 DEFINING TEXT MINING

Text mining can be broadly defined as a knowledge-intensive process in which a user interacts with a document collection over time by using a suite of analysis tools. In a manner analogous to data mining, text mining seeks to extract useful information from data sources through the identification and exploration of interesting patterns. In the case of text mining, however, the data sources are document collections, and interesting patterns are found not among formalized database records but in the unstructured textual data in the documents in these collections.

Certainly, text mining derives much of its inspiration and direction from seminal research on data mining. Therefore, it is not surprising to find that text mining and data mining systems evince many high-level architectural similarities. For instance, both types of systems rely on preprocessing routines, pattern-discovery algorithms, and presentation-layer elements such as visualization tools to enhance the browsing of answer sets. Further, text mining adopts many of the specific types of patterns in its core knowledge discovery operations that were first introduced and vetted in data mining research.

Because data mining assumes that data have already been stored in a structured format, much of its preprocessing focus falls on two critical tasks: Scrubbing and normalizing data and creating extensive numbers of table joins. In contrast, for text mining systems, preprocessing operations center on the identification and extraction of representative features for natural language documents. These preprocessing operations are responsible for transforming unstructured data stored in document collections into a more explicitly structured intermediate format, which is a concern that is not relevant for most data mining systems.

Moreover, because of the centrality of natural language text to its mission, text mining also draws on advances made in other computer science disciplines concerned with the handling of natural language. Perhaps most notably, text mining exploits techniques and methodologies from the areas of information retrieval, information extraction, and corpus-based computational linguistics.

I.1.1 The Document Collection and the Document

A key element of text mining is its focus on the *document collection*. At its simplest, a document collection can be any grouping of text-based documents. Practically speaking, however, most text mining solutions are aimed at discovering patterns across very large document collections. The number of documents in such collections can range from the many thousands to the tens of millions.

Document collections can be either *static*, in which case the initial complement of documents remains unchanged, or *dynamic*, which is a term applied to document collections characterized by their inclusion of new or updated documents over time. Extremely large document collections, as well as document collections with very high rates of document change, can pose performance optimization challenges for various components of a text mining system.

An illustration of a typical real-world document collection suitable as initial input for text mining is PubMed, the National Library of Medicine's online repository of citation-related information for biomedical research papers. PubMed has received significant attention from computer scientists interested in employing text mining techniques because this online service contains text-based document abstracts for more than 12 million research papers on topics in the life sciences. PubMed represents the most comprehensive online collection of biomedical research papers published in the English language, and it houses data relating to a considerable selection of publications in other languages as well. The publication dates for the main body of PubMed's collected papers stretch from 1966 to the present. The collection is dynamic and growing, for an estimated 40,000 new biomedical abstracts are added every month.

Even subsections of PubMed's data repository can represent substantial document collections for specific text mining applications. For instance, a relatively recent PubMed search for only those abstracts that contain the words *protein* or *gene* returned a result set of more than 2,800,000 documents, and more than 66 percent of these documents were published within the last decade. Indeed, a very narrowly defined search for abstracts mentioning *epidermal growth factor receptor* returned more than 10,000 documents.

The sheer size of document collections like that represented by PubMed makes manual attempts to correlate data across documents, map complex relationships, or identify trends at best extremely labor-intensive and at worst nearly impossible to achieve. Automatic methods for identifying and exploring interdocument data relationships dramatically enhance the speed and efficiency of research activities. Indeed, in some cases, automated exploration techniques like those found in text mining are not just a helpful adjunct but a baseline requirement for researchers to be able, in a practicable way, to recognize subtle patterns across large numbers of natural language documents.

Text mining systems, however, usually do not run their knowledge discovery algorithms on unprepared document collections. Considerable emphasis in text mining is devoted to what are commonly referred to as *preprocessing operations*. Typical text mining preprocessing operations are discussed in detail in Chapter III.

Text mining preprocessing operations include a variety of different types of techniques culled and adapted from information retrieval, information extraction, and computational linguistics research that transform raw, unstructured, original-format content (like that which can be downloaded from PubMed) into a carefully structured, intermediate data format. Knowledge discovery operations, in turn, are operated against this specially structured intermediate representation of the original document collection.

The Document

Another basic element in text mining is the *document*. For practical purposes, a document can be very informally defined as a unit of discrete textual data within a collection that usually, but not necessarily, correlates with some real-world document such as a business report, legal memorandum, e-mail, research paper, manuscript, article, press release, or news story. Although it is not typical, a document can be defined a little less arbitrarily within the context of a particular document collection by describing a *prototypical document* based on its representation of a similar class of entities within that collection.

One should not, however, infer from this that a given document necessarily exists only within the context of one particular collection. It is important to recognize that a document can (and generally does) exist in any number or type of collections – from the very formally organized to the very ad hoc. A document can also be a member of different document collections, or different subsets of the same document collection, and can exist in these different collections at the same time. For example, a document relating to Microsoft's antitrust litigation could exist in completely different document collections oriented toward current affairs, legal affairs, antitrust-related legal affairs, and software company news.

"Weakly Structured" and "Semistructured" Documents

Despite the somewhat misleading label that it bears as *unstructured data*, a text document may be seen, from many perspectives, as a structured object. From a linguistic perspective, even a rather innocuous document demonstrates a rich amount of semantic and syntactical structure, although this structure is implicit and to some degree hidden in its textual content. In addition, typographical elements such as punctuation marks, capitalization, numerics, and special characters – particularly when coupled with layout artifacts such as white spacing, carriage returns, underlining, asterisks, tables, columns, and so on – can often serve as a kind of "soft markup" language, providing clues to help identify important document subcomponents such as paragraphs, titles, publication dates, author names, table records, headers, and footnotes. Word sequence may also be a structurally meaningful dimension to a document. At the other end of the "unstructured" spectrum, some text documents, like those generated from a WYSIWYG HTML editor, actually possess from their inception more overt types of embedded metadata in the form of formalized markup tags.

Documents that have relatively little in the way of strong typographical, layout, or markup indicators to denote structure – like most scientific research papers, business reports, legal memoranda, and news stories – are sometimes referred to as *free-format* or *weakly structured* documents. On the other hand, documents with extensive and consistent format elements in which field-type metadata can be more easily inferred – such as some e-mail, HTML Web pages, PDF files, and word-processing files with heavy document templating or style-sheet constraints – are occasionally described as *semistructured* documents.

I.1.2 Document Features

The preprocessing operations that support text mining attempt to leverage many different elements contained in a natural language document in order to transform it from an irregular and implicitly structured representation into an explicitly structured representation. However, given the potentially large number of words, phrases, sentences, typographical elements, and layout artifacts that even a short document may have – not to mention the potentially vast number of different senses that each of these elements may have in various contexts and combinations – an essential task for most text mining systems is the identification of a simplified subset of document features that can be used to represent a particular document as a whole. We refer to such a set of features as the *representational model* of a document and say that individual documents are *represented by* the set of features that their representational models contain.

Even with attempts to develop efficient representational models, each document in a collection is usually made up of a large number – sometimes an exceedingly large number – of features. The large number of features required to represent documents in a collection affects almost every aspect of a text mining system's approach, design, and performance.

Problems relating to high *feature dimensionality* (i.e., the size and scale of possible combinations of feature values for data) are typically of much greater magnitude in text mining systems than in classic data mining systems. Structured representations of natural language documents have much larger numbers of potentially representative features – and thus higher numbers of possible combinations of feature values – than one generally finds with records in relational or hierarchical databases.

For even the most modest document collections, the number of word-level features required to represent the documents in these collections can be exceedingly large. For example, in an extremely small collection of 15,000 documents culled from Reuters news feeds, more than 25,000 nontrivial word stems could be identified.

Even when one works with more optimized feature types, tens of thousands of concept-level features may still be relevant for a single application domain. The number of attributes in a relational database that are analyzed in a data mining task is usually significantly smaller.

The high dimensionality of potentially representative features in document collections is a driving factor in the development of text mining preprocessing operations aimed at creating more streamlined representational models. This high dimensionality also indirectly contributes to other conditions that separate text mining systems from data mining systems such as greater levels of pattern overabundance and more acute requirements for postquery refinement techniques.

Another characteristic of natural language documents is what might be described as *feature sparsity*. Only a small percentage of all possible features for a document collection as a whole appears in any single document, and thus when a document is represented as a binary vector of features, nearly all values of the vector are zero.

The tuple dimension is also sparse. That is, some features often appear in only a few documents, which means that the support of many patterns is quite low.

Commonly Used Document Features: Characters, Words, Terms, and Concepts

Because text mining algorithms operate on the feature-based representations of documents and not the underlying documents themselves, there is often a trade-off between two important goals. The first goal is to achieve the correct calibration of the volume and semantic level of features to portray the meaning of a document accurately, which tends to incline text mining preprocessing operations toward selecting or extracting relatively more features to represent documents. The second goal is to identify features in a way that is most computationally efficient and practical for pattern discovery, which is a process that emphasizes the streamlining of representative feature sets; such streamlining is sometimes supported by the validation, normalization, or cross-referencing of features against controlled vocabularies or external knowledge sources such as dictionaries, thesauri, ontologies, or knowledge bases to assist in generating smaller representative sets of more semantically rich features.

Although many potential features can be employed to represent documents,[1] the following four types are most commonly used:

- ***Characters.*** The individual component-level letters, numerals, special characters and spaces are the building blocks of higher-level semantic features such as words, terms, and concepts. A character-level representation can include the full set of all characters for a document or some filtered subset. Character-based representations without positional information (i.e., bag-of-characters approaches) are often of very limited utility in text mining applications. Character-based representations that include some level of positional information (e.g., bigrams or trigrams) are somewhat more useful and common. In general, however, character-based representations can often be unwieldy for some types of text processing techniques because the feature space for a document is fairly unoptimized. On the other hand, this feature space can in many ways be viewed as the most complete of any representation of a real-world text document.
- ***Words.*** Specific words selected directly from a "native" document are at what might be described as the basic level of semantic richness. For this reason, word-level features are sometimes referred to as existing in the *native feature space* of a document. In general, a single word-level feature should equate with, or have the value of, no more than one linguistic token. Phrases, multiword expressions, or even multiword hyphenates would not constitute single word-level features. It is possible for a word-level representation of a document to include a feature for each word within that document – that is the "full text," where a document is represented by a complete and unabridged set of its word-level features. This can

[1] Beyond the three feature types discussed and defined here – namely, words, terms, and concepts – other features that have been used for representing documents include linguistic phrases, nonconsecutive phrases, keyphrases, character bigrams, character trigrams, frames, and parse trees.

lead to some word-level representations of document collections having tens or even hundreds of thousands of unique words in its feature space. However, most word-level document representations exhibit at least some minimal optimization and therefore consist of subsets of representative features filtered for items such as stop words, symbolic characters, and meaningless numerics.

- ***Terms.*** *Terms* are single words and multiword phrases selected directly from the corpus of a native document by means of *term-extraction* methodologies. Term-level features, in the sense of this definition, can *only* be made up of specific words and expressions found within the native document for which they are meant to be generally representative. Hence, a term-based representation of a document is necessarily composed of a subset of the terms in that document. For example, if a document contained the sentence

  > President Abraham Lincoln experienced a career that took him from log cabin to White House,

  a list of terms to represent the document could include single word forms such as "Lincoln," "took," "career," and "cabin" as well as multiword forms like "President Abraham Lincoln," "log cabin," and "White House."

  Several of term-extraction methodologies can convert the raw text of a native document into a series of *normalized terms* – that is, sequences of one or more tokenized and lemmatized word forms associated with part-of-speech tags. Sometimes an external lexicon is also used to provide a controlled vocabulary for term normalization. Term-extraction methodologies employ various approaches for generating and filtering an abbreviated list of most meaningful *candidate terms* from among a set of normalized terms for the representation of a document. This culling process results in a smaller but relatively more semantically rich document representation than that found in word-level document representations.
- ***Concepts.***[2] *Concepts* are features generated for a document by means of manual, statistical, rule-based, or hybrid *categorization* methodologies. Concept-level features can be manually generated for documents but are now more commonly extracted from documents using complex preprocessing routines that identify single words, multiword expressions, whole clauses, or even larger syntactical units that are then related to specific *concept identifiers*. For instance, a document collection that includes reviews of sports cars may not actually include the specific word "automotive" or the specific phrase "test drives," but the concepts "automotive" and "test drives" might nevertheless be found among the set of concepts used to to identify and represent the collection.

  Many categorization methodologies involve a degree of cross-referencing against an external knowledge source; for some statistical methods, this source might simply be an annotated collection of training documents. For manual and rule-based categorization methods, the cross-referencing and validation of prospective concept-level features typically involve interaction with a "gold standard" such as a preexisting domain ontology, lexicon, or formal concept

[2] Although some computer scientists make distinctions between keywords and concepts (e.g., Blake and Pratt 2001), this book recognizes the two as relatively interchangeable labels for the same feature type and will generally refer to either under the label *concept*.

hierarchy – or even just the mind of a human domain expert. Unlike word- and term-level features, concept-level features can consist of words not specifically found in the native document.

Of the four types of features described here, terms and concepts reflect the features with the most condensed and expressive levels of semantic value, and there are many advantages to their use in representing documents for text mining purposes. With regard to the overall size of their feature sets, term- and concept-based representations exhibit roughly the same efficiency but are generally much more efficient than character- or word-based document models. Term-level representations can sometimes be more easily and automatically generated from the original source text (through various term-extraction techniques) than concept-level representations, which as a practical matter have often entailed some level of human interaction.

Concept-level representations, however, are much better than any other feature-set representation at handling synonymy and polysemy and are clearly best at relating a given feature to its various hyponyms and hypernyms. Concept-based representations can be processed to support very sophisticated concept hierarchies, and arguably provide the best representations for leveraging the domain knowledge afforded by ontologies and knowledge bases.

Still, concept-level representations do have a few potential drawbacks. Possible disadvantages of using concept-level features to represent documents include (a) the relative complexity of applying the heuristics, during preprocessing operations, required to extract and validate concept-type features and (b) the domain-dependence of many concepts.[3]

Concept-level document representations generated by categorization are often stored in vector formats. For instance, both CDM-based methodologies and Los Alamos II–type concept extraction approaches result in individual documents being stored as vectors.

Hybrid approaches to the generation of feature-based document representations can exist. By way of example, a particular text mining system's preprocessing operations could first extract terms using term extraction techniques and then match or normalize these terms, or do both, by winnowing them against a list of meaningful entities and topics (i.e., concepts) extracted through categorization. Such hybrid approaches, however, need careful planning, testing, and optimization to avoid having dramatic – and extremely resource-intensive – growth in the feature dimensionality of individual document representations without proportionately increased levels of system effectiveness.

For the most part, this book concentrates on text mining solutions that rely on documents represented by concept-level features, referring to other feature types where necessary to highlight idiosyncratic characteristics or techniques. Nevertheless, many of the approaches described in this chapter for identifying and browsing patterns within document collections based on concept-level representations can also

[3] It should at least be mentioned that there are some more distinct disadvantages to using manually generated concept-level representations. For instance, manually generated concepts are fixed, labor-intensive to assign, and so on. See Blake and Pratt (2001).

be applied – perhaps with varying results – to document collections represented by other feature models.

Domains and Background Knowledge

In text mining systems, concepts belong not only to the descriptive attributes of a particular document but generally also to *domains*. With respect to text mining, a domain has come to be loosely defined as a specialized area of interest for which dedicated *ontologies, lexicons*, and *taxonomies* of information may be developed.

Domains can include very broad areas of subject matter (e.g., *biology*) or more narrowly defined specialisms (e.g., *genomics or proteomics*). Some other noteworthy domains for text mining applications include financial services (with significant subdomains like corporate finance, securities trading, and commodities.), world affairs, international law, counterterrorism studies, patent research, and materials science. Text mining systems with some element of domain-specificity in their orientation – that is, most text mining systems designed for a practical purpose – can leverage information from formal external knowledge sources for these domains to greatly enhance elements of their preprocessing, knowledge discovery, and presentation-layer operations.

Domain knowledge, perhaps more frequently referred to in the literature as *background knowledge*, can be used in text mining preprocessing operations to enhance concept extraction and validation activities. Access to background knowledge – although not strictly necessary for the creation of concept hierarchies within the context of a single document or document collection – can play an important role in the development of more meaningful, consistent, and normalized concept hierarchies.

Text mining makes use of background knowledge to a greater extent than, and in different ways from, data mining. For advanced text mining applications that can take advantage of background knowledge, features are not just elements in a flat set, as is most often the case in structured data applications. By relating features by way of lexicons and ontologies, advanced text mining systems can create fuller representations of document collections in preprocessing operations and support enhanced query and refinement functionalities.

Indeed, background knowledge can be used to inform many different elements of a text mining system. In preprocessing operations, background knowledge is an important adjunct to classification and concept-extraction methodologies. Background knowledge can also be leveraged to enhance core mining algorithms and browsing operations. In addition, domain-oriented information serves as one of the main bases for search refinement techniques.

In addition, background knowledge may be utilized by other components of a text mining system. For instance, background knowledge may be used to construct meaningful constraints in knowledge discovery operations. Likewise, background knowledge may also be used to formulate constraints that allow users greater flexibility when browsing large result sets.

I.1.3 The Search for Patterns and Trends

Although text mining preprocessing operations play the critical role of transforming unstructured content of a raw document collection into a more tractable concept-level data representation, the core functionality of a text mining system resides in the analysis of *concept co-occurrence* patterns across documents in a collection. Indeed, text mining systems rely on algorithmic and heuristic approaches to consider *distributions, frequent sets*, and various *associations* of concepts at an *interdocument* level in an effort to enable a user to discover the nature and relationships of concepts as reflected in the collection as a whole.

For example, in a collection of news articles, a large number of articles on politician X and "scandal" may indicate a negative image of the character of X and alert his or her handlers to the need for a new public relations campaign. Or, a growing number of articles on company Y and product Z may indicate a shift of focus in company Y's interests – a shift that should be noted by its competitors. In another example, a potential relationship might be inferred between two proteins P_1 and P_2 by the pattern of (a) several articles mentioning the protein P_1 in relation to the enzyme E_1, (b) a few articles describing functional similarities between enzymes E_1 and E_2 without referring to any protein names, and (c) several articles linking enzyme E_2 to protein P_2. In all three of these examples, the information is not provided by any single document but rather from the totality of the collection. Text mining's methods of pattern analysis seek to discover co-occurrence relationships between concepts as reflected by the totality of the corpus at hand.

Text mining methods – often based on large-scale, brute-force search directed at large, high-dimensionality feature sets – generally produce very large numbers of patterns. This results in an overabundance problem with respect to identified patterns that is usually much more severe than that encountered in data mining applications aimed at structured data sources.

A main operational task for text mining systems is to enable a user to limit pattern overabundance by providing refinement capabilities that key on various specifiable measures of "interestingness" for search results. Such refinement capabilities prevent system users from getting overwhelmed by too many uninteresting results.

The problem of pattern overabundance can exist in all knowledge discovery activities. It is simply heightened when interacting with large collections of text documents, and, therefore, text mining operations must necessarily be conceived to provide not only relevant but also manageable result sets to a user.

Text mining also builds on various data mining approaches first specified in Lent, Agrawal, and Srikant (1997) to identify trends in data. In text mining, *trend analysis* relies on date-and-time stamping of documents within a collection so that comparisons can be made between a subset of documents relating to one period and a subset of documents relating to another.

Trend analysis across document subsets attempts to answer certain types of questions. For instance, in relation to a collection of news stories, Montes-y-Gomez, Gelbukh, and Lopez-Lopez (2001b) suggests that trend analysis concerns itself with questions such as the following:

- *What is the general trend of the news topics between two periods (as represented by two different document subsets)?*
- *Are the news topics nearly the same or are they widely divergent across the two periods?*
- *Can emerging and disappearing topics be identified?*
- *Did any topics maintain the same level of occurrence during the two periods?*

In these illustrative questions, individual "news topics" can be seen as specific concepts in the document collection. Different types of trend analytics attempt to compare the frequencies of such concepts (i.e., number of occurrences) in the documents that make up the two periods' respective document subcollections. Additional types of analysis, also derived from data mining, that can be used to support trend analysis are *ephemeral association discovery* and *deviation detection*. Some specific methods of trend analysis are described in Section II.1.5.

I.1.4 The Importance of the Presentation Layer

Perhaps the key presentation layer functionality supported by text mining systems is *browsing*. Most contemporary text mining systems support browsing that is both dynamic and *content-based*, for the browsing is guided by the actual textual content of a particular document collection and not by anticipated or rigorously prespecified structures. Commonly, user browsing is facilitated by the graphical presentation of concept patterns in the form of a hierarchy to aid interactivity by organizing concepts for investigation.

Browsing is also *navigational*. Text mining systems confront a user with extremely large sets of concepts obtained from potentially vast collections of text documents. Consequently, text mining systems must enable a user to move across these concepts in such a way as to always be able to choose either a "big picture" view of the collection in toto or to drill down on specific – and perhaps very sparsely identified – concept relationships.

Visualization tools are often employed by text mining systems to facilitate navigation and exploration of concept patterns. These use various graphical approaches to express complex data relationships. In the past, visualization tools for text mining sometimes generated static maps or graphs that were essentially rigid snapshots of patterns or carefully generated reports displayed on the screen or printed by an attached printer. State-of-the-art text mining systems, however, now increasingly rely on highly interactive graphic representations of search results that permit a user to drag, pull, click, or otherwise directly interact with the graphical representation of concept patterns. Visualization approaches, like that seen in Figure I.1, are discussed more fully in Chapter X.

Several additional types of functionality are commonly supported within the front ends of text mining systems. Because, in many respects, the presentation layer of a text mining system really serves as the front end for the execution of the system's core knowledge discovery algorithms, considerable attention has been focused on providing users with friendlier and more powerful methods for executing these algorithms. Such methods can become powerful and complex enough to necessitate developing dedicated *query languages* to support the efficient parameterization and execution of specific types of pattern discovery queries. The use of the presentation layer for query execution and simple browsing is discussed in Chapter IX.

At the same time, consistent with an overall emphasis on user empowerment, the designers of many text mining systems have moved away from limiting a user to running only a certain number of fixed, preprogrammed search queries. Instead, these text mining systems are designed to expose much of their search functionality to the user by opening up direct access to their query languages by means of *query language interfaces* or *command-line query interpreters*.

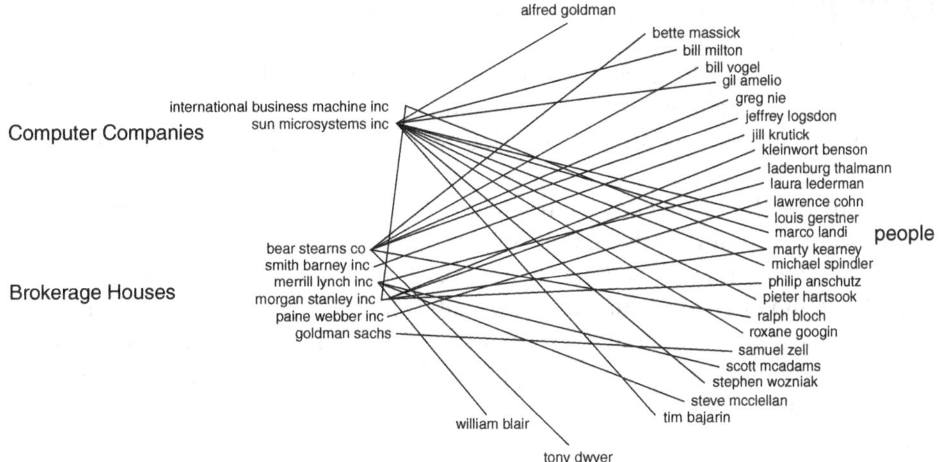

Figure I.1. Example of a visualization tool – mapping concepts (keywords) within the context of categories by means of a "category graph." (From Feldman, Kloesgen, Ben-Yehuda, et al. 1997.)

Furthermore, text mining front ends may offer a user the ability to *cluster* concepts through a suite of *clustering tools* (discussed in Chapter V) in ways that make the most cognitive sense for a particular application or task. Text mining systems can also allow a user to create customized *profiles* for concepts or concept relationships to produce a richer knowledge environment for interactive exploration.

Finally, some text mining systems offer users the ability to manipulate, create, or concatenate *refinement constraints* to assist in producing more manageable and useful result sets for browsing. Like other aspects relating to the creation, shaping, and parameterization of queries, the use of such refinement constraints can be made much more user-friendly by incorporating graphical elements such as pull-downs, radio boxes, or context- or query-sensitive pick lists.

I.1.5 Citations and Notes

Sections I.1–I.1.1

Useful introductions to text mining include Feldman and Dagan (1995), Dixon (1997), Rajman and Besancon (1997b), Feldman (1998), Rajman and Besancon (1998), Hearst (1999a), Tan (1999), and Porter (2002).

Feldman (1998) points out some of the distinctions between classic data mining preprocessing operations, such as table joins, and those of text mining systems. Feldman and Hirsh (1996) discusses text mining's indebtedness to information retrieval. Feldman, Fresko, Hirsh et al. (1998) and Nahm and Mooney (2000), among other works, indicate text mining's dependence on information extraction methodologies – especially in terms of preprocessing operations. Hearst (1999) notes text mining's relatedness to some elements of corpus-based computational linguistics.

PubMed, developed by the National Center for Biotechnology Information (NCBI) at the National Library of Medicine (NLM), a division of the U.S. National Institutes of Health (NIH), is the overall name given to the NLM's database access system, which provides access to resources such as the MEDLINE and

OLDMEDLINE databases. Full information on PubMed can be found at <www.ncbi.nih.gov/entrez/ query.fcgi>.

Hirschman et al. (2002) and Blake and Pratt (2001) both highlight PubMed's attractiveness as a data source for text mining systems. The estimate that 40,000 new biomedical abstracts are being added to PubMed every month comes from Pustejovsky et al. (2002).

Rajman and Besancon (1998) introduced the notion of a prototypical document with respect to text mining document collections.

Freitag (1998b) makes the point that a text document can be viewed as a structured object and discusses many of the semantic and syntactical structures that lend structure to a document. Freitag (1998b) and Zaragoza, Massih-Reza, and Gallinari (1999) both indicate that word sequence may also be a structurally meaningful dimension in documents.

Section I.1.2

Blake and Pratt (2001) presents a discussion of document features in a light useful to understanding text mining considerations. The definition of feature dimensionality that we rely on in Chapter II is shaped by the notion as it is described in Pedersen and Bruce (1997). Statistics for the number of word-level features in a collection of 15,000 documents come from Feldman (1998). Yang and Pedersen (1997) points out that tens of thousands of concept-level features may be relevant for a single application domain.

Blake and Pratt (2001) and Yang and Pedersen (1997) are generally valuable for understanding some distinctions between different types of document features. The phrase *native feature space* was borrowed from Yang and Pedersen (1997). Term-extraction methodologies in text mining are fully treated in Feldman, Fresko, Hirsh et al. (1998). Feldman et al. (2002), Hull (1996), and Brill (1995) are classic works on information extraction useful for understanding lemmatized forms, normalized terms, and so on.

Although some computer scientists make distinctions between keywords and concepts (e.g., Blake and Pratt 2001), this book recognizes the two as relatively interchangeable labels for the same feature type and will generally refer to either under the label *concept*.

It should at least be mentioned that there are some more distinct disadvantages to using manually generated concept-level representations. Manually generated concepts, for example, are fixed and labor-intensive to assign (Blake and Pratt 2001). CDM-based methodologies are discussed in Goldberg (1996).

Feldman and Hirsh (1996a) presents one of the first formal discussions regarding the use of background knowledge in text mining. Other relevant works include Kosmynin and Davidson (1996); Zelikovitz and Hirsh (2000); and Hotho, Staab, and Stumme (2003).

Section I.1.3

Feldman, Kloesgen, Ben-Yehuda, et al. (1997) provides an early treatment of knowledge discovery based on co-occurrence relationships between concepts in documents within a document collection. Lent, Agrawal, and Srikant (1997) is the seminal early work for identifying trends in large amounts of textual data. The high-level questions important to trend analysis identified in Section I.1.3 are based on similar questions presented in Montes-y-Gomez et al. (2001b). The terms *ephemeral association discovery* and *deviation detection* are used here in the manner introduced in Montes-y-Gomez et al. (2001b).

Section I.1.4

Treatments of browsing germane to text mining and related applications include Chang and Rice (1993); Dagan, Feldman, and Hirsh (1996); Feldman, Kloesgen, Ben-Yehuda, et al. (1997); Smith (2002); and Dzbor, Domingue, and Motta (2004). Browsing is discussed in Chapter IX, while a detailed discussion of more elaborate visualization approaches for supporting user interactivity in text mining applications can be found in Chapter X.

I.2 GENERAL ARCHITECTURE OF TEXT MINING SYSTEMS

At an abstract level, a text mining system takes in input (raw documents) and generates various types of output (e.g., patterns, maps of connections, trends). Figure I.2 illustrates this basic paradigm. A human-centered view of knowledge discovery, however, yields a slightly more complex input–output paradigm for text mining (see Figure I.3). This paradigm is one in which a user is part of what might be seen as a prolonged interactive loop of querying, browsing, and refining, resulting in answer sets that, in turn, guide the user toward new iterative series of querying, browsing, and refining actions.

I.2.1 Functional Architecture

On a functional level, text mining systems follow the general model provided by some classic data mining applications and are thus roughly divisible into four main areas: (a) preprocessing tasks, (b) core mining operations, (c) presentation layer components and browsing functionality, and (d) refinement techniques.

- ***Preprocessing Tasks*** include all those routines, processes, and methods required to prepare data for a text mining system's core knowledge discovery operations. These tasks typically center on data source preprocessing and categorization

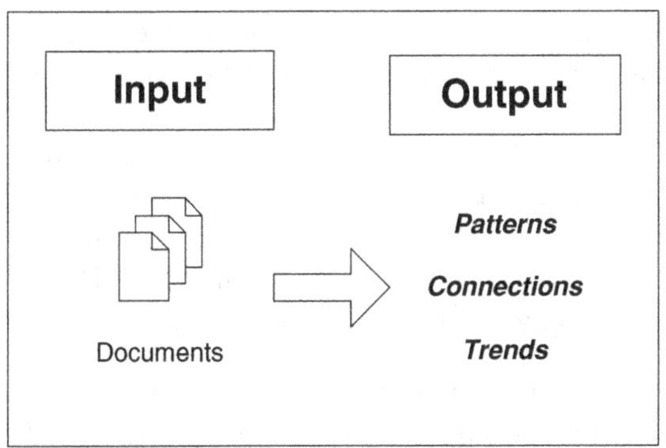

Figure I.2. Simple input–output model for text mining.

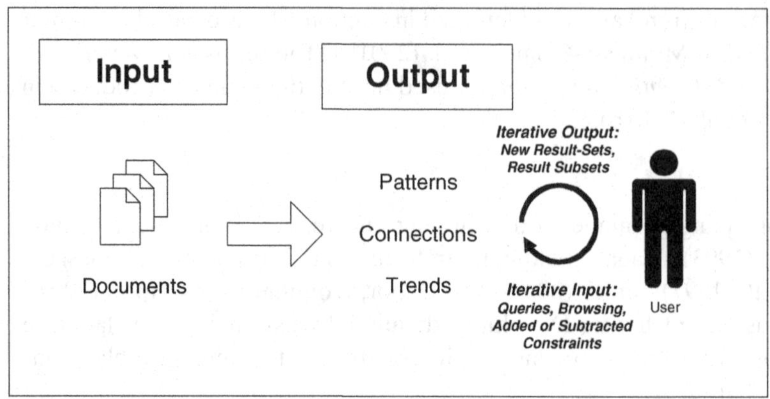

Figure I.3. Iterative loop for user input and output.

activities. Preprocessing tasks generally convert the information from each original data source into a canonical format before applying various types of feature extraction methods against these documents to create a new collection of documents fully represented by concepts. Where possible, preprocessing tasks may also either extract or apply rules for creating document date stamps, or do both. Occasionally, preprocessing tasks may even include specially designed methods used in the initial fetching of appropriate "raw" data from disparate original data sources.

- ***Core Mining Operations*** are the heart of a text mining system and include pattern discovery, trend analysis, and incremental knowledge discovery algorithms. Among the commonly used patterns for knowledge discovery in textual data are distributions (and proportions), frequent and near frequent concept sets, and associations. Core mining operations can also concern themselves with comparisons between – and the identification of levels of "interestingness" in – some of these patterns. Advanced or domain-oriented text mining systems, or both, can also augment the quality of their various operations by leveraging background knowledge sources. These core mining operations in a text mining system have also been referred to, collectively, as *knowledge distillation* processes.
- ***Presentation Layer Components*** include GUI and pattern browsing functionality as well as access to the query language. Visualization tools and user-facing query editors and optimizers also fall under this architectural category. Presentation-layer components may include character-based or graphical tools for creating or modifying concept clusters as well as for creating annotated profiles for specific concepts or patterns.
- ***Refinement Techniques***, at their simplest, include methods that filter redundant information and cluster closely related data but may grow, in a given text mining system, to represent a full, comprehensive suite of suppression, ordering, pruning, generalization, and clustering approaches aimed at discovery optimization. These techniques have also been described as *postprocessing*.

Preprocessing tasks and core mining operations are the two most critical areas for any text mining system and typically describe serial processes within a generalized view of text mining system architecture, as shown in Figure I.4.

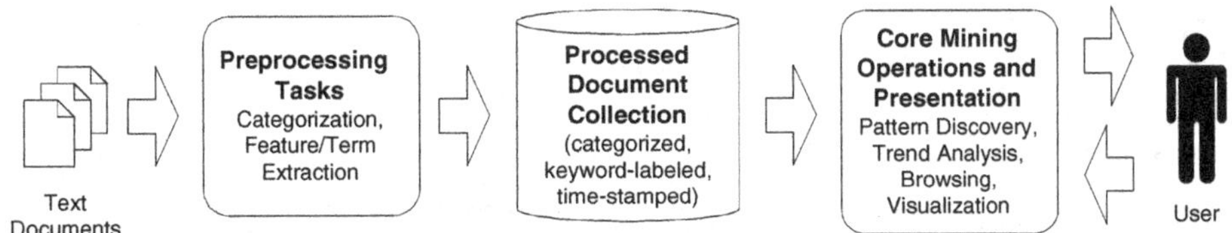

Figure I.4. High-level text mining functional architecture.

At a slightly more granular level of detail, one will often find that the processed document collection is, itself, frequently intermediated with respect to core mining operations by some form of flat, compressed or hierarchical representation, or both, of its data to better support various core mining operations such as hierarchical tree browsing. This is illustrated in Figure I.5. The schematic in Figure I.5 also factors in the typical positioning of refinement functionality. Further, it adds somewhat more

WWW & FTP Resources
News and Email
Other Online Resources
Document Fetching/ Crawling Techniques
Preprocessing Tasks
Categorization, Feature/Term Extraction
Processed Document Collection
(categorized, keyword-labeled, time-stamped)
Compressed or Hierarchical Representation
Text Mining Discovery Algorithms
Pattern Identification, Trend Analysis
Refinement Techniques
Suppression, Ordering, Pruning, Generalization, Clustering
Browsing Functionality
Simple Filters, Query Interpreter, Search Interpreter, Visualization Tools, GUI, Graphing
User

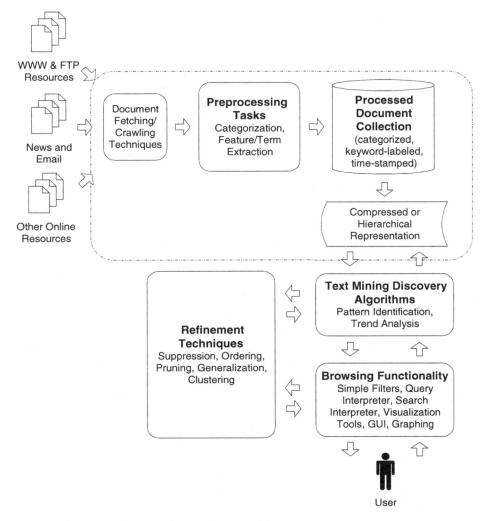

Figure I.5. System architecture for generic text mining system.

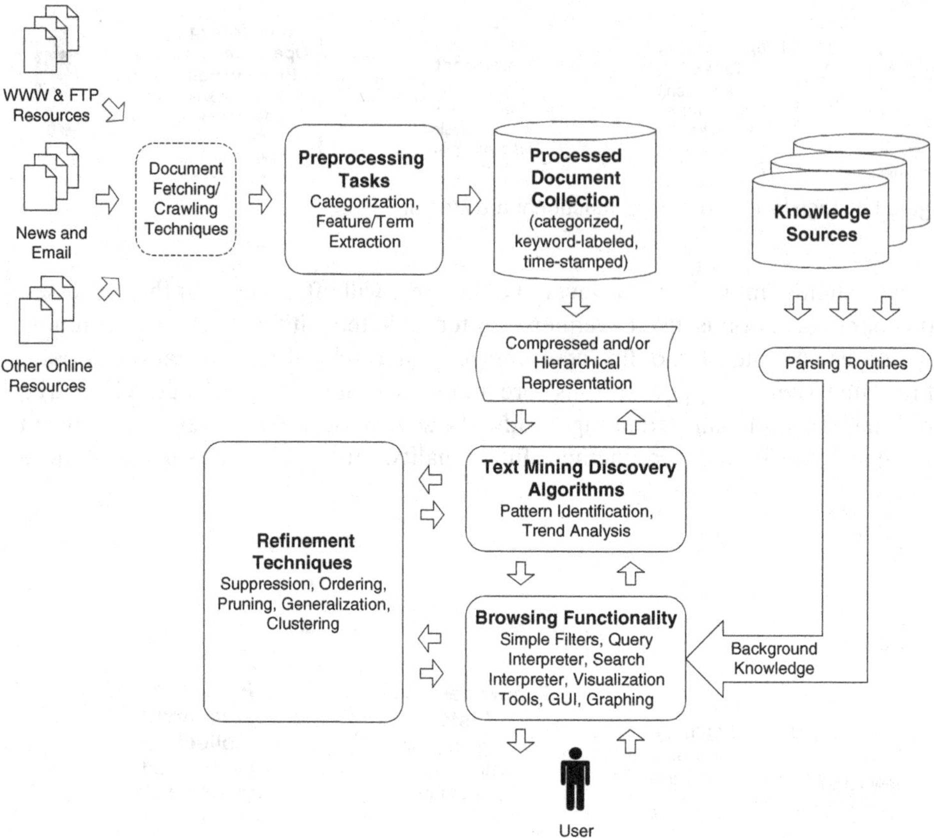

Figure I.6. System architecture for an advanced or domain-oriented text mining system.

detail with respect to relative functioning of core data mining algorithms. Many text mining systems – and certainly those operating on highly domain-specific data sources, such as medicine, financial services, high tech, genomics, proteomics, and chemical compounds – can benefit significantly from access to special background or domain-specific data sources. See Figure I.6.

Background knowledge is often used for providing constraints to, or auxiliary information about, concepts found in the text mining collection's document collection. The background knowledge for a text mining system can be created in various ways. One common way is to run parsing routines against external knowledge sources, such as formal ontologies, after which unary or binary predicates for the concept-labeled documents in the text mining system's document collection are identified. These unary and binary predicates, which describe properties of the entities represented by each concept deriving from the expert or "gold standard" information sources, are in turn put to use by a text mining system's query engine. In addition, such constraints can be used in a text mining system's front end to allow a user to either (a) create initial queries based around these constraints or (b) refine queries over time by adding, substracting, or concatenating constraints.

Commonly, background knowledge is preserved within a text mining system's architecture in a persistent store accessible by various elements of the system. This type of persistent store is sometimes loosely referred to as a system's

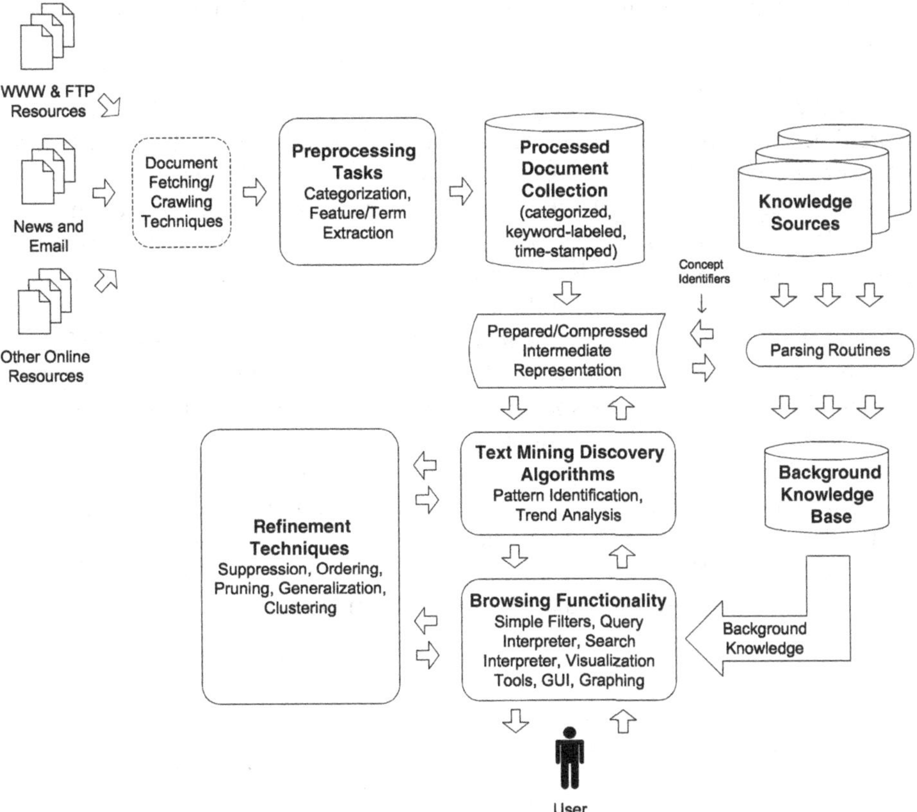

Figure I.7. System architecture for an advanced text mining system with background knowledge base.

knowledge base. The typical position of a knowledge base within the system architecture of a text mining system can be seen in Figure I.7.

These generalized architectures are meant to be more descriptive than prescriptive in that they represent some of the most common frameworks found in the present generation of text mining systems. Good sense, however, should be the guide for prospective system architects of text mining applications, and thus significant variation on the general themes that have been identified is possible. System architects and developers could include more of the filters typically found in a text mining system's browser or even within subroutines contained among the system's store of refinement techniques as "preset" options within search algorithms included in its main discovery algorithms. Likewise, it is conceivable that a particular text mining system's refinement techniques or main discovery algorithms might later find a very fruitful use for background knowledge.

I.2.2 Citations and Notes

Section I.2

The view of human-centered knowledge discovery introduced in Brachman and Anand (1996) and to some degree echoed in Grinstein (1996) influences much of the discussion of text mining systems in Chapter II and indeed throughout this book.

Section I.2.1

The architectural elements of the systems elaborated on here reflect a composite of operations developed in several widely described real-world text mining applications, most especially the KDT (Feldman and Dagan 1995), FACT (Feldman and Hirsh 1996a; Feldman and Hirsh 1996b; Feldman and Hirsh 1997), and Document Explorer (Feldman, Kloesgen, Ben Yehuda, et al. 1997; Feldman, Kloesgen, and Zilberstein 1997a) systems. Besides these text mining applications, other systems at least referentially contributing in some way to this composite include the TEXTRISE system (Nahm and Mooney 2000), the SYNDICATE system (Hahn and Schnattinger 1997), the Explora System (Kloesgen 1995b), and the LINDI project (Hearst 1999).

In particular, Feldman, Kloesgen, and Zilberstein (1997a) includes a pertinent discussion of the architecture of the Document Explorer System. Tan (1999) also proposes a generalized architecture for text mining systems, using the term "knowledge distillation processes" in roughly the same way as this section refers to "core mining operations." The term "postprocessing" – as a general label for what this book refers to as refinement techniques – comes from Hotho et al. (2002).

II

Core Text Mining Operations

Core mining operations in text mining systems center on the algorithms that underlie the creation of queries for discovering patterns in document collections. This chapter describes most of the more common – and a few useful but less common – forms of these algorithms. Pattern-discovery algorithms are discussed primarily from a high-level definitional perspective. In addition, we examine the incorporation of background knowledge into text mining query operations. Finally, we briefly treat the topic of text mining query languages.

II.1 CORE TEXT MINING OPERATIONS

Core text mining operations consist of various mechanisms for discovering patterns of concept occurrence within a given document collection or subset of a document collection. The three most common types of patterns encountered in text mining are *distributions* (and *proportions*), *frequent and near frequent sets*, and *associations*.

Typically, when they offer the capability of discovering more than one type of pattern, text mining systems afford users the ability to toggle between displays of the different types of patterns for a given concept or set of concepts. This allows the richest possible exploratory access to the underlying document collection data through a browser.

II.1.1 Distributions

This section defines and discusses some of text mining's most commonly used distributions. We illustrate this in the context of a hypothetical text mining system that has a document collection *W* composed of documents containing news wire stories about world affairs that have all been preprocessed with concept labels.

Whether as an initial step, to create a baseline, or to create more meaningful subdivisions of a single document collection for comparison purposes, text mining systems generally need to refer to some subcollection of a complete document collection. This activity is commonly referred to as *concept selection*. Given some collection of documents D, a text mining system will have a requirement to refer to some subcollection of D that is labeled by one or more given concepts.

Definition II.1. Concept Selection: If D is a collection of documents and K is a set of concepts, D/K is the subset of documents in D labeled with all of the concepts in K. When it is clear from the context, given a single concept k, rather than writing $D/\{k\}$ we use the notation D/k.

For example, the collection W contains a subset of the World Affairs collection – namely those documents that are labeled with the concepts *iran, nicaragua,* and *reagan; W/bush* contains the subset of documents that are labeled (at least) with *reagan*; and $W/G8$ contains those documents that are labeled with any terminal node under *G8* (i.e., labeled with any *G8* country). *G8* is treated as a concept here when is being performed concept selection (rather than being viewed as the set of concepts under it, in which case it would have required *all* of its descendants to be present).

Text mining systems often need to identify or examine the proportion of a set of documents labeled with a particular concept. This analytic is commonly referred to as *concept proportion.*

Definition II.2. Concept Proportion: If D is a collection of documents and K is a set of concepts, $f(D, K)$ is the fraction of documents in D labeled with all of the concepts in K, that is, $f(D, K) = \frac{|D/k|}{|D|}$. Given one concept k, rather than writing $f(D, \{k\})$, we use the notation $f(D, k)$. When D is clear from context, we drop it and write $f(k)$.

Thus, for example, f(W, {*iran, nicaragua, reagan*} is the fraction of documents in the World Affairs collection labeled with *iran, nicaragua*, and reagan; $f(reagan)$ is the proportion of the collection labeled with the concept *reagan*; and $f(G8)$ is the proportion labeled with any ($G8$) country.

By employing definitions of selection and proportion, text mining systems can already begin identifying some useful quantities for analyzing a set of documents. For example, a text mining system might want to identify the proportion of those documents labeled with K_2 that are also labeled by K_1, which could be designated by expression $f(D/K_2, K_1)$.

This type of proportion occurs regularly enough that it has received an explicit name and notation: *conditional concept proportion.*

Definition II.3. Conditional Concept Proportion: If D is a collection of documents and K_1 and K_2 are sets of concepts, $f(D, K_1 \mid K_2)$ is the proportion of all those documents in D labeled with K_2 that are also labeled with K_1, that is, $f(D, K_1 \mid K_2) = f(D/K_2, K_1)$. When D is clear from context, we will write this as $f(K_1 \mid K_2)$.

Applying this definition, we find that $f(reagan \mid iran)$ would represent the proportion of all documents labeled by the concept *iran* that are also labeled by the concept *reagan.*

Commonly, a text mining system needs to analyze the distribution of concepts that are descendents of a particular node in a concept hierarchy. For example, a text mining system might need to allow the analysis of the distribution of concepts denoting *finance topics* – that is, descendents of the *finance topics* node in an example concept hierarchy. To accomplish this, a text mining system could use the expression

$P_K(x)$ to refer to such distributions – it will assign to any concept x in K a value between 0 and 1 – where the values are not required to add up to 1.

This type of proportion can be referred to as a *concept distribution*. In the following sections we present several specific examples of such $P_K(x)$ distributions.

One particularly important concept distribution for knowledge discovery operations is the *concept proportion distribution*, which gives the proportion of documents in some collection that are labeled with each of a number of selected concepts:

Definition II.4. Concept Proportion Distribution: If D is a collection of documents and K is a set of concepts, $F_K(D, x)$ is the proportion of documents in D labeled with x for any x in K. When D is clear from context, we will write this as $F_K(x)$.

Note the distinction between $P_K(x)$ and $F_K(x)$. $P_K(x)$ refers generically to any function that is a concept distribution. $F_K(x)$ is a specific concept distribution defined by a particular concept-labeled set of documents.

Thus, for example $F_{\text{topics}}(R, x)$ would represent the proportions of documents in W labeled with keywords under the *topics* node in the concept hierarchy. In this expression, *topics* is used as shorthand for referring to a set of concepts – namely, all those that occur under the *topics* node – instead of explicitly enumerating them all.

Also, note that $F_{\{k\}}(D, k) = f(D, k)$ – that is, F_K subsumes the earlier defined f when it is applied to a single concept. Unlike f, however, F_K is restricted to refer only to the proportion of occurrences of *individual* concepts (those occurring in the set K).[1] Thus f and F are not comparable.

Mathematically, F is not a true frequency distribution, for each document may be labeled by multiple items in the set K. Thus, for example, a given document may be labeled by two (or more) *G8* countries because occurrences of concepts are not disjoint events. Therefore, the sum of values in F_{G8} may be greater than one.

In the worst case, if all concepts in K label all documents, the sum of the values in a distribution F can be as large as $|K|$. Furthermore, because some documents may contain none of the concepts in a given K, the sum of frequencies in F might also be smaller than one – in the worst case, zero. Nonetheless, the term "distribution" is used for F, for many of the connotations this term suggests still hold true.

Just as was the case for concept proportions, text mining systems can also leverage conditional keyword-proportion distributions, which are probably one of the most used concept distributions in text mining systems.

Definition II.5. Conditional Concept Proportion Distribution: If D is a collection of documents and K and K' are sets of concepts, $F_K(D, x \mid K')$ is the proportion of those documents in D labeled with all the concepts in K' that are also labeled with concept x (with x in K), that is, $F_K(D, x \mid K') = F_K(D/K \mid K', x)$. We often write this as $F_K(x \mid K')$ when D is clear from context.

Thus, for example, $F_{\text{topics}}(x \mid Argentina)$ would assign any concept x under *topics* in the hierarchy with the proportion of documents labeled by x within the set of all documents labeled by the concept *Argentina*, and $F_{\text{topics}}(x \mid \{UK, USA)$ is the similar distribution for those documents labeled with both the *UK* and *USA* concepts.

[1] It is also quite simple to define a similar notion for *sets* of concepts, for example, by computing the proportions for each subset of a set K (Feldman, Dagan, and Hirsh, 1998).

One of the baseline distributions text mining systems use to compare distributions is the average distribution over a set of sibling nodes in the hierarchy. For example, when looking at the proportions of *loan* within South American countries such as $f(W, \textit{loan} \mid \textit{Argentina})$, $f(W, \textit{loan} \mid \textit{Brazil})$, and $f(W, \textit{loan} \mid \textit{Columbia})$), an end user may be interested in the average of all proportions of this form for all the South American countries – that is, the average of all proportions of the form $f(W, \textit{loan} \mid k)$, where k ranges over all South American countries.

Definition II.6. Average Concept Proportion: Given a collection of documents D, a concept k, and an internal node in the hierarchy n, an *average concept proportion*, denoted by $a(D, k \mid n)$, is the average value of $f(D, k \mid k')$, where k' ranges over all immediate children of n – that is, $a(D, k \mid n) = \text{Avg}_{\{k' \text{ is a child of } n\}}\{f(D, k \mid k')\}$. When D is clear from context, this will be written $a(k|n)$.

For example, $a(\textit{loan} \mid \textit{South\_America})$ is the average concept proportion of $f(\textit{loan} \mid k')$ as k' varies over each child of the node *South_America* in the concept hierarchy; that is, it is the average conditional keyword proportion for *loan* within South American countries.

This quantity does *not* average the values weighted by the number of documents labeled by each child of n. Instead, it equally represents each descendant of n and should be viewed as a summary of what a typical concept proportion is for a child of n.

An end user may be interested in the distribution of averages for each economic topic within South American countries. This is just another keyword distribution referred to as an *average concept distribution.*

Definition II.7. Average Concept Distribution: Given a collection of documents D and two internal nodes in the hierarchy n and n', an *average concept distribution*, denoted by $A_n(Dx \mid n')$, is the distribution that, for any x that is a child of n, averages x's proportions over all children of n' – that is, $A_n(D, x \mid n') = \text{Avg}_{\{k' \text{ is a child of } n'\}}\{F_n(D, x \mid k')\}$. When clear from context, this will be written $A_n(x \mid n')$.

For example $A_{\text{topics}}(x|\textit{South\_America})$, which can be read as "the average distribution of topics within South American countries," gives the average proportion within all South American countries for any topic x.

A very basic operation for text mining systems using concept-distributions is the display of conditional concept-proportion distributions. For example, a user may be interested in seeing the proportion of documents labeled with each child of *topics* for all those documents labeled by the concept *Argentina*, that is, the proportion of *Argentina* documents that are labeled with each topic keyword.

This distribution would be designated by $F_{\text{topics}}(W, x \mid \textit{Argentina})$, and a correlating graph could be generated, for instance, as a bar chart, which might display the fact that 12 articles among all articles of *Argentina* are annotated with *sorghum*, 20 with *corn*, 32 with *grain*, and so on, providing a summary of the areas of economical activity of Argentina as reflected in the text collection. Conditional concept-proportion distributions can also be conditioned on *sets* of concepts.

In some sense, this type of operation can be viewed as a more refined form of traditional concept-based retrieval. For example, rather than simply requesting all documents labeled by *Argentina* or by both *UK* and *USA*, the user can see the documents at a higher level by requesting documents labeled by *Argentina* for example, and first seeing what proportions are labeled by concepts from some secondary set of concepts of interest with the user being able to access the documents through this more fine-grained grouping of *Argentina*-labeled documents.

Comparing with Average Distributions

Consider a conditional proportion of the form $F_k(D, x \mid k) f$, the distribution over K of all documents labeled with some concept k (not necessarily in K). It is natural to expect that this distribution would be similar to other distributions of this form over conditioning events k' that are siblings of k. When they differ substantially it is a sign that the documents labeled with the conditioning concept k may be of interest.

To facilitate this kind of comparison of concept-labeled documents with the average of those labeled with the concept and its siblings, a user can specify two internal nodes of the hierarchy and compare individual distributions of concepts under one of the nodes conditioned on the concept set under the other node – that is, compute $D(F_n(x \mid k) || A_n(x \mid n'))$ for each k that is a child of n'.

In addition to their value in finding possible interesting concept labelings, comparisons of this type also provide a hierarchical browsing mechanism for concept co-occurrence distributions. For example, an analyst interested in studying the topic distribution in articles dealing with *G8* countries may first browse the average class distribution for *G8*. This might reveal the major topics that are generally common for *G8* countries. Then, an additional search could be used to reveal the major characteristics specific for each country.

Comparing Specific Distributions

The preceding mechanism for comparing distributions with an average distribution is also useful for comparing conditional distributions of two specific nodes in the hierarchy. For example, one could measure the distance from the average topic distribution of *Arab_League* countries to the average topic distribution of *G8* countries. An answer set could be returned from a query into a table with countries sorted in decreasing order of their contribution to the distance (second column) – namely $d(A_{\text{topics}}(K \mid Arab\_League) \mid\mid A_{\text{topics}}(k \mid G8))$.

Additional columns could show, respectively, the percentage of the topic in the average topic distribution of the *Arab_League* countries $(A_{\text{topics}}(x \mid G8))$ and in the average topic distribution of the *G8* countries $(A_{\text{topics}}(x \mid G8))$. One could also show the total number of articles in which the topic appears with any *Arab_League* country and any *G8* country. This would reveal the topics with which *Arab_League* countries are associated much more than *G8* countries such as grain, wheat, and crude oil. Finally, one could show the comparison in the opposite direction, revealing the topics with which *G8* countries are highly associated relative to the *Arab_League*.

II.1.2 Frequent and Near Frequent Sets

Frequent Concept Sets

In addition to proportions and distributions, another basic type of pattern that can be derived from a document collection is a *frequent concept set*. This is defined as a set of concepts represented in the document collection with co-occurrences at or above a minimal support level (given as a threshold parameter s; i.e., all the concepts of the frequent concept set appear together in at least s documents). Although originally defined as an intermediate step in finding *association rules* (see Section II.1.3), frequent concept sets contain a great deal of information of use in text mining.

The search for frequent sets has been well treated in data mining literature, stemming from research centered on investigating *market basket*–type associations first published by Agrawal et al. in 1993. Essentially, a document can be viewed as a market basket of named entities. Discovery methods for frequent concept sets in text mining build on the *Apriori* algorithm of Agrawal et al. (1993) used in data mining for market basket association problems. With respect to frequent sets in natural language application, *support* is the number (or percent) of documents containing the given rule – that is, the co-occurrence frequency. *Confidence* is the percentage of the time that the rule is true.

L_1 = {large 1 – itemsets}
for ($k = 2$; $L_{k-1} \neq \emptyset$; k++) **do begin**
    C_k = apriori-gen (L_{k-1}) // new candidates
    forall transactions $t \in D$ **do begin**
        C_1 = subset (C_k, t) // candidates contained in t
        forall candidates $c \in C_t$ **do**
            c.count ++;
        end
        $L_k = \{c \in C_k \mid c.count \geq minsupport\}$
end
Answer $= \bigcup_k L_k$;

Algorithm II.1: The Apriori Algorithm (Agrawal and Srikant 1994)[2]

A frequent set in text mining can be seen directly as a query given by the conjunction of concepts of the frequent set. Frequent sets can be partially ordered by their generality and hold the simple but useful pruning property that each subset of a frequent set is a frequent set. The discovery of frequent sets can be useful both as a type of search for patterns in its own right and as a preparatory step in the discovery of *associations*.

Discovering Frequent Concept Sets

As mentioned in the previous section, frequent sets are generated in relation to some support level. Because support (i.e., the frequency of co-occurrence) has been by convention often expressed as the variable σ, frequent sets are sometimes also referred to as *σ-covers*, or *σ-cover sets*. A simple algorithm for generating frequent sets relies on incremental building of the group of frequent sets from singleton *σ-covers*, to which additional elements that continue to satisfy the support constraint

[2] In data mining, the expression *item* is commonly used in a way that is roughly analogous to the expression *feature* in text mining. Therefore, the expression *item set* can be seen here, at least, as analogous to the expression *concept set*.

are progressively added. Algorithm II.2 is a typical algorithm for discovering frequent concept sets.

$L_1 = \{\{A\} \mid A \in R \text{ and } [A] \geq \sigma\}$
$i = 1$
While $L_i \neq \emptyset$ **do**
$L_{i+1} = \{S1 \cup S2 \mid S1, S2 \in L_i, \mid S1 \cup S2 \mid = i + 1,$
all subsets of $S1 \cup S2$ are in $L_i\}$
$i = i + 1$
end do
return $(\{X \mid X \in \bigcup_i L_i \text{ and } |[X]| \geq \sigma\})$

Algorithm II.2: Algorithm for Frequent Set Generation

Near Frequent Concept Sets

Near frequent concept sets establish an undirected relation between two frequent sets of concepts. This relation can be quantified by measuring the degree of overlapping, for example, on the basis of the number of documents that include all the concepts of the two concept sets. This measure can be regarded as a distance function between the concept sets. Several distance functions can be introduced (e.g., based on the cosine of document vectors, Tanimoto distance, etc.).

Directed relations between concept sets can also be identified. These are considered types of *associations* (see Section II.1.3).

II.1.3 Associations

A formal description of association rules was first presented in the same research on "market basket" problems that led to the identification of *frequent sets* in data mining. Subsequently, associations have been widely discussed in literature on knowledge discovery targeted at both structured and unstructured data.

In text mining, *associations* specifically refer to the directed relations between concepts or sets of concepts. An *association rule* is generally an expression of the form $A \Rightarrow B$, where A and B are sets of features. An association rule $A \Rightarrow B$ indicates that transactions that involve A tend also to involve B.

For example, from the original market-basket problem, an association rule might be *25 percent of the transactions that contain pretzels also contain soda; 8 percent of all transactions contain both items*. In this example, 25 percent refers to the *confidence* level of the association rule, and 8 percent refers to the rule's level of *support*.

With respect to concept sets, association rule $A \Rightarrow B$, relating two frequent concept sets A and B, can be quantified by these two basic measures of support and confidence. *Confidence* is the percentage of documents that include all the concepts in B within the subset of those documents that include all the concepts in A. *Support* is the percentage (or number) of documents that include all the concepts in A and B.

More precisely, we can describe association rules as follows:

- Let $r = \{t_1, \ldots, t_n\}$ be a collection of documents, each labeled with some subset of concepts from the m-concept set $R = \{I_1, I_2, \ldots, I_m\}$.

- Given a concept A and document t, we write $t(A) = 1$ if A is one of the concepts labeling t, and $t(A) = 0$ otherwise.
- If W is a subset of the concepts in R, $t(W) = 1$ represents the case that $t(A) = 1$ for every concept $A \in W$.
- Given a set X of concepts from R, define $(X) = \{i \mid t_i(X) = 1\}$; (X) is the set of all documents t_i that are labeled (at least) with all the concepts in X.
- Given some number σ (the support threshold), X is called a σ-covering if $|(X)| \geq \sigma$.

$W \Rightarrow B$ is an association rule over r if $W \subseteq R$ and $B \subseteq R \backslash W$. We refer to W as the *left-hand side* (LHS) of the association and B as the *right-hand side* (RHS).

Finally, we say that r satisfies $W \Rightarrow B$ with respect to $0 < \gamma \leq 1$ (the confidence threshold) and σ (the support threshold) if $W \cup B$ is a σ-covering (i.e., $|(W \cup B)| \geq \sigma$ and $|(W \cup B)|/|(W)| \geq \gamma$). Intuitively, this means that, of all documents labeled with the concepts in W, at least a proportion γ of them are also labeled with the concepts in B; further, this rule is based on at least σ documents labeled with all the concepts in both W and B.

For example, a document collection has documents labeled with concepts in the following tuples: {x, y, z, w}, {x, w}, {x, y, p}, {x, y, t}. If $\gamma = 0.8$ and $\sigma = 0.5$, and {x}, {y}, {w}, {x, w}, and {x, y} are coverings, then {y} ⇒ {x} and {w} ⇒ {x} are the only associations.

Discovering Association Rules

The discovery of association rules is the problem of finding all the association rules with a confidence and support greater than the user-identified values *minconf* (i.e., γ, or the minimum confidence level) and *minsup* (i.e., σ, or the minimum support level) thresholds.

The basic approach to discovering associations is a generally straightforward two-step process as follows:

- Find all frequent concept sets X (i.e., all combinations of concepts with a support greater than *minsup*);
- Test whether $X \backslash B \Rightarrow B$ holds with the required confidence.

The first step – namely the generation of frequent concept sets (see Algorithm II.2) – has usually been found to be by far the most computationally expensive operation. A typical simple algorithm for the second step – generating associations (after the generation of maximal frequent concept sets has been completed) – can be found below in Algorithm II.3.

foreach *X maximal frequent set* **do**

generate all the rules $X \setminus \{b\} \Rightarrow \{b\}$, where $b \in X$, such that

$$\frac{|[X \backslash \{b\}]|}{|[X]|} \geq \sigma$$

endfch

Algorithm II.3: Simple Algorithm for Generating Associations (Rajman and Besancon 1998)

Thus, essentially, if {w, x} and {w, x, y, z} are frequent concept sets, then the association rule {w, x} ⇒ {y, z} can be computed by the following ratio:

$$c = \frac{support\ (\{w, x, y, z\})}{support\ (\{w, x\})}.$$

Again, however, in this case the association rule will only hold if $c \geq \sigma$.

Given these steps, if there are m concepts in a document collection, then, in a single pass, all possible 2^m subsets for that document collection can be checked. Of course, in extremely large, concept-rich document collections, this can still be a nontrivial computational task. Moreover, because of the implications of generating an overabundance of associations, additional procedures – such as structural or statistical pruning, redundancy elimination, and so on – are sometimes used to supplement the main association rule extraction procedure in order to limit the number of generated associations.

Maximal Associations

Association rules are very useful in helping to generally describe associations relevant between concepts. *Maximal associations* represent a more specialized type of relationship between concepts in which associations are identified in terms of their relevance to one concept and their lack of relevance to another. These associations help create solutions in the particular problem space that exists within text document collections, where closely related items frequently appear together. Conventional association rules fail to provide a good means for allowing the specific discovery of associations pertaining to concepts that most often do not appear alone (but rather together with closely related concepts) because associations relevant only to these concepts tend to have low confidence. Maximal association rules provide a mechanism for discovering these types of specialized relations.

For example, in a document collection, the concept "Saddam Hussein" may most often appear in association with "Iraq" and "Microsoft" most often with "Windows." Because of the existence of these most common relationships, associations especially relevant to the first concept in the association, but not the other, will tend to have low confidence. For instance, an association between "Iraq" and the "Arab League" would have low confidence because of the many instances in which "Iraq" appears with "Saddam Hussein" (and not "Arab League"). Likewise, an association between "Microsoft" and "Redmond" would potentially be left unidentified because of the many more instances in which "Microsoft" appears with "Windows." Maximal associations identify associations relevant to one concept but not the other – that is, associations relating to "Iraq" or "Microsoft" alone.

Maximal Association Rules: Defining M-Support and M-Confidence

Fundamentally, a maximal association rule $X \overset{max}{\Rightarrow} Y$ states that, whenever X is the only concept of its type in a transaction (i.e., when X appears *alone*), then Y also appears with some confidence. To understand the notion of a maximal association rule it is important define the meaning of *alone* in this context. We can do so with respect to categories of G:

Definition II.8. Alone with Respect to Maximal Associations: For a transaction t, a category g, and a concept-set $X \subseteq g_i$, one would say that X is alone in t if $t \cap g_i = X$.

That is, X is alone in t if X is the largest subset of g_i that is in t. In such a case, one would say that X is maximal in t and that t *M-supports* X. For a document collection D, the *M-support* of X in D, denoted as $s_{\underset{D}{max}}(X)$, is the number of transactions $t \in D$ that *M-support* X.

A maximal association rule, or *M-association*, is a rule of the form $X \overset{max}{\Rightarrow} Y$, where X and Y are subsets of distinct categories that could be identified as $g\ (X)$ and $g\ (Y)$, respectively. The *M-support* for the maximal association $X \overset{max}{\Rightarrow} Y$, which can be denoted as $s_{\underset{D}{max}}(X \overset{max}{\Rightarrow} Y)$, can be defined as

$$s_{\underset{D}{max}}(X \overset{max}{\Rightarrow} Y) = |\{t : t \text{ M-supports } X \text{ and } t \text{ supports } Y\}|.$$

That is, $(X \overset{max}{\Rightarrow} Y)$ is equal to the number of transactions in D that M-support X and also support Y in the conventional sense, which suggests that, whenever a transaction M-supports X, then Y also appears in the transaction with some probability.

In measuring this probability, we are generally interested only in those transactions in which some element of $g(Y)$ (i.e., the category of Y) appears in the transaction. Thus, we define confidence in the following manner. If $D(X, g(Y))$ is the subset of the document collection D consisting of all the transactions that M-support X and contain at least one element of $g(Y)$, then the M-confidence of the rule $X \overset{max}{\Rightarrow} Y$, denoted by $c_{\underset{D}{max}}(X \overset{max}{\Rightarrow} Y)$, is

$$c_{\underset{D}{max}}(X \overset{max}{\Rightarrow} Y) = \frac{s_{\underset{D}{max}}(X \overset{max}{\Rightarrow} Y)}{|D(X, g(Y))|}.$$

A text mining system can search for associations in which the M-support is higher than some user-specified *minimum M-support*, which has been denoted by the designation s, and the M-confidence is higher than some user-specified minimum M-confidence, which has been denoted by c. A set X that has M-support of at least s is said to be *M-frequent*.

M-Factor

Any maximal association rule is also a conventional association with perhaps different levels of support and confidence. The *M-factor* of the rule $X \overset{max}{\Rightarrow} Y$ is the ratio between the M-confidence of the maximal association $X \overset{max}{\Rightarrow} Y$ and the confidence of the *corresponding* conventional association $X \Rightarrow Y$. Specifically, if D is a subset of the transaction that contains at least one concept of $g(Y)$, then, the M-factor of the association $X \overset{max}{\Rightarrow} Y$ is

$$\text{M-factor } (X \overset{max}{\Rightarrow} Y) = c_{\underset{D}{max}}(X \overset{max}{\Rightarrow} Y) = \frac{c_{\underset{D}{max}}(X \overset{max}{\Rightarrow} Y)}{c_{D'}(X \Rightarrow Y)}.$$

Here, the denominator is the confidence for the rule $X \Rightarrow Y$ with respect to D'. This is because, given that the M-confidence is defined with respect to D', the comparison to conventional associations must also be with respect to the set.

From a practical perspective, one generally seeks M-associations with a higher M-factor. Such M-associations tend to represent more interesting rules.

II.1.4 Isolating Interesting Patterns

The notion of *interestingness* with respect to knowledge discovery in textual data has been viewed from various subjective and contextual perspectives. The most common method of defining interestingness in relation to patterns of distributions, frequent sets, and associations has been to enable a user to input expectations into a system and then to find some way of measuring or ranking patterns with respect to how far they differ from the user's expectations.

Text mining systems can quantify the potential degree of "interest" in some piece of information by comparing it to a given "expected" model. This model then serves as a baseline for the investigated distribution.

For example, a user may want to compare the data regarding Microsoft with an averaged model constructed for a group of computer software vendors. Alternatively, a user may want to compare the data relating to Microsoft in the last year with a model constructed from the data regarding Microsoft in previous years.

Interestingness with Respect to Distributions and Proportions

Because text mining systems rely on concept proportions and distributions to describe the data, one therefore requires measures for quantifying the distance between an investigated distribution and another distribution that serves as a baseline model (Feldman, Dagan, and Hirsh 1998). So long as the distributions are discrete, one can simply use sum-of-squares to measure the distance between two models:

$$D(p' \parallel p) = \sum_{x} (p'(x) - p(x))^2,$$

where the target distribution is designated by p and the approximating distribution by p' and the x in the summation is taken over all objects in the domain. This measure is always nonnegative and is 0 if and only if $p' = p$.

Given this measure, one can use it as a heuristic device. With respect to distribution-based patterns, this could be used as a heuristic for judging concept-distribution similarities. This measure is referred to as *concept distribution distance.*

Definition II.9. Concept Distribution Distance: Given two concept distributions $P'_K(x)$ and $P_K(x)$, the distance $D(P'_K \parallel P_K)$ between them is defined by $D(P'_K(x) \parallel P_K(x)) = \sum_{x \in K} (P'_K(x) - P_K(x))^2$.

Text mining systems are also sometimes interested in the value of the difference between two distributions at a particular point. This measure is called *concept proportion distance.*

Definition II.10. Concept Proportion Distance: Given two concept distributions $P'_K(x)$ and $P_K(x)$, and a concept k in K, the distance $d(P'_K(k) \parallel P_K(k))$ between them is defined by $D(P'_K(k) \parallel P_K(k)) = P'_K(k) - P_K(k)$.

Thus, another way to state $D(P'_K \parallel P_K)$ would be

$$\sum_{x \in K} [d(P_K(x) \parallel P_K(x))]^2.$$

As an example, the distance between the distribution of *topics* within *Argentina* and the distribution of *topics* within *Brazil* would be written as $D(F_{\text{topics}}(x \mid Argentina) \,||\, F_{\text{topics}}(x \mid Brazil))$, and the distance between the distribution of *topics* within *Argentina* and the average distribution of *topics* within *South_America* would be written as $D(F_{\text{topics}}(x \mid Argentina) \,||\, A_{\text{topics}}(x \mid South\_America))$.

II.1.5 Analyzing Document Collections over Time

Early text mining systems tended to view a document collection as a single, monolithic entity – a unitary corpus consisting of one coherent and largely *static* set of textual documents. Many text mining applications, however, benefit from viewing the document collection not as a monolithic corpus but in terms of subsets or divisions defined by the date and time stamps of documents in the collection. This type of view can be used to allow a user to analyze similarities and differences between concept relationships across the various subdivisions of the corpus in a way that better accounts for the change of concept relationships over time.

Trend analysis, in text mining, is the term generally used to describe the analysis of concept distribution behavior across multiple document subsets over time. Other time-based analytics include the discovery of *ephemeral associations*, which focuses on the influence or interaction of the most frequent or "peak" concepts in a period on other concepts, and *deviation*, which concentrates on irregularities such as documents that have concepts differing from more typical documents in a document collection (or subcollection) over time. In addition, text mining systems can enable users to explore the evolution of concept relationships through *temporal context graphs* and context-oriented *trend graphs*.

Although trend analysis and related time-based analytics attempt to better account for the evolving nature of concept relationships in a document collection, text mining systems have also developed practical approaches to the real-world challenges inherent in supporting truly dynamic document collections that add, modify, or delete documents over time. Such algorithms have been termed *incremental algorithms* because they tend to be aimed at more efficient incremental update of the search information that has already been mined from a document collection to account for new data introduced by documents added to this collection over time.

Both trend analysis and incremental algorithms add a certain dynamism to text mining systems, allowing these systems to interact with more dynamic document collections. This can be critical for developing useful text mining applications targeted at handling time series–type financial reports, topical news feeds, text-based market data, time-sensitive voter or consumer sentiment commentary, and so on.

Trend Analysis

The origin of the problem of discovering trends in textual data can be traced to research on methods for detecting and presenting trends in word phrases. These methods center on a two-phase process in which, in the first phase, phrases are created as frequent *sequences* of words using the sequential patterns mining algorithm first mooted for mining structured databases and, in the second phase, a user can query the system to obtain all phrases whose trend matches a specified pattern (i.e., "recent upward trend").

More recent methods for performing trend analysis in text mining have been predicated on the notion that the various types of concept distributions are functions of document collections. It is therefore possible to compare two distributions that are otherwise identical except that they are for different subcollections. One notable example of this is having two collections from the same source (such as from a news feed) but from different points in time.

For instance, one can compare the distribution of *topics* within *Argentina*-labeled documents, as formed by documents published in the first quarter of 1987, with the same distribution formed by documents from the second quarter of 1987. This comparison will highlight those topics whose proportion changed between the two time points, directing the attention of the user to specific trends or events in these topics with respect to Argentina. If R_1 is used to designate a portion of a Reuters newswire data collection from the first quarter of 1987, and R_2 designates the portion from the second quarter of 1987, this would correspond to comparing $F_{\text{topics}}(R_1, x \mid Argentina)$ and $F_{\text{topics}}(R_2, x \mid Argentina)$.

This knowledge discovery operation can be supplemented by listing trends that were identified across different quarters in the time period represented by the Reuters collection by computing $R(F_{\text{countries}}(R_1, x \mid countries) \mid\mid F_{\text{countries}}(R_2, x \mid countries))$, where R_1 and R_2 correspond to different subcollections from different quarters.[3] A text mining system could also calculate the percentage and absolute frequency for $F_{\text{countries}}(x \mid countries)$ for each such pair of collections.

Ephemeral Associations

An *ephemeral association* has been defined by Montes-y-Gomez et al. (2001b) as a direct or inverse relation between the probability distributions of given topics (concepts) over a fixed time span. This type of association differs notionally from the more typical association form $A \Rightarrow B$ because it not only indicates the co-occurrence of two topics or sets of topics but primarily indicates how these topics or sets of topics are related within the fixed time span.

Examples of ephemeral associations can be found in news feeds in which one very frequently occurring or "peak" topic during a period seems to influence either the emergence or disappearance of other topics. For instance, news stories (documents) about a close election that involve allegations of election machine fraud may correlate with the emergence of stories about election machine technology or vote fraud stories from the past. This type of ephemeral association is referred to as a *direct ephemeral association*.

On the other hand, news stories relating to the victory of a particular tennis player in a major tournament may correlate with a noticeable and timely decrease in stories mentioning other tennis players who were formerly widely publicized. Such

[3] It would also be quite fair to ask for a distribution $F_K(x \mid K)$, which analyzes the co-occurrences of different keywords under the same node of the hierarchy. Thus, for example, $F_{\text{countries}}(x \mid countries)$ would analyze the co-occurrences of country labels on the various documents.

momentary negative influence between one topic and another is referred to as an *inverse ephemeral association.*

One statistical method suggested by Montes-y-Gomez et al. (2001b) to detect ephemeral associations has been the correlation measure r. This method has been expressed as

$$r = \frac{S_{01}}{\sqrt{S_{00}S_{01}}},$$

$$S_{kl} = \sum_{i=1}^{n} (p_k^i, p_l^i) - \frac{1}{n}\left(\sum_{i=1}^{n} p_k^i\right)\left(\sum_{i=1}^{n} p_l^i\right),$$

$$k, l = 0, 1.$$

Within this method, p_0^i is the probability of the peak topic, and p_1^i is the probability of the other topic in the period i. The correlation coefficient r attempts to measure how well two variables – here, topics or concepts – are related to one another. It describes values between −1 and 1; the value −1 means there is a perfect inverse relationship between two topics, whereas the value 1 denotes a perfect direct relationship between two topics. The value 0 indicates the absence of a relation.

Deviation Detection

Users of text mining systems are sometimes interested in deviations – that is, the identification of anomalous instances that do not fit a defined "standard case" in large amounts of data. The normative case is a representation of the average element in a data collection. For instance, in news feed documents and the topics (concepts) that they contain, a particular topic can be considered a deviation if its probability distribution greatly diverges from distributions of other topics in the same sample set.

Research into deviation detection for text mining is still in its early, formative stages, and we will not discuss it in detail here. However, work has been done by Montes-y-Gomez, Gelbukh, and Lopez-Lopez (Montes-y-Gomez et al. 2001b) and others to examine the difficult task of detecting deviations among documents in large collections of news stories, which might be seen as an application of knowledge discovery for distribution-type patterns. In such applications, time can also be used as an element in defining the norm.

In addition, one can compare norms for various time-based subsets of a document collection to find individual news documents whose topics substantially deviate from the topics mentioned by other news sources. Sometimes such deviating individual documents are referred to as *deviation sources.*

From Context Relationships to Trend Graphs

Another approach to to exploring the evolution of concept relationships is to examine *temporal context relationships.* Temporal context relationships are most typically represented by two analytical tools: the *temporal context graph* and the *trend graph.*

Before describing these time-based, context-oriented analytical tools, we expend a little effort explicating the more general notions of *context* in document collections.

Indeed, both temporal context graphs and trend graphs build on the notion of the *context relationship* and its typical visual representation in the form of the *context graph*.

Context Phrases and Context Relationships

Generally, a *context relationship* in a document collection is the relationship within a set of concepts found in the document collection in relation to a separately specified concept (sometimes referred to as the *context* or the *context concept*). A context relationship search might entail identifying all relationships within a set of company names within the context of the concept "bankruptcy." A *context phrase* is the name given to a subset of documents in a document collection that is either labeled with all, or at least one, of the concepts in a specified set of concepts.

Formal definitions for both *context phrases* and the *context relationship* are as follows:

Definition II.11. Context Phrase: If D is a collection of documents and C is a set of concepts, $D/A(C)$ is the subset of documents in D labeled with all the concepts in C, *and $D/O(C)$ is the subset of documents in D labeled with at least one of the concepts in C. Both $A(C)$ and $O(C)$ are referred to as context phrases.*

Definition II.12. Context Relationship: If D is a collection of documents, c_1 and c_2 are individual concepts, and P is a context phrase, $R(D, c_1, c_2 \mid P)$ is the number of documents in D/P which include both c_1 and c_2. Formally, $R(D, c_1, c_2 \mid P) = |(D/A(\{c_1, c_2\}))|P|$.

The Context Graph

Context relationships are often represented by a *context graph*, which is a graphic representation of the relationship between a set of concepts (e.g., *countries*) as reflected in a corpus respect to a given context (e.g., *crude_oil*).

A context graph consists of a set of *vertices* (also sometimes referred to as *nodes*) and *edges*. The vertices (or nodes) of the graph represent concepts. Weighted "edges" denote the affinity between the concepts.

Each vertex in the context graph signifies a single concept, and two concepts are connected by an edge if their similarity, with respect to a predefined similarity function, is larger than a given threshold (similarity functions in graphing are discussed in greater detail in Chapter X). A context graph is defined with respect to a given context, which determines the context in which the similarity of concepts is of interest (see Figure II.1).

A context graph also has a formal definition:

Definition II.13. Context Graph: If D is a collection of documents, C is a set of concepts, and P is a context phrase, the *concept graph* of D, C, P is a weighted graph $G = (C, E)$, with nodes in C and a set of edges $E = (\{c_1, c_2\} \mid R(D, c_1, c_2 \mid P) > 0)$. For each edge, $\{c_1, c_2\} \in E$, one defines the weight of the edge, $w\{c_1, c_2\} = R(D, c_1, c_2 \mid P)$.

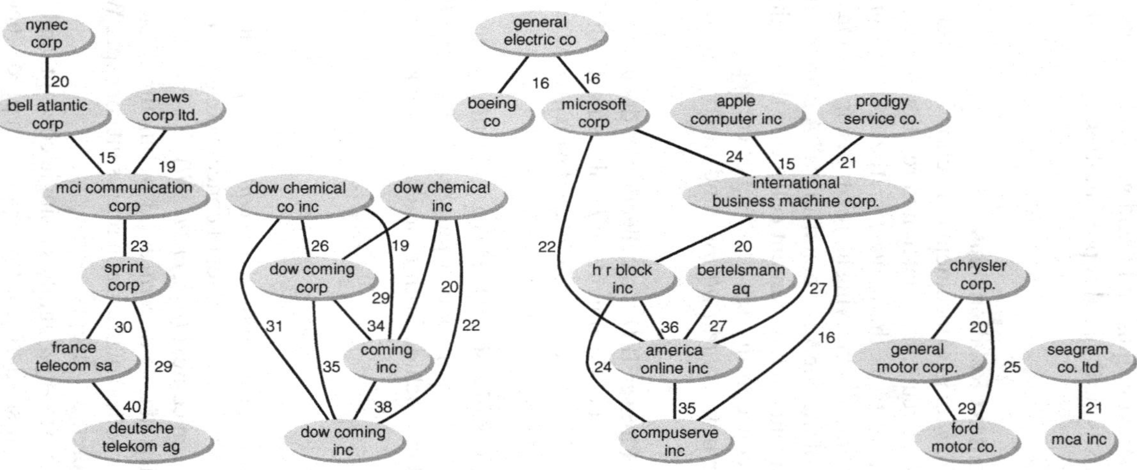

Figure II.1. Context graph for companies in the context of "joint venture." (From Feldman, Fresko, Hirsh, et al. 1998.)

It is often useful to be able to examine not just concept relationships within a given concept context but also to analyze the similarities and differences in context relationships across different temporal segments of the corpus. A *temporal context relationship* refers specifically to the relationship between a set of concepts, as reflected across these segments (identified by individual document date and time stamps) with respect to specified contexts over time. For investigation across segments, a selected subset of documents must be created that constitute a given temporal "segment" of the document collection as a whole.

Definition II.14. Temporal Selection ("Time Interval"): If D is a collection of documents and I is a time range, date range, or both, D_I is the subset of documents in D whose time stamp, date stamp, or both, is within I. The resulting selection is sometimes referred to as the *time interval.*

The formal definition for temporal context relationship builds on both this definition and that supplied earlier for a generic concept relationship (Definition II.12).

Definition II.15. Temporal Context Relationship: If D is a collection of documents, c_1 and c_2 are individual concepts, P is a context phrase, and I is the time interval, then $R_I(D, c_1, c_2 \mid P)$ is the number of documents in D_I in which c_1 and c_2 co-occur in the context of P – that is, $R_I(D, c_1, c_2 \mid P)$ is the number of D_I/P that include both c_1 and c_2.

A *temporal context graph*, then, can be defined as follows:

Definition II.16. Temporal Context Graph: If D is a collection of documents, C is a set of concepts, P is a context phrase, and I is the time range, the *temporal concept graph* of D, C, P, I is a weighted graph $G = (C, E_I)$ with set nodes in C and a set of edges E_I, where $E_I = (\{c_1, c_2\} \mid R(D, c_1, c_2 \mid P) > 0)$. For each edge, $\{c_1, c_2\} \in E$, one defines the weight of the edge by $w_I\{c_1, c_2\} = R_I(D, c_1, c_2 \mid P)$.

The Trend Graph

A *trend graph* is a very specialized representation that builds on the temporal context graph as informed by the general approaches found in trend analysis. A trend graph can be obtained by partitioning the entire timespan covered by a time- or date-stamped document collection, or both, into a series of consecutive time intervals. These intervals can then be used to generate a corresponding sequence of temporal context graphs.

This sequence of temporal context graphs can be leveraged to create combined or cumulative trend graphs that display the evolution of concept relationships in a given context by means of visual cues such as the character and relative weight of edges in the graph. For instance, several classes of edges may be used to indicate various conditions:

- ***New Edges*:** edges that did not exist in the previous graph.
- ***Increased Edges*:** edges that have a relatively higher weight in relation to the previous interval.

- ***Decreased Edges*:** edges that have a relatively decreased weight than the previous interval.
- ***Stable Edges*:** edges that have about the same weight as the corresponding edge in the previous interval.

Handling Dynamically Updated Data

There are many situations in which the document collection for a text mining system might require frequent – perhaps even constant – updating. This regularly occurs in environments in which the maintenance of data *currency* is at a premium such as when a user wants iteratively run searches on topical news, time-sensitive financial information, and so on. In such situations, there is a need for documents to be added dynamically to the document collection and a concurrent need for a user of the text mining system always – that is to say, at every instance of a new document's being added to the collection – to know the full and *current* set of patterns for the searches that he or she has run.

An obvious solution is simply to rerun the search algorithm the user is employing from scratch whenever there is a new data update. Unfortunately, this approach is computationally inefficient and resource intensive (e.g., I/O, memory capacity, disk capacity), resulting in unnecessary performance drawbacks. Additionally, users of text mining systems with large document collections or frequent updates would have to endure more significant interruptions in their knowledge mining activities than if a quicker updating mechanism employing methods of modifying search results on an increment-by-increment basis were implemented.

The more useful and sophisticated approach is to leverage knowledge from previous search runs as a foundation to which new information can be added incrementally. Several algorithms have been described for handling the incremental update situations in data mining, and these algorithms also have applicability in text mining. These include the *FUP*, FUP_2, and *Delta* algorithms, which all attempt to minimize the recomputation required for incremental updating of Apriori-style, frequent set, and association rule search results. Another algorithm, based on the notion of *border sets* in data mining, however, also offers a very efficient and robust mechanism for treating the incremental case when dealing with discovered frequent sets and associations from natural language documents.

The Borders Incremental Text Mining Algorithm

The Borders algorithm can be used to update search pattern results incrementally. It affords computational efficiency by reducing the number of scans for relations, reducing the number of candidates, and then performing no scan if there is no frequent set. This algorithm is also robust because it supports insertions and deletions as well as absolute and percentage-based thresholds.

The Borders algorithm is based on the notions of *border sets* and *negative borders*. In a sense, a border set can be seen as a notion related to that of a frequent set and may be defined as follows:

Definition II.17. Border Set: X is a border set if it is not a frequent set, but any proper subset $Y \subset X$ is a frequent set (see also Figure II.2).

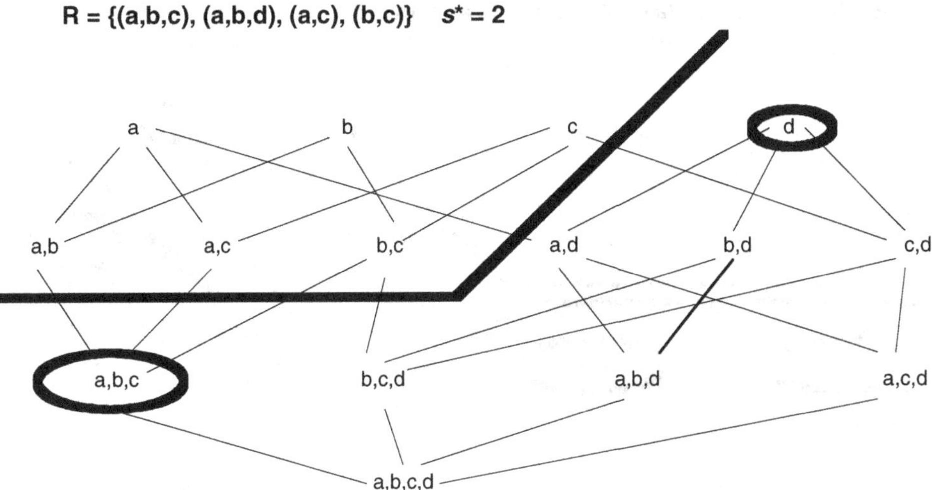

Figure II.2. Illustration of border sets.

The full benefit of the Borders algorithm can be appreciated when one attempts to accommodate incremental data updates of association rules. The Apriori algorithm for generating associations entails two main steps, beginning with the discovery of frequent sets through multiple scans of relations. This "first-step" search for frequent sets is very often the most computationally expensive part of association discovery. For each of the relation scans, a set of *candidates* is assembled and, during each scan, the support of each candidate is computed. The Borders algorithm functions initially to reduce the number of relation scans. Generally this serves to reduce the number of candidates. In addition, the algorithm does not perform a scan if no frequent set is identified.

Some important notational elements for discussing of the Borders algorithm are described below.

- Concept set $A = \{A_1, \ldots, A_m\}$
- Relations over A:
  - R_{old}: old relation
  - R_{inc}: increment
  - R_{new}: new combined relation
- $s(X/R)$: support of concept set X in the relation R
- s^*: minimum support threshold (*minsup*).

The Borders algorithm also makes use of two fundamental properties.

- ***Property 1***: if X is a new frequent set in R_{new}, then there is a subset $Y \subseteq X$ such that Y is a *promoted border*.
- ***Property 2***: if X is a new k-sized frequent set in R_{new}, then for each subset $Y \subseteq X$ of size $k-1$, Y is one of the following: (a) a promoted border, (b) a frequent set, or (c) an old frequent set with additional support in R_{inc}.

The Borders algorithm itself can be divided into two stages.

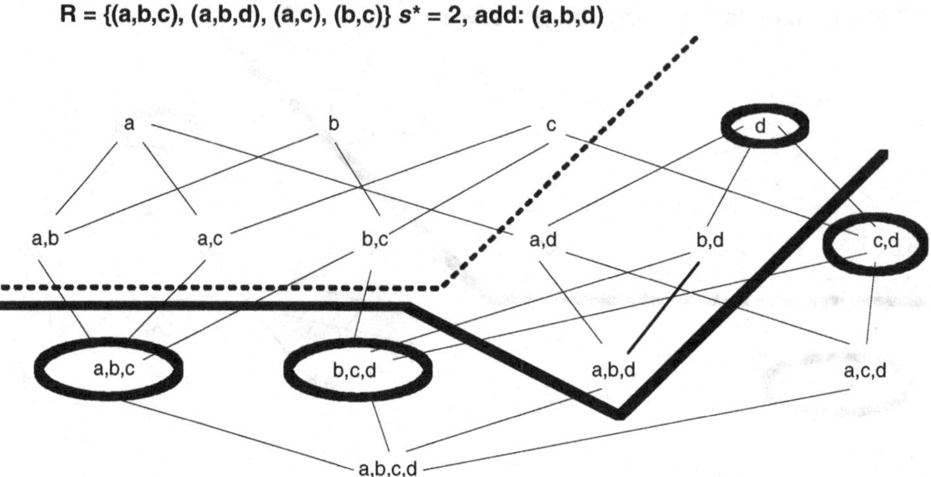

Figure II.3. Illustration of promoted borders and new borders.

- ***Stage 1: Finding Promoted Borders and Generating Candidates.***
  - Maintain the support for all borders and frequent sets.
  - When new data arrive for each border B of R_{old},
    - Compute $s(B, R_{\text{inc}})$
    - $s(B, R_{\text{new}}) = s(B, R_{\text{old}}) + s(B, R_{\text{inc}})$
  - If $s(B, R_{\text{new}}) \geq s^*$, then B is a *promoted border.*
    - If a *promoted border* does exist,
      - Run an Apriori-like algorithm, and
      - Generate *candidates* using the Property 1 and Property 2.
- ***Stage 2: Processing Candidates.***
  - $L_0 = PB(1), i = 1$
  - Although ($L_1 \neq \emptyset$ or $i \leq$ the largest promoted border)
    - Candidates $(I + 1) = \{X \mid |X| = i + 1$
      - $\exists \quad Y \subset X, |Y| = 1, Y \in PB(i) \cup L_i$
      - $\forall \quad Z \subset X, |Z| = 1, Z \in PB(i) \cup F(i) \cup L_i\}$
    - Scan relation and compute $s(X, R_{\text{new}})$ for each candidate X
    - $L_{i+1} = \{X \text{ candidate: } s(X, R_{\text{new}}) \geq s^*\}$.

See Figure II.3 for an illustration of promoted borders. With the Borders algorithm, full relations are never scanned if there is no new frequent set. Moreover, because of its parsimony in scanning for relations, the algorithm is likely to yield a small candidate set.

Percentage thresholds can be incorporated into incremental update schemes for text mining systems in conjunction with the Borders algorithm. For instance, we can define a threshold as σ percent of the size of the relations, and thus $S^* = \sigma|R|$. The key point for this type of operation is to redetermine the type of each set according to the new threshold before running the algorithm.

Deletions with absolute thresholds for incremental data can be accommodated relatively straightforwardly:

$$s(X, R_{\text{new}}) = s(X, R_{\text{old}}) - s(X, R_{\text{inc}}).$$

For percentage-type thresholds, the approach to handling deletions is perhaps a bit less intuitive but not too complex. In these cases, one can simply look at a deletion as a decrease in the absolute threshold and approach the deletion with the following equation:

$$s^*_{\text{new}} = \sigma(|R_{\text{old}}| + |R_{\text{inc}}|) = s^*_{\text{old}} - s^*_{\text{inc}}.$$

General changes to the threshold value should also be generally supported. Increasing the threshold is relatively easy, for only *borders* and *frequent sets* need be considered. On the other hand, an approach to decreasing the threshold might be to view border X with $s(B, R_{\text{new}}) \geq s^*_{\text{new}}$ as a promoted border before running the Borders algorithm.

II.1.6 Citations and Notes

Section II.1.–II.1.1

The primary source leveraged for information throughout Section II.1 is Feldman, Dagan, et al. (1998). Although focused more on visualization, Hearst (1995) also provides some interesting general background for the topic. Definitions II.1. through II.7. derive from descriptions of distribution and proportion types identified in Feldman, Dagan, et al. (1998).

Section II.1.2

Agrawal, Imielinski, and Swami (1993) and Agrawal and Srikant (1994) introduce the generation of frequent sets as part of the Apriori algorithm. Beyond Agrawal et al.'s seminal research on investigating *market basket*–type associations (Agrawal et al. 1993), other important works shaping the present-day understanding of frequent concept sets include Agrawal and Srikant (1994) and Silverstein, Brin, and Motwani (1999). In addition, Clifton and Cooley (1999) provides a useful treatment of market basket problems and describes how a document may be viewed as a market basket of named entities. Feldman, Aumann, Amir, et al. (1997); Rajman and Besancon (1997b); and Rajman and Besancon (1998) discuss the application of elements of the Apriori algorithm to textual data.

Algorithm 1 in Section II.1.2. was taken from Agrawal and Srikant (1994).

Rajman and Besancon (1997b) provides the background for Section II.1.2.'s discussion of the discovery of frequent concept sets. Although Algorithm 2 in Section II.1.2 is a generalized and simple one for frequent set generation based on the notions set forth in Agrawal et al. (1993) and Agrawal and Srikant (1994), Rajman and Besancon (1997b) provides a slightly different but also useful algorithm for accomplishing the same task.

Section II.1.3

In addition to presenting the framework for generating frequent sets, the treatment of the Apriori algorithm by Agrawal et al. (1993) also provided the basis for generating associations from large (structured) data sources. Subsequently, associations have been widely discussed in literature relating to knowledge discovery targeted at both structured and unstructured data (Agrawal and Srikant 1994; Srikant and Agrawal 1995; Feldman, Dagan, and Kloesgen 1996a; Feldman and Hirsh 1997; Feldman and Hirsh 1997; Rajman and Besancon 1998; Nahm and Mooney 2001; Blake and Pratt 2001; Montes-y-Gomez et al. 2001b; and others).

The definitions for association rules found in Section II.1.3. derive primarily from Agrawal et al. (1993), Montes-y-Gomez et al. (2001b), Rajman and Besancon (1998), and Feldman and Hirsh (1997). Definitions of minconf and minsup thresholds have been taken from Montes-y-Gomez et al. (2001b) and Agrawal et al. (1993). Rajman and Besancon (1998) and Feldman and Hirsh (1997) both point out that the discovery of frequent sets is the most computationally intensive stage of association generation.

The algorithm example for the discovery of associations found in Section II.3.3's Algorithm 3 comes from Rajman and Besancon (1998); this algorithm was directly inspired by Agrawal et al. (1993). The ensuing discussion of this algorithm's implications was influenced by Rajman and Besancon (1998), Feldman, Dagan, and Kloesgen (1996a), and Feldman and Hirsh (1997).

Maximal associations are most recently and comprehensively treated in Amir et al. (2003), and much of the background for the discussion of maximal associations in Section II.1.3 derives from this source. Feldman, Aumann, Amir, et al. (1997) is also an important source of information on the topic. The definition of a maximal association rule in Section II.1.3, along with Definition II.8 and its ensuing discussion, comes from Amir, Aumann, et al. (2003); this source is also the basis for Section II.1.3's discussion of the *M-factor* of a maximal association rule.

Section II.1.4

Silberschatz and Tuzhilin (1996) provides perhaps one of the most important discussions of interestingness with respect to knowledge discovery operations; this source has influenced much of Section II.1.5. Blake and Pratt (2001) also makes some general points on this topic.

Feldman and Dagan (1995) offers an early but still useful discussion of some of the considerations in approaching the isolation of interesting patterns in textual data, and Feldman, Dagan, and Hirsh (1998) provides a useful treatment of how to approach the subject of interestingness with specific respect to distributions and proportions. Definitions II.9 and II.10 derive from Feldman, Dagan, and Hirsh (1998).

Section II.1.5

Trend analysis in text mining is treated by Lent et al. (1997); Feldman and Dagan (1995); Feldman, Dagan, and Hirsh (1998); and Montes-y-Gomez et al. (2001b). Montes-y-Gomez et al. (2001b) offers an innovative introduction to the notions of *ephemeral associations* and *deviation detection*; this is the primary recent source for information relating to these two topics in Section II.1.5.

The analysis of sequences and trends with respect to knowledge discovery in structured data has been treated in several papers (Mannila, Toivonen, and Verkamo 1995;

Srikant and Agrawal 1996; Keogh and Smyth 1997; Bettini, Wang, and Joiodia 1996; Mannila et al. 1995; and Mannila, Toivonen, and Verkamo 1997). Algorithms based on the identification of *episodes* (Mannila et al. 1995) and *sequential patterns* (Srikant and Agrawal 1996) in large data repositories have been described as mechanisms for better mining of implicit trends in data over time. Related work on the discovery of time series analysis has also been discussed (Agrawal and Srikant 1995; Keogh and Smyth 1997).

Lent et al. (1997) and Feldman, Aumann, Zilberstein, et al. (1997) emphasize that trend analysis focused on text mining relates to collections of documents that can be viewed as subcollections defined, in part, by time. These two works are among the most important entry points for the literature of trend analysis in text mining. Montes-y-Gomez et al. (2001b) also makes very interesting contributions to the discussion of the topic.

Definitions related to ephemeral associations come from Montes-y-Gomez et al. (2001b); the terms *ephemeral association* and *deviation detection* are used in this chapter within the general definitional context of this source. Use of the correlation measure *r* in the detection of ephemeral associations also comes from this source, building on original work found in Freund and Walpole (1990). Finally, the examples used to illustrate direct and inverse ephemeral associations are based on the discussions contained in Montes-y-Gomez et al. (2001b).

The discussion of deviation detection in Section II.1.5 has been shaped by several sources, including Montes-y-Gomez et al. (2001b); Knorr, Ng, and Tucatov (2000); Arning, Agrawal, Raghavan (1996); Feldman and Dagan (1995); and Feldman, Aumann, Zilberstein, et al. (1997). Much of the terminology in this section derives from Montes-y-Gomez et al. (2001b). The term *deviation sources* was coined in Montes-y-Gomez et al. (2001b).

Much of Section II.1.5's discussion of context and trend graphs derives directly from Feldman, Aumann, Zilberstein, et al. (1997) as do Definitions II.11, II.12, II.13, II.14, II.15, and II.16. The trend graph described in Section II.3.5 has also, in a general way, been influenced by Lent et al. (1997).

Feldman, Amir, et al. (1996) was an early work focusing on measures that would support a text mining system's ability to handle dynamically updated data. The *FUP* incremental updating approach comes from Cheung et al. (1996), the FUP_2 is formalized in Cheung, Lee, and Kao (1997), and the *Delta* algorithms were identified in Feldman, Amir, et al. (1996).

The notion of border sets was introduced, with respect to data mining, in Mannila and Toivonen (1996). Much of the discussion of border sets in this section is an application of the border set ideas of Mannila and Toivonen (1996) to collections of text documents. The Apriori algorithm for generating associations was identified in Agrawal et al. (1993) and Agrawal and Srikant (1994).

II.2 USING BACKGROUND KNOWLEDGE FOR TEXT MINING

II.2.1 Domains and Background Knowledge

As has already been described in Section II.1, concepts derived from the representations of documents in text mining systems belong not only to the descriptive attributes of particular documents but generally also to *domains*. A domain can be loosely defined as a specialized area of interest for which formal *ontologies, lexicons*, and *taxonomies* of information may be created. Domains can exist for very broad areas of interest (e.g., *economics* or *biology*) or for more narrow niches (e.g., *macroeconomics, microeconomics, mergers, acquisitions, fixed income, equities, genomics, proteomics, zoology, virology, immunology*, etc.).

Much of what has been written about the use of *domain knowledge* (also referred to as *background knowledge*) in classic data mining concerns its use as a mechanism for constraining knowledge discovery search operations. From these works, it is possible to generalize three primary forms of usable background knowledge from external sources for data mining applications: (a) constraints, (b) attribute relationship rules, and (c) "hierarchical trees" or "category domain knowledge." More recent literature, however, suggests that other types and implementations of background knowledge may also be useful in data mining operations.

Text mining systems, particularly those with some pronounced elements of domain specificity in their orientation, can leverage information from formal external knowledge sources for these domains to greatly enhance a wide variety of elements in their system architecture. Such elements include those devoted to preprocessing, knowledge discovery, and presentation-layer operations. Even text mining systems without pronounced elements of domain specificity in their design or usage, however, can potentially benefit by the inclusion of information from knowledge sources relating to broad but still generally useful domains such as *the English language* or *world almanac–type facts*.

Indeed, background knowledge can be used in text mining preprocessing operations to enhance concept extraction and validation activities. Furthermore, access to background knowledge can play a vital role in the development of meaningful, consistent, and normalized concept hierarchies.

Background knowledge, in addition, may be utilized by other components of a text mining system. For instance, one of the most clear and important uses of background knowledge in a text mining system is the construction of meaningful constraints for knowledge discovery operations. Likewise, background knowledge may also be used to formulate constraints that allow users greater flexibility when browsing large result sets or in the formatting of data for presentation.

II.2.2 Domain Ontologies

Text mining systems exploit background knowledge that is encoded in the form of *domain ontologies*. A domain ontology, sometimes also referred to less precisely as a *background knowledge source* or *knowledge base*, might be informally defined as the set of all the classes of interest and all the relations between these classes for a given domain. Perhaps another way of describing this is to say that a domain ontology houses all the facts and relationships for the domain it supports. Some see a grouping of facts and relationships as a *vocabulary* constructed in such a way as to be both understandable by humans and readable by machines.

A more formal – albeit very generic – definition for a domain ontology can be attempted with the following notation proposed by Hotho et al. (2003) derived generally from research into formal concept analysis:

Definition II.18. Domain Ontology with Domain Hierarchy: A *domain ontology* is a tuple $O := (C, \leq c)$ consisting of a set C whose elements are called *concepts* and a partial order $\leq c$ on C, which is labeled a *concept hierarchy* or *taxonomy*.

One example of a real-world ontology for a broad area of interest can be found in *WordNet*, an online, public domain ontology originally created at Princeton University that has been designed to model the domain of the English language. Version 1.7 of WordNet contains approximately 110,000 unique concepts (referred to as *synsets* by WordNet's designers); the ontology also has a sophisticated concept hierarchy that supports relation-type information.

WordNet can be used as a "terminological knowledge base" of concepts, concept types, and concept relations to provide broadly useful background knowledge relating to the domain of the English language. A WordNet *synset* represents a single unique instance of a concept meaning related to other *synsets* by some type of specified relation.

Interestingly, WordNet also supports a lexicon of about 150,000 lexical entries (in WordNet's terminology "words") that might more generally be viewed as a list of lexical identifiers or "names" for the concepts stored in the WordNet ontology. Users of WordNet can query both its ontology and its lexicon.

Another ontology implementation that models a narrower subject area domain is the Gene Ontology™ or GO knowledge base administered by the Gene Ontology Consortium. The GO knowledge base serves as a controlled vocabulary that describes gene products in terms of their associated biological processes, cellular components, and molecular functions. In this controlled vocabulary, great care is taken both to construct and define concepts and to specify the relationships between them. Then, the controlled vocabulary can be used to annotate gene products.

GO actually comprises several different structured knowledge bases of information related to various species, coordinates, synonyms and so on. Each of these ontologies constitutes structured vocabularies in the form of directed acyclic graphs (DAGs) that represent a network in which each concept ("term" in the GO terminology) may be the "child" node of one or more than one "parent" node. An example of this from the GO molecular function vocabulary is the function concept *transmembrane receptor protein-tyrosine kinase* and its relationship to other function concepts; it is a subclass both of the parent concept *transmembrane receptor* and of the parent concept *protein tyrosine kinase*. Figure II.4 provides a high-level view of the Gene Ontology structure.

Several researchers have reported that the GO knowledge base has been used for background knowledge and other purposes. Moreover, the Gene Ontology Consortium has developed various specialized browsers and mapping tools to help developers of external systems leverage the background knowledge extractable from the GO knowledge base.

II.2.3 Domain Lexicons

Text mining systems also leverage background knowledge contained in *domain lexicons*. The names of domain concepts – and the names of their relations – make up a domain ontology's lexicon. The following definitions come from Hotho et al. (2003).

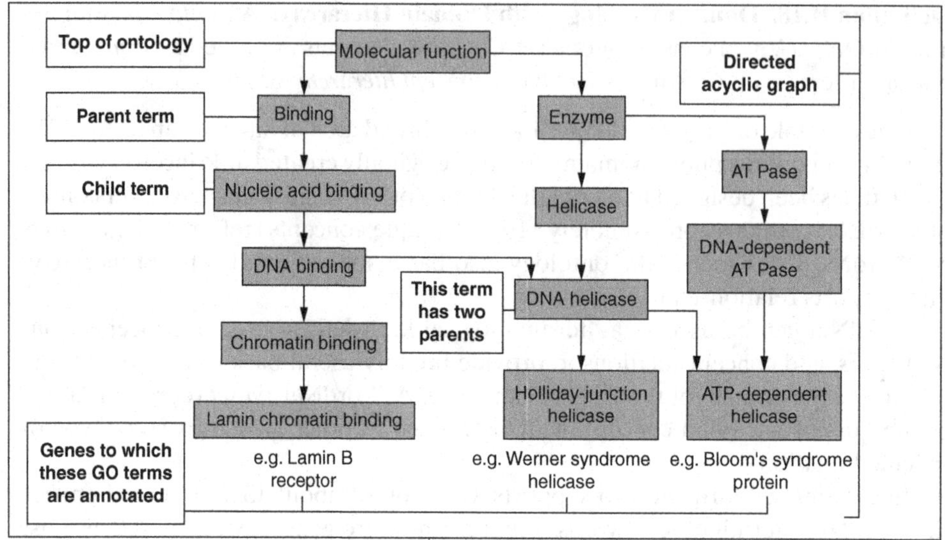

Figure II.4. Schematic of the Gene Ontology structure. (From GO Consortium 2001.)

Definition II.19. Domain Lexicon: A lexicon for an ontology O is a tuple Lex: $= (S_C, Ref_C)$ consisting of a set S_C, whose elements are called *names of concepts*, and a relation $Ref_C \subseteq S_C \times c$ called *lexical reference for concepts* for which $(c, c) \in Ref_C$ holds for all $c \in C \cap S_C$.

Based on Ref_C, we define, for $s \in S_C$, $Ref_C\ (s)$: $= \{c \in C \mid (s, c) \in Ref_C\}$ and, for $c \in C$, $Ref^{-1}{}_C\ (c)$: $= \{s \in S_C \mid (s, c) \in Ref_C\}$.

For the typical situation – such as the WordNet example – of an ontology with a lexicon, one could also use a simple notation:

Definition II.20. Domain Ontology with Lexicon: An *ontology with lexicon* is a pair (O, Lex), where O is an ontology and Lex is a lexicon for O.

A lexicon such as that available with WordNet can serve as the entry point to background knowledge. Using a lexicon, a text mining system could normalize the concept identifiers available for annotation of documents in its corpus during preprocessing in a way that supports, by means of the lexicon's related ontology, both the resolution of synonyms and the extraction of rich semantic relationship information about concepts.

II.2.4 Introducing Background Knowledge into Text Mining Systems

Background knowledge can be introduced into text mining systems in various ways and at various points in a text mining system's architecture. Although there are may be any number of arguments about how background knowledge can enrich the value of knowledge discovery operations on document collections, there are three main *practical* reasons why background information is so universally important in text mining systems.

First, background knowledge can be used in a text mining system to limit pattern abundance. Background knowledge can be crafted into constraints that allow for more efficient and meaningful queries; such constraints can be used for a variety of other purposes as well. Second, background knowledge is an extremely efficient mechanism for resolving questions of concept synonymy and polysemy at the level of search. Access to an ontology that stores both lexical references and relations allows for various types of resolution options. Third, background knowledge can be leveraged in preprocessing operations to create both a consistent lexical reference space and consistent hierarchies for concepts that will then be useful throughout other subsequent query, presentation, and refinement operations.

Perhaps the simplest method to integrate background knowledge into a text mining system is by using it in the construction of meaningful query constraints. For instance, with respect to association discovery, concepts in a text mining system can be preprocessed into either some hierarchical form or clusters representing some limited number of categories or classes of concepts. These categories can then be compared against some relevant external knowledge source to extract interesting attributes for these categories and relations between categories.

A tangible example of this kind of category- or class-oriented background knowledge constraint is a high-level category like *company*, which might, after reference to some commercial ontology of company information, be found to have commonly occurring attributes such as *ProductType, Officers*, *CEO*, *CFO*, *BoardMembers, CountryLocation, Sector, Size*, or *NumberOfEmployees*. The category *company* could also have a set of relations to other categories such as *IsAPartnerOf, IsACustomerOf, IsASupplierTo, IsACompetitorTo,* or *IsASubsidiaryOf*. These category attributes and relations could then be used as constraints available to a user on a pick list when forming a specific association-discovery query relating either to the class *company* or to a concept that is a particular member of that class.

The resulting query expression (with constraint parameter) would allow the user to specify the LHS and RHS of his or her query more carefully and meaningfully. The inclusion of these types of constraints not only increases user interactivity with a text mining system because the user will be more involved in specifying interesting query parameters but can also limit the amount of unwanted patterns resulting from underspecified or inappropriately specified initial queries.

Further, background information constraints can be used in an entirely different way – namely, in the formatting of presentation-level displays of query results. For instance, even if a user did not specify particular constraints as parameters to his or her query expression, a text mining system could still "add value" to the display of the result set by, for instance, highlighting certain associations for which particular preset constraint conditions have been met. An example of this might be that, in returning a result set to a query for all *companies* associated with *crude oil*, the system could highlight those companies identified as suppliers of crude oil in blue whereas those companies that are buyers of crude oil could be highlighted in red. Such color coding might aid in users' exploration of data in the result set because these data provide more information to the user than simply presenting a bland listing of associations differentiated only by confidence level.

Another common use of background knowledge is in the creation of consistent hierarchical representations of concepts in the document collection. During preprocessing – or even during a query – groups of concepts can be compared against some normalized hierarchical form generated from an ontology. The resulting concept hierarchy has the benefit of being both informed by the domain knowledge about relationships collected in the ontology and more consistently integrated with the external source in the event that other types of system operations require reference to information contained in the ontology.

II.2.5 Real-World Example: FACT

FACT (Finding Associations in Collections of Text) was a text mining system developed by Feldman and others during the late 1990s. It represented a focused effort at enhancing association discovery by means of several constraint types supplied by a background knowledge source. In this, it created a very straightforward example of how background knowledge could be leveraged to clear practical effect in knowledge discovery operations on document collections.

General Approach and Functionality

The FACT system might essentially be seen as an advanced tool focused specifically on the discovery of associations in collections of keyword (concept)-labeled text documents. Centering on the association discovery query, the FACT system provided a robust query language through which a user could specify queries over the implicit collection of possible query results supported by the documents in the collection.

Rather than requiring the specification of an explicit query expression in this language, FACT presented the user with a simple-to-use graphical interface in which a user's various discovery tasks could be specified, and the underlying query language provided a well-defined semantics for the discovery actions performed by the user through the interface (see Figure II.5).

Perhaps most importantly, FACT was able to exploit some basic forms of background knowledge. Running against a document collection of newswire articles, FACT used a simple textual knowledge source (the CIA World Factbook) to exploit knowledge relating to countries. FACT was able to leverage several attributes relating to a country (size, population, export commodities, organizational memberships, etc.) as well as information about relationships between countries (e.g., whether countries were neighbors or trading partners, had a common language, had a common border, etc.).

Using this background knowledge to construct meaningful constraints, FACT allowed a user, when making a query, to include constraints over the set of desired results. Finally, FACT also exploited these constraints in how it structured its search for possible results. This background knowledge thus enabled FACT to, for example, discover associations between a *G7* country, for instance, that appeared as a concept label of a document and some other *nonbordering G7* countries that also appeared as concept labels of the document.

System Architecture

FACT's system architecture was straightforward. In a sense, all system components centered around the execution of a query (see Figure II.6). The system's query

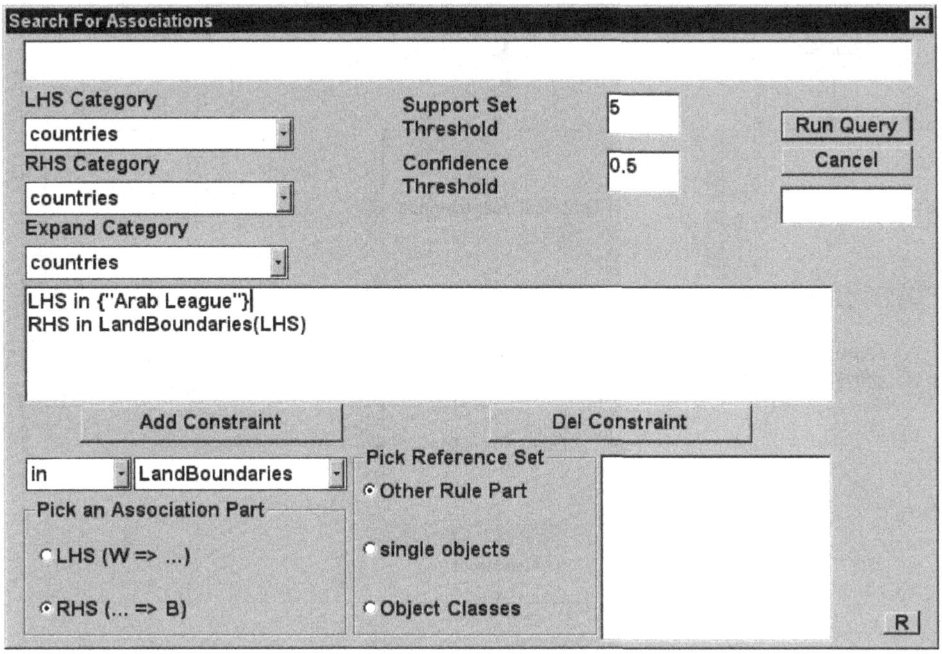

Figure II.5. FACT's query specification interface. (From Feldman and Hirsh 1997. Reprinted with permission of John Wiley and Sons.)

execution core operations took three inputs – the annotated document collection, distilled background knowledge, and a user's knowledge-discovery query – to create output that was passed to a presentation-layer tool that formatted the result set for display and user browsing.

The system provided an easy-to-use interface for a user to compose and execute an association discovery query, supplemented by constraints for particular types of keywords that had been derived from an external knowledge source. The system then ran the fully constructed query against a document collection whose documents were represented by keyword annotations that had been pregenerated by a series of text categorization algorithms.

Result sets could be returned in ways that also took advantage of the background knowledge–informed constraints. A user could explore a result set for a query and then refine it using a different combination of constraints.

Implementation

The document collection for the FACT system was created from the Reuters-22173 text categorization test collection, a collection of documents that appeared on the Reuters newswire in 1987. This collection obviated the need to build any system elements to preprocess the document data by using categorization algorithms.

The Reuters-22173 documents were preassembled and preindexed with categories by personnel from Reuters Ltd. and Carnegie Group, Inc., and some final formatting was manually applied. The Reuters personnel tagged each document

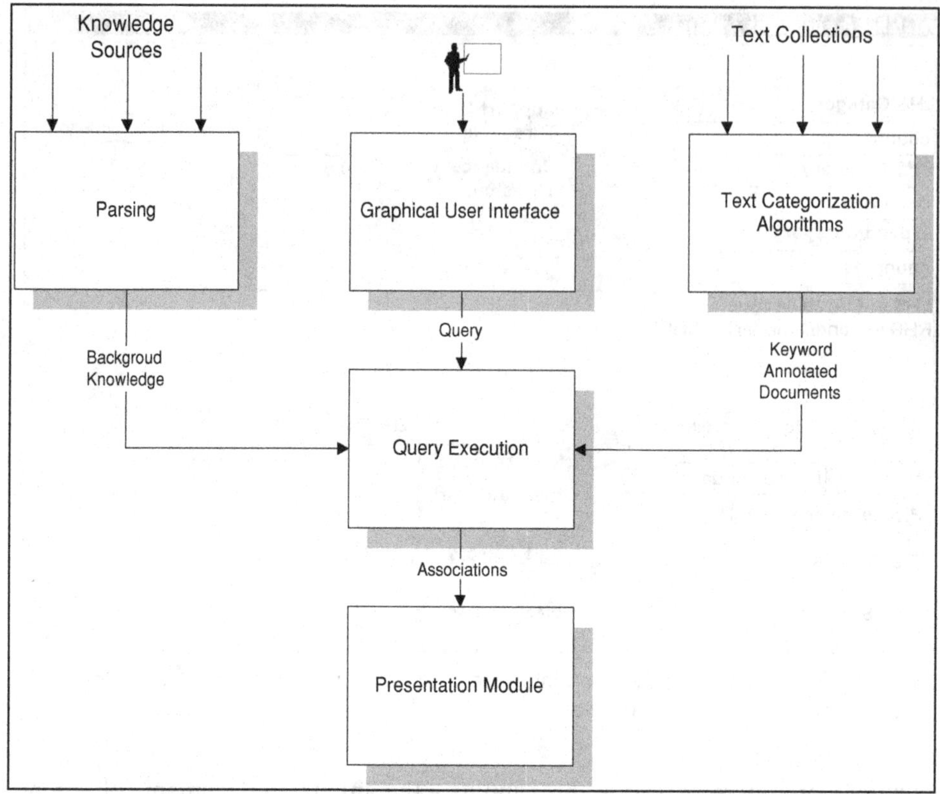

Figure II.6. System architecture of FACT. (From Feldman and Hirsh 1997. Reprinted with permission of John Wiley and Sons.)

with a subset of 135 keywords that fell into five overarching categories: *countries*, *topics*, *people*, *organizations*, and *stock exchanges*.

The 1995 CIA World Factbook that served as the FACT system's ostensible ontology amd background knowledge source was a structured document containing information about each of the countries of the world and was divided into six sections: Geography, People, Government, Economy, Communications, and Defense Forces. For experimentation with the Reuters-22173 data, the following background information was extracted for each country *C*:

- **MemberOf:** all organizations of which *C* is a member (e.g., G7, Arab League, EC),
- **LandBoundaries:** the countries that have a land border with *C*,
- **NaturalResources:** the natural resources of *C* (e.g., crude, coal, copper, gold),
- **ExportCommodities:** the main commodities exported by *C* (e.g., meat, wool, wheat),
- **ExportPartners:** the principal countries to which *C* exports its ExportCommodities,
- **ImportCommodities:** the main commodities imported by *C* (e.g., meat, wool, wheat),

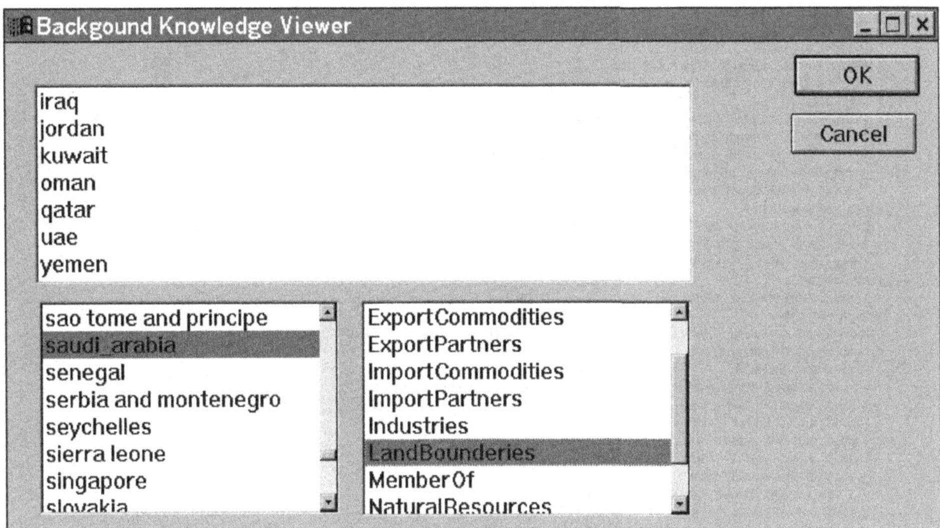

Figure II.7. FACT's background knowledge viewer showing the countries having land boundaries with Saudi Arabia. (From Feldman and Hirsh 1997. Reprinted with permission of John Wiley and Sons.)

- **ImportPartners:** the principal countries from which C imports its Import Commodities,
- **Industries:** the main industries of C (e.g., iron, steel, machines, textiles, chemicals), and
- **Agriculture:** the main agricultural products of C (e.g., grains, fruit, potatoes, cattle).

The first boldfaced element before the colon defines a unary predicate, and the remainder of each entry constitutes a binary predicate over the set of keywords that can label the documents in the Reuters-22173 collection. Users could browse this background knowledge in FACT by means of a utility (see Figure II.7).

For its main association-discovery algorithm, FACT implemented a version of the two-phase Apriori algorithm. After generating σ-covers, however, FACT modified the traditional association-discovery phase to handle the various types of constraints that had been generated from the CIA World Factbook.

Upon completion of a query, FACT executed its query code and passed a result set back to a specialized presentation tool, the FACT system's association browser. This browser performed several functions. First, it filtered out redundant results. Second, it organized results hierarchically – identifying commonalties among the various discovered associations and sorting them in decreasing order of confidence.

Further, the tool housed this hierarchical, sorted representation of the result set in a screen presentation that enabled a user to browse the titles of documents supporting each of the individual associations in the result set simply by pointing and clicking on that association (see Figure II.8).

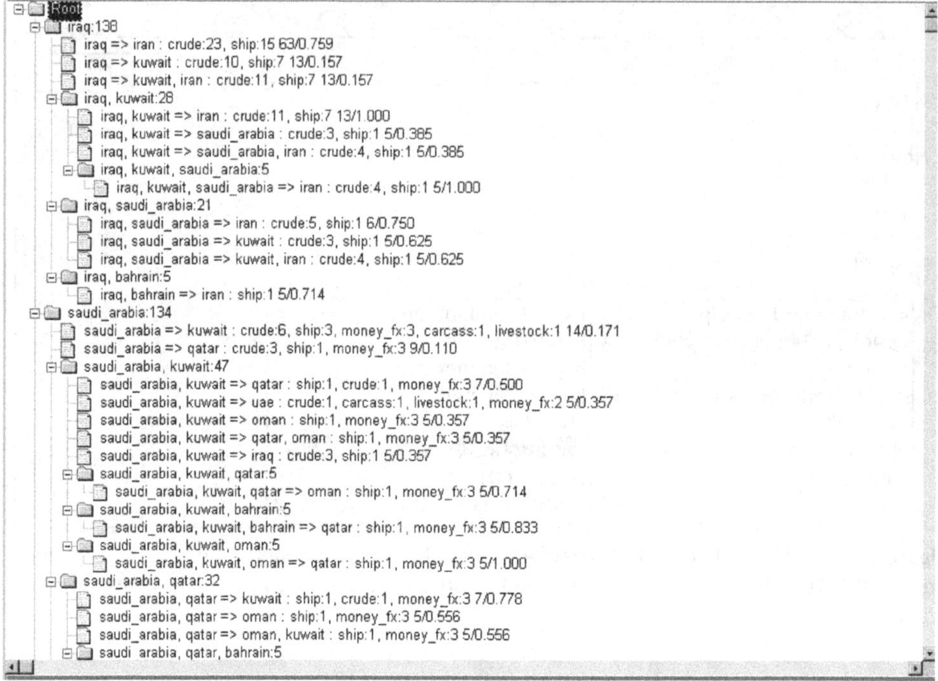

Figure II.8. FACT's association browser presentation module showing a result set for associations of Arab League countries with countries sharing a border. (From Feldman and Hirsh 1997. Reprinted with permission of John Wiley and Sons.)

Experimental Performance Results

FACT appeared to perform well on queries of the form "find all associations between a set of countries including *Iran* and any person" and "find all associations between a set of topics including *Gold* and any country" as well as more complex queries that included constraints. One interesting – albeit still informal and crude – experiment performed on the system was to see if there was any performance difference (based on a comparison of CPU time) between query templates with and without constraints. In most cases, the queries involving constraints extracted from background knowledge appeared to be noticeably more efficient in terms of CPU time consumption.

Some practical difficulties were encountered when trying to convert the CIA World Factbook into unary and binary predicates when the vocabulary in the Factbook differed from the universe of keywords labeling the Reuters documents (Feldman and Hirsh 1997). This is a problem that can creep into almost any text mining system that attempts to integrate background knowledge. FACT's designers put in place a point solution to resolve this problem by including additional background knowledge from a standard reference dictionary to help at least provide a basic definition of synonyms.

Obviously, today, advanced text mining systems involving background knowledge can integrate with more sophisticated dictionary-type ontologies like WordNet to resolve problems with synonymy. Further, today's designers of text mining systems can also consider various strategies for including background knowledge in preprocessing routines to help create more consistency in the concept tags that annotate document collections before the execution of any knowledge discovery algorithms.

II.2.6 Citations and Notes

Section II.2.1

For general discussion of the use of background knowledge to construct constraints in classic data mining, see Anand, Bell, and Hughes (1995) and Yoon et al. (1999). Kopanis, Avouris, and Daskalaki (2002) discusses other uses for background knowledge in data mining systems. Feldman and Hirsh (1996a) provides an early discussion of various uses of background knowledge within a text mining system.

Section II.2.2

The informal definition for a domain ontology in Section II.2.2 comes from Craven and Kumlien (1999). The definition for a domain vocabulary was derived from Gruber (1993). Definition II.18 has been taken from Hotho et al. (2003); this source provides much of the background and definitional information for the topics discussed throughout Sections II.2.2 through II.2.4.

A large body of literature exists on the subject of WordNet, but the basic overview is contained in Martin (1995); the identification of WordNet as a "terminological knowledge base" also comes from this source. Descriptions of WordNet's lexicon, concept hierarchy, and ontological structure rely on information published in Rodriguez, Gomez-Hidalgo, and Diaz-Agudo (1997) and Hotho et al. (2003).

The Gene Ontology knowledge base is described in GO Consortium (2000). The schematic of the GO knowledge base displayed in Figure II.4 comes from GO Consortium (2001); the example in Section II.2.2 involving the function concept *transmembrane receptor protein-tyrosine kinase* was also taken from this source. Hill et al. (2002) and Hirschman et al. (2002) have both reported use of the GO knowledge base for background knowledge purposes in knowledge discovery systems.

Section II.2.3

Definitions II.19 and II.20 as well as the WordNet examples used in discussing these definitions come from Hotho et al. (2003).

Sections II.2.4.–II.2.5

The FACT system is described in Feldman and Hirsh (1996a), Feldman and Hirsh (1996b), and Feldman and Hirsh (1997), and it influenced a substantial amount of later discussion of text mining systems (Landau, Feldman, Aumann, et al. 1998; Blake and Pratt 2001; Montes-y-Gomez et al. 2001b; Nahm and Mooney 2001; and others). Most of the descriptions of the FACT system found in Section II.2.5 derive from Feldman and Hirsh (1997).

II.3 TEXT MINING QUERY LANGUAGES

Query languages for the type of generalized text mining system described in this chapter must serve several straightforward purposes. First, these languages must allow for the specification and execution of one of the text mining system's search algorithms. Second, they generally need to allow for multiple constraints to be appended to a search argument; such constraints need to be specifiable by a user. Third, the query languages typically also need to perform some types of auxiliary filtering and redundancy to minimize pattern overabundance in result sets.

Most text mining systems offer access to their query language either through a more abstracted and "friendly" interface that acts to assist the user by means of pick lists, pull-down menus, and scroll bars containing preset search types and constraints or through more direct "command-line" access to the query language that exposes query language expressions in their full syntax. Some text mining systems offer both.

It is important in any implementation of a query language interface for designers of text mining systems to consider carefully the usage situations for the interfaces they provide. For instance, having a user-friendly, graphically oriented tool may greatly enhance a system's ease of use, but if this tool severely limits the types of queries that may be performed it may not meet a strict cost–benefit analysis.

Similarly, direct access to a text mining system's query language to support the construction of ad hoc queries can be very advantageous for some users trying to experiment with queries involving complex combinations of constraints. If, however, such a direct query interface does not allow for robust storage, reuse, renaming, and editing of ad hoc queries as query templates, such "low level" access to the query language can become very inefficient and frustrating for users.

II.3.1 Real World Example: KDTL

The text mining query language KDTL (knowledge discovery in text language) was first introduced in 1996 as the query language engine supporting the FACT system and was subsequently more fully described as a central element of Feldman, Kloesgen, et al.'s later Document Explorer system.

KDTL's primary function is to provide a mechanism for performing queries that isolate interesting patterns. A Backus Naur Form (BNF) description of KDTL is shown in Figure II.9.

KDTL supports all three main patter-discovery query types (i.e., distributions, frequent sets, and associations) as well as less common graphing outputs (i.e., keyword graph, directed keyword graph). Also notice that each query contains one algorithmic statement and several constraint statements.

The constraint part of the query is structured in such a way that the user needs first to select a single relevant component – that is, the left-hand side (LHS) of the association, right-hand side (RHS), frequent set, or a path in a keyword graph. Then, all subsequent constraint statements are applied to this component.

When specifying set relations, the user can optionally specify background predicates to be applied to the given expressions. KDTL intentionally contains some redundancy in the constraints statements to facilitate easier specification of queries.

II.3.2 KDTL Query Examples

Here are some typical examples of KDTL queries executed on the Reuters-22173 document collection used by FACT and described in Section II.5.

```
Algorithmic statements:

gen_rule() : generate all matching association rules
gen_frequent_set(): generate all matching frequent sets
gen_kg() : generate a keyword graph
gen_dkg() : generate a directed keyword graph
gen_dist() : generate a distribution

Constraint statements:

set_filter(<Set>) - the set MUST meet the following
constraints
set_not_filter(<Set>) - the set MUST NOT meet the following
constraints

<Set> ::=  frequent_set | left | right | path

contain([<background predicate>], <Expression>) -
      the designated set must contain <expression> (or
      <background predicate>(<expression>))
subset([<background predicate>],<Expression>) -
     the designated set is a subset of <expression> (or
      <background predicate>(<expression>))
disjoint([<background predicate>],<Expression>) -
     the designated set and <expression> are disjoint (or
      <background predicate>(<expression>))
equal([<background predicate>],<Expression>) -
     the designated set is equal to <expression> (or
      <background predicate>(<expression>))

all_has(<Expression>) -
     all members of the designated set are descendents of
      <expression> in the taxonomy
one_has(<Expression>) -
     at least one of the members of the designated set is a
      descendent of <expression>

property_count(<Expression>,<low>,<high>) -
     # of members that are descendents of <expression> is in
      the specified range
size(<Expression>,<low>,<high>) -
     size of the designated set is in the specified range

Set_conf(real)
Set_supp(integer)

<Expression> ::= Keyword | Category |
     <Expression>,<Expression> |
                         <Expression> ; <Expression>
<high> ::= integer
<low>  ::= integer
```

Figure II.9. BNF description of KDTL. (From Feldman, Kloesgen, and Zilberstein 1997a. Reprinted with permission of Springer Science and Business Media.)

In order to query only those associations that correlate between a set of countries including Iran and a person, the KDTL query expression would take the following form:

set_filter(left); all_has({"countries"}); contain({"iran"});
set_filter(right); all_has({"people"}); property_count("people",1,1);
set_supp(4); set_conf(0.5); gen_rule();

Run against the Reuters collection, the system would find four associations as a result of this particular query, all of which would have Reagan in the RHS.

(6.54%) Iran, Nicaragua, USA ⇒ Reagan
(6.50%) Iran, Nicaragua ⇒ Reagan
(18.19%) Iran, USA ⇒ Reagan
(19.10%) Iran ⇒ Reagan

The interesting associations are those that include Iran and Nicaragua on the LHS. Upon querying the document collection, one can see that, when Iran and Nicaragua are in the document, then, if there is any person in the document, Reagan will be in that document too. In other words, the association Iran, Nicaragua, <person> ⇒ Reagan has 100-percent confidence and is supported by six documents. The <person> constraint means that there must be at least one person name in the document.

As another example, if one wanted to infer which people were highly correlated with West Germany (Reuters collection was from a period before the reunion of Germany), a query that looked for correlation between groups of one to three people and West Germany would be formulated.

set_filter("left"); size(1,3); all_has({"people"});
set_filter("right"); equal({"west_germany"});
set_supp(10); set_conf(0.5); gen_rule();

The system found five such associations; in all them the people on the LHS were senior officials of the West German government. Kohl was the Chancellor, Poehl was the president of the Central Bank, Bangemann was the Economic Minister, and Stoltenberg was the Finance Minister. If one wanted to infer from a document collection who the high officials of a given country are, a similar query would probably yield a reasonably accurate answer.

This type of example can also be used to show how background knowledge can be leveraged to eliminate trivial associations. For instance, if a user is very familiar with German politics and not interested in getting these particular associations, he or she might like to see associations between people who are not German citizens and Germany. Adding the constraints *set_filter_not("left"); equal(nationality, "west_germany");* will eliminate all the associations shown below.

(8.100%) Poehl, Stoltenberg ⇒ West Germany
(6.100%) Bangemann ⇒ West Germany
(11.100%) Kohl ⇒ West Germany
(21.80%) Poehl ⇒ West Germany
(44.75%) Stoltenberg ⇒ West Germany

II.3.3 KDTL Query Interface Implementations

In Figures II.10 and II.11, one can see two elements of a sample GUI for defining KDTL queries. In the KDTL Query Editor (see Figure II.10), a user builds a query expression with one constraint at a time.

The tabbed dialog boxes in Figure II.11 demonstrate how the user defines a single constraint. Several different types of set constraints are supported, including background and numerical size constraints.

The results of a typical query – of the kind defined in Figures II.10 and II.11 – can be seen in Figure II.12.

In this query, the object was to find all associations that connect a set of countries and a set of economical indicator topics if trade is not in the set. Only one association satisfies all these constraints. If the last constraint had been lifted – and one allowed "trade" to be in the RHS of the association – the system would have returned 18 associations.

II.3.4 Citations and Notes

Sections II.3–II.3.2

The descriptions of KDTL in Section II.3, as well as the example of the language and the various screen shots of query interfaces, primarily come from Feldman, Kloesgen, and Zilberstein (1997a). See also Feldman and Hirsh (1997).

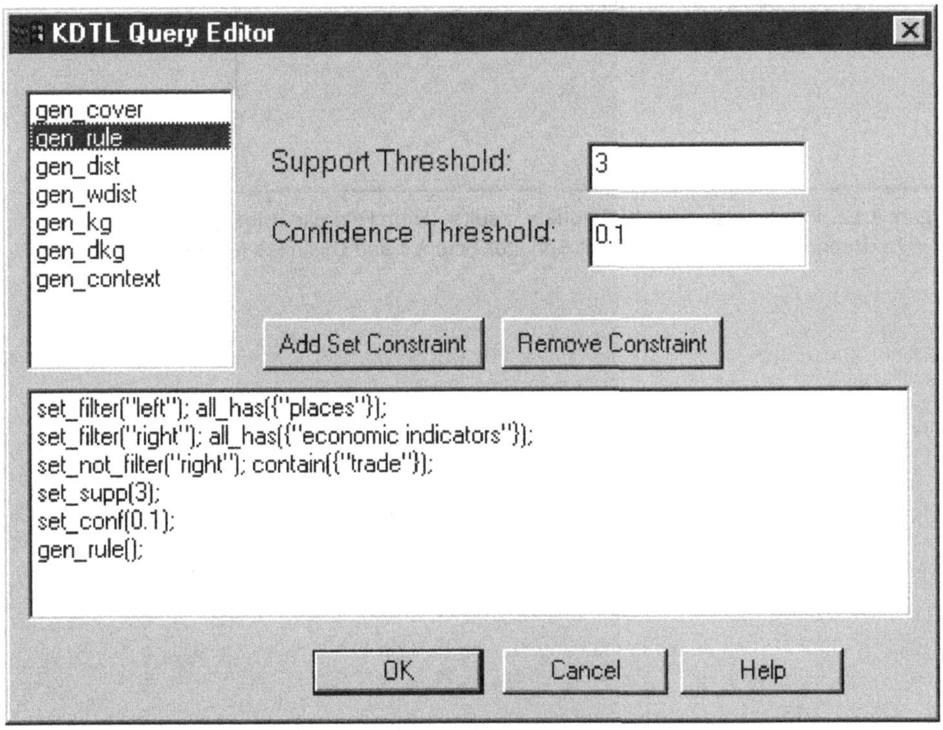

Figure II.10. Defining a KDTL query. (From Feldman, Kloesgen, and Zilberstein 1997a. Reprinted with permission of Springer Science and Business Media.)

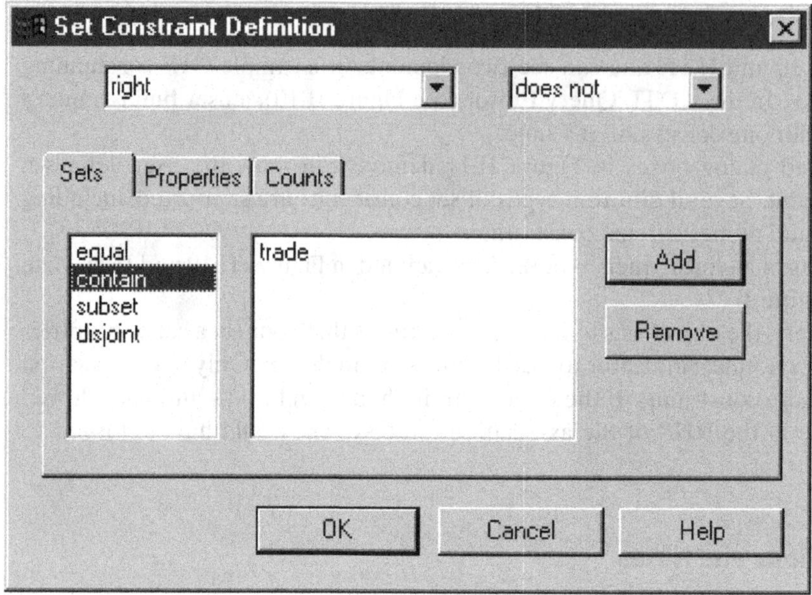

Figure II.11. Defining a KDTL set constraint. (From Feldman, Kloesgen, and Zilberstein 1997a. Reprinted with permission of Springer Science and Business Media.)

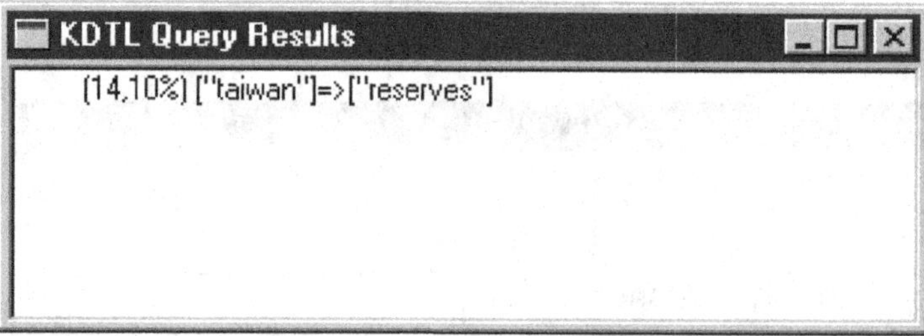

Figure II.12. Interface showing KDTL query results. (From Feldman, Kloesgen, and Zilberstein 1997a. Reprinted with permission of Springer Science and Business Media.)

Text Mining Preprocessing Techniques

Effective text mining operations are predicated on sophisticated data preprocessing methodologies. In fact, text mining is arguably so dependent on the various preprocessing techniques that infer or extract structured representations from raw unstructured data sources, or do both, that one might even say text mining is to a degree *defined* by these elaborate preparatory techniques. Certainly, very different preprocessing techniques are required to prepare raw unstructured data for text mining than those traditionally encountered in knowledge discovery operations aimed at preparing structured data sources for classic data mining operations.

A large variety of text mining preprocessing techniques exist. All in some way attempt to structure documents – and, by extension, document collections. Quite commonly, different preprocessing techniques are used in tandem to create structured document representations from raw textual data. As a result, some typical combinations of techniques have evolved in preparing unstructured data for text mining.

Two clear ways of categorizing the totality of preparatory document structuring techniques are *according to their task* and *according to the algorithms and formal frameworks that they use.*

Task-oriented preprocessing approaches envision the process of creating a structured document representation in terms of tasks and subtasks and usually involve some sort of preparatory goal or problem that needs to be solved such as extracting titles and authors from a PDF document. Other preprocessing approaches rely on techniques that derive from formal methods for analyzing complex phenomena that can be also applied to natural language texts. Such approaches include classification schemes, probabilistic models, and rule-based systems approaches.

Categorizing text mining preprocessing techniques by either their task orientation or the formal frameworks from which they derive does not mean that "mixing and matching" techniques from either category for a given text mining application are prohibited. Most of the algorithms in text mining preprocessing activities are not specific to particular tasks, and most of the problems can be solved by several quite different algorithms.

Each of the preprocessing techniques starts with a partially structured document and proceeds to enrich the structure by refining the present features and adding new ones. In the end, the most advanced and meaning-representing features are used for the text mining, whereas the rest are discarded.

The nature of the input representation and the output features is the principal difference between the preprocessing techniques. There are natural language processing (NLP) techniques, which use and produce domain-independent linguistic features. There are also *text categorization* and *IE* techniques, which directly deal with the domain-specific knowledge.

Often the same algorithm is used for different tasks, constituting several different techniques. For instance, hidden Markov models (HMMs) can successfully be used for both part-of-speech (POS) tagging and named-entity extraction.

One of the important problems, yet unsolved in general, is to combine the *processes* of different techniques as opposed simply to combining the results. For instance, frequently part-of-speech ambiguities can easily be resolved by looking at the syntactic roles of the words. Similarly, structural ambiguities can often be resolved by using domain-specific information.

Also, the bulk of any document does not contain relevant information but still must pass all of the processing stages before it can be discarded by the final one, which is extremely inefficient. It is impossible to use *latter* information for influencing the *former* processes. Thus, the processes must run simultaneously, influencing each other.

The algorithms used for different tasks are, however, usually very different and are difficult to redesign to run together. Moreover, such redesigning makes the algorithms strongly coupled, precluding any possibility of changing them later.

Because there are several widely different algorithms for each of the separate tasks, all performing at more or less the same level, the designers of preprocessing architectures are very reluctant to commit themselves to any specific one and thus try to design their systems to be modular. Still, there have recently been some attempts to find an algorithm, or a mutually consistent set of algorithms, to perform most of the preprocessing task in a single big step.

III.1 TASK-ORIENTED APPROACHES

A document is an abstract entity that has a variety of possible actual representations. Informally, the task of the document structuring process is to take the most "raw" representation and convert it to the representation through which the essence (i.e., the meaning) of the document surfaces.

A divide-and-conquer strategy is typically employed to cope with this extremely difficult problem. The problem is separated into a set of smaller subtasks, each of which is solved separately. The subtasks can be divided broadly into three classes – preparatory processing, general purpose NLP tasks, and problem-dependent tasks. The complete hierarchy of text mining subtasks is shown in Figure III.1. Preparatory processing converts the raw representation into a structure suitable for further linguistic processing. For example, the raw input may be a PDF document, a scanned page, or even recorded speech. The task of the preparatory processing is to convert the raw input into a stream of text, possibly labeling the internal text zones such

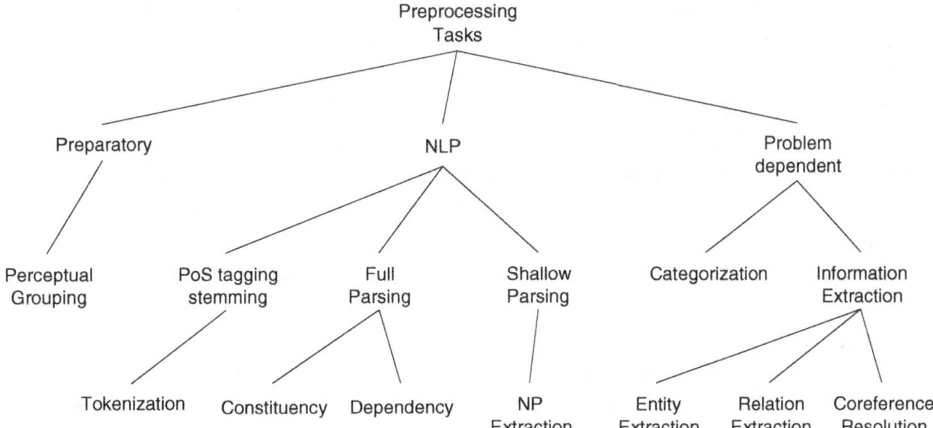

Figure III.1. A taxonomy of text preprocessing tasks.

as paragraphs, columns, or tables. It is sometimes also possible for the preparatory processing to extract some document-level fields such as *<Author>* or *<Title>* in cases in which the visual position of the fields allows their identification.

The number of possible sources for documents is enormous, and the number of possible formats and raw representations is also huge. Very complex and powerful techniques are sometimes required to convert some of those formats into a convenient form. Optical character recognition (OCR), speech recognition, and conversion of electronic files from proprietary formats are described elsewhere at length and are beyond the scope of the discussion here. However, one generic task that is often critical in text mining preprocessing operations and not widely covered in the literature of knowledge discovery might be called perceptual grouping.

The general purpose NLP tasks process text documents using the general knowledge about natural language. The tasks may include tokenization, morphological analysis, POS tagging, and syntactic parsing – either shallow or deep. The tasks are general purpose in the sense that their output is not specific for any particular problem. The output can rarely be relevant for the end user and is typically employed for further problem-dependent processing. The domain-related knowledge, however, can often enhance the performance of the general purpose NLP tasks and is often used at different levels of processing.

Finally, the problem-dependent tasks prepare the final representation of the document meaning. In text mining, *categorization* and *information extraction* are typically used.

III.1.1 General Purpose NLP Tasks

It is currently an orthodox opinion that language processing in humans cannot be separated into independent components. Various experiments in psycholinguistics clearly demonstrate that the different stages of analysis – phonetic, morphological, syntactical, semantical, and pragmatical – occur simultaneously and depend on each other.

The precise algorithms of human language-processing are unknown, however, and although several systems do try to combine the stages into a coherent single process, the complete satisfactory solution has not yet been achieved. Thus, most of the text understanding systems employ the traditional divide-and-conquer strategy, separating the whole problem into several subtasks and solving them independently.

In particular, it is possible to get quite far using only linguistics and no domain knowledge. The NLP components built in this way are valued for their generality. The tasks they are able to perform include tokenization and zoning, part-of-speech tagging and stemming, and shallow and deep syntactic parsing.

Tokenization

Prior to more sophisticated processing, the continuous character stream must be broken up into meaningful constituents. This can occur at several different levels. Documents can be broken up into chapters, sections, paragraphs, sentences, words, and even syllables or phonemes.

The approach most frequently found in text mining systems involves breaking the text into sentences and words, which is called *tokenization*. The main challenge in identifying sentence boundaries in the English language is distinguishing between a period that signals the end of a sentence and a period that is part of a previous token like Mr., Dr., and so on.

It is common for the tokenizer also to extract *token features*. These are usually simple categorical functions of the tokens describing some superficial property of the sequence of characters that make up the token. Among these features are types of capitalization, inclusion of digits, punctuation, special characters, and so on.

Part-of-Speech Tagging

POS tagging is the annotation of words with the appropriate POS tags based on the context in which they appear. POS tags divide words into categories based on the role they play in the sentence in which they appear. POS tags provide information about the semantic content of a word. Nouns usually denote "tangible and intangible things," whereas prepositions express relationships between "things."

Most POS tag sets make use of the same basic categories. The most common set of tags contains seven different tags (Article, Noun, Verb, Adjective, Preposition, Number, and Proper Noun). Some systems contain a much more elaborate set of tags. For example, the complete Brown Corpus tag set has no less than 87 basic tags.

Usually, POS taggers at some stage of their processing perform morphological analysis of words. Thus, an additional output of a POS tagger is a sequence of stems (also known as "lemmas") of the input words.

Syntactical Parsing

Syntactical parsing components perform a full syntactical analysis of sentences according to a certain grammar theory. The basic division is between the *constituency* and *dependency* grammars.

Constituency grammars describe the syntactical structure of sentences in terms of recursively built *phrases* – sequences of syntactically grouped elements. Most constituency grammars distinguish between noun phrases, verb phrases, prepositional phrases, adjective phrases, and clauses. Each phrase may consist of zero or smaller phrases or words according to the rules of the grammar. Additionally, the syntactical structure of sentences includes the *roles* of different phrases. Thus, a noun phrase may be labeled as the subject of the sentence, its direct object, or the complement.

Dependency grammars, on the other hand, do not recognize the constituents as separate linguistic units but focus instead on the direct relations between words. A typical dependency analysis of a sentence consists of a labeled DAG with words for nodes and specific relationships (dependencies) for edges. For instance, a subject and direct object nouns of a typical sentence depend on the main verb, an adjective depends on the noun it modifies, and so on.

Usually, the phrases can be recovered from a dependency analysis – they are the connected components of the sentence graph. Also, pure dependency analyses are very simple and convenient to use by themselves. Dependency grammars, however, have problems with certain common language constructions such as conjunctions.

Shallow Parsing

Efficient, accurate parsing of unrestricted text is not within the reach of current techniques. Standard algorithms are too expensive for use on very large corpora and are not robust enough. Shallow parsing compromises speed and robustness of processing by sacrificing depth of analysis.

Instead of providing a complete analysis (a parse) of a whole sentence, shallow parsers produce only parts that are easy and unambiguous. Typically, small and simple noun and verb phrases are generated, whereas more complex clauses are not formed. Similarly, most prominent dependencies might be formed, but unclear and ambiguous ones are left unresolved.

For the purposes of information extraction, shallow parsing is usually sufficient and therefore preferable to full analysis because of its far greater speed and robustness.

III.1.2 Problem-Dependent Tasks: Text Categorization and Information Extraction

The final stages of document structuring create representations that are meaningful for either later (and more sophisticated) processing phases or direct interaction of the text mining system user. The text mining techniques normally expect the documents to be represented as sets of features, which are considered to be structureless atomic entities possibly organized into a taxonomy – an *IsA*-hierarchy. The nature of the features sharply distinguishes between the two main techniques: *text categorization* and *information extraction* (IE). Both of these techniques are also popularly referred to as "tagging" (because of the tag-formatted structures they introduce in a processed document), and they enable one to obtain formal, structured representations of documents. Text categorization and IE enable users to move from a "machine readable" representation of the documents to a "machine understandable" form of the documents. This view of the tagging approach is depicted in Figure III.2.

Text categorization (sometime called text classification) tasks tag each document with a small number of concepts or keywords. The set of all possible concepts or keywords is usually manually prepared, closed, and comparatively small. The hierarchy relation between the keywords is also prepared manually.

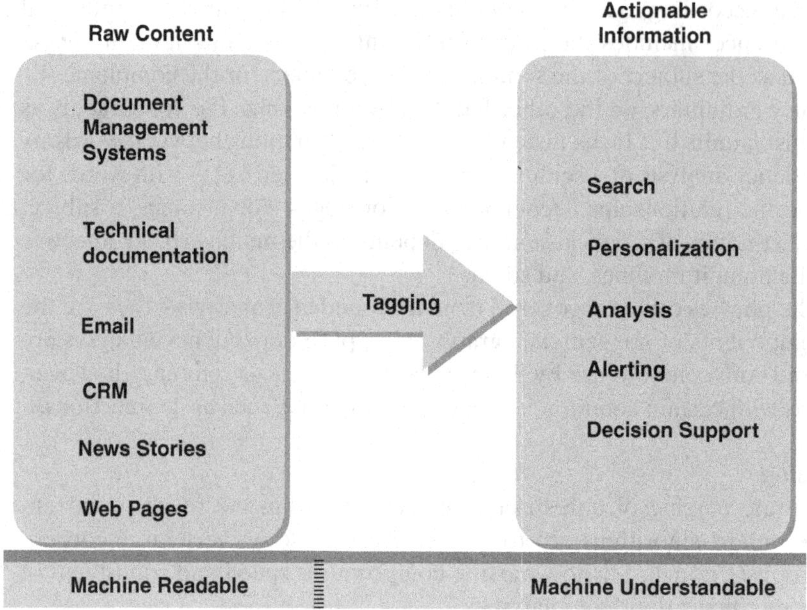

Figure III.2. Bridging the gap between raw data and actionable information.

IE is perhaps the most prominent technique currently used in text mining preprocessing operations. Without IE techniques, text mining systems would have much more limited knowledge discovery capabilities.

IE must often be distinguished from information retrieval or what is more informally called "search." Information retrieval returns documents that match a given query but still requires the user to read through these documents to locate the relevant information. IE, on the other hand, aims at pinpointing the relevant information and presenting it in a structured format – typically in a tabular format. For analysts and other knowledge workers, IE can save valuable time by dramatically speeding up discovery-type work.

III.2 FURTHER READING

POS Tagging

Please refer to Maltese and Mancini (1991), Brill (1992), Kupiec (1992), Schutze (1993), and Brill (1995) for further details about POS tagging.

Shallow Parsing

The following papers discuss how to perform shallow parsing of documents: Tzoukermann, Klavans, and Jacquemin (1997); Lager (1998); Daelemans, Buchholz, and Veenstra (1999); Lewin et al. (1999); Munoz et al. (1999); and Punyakanok and Roth (2000).

Constituency Grammars

Information on constituency grammers can be found in Reape (1989), Keller (1992), and Pollard and Sag (1994).

Dependency Grammars

The following papers provide more information about dependency grammars: Lombardo (1991), Carroll and Charniak (1992), Rambow and Joshi (1994), Lin (1995), and Neuhaus and Broker (1997).

General Information Extraction

A general overview of the information extraction field can be found in Cowie and Lehnert (1996), Grishman (1996), Cardie (1997), and Grishman (1997).

IV

Categorization

Probably the most common theme in analyzing complex data is the classification, or categorization, of elements. Described abstractly, the task is to classify a given data instance into a prespecified set of categories. Applied to the domain of document management, the task is known as *text categorization* (TC) – given a set of categories (subjects, topics) and a collection of text documents, the process of finding the correct topic (or topics) for each document.

The study of automated text categorization dates back to the early 1960s (Maron 1961). Then, its main projected use was for indexing scientific literature by means of controlled vocabulary. It was only in the 1990s that the field fully developed with the availability of ever increasing numbers of text documents in digital form and the necessity to organize them for easier use. Nowadays automated TC is applied in a variety of contexts – from the classical automatic or semiautomatic (interactive) indexing of texts to personalized commercials delivery, spam filtering, Web page categorization under hierarchical catalogues, automatic generation of metadata, detection of text genre, and many others.

As with many other artificial intelligence (AI) tasks, there are two main approaches to text categorization. The first is the *knowledge engineering* approach in which the expert's knowledge about the categories is directly encoded into the system either declaratively or in the form of procedural classification rules. The other is the *machine learning* (ML) approach in which a general inductive process builds a classifier by learning from a set of preclassified examples. In the document management domain, the knowledge engineering systems usually outperform the ML systems, although the gap in performance steadily shrinks. The main drawback of the knowledge engineering approach is what might be called the *knowledge acquisition bottleneck* – the huge amount of highly skilled labor and expert knowledge required to create and maintain the knowledge-encoding rules. Therefore, most of the recent work on categorization is concentrated on the ML approach, which requires only a set of manually classified training instances that are much less costly to produce.

This chapter is organized as follows. We start with the description of several common applications of text categorization. Then the formal framework and the issues of problem representation are described. Next we survey the most commonly used algorithms solving the TC problem and wrap up with the issues of experimental evaluation and a comparison between the different algorithms.

IV.1 APPLICATIONS OF TEXT CATEGORIZATION

Three common TC applications are text indexing, document sorting and text filtering, and Web page categorization. These are only a small set of possible applications, but they demonstrate the diversity of the domain and the variety of the TC subcases.

IV.1.1 Indexing of Texts Using Controlled Vocabulary

The topic of most of the early research in the TC field is text indexing. In Boolean information retrieval (IR) systems, each document in a big collection is assigned one or more key terms describing its content. Then, the IR system is able to retrieve the documents according to the user queries, which are based on the key terms. The key terms all belong to a finite set called *controlled vocabulary*, which is often a thematic hierarchical thesaurus such as the NASA aerospace thesaurus or the MESH thesaurus for medicine.

The task of assigning keywords from a controlled vocabulary to text documents is called *text indexing*. If the keywords are viewed as categories, then text indexing is an instance of the general TC problem and can be addressed by the automatic techniques described in this chapter.

Typically, each document should receive at least one, and not more than k, keywords. Also, the task can be solved either fully automatically or semiautomatically, in which case the user selects a set of keywords from a ranked list supplied by a TC system.

Automatic indexing can be a part of *automated extraction of metadata*. The metadata describe a document in a variety of aspects, some of which are thematic – related to the contents of the document – the bibliographic codes, key terms, and so on. Extraction of this metadata can be viewed as a document indexing problem, which can be tackled by TC techniques.

IV.1.2 Document Sorting and Text Filtering

Another common problem related but distinct from document indexing is sorting the given collection of documents into several "bins." For instance, in a newspaper, the classified ads may need to be categorized into "Personal," "Car Sale," "Real Estate," and so on. Another example is e-mail coming into an organization, which may need to be sorted into categories such as "Complaints," "Deals," "Job applications," and others.

The document sorting problem has several features that distinguish it from the related tasks. The main difference is the requirement that each document belong to exactly one category. Other typical features are relatively small numbers of categories and the "online" nature of the task: The documents to be categorized are usually presented to the classifier one by one, not as a single batch.

Text filtering activity can be seen as document sorting with only two bins – the "relevant" and "irrelevant" documents. Examples of text filtering abound. A sports-related online magazine should filter out all nonsport stories it receives from the news feed. An e-mail client should filter away spam. A personalized ad filtering system should block any ads that are uninteresting to the particular user.

For most of the TC systems, recall errors (which arise when a category is missing some document that should have been assigned to it) and precision errors (which occur when a category includes documents that should not belong to it) are considered to have about the same cost. For many of the filtering tasks, however, the recall errors (e.g., an important letter is considered spam and hence is missing from the "good documents" category) are much more costly than precision errors (some of the spam still passes through, and thus the "good documents" category contains some extra letters).

For personalized filtering systems it is common for the user to provide the feedback to the system – by marking received documents as relevant or irrelevant. Because it is usually computationally unfeasible to fully retrain the system after each document, *adaptive* learning techniques are required (see Bibliography).

IV.1.3 Hierarchical Web Page Categorization

A common use of TC is the automatic classification of Web pages under the hierarchical catalogues posted by popular Internet portals such as Yahoo. Such catalogues are very useful for direct browsing and for restricting the query-based search to pages belonging to a particular topic.

The other applications described in this section usually constrain the number of categories to which a document may belong. Hierarchical Web page categorization, however, constrains the number of documents belonging to a particular category to prevent the categories from becoming excessively large. Whenever the number of documents in a category exceeds k, it should be split into two or more subcategories. Thus, the categorization system must support adding new categories and deleting obsolete ones.

Another feature of the problem is the hypertextual nature of the documents. The Web documents contain links, which may be important sources of information for the classifier because linked documents often share semantics.

The hierarchical structure of the set of categories is also uncommon. It can be dealt with by using a separate classifier at every branching point of the hierarchy.

IV.2 DEFINITION OF THE PROBLEM

The general text categorization task can be formally defined as the task of approximating an unknown category assignment function $F : D \times C \rightarrow \{0, 1\}$, where D is the set of all possible documents and C is the set of predefined categories. The value of $F(d, c)$ is 1 if the document d belongs to the category c and 0 otherwise. The approximating function $M : D \times C \rightarrow \{0, 1\}$ is called a *classifier*, and the task is to build a classifier that produces results as "close" as possible to the true category assignment function F.

IV.2.1 Single-Label versus Multilabel Categorization

Depending on the properties of F, we can distinguish between *single-label* and *multilabel* categorization. In multilabel categorization the categories overlap, and a document may belong to any number of categories. In single-label categorization, each document belongs to exactly one category. *Binary* categorization is a special case of single-label categorization in which the number of categories is two. The binary case is the most important because it is the simplest, most common, and most often used for the demonstration of categorization techniques. Also, the general single-label case is frequently a simple generalization of the binary case. The multilabel case can be solved by $|C|$ binary classifiers ($|C|$ is the number of categories), one for each category, provided the decisions to assign a document to different categories are independent from each other.

IV.2.2 Document-Pivoted versus Category-Pivoted Categorization

Usually, the classifiers are used in the following way: Given a document, the classifier finds all categories to which the document belongs. This is called a *document-pivoted categorization*. Alternatively, we might need to find all documents that should be filed under a given category. This is called a *category-pivoted categorization*. The difference is significant only in the case in which not all documents or not all categories are immediately available. For instance, in "online" categorization, the documents come in one-by-one, and thus only the document-pivoted categorization is possible. On the other hand, if the categories set is not fixed, and if the documents need to be reclassified with respect to the newly appearing categories, then category-pivoted categorization is appropriate. However, most of the techniques described in this chapter allow both.

IV.2.3 Hard versus Soft Categorization

A fully automated categorization system makes a binary decision on each document-category pair. Such a system is said to be doing the *hard* categorization. The level of performance currently achieved by fully automatic systems, however, may be insufficient for some applications. Then, a semiautomated approach is appropriate in which the decision to assign a document to a category is made by a human for whom the TC system provides a list of categories arranged by the system's estimated appropriateness of the category for the document. In this case, the system is said to be doing the *soft* or *ranking* categorization. Many classifiers described in this chapter actually have the whole segment [0, 1] as their range – that is, they produce a real value between zero and one for each document-category pair. This value is called a *categorization status value* (CSV). Such "continuous" classifiers naturally perform ranking categorization, but if a binary decision is needed it can be produced by checking the CSV against a specific threshold.

Various possible policies exist for setting the threshold. For some types of classifiers it is possible to calculate the thresholds analytically, using decision-theoretic measures such as utility. There are also general classifier-independent methods. *Fixed thresholding* assigns exactly k top-ranking categories to each document. *Proportional thresholding* sets the threshold in such a way that the same fraction of the test set belongs to a category as to the corresponding fraction of the training set. Finally, the most common method is to set the value of the threshold in such a way as to maximize the performance of the classifier on a validation set. The validation set is some portion of the training set that is not used for creating the model. The sole purpose of the validation set is to optimize some of the parameters of the classifier (such as the threshold). Experiments suggest that the latter method is usually superior to the others in performance (Lewis 1992a, 1992b; Yang 1999).

IV.3 DOCUMENT REPRESENTATION

The common classifiers and learning algorithms cannot directly process the text documents in their original form. Therefore, during a preprocessing step, the documents are converted into a more manageable representation. Typically, the documents are represented by *feature vectors.* A feature is simply an entity without internal structure – a dimension in the feature space. A document is represented as a vector in this space – a sequence of features and their weights.

The most common *bag-of-words* model simply uses all words in a document as the features, and thus the dimension of the feature space is equal to the number of different words in all of the documents. The methods of giving weights to the features may vary. The simplest is the *binary* in which the feature weight is either one – if the corresponding word is present in the document – or zero otherwise. More complex weighting schemes are possible that take into account the frequencies of the word in the document, in the category, and in the whole collection. The most common TF-IDF scheme gives the word w in the document d the weight

$$\textit{TF-IDF\_Weight}\,(w, d) = \textit{TermFreq}(w, d) \cdot \log\,(N \,/\, \textit{DocFreq}(w)),$$

where $\textit{TermFreq}(w, d)$ is the frequency of the word in the document, N is the number of all documents, and $\textit{DocFreq}(w)$ is the number of documents containing the word w.

IV.3.1 Feature Selection

The number of different words is large even in relatively small documents such as short news articles or paper abstracts. The number of different words in big document collections can be huge. The dimension of the bag-of-words feature space for a big collection can reach hundreds of thousands; moreover, the document representation vectors, although sparse, may still have hundreds and thousands of nonzero components.

Most of those words are irrelevant to the categorization task and can be dropped with no harm to the classifier performance and may even result in improvement owing to noise reduction. The preprocessing step that removes the irrelevant words is called *feature selection*. Most TC systems at least remove the *stop words* – the function words and in general the common words of the language that usually do not contribute to the semantics of the documents and have no real added value. Many systems, however, perform a much more aggressive filtering, removing 90 to 99 percent of all features.

In order to perform the filtering, a measure of the relevance of each feature needs to be defined. Probably the simplest such measure is the document frequency *DocFreq*(w). Experimental evidence suggests that using only the top 10 percent of the most frequent words does not reduce the performance of classifiers. This seems to contradict the well-known "law" of IR, according to which the terms with low-to-medium document frequency are the most informative. There is no contradiction, however, because the large majority of all words have a *very* low document frequency, and the top 10 percent do contain all low-to-medium frequency words.

More sophisticated measures of feature relevance exist that take into account the relations between features and the categories. For instance, the *information gain*

$$IG(w) = \sum_{c \in C \cup \overline{C}} \sum_{f \in \{w, \overline{w}\}} P(f, c) \cdot \log \frac{P(c \mid f)}{P(c)}$$

measures the number of bits of information obtained for the prediction of categories by knowing the presence or absence in a document of the feature f. The probabilities are computed as ratios of frequencies in the training data. Another good measure is the chi-square

$$\chi^2_{\max}(f) = \max_{c \in C} \frac{|Tr| \cdot (P(f, c) \cdot P(\bar{f}, \bar{c}) - P(f, \bar{c}) \cdot P(\bar{f}, c))^2}{P(f) \cdot P(\bar{f}) \cdot P(c) \cdot P(\bar{c})},$$

which measures the maximal strength of dependence between the feature and the categories. Experiments show that both measures (and several other measures) can reduce the dimensionality by a factor of 100 without loss of categorization quality – or even with a small improvement (Yang and Pedersen 1997).

IV.3.2 Dimensionality Reduction by Feature Extraction

Another way of reducing the number of dimensions is to create a new, much smaller set of synthetic features from the original feature set. In effect, this amounts to creating a transformation from the original feature space to another space of much lower dimension. The rationale for using synthetic features rather than naturally occurring words (as the simpler feature filtering method does) is that, owing to polysemy, homonymy, and synonymy, the words may not be the optimal features. By transforming the set of features it may be possible to create document representations that do not suffer from the problems inherent in those properties of natural language.

Term clustering addresses the problem of synonymy by grouping together words with a high degree of semantic relatedness. These word groups are then used as features instead of individual words. Experiments conducted by several groups of researchers showed a potential in this technique only when the background information about categories was used for clustering (Baker and McCallum 1998; Slonim and Tishby 2001). With unsupervised clustering, the results are inferior (Lewis 1992a, 1992b; Li and Jain 1998).

A more systematic approach is latent semantic indexing (LSI). The details of this method are described in Chapter V. For the TC problem, the performance of the LSI also improves if the categories information is used. Several LSI representations, one for each category, outperform a single global LSI representation. The experiments also show that LSI usually performs better than the chi-square filtering scheme.

IV.4 KNOWLEDGE ENGINEERING APPROACH TO TC

The knowledge engineering approach to TC is focused around manual development of classification rules. A domain expert defines a set of sufficient conditions for a document to be labeled with a given category. The development of the classification rules can be quite labor intensive and tedious.

We mention only a single example of the knowledge engineering approach to the TC – the well-known CONSTRUE system (Hayes, Knecht, and Cellio 1988; Hayes et al. 1990; Hayes and Weinstein 1990; Hayes 1992) built by the Carnegie group for Reuters. A typical rule in the CONSTRUE system is as follows:

if DNF (disjunction of conjunctive clauses) formula ***then*** category ***else*** ¬category

Such rule may look like the following:

If ((wheat & farm) or
(wheat & commodity) or
(bushels & export) or
(wheat & tonnes) or
(wheat & winter & ¬soft))
then Wheat
else ¬Wheat

The system was reported to produce a 90-percent breakeven between precision and recall on a small subset of the Reuters collection (723 documents). It is unclear whether the particular chosen test collection influenced the results and whether the system would scale up, but such excellent performance has not yet been unattained by machine learning systems.

However, the knowledge acquisition bottleneck that plagues such expert systems (it took several man-years to develop and fine-tune the CONSTRUE system for Reuters) makes the ML approach attractive despite possibly somewhat lower quality results.

IV.5 MACHINE LEARNING APPROACH TO TC

In the ML approach, the classifier is built automatically by learning the properties of categories from a set of preclassified training documents. In the ML terminology, the learning process is an instance of *supervised* learning because the process is guided by applying the known true category assignment function on the training set. The unsupervised version of the classification task, called *clustering*, is described in Chapter V. There are many approaches to classifier learning; some of them are variants of more general ML algorithms, and others have been created specifically for categorization.

Four main issues need to be considered when using machine learning techniques to develop an application based on text categorization. First, we need to decide on the categories that will be used to classify the instances. Second, we need to provide a training set for each of the categories. As a rule of thumb, about 30 examples are needed for each category. Third, we need to decide on the features that represent each of the instances. Usually, it is better to generate as many features as possible because most of the algorithms will be able to focus just on the relevant features. Finally, we need to decide on the algorithm to be used for the categorization.

IV.5.1 Probabilistic Classifiers

Probabilistic classifiers view the categorization status value CSV(d, c) as the probability $P(c \mid d)$ that the document d belongs to the category c and compute this probability by an application of Bayes' theorem:

$$P(c \mid d) = \frac{P(d \mid c)P(c)}{P(d)}.$$

The marginal probability $P(d)$ need not ever be computed because it is constant for all categories. To calculate $P(d \mid c)$, however, we need to make some assumptions about the structure of the document d. With the document representation as a feature vector $\mathbf{d} = (w_1, w_2, \ldots)$, the most common assumption is that all coordinates are independent, and thus

$$P(d \mid c) = \prod_i P(w_i \mid c).$$

The classifiers resulting from this assumption are called *Naïve Bayes* (NB) classifiers. They are called "naïve" because the assumption is never verified and often is quite obviously false. However, the attempts to relax the naïve assumption and to use the probabilistic models with dependence so far have not produced any significant improvement in performance. Some theoretic justification to this unexpected robustness of the Naïve Bayes classifiers is given in Domingos and Pazzani (1997).

IV.5.2 Bayesian Logistic Regression

It is possible to model the conditional probability $P(c \mid d)$ directly. Bayesian logistic regression (BLR) is an old statistical approach that was only recently applied to the TC problem and is quickly gaining popularity owing to its apparently very high performance.

Assuming the categorization is binary, we find that the logistic regression model has the form

$$P(c \mid \mathbf{d}) = \varphi(\boldsymbol{\beta} \cdot \mathbf{d}) = \varphi\left(\textstyle\sum_i \beta_i d_i\right),$$

where $c = \pm 1$ is the category membership value (± 1 is used instead of $\{0, 1\}$ for simpler notation), $\mathbf{d} = (d_1, d_2, \ldots)$ is the document representation in the feature space, $\boldsymbol{\beta} = (\beta_1, \beta_2, \ldots)$ is the model parameters vector, and φ is the *logistic link* function

$$\varphi(x) = \frac{\exp(x)}{1 + \exp(x)} = \frac{1}{1 + \exp(-x)}.$$

Care must be taken in order for a logistic regression model not to overfit the training data. The Bayesian approach is to use a prior distribution for the parameter vector $\boldsymbol{\beta}$ that assigns a high probability to each β_i's being at or near zero. Different priors are possible, and the commonly used are Gaussian and Laplace priors.

The simplest is the Gaussian prior with zero mean and variance τ:

$$p(\beta_i \mid \tau) = N(0, \tau) = \frac{1}{\sqrt{2\pi\tau}} \exp\left(\frac{-\beta_i^2}{2\tau}\right).$$

If the a priori independence of the components of $\boldsymbol{\beta}$ and the equality of variances τ for all components are assumed, the overall prior for $\boldsymbol{\beta}$ is the product of the priors for β_i. With this prior, the maximum a posteriori (MAP) estimate of $\boldsymbol{\beta}$ is equivalent to ridge regression for the logistic model.

The disadvantage of the Gaussian prior in the TC problem is that, although it favors the parameter values' being close to zero, the MAP estimates of the parameters will rarely be exactly zero; thus, the model will not be sparse. The alternative Laplace prior does achieve sparseness:

$$p(\beta_i \mid \lambda) = \frac{\lambda}{2} \exp(-\lambda \, |\beta_i|).$$

Using this kind of prior represents a belief that a small portion of the input variables has a substantial effect on the outcome, whereas most of the other variables are unimportant. This belief is certainly justifiable for the TC task. The particular value of the hyperparameter λ (and τ for the Gaussian prior) can be chosen a priori or optimized using a validation set.

In an "ideal" setting, the posterior distribution of $\boldsymbol{\beta}$ would be used for the actual prediction. Owing to computational cost constraints, however, it is common to use a point estimate of $\boldsymbol{\beta}$, of which the *posterior mode* (any value of $\boldsymbol{\beta}$ at which the posterior distribution of $\boldsymbol{\beta}$ takes on its maximal value) is the most common.

The log-posterior distribution of $\boldsymbol{\beta}$ is

$$l(\boldsymbol{\beta}) = p(\boldsymbol{\beta} \mid D) = -\left(\sum_{(\mathbf{d},c)\in D} \ln(\exp(-c\,\boldsymbol{\beta}\cdot\mathbf{d}) + 1)\right) + \ln p(\boldsymbol{\beta}),$$

where $D = \{(\mathbf{d}_1, c_1), (\mathbf{d}_2, c_2)\ldots\}$ is the set of training documents $\mathbf{d}_i$ and their true category membership values $c_i = \pm 1$, and $p(\boldsymbol{\beta})$ is the chosen prior:

$$\ln p(\boldsymbol{\beta}) = -\left(\sum_i \left(\ln\sqrt{\tau} + \frac{\ln 2\pi}{2} + \frac{\beta_i^2}{\tau}\right)\right), \text{ for Gaussian prior, and}$$

$$\ln p(\boldsymbol{\beta}) = -\left(\sum_i (\ln 2 - \ln\lambda + \lambda \mid \beta_i \mid)\right), \text{ for Laplace prior.}$$

The MAP estimate of $\boldsymbol{\beta}$ is then simply $\arg\max_{\boldsymbol{\beta}} l(\boldsymbol{\beta})$, which can be computed by any convex optimization algorithm.

IV.5.3 Decision Tree Classifiers

Many categorization methods share a certain drawback: The classifiers cannot be easily understood by humans. The *symbolic* classifiers, of which the decision tree classifiers are the most prominent example, do not suffer from this problem.

A decision tree (DT) classifier is a tree in which the internal nodes are labeled by the features, the edges leaving a node are labeled by tests on the feature's weight, and the leaves are labeled by categories. A DT categorizes a document by starting at the root of the tree and moving successively downward via the branches whose

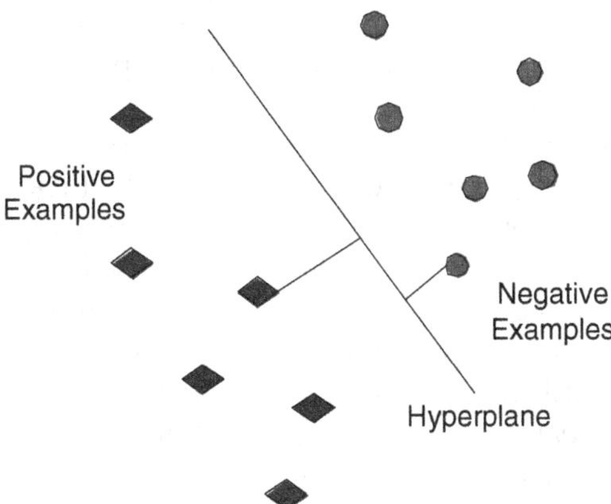

Figure IV.1. A Decision Tree classifier.

conditions are satisfied by the document until a leaf node is reached. The document is then assigned to the category that labels the leaf node. Most of the DT classifiers use a binary document representation, and thus the trees are binary. For example, the tree that corresponds to the CONSTRUE rule mentioned in Section IV.4 may look like Figure IV.1.

Most of the DT-based systems use some form of general procedure for a DT induction such as ID3, C4.5, and CART. Typically, the tree is built recursively by picking a feature f at each step and dividing the training collection into two subcollections, one containing f and another not containing f, until only documents of a single category remain – at which point a leaf node is generated. The choice of a feature at each step is made by some information-theoretic measure such as information gain or entropy. However, the trees generated in such a way are prone to overfit the training collection, and so most methods also include *pruning* – that is, removing the too specific branches.

The performance of a DT classifier is mixed but is inferior to the top-ranking classifiers. Thus it is rarely used alone in tasks for which the human understanding of the classifier is not essential. DT classifiers, however, are often used as a baseline for comparison with other classifiers and as members of classifier committees.

IV.5.4 Decision Rule Classifiers

Decision rule (DR) classifiers are also symbolic like decision trees. The rules look very much like the disjunctive normal form (DNF) rules of the CONSTRUE system but are built from the training collection using *inductive rule learning*. Typically, the rule learning methods attempt to select the best rule from the set of all possible covering rules (i.e., rules that correctly classify all training examples) according to some optimality criterion. DNF rules are often built in a bottom-up fashion. The initial most specific classifier is built from the training set by viewing each training document as a clause

$$d_1 \wedge d_2 \wedge \ldots \wedge d_n \rightarrow c,$$

where d_i are the features of the document and c its category. The learner then applies a series of generalizations (e.g., by removing terms from the clauses and by merging rules), thus maximizing the compactness of the rules while keeping the *covering* property. At the end of the process, a *pruning* step similar to the DT pruning is applied that trades covering for more generality.

Rule learners vary widely in their specific methods, heuristics, and optimality criteria. One of the prominent examples of this family of algorithms is RIPPER (repeated incremental pruning to produce error reduction) (Cohen 1995a; Cohen 1995b; Cohen and Singer 1996). Ripper builds a rule set by first adding new rules until all positive category instances are covered and then adding conditions to the rules until no negative instance is covered. One of the attractive features of Ripper is its ability to bias the performance toward higher precision or higher recall as determined by the setting of the *loss ratio* parameter, which measures the relative cost of "false negative" and "false positive" errors.

IV.5.5 Regression Methods

Regression is a technique for approximating a real-valued function using the knowledge of its values on a set of points. It can be applied to TC, which is the problem of approximating the category assignment function. For this method to work, the assignment function must be considered a member of a suitable family of continuous real-valued functions. Then the regression techniques can be applied to generate the (real-valued) classifier.

One regression method is the linear least-square fit (LLSF), which was first applied to TC in Yang and Chute (1994). In this method, the category assignment function is viewed as a $|C| \times |F|$ matrix, which describes some linear transformation from the feature space to the space of all possible category assignments. To build a classifier, we create a matrix that best accounts for the training data. The LLSF model computes the matrix by minimizing the error on the training collection according to the formula

$$M = \arg\min_M ||MD - O||_F,$$

where D is the $|F| \times |TrainingCollection|$ matrix of the training document representations, O is the $|C| \times |TrainingCollection|$ matrix of the true category assignments, and the $||\cdot||_F$ is the *Frobenius norm*

$$||A||_F = \sqrt{\sum A_{ij}^2}.$$

The matrix M can be computed by performing singular value decomposition on the training data. The matrix element m_{ij} represents the degree of association between the ith feature and the jth category.

IV.5.6 The Rocchio Methods

The Rocchio classifier categorizes a document by computing its distance to the prototypical examples of the categories. A prototypical example for the category c is a vector $(w_1, w_2, \ldots)$ in the feature space computed by

$$w_i = \frac{\alpha}{|\text{POS}(c)|} \sum_{d \in \text{POS}(c)} w_{di} - \frac{\beta}{|\text{NEG}(c)|} \sum_{d \in \text{NEG}(c)} w_{di},$$

where POS(c) and NEG(c) are the sets of all training documents that belong and do not belong to the category c, respectively, and w_{di} is the weight of ith feature in the document d. Usually, the positive examples are much more important than the negative ones, and so $\alpha >> \beta$. If $\beta = 0$, then the prototypical example for a category is simply the centroid of all documents belonging to the category.

The Rocchio method is very easy to implement, and it is cheap computationally. Its performance, however, is usually mediocre – especially with categories that are unions of disjoint clusters and in, general, with the categories that are not linearly separable.

IV.5.7 Neural Networks

Neural network (NN) can be built to perform text categorization. Usually, the input nodes of the network receive the feature values, the output nodes produce the categorization status values, and the link weights represent dependence relations. For classifying a document, its feature weights are loaded into the input nodes; the activation of the nodes is propagated forward through the network, and the final values on output nodes determine the categorization decisions.

The neural networks are trained by *back propagation*, whereby the training documents are loaded into the input nodes. If a misclassification occurs, the error is propagated back through the network, modifying the link weights in order to minimize the error.

The simplest kind of a neural network is a perceptron. It has only two layers – the input and the output nodes. Such network is equivalent to a linear classifier. More complex networks contain one or more *hidden* layers between the input and output layers. However, the experiments have shown very small – or no – improvement of nonlinear networks over their linear counterparts in the text categorization task (Schutze, Hull, and Pederson 1995; Wiener 1995).

IV.5.8 Example-Based Classifiers

Example-based classifiers do not build explicit declarative representations of categories but instead rely on directly computing the similarity between the document to be classified and the training documents. Those methods have thus been called lazy learners because they defer the decision on how to generalize beyond the training data until each new query instance is encountered. "Training" for such classifiers consists of simply storing the representations of the training documents together with their category labels.

The most prominent example of an example-based classifier is kNN (k-nearest neighbor). To decide whether a document d belongs to the category c, kNN checks whether the k training documents most similar to d belong to c. If the answer is positive for a sufficiently large proportion of them, a positive decision is made; otherwise, the decision is negative. The distance-weighted version of kNN is a variation that weighs the contribution of each neighbor by its similarity to the test document.

In order to use the algorithm, one must choose the value of k. It can be optimized using a validation set, but it is probable that a good value can be picked a priori.

Larkey and Croft (Larkey and Croft 1996) use $k = 20$, whereas Yang (Yang 2001) has found $30 \leq k \leq 45$ to yield the best effectiveness. Various experiments have shown that increasing the value of k does not significantly degrade the performance.

The kNN is one of the best-performing text classifiers to this day. It is robust in the sense of not requiring the categories to be linearly separated. Its only drawback is the relatively high computational cost of classification – that is, for each test document, its similarity to all of the training documents must be computed.

IV.5.9 Support Vector Machines

The support vector machine (SVM) algorithm is very fast and effective for text classification problems.

In geometrical terms, a binary SVM classifier can be seen as a hyperplane in the feature space separating the points that represent the positive instances of the category from the points that represent the negative instances. The classifying hyperplane is chosen during training as the unique hyperplane that separates the known positive instances from the known negative instances with the maximal margin. The margin is the distance from the hyperplane to the nearest point from the positive and negative sets. The diagram shown in Figure IV.2 is an example of a maximal margin hyperplane in two dimensions.

It is interesting to note that SVM hyperplanes are fully determined by a relatively small subset of the training instances, which are called the *support vectors*. The rest of the training data have no influence on the trained classifier. In this respect, the SVM algorithm appears to be unique among the different categorization algorithms.

The SVM classifier has an important advantage in its theoretically justified approach to the overfitting problem, which allows it to perform well irrespective of the dimensionality of the feature space. Also, it needs no parameter adjustment

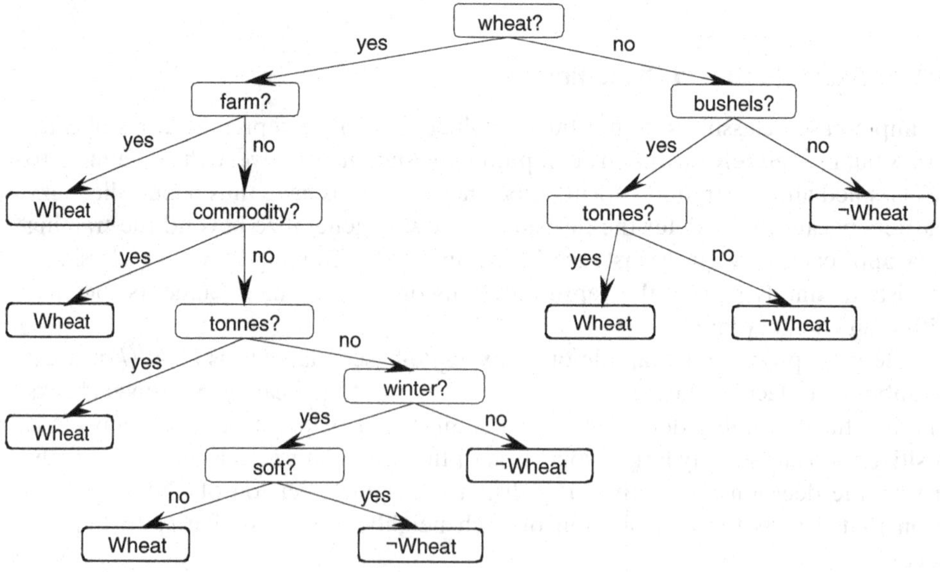

Figure IV.2. Diagram of a 2-D Linear SVM.

because there is a theoretically motivated "default" choice of parameters that has also been shown experimentally to provide the best performance.

IV.5.10 Classifier Committees: Bagging and Boosting

The idea of using committees of classifiers stems from the intuition that a team of experts, by combining their knowledge, may produce better results than a single expert alone. In the *bagging* method of building committees, the individual classifiers are trained in parallel on the same training collection. In order for the committee to work, the classifiers must differ significantly from each other – either in their document representation or in their learning methods. In text categorization, the latter method is usually chosen. As this chapter suggests, there is certainly no shortage of widely different learning methods.

Assume there are k different classifiers. To build a single committee classifier, one must choose the method of combining their results. The simplest method is the *majority vote* in which a category is assigned to a document iff at least $(k+1)/2$ classifiers decide this way (k must be an odd number, obviously). Another possibility, suited for continuous output, is the *weighted linear combination*, whereby the final CSV is given by a weighted sum of the CSVs of the k classifiers. The weights can be estimated on a validation dataset. Other methods of combining classifiers are also possible.

Boosting is another method of improving the quality of categorization by using several classifiers. Unlike the bagging method, in boosting the classifiers are trained sequentially. Before training the ith classifier, the training set is reweighed with greater weight given to the documents that were misclassified by the previous classifiers. The AdaBoost algorithm is the best known example of this approach. It is defined as follows:

Let X be the feature space, and let $D = \{(d_1, c_1), (d_2, c_3), \ldots\}$ be the training data, where $d_i \in X$ are the training document representations and $c_i \in \{+1, -1\}$ the category assignment (binary). A *weak learner* is some algorithm that is able to produce a *weak hypothesis* (classifier) $h : X \to \{\pm 1\}$ given the training data D together with a weight distribution W upon it. The "goodness" of a hypothesis is measured by its *error*

$$\varepsilon(h, W) = \sum_{i : h(d_i) \neq c_i} W(i),$$

which is the sum of weights of misclassified documents.

The AdaBoost algorithm

- Initializes weights distribution $W_1(i) = 1/|\mathrm{D}|$for all i, and
- Repeats for $t = 1, \ldots, k$.
  Train a weak classifier h_t using the current weights W_t.
  Let $\alpha_t = \frac{1}{2} \ln \frac{1-\varepsilon(h_t, W_t)}{\varepsilon(h_t, W_t)}$.

Update the weights: $W_{t+1}(i) = Z_t \cdot W_t(i) \cdot$

$$\begin{cases} \exp(-\alpha_t), & \text{if } h_t(d_i) = c_i, \\ \exp(\alpha_t), & \text{otherwise.} \end{cases}$$

(Z_t is the normalization factor chosen so that $\sum_i W_{t+1}(i) = 1$).

- The final classifier is $H(d) = \text{sign}\left(\sum_{t=1..k} \alpha_t h_t(d)\right)$.

It can be proved that, if the weak learner is able to generate classifiers with error $\varepsilon < \frac{1}{2} - \lambda$ for any fixed $\lambda > 0$ (which means, if the weak classifiers are any better than random), then the training error for the final classifier drops exponentially fast with the number k of algorithm steps. It can also be shown that AdaBoost has close relations with SVM, for it also maximizes the margin between training instances. Because of this, AdaBoost also has a similar resistance to overfitting.

IV.6 USING UNLABELED DATA TO IMPROVE CLASSIFICATION

All of the ML classifiers require fairly large training collections of preclassified documents. The task of manually labeling a large number of documents, although much less costly than manually creating a classification knowledge base, is still usually quite a chore. On the other hand, unlabeled documents usually exist in abundance, and any amount of them can be acquired with little cost. Therefore, the ability to improve the classifier performance by augmenting a relatively small number of labeled documents with a large number of unlabeled ones is very useful for applications. The two common ways of incorporating knowledge from unlabeled documents are expectation maximization (EM) and cotraining.

EM works with probabilistic generative classifiers such as Naïve Bayes. The idea is to find the most probable model given both labeled and unlabeled documents. The EM algorithm performs the optimization in a simple and appealing way:

- First, the model is trained over the labeled documents.
- Then the following steps are iterated until convergence in a local maximum occurs:

  E-step: the unlabeled documents are classified by the current model.
  M-step: the model is trained over the combined corpus.

In the M-step, the category assignments of the unlabeled documents are assumed to be fractional according to the probabilities produced by the E-step.

Cotraining works with the documents, for which two *views* are available, providing two different document representations, both of which are sufficient for classification. For example, a Web page may have its content as one view and the anchor text appearing in the hyperlinks to the page as another. In the domain of MedLine papers, the abstract may be one view and the whole text another. The cotraining is a bootstrapping strategy in which the unlabeled documents classified by means of one of the views are then used for training the classifier using the other view, and vice versa.

Both EM and cotraining strategies have experimentally shown a significant reduction (up to 60%) in the amount of labeled training data required to produce the same classifier performance.

IV.7 EVALUATION OF TEXT CLASSIFIERS

Because the text categorization problem is not sufficiently well-defined, the performance of classifiers can be evaluated only experimentally.

Any TC experiment requires a document collection labeled with a set of categories. This collection is divided into two parts: the *training* and *test* document sets. The training set, as the name suggests, is used for training the classifier, and the test set is the one on which the performance measures are calculated. Usually, the test set is the smaller of the two. It is very important not to use the test set in any way during the classifier training and fine-tuning. When there is a need to optimize some classifier parameters experimentally, the training set is further divided into two parts – the training set proper and a *validation* set, which is used for the parameter optimizations.

A commonly used method to smooth out the variations in the corpus is the *n-fold cross-validation*. In this method, the whole document collection is divided into n equal parts, and then the training-and-testing process is run n times, each time using a different part of the collection as the test set. Then the results for n folds are averaged.

IV.7.1 Performance Measures

The most common performance measures are the classic IR measures of *recall* and *precision*. A recall for a category is defined as the percentage of correctly classified documents among all documents belonging to that category, and precision is the percentage of correctly classified documents among all documents that were assigned to the category by the classifier.

Many classifiers allow trading recall for precision or vice versa by raising or lowering parameter settings or the output threshold. For such classifiers there is a convenient measure, called the *breakeven* point, which is the value of recall and precision at the point on the recall-versus-precision curve where they are equal. Alternatively, there is the F_1 measure, equal to $2/(1/\text{recall} + 1/\text{precision})$, which combines the two measures in an ad hoc way.

IV.7.2 Benchmark Collections

The most known publicly available collection is the Reuters set of news stories, classified under economics-related categories. This collection accounts for most of the experimental work in TC so far. Unfortunately, this does not mean that the results produced by different researchers are directly comparable because of subtle differences in the experimental conditions.

In order for the results of two experiments to be directly comparable, the following conditions must be met:

(1) The experiments must be performed on exactly the same collection (meaning the same documents and same categories) using the same split between training and test sets.
(2) The same performance measure must be chosen.

(3) If a particular part of a system is compared, all other parts must be exactly the same. For instance, when comparing learning algorithms, the document representations must be the same, and when comparing the dimension reduction methods, the learning algorithms must be fixed together with their parameters.

These conditions are very difficult to meet – especially the last one. Thus, in practice, the only reliable comparisons are those done by the same researcher.

Other frequently used benchmark collections are the OHSUMED collection of titles and abstracts of papers from medical journals categorized with MESH thesaurus terms, 20 Newsgroups collection of messages posted to newsgroups with the newsgroups themselves as categories, and the TREC-AP collection of newswire stories.

IV.7.3 Comparison among Classifiers

Given the lack of a reliable way to compare classifiers across researchers, it is possible to draw only very general conclusions in reference to the question Which classifier is the best?

- According to most researchers, the top performers are SVM, AdaBoost, *k*NN, and Regression methods. Insufficient statistical evidence has been compiled to determine the best of these methods. Efficiency considerations, implementation complexity, and other application-related issues may assist in selecting from among these classifiers for specific problems.
- Rocchio and Naïve Bayes have the worst performance among the ML classifiers, but both are often used as baseline classifiers. Also, NB is very useful as a member of classifier committees.
- There are mixed results regarding the neural networks and decision tree classifiers. Some of the experiments have demonstrated rather poor performance, whereas in other experiments they performed nearly as well as SVM.

IV.8 CITATIONS AND NOTES

Section IV.1

Applications of text categorization are described in Hayes et al. (1988); Ittner, Lewis, and Ahn (1995); Larkey (1998); Lima, Laender, and Ribeiro-Neto (1998); Attardi, Gulli, and Sebastiani (1999); Drucker, Vapnik, and Wu (1999); Moens and Dumortier (2000); Yang, Ault, Pierce, and Lattimer (2000); Gentili et al. (2001); Krier and Zaccà (2002); Fall et al. (2003); and Giorgetti and Sebastiani (2003a, 2003b).

Section IV.2

For a general introduction to text categorization, refer to Sebastiani (2002) and Lewis (2000), which provides an excellent tutorial on the subject.

Section IV.3

Approaches that integrate linguistic and background knowledge into the categorization process can be found in Jacobs (1992); Rodriguez et al. (1997); Aizawa (2001); and Benkhalifa, Mouradi, and Bouyakhf (2001a, 2001b).

Section IV.5.3–IV.5.4

The following papers discuss how to use decision trees and decision lists for text categorization: Apte, Damerau, and Weiss (1994a, 1994b, 1994c); Li and Yamanishi (1999); Chen and Ho (2000); and Li and Yamanishi (2002).

Section IV.5.5

The use of regression for text categorization is discussed in Zhang and Oles (2001), Zhang et al. (2003), and Zhang and Yang (2003).

Section IV.5.8

The *k*NN algorithm is discussed and described in Yavuz and Guvenir (1998); Han, Karypis, and Kumar (2001); Soucy and Mineau (2001b); and Kwon and Lee (2003).

Section IV.5.9

The SVM algorithm is described and discussed in Vapnik (1995); Joachims (1998); Kwok (1998); Drucker, Vapnik, et al. (1999); Joachims (1999); Klinkenberg and Joachims (2000); Siolas and d'Alche-Buc (2000); Tong and Koller (2000); Joachims (2001); Brank et al. (2002); Joachims (2002); Leopold and Kindermann (2002); Diederich et al. (2003); Sun, Naing, et al. (2003); Xu et al. (2003); and Zhang and Lee (2003).

Section IV.5.10

Approaches that combine several algorithms by using committees of algorithms or by using boosting are described in Larkey and Croft (1996); Liere and Tadepalli (1997); Liere and Tadepalli (1998); Forsyth (1999); Ruiz and Srinivasan (1999a, 1999b); Schapire and Singer (2000); Sebastiani, Sperduti, and Valdambrini (2000); Al-Kofahi et al. (2001); Bao et al. (2001); Lam and Lai (2001); Taira and Haruno (2001); and Nardiello, Sebastiani, and Sperduti (2003).

Additional Algorithms

There are several *adaptive* (or *online*) algorithms that build classifiers incrementally without requiring the whole training set to be present at once. A simple *perceptron* is described in Schutze et al. (1995) and Wiener (1995). A WINNOW algorithm, which is a multiplicative variant of perceptron, is described in Dagan, Karov, and Roth (1997). Other online algorithms include WIDROW_HOFF, EXPONENTIATED GRADIENT (Lewis et al. 1996), and SLEEPING EXPERTS (Cohen and Singer 1999).

Relational and rule-based approaches to text categorization are discussed in Cohen (1992); Cohen (1995a, 1995b); and Cohen and Hirsh (1998).

Section IV.7

Comparisons between the categorization algorithms are discussed in Yang (1996) and Yang (1999).

Clustering

Clustering is an unsupervised process through which objects are classified into groups called clusters. In categorization problems, as described in Chapter IV, we are provided with a collection of preclassified training examples, and the task of the system is to learn the descriptions of classes in order to be able to classify a new unlabeled object. In the case of clustering, the problem is to group the given unlabeled collection into meaningful clusters without any prior information. Any labels associated with objects are obtained solely from the data.

Clustering is useful in a wide range of data analysis fields, including data mining, document retrieval, image segmentation, and pattern classification. In many such problems, little prior information is available about the data, and the decision-maker must make as few assumptions about the data as possible. It is for those cases the clustering methodology is especially appropriate.

Clustering techniques are described in this chapter in the context of textual data analysis. Section V.1 discusses the various applications of clustering in text analysis domains. Sections V.2 and V.3 address the general clustering problem and present several clustering algorithms. Finally Section V.4 demonstrates how the clustering algorithms can be adapted to text analysis.

V.1 CLUSTERING TASKS IN TEXT ANALYSIS

One application of clustering is the analysis and navigation of big text collections such as Web pages. The basic assumption, called the *cluster hypothesis*, states that relevant documents tend to be more similar to each other than to nonrelevant ones. If this assumption holds for a particular document collection, the clustering of documents based on the similarity of their content may help to improve the search effectiveness.

V.1.1 Improving Search Recall

Standard search engines and IR systems return lists of documents that match a user query. It is often the case that the same concepts are expressed by different terms in different texts. For instance, a "car" may be called "automobile," and a query for "car" would miss the documents containing the synonym. However, the overall word contents of related texts would still be similar despite the existence of many synonyms. Clustering, which is based on this overall similarity, may help improve the recall of a query-based search in such a way that when a query matches a document its whole cluster can be returned.

This method alone, however, might significantly degrade precision because often there are many ways in which documents are similar, and the particular way to cluster them should depend on the particular query.

V.1.2 Improving Search Precision

As the number of documents in a collection grows, it becomes a difficult task to browse through the lists of matched documents given the size of the lists. Because the lists are unstructured, except for a rather weak relevance ordering, he or she must know the exact search terms in order to find a document of interest. Otherwise, the he or she may be left with tens of thousands of matched documents to scan.

Clustering may help with this by grouping the documents into a much smaller number of groups of related documents, ordering them by relevance, and returning only the documents from the most relevant group or several most relevant groups.

Experience, however, has shown that the user needs to guide the clustering process so that the clustering will be more relevant to the user's specific interest. An interactive browsing strategy called scatter/gather is the development of this idea.

V.1.3 Scatter/Gather

The scatter/gather browsing method (Cutting et al. 1992; Hearst and Pedersen 1996) uses clustering as a basic organizing operation. The purpose of the method is to enhance the efficiency of human browsing of a document collection when a specific search query cannot be formulated. The method is similar to the techniques used for browsing a printed book. An index, which is similar to a very specific query, is used for locating specific information. However, when a general overview in needed or a general question is posed, a table of contents, which presents the logical structure of the text, is consulted. It gives a sense of what sorts of questions may be answered by more intensive exploration of the text, and it may lead to the particular sections of interest.

During each iteration of a scatter/gather browsing session, a document collection is *scattered* into a set of clusters, and the short descriptions of the clusters are presented to the user. Based on the descriptions, the user selects one or more of the clusters that appear relevant. The selected clusters are then *gathered* into a new subcollection with which the process may be repeated. In a sense, the method dynamically generates a table of contents for the collection and adapts and modifies it in response to the user's selection.

V.1.4 Query-Specific Clustering

Direct approaches to making the clustering query-specific are also possible. The hierachical clustering is especially appealing because it appears to capture the essense of the cluster hypothesis best. The most related documents will appear in the small tight clusters, which will be nested inside bigger clusters containing less similar documents. The work described in Tombros, Villa, and Rijsbergen (2002) tested the cluster hypothesis on several document collections and showed that it holds for query-specific clustering.

Recent experiments with cluster-based retrieval (Liu and Croft 2003) using language models show that this method can perform consistently over document collections of realistic size, and a significant improvement in document retrieval can be obtained using clustering without the need for relevance information from by the user.

V.2 THE GENERAL CLUSTERING PROBLEM

A clustering task may include the following components (Jain, Murty, and Flynn 1999):

- Problem representation, including feature extraction, selection, or both,
- Definition of proximity measure suitable to the domain,
- Actual clustering of objects,
- Data abstraction, and
- Evaluation.

Here we describe the representation of a general clustering problem and several common general clustering algorithms. Data abstraction and evaluation of clustering results are usually very domain-dependent and are discussed in Section V.4, which is devoted to clustering of text data.

V.2.1 Problem Representation

All clustering problems are, in essence, optimization problems. The goal is to select the best among all possible groupings of objects according to the given clustering quality function. The quality function maps a set of possible groupings of objects into the set of real numbers in such a way that a better clustering would be given a higher value.

A good clustering should group together similar objects and separate dissimilar ones. Therefore, the clustering quality function is usually specified in terms of a *similarity* function between objects. In fact, the exact definition of a clustering quality function is rarely needed for clustering algorithms because the computational hardness of the task makes it infeasible to attempt to solve it exactly. Therefore, it is sufficient for the algorithms to know the similarity function and the basic requirement – that similar objects belong to the same clusters and dissimilar to separate ones.

A similarity function takes a pair of objects and produces a real value that is a measure of the objects' proximity. To do so, the function must be able to compare the internal structure of the objects. Various *features* of the objects are used for this purpose. As was mentioned in Chapter I, *feature extraction* is the process of generating the sets of features representing the objects, and *feature selection* is the process of identifying the most effective subset of the extracted features.

The most common *vector space model* assumes that the objects are vectors in the high-dimensional *feature space*. A common example is the bag-of-words model of text documents. In a vector space model, the similarity function is usually based on the distance between the vectors in some metric.

V.2.2 Similarity Measures

The most popular metric is the usual Euclidean distance

$$D(\mathbf{x_i}, \mathbf{x_j}) = \sqrt{\sum_k (x_{ik} - x_{jk})^2},$$

which is a particular case with $p = 2$ of Minkowski metric

$$D_p(\mathbf{x_i}, \mathbf{x_j}) = \left(\sum_k (x_{ik} - x_{jk})^p \right)^{1/p}.$$

For the text documents clustering, however, the cosine similarity measure is the most common:

$$Sim(\mathbf{x_i}, \mathbf{x_j}) = (x'_i \cdot x'_j) = \sum_k x'_{ik} \cdot x'_{jk},$$

where x' is the normalized vector $\mathbf{x} = x/|x|$.

There are many other possible similarity measures suitable for their particular purposes.

V.3 CLUSTERING ALGORITHMS

Several different variants of an abstract clustering problem exist. A *flat (or partitional)* clustering produces a single partition of a set of objects into disjoint groups, whereas a *hierarchical* clustering results in a nested series of partitions.

Each of these can either be a *hard* clustering or a *soft* one. In a hard clustering, every object may belong to exactly one cluster. In soft clustering, the membership is fuzzy – objects may belong to several clusters with a fractional degree of membership in each.

Irrespective of the problem variant, the clustering optimization problems are computationally very hard. The brute-force algorithm for a hard, flat clustering of n-element sets into k clusters would need to evaluate $k^n / k!$ possible partitionings. Even enumerating all possible single clusters of size l requires $n!/l!(n-l)!$, which is exponential in both n and l. Thus, there is no hope of solving the general optimization problem exactly, and usually some kind of a greedy approximation algorithm is used.

Agglomerative algorithms begin with each object in a separate cluster and successively merge clusters until a stopping criterion is satisfied. *Divisive* algorithms begin with a single cluster containing all objects and perform splitting until a stopping criterion is met. "*Shuffling*" algorithms iteratively redistribute objects in clusters.

The most commonly used algorithms are the K-means (hard, flat, shuffling), the EM-based mixture resolving (soft, flat, probabilistic), and the HAC (hierarchical, agglomerative).

V.3.1 K-Means Algorithm

The K-means algorithm partitions a collection of vectors $\{x_1, x_2, \ldots x_n\}$ into a set of clusters $\{C_1, C_2, \ldots C_k\}$. The algorithm needs k cluster seeds for initialization. They can be externally supplied or picked up randomly among the vectors.

The algorithm proceeds as follows:

Initialization:

k seeds, either given or selected randomly, form the core of k clusters. Every other vector is assigned to the cluster of the closest seed.

Iteration:

The *centroids* M_i of the current clusters are computed:

$$M_i = |C_i|^{-1} \sum_{x \in c_i} x.$$

Each vector is reassigned to the cluster with the closest centroid.

Stopping condition:

At convergence – when no more changes occur.

The K-means algorithm maximizes the clustering quality function Q:

$$Q(C_1, C_2, \ldots, C_k) = \sum_{C_1} \sum_{x \in C_i} Sim(x - M_i).$$

If the distance metric (inverse of the similarity function) behaves well with respect to the centroids computation, then each iteration of the algorithm increases the value of Q. A sufficient condition is that the centroid of a set of vectors be the vector that maximizes the sum of similarities to all the vectors in the set. This condition is true for all "natural" metrics. It follows that the K-means algorithm always converges to a local maximum.

The K-means algorithm is popular because of its simplicity and efficiency. The complexity of each iteration is $O(kn)$ similarity comparisons, and the number of necessary iterations is usually quite small.

A major problem with the K-means algorithm is its sensitivity to the initial selection of seeds. If a bad set of seeds is used, the generated clusters are often very much suboptimal. Several methods are known to deal with this problem. The simplest way is to make several clustering runs with different random choices of seeds. Another possibility is to choose the initial seeds utilizing external domain-dependent information.

Several algorithmic methods of dealing with the K-means suboptimality also exist. One possibility is to allow *postprocessing* of the resulting clusters. For instance, the ISO-DATA algorithm (Jensen 1996) merges clusters if the distance between their centroids is below a certain threshold, and this algorithm splits clusters having excessively high variance. Another possibility is employed by the Buckshot algorithm described at the end of this section.

The best number of clusters, in cases where it is unknown, can be computed by running the K-means algorithm with different values of k and choosing the best one according to any clustering quality function.

V.3.2 EM-based Probabilistic Clustering Algorithm

The underlying assumption of *mixture-resolving* algorithms is that the objects to be clustered are drawn from k distributions, and the goal is to identify the parameters of each that would allow the calculation of the probability $P(C_i \mid x)$ of the given object's belonging to the cluster C_i.

The expectation maximization (EM) is a general purpose framework for estimating the parameters of distribution in the presence of hidden variables in observable data. Adapting it to the clustering problem produces the following algorithm:

Initialization:
The initial parameters of k distributions are selected either randomly or externally.
Iteration:
E-Step: Compute the $P(C_i \mid x)$ for all objects x by using the current parameters of the distributions. Relabel all objects according to the computed probabilities.
M-Step: Reestimate the parameters of the distributions to maximize the likelihood of the objects' assuming their current labeling.
Stopping condition:
At convergence – when the change in log-likelihood after each iteration becomes small.

After convergence, the final labelings of the objects can be used as the fuzzy clustering. The estimated distributions may also be used for other purposes.

V.3.3 Hierarchical Agglomerative Clustering (HAC)

The HAC algorithm begins with each object in separate cluster and proceeds to repeatedly merge pairs of clusters that are most similar according to some chosen criterion. The algorithm finishes when everything is merged into a single cluster. The history of merging provides the binary tree of the clusters hierarchy.

Initialization:
Every object is put into a separate cluster.
Iteration:
Find the pair of most similar clusters and merge them.
Stopping condition:
When everything is merged into a single cluster.

Different versions of the algorithm can be produced as determined by how the similarity between clusters is calculated. In the *single-link* method, the similarity between two clusters is the maximum of similarities between pairs of objects from the two clusters. In the *complete-link* method, the similarity is the minimum of similarities of such pairs of objects. The single-link approach may result in long and thin chainlike clusters, whereas the complete-link method results in tight and compact clusters. Although the single-link method is more versatile, experience suggests that the complete-link one produces more useful results.

Other possible similarity measures include "center of gravity" (similarity between centroids of clusters), "average link" (average similarity between pairs of objects of clusters), and a "group average" (average similarity between all pairs of objects in a merged cluster), which is a compromise between the single- and complete-link methods.

The complexity of HAC is $O(n^2s)$, where n is the number of objects and s the complexity of calculating similarity between clusters. For some object similarity measures it is possible to compute the group average cluster similarity in constant time, making the complexity of HAC truly quadratic. By definition, the group average similarity between clusters C_i and C_j is

$$Sim(C_i, C_j) = \frac{1}{|C_i \cup C_j|(|C_i \cup C_j| - 1)} \sum_{x,y \in C_i \cup C_j, x \neq y} Sim(x, y).$$

Assuming that the similarity between individual vector is the cosine similarity, we have

$$Sim(C_i, C_j) = \frac{(S_i + S_j) \cdot (S_i + S_j) - (|C_i| + |C_j|)}{|C_i \cup C_j|(|C_i \cup C_j| - 1)},$$

where $S_i = \sum_{x \in Ci} x$ is the sum of all vectors in the ith cluster. If all S_i's are always maintained, the cosine similarity between clusters can always be computed in a constant time.

V.3.4 Other Clustering Algorithms

Several graph-theoretic clustering algorithms exist. The best known is based on construction of the minimal spanning tree (MST) of the objects and then deleting the edges with the largest lengths to generate clusters. In fact, the hierarchical approaches are also related to graph theoretic clustering. Single-link clusters are subgraphs of the MST, which are also the connected components (Gotlieb and Kumar 1968). Complete-link clusters are the maximal complete subgraphs (Backer and Hubert 1976).

The nearest neighbor clustering (Lu and Fu 1978) assigns each object to the cluster of its nearest labeled neighbor object provided the similarity to that neighbor is sufficiently high. The process continues until all objects are labeled.

The Buckshot algorithm (Cutting et al. 1992) uses the HAC algorithm to generate a good initial partitioning for use by the K-means algorithm. For this purpose, $\sqrt{kn}$ objects are randomly selected, and the group-average HAC algorithm is run on the set. The k clusters generated by HAC are used to initialize the K-means algorithm, which is then run on the whole set of n objects. Because the complexity of HAC is quadratic, the overall complexity of Buckshot remains $O(kn)$ linear in the number of objects.

V.4 CLUSTERING OF TEXTUAL DATA

The clustering of textual data has several unique features that distinguish it from other clustering problems. This section discusses the various issues of representation, algorithms, data abstraction, and evaluation of text data clustering problems.

V.4.1 Representation of Text Clustering Problems

The most prominent feature of text documents as objects to be clustered is their very complex and rich internal structure. In order to be clustered, the documents must be converted into vectors in the feature space. The most common way of doing this, the bag-of-words document representation, assumes that each word is a dimension in the feature space. Each vector representing a document in this space will have a component for each word. If a word is not present in the document, the word's component of the document vector will be zero. Otherwise, it will be some positive value, which may depend on the frequency of the word in the document and in the whole document collection. The details and the different possibilities of the bag-of-words document representation are discussed in Section IV. One very important problem arises for clustering – feature selection.

With big document collections, the dimension of the feature space may easily range into the tens and hundreds of thousands. Because of this, feature selection methods are very important for performance reasons. Many good feature selection methods are available for categorization, but they make use of the distribution of features in classes as found in the training documents. This distribution is not available for clustering.

There are two possible ways of reducing the dimensionality of documents. *Local* methods do not reduce the dimension of the whole feature space but simply delete "unimportant" components from individual document vectors. Because the complexity of calculating the similarity between documents is proportional to the number of nonzero components in the document vectors, such truncation is effective. In practice, the document vectors themselves are already quite sparse, and only the centroids, which can be very dense, need truncation.

The alternative approach is a global *dimension reduction*. Its disadvantage is that it does not adapt to unique characteristics of each document. The advantage is that this method better preserves the ability to compare dissimilar documents because every document undergoes identical transformation. One increasingly popular technique of dimension reduction is based on latent semantic indexing (LSI).

V.4.2 Dimension Reduction with Latent Semantic Indexing

Latent semantic indexing linearly maps the N-dimensional feature space F onto a lower dimensional subspace in a provably optimal way, in the following sense: among all possible subspaces V ∈ F of dimension k, and all possible linear maps M from F onto V, the map given by the LSI perturbs the documents the least, so that the $\sum_{d \in \text{documents}} |D - M(d)|^2$ is minimal. LSI is based upon applying the singular value decomposition (SVD) to the term-document matrix.

V.4.3 Singular Value Decomposition

An SVD of a real $m \times n$ matrix A is a representation of the matrix as a product

$$A = UDV^{\mathrm{T}},$$

where U is a column-orthonormal $m \times r$ matrix, D is a diagonal $r \times r$ matrix, and V is a column-orthonormal $n \times r$ matrix in which r denotes the rank of A. The term "column-orthonormal" means that the column vectors are normalized and have a zero dot-product; thus,

$$UU^{\mathrm{T}} = V^{\mathrm{T}}V = I.$$

The diagonal elements of D are the singular values of A and can all be chosen to be positive and arranged in a descending order. Then the decomposition becomes unique.

There are many methods of computing the SVD of matrices. See Berry (1992) for methods adapted to large but sparse matrices.

Using SVD for Dimension Reduction

The dimension reduction proceeds in the following steps. First, a terms-by-documents rectangular matrix A is formed. Its columns are the vector representations of documents. Thus, the matrix element A_{td} is nonzero when the term t appears in the document d.

Then, the SVD of the matrix A is calculated:

$$A = UDV^{\mathrm{T}}.$$

Next the dimension reduction takes place. We keep the k highest values in the matrix D and set others to zero, resulting in the matrix D'. It can be shown that the matrix

$$A' = UD'V^{\mathrm{T}}$$

is the matrix of rank k that is closest to A in the least-squares sense.

The cosine similarity between the original document vectors is given by the dot product of their corresponding columns in the A matrix. The reduced-dimensional approximation is calculated as the dot product of the columns of A'. Of course, the A' itself need never be calculated. Instead, we can see that

$$A'^{\mathrm{T}} A' = VD'^{\mathrm{T}} U^{\mathrm{T}} UD'V^{\mathrm{T}} = VD'^{\mathrm{T}} D'V^{\mathrm{T}},$$

and thus the representation of documents in the low-dimensional LSI space is given by the rows of the VD^{T} matrix, and the dot product can be calculated between those k-dimensional rows.

Medoids

It is possible to improve the speed of text clustering algorithms by using *medoids* instead of centroids (mentioned in Section V.3). Medoids are actual documents that are most similar to the centroids. This improves the speed of algorithms in a way similar to feature space dimensionality reduction because sparse document vectors are substituted for dense centroids.

Using Naïve Bayes Mixture Models with the EM Clustering Algorithm

For the EM-based fuzzy clustering of text documents, the most common assumption is the Naïve Bayes model of cluster distribution. This model has the following parameters: the prior cluster probability $P(C_i)$ and the probabilities $P(f_i \mid C_i)$ of features in the cluster.

Given the model parameters, the probability that a document belongs to a cluster is

$$P(C_i|x) = P(C_i)\prod_f P(f|C_i) \Big/ \sum_C P(C)\prod_f P(f|C).$$

On the assumption that the current document labeling is $L(x)$, the maximum likelihood estimation of the parameters is

$$P(C_i) = |\{x : L(x) = C_i\}|/N,$$

$$P(f|C_i) = |\{x : L(x) = C_i \quad \text{and} \quad f \in x\}|/|\{x : L(x) = C_i\}|,$$

where N is the number of documents.

Using this method it is possible to improve *categorization* systems in cases in which the number of labeled documents is small but many unlabeled documents are available. Then the labeled documents can be used to train the initial NB models, which are then used within the EM algorithm to cluster the unlabeled documents. The final cluster models are the output classifiers produced by this technique. The experiments have shown a significant improvement in accuracy over the classifiers that are trained only on labeled data (Nigam et al. 2000).

V.4.4 Data Abstraction in Text Clustering

Data abstraction in clustering problems entails generating a meaningful and concise description of the cluster for the purposes of further automatic processing or for user consumption. The machine-usable abstraction is usually easiest; natural candidates are cluster centroids or probabilistic models of clusters.

In the case of text clustering, the problem is to give the user a meaningful cluster label. For some applications, such as scatter/gather browsing, a good label is almost as important as good clustering. A good label would consist of a very small number of terms precisely distinguishing the cluster from the others. For instance, after clustering documents about "jaguar," we would like one cluster to be named "Animal" and another "Car."

There are many possibilities of generating cluster labels automatically:

- A title of the medoid document or several typical document titles can be used.
- Several words common to the cluster documents can be shown. A common heuristic is to present the five or ten most frequent terms in the centroid vector of the cluster.
- A distinctive noun phrase, if it can be found, is probably the best label.

V.4.5 Evaluation of Text Clustering

Measuring the quality of an algorithm is a common problem in text as well as data mining. It is easy to compare the exact measures, such as time and space complexity, but the quality of the results needs human judgment, which introduces a high degree of subjectivity.

The "internal" measures of clustering quality are essentially the functions we would like to optimize by the algorithms. Therefore, comparing such measures for clusterings produced by different algorithms only shows which algorithm results in a better approximation of the general optimization problem for the particular case. This makes some sense, but what we would like to see is a measure of how good the clustering is for human consumption or for further processing.

Given a set of categorized (manually classified) documents, it is possible to use this benchmark labeling for evaluation of clusterings. The most common measure is *purity*. Assume $\{L_1, L_2, \ldots, L_n\}$ are the manually labeled classes of documents, and $\{C_1, C_2, \ldots, C_m\}$ are the clusters returned by the clustering process. Then,

$$Purity(C_i) = \max_j |L_j \cap C_i| / |C_i|.$$

Other measures include the *entropy* of classes in clusters, *mutual information* between classes and clusters, and so on. However, all these measures suffer from the limitation that there is more than one way to classify documents – all equally right.

Probably the most useful evaluation is the straightforward measure of the utility of the resulting clustering in its intended application. For instance, assume the clustering is used for improving the navigation of search results. Then it is possible to prepare a set of queries and the intended results manually and to measure the improvement produced by clustering directly using simulated experiments.

V.5 CITATIONS AND NOTES

Section V.1

The scatter/gather method was introduced by Cutting in Cutting et al. (1992) and further expanded in Cutting, Karger, et al. (1993). Application and analysis of the scatter/gather methods are described in Cutting, Karger, et al. (1992); Cutting, Karger, and Pedersen (1993); Hearst, Karger, and Pedersen (1995); and Hearst and Pedersen (1996).

Section V.3

Descriptions of general clustering algorithms and comparisons between them can be found in the following papers: Mock (1998); Zhong and Ghosh (2003); Jain and Dubes (1988); Goldszmidt and Sahami (1998); Jain et al. (1999); and Steinbach, Karypis, and Kumar (2000). Algorithms for performing clustering on very large amount of data are described in Bradley, Fayyad, and Reina (1998) and Fayyad, Reina, and Bradley (1998).

Section V.4

Clustering by using latent semantic indexing (LSI) is described in the following papers: Deerwester et al. (1990); Hull (1994); and Landauer, Foltz, and Laham (1998). In many cases there is a need to utilize background information and external knowledge bases. Clustering using backround information is described in Hotho et al.

(2003), and clustering using ontologies is described in Hotho, Staab, and Maedche (2001). Clustering using the popular WordNet resource is mentioned in Benkhalifa, Mouradi, and Bouyakhf (2001a, 2000b).

Specific clustering algorithms adapted for textual data are described in Iwayama and Tokunaga (1995a, 1995b); Goldszmidt and Sahami (1998); Zamir and Etzioni (1999); El-Yaniv and Souroujon (2001); and Dhillon, Mallela, and Kumar (2002).

Information Extraction

VI.1 INTRODUCTION TO INFORMATION EXTRACTION

A mature IE technology would allow rapid creation of extraction systems for new tasks whose performance would approach a human level. Nevertheless, even systems without near perfect recall and precision can be of real value. In such cases, the results of the IE system would need to be fed into an auditing environment to allow auditors to fix the system's precision (an easy task) and recall (much harder) errors. These types of systems would also be of value in cases in which the information is too vast for the users to be able to read all of it; hence, even a partially correct IE system would be preferable to the alternative of not obtaining any potentially relevant information. In general, IE systems are useful if the following conditions are met:

- The information to be extracted is specified explicitly and no further inference is needed.
- A small number of templates are sufficient to summarize the relevant parts of the document.
- The needed information is expressed relatively locally in the text (check Bagga and Biermann 2000).

As a first step in tagging documents for text mining systems, each document is processed to find (i.e., extract) *entities* and *relationships* that are likely to be meaningful and content-bearing. The term *relationships* here denotes *facts* or *event*s involving certain *entities*.

By way of example, a possible *event* might be a company's entering into a joint venture to develop a new drug. An example of a *fact* would be the knowledge that a gene causes a certain disease. *Facts* are static and usually do not change; events are more dynamic and generally have a specific time stamp associated with them. The extracted information provides more concise and precise data for the mining process than the more naive word-based approaches such as those used for text categorization, and the information tends to represent concepts and relationships that are more meaningful and relate directly to the examined document's domain.

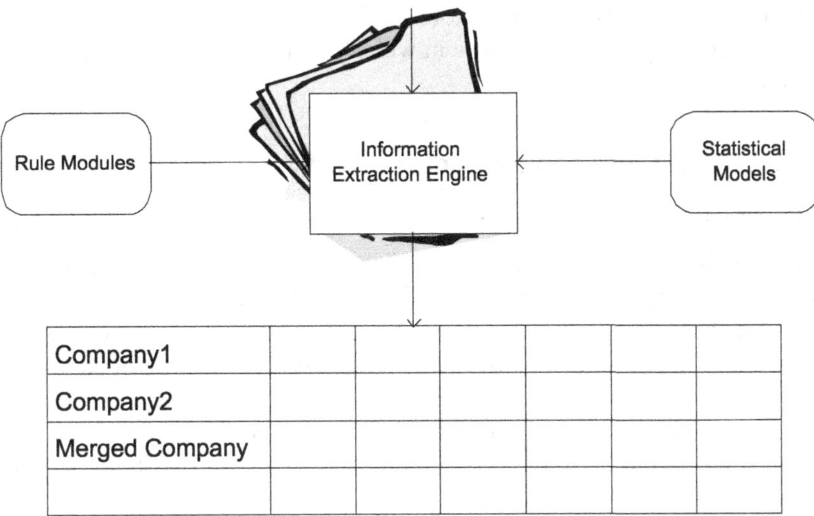

Figure VI.1. Schematic view of the information extraction process.

Consequently, IE methods allow for mining of the actual information present within the text rather than the limited set of tags associated with the documents. The IE process makes the number of different relevant *entities* and *relationships* on which the text mining is performed unbounded – typically thousands or even millions, which would be far beyond the number of tags any automated categorization system could handle. Thus, preprocessing techniques involving IE tend to create more rich and flexible representation models for documents in text mining systems.

IE can be seen as a limited form of "complete text comprehension." No attempt is made to understand the document at hand fully. Instead, one defines a priori the types of semantic information to be extracted from the document. IE represents documents as sets of entities and frames that are another way of formally describing the relationships between the entities.

The set of all possible entities and frames is usually open and very big compared with the set of categorization keywords. It cannot be created manually. Instead, the features are extracted directly from the text. The hierarchy relation between the entities and frames is usually a simple tree. The root has several children – the entity types (e.g., "*Company*," "*Person*," "*Gene*," etc.) under which the actual entities are automatically added as they are being discovered.

The frames constitute structured objects, and so they cannot be directly used as features for text mining. Instead, the frame attributes and its label are used for features. The frame itself, however, may bypass the regular text mining operations and may be fed directly to the querying and visualization components.

The simplest kind of information extraction is called *term extraction*. There are no frames, and there is only one entity type – simply "*term*."

Figure VI.1 gives a schematic view of the IE process. At the heart of the process we have the IE engine that takes a set of documents as input. The engine works by using a statistical model, a rule module, or a mix of both.

The output of the engine is a set of annotated frames extracted from the documents. The frames actually populate a table in which the fields of the frame are the rows of the table.

VI.1.1 Elements That Can Be Extracted from Text

There are four basic types of elements that can, at present, be extracted from text.

- ***Entities.*** Entities are the basic building blocks that can be found in text documents. Examples include people, companies, locations, genes, and drugs.
- ***Attributes.*** Attributes are features of the extracted entities. Some examples of attributes are the title of a person, the age of a person, and the type of an organization.
- ***Facts.*** Facts are the relations that exist between entities. Some examples are an employment relationship between a person and a company or phosphorylation between two proteins.
- ***Events.*** An event is an activity or occurrence of interest in which entities participate such as a terrorist act, a merger between two companies, a birthday and so on.

Figure VI.2 shows a full news article that demonstrates several tagged entities and relationships.

VI.2 HISTORICAL EVOLUTION OF IE: THE MESSAGE UNDERSTANDING CONFERENCES AND TIPSTER

The Defense Advanced Research Project Agency (DARPA) has been sponsoring efforts to codify and expand IE tasks, and the most comprehensive work has arisen from MUC-6 (Message Understanding Conference) and MUC-7 conferences. We now describe the various tasks introduced during the MUC conferences.

VI.2.1 Named Entity Recognition

The named entity recognition (NE, sometimes denoted also as NER) phase is the basic task-oriented phase of any IE system. During this phase the system tries to identify all mentions of proper names and quantities in the text such as the following types taken from MUC-7:

- People names, geographic locations, and organizations;
- Dates and times; and
- Monetary amounts and percentages.

The accuracy (F1) of the extraction results obtained on the NE task is usually quite high, and the best systems manage to get even up to 95-percent breakeven between precision and recall.

The NE task is weakly domain dependent – that is, changing the domain of the texts being analyzed may or may not induce degradation of the performance levels. Performance will mainly depend on the level of generalization used while developing the NE engine and on the similarity between the domains.

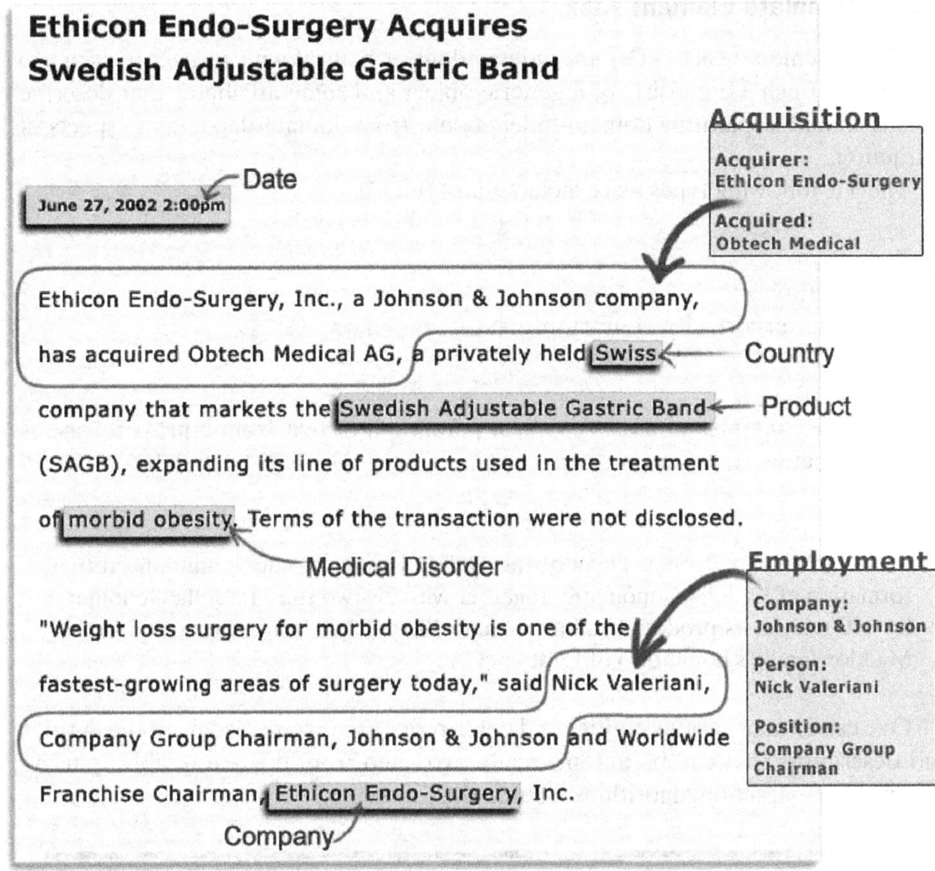

Figure VI.2. A tagged news article.

Proper names usually account for 70 percent of the named entities in the MUC corpuses, dates and times account for 25 percent, and monetary amounts and percentages account for less than 5 percent of the total named entities. Out of the named entities, about 45–50 percent are organization names, 12–32 percent are location tags, and 23–39 percent are people tags.

The MUC committee stipulated that the following types of noun phrases should not be extracted because they do not refer to any specific entity:

- Artifacts (e.g., *Wall Street Journal*, MTV, etc.),
- Common nouns used in anaphoric reference (such as the plane, the company, etc.),
- Names of groups of people and laws named after people (e.g., Republicans, "Gramm–Rudman amendment," "the Nobel Prize," etc.),
- Adjectival forms of location names (e.g., "American," "Japanese," etc.), and
- Miscellaneous uses of numbers that are not specifically currency or percentages.

VI.2.2 Template Element Task

Template element tasks (TEs) are independent or neutral with respect to scenario or domain. Each TE consists of a generic object and some attributes that describe it. This enables separating domain-independent from domain-dependent aspects of extraction.

The TE following types were included in MUC-7:

- Person
- Organization
- Location (airport, city, country, province, region, water)
- Artifact.

Here are examples of TEs. A typical paragraph of text from a press release is as follows below (taken from <http://www.itl.nist.gov/iaui/894.02/related_projects/muc/>):

> Fletcher Maddox, former Dean of the UCSD Business School, announced the formation of La Jolla Genomatics together with his two sons. La Jolla Genomatics will release its product Geninfo in June 1999. L.J.G. is headquartered in the Maddox family's hometown of La Jolla, CA.

One can extract various entities and descriptors. For instance, some of the entities and descriptors that can be automatically extracted from this paragraph by using information extraction algorithms include the following:

```
entity {
ID = 1,
NAME = "Fletcher Maddox"
DESCRIPTOR = "Former Dean of USCD Business School"
CATEGORY = person
}
entity {
ID = 2
NAME = "La Jolla Genomatics"
ALIAS = "LJG"
DESCRIPTOR = ""
CATEGORY = organization
}
entity {
ID = 3
NAME = "La Jolla"
DESCRIPTOR = "the Maddox family hometown"
CATEGORY = location
}
```

VI.2.3 Template Relationship (TR) Task

The Template relationship task (TR) expresses a domain-independent relationship between entities as compared with TEs, which just identify entities themselves. The goal of the TR task is to find the relationships that exist between the template elements extracted from the text (during the TE task). Just like the definition of an entity, entity attributes depend on the problem and the nature of the texts being analyzed; the relationships that may exist between template elements is domain dependent too. For example, persons and companies may be related by employee_of relation, companies and locations may be related by located_of relations, and companies may be interrelated by subdivision_of relations.

The following TRs were extracted from the sample text:

employee_of (Fletcher Maddox, UCSD Business School)
employee_of (Fletcher Maddox, La Jolla Genomatics)
product_of (Geninfo, La Jolla Genomatics)
location_of (La Jolla, La Jolla Genomatics)
location_of (CA, La Jolla Genomatics)

VI.2.4 Scenario Template (ST)

Scenario templates (STs) express domain and task-specific entities and relations. The main purpose of the ST tasks is to test portability to new extraction problems quickly. This task gives advantage to technologies that are not so labor intensive and hence can port the extraction engine to a new domain in a short time (couple of weeks).

Here are a few events that were extracted from the sample text:

```
company-formation-event {
PRINCIPAL = "Fletcher Maddox"
DATE = ""
CAPITAL = ""
}
product-release-event {
COMPANY = "La Jolla Genomatics"
PRODUCS = "Geninfo"
DATE = "June 1999"
COST = ""
}
```

VI.2.5 Coreference Task (CO)

The coreference task (CO) captures information on coreferring expressions (e.g., pronouns or any other mentions of a given entity), including those tagged in the NE, TE tasks. This CO focuses on the IDENTITY (IDENT) relation, which is symmetrical and transitive. It creates equivalence classes (or coreference chains) used for scoring. The task is to mark nouns, noun phrases, and pronouns.

```
"It's a chance to think about first-level
questions", said Ms. <enamex type=
"PERSON">Cohn</enamex>, a partner in the <enamex type=
"ORGANIZATION"> McGlashan & Sarrail</enamex> firm in
<enamex type= "LOCATION">San Mateo</enamex>, Senamex
type= "LOCATION">Calif.</enamex>
```

Figure VI.3. MUC-style annotation.

Consider the following sentence:

David$_1$ came home from school, and saw his$_1$ mother$_2$,
Rachel$_2$. She$_2$ told him$_1$ that his$_1$ father will be late.

The correctly identified pronominal coreference chains are (**David**$_1$, **his**$_1$, **him**$_1$, **his**$_1$) and (**mother**$_2$, **Rachel**$_2$, **She**$_2$).

This is not a high-accuracy task for IE systems but properly resolving some kinds of coreference is usually difficult even for humans annotators, who achieved about 80 percent.

An MUC-style tagging is shown in Figure VI.3, and a sample template extracted from that text fragment is shown in Figure VI.4.

VI.2.6 Some Notes about IE Evaluation

We follow here the discussion of Lavelli et al. (2004) about various problems in the common evaluation methodology of information extraction. The main problem is that it is very hard to compare different IE experiments without comparing the exact settings of each experiment. In particular the following problems were raised:

- The exact split between the training set and test set: considering both the proportions between the two sets (e.g., a 50/50 versus a 90/10 split) and the repetition procedure adopted in the experiment (e.g., a single specific split between training and test versus n repeated random splits versus n-fold cross-validations).
- Determining the test set: the test set for each point on the learning curve can be the same (hold-out set) or be different and based on the exact split.
- What constitutes an exact match: how to treat an extraneous or a missing comma – that is, should it be counted as a mistake or is it close enough and does not miss any critical information.
- Feature Selection: many different types of features can be used, including orthographic features, linguistic features (such as POS, stemming, etc.), and semantic features based on external ontologies. In order to compare any two algorithms properly they must operate on the same set of features.

```
<ORGANIZATION-9303020074-1> :=
    ORG_NAME: "McGlashan & Sarrail"
    ORG_ALIAS: "M & S"
    ORG_LEADER: <PERSON-9303020074-57>
    ORG_TYPE: COMPANY
```

Figure VI.4. MUC-style templates.

Counting the Correct Results

- Exact Matches: Instances generated by the extractor that perfectly match actual instances annotated by the domain expert.
- Contained Matches: Instances generated by the extractor that contain actual instances annotated by the domain expert and some padding from both sides.
- Overlapped Matches: Instances generated by the extractor that overlap actual instances annotated by the domain expert (at least one word is in the intersection of the instances).

Another aspect is how to treat entities that appear multiple times in a document. One option is to extract all of them, and then any omission will result in lower recall. Another option is to extract each entity just once; hence, it is enough just to identify one occurrence of each entity. There are situations in which the latter option will actually make sense if we are just interested in knowing which entities appear in each document (and we do not care how many times it appears).

VI.3 IE EXAMPLES

This section provides several real-world examples of input documents and the results obtained by performing information extraction on them. The examples have been culled from a variety of domains and demonstrate a broad range tagging standards to give the reader an exposure to the different ways to approach coding the information exaction process.

VI.3.1 Case 1: Simplistic Tagging, News Domain

Consider a system that extracts business events from news articles. Such a system is useful for business analysts or even casual users interested in keeping abreast of the current business events. Consider the following text fragment:

> "TeliaSonera, the Nordic region's largest telecoms operator, was formed in 2002 from the cross-border merger between Telia and Finland's Sonera,"

One can extract the following frame from it:

FrameName: Merger
Company1: Telia
Company2: Sonera
New Company: TeliaSonera

This frame actually provides a concise summary of the previous text fragment. The following cases will show the types of summary information that can be extracted from other text fragments.

VI.3.2 Case 2: Natural Disasters Domain

> **4 Apr Dallas** – Early last evening, a tornado swept through an area northwest of Dallas, causing extensive damage. Witnesses confirm that the twister occurred without warning at approximately 7:15 p.m. and destroyed the mobile homes.

The Texaco station, at 102 Main Street, Farmers Branch, TX, was severely damaged, but no injuries were reported. Total property damages are estimated at $350,000.

Event:	tornado
Date:	4/3/97
Time:	19:15
Location:	Farmers Branch : "northwest of Dallas" : TX : USA
Damage:	mobile homes
	Texaco station
Estimated Losses:	$350,000
Injuries:	none

VI.3.3 Case 3: Terror-Related Article, MUC-4

19 March – a bomb went off this morning near a power tower in San Salvador leaving a large part of the city without energy, but no causalities have been reported. According to unofficial sources, the bomb – allegedly detonated by urban guerrilla commandos – blew up a power tower in the northwestern part of San Salvador at 0650 (1250 GMT).

Incident Type:	Bombing
Date:	March 19th
Location:	El Salvador: San Salvador (City)
Perpetrator:	urban guerrilla commandos
Physical Target:	power tower
Human Target:	–
Effect of Physical Target:	destroyed
Effect on Human Target:	no injury or death
Instrument	bomb

VI.3.4 Technology-Related Article, TIPSTER-Style Tagging

Here is an article from the MUC-5 evaluation dealing with microelectronics.

```
<doc>
<REFNO> 000019641 </REFNO>
<DOCNO> 3560177 </DOCNO>
<DD> November 25, 1991 </DD>
<SO> News Release </SO>
<TXT>
Applied Materials, Inc. today announced its newest source technology, called
the Durasource, for the Endura(TM) 5500 PVD system. This enhanced source
includes new magnet configurations, giving the industry's most advanced
```

sputtered aluminum step coverage in sub-micron contacts, and a new one piece target that more than doubles target life to approximately 8000 microns of deposition compared to conventional two-piece "bonded" targets. The Durasource enhancement is fully retrofittable to installed Endura 5500 PVD systems. The Durasource technology has been specially designed for 200 mm wafer applications, although it is also available for 125 mm and 1sOmm wafer sizes. For example, step coverage symmetry is maintained within 3% between the inner and outer walls of contacts across a 200 mm wafer. Film thickness uniformity averages 3% (3 sigma) over the life of the target.
</TXT>
</doc>

```
<TEMPLATE-3560177-1> :=
        DOC NR: 3560177
        DOC DATE: 251192
        DOCUMENT SOURCE: "News Release"
        CONTENT:
        <MICROELECTRONICS_CAPABILITY-3560177-1>
        DATE TEMPLATE COMPLETED: 021292
        EXTRACTION TIME: 5
        COMMENT: "article focuses on nonreportable target source
        but reportable info available"
        /"TOOL_VERSION: LOCKE.3.4"
        /"FILLRULES_VERSION: EME.4.0"
<MICROELECTRONICS_CAPABILITY-3560177-1> :=
        PROCESS: <LAYERING-3560177-1>
        MANUFACTURER: <ENTITY-3560177-1>
<ENTITY-3560177-1> :=
        NAME: Applied Materials, INC
        TYPE: COMPANY
<LAYERING-3560177-1> :=
        TYPE: SPUTTERING
        FILM: ALUMINUM
        EQUIPMENT: <EQUIPMENT-3560177-1>
<EQUIPMENT-3560177-1> :=
        NAME_OR_MODEL: "Endura(TM) 5500"
        MANUFACTURER: <ENTITY-3560177-1>
        EQUIPMENT_TYPE: PVD_SYSTEM
        STATUS: IN_USE
        WAFER_SIZE: (200 MM)
                    (125 MM)
        COMMENT: "actually three wafer sizes, third is error 1sOmm"
```

VI.3.5 Case 5: Comprehensive Stage-by-Stage Example

- ***Original Sentence*:** Mr. Eskew was Vice President of Worldwide Sales for Sandpiper Networks, which was recently acquired by Digital Island where he created the worldwide sales strategy.
- ***After Part of Speech Tagging*:**
  <Prop>Mr. Eskew</Prop> <Verb>was</Verb> <Prop>Vice President</Prop> <Prep>of</Prep> <Prop>Worldwide Sales</Prop> <Prep>for</Prep> <Prop>Sandpiper Networks</Prop> which <Verb>was</Verb> <Adv>recently</Adv> <Verb>acquired</Verb> <Prep>by</Prep> <Prop>Digital Island</Prop> where <Pron>he</Pron> <Verb>created</Verb> <Det>the</Det> <Adj>worldwide</Adj> <Nn>sales strategy.</Nn>
- ***After Shallow Parsing*:**
  NP:{Mr. Eskew} was NP:{Vice President of Worldwide Sales} for NP:{Sandpiper Networks} which was ADV:{recently} V:{acquired} by NP:{Digital Island} where NP:{he} V:{created} NP:{the worldwide sales strategy}
- ***After Named Entity Recognition*:**
  Person:{Mr. Eskew} was Position:{Vice President of Worldwide Sales} for Company:{Sandpiper Networks} which was ADV:{recently} V:{acquired} by Company:{Digital Island} where Person:{he} V:{created} NP:{the worldwide sales strategy}
- ***After Merging (Anaphora Resolution)*:**
  Person:{Mr. Eskew} was Position:{Vice President of Worldwide Sales} for Company:{Sandpiper Networks} which was ADV:{recently} V:{acquired} by Company:{Digital Island} where Person:{Mr. Eskew} V:{created} NP:{the worldwide sales strategy}
- ***Frames Extracted*:**
  Frame Type: **Acquisition**
  Acquiring Company: Digital Island
  Acquired Company: Sandpiper Networks
  Acquisition Status: Historic

  FrameType: **PersonPositionCompany**
  Person: Mr. Eskew
  Position: Vice President of Worldwide Sales
  Company: Sandpiper Networks
  Status: Past

VI.4 ARCHITECTURE OF IE SYSTEMS

Figure VI.5 shows the generalized architecture for a basic IE system of the type that would be used for text mining preprocessing activities. The subcomponents are colored according to their necessity within the full system.

A typical general-use IE system has three to four major components. The first component is a tokenization or *zoning* module, which splits an input document into its basic building blocks. The typical building blocks are words,

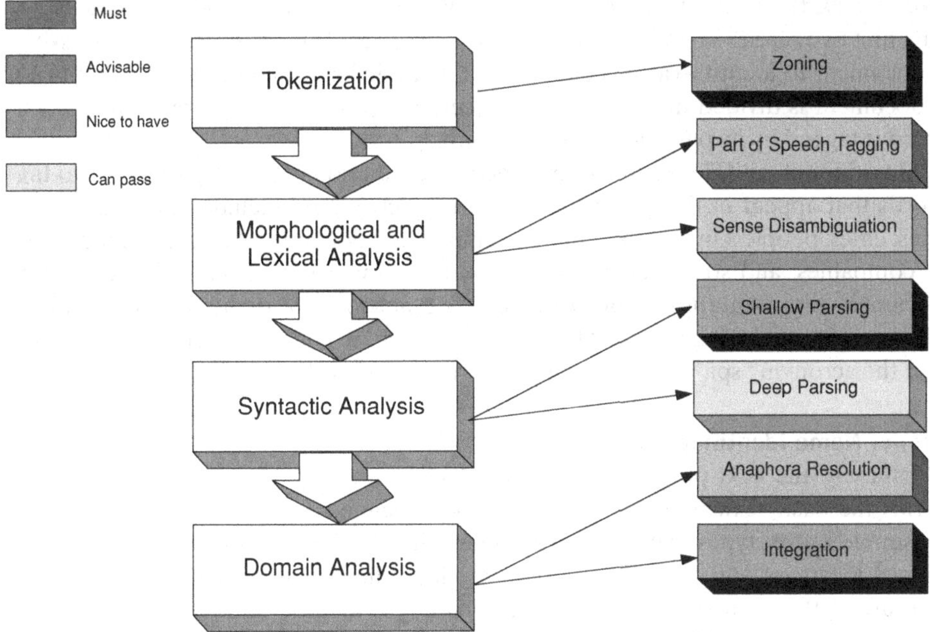

Figure VI.5. Architecture of a typical information extraction system.

sentences and paragraphs. Rarely we may have higher building blocks like sections and chapters.

The second component is a module for performing *morphological and lexical analysis*. This module handles activities such as assigning POS tags to the document's various words, creating basic phrases (like noun phrases and verb phrases), and disambiguating the sense of ambiguous words and phrases.

The third component is a module for *syntactic analysis*. This part of an IE system establishes the connection between the different parts of each sentence. This is done either by doing full parsing or shallow parsing.

A fourth and increasingly more common component in IE systems performs what might be termed *domain analysis*, which is a function in which the system combines all the information collected from the previous components and creates complete frames that describe relationships between entities. Advanced domain analysis modules also possess an anaphora resolution component. Anaphora resolution concerns itself with resolving indirect (and usually pronomic) references for entities that may appear in sentences other than the one containing the primary direct reference to an entity.

VI.4.1 Information Flow in an IE System

Most information extraction systems use a deterministic bottom-up approach to analyzing the document. Initially, one identifies the low-level elements and then identifies higher level features that are based on the low-level features identified in the previous phases.

Processing the Initial Lexical Content: Tokenization and Lexical Analysis

The first two phases of an IE system really both concern themselves with processing a document to identify various elements of its basic lexical content. As a first pass, a document is divided into tokens, sentences, and possibly paragraphs. Then, each word is tagged by its part of speech and lemma.

In addition, an IE system can use specialized dictionaries and gazetteers to tag words that appear in those word lists. Typical dictionaries include names of countries, cities, people's first names, public companies, company suffixes, common titles in companies, and so on. Dictionary support during initial tagging creates richer document representations. For example, using appropriate dictioniaries, the word "Robert" would be tagged as a "first name," "IBM" would be tagged as a company, and the acronym "spa" could be tagged as "company suffix."

Proper Name Identification

Commonly, the next phase is proper name identification. After an IE system performs the basic lexical analysis, it is typically designed to try to identify a variety of simple entity types such as dates, times, e-mail address, organizations, people names, locations, and so on. The entities are identified by using regular expressions that utilize the context around the proper names to identify their type. The regular expressions can use POS tags, syntactic features, and orthographic features such as capitalization.

Proper name identification is performed by scanning the words in the sentence while trying to match one of the patterns in the predefined set of regular expressions. Each proper name type has its associated set of regular expressions. All patterns are attempted for each word. If more than one pattern is matched, the IE system picks the pattern that matches the longest word sequence. If there is a tie, the IE system usually just uses the first pattern. If no pattern matches, the IE system moves to the next word and reapplies the entire set of patterns. The process continues until the end of the sentence is reached.

To illustrate how such regular expressions are constructed, we present several regular expressions for identifying people names below.

1. @Honorific CapitalizedWord CapitalizedWord
   a. @Honorific is a list of honorific titles such as {Dr., Prof., Mr., Ms., Mrs. etc.)
   b. Example: Mr. John Edwards
2. @FirstNames CapitalizedWord
   a. @FirstNames is a list of common first names collected from sites like the U.S. census and other relevant sites
   b. Example: Bill Hellman
3. CapitalizedWord CapitalizedWord [,] @PersonSuffix
   a. @PersonSuffix is a list of common suffixes such as {Jr., Sr., II, III, etc.}
   b. Example: Mark Green, Jr.
4. CapitalizedWord CapitalLetter [.] CapitalizedWord
   a. CapitalLetter followed by an optional period is a middle initial of a person and a strong indicator that this is a person name
   b. Example: Nancy M. Goldberg

Element	Grammatical Function	Type
E1	NP	Company
E2	VG	
E3	NP	Person
E4	NP	Position
E5	NP	Position
E6	NP	Company
E7	NP	Location
E8	VG	
E9	NP	Position

Figure VI.6. Identifying a text element's grammatic function and type.

5. CapitalizedWord CapitalLetter @PersonVerbs
   a. @PersonVerbs is a list of common verbs that are strongly associated with people such as {said, met, walked, etc.}

A more expansive treatment of the topic of manual rule writing and pattern development is offered in Appendix A.

Shallow Parsing

After identifying the basic entities, an IE system moves to shallow parsing and identification of noun and verb groups. These elements will be used as building blocks for the next phase that identifies relations between these elements. As an example, consider the following annotated text fragment:

> Associated Builders and Contractors (ABC)$_{\mathbf{E1}}$ today announced$_{\mathbf{E2}}$ that Bob Piper$_{\mathbf{E3}}$, co-owner$_{\mathbf{E4}}$ and vice president of corporate operations$_{\mathbf{E5}}$, Piper Electric Co., Inc.$_{\mathbf{E6}}$, Arvada, Colo.$_{\mathbf{E7}}$, has been named$_{\mathbf{E8}}$ vice president of workforce development$_{\mathbf{E9}}$.

Essentially, at this point, an IE system focuses on creating a comprehensive listing of the types of elements found in such a text fragment in the manner shown in Figure VI.6.

The next step performed by an IE system is the construction of noun groups based on the noun phrases (NPs) that were constructed before. The construction is based on common patterns developed manually. Essentially, this works in the following manner. On the basis of a few typical patterns such as

1. Position and Position, Company
2. Company, Location,

one can construct the following noun groups (NGs):

1. co-owner$_{\mathbf{E4}}$ and vice president of corporate operations$_{\mathbf{E5}}$, Piper Electric Co., Inc.$_{\mathbf{E6}}$
2. Piper Electric Co., Inc.$_{\mathbf{E6}}$, Arvada, Colo.$_{\mathbf{E7}}$.

Already, even at the conclusion of the initial tokenization and lexical analysis stages of the IE system's preprocessing operations, a relatively rich amount of structure has been created to represent the text of a particular document. This structure will be useful as a building block for further phases of IE-related preprocessing operations.

Building Relations

The construction of relations between entities is done by using domain-specific patterns. The generality of the patterns depends on the depth of the linguistic analysis performed at the sentence level. If one just performs this analysis against individual noun or verb phrases, or both, then one will need to develop five to six times more patterns than if simply the subject, verb, and object of each sentence were identified. To extract an executive appointment event from the text fragment above, one could use the following pattern:

Company [Temporal] @Announce Connector Person PersonDetails @Appoint Position

This pattern can be broken down in the following way:

- ***Temporal*** is a phrase indicating a specific date and/or time such as {yesterday, today, tomorrow, last week, an hour ago}
- ***@Announce*** is a set of phrases that correspond to the activity of making a public announcement like {announced, notified, etc.}
- ***Connector*** is a set of connecting words like {that, ... }
- ***PersonDetails*** is a phrase describing some fact about a person (such as his or her age, current position, etc.); it will be usually surrounded by commas
- ***@Appoint*** is a set of phrases that correspond to the activity of appointing a person to a position like {appointed, named, nominated, etc.}

One of the main tasks during the relation extraction is coreference resolution, which is introduced in Section VI.5. We expand on coreference resolution in Section VI.5.

Inferencing

In many cases, an IE system has to resort to some kind of common sense reasoning and infer missing values to complete the identification of events. The inference rules are written as a formalism similar to Prolog clauses. Common examples include family relations, management changes, spatial relations, and so on.

Below are two examples, one related to location of a person and the other to the position a person is going to fill. The first example is a simple two-sentence text fragment.

Example 1: John Edgar was reported to live with Nancy Leroy. His Address is 101 Forest Rd., Bethlehem, PA.

From this, it is possible to extract the following entities and events:

1. person(John Edgar)
2. person(Nancy Leroy)
3. livetogether(John Edgar, Nancy Leroy)
4. address(John Edgar, 101 Forest Rd., Bethlehem, PA)

Using the following rule, one can infer that Nancy Leroy lives at 101 Forest Rd., Bethlehem, PA.

address(P1,A) :- person(P1), person(P2), livetogether(P1,P2), address(P1,A).

The second example is also a two-sentence text fragment.

Example 2: RedCarpet Inc. announced that its President, JayGoldman, has resigned. The company appointed Fred Robbins to the position.

From this one can extract the following entities and events:

1. company(RedCarpet)
2. person(Jay Goldman)
3. personLeftPosition(Jay Goldman, RedCarpet, President)
4. personReplacesPerson(Fred Robbins, Jay Goldman)

Using the following rule in this second example, one can infer that Fred Robbins is the new President of RedCarpet:

newposition(P2,Pos) :- person(P1), person(P2), company(C1), personLeftPosition(P1,C1,Pos), personReplacesPerson (P2,P1).

VI.5 ANAPHORA RESOLUTION

Anaphora or *coreference resolution* is the process of matching pairs of NLP expressions that refer to the same entity in the real world. It is a process that is critical to the proper function of advanced text mining preprocessing systems.

Below is an example of an annotated text fragment that includes chains of coreffering phrases. We can see here two chains referring to a person (#1, #5), one chain referring to an incident (#2), one chain referring to groups of people (#4), two chains referring to locations (#3, #7), and one chain referring to an organization (#6).

HADERA, Israel$_3$ (AP) – A Palestinian gunman$_1$ walked into a wedding hall in northern Israel$_3$ late Thursday and opened fire, killing six people and injuring 30$_2$, police$_6$ said.... Police$_6$ earlier said the attacker$_1$ threw hand grenades but witnesses and later police$_6$ accounts said the attacker$_1$ opened fire with an M-16 and was$_1$ stopped before he$_1$ could throw a grenade. The Al Aqsa Brigades$_4$, a militia$_4$ linked to Yasser Arafat's Fatah claimed responsibility. The group$_4$ said that Abed Hassouna$_1$ from a village$_7$ near the Palestinian town of Nablus carried out the attack$_2$ to avenge the death of Raed Karmi$_5$, (the militia)$_4$'s leader$_5$ in the town of Tulkarem. Hassouna$_1$ had been a Palestinian policeman$_1$ but left$_1$ the force two years ago, residents of his$_1$ village$_7$ said.

There are two main approaches to anaphora resolution. One is a knowledge-based approach based on linguistic analysis of the sentences and is coded as a rigid algorithm. The other approach is a machine learning approach based on an annotated corpus.

VI.5.1 Pronominal Anaphora

Pronominal anaphora deals with resolving pronouns such as he, she, and they, It is the most common type of coreference. There are three types of pronouns:

- ***Reflexive pronouns***: himself, herself
- ***Personal pronouns***: he, him, you
- ***Possessive pronouns***: her, his, hers

It should be pointed out that not all pronouns in English are anaphoric. For instance, "it" can often be nonanaphoric as in the case of the previous sentence. Other examples of nonanaphoric "it" include expressions such as "It is important," "It is necessary," or "It has to be taken into account." A nonanaphoric "it" is described as *pleonastic*.

VI.5.2 Proper Names Coreference

The task here is to link together all the variations of a proper name (person, organization, location) that are observed in text. For example,

> Former President $Bush_1$ defended the U.S. military Thursday during a speech at one of the nation's largest Army posts, where one private accused of abusing Iraqi prisoners awaits a court-martial. "These are difficult times for the Army as the actions of a handful in Iraq violate the soldier's code," said George H. W. $Bush_1$.

Additional examples can be observed in the example above.

VI.5.3 Apposition

Appositives are used to provide auxiliary information for a named entity. This information is separated from the entity by a comma and either precedes it or comes directly after it as in the following example:

> said George H. W. $Bush_1$, the father of President $Bush_1$. the father of President $Bush_1$, George H. W. $Bush_1$ said. . . .

A necessary condition for an appositional phrase to corefer to a named entity is that they occur in different noun phrases. If the apposition is a modifier of the named entity within the same noun phrase, then they are not considered coreferring as in the following phrase "Former President Bush." In this case *Former President* is not coreferring to Bush.

VI.5.4 Predicate Nominative

A predicate nominative occurs after a copulative verb (is, seems, looks like, appears, etc.) and completes a reference to the subject of a clause.

An example follows:

> Bill $Gates_1$ is the Chairman of Microsoft $Corporation_1$
> Subject: Bill Gates
> Predicate Nominative: the Chairman of Microsoft Corporation

A predicate nominative is a candidate for coreference only if it is stated in a firm way. If it is stated in a speculative or negative way, then it is not a candidate for coreference.

VI.5.5 Identical Sets

In this type of coreference the anaphor and the antecedent both refer to sets that are identical or to identical types. In the following example, "The Al Aqsa Brigades," "a militia," and "The group" all refer to the same set of people.

> The Al Aqsa Brigades$_4$, a militia$_4$ linked to Yasser Arafat's Fatah claimed responsibility. The group$_4$ said that Abed Hassouna$_1$ from a village$_7$ near the Palestinian town of Nablus carried out the attack$_2$ to avenge the death of Raed Karmi$_5$, (the militia)$_4$'s leader$_5$

Identifying identical sets is usually extremely difficult because deep knowledge about the domain is needed.

If we have a lexical dictionary such as WordNet that include hyponyms and hypernyms, we may be able to identify identical sets. We can deduce, for instance, that "militia" is a kind of "group."

VI.5.6 Function–Value Coreference

A function–value coreference is characterized by phrases that have a function–value relationship. Typically, the function will be descriptive and the value will be numeric.

In the following text there are two function–value pairs:

> Evolved Digital Systems's Revenues$_1$ were \$4.1M$_1$ for the quarter, up 61% compared to the first quarter of 2003. Net Loss$_2$ declined by 34% to \$5.6M$_2$.

Function: Evolved Digital Systems's Revenues
Value: $4.1M
Function: Net Loss
Value: $5.6M

VI.5.7 Ordinal Anaphora

Ordinal anaphora involves a cardinal number like *first* or *second* or an adjective such as *former* or *latter* as in the following example:

> IBM and Microsoft$_1$ were the final candidates, but the agency preferred the latter company$_1$.

VI.5.8 One-Anaphora

A one-anaphora consists of an anaphoric expression realized by a noun phrase containing the word "one" as in the following:

> If you cannot attend a tutorial$_1$ in the morning, you can go for an afternoon one$_1$.

VI.5.9 Part–Whole Coreference

Part–whole coreference occurs when the anaphor refers to a part of the antecedent as in the following:

> John has bought a new car$_1$. The indicators$_1$ use the latest laser technology.

As in the case of identifying identical sets discussed in Section VI.5.5, a lexical resource such WordNet is needed. In particular, WordNet includes the meronymy–holonymy relationship, which can help us identify that indicators are a part of a car.

VI.5.10 Approaches to Anaphora Resolution

Most of the work on coreference resolution focuses on pronominal resolution because that is the most common type of coreference and is also one of the easier types to resolve.

Most of the approaches to pronominal resolution share a common overall structure:

- Identify the relevant paragraphs (or sentences) around the pronoun in which one will search for candidates antecedents.
- Using a set of consistency checks, delete the candidates that to do meet any of the checks.
- Assign salience values to each of the surviving candidates according to a set of predefined rules.
- Pick the candidate with the highest salience value.

Some of these approaches require heavy preprocessing and rely on full parsers, whereas others are fairly knowledge-poor and rely on shallow parsing. The focus here will be on approaches that do not require full parsing of the sentences because doing this is too time-consuming and hence prohibitive in a real-world IE system.

VI.5.10.1 Hobbs Algorithm

The most simplistic algorithm is the *Hobbs algorithm*, which is also called the *Naive algorithm* (Hobbs 1986). This algorithm works by specifying a total order on noun phrases in the prior discourse and comparing each noun phrase against a set of constraints imposed by the features of the anaphor (i.e., gender, number). The first antecedent to satisfy all the constraints is chosen.

A few points to note about this algorithm are as follows:

- For two candidate antecedents *a* and *b*, if *a* is encountered before *b* in the search space, then *a* is preferred over *b*.
- The salience given to the candidate antecedents imposes a total ordering on the antecedents – that is, no two antecedents will have the same salience.
- The algorithm can not handle ambiguity and will resolve a pronoun as if there were at least one possible antecedent.

VI.5.11 CogNIAC (Baldwin 1995)

CogNIAC is a pronoun resolution engine designed around the assumption that there is a subclass of anaphora that does not require general purpose reasoning. Among the kinds of information CogNIAC does require are POS tagging, simple noun phrase recognition, and basic semantic category information like gender and number.

The system is based on a set of high-confidence rules that are successively applied over the pronoun under consideration. The rules are ordered according to their importance and relevance to anaphora resolution. The processing of a pronoun stops when one rule is satisfied. Below are listed the six rules used by the system. For each of them, the ***sentence prefix of anaphor*** is defined as the text portion of the sentence from the beginning of the sentence to the position of the anaphor.

1. ***Unique Antecedent.***
   Condition: If there is a single valid antecedent ***A*** in the relevant discourse.
   Action: A is the selected antecedent.
2. ***Reflexive Pronoun.***
   Condition: If the anaphor is a reflexive pronoun.
   Action: Pick the nearest valid antecedent in the anaphor prefix of the current sentence.
3. ***Unique in Current + Preceding.***
   Condition: If there is a single valid antecedent A in the preceding sentence and anaphor prefix of the current sentence.
   Action: A is the selected antecedent.
   Example: **Rupert Murdock**'s News Corp. confirmed his interest in buying back the ailing New York Post. But analysts said that if **he** winds up bidding for the paper, ...
4. ***Possessive Pronoun.***
   Condition: If the anaphor is a possessive pronoun and there is a single exact copy of the possessive phrase in the previous sentence.
   Action: The antecedent of the latter copy is the same as the former.
   Example: After he was dry, Joe carefully laid out the damp towel in front of **his locker**. Travis went over to **his locker**, took out a towel and started to dry off.
5. ***Unique in Current Sentence.***
   Condition: If there is a single valid antecedent ***A*** in the anaphor-prefix of the current sentence
   Action: A is the selected antecedent.
6. ***Unique Subject–Subject Pronoun.***
   Condition: If the subject of the previous sentence is a valid antecedent *A* and the anaphor is the subject of the current sentence.
   Action: A is the selected antecedent.

VI.5.11.1 Kennedy and Boguraev

This approach is based on Lappin and Leass's (1994) method but without the need for full parsing. This algorithm was used to resolve personal pronouns, reflexives, and possessives. The algorithm works by constructing coreference equivalence classes.

Each such class has a salience that is computed based on a set of 10 factors. Each pronoun is resolved to the antecedent that belongs to the class with the highest salience.

Here are the factors used by the salience algorithm. All the conditions refer to the current candidate for which we want to assign salience. *GFUN* is the grammatical function of the candidate

SENT-S: 100 iff in the current sentence
CNTX-S: 50 iff in the current context
SUBJ-S: 80 iff GFUN = *subject*
EXST-S: 70 iff in an existential construction
POSS-S: 65 iff GFUN = *possessive*
ACC-S: 50 iff GFUN = *direct object*
DAT-S: 40 iff GFUN = *indirect object*
OBLQ-S: 30 iff the complement of a preposition
HEAD-S: 80 iff EMBED = NIL
ARG-S: 50 iff ADJUNCT = NIL

As an example of the salience assignment, consider the following text fragment:

> Sun's prototype Internet access device uses a 110-Mhz MicroSPARCprocessor, and is diskless. Its dimensions are 5.5 inches × 9 inches × 2 inches.

Anaphors and candidates are represented using their offset in the text (from the beginning of the document), their grammatical function, and several other syntactic features.

The structure of each candidate is Element: Offset/Salience

ANAPHOR:	Its : 347
CANDIDATES:	
Internet access device:	335/180 (=50+85+50)
MicroSPARCprocessor:	341/165 (=50+65+50)
Sun's:	333/140 (=50+40+50)

The first sentence in this fragment includes three candidates with different grammatical functions. The second sentence, which includes that anaphor, does not include any candidate satisfying the basic constraints. The three candidates in the first sentence are ranked according to their salience.

The main factor determining the salience is the grammatical function of each candidate. *Internet access device* is the subject of the sentence and hence satisfies the SUBJ-S condition, is the optimal candidate, and is selected as the antecedent of Its.

VI.5.11.2 Mitkov

In contrast to the previous approaches that use mostly positive rules, Mitkov's approach (Mitkov 1998) is based on a set of boosting and impeding indicators applied to each candidate. The approach takes as an input the output of a text processed by a part-of-speech tagger, identifies the noun phrases that precede the anaphor within a distance of two-sentences, checks them for gender and number agreement with the anaphor, and then applies the genre-specific antecedent indicators to the remaining candidates.

The boosting indicators assign a positive score to a matching candidate, reflecting a positive likelihood that it is the antecedent of the current pronoun. In contrast, the impeding indicators apply a negative score to the matching candidate, reflecting a lack of confidence that it is the antecedent of the current pronoun. The candidate with the highest combined score is selected.

Here are some of the indicators used by Mitkov:

- ***Definiteness.*** Definite noun phrases in previous sentences are more likely antecedents of pronominal anaphors than indefinite ones (definite noun phrases score 0 and indefinite ones are penalized by –1).
- ***Givenness.*** Noun phrases in previous sentences representing the "given information" are deemed good candidates for antecedents and score 1 (candidates not representing the theme score 0). The given information is usually the first noun phrase in a nonimperative sentence.
- ***Indicating Verbs.*** If a verb in the sentence has a stem that is a member of {discuss, present, illustrate, identify, summarize, examine, describe, define, show, check, develop, review, report, outline, consider, investigate, explore, assess, analyze, synthesize, study, survey, deal, cover}, then the first NP following the verb is the preferred antecedent.
- ***Lexical Reiteration.*** Lexically reiterated noun phrases are preferred as candidates for antecedent (an NP scores 2 if is repeated within the same paragraph twice or more, 1 if repeated once, and 0 if it is not repeated). The matching is done in a loose way such that synonyms and NPs sharing the same head are considered identical.
- ***Section Heading Preference.*** If a noun phrase occurs in the heading of the section containing the current sentence, then we consider it the preferred candidate.
- "***Nonprepositional***" ***Noun Phrases.*** A "nonprepositional" noun phrase is given a higher preference than a noun phrase that is part of a prepositional phrase (0, –1). Example: `Insert the cassette into the VCR making sure it is suitable for the length of recording`. Here VCR is penalized for being part of a prepositional phrase and is resolved to the cassette.
- ***Collocation Pattern Preference.*** This preference is given to candidates having an identical verb collocation pattern with a pronoun of the pattern "noun phrase (pronoun), verb" and "verb, noun phrase (pronoun)." *Example*: `Press the key down and turn the volume up... Press it again`. Here key is preferred antecedent because it shares the same verb (press) with the pronoun ("it").
- ***Immediate Reference.*** Given a pattern of the form "... You? V1 NP... con you? V2 it (*con* you? V3 it)", where *con* ∈ {and/or/before/after...}, the noun phrase immediately after V1 is a very likely candidate for the antecedent of the pronoun "it" immediately following V2 and is therefore given preference (scores 2 and 0). Example:

> To print the $\underline{\text{paper}}_1$, you can stand the $\underline{\text{printer}}_2$ up or lay $\underline{\text{it}}_2$ flat. To turn on the $\underline{\text{printer}}_2$, press the $\underline{\text{Power button}}_3$ and hold $\underline{\text{it}}_3$ down for a moment. Unwrap the the paper_1, form $\underline{\text{it}}_1$ and align $\underline{\text{it}}_1$ then load $\underline{\text{it}}_1$ into the drawer.

- ***Referential distance.*** In complex sentences, noun phrases receive the following scores based on how close they are to the anaphor:
  - previous clause: 2
  - previous sentence: 1
  - 2 sentences: 0
  - 3 sentences further back: –1

  In simple sentences, the scores are as follows:
  - previous sentence: 1
  - 2 sentences: 0
  - 3 sentences further back: –1
- ***Domain Terminology Preference.*** NPs representing domain terms are more likely to be the antecedent (score 1 if the NP is a term and 0 if not).

VI.5.11.3 Evaluation of Knowledge-Poor Approaches

For many years, one of the main problems in contrasting the performance of the various systems and algorithms had been that there was no common ground on which such a comparison could reasonably be made. Each algorithm used a different set of documents and made different types of assumptions.

To solve this problem, Barbu (Barbu and Mitkov 2001) proposed the idea of the "evaluation workbench" – an open-ended architecture that allows the incorporation of different algorithms and their comparison on the basis of the same preprocessing tools and data. The three algorithms just described were all implemented and compared using the same workbench.

The three algorithms implemented receive as input the same representation of the input file. This representation is generated by running an XML parser over the file resulting from the preprocessing phase. Each noun phrase receives the following list of features:

- the original word form
- the lemma of the word or of the head of the noun phrase
- the starting and ending position in the text
- the part of speech
- the grammatical function (subject, object...)
- the index of the sentence that contains the referent
- the index of the verb related to the referent.

In addition, two definitions should be highlighted as follows:

- ***Precision*** = number of correctly resolved anaphors / number of anaphors attempted to be resolved
- ***Success Rate*** = number of correctly resolved anaphors / number of all anaphors.

The overall results as reported in Mitkov are summarized in the following table:

	K&B	Cogniac	Mitkov
Precision	52.84%	42.65%	48.81%
Success	61.6%	49.72%	56.9%

VI.5.11.4 Machine Learning Approaches

One of the learning approaches (Soon et al. 2001) is based on building a classifier based on the training examples in the annotated corpus. This classifier will be able to take any pair of NLP elements and return true if they refer to the same real-world entity and false otherwise. The NLP elements can be nouns, noun phrases, or pronouns and will be called *markables*.

The markables are derived from the document by using the regular NLP preprocessing steps as outlined in the previous section (tokenization, zoning, part of speech tagging, noun phrase extraction and entity extraction). In addition to deriving the markables, the preprocessing steps make it possible to create a set of features for each of the markables. These features are used by the classifier to determine if any two markables have a coreference relation.

Some Definitions

- ***Indefinite Noun Phrase.*** An indefinite noun phrase is a phrase that is used to introduce a specific object or set of objects believed to be new to the addressee (e.g., a new automobile, some sheep, and five accountants).
- ***Definite Noun Phrase.*** This is a noun phrase that starts with the article "the."
- ***Demonstrative Noun Phrase.*** This is a noun phrase that starts with "this," "that," "those," or "these."

Features of Each Pair of Markables

- Sentence Distance: 0 if the markables are in the same sentence.
- Pronoun: 1 if one of the markables is a pronoun; 0 otherwise.
- Exact Match: 1 if the two markables are identical; 0 otherwise.
- Definite Noun Phrase: 1 if one of the markables if a definite noun phrase; 0 otherwise.
- Demonstrative Noun Phrase: 1 if one of the markables is a demonstrative noun phrase.
- Number Agreement: 1 if the both markables are singular or plural; 0 otherwise.
- Semantic Agreement: 1 if the markables belong to the same semantic class (based on the entity extraction component).
- Gender Agreement: 1 if the two markables have the same gender (male, female), 0 if not, and 2 if it is unknown.
- Proper Name: 1 if both markables are proper names; 0 otherwise.
- Alias: 1 if one markable is an alias of the other entity (like GE and General Motors).

Generating Training Examples

- ***Positive Examples.*** Assume that in a given document we have found four markables that refer to the same real-world entity, {M1,M2,M3,M4}. For each adjacent pair of markables we will generate a positive example. In this case, we will have three positive examples – namely {M1,M2}, {M2,M3} and {M3,M4}.
- ***Negative Examples.*** Assume that markables a,b,c appear between M1 and M2; then, we generate three negative examples {a,M2}, {b,M2}, {c,M2}.

The Algorithm

```
Identify all markables
For each anaphor A
    Let M1 to Mn be all markables from the
beginning of the document till A
    For i=n;i=1;i - -
        if PairClassifier(A,Mi)=true then
            A, Mi is an anaphoric pair
            exit
          end if
        end for
    end for
```

Evaluation

Training on 30 documents yielded a classifier that was able to achieve precision of 68 percent and recall of 52 percent (F1 = 58.9%).

Ng and Cardie (Ng and Cardie 2002) have suggested two types of extensions to the Soon et al. corpus-based approach. First, they applied three extralinguistic modifications to the machine learning framework, which together provided substantial and statistically significant gains in coreference resolution precision. Second, they expanded the Soon et al. feature set from 12 features to an arguably deeper set of 53.

Ng and Cardie have also proposed additional lexical, semantic, and knowledge-based features – most notably, 26 additional grammatical features that include a variety of linguistic constraints and preferences. The main modifications that were suggested by Ng and Cardie are as follows:

- ***Best-first Clustering.*** Rather than a right-to-left search from each anaphoric NP for the first coreferent NP, a right-to-left search for a *highly likely antecedent* was performed. As a result, the coreference clustering algorithm was modified to select as the antecedent of NP the NP with the highest coreference likelihood value from among preceding NPs with coreference class values above 0.5.
- ***Training Set Creation.*** Rather than generate a positive training example for each anaphoric NP and its **closest** antecedent, a positive training example was generated for its **most confident** antecedent. For a nonpronominal NP, the closest **nonpronominal** preceding antecedent was selected as the most confident antecedent. For pronouns, the closest preceding antecedent was selected as the most confident antecedent.
- ***String Match Feature.*** Soon's string match feature (SOON STR) tests whether the two NPs under consideration are the same string after removing determiners from each. Rather than using the same string match for all types of anaphors, finer granularity is used. Exact string match is likely to be a better coreference predictor for proper names than it is for pronouns, for example. Specifically, the SOON STR feature is replaced by three features – PRO STR, PN STR, and WORDS STR – that restrict the application of string matching to pronouns, proper names, and nonpronominal NPs, respectively.

Overall, the learning framework and linguistic knowledge source modifications boost performance of Soon's learning-based coreference resolution approach from an F-measure of 62.6 to 70.4 on MUC-6 and from 60.4 to 63.4 on MUC-7.

VI.6 INDUCTIVE ALGORITHMS FOR IE

Rule Induction algorithms produce symbolic IE rules based on a corpus of annotated documents.

VI.6.1 WHISK

WHISK is a supervised learning algorithm that uses hand-tagged examples for learning information extraction rules. WHISK learns regular expressions for each of the fields it is trying to extract. The algorithm enables the integration of user-defined semantic classes. Such classes enable the system to adjust to the specific jargon of a given domain. As an example, consider the domain of apartment rental ads. We want to accommodate all types of spellings of bedroom, and hence we introduce the following semantic class: Bdrm = (brs |br |bds | bdrm | bd| bedroom| bed). WHISK learns the regular expressions by using an example-covering algorithm that tries to cover as many positive examples while not covering any negative example. The algorithm begins learning a single rule by starting with an empty rule; then we add one term at a time until either no negative examples are covered by the rule or the prepruning criterion has been satisfied. Each time we add the term that minimizes the Laplacian, which is $(e + 1)/(n + 1)$, where e is the number of negative examples covered by the rule as a result of the addition of the term and n is the number of positive examples covered by the rule as a result of the term addition. The process of adding rules repeats until the set of learned rules covers all the positive training instances. Finally, postpruning removes some of the rules to prevent overfitting.

Here is an example of a WHISK rule:

ID::1
Input:: * (Digit) 'BR' * '$' (number)
Output:: Rental {Bedrooms $1} {Price $2}

For instance, from the text "3 BR, upper flr of turn of ctry. Incl gar, grt N. Hill loc 995$. (206)-999-9999," the rule would extract the frame Bedrooms – 3, Price – 995.

The "*" char in the pattern will match any number of characters (unlimited jump). Patterns enclosed in parentheses become numbered elements in the output pattern, and hence (Digit) is $1 and (number) is $2.

VI.6.2 BWI

The BWI (boosted wrapper induction) is a system that utilizes wrapper induction techniques for traditional Information Extraction. IE is treated as a classification problem that entails trying to approximate two boundary functions $X_{\text{begin}}(i)$ and $X_{\text{end}}(i)$. $X_{\text{begin}}(i)$ is equal to 1 if the ith token starts a field that is part of the frame to be extracted and 0 otherwise. $X_{\text{end}}(i)$ is defined in a similar way for tokens that end a field. The learning algorithm approximates each X function by taking a set of pairs of the form $\{i, X\}(i)$ as training data. Each field is extracted by a wrapper $W = <F, A, H>$ where

F is a set of begin boundary detectors
A is a set of end boundary detectors
$H(k)$ is the probability that the field has length k

A boundary detector is just a sequence of tokens with wild cards (some kind of a regular expression).

$$W(i, j) = \begin{cases} 1 & \text{if} \quad F(i)A(j)H(j-i+1) > \sigma \\ 0 & \quad\text{otherwise} \end{cases}$$

$$F(i) = \sum_k C_{F_k} F_k(i), \quad A(i) = \sum_k C_{A_k} A_k(i).$$

$W(i, j)$ is a nave Bayesian approximation of the probability that we have a field between token i and j with uniform priors. Clearly, as σ is set to be higher we get better precision and lower recall, and if we set σ to be 0 we get the highest recall but compromise precision.

The BWI algorithm learns two detectors by using a greedy algorithm that extends the prefix and suffix patterns while there is an improvement in the accuracy. The sets $F(i)$ and $A(i)$ are generated from the detectors by using the AdaBoost algorithm. The detector pattern can include specific words and regular expressions that work on a set of wildcards such as <num>, <Cap>, <LowerCase>, <Punctuation> and <Alpha>.

When the BWI algorithm was evaluated on the acquisition relations from the Reuters news collection, it achieved the following results compared with HMM:

Slot	**BWI**	**HMM**
Acquiring Company	34.1%	30.9%
Dollar Amount	50.9%	55.5%

VI.6.3 The $(LP)^2$ Algorithm

The $(LP)^2$ algorithm learns from an annotated corpus and induces two sets of rules: tagging rules generated by a bottom-up generalization process and correction rules that correct mistakes and omissions done by the tagging rules.

A tagging rule is a pattern that contains conditions on words preceding the place where a tag is to be inserted and conditions on the words that follow the tag. Conditions can be either words, lemmas, lexical categories (such as digit, noun, verb, etc), case (lower or upper), and semantic categories (such as time-id, cities, etc).

The $(LP)^2$ algorithm is a covering algorithm that tries to cover all training examples. The initial tagging rules are generalized by dropping conditions.

A sample rule for tagging the stime (start time of a seminar) is shown below.

	Condition					
Word Index	**word**	**lemma**	**LexCat**	**Case**	**SemCat**	**Tag Inserted**
3		at				<stime>
4			digit			
5					time-id	

The correction rules take care of incorrect boundaries set for the tags and shift them to fix the errors. An example is "at <stime> 4 </stime> pm," where the </stime> tag should be shifted one token to the right. The correction rules learn from the mistakes of the tagging processing on the training corpus. The action taken by a correction rule is just to shift the tag rather than introduce a new tag. The same covering algorithm used for learning the tagging rules is used for learning the correction rules.

$(LP)^2$ was also tested on extracting information from financial news articles and managed to obtain the following results:

Tag	F1	Tag	F1
Location	70%	Organization	86%
Currency	85%	Stock Name	85%
Stock Exchange Name	91%	Stock Category	86%
Stock Exchange Index	97%	Stock Type	92%

These results are not on par with the results achieved by the probabilistic extraction algorithms such as HMM, CRF, and MEMM. It seems that the inductive algorithms are suitable for semistructured domains, where the rules are fairly simple, whereas when dealing with free text documents (such as news articles) the probabilistic algorithms perform much better.

VI.6.4 Experimental Evaluation

All four algorithms were evaluated on the CMU seminar announcement database and achieved the following results (F1results):

Slot	BWI	HMM	$(LP)^2$	WHISK
Speaker	67.7%	76.6%	77.6	18.3%
Location	76.7%	78.6%	75.0%	66.4%
Start Time	99.6%	98.5%	99.0%	92.6%
End Time	93.9%	62.1%	95.5%	86%

VI.7 STRUCTURAL IE

VI.7.1 Introduction to Structural IE

Most text mining systems simplify the structure of the documents they process by ignoring much of the structural or visual characteristics of the text (e.g., font type, size, location, etc.) and process the text either as a linear sequence or as a bag of words. This allows the algorithms to focus on the semantic aspects of the document. However, valuable information is lost in these approaches, which ignore information contained in the visual elements of a document.

Consider, for example, an article in a journal. The title is readily identifiable based on its special font and location but less so based on its semantic content alone, which may be similar to the section headings. This holds true in the same way for the author names, section headings, running title,and so on. Thus, much important information is provided by the visual layout of the document – information that is ignored by most text mining and other document analysis systems.

One can, however, leverage preprocessing techniques that do not focus on the semantic content of the text but instead on the visual layout alone in an effort to extract the information contained in layout elements. These type of techniques entail an IE task in which one is provided a document and seeks to discover specific fields of the document (e.g., the title, author names, publication date, figure captions, bibliographical citings, etc.). Such techniques have been termed *structural* or *visual information extraction.*

Of course, it goes without saying that, within the overall context of text mining preprocessing, a structural or visual IE approach is not aimed at replacing the semantic one. Instead, the structural IE approach can be used to complement other more conventional text mining preprocessing processes.

This section describes a recently developed general algorithm that allows the IE task to be performed based on the visual layout of the document. The algorithm employs a machine learning approach whereby the system is first provided with a set of training documents in which the desired fields are manually tagged. On the basis of these training examples, the system automatically learns how to find the corresponding fields in future documents.

VI.7.2 Overall Problem Definition

A document D is a set of primitive elements $D = \{e_1, \ldots, e_n\}$. A primitive element can be a character, a line, or any other visual object as determined by the document format. A primitive element can have any number of visual attributes such as font size and type, physical location, and so on. The *bounding box* attribute, which provides the size and location of the bounding box of the element, is assumed to be available for all primitive elements. We define an *object* in the document to be any set of primitive elements.

The *visual information extraction (VIE)* task is as follows. We are provided with a set of *target fields* $F = \{f_1, \ldots, f_k\}$ to be extracted and a set of *training documents* $T = \{T_1, \ldots, T_m\}$ wherein all occurrences of the target fields are annotated. Specifically, for each target field f and training document T, we are provided with the object

$f(T)$ of T that is of type f ($f(T) = 0$ if f does not appear in T). The goal, when presented with an unannotated query document Q, is to annotate the occurrences of target fields that exist in Q (not all target fields need be present in each document).

Practically, the VIE task can be decomposed into two subtasks. First, for each document (both training and query) one must group the primitive elements into meaningful objects (e.g., lines, paragraphs, etc.) and establish the hierarchical structure among these objects. Then, in the second stage, the structure of the query document is compared with the structures of the training documents to find the objects corresponding to the target fields.

It has also proven possible to enhance the results by introducing the notion of *templates*, which are groups of training documents with a similar layout (e.g., articles from the same journal). Using templates, one can identify the essential features of the page layout, ignoring particularities of any specific document. Templates are discussed in detail in the sections that follow.

A brief examination is also made of a real-world system that was implemented for a typical VIE task involving a set of documents containing financial analyst reports. The documents were in PDF format. Target fields included the title, authors, publication dates, and others.

VI.7.3 The Visual Elements Perceptual Grouping Subtask

Recall that a document is a set of primitive elements such as characters, figures, and so on. The *objects* of a document are sets of primitive elements. Target fields, in general, are objects.

Thus, the first step in the visual IE task is to group the primitive elements of the documents into higher level objects. The grouping should provide the conceptually meaningful objects of the document such as paragraphs, headings, and footnotes.

For humans, the grouping process is easy and is generally performed unconsciously based on the visual structure of the document. As with other types of IE perceptual grouping requirements, the goal is to mimic the human perceptual grouping process.

VI.7.4 Problem Formulation for the Perceptual Grouping Subtask

One can model the structure of the objects of a document as a tree, of which the leaves are primitive elements and the internal nodes are (composite) objects. This structure is called the object tree or *O-Tree* of the document.

The O-Tree structure creates a hierarchal structure among objects in which higher level objects consist of groups of lower level objects. This hierarchal structure reflects the conceptual structure of documents in which objects such as columns are groups of paragraphs, which, in turn, are groups of lines, and so on. The exact levels and objects represented in the O-Tree are application and format dependent.

For an HTML document, for example, the O-Tree may include objects representing tables, menus, the text body, and other elements, whereas for PDF documents the O-Tree may include objects representing paragraphs, columns, lines, and so on. Accordingly, for each file format and application we define the *object hierarchy, H*, which determines the set of possible *object types*, and a hierarchy among these objects. Any object hierarchy must contain an object of type document, which is at the root of the hierarchy. When constructing an O-Tree for a document, each object is labeled by one of the *object types* defined in the object hierarchy, and the tree structure must correspond to the hierarchical structure defined in the hierarchy.

Formally, an object hierarchy H is a rooted DAG that satisfies the following:

- The leaf nodes are labeled by primitive element types.
- Internal nodes are labeled by objects types.
- The root node is labeled by the document object type.
- For object types x and y, type y is a child of x if an object of type x can (directly) contain an object type y.

For a document $D = \{e_1, \ldots, e_n\}$ and an object hierarchy H, an *O-Tree of D* according to H is a tree O with the following characteristics:

- The leaves of O consist of all primitive elements of D.
- Internal nodes of O are objects of D.
- If X and X' are nodes of O (objects or primitive elements) and $X \subset X'$, then X' is an ancestor (or parent) of X.
- Each node X is labeled by a label from H denoted *label*(X).
- If X' is a parent of X in T, then *label*(X') is a parent of *label*(X) in H.
- *label*(*root*) = Document.

VI.7.5 Algorithm for Constructing a Document O-Tree

Given a document, one constructs an O-Tree for the document. In doing so, the aim is to construct objects best reflecting the true grouping of the elements into "meaningful" objects (e.g., paragraphs, columns, etc.). When constructing an object we see to it that the following requirements are met:

- The elements of the objects are within the same physical area of the page. Specifically, each object must be *connected* – that is, an object X cannot be decomposed into two separate objects $X1$ and $X2$ such that any line connecting $X1$ and $X2$ necessarily crosses an element in a different object.
- The elements of the object have similar characteristics (e.g., similar font type, similar font size, etc.). Specifically, one must assume a *fitness function fit*(.,.) such that for any two objects X and Y, where *label*(Y) is child of *label*(X), *fit*(Y,X) provides a measure of how fit Y is as an additional member to X (e.g., if X is a paragraph and Y a line, then how similar is Y the other lines in X). One adds Y to X only if *fit*(Y;X) is above some threshold value, °. The exact nature of the function *fit*(¢; ¢) and the threshold value are format and domain dependent.

Given these two criteria, the O-Tree can be constructed in a greedy fashion, from the bottom up, layer by layer. In doing so, one should always prefer to enlarge existing objects of the layer, starting with the largest object. If no existing object can be enlarged, and there are still "free" objects of the previous layer, a new object is created. The procedure terminates when the root object, labeled Document, is completed. A description of the algorithm is provided in the following pseudocode algorithm:

```
Input: D - Document
Output: O-Tree for D

 1. For each type t ∈ H do
    let level(t) be the length of the longest path from t to a leaf
 2. Let h = level(Document)
 3. Objects(0) ← D
 4. For i = 1 to h do
 5. Objects(i) ← 0
 6. free ← Objects(i − 1)
 7. While free ≠ 0 do
 8. For each X ∈ Objects(i) in order of descending size do
 9. For each Y ∈ free in order of increasing distance from X do
10. If Y is a neighbor of X and fit(Y, X) ≥ γ then
11. X ← X ∪ Y
12. make Y a child of X
13. Remove Y from free
14. Break (go to line 7)
15. For each t ∈ H such that level(t) = i do
16. if Objects(i) does not include an empty object of type t
17. Add an empty set of type t to Objects(i)
18. end while
19. Remove empty objects from Objects(i)
20. end for
21. return resulting O-Tree
```

VI.7.6 Structural Mapping

Given a Visual Information Extraction task, one first constructs an O-Tree for each of the training documents as well as for the query document, as described in the previous section. Once all the documents have been structured as O-Trees, it is necessary to find the objects of Q (the query document) that correspond to the target fields. This is done by comparing the O-Tree of Q, and the objects therein, to those of the training documents.

This comparison is performed in two stages. First, the training document that is visually most similar to the query document is found. Then, one maps between the objects of the two documents to discover the targets fields in the query document.

VI.7.6.1 Basic Algorithm

- ***Document Similarity.*** Consider a query document Q and training documents $T = \{T_1, \ldots, T_n\}$. We seek to find the training document T_{opt} that is *visually* most similar to the query document. We do so by comparing the O-Trees of the documents. In the comparison we only concentrate on similarities between the top levels of the O-Tree. The reason is that even similar documents may still differ in the details.

Let $O(Q)$ and $O(T_1),\ldots,O(T_n)$ be the O-Trees, the query document and the training documents, respectively, and let H be the type hierarchy. We define a subgraph of H, which we call the *Signature Hierarchy*, consisting of the types in H that determine features of the global layout of the page (e.g., columns, tables). The types that are included in the signature is implementation dependent, but generally the signature would include the top one or two levels of the type hierarchy. For determining the similarity between the objects we assume the existence of a similarity function $sim(X,Y)$, which provides a measure of similarity between objects of the same type based on object characteristics such as size, location, and fonts ($sim(X,Y)$ is implementation dependent).

Given a query document Q and a training document T, for each object X in the signature of T we find the object $X0$ of Q (of the same type as X) that is most similar to X. We then compute the average similarity for all objects in the signature of T to obtain the overall similarity score between the documents. We choose the document with the highest similarity score. A description of the procedure is provided below.

```
Input: Q, T1..., T n., and their respective O-Trees
Output: Topt (training document most similar to query document)
for i = 1 to n do
total ← 0
count ← 0
For each t ∈ S do
For each X ∈ O(Ti) of type t do
s(X) ← max {sim(X,X') | X' ∈ O(Q), X' of type t}
total ← total + s(X)
count ← count + 1
score (i) ← total = count
end for
opt ← argmax{score (i) g}
return Topt
```

- ***Finding the Target Fields.*** Once the most similar training document T_{opt} has been determined, it remains to find the objects of Q that correspond to the target fields, as annotated in the document T_{opt}. One does so by finding, for each target field f, the object within $O(Q)$ that is most similar to $f(T_{opt})$ (the object in $O(T_{opt})$ annotated as f). Finding this object is done in an exhaustive manner, going over all objects of $O(Q)$. One also makes sure that the similarity between this object and the corresponding object of T_{opt} is beyond a certain threshold α, or else one decides that the field f has not been found in Q (either because it is not there or we have failed to find it).

A description of the procedure for finding the target fields is provided in the algorithm below. Note that the annotation of the training documents is performed before (and independent) of the construction of the O-Trees. Thus, annotated objects need not appear in the O-Tree. If this is the case, line 2 sees to it that one takes the minimal object of the $O(T_{opt})$ that fully contains the annotated object.

Input:
- Q, T_{opt} (and their respective O-Trees)
- $\{f(T_{opt}) \mid f \in F\}$(target fields in T_{opt})

Output: $\{f(Q) \mid f \in F\}$(Target fields in Q)
1 *For each* $f \in F$ do
1. Let $f(T_{opt}) \in O(T_{opt})$ be minimal such that $f(T_{opt}) \subseteq {}^{-}f(T_{opt})$
2. $f(Q) \leftarrow \text{argmax}\{sim(f(T_{opt}), X) \mid X \in O(Q); X \text{ of type } t\}$
3. if $sim({}^{-}f(T_{opt}), f(Q)) < \alpha$ then $f(Q) \leftarrow 0$

VI.7.7 Templates

The preceding algorithm is based on finding the single most similar document to the query document and then extracting all the target fields based on this document alone. Although this provides good results in most cases, there is the danger that particularities of any single document may reduce the effectiveness of the algorithm.

To overcome this problem, the notion of *templates* has been introduced; these templates permit comparison of the query document with a *collection* of similar documents. A *template* is a set of training documents that have the same general visual layout (e.g., articles from the same journal, Web pages from the same site, etc.). The documents in each template may be different in details but share the same overall structure.

Using templates, one finds the template most similar to the query document (rather than the document most similar). This is accomplished by – for each template – averaging the similarity scores between the query document and all documents in the template.

One then picks the template with the highest average similarity. Once the most similar template is determined, the target fields are provided by finding the object of Q most similar to a target field in *any* of the documents in the template. A description of the process by which one can find target fields through the use of templates is provided below.

Input:
- Q and its O-Tree
- $T_{opt} = \{T_1, \ldots, T_{k\cdot}\}$(most similar template) and respective O-Trees
- $\{f(T) \mid f \in F, T \in T_{opt}\}$(target fields in T_{opt})

Output: $\{f(Q) \mid f \in F\}$(Target fields in Q)
1 For each $f \in F$ do
1. For each $T \in T_{opt}$ do

2. Let $^{-}f(T) \in O(T)$ be minimal such that $f(T) \subseteq {}^{-}f(T)$
3. $X_T \leftarrow$ (argmax$\{sim(^{-}f(T), X) \mid X \in O(Q), X$ of type $t\}$
4. $s(T) \leftarrow sim(^{-}f(T), X_T)$
5. if $\max\{s(T) \mid T \in T_{opt}\} \geq \alpha$ then
6. $f(Q) \leftarrow$ (argmax$\{s(X_T) \mid T \in T_{opt}\}$
7. else $f(Q) \leftarrow 0$

VI.7.8 Experimental Results

A system for Visual Information Extraction, as described above, was recently implemented on documents that are analyst reports from several leading investment banks. The training data consisted of 130 analyst reports from leading investment banks: 38 from Bear Stearns, 14 from CSFB, 15 from Dresdner, and 63 from Morgan Stanley. All the documents were in PDF format. The training documents were divided into a total of 30 templates: 7 from the Bear Stearns data, 4 from the CSFB data, 5 from the Dresdner data, and 14 in the Morgan Stanley data. All the training documents were manually annotated for the target fields. The target fields included the following fields: Author, Title, Subtitle, Company, Ticker, Exchange, Date, Geography, Industry Info. Not all documents included all target fields, but within each template documents had the same target fields.

The system was tested on 255 query documents: 33 from Bear Stearns, 12 from CSFB, 14 from Dresdner, and 196 from Morgan Stanley. With regard to the implementation, the type hierarchy (H) used in the system is provided in Figure VI.7. The signature hierarchy contained the objects of type column and paragraph. The implementation of the fitness function *fit*(.,.) (for the fitness of one object within the other) takes into account the distance between the objects and the similarity of font type.

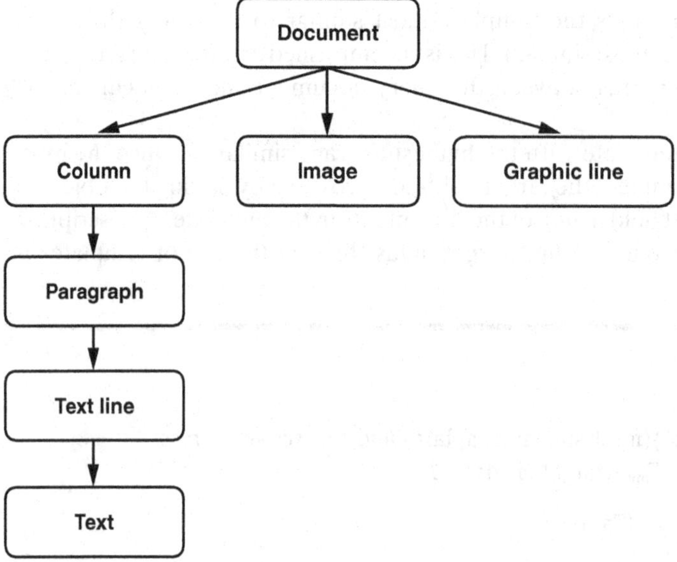

Figure VI.7. The type hierarchy.

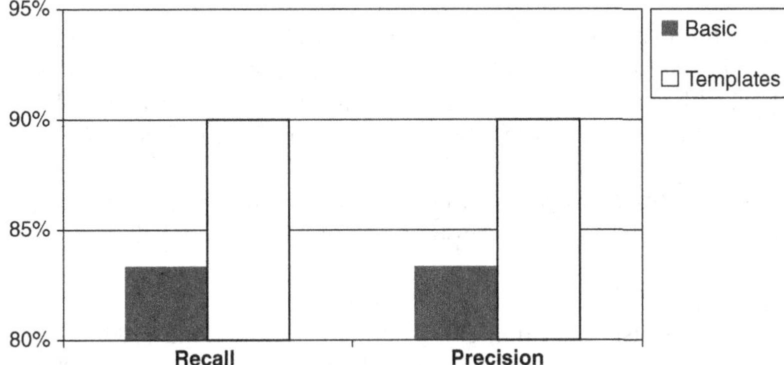

Figure VI.8. Overall recall and precision rates for basic algorithm and for algorithm using templates.

For the fitness of a line within an existing paragraph, it also takes into account the distance between lines. The similarity function *sim*(.,.), which measures the similarity between objects in different documents, is primarily based on similarity between the sizes and locations of the respective objects.

With an emphasis on the results, the performance of the system was measured with the basic algorithm and the use of templates. The overall average recall and precision values are given in Figure VI.8.

On the whole the introduction of templates improved the performance of the algorithm, increasing the average accuracy from 83 to 90 percent. Note that for both algorithms the recall and precision values are essentially identical. The reason for this is that, for any target field *f*, on the one hand, each document contains only one object of type *f*, and, on the other hand, the algorithm marks one object as being of type *f*. Thus, for every recall error there is a corresponding precision error. The slight difference that does exist between the recall and precision marks is due to the cases in which the algorithm decided not to mark any element, signifying a recall error but not a precision error.

Some target fields are harder to detect than others. It is interesting to note that, although the introduction of templates improves accuracy in most cases, there are some target fields for which it reduces accuracy. Understanding the exact reasons for this and how to overcome such problems is a topic for further research.

VI.8 FURTHER READING

Section VI.1

For a full list of definitions related to information extraction, see <http://www.itl.nist.gov/iaui/894.02/related˙projects/muc/info/definitions.html>.

Section VI.4

Descriptions of rule-based information extraction systems can be found in Hobbs et al. (1991); Appelt, Hobbs, Bear, Israel, and Tyson (1993); Grishman (1996); Freitag (1997); Grishman (1997); Wilks (1997); and Ciravegna et al. (1999).

Section VI.5

Algorithms on anaphora resolutions can be found in Rich and LuperFoy (1988); Lappin and Leass (1994); McCarthy and Lehnert (1995); Humphreys, Gaizauskas, and Azzam (1997); Kehler (1997); Kennedy and Boguraev (1997); Barbu and Mitkov (2001); Klebanov and Wiemer-Hastings (2002); Ng and Cardie (2002); and Ng and Cardie (2003).

Discussions about evaluation of anaphora resolution algorithms can be found in Aone and Bennett (1995) and Azzam, Humphreys, and Gaizauskas (1998).

Section VI.6

More details about the whisk algorithm can be found in Soderland (1999). The description of the BWI algorithm can be found in Freitag and Kushmerick (2000). The $(LP)^2$ algorithm is described in Ciravegna (2001).

VII

Probabilistic Models for Information Extraction

Several common themes frequently recur in many tasks related to processing and analyzing complex phenomena, including natural language texts. Among these themes are classification schemes, clustering, probabilistic models, and rule-based systems.

This section describes some of these techniques generally, and the next section applies them to the tasks described in Chapter VI.

Research has demonstrated that it is extremely fruitful to model the behavior of complex systems as some form of a random process. Probabilistic models often show better accuracy and robustness against the noise than categorical models. The ultimate reason for this is not quite clear and is an excellent subject for a philosophical debate.

Nevertheless, several probabilistic models have turned out to be especially useful for the different tasks in extracting meaning from natural language texts. Most prominent among these probabilistic approaches are hidden Markov models (HMMs), stochastic context-free grammars (SCFG), and maximal entropy (ME).

VII.1 HIDDEN MARKOV MODELS

An HMM is a finite-state automaton with stochastic state transitions and symbol emissions (Rabiner 1990). The automaton models a probabilistic generative process. In this process, a sequence of symbols is produced by starting in an initial state, emitting a symbol selected by the state, making a transition to a new state, emitting a symbol selected by the state, and repeating this transition–emission cycle until a designated final state is reached.

Formally, let $O = \{o_1, \dots o_M\}$ be the finite set of observation symbols and $Q = \{q_1, \dots q_N\}$ be the finite set of states. A first-order Markov model λ is a triple (π, A, B), where $\pi : Q \to [0, 1]$ defines the starting probabilities, $A : Q \times Q \to [0, 1]$ defines the transition probabilities, and $B : Q \times O \to [0, 1]$ denotes the emission probabilities. Because the functions π, A, and B define true probabilities, they must satisfy

$$\Sigma_{q \in Q}\, \pi(q) = 1,$$

$$\Sigma_{q' \in Q} A(q, q') = 1 \quad \text{and} \quad \Sigma_{o \in O} B(q, o) = 1 \text{ for all states } q.$$

A model λ together with the random process described above induces a probability distribution over the set O^* of all possible observation sequences.

VII.1.1 The Three Classic Problems Related to HMMs

Most applications of hidden Markov models can be reduced to three basic problems:

1. Find $P(T \mid \lambda)$ – the probability of a given observation sequence T in a given model λ.
2. Find $\text{argmax}_{S\in Q^{|T|}} P(T, S \mid \lambda)$ – the most likely state trajectory given λ and T.
3. Find $\text{argmax}_{\lambda} P(T, \mid \lambda)$ – the model that best accounts for a given sequence.

The first problem allows us to compute the probability distribution induced by the model. The second finds the most probable states sequence for a given observation sequence. These two tasks are typically used for analyzing a given observation.

The third problem, on the other hand, adjusts the model itself to maximize the likelihood of the given observation. It can be viewed as an HMM training problem.

We now describe how each of these three problems can be solved. We will start by calculating $P(T \mid \lambda)$, where T is a sequence of observation symbols $T = t_1t_2 \ldots t_k \in O^*$. The most obvious way to do that would be to enumerate every possible state sequence of length $|T|$. Let $S = s_1s_2 \ldots s_{|T|} \in Q^{|T|}$ be one such sequence. Then we can calculate the probability $P(T \mid S, \lambda)$ of generating T knowing that the process went through the states sequence S. By Markovian assumption, the emission probabilities are all independent of each other. Therefore,

$$P(T \mid S, \lambda) = \pi_{i=1..|T|} B(s_i, t_i).$$

Similarly, the transition probabilities are independent. Thus the probability $P(S|\lambda)$ for the process to go through the state sequence S is

$$P(S \mid \lambda) = \pi(s_1) \cdot \pi_{i=1..|T|-1} A(s_i, s_{i+1}).$$

Using the above probabilities, we find that the probability $P(T|\lambda)$ of generating the sequence can be calculated as

$$P(T \mid \lambda) = \Sigma^{|T|}_{S\in Q} P(T \mid S, \lambda) \cdot P(S \mid \lambda).$$

This solution is of course infeasible in practice because of the exponential number of possible state sequences. To solve the problem efficiently, we use a dynamical programming technique. The resulting algorithm is called the *forward–backward* procedure.

VII.1.2 The Forward–Backward Procedure

Let $\alpha_m(q)$, the *forward variable*, denote the probability of generating the initial segment $t_1t_2 \ldots t_m$ of the sequence T and finishing at the state q at time m. This forward variable can be computed recursively as follows:

1. $\alpha_1(q) = \pi(q) \cdot B(q, t_1)$,
2. $\alpha_{n+1}(q) = \Sigma_{q'\in Q} \alpha_n(q') \cdot A(q', q) \cdot B(q, t_{n+1})$.

Then, the probability of the whole sequence T can be calculated as

$$P(T \mid \lambda) = \Sigma_{q \in Q} \alpha_{|T|}(q).$$

In a similar manner, one can define $\beta_m(q)$, the *backward variable*, which denotes the probability of starting at the state q and generates the final segment $t_{m+1} \ldots t_{|T|}$ of the sequence T. The backward variable can be calculated starting from the end and going backward to the beginning of the sequence:

1. $\beta_{|T|}(q) = 1$,
2. $\beta_{n-1}(q) = \Sigma_{q' \in Q} A(q, q') \cdot B(q', t_n) \cdot \beta_n(q')$.

The probability of the whole sequence is then

$$P(T \mid \lambda) = \Sigma_{q \in Q}\, \pi(q) \cdot B(q, t_1) \cdot \beta_1(q).$$

VII.1.3 The Viterbi Algorithm

We now proceed to the solution of the second problem – finding the most likely state sequence for a given sequence T. As with the previous problem, enumerating all possible state sequences S and choosing the one maximizing $P(T, S \mid \lambda)$ is infeasible. Instead, we again use dynamical programming, utilizing the following property of the optimal states sequence: if T' is some initial segment of the sequence $T = t_1 t_2 \ldots t_{|T|}$ and $S = s_1 s_2 \ldots s_{|T|}$ is a state sequence maximizing $P(T, S \mid \lambda)$, then $S' = s_1 s_2 \ldots s_{|T'|}$ maximizes $P(T', S' \mid \lambda)$ among all state sequences of length $|T'|$ ending with $s_{|T|}$. The resulting algorithm is called the *Viterbi* algorithm.

Let $\gamma_n(q)$ denote the state sequence ending with the state q, which is optimal for the initial segment $T_n = t_1 t_2 \ldots t_n$ among all sequences ending with q, and let $\delta_n(q)$ denote the probability $P(T_n, \gamma_n(q) \mid \lambda)$ of generating this initial segment following those optimal states. Delta and gamma can be recursively calculated as follows:

1. $1.\delta_1(q) = \pi(q) \cdot B(q, t_1), \gamma_1(q) = q$,
2. $\delta_{n+1}(q) = \max_{q' \in Q} \delta_n(q') \cdot A(q', q) \cdot B(q, t_{n+1}), \gamma_{n+1}(q) = \gamma_1(q')q$,
   where $q' = \operatorname{argmax}_{q' \in Q} \delta_n(q') \cdot A(q', q) \cdot B(q, t_{n+1})$.

Then, the best states sequence among $\{\gamma_{|T|}(q) : q \in Q\}$ is the optimal one:

$$\operatorname{argmax}_{S \in Q^{|T|}} P(T, S \mid \lambda) = \gamma_{|T|}(\operatorname{argmax}_{q \in Q} \delta_{|T|}(q)).$$

Example of the Viterbi Computation

Using the HMM described in Figure VII.1 with the sequence (a, b, a), one would take the following steps in using the Viterbi algorithm:

$$\pi_i = \begin{pmatrix} 0.5 & 0 & 0.5 \end{pmatrix}, \qquad A_{ij} = \begin{pmatrix} 0.1 & 0.4 & 0.4 \\ 0.4 & 0.1 & 0.5 \\ 0.4 & 0.5 & 0.1 \end{pmatrix},$$

$$B_i(a) = \begin{pmatrix} 0.5 & 0.8 & 0.2 \end{pmatrix}, \qquad B_i(b) = \begin{pmatrix} 0.5 & 0.2 & 0.8 \end{pmatrix}$$

First Step (a):

- $\delta_1(S1) = \pi(S1) \cdot B(S1, a) = 0.5 \cdot 0.5 = 0.25$

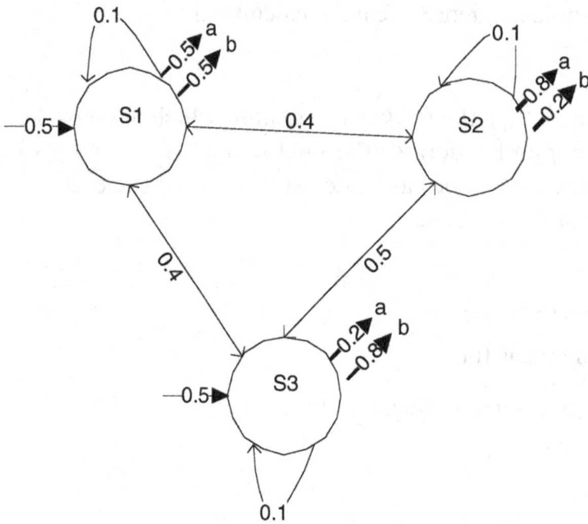

Figure VII.1. A sample HMM.

- $\delta_1(S2) = \pi(S2) \cdot B(S2, a) = 0$
- $\delta_1(S3) = \pi(S3) \cdot B(S3, a) = 0.5 \cdot 0.2 = 0.1$

Second Step (b):

- $$\begin{aligned}\delta_2(S1) &= \max_{q' \in Q} \delta_1(q') \cdot A(q', S1) \cdot B(S1, b) \\ &= \max(\delta_1(S1) \cdot A(S1, S1) \cdot B(S1, b), \\ &\quad \delta_1(S2) \cdot A(S2, S1) \cdot B(S1, b), \\ &\quad \delta_1(S3) \cdot A(S3, S1) \cdot B(S1, b)) \\ &= \max(0.25 \cdot 0.1 \cdot 0.5, \\ &\quad 0, \\ &\quad 0.1 \cdot 0.4 \cdot 0.5) \\ &= \max(0.0125, 0, 0.02) = 0.02\end{aligned}$$
- $\gamma_2(S1) = S3$

In a similar way, we continue to calculate the other δ and γ factors. Upon reaching t_3 we can see that $S1$ and $S3$ have the highest probabilities; hence, we trace back our steps from both states using the γ variables. We have in this case two optimal paths: $\{S1, S3, S1\}$ and $\{S3, S2, S3\}$. The diagram of the computation of the Viterbi Algorithm is shown in Figure VII.2.

Note that, unlike the forward–backward algorithm described in Section VII.1.2 the Viterbi algorithm does not use summation of probabilities. Only multiplications are involved. This is convenient because it allows the use of logarithms of probabilities instead of the probabilities themselves and to use summation instead of multiplication. This can be important because, for large sequences, the probabilities soon become infinitesimal and leave the range of the usual floating-point numbers.

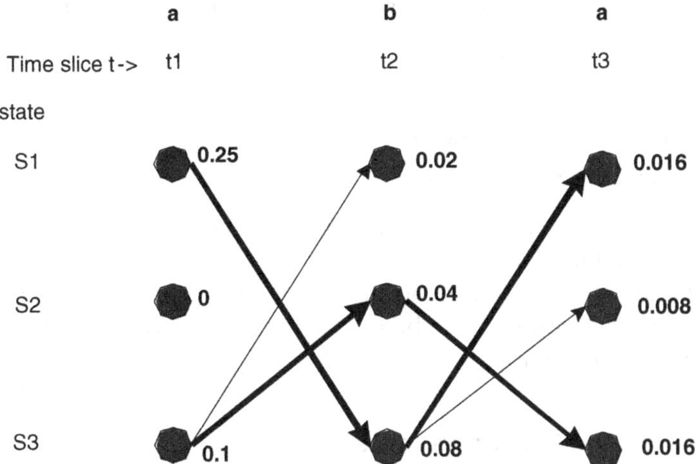

Figure VII.2. Computation of the optimal path using the Viterbi algorithm.

VII.1.4 The Training of the HMM

The most difficult problem of the three involves training the HMM. In this section, only the problem of estimating the parameters of HMM is covered, leaving the topology of the finite-state automaton fixed.

The training algorithm is given some initial HMM and adjusts it so as to maximize the probability of the training sequence. However, the set of states is given in advance, and the transition and emission probabilities, which are initially zero, remain zero. The adjustment formulas are called *Baum–Welsh reestimation formulas.*

Let $\mu_n(q)$ be the probability $P(s_n = q \mid T, \lambda)$ of being in the state q at time n while generating the observation sequence T. Then $\mu_n(q) \cdot P(T \mid \lambda)$ is the probability of generating T passing through the state q at time n. By definition of the forward and backward variables presented in Section VII.1.2, this probability is equal to $\alpha_n(q) \cdot \beta_n(q)$. Thus,

$$\mu_n(q) = \alpha_n(q) \cdot \beta_n(q) \,/\, P(T \mid \lambda).$$

Also let $\varphi_n(q, q')$ be the probability $P(s_n = q, s_{n+1} = q' \mid T, \lambda)$ of passing from state q to state q' at time n while generating the observation sequence T. As in the preceding equation,

$$\varphi_n(q, q') = \alpha_n(q) \cdot A(q, q') \cdot B(q', o_{n+1}) \cdot \beta_n(q) / P(T \mid \lambda).$$

The sum of $\mu_n(q)$ over all $n = 1 \ldots \mid T \mid$ can be seen as the expected number of times the state q was visited while generating the sequence T. Or, if one sums over $n = 1 \ldots \mid T \mid -1$, the expected number of transitions out of the state q results because there is no transition at time $|T|$. Similarly, the sum of $\varphi_n(q, q')$ over all $n = 1 \ldots \mid T \mid -1$ can be interpreted as the expected number of transitions from the state q to q'.

The Baum–Welsh formulas reestimate the parameters of the model λ according to the expectations

$$\pi'(q) := \mu_1(q),$$
$$A'(q, q') := \Sigma_{n=1..|T|-1}\varphi_n(q, q')/\Sigma_{n=1..|T|-1}\mu_n(q),$$
$$B'(q, o) := \Sigma_{n:Tn=o}\mu_n(q)/\Sigma_{n=1..|T|}\mu_n(q).$$

It can be shown that the model $\lambda' = (\pi', A', B')$ is equal either to λ, in which case the λ is the critical point of the likelihood function $P(T \mid \lambda)$, or λ', which better accounts for the training sequence T than the original model λ in the sense that $P(T \mid \lambda') > P(T \mid \lambda)$. Therefore, the training problem can be solved by iteratively applying the reestimation formulas until convergence.

VII.1.5 Dealing with Training Data Sparseness

It is often the case that the amount of training data – the length of the training sequence T – is insufficient for robust estimation of parameters of a complex HMM. In such cases, there is often a trade-off between constructing complex models with many states and constructing simple models with only a few states.

The complex model is better able to represent the intricate structure of the task but often results in a poor estimation of parameters. The simpler model, on the other hand, yields a robust parameter estimation but performs poorly because it is not sufficiently expressive to model the data.

Smoothing and *shrinkage* (Freitag and McCallum 1999) are the techniques typically used to take the sting out of data sparseness problems in probabilistic modeling. This section describes the techniques with regard to HMM, although they apply in other contexts as well such as SCFG.

Smoothing is the process of flattening a probability distribution implied by a model so that all reasonable sequences can occur with some probability. This often involves broadening the distribution by redistributing weight from high-probability regions to zero-probability regions. Note that smoothing may change the topology of an HMM by making some initially zero probability nonzero.

The simplest possible smoothing method is just to pretend that every possible training event occurrs one time more than it actually does. Any constant can be used instead of "one." This method is called *Laplace smoothing*. Other possible methods may include back-off smoothing, deleted interpolation, and others.[1]

Shrinkage is defined in terms of some hierarchy representing the expected similarity between parameter estimates. With respect to HMMs, the hierarchy can be defined as a tree with the HMM states for the leaves – all at the same depth.

This hierarchy is created as follows. First, the most complex HMM is built and its states are used for the leaves of the tree. Then the states are separated into disjoint classes within which the states are expected to have similar probability distributions. The classes become the parents of their constituent states in the hierarchy. Note that the HMM structure at the leaves induces a simpler HMM structure at the level of

[1] Full details outlining the smoothing technique can be found in Manning and Schutze (1999).

the classes. It is generated by summing the probabilities of emissions and transitions of all states in a class. This process may be repeated until only a single-state HMM remains at the root of the hierarchy.

Training such a hierarchy is straightforward. The emission and transition probabilities of the states in the internal levels of the hierarchy are calculated by summing the corresponding probabilities of their descendant leaves. Modeling using the hierarchy is also simple. The topology of the most complex HMM is used. However, the transition and emission probabilities of a given state are calculated by linearly interpolating between the corresponding probabilities for all ancestors of the state in the shrinkage hierarchy. The weights of the different models in the interpolation can be fixed at some reasonable value, like $\frac{1}{2}$, or can be optimized using held-out training data.

VII.2 STOCHASTIC CONTEXT-FREE GRAMMARS

An SCFG is a quintuple $G = (T, N, S, R, P)$, where T is the alphabet of terminal symbols (tokens), N is the set of nonterminals, S is the starting nonterminal, R is the set of rules, and $P : R \to [0.1]$ defines their probabilities. The rules have the form

$$n \to s_1 s_2 \ldots s_k,$$

where n is a nonterminal and each s_i is either a token or another nonterminal. As can be seen, SCFG is a usual context-free grammar with the addition of the P function.

As is true for a canonical (nonstochastic) grammar, SCFG is said to *generate* (or *accept*) a given string (sequence of tokens) if the string can be produced starting from a sequence containing just the starting symbol S and expanding nonterminals one by one in the sequence using the rules from the grammar. The particular way the string was generated can be naturally represented by a *parse tree* with the starting symbol as a root, nonterminals as internal nodes, and the tokens as leaves.

The semantics of the probability function P are straightforward. If r is the rule $n \to s_1 s_2 \ldots s_k$, then $P(r)$ is the frequency of expanding n using this rule, or, in Bayesian terms, if it is known that a given sequence of tokens was generated by expanding n, then $P(r)$ is the a priori likelihood that n was expanded using the rule r. Thus, it follows that for every nonterminal n the sum $\sum P(r)$ of probabilities of all rules r headed by n must be equal to one.

VII.2.1 Using SCFGs

Usually, some of the nonterminal symbols of a grammar correspond to meaningful language concepts, and the rules define the allowed syntactic relations between these concepts. For instance, in a parsing problem, the nonterminals may include S, NP, VP, and others, and the rules would define the syntax of the language. For example, $S \to NP\ VP$. Then, when the grammar is built, it is used for parsing new sentences.

In general, grammars are ambiguous in the sense that a given string can be generated in many different ways. With nonstochastic grammars there is no way to compare different parse trees, and thus the only information we can gather for a given sentence is whether or not it is *grammatical* – that is whether it can be produced by any parse. With SCFG, different parses have different probabilities; therefore, it is possible to find the best one, resolving the ambiguity.

In designing preprocessing systems around SCFGs, it has been found neither necessary nor desirable (for performance reasons) to perform a full syntactic parsing of all sentences in the document. Instead, a very basic "parsing" can be employed for the bulk of a text, but within the relevant parts the grammar is much more detailed. Thus, the extraction grammars can be said to define *sublanguages* for very specific domains.

In the classical definition of SCFG it is assumed that the rules are all independent. In this case it is possible to find the (unconditional) probability of a given parse tree by simply multiplying the probabilities of all rules participating in it. Then the usual parsing problem is formulated as follows: Given a sequence of tokens (a *string*), find the most probable parse tree that could generate the string. A simple generalization of the Viterbi algorithm is able to solve this problem efficiently.

In practical applications of SCFGs, it is rarely the case that the rules are truly independent. Then, the easiest way to cope with this problem while leaving most of the formalism intact is to let the probabilities $P(r)$ be conditioned on the context where the rule is applied. If the conditioning context is chosen reasonably, the Viterbi algorithm still works correctly even for this more general problem.

VII.3 MAXIMAL ENTROPY MODELING

Consider a random process of an unknown nature that produces a single output value y, a member of a finite set Y of possible output values. The process of generating y may be influenced by some contextual information x – a member of the set X of possible contexts. The task is to construct a statistical model that accurately represents the behavior of the random process. Such a model is a method of estimating the conditional probability of generating y given the context x.

Let $P(x, y)$ be denoted as the unknown true joint probability distribution of the random process, and let $p(y \mid x)$ be the model we are trying to build taken from the class $\wp$ of all possible models. To build the model we are given a set of training samples generated by observing the random process for some time. The training data consist of a sequence of pairs (x_i, y_i) of different outputs produced in different contexts.

In many interesting cases the set X is too large and underspecified to be used directly. For instance, X may be the set of all dots "." in all possible English texts. For contrast, the Y may be extremely simple while remaining interesting. In the preceding case, the Y may contain just two outcomes: "SentenceEnd" and "NotSentenceEnd." The target model $p(y \mid x)$ would in this case solve the problem of finding sentence boundaries.

In such cases it is impossible to use the context x directly to generate the output y. There are usually many regularities and correlations, however, that can be exploited. Different contexts are usually similar to each other in all manner of ways, and similar contexts tend to produce similar output distributions.

To express such regularities and their statistics, one can use *constraint functions* and their expected values. A constraint function $f: X \times Y \to R$ can be any real-valued function. In practice it is common to use binary-valued *trigger* functions of the form

$$f(x, y) = \begin{cases} 1, & \text{if } C(x) \text{ and } y = y_i, \\ 0, & \text{otherwise.} \end{cases}$$

Such a trigger function returns one for pair (x, y) if the context x satisfies the condition predicate C and the output value y is y_i. A common short notation for such a trigger function is $C \to y_i$. For the example above, useful triggers are

previous token is "Mr" → NotSentenceEnd,
next token is capitalized → SentenceEnd.

Given a constraint function f, we express its importance by requiring our target model to reproduce f's expected value faithfully in the true distribution:

$$p(f) = \Sigma_{x,y} p(x, y) f(x, y) = P(f) = \Sigma_{x,y} P(x, y) f(x, y).$$

In practice we cannot calculate the true expectation and must use an *empirical* expected value calculated by summing over the training samples:

$$p_E(f) = \Sigma_{i=1..N} \Sigma_{y \in Y} p(y \mid x_i) f(x_i, y)/N = P_E(f) = \Sigma_{i=1..N} f(x_i, y_i)/N.$$

The choice of feature functions is of course domain dependent. For now, let us assume the complete set of features $F = \{f_k\}$ is given. One can express the completeness of the set of features by requiring that the model agree with all the expected value constraints

$$p_E(f_k) = P_E(f_k) \text{ for all } f_k \in F$$

while otherwise being as uniform as possible. There are of course many models satisfying the expected values constraints. However, the uniformity requirement defines the target model uniquely. The degree of uniformity of a model is expressed by its *conditional entropy*

$$H(p) = -\sum_{x,y} p(x) \cdot p(y \mid x) \cdot \log p(y \mid x).$$

Or, empirically,

$$H_E(p) = -\Sigma_{i=1..N} \Sigma_{y \in Y} p(y \mid x_i) \cdot \log p(y \mid x_i)/N.$$

The constrained optimization problem of finding the maximal-entropy target model is solved by application of Lagrange multipliers and the Kuhn–Tucker theorem. Let us introduce a parameter λ_k (the Lagrange multiplier) for every feature. Define the Lagrangian $\Lambda(p, \lambda)$ by

$$\Lambda(p, \lambda) \equiv H_E(p) + \Sigma_k \lambda_k (p_E(f_k) - P_E(f_k)).$$

Holding λ fixed, we compute the unconstrained maximum of the Lagrangian over all $p \in \wp$. Denote by p_λ the p where $\Lambda(p, \lambda)$ achieves its maximum and by $\Psi(\lambda)$ the value of Λ at this point. The functions p_λ and $\Psi(\lambda)$ can be calculated using simple calculus:

$$p_\lambda(y \mid x) = \frac{1}{Z_\lambda(x)} \exp\left(\sum_k \lambda_k f_k(x, y)\right),$$
$$\Psi(\lambda) = -\sum_{i=1..N} \log Z_\lambda(x)/N + \sum_k \lambda_k P_E(f_k),$$

where $Z_\lambda(x)$ is a normalizing constant determined by the requirement that $\Sigma_{y \in Y} p_\lambda(y \mid x) = 1$. Finally, we pose the *dual* optimization problem

$$\lambda^* = \text{argmax}_\lambda \Psi(\lambda).$$

The Kuhn–Tucker theorem asserts that, under certain conditions, which include our case, the solutions of the primal and dual optimization problems coincide. That is, the model p, which maximizes $H_E(p)$ while satisfying the constraints, has the parametric form p_{λ^*}.

It is interesting to note that the function $\Psi(\lambda)$ is simply the log-likelihood of the training sample as predicted by the model p_λ. Thus, the model p_{λ^*} maximizes the likelihood of the training sample among all models of the parametric form p_λ.

VII.3.1 Computing the Parameters of the Model

The function $\Psi(\lambda)$ is well behaved from the perspective of numerical optimization, for it is smooth and concave. Consequently, various methods can be used for calculating λ^*. Generalized iterative scaling is the algorithm specifically tailored for the problem. This algorithm is applicable whenever all constraint functions are non-negative: $f_k(x, y) \geq 0$.

The algorithm starts with an arbitrary choice of λ's – for instance $\lambda_k = 0$ for all k. At each iteration the λ's are adjusted as follows:

1. For all k, let $\Delta\lambda_k$ be the solution to the equation

   $$P_E(f_k) = \Sigma_{i=1..N} \Sigma_{y \in Y} p_\lambda(y \mid x_i) \cdot f_k(x_i, y) \cdot \exp(\Delta\lambda_k f^\#(x_i, y))/N,$$

   where $f^\#(x, y) = \Sigma_k f_k(x, y)$.
2. For all k, let $\lambda_k := \lambda_k + \Delta\lambda_k$.

In the simplest case, when $f^\#$ is constant, $\Delta\lambda_k$ is simply $(1/f^\#) \cdot \log P_E(f_k)/p_{\lambda E}(f_k)$. Otherwise, any numerical algorithm for solving the equation can be used such as Newton's method.

VII.4 MAXIMAL ENTROPY MARKOV MODELS

For many tasks the conditional models have advantages over generative models like HMM. Maximal entropy Markov models (McCallum, Freitag, and Pereira 2000), or MEMM, is one class of such a conditional model closest to the HMM.

A MEMM is a probabilistic finite-state acceptor. Unlike HMM, which has separate transition and emission probabilities, MEMM has only transition probabilities, which, however, depend on the observations. A slightly modified version of the

Viterbi algorithm solves the problem of finding the most likely state sequence for a given observation sequence.

Formally, a MEMM consists of a set $Q = \{q_1, \ldots, q_N\}$ of states, and a set of transition probabilities functions $A_q : X \times Q \rightarrow [0, 1]$, where X denotes the set of all possible observations. $A_q(x, q')$ gives the probability $P(q' \mid q, x)$ of transition from q to q', given the observation x. Note that the model does not generate x but only conditions on it. Thus, the set X need not be small and need not even be fully defined. The transition probabilities A_q are separate exponential models trained using maximal entropy.

The task of a trained MEMM is to produce the most probable sequence of states given the observation. This task is solved by a simple modification of the Viterbi algorithm. The forward–backward algorithm, however, loses its meaning because here it computes the probability of the observation being generated by *any* state sequence, which is always one. However, the forward and backward variables are still useful for the MEMM training. The forward variable [Ref->HMM] $\alpha_m(q)$ denotes the probability of being in state q at time m given the observation. It is computed recursively as

$$\alpha_{n+1}(q) = \Sigma_{q' \in Q} \alpha_n(q') \cdot A_q(x, q').$$

The backward variable β denotes the probability of starting from state q at time m given the observation. It is computed similarly as

$$\beta_{n-1}(q) = \Sigma_{q' \in Q} A_q(x, q') \cdot \beta_n(q').$$

The model A_q for transition probabilities from a state is defined parametrically using constraint functions. If $f_k : X \times Q \rightarrow \mathbf{R}$ is the set of such functions for a given state q, then the model A_q can be represented in the form

$$A_q(x, q') = Z(x, q)^{-1} \exp(\Sigma_k \lambda_k f_k(x, q')),$$

where λ_k are the parameters to be trained and $Z(x, q)$ is the normalizing factor making probabilities of all transitions from a state sum to one.

VII.4.1 Training the MEMM

If the true states sequence for the training data is known, the parameters of the models can be straightforwardly estimated using the GIS algorithm for training ME models.

If the sequence is not known – for instance, if there are several states with the same label in a fully connected MEMM – the parameters must be estimated using a combination of the Baum–Welsh procedure and iterative scaling. Every iteration consists of two steps:

1. Using the forward–backward algorithm and the current transition functions to compute the state occupancies for all training sequences.
2. Computing the new transition functions using GIS with the feature frequencies based on the state occupancies computed in step 1.

It is unnecessary to run GIS to convergence in step 2; a single GIS iteration is sufficient.

VII.5 CONDITIONAL RANDOM FIELDS

Conditional random fields (CRFs) (Lafferty, McCallum, et al. 2001) constitute another conditional model based on maximal entropy. Like MEMMs, which are described in the previous section, CRFs are able to accommodate many possibly correlated features of the observation. However, CRFs are better able to trade off decisions at different sequence positions. MEMMs were found to suffer from the so-called label bias problem.

The problem appears when the MEMM contains states with different output degrees. Because the probabilities of transitions from any given state must sum to one, transitions from lower degree states receive higher probabilities than transitions from higher degree states. In the extreme case, transition from a state with degree one always gets probability one, effectively ignoring the observation.

CRFs do not have this problem because they define a single ME-based distribution over the whole label sequence. On the other hand, the CRFs cannot contain "hidden" states – the training data must define the sequence of states precisely. For most practical sequence labeling problems this limitation is not significant.

In the description of CRFs presented here, attention is restricted to their simplest form – linear chain CRFs, which generalize finite-state models like HMMs and MEMMs. Such CRFs model the conditional probability distribution of sequences of labels given the observation sequences. More general formulations are possible (Lafferty et al. 2001; McCallum and Jensen 2003).

Let X be a random variable over the observation sequences and Y a random variable over the label sequences. All components Y_i of Y are assumed to range over a finite set L of labels. The labels roughly correspond to states in finite-state models. The variables X and Y are jointly distributed, but CRF constructs a conditional model $p(Y \mid X)$ without explicitly modeling the margin $p(X)$.

A CRF on (X, Y) is specified by a vector $\mathbf{f} = (f_1, f_2, \ldots f_m)$ of *local features* and a corresponding *weight vector* $\boldsymbol{\lambda} = (\lambda_1, \lambda_2, \ldots \lambda_m)$. Each local feature $f_j(\mathbf{x}, \mathbf{y}, i)$ is a real-valued function of the observation sequence $\mathbf{x}$, the labels sequence $\mathbf{y} = (y_1, y_2, \ldots y_n)$, and the sequence position i. The value of a feature function at any given position i may depend only on y_i or on y_i and y_{i+1} but not on any other components of the label sequence $\mathbf{y}$. A feature that depends only on y_i at any given position i is called a *state feature*, and if it depends on y_i and y_{i+1} it is called a *transition feature*.

The *global feature vector* $\mathbf{F}(\mathbf{x}, \mathbf{y})$ is a sum of local features at all positions:

$$\mathbf{F}(\mathbf{x}, \mathbf{y}) = \Sigma_{i=1..n}\mathbf{f}(\mathbf{x}, \mathbf{y}, i).$$

The conditional probability distribution defined by the CRF is then

$$p_\lambda(\mathbf{y} \mid \mathbf{x}) = Z_\lambda(\mathbf{x})^{-1}\exp(\boldsymbol{\lambda} \cdot \mathbf{F}(\mathbf{x}, \mathbf{y})),$$

where

$$Z_\lambda(\mathbf{x}) = \Sigma_y \exp(\boldsymbol{\lambda} \cdot \mathbf{F}(\mathbf{x}, \mathbf{y})).$$

It is a consequence of a fundamental theorem about random Markov fields (Kindermann and Snell 1980; Jain and Chellappa 1993) that any conditional distribution $p(\mathbf{y}/\mathbf{x})$ obeying the Markov property $p(y_i \mid x, \{y_j\}_{j \neq i}) = p(y_i \mid x, y_{i-1}, y_{i+1})$

can be written in the exponential form above with a suitable choice of the feature functions and the weights vector.

Notice also that any HMM can be represented in the form of CRF if its set of states Q coincide with the set of labels L. If $A : L \times L \to [0, 1]$ denotes the transition probability and $B : L \times O \to [0, 1]$ denotes is the emission probability functions, the corresponding CRF can be defined by the set of state features

$$f_{yo}(\mathbf{x}, \mathbf{y}, k) \equiv (y_k = y) \text{ and } (x_k = o)$$

and transition features

$$f_{yy'}(\mathbf{x}, \mathbf{y}, k) \equiv (y_k = y) \text{ and } (y_{k+1} = y')$$

with the weights $\lambda_{yo} = \log B(y, o)$ and $\lambda_{yy'} = \log A(y, y')$.

VII.5.1 The Three Classic Problems Relating to CRF

As with HMMs, three main problems are associated with CRFs:

1. Given a CRF λ, an observation sequence $\mathbf{x}$, and a label sequence $\mathbf{y}$, find the conditional probability $p_\lambda(\mathbf{y} \mid \mathbf{x})$.
2. Given a CRF λ and an observation sequence $\mathbf{x}$, find the most probable label sequence $\mathbf{y} = \text{argmax}_{\mathbf{y}}\, p_\lambda(\mathbf{y} \mid \mathbf{x})$.
3. Given a set of training samples $(\mathbf{x}^{(k)}, \mathbf{y}^{(k)})$, find the CRF parameters λ that maximize the likelihood of the training data.

At least a basic attempt will be made here to explain the typical approaches for each of these problems.

VII.5.2 Computing the Conditional Probability

For a given $\mathbf{x}$ and a given position i define a $|L| \times |L|$ *transition matrix* $M_i(\mathbf{x})$ by

$$M_i(\mathbf{x})[y, y'] = \exp\left(\boldsymbol{\lambda} \cdot \mathbf{f}(\mathbf{x}, \{y_i = y, y_{i+1} = y'\}, i)\right).$$

Then, the conditional probability $p_\lambda(\mathbf{y} \mid \mathbf{x})$ can be decomposed as

$$p_\lambda(\mathbf{y} \mid \mathbf{x}) = Z_\lambda(\mathbf{x})^{-1} \pi_{i=1..n} M_i(\mathbf{x})[y_i, y_{i+1}].$$

The normalization factor $Z_\lambda(\mathbf{x})$ can be computed by a variant of the forward–backward algorithm. The forward variables $\alpha_i(\mathbf{x}, y)$ and the backward variables $\beta_i(\mathbf{x}, \mathbf{y})$, for $y \in L$, can be computed using the recurrences

$$\begin{aligned}
&\alpha_0(x, y) = 1, \\
&\alpha_{i+1}(\mathbf{x}, y) = \Sigma_{y' \in L} \alpha_i(\mathbf{x}, y') M_i(y', y, \mathbf{x}), \\
&\beta_n(\mathbf{x}, y) = 1, \\
&\beta_{i-1}(\mathbf{x}, y) = \Sigma_{y' \in L} M_{i-1}(y, y', \mathbf{x}) \beta_i(\mathbf{x}, y').
\end{aligned}$$

Finally, $Z_\lambda(\mathbf{x}) = \Sigma_{y \in L} \alpha_n(\mathbf{x}, y)$.

VII.5.3 Finding the Most Probable Label Sequence

The most probable label sequence $\mathbf{y} = \text{argmax}_{\mathbf{y}}\ p_\lambda(\mathbf{y} \mid \mathbf{x})$ can be found by a suitable adaptation of the Viterbi algorithm. Note that

$$\text{argmax}_y p_\lambda(\mathbf{y} \mid \mathbf{x}) = \text{argmax}_y\ (\boldsymbol{\lambda} \cdot \mathbf{F}(\mathbf{x}, \mathbf{y}))$$

because the normalizer $Z_\lambda(\mathbf{x})$ does not depend on $\mathbf{y}$. $\mathbf{F}(\mathbf{x}, \mathbf{y})$ decomposes into a sum of terms for consecutive pairs of labels, making the task straightforward.

VII.5.4 Training the CRF

CRF is trained by maximizing the log-likelihood of a given training set $\{(\mathbf{x}^{(k)}, \mathbf{y}^{(k)})\}$:

$$L(\lambda) = \Sigma_k \log p_\lambda(\mathbf{y}^{(k)} \mid \mathbf{x}^{(k)}) = \Sigma_k[\lambda \cdot \mathbf{F}(\mathbf{x}^{(k)}, \mathbf{y}^{(k)}) - \log Z_\lambda(\mathbf{x}^{(k)})].$$

This function is concave in λ, and so the maximum can be found at the point where the gradient L is zero:

$$0 = \nabla L = \Sigma_k[\mathbf{F}(\mathbf{x}^{(k)}, \mathbf{y}^{(k)}) - \Sigma_y \mathbf{F}(\mathbf{x}^{(k)}, \mathbf{y}) p_\lambda(\mathbf{y} \mid \mathbf{x}^{(k)})].$$

The left side is the empirical average of the global feature vector, and the right side is its model expectation. The maximum is reached when the two are equal:

$$(^*)\Sigma_k \mathbf{F}(\mathbf{x}^{(k)}, \mathbf{y}^{(k)}) = \Sigma_k \Sigma_y \mathbf{F}(\mathbf{x}^{(k)}, \mathbf{y}) p_\lambda(\mathbf{y} \mid \mathbf{x}^{(k)}).$$

Straightforwardly computing the expectations on the right side is infeasible, because of the necessity of summing over an exponential number of label sequences $\mathbf{y}$. Fortunately, the expectations can be rewritten as

$$\Sigma_y \mathbf{F}(\mathbf{x}, \mathbf{y}) p_\lambda(\mathbf{y} \mid \mathbf{x}) = \Sigma_{i=1,n} \Sigma_{y,y' \in L} p_\lambda(y_i = y, y_{i+1} = y' \mid \mathbf{x}) \mathbf{f}(\mathbf{x}, \mathbf{y}, i),$$

which brings the number of summands down to polynomial size. The probabilities $p_\lambda(y_i = y, y_{i+1} = y' \mid \mathbf{x})$ can be computed using the forward and backward variables:

$$p_\lambda(y_i = y, y_{i+1} = y' \mid \mathbf{x}) = Z(\mathbf{x})^{-1} \alpha_i(\mathbf{x}, y) M_i(y', y, \mathbf{x}) \beta_{i+1}(\mathbf{x}, y').$$

GIS can be used to solve the equation (*). A particularly simple form of it further requires that the total count of all features in any training sequence be constant. If this condition does not hold, a new *slack* feature can be added, making the sum equal to a predefined constant S:

$$s(\mathbf{x}, \mathbf{y}, i) = S - \Sigma_i \Sigma_j f_j(\mathbf{x}, \mathbf{y}, i).$$

If the condition holds, the parameters λ can be adjusted by

$$\lambda: = \lambda + \Delta\lambda,$$

where the $\boldsymbol{\Delta\lambda}$ are calculated by

$$\Delta\lambda_j = S^{-1} \log \text{ (empirical average of } f_j / \text{ modelexpectation of } f_j).$$

VII.6 FURTHER READING

Section VII.1

For a great introduction on hidden Markov models, refer to Rabiner (1986) and Rabiner (1990).

Section VII.2

Stochastic context-free grammars are described in Collins (1997) and Collins and Miller (1998).

Section VII.3

The following papers elaborate more on maximal entropy with regard to text processing: Reynar and Ratnaparkhi (1997); Borthwick (1999); and Charniak (2000).

Section VII.4

Maximal entropy Markov models are described in McCallum et al. (2000).

Section VII.5

Random markov fields are described in Kindermann and Snell (1980) and Jain and Chellappa (1993). Conditional random fields are described in Lafferty et al. (2001) and Sha and Pereira (2003).

Preprocessing Applications Using Probabilistic and Hybrid Approaches

The related fields of NLP, IE, text categorization, and probabilistic modeling have developed increasingly rapidly in the last few years. New approaches are tried constantly and new systems are reported numbering thousands a year. The fields largely remain experimental science – a new approach or improvement is conceived and a system is built, tested, and reported. However, comparatively little work is done in analyzing the results and in comparing systems and approaches with each other. Usually, it is the task of the authors of a particular system to compare it with other known approaches, and this presents difficulties – both psychological and methodological.

One reason for the dearth of analytical work, excluding the general lack of sound theoretical foundations, is that the comparison experiments require software, which is usually either impossible or very costly to obtain. Moreover, the software requires integration, adjustment, and possibly training for any new use, which is also extremely costly in terms of time and human labor.

Therefore, our description of the different possible solutions to the problems described in the first section is incomplete by necessity. There are just too many reported systems, and there is often no good reason to choose one approach against the other. Consequently, we have tried to describe in depth only a small number of systems. We have chosen as broad a selection as possible, encompassing many different approaches. And, of course, the results produced by the systems are state of the art or sufficiently close to it.

VIII.1 APPLICATIONS OF HMM TO TEXTUAL ANALYSIS

VIII.1.1 Using HMM to Extract Fields from Whole Documents

Freitag and McCallum (Freitag and McCallum 1999, 2000) implemented a fields extraction system utilizing no general-purpose NLP processing. The system is designed to solve a general problem that can be specified as follows: *find the best unbroken fragment of text from a document that answers some domain-specific*

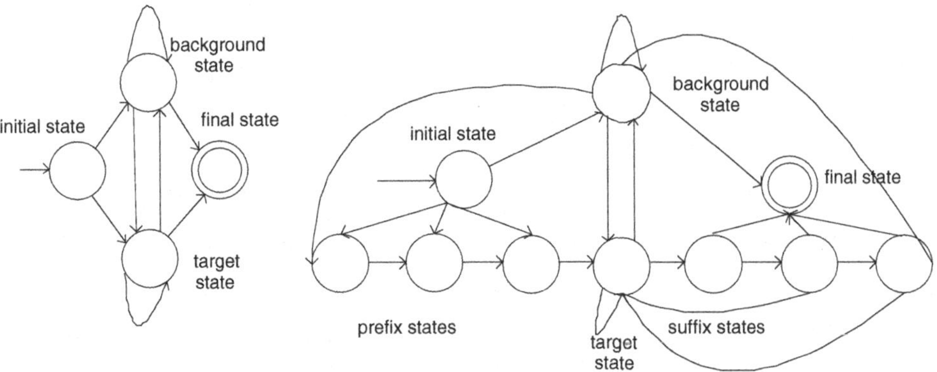

Figure VIII.1. Possible topologies of a simple HMM.

question. The question is stated implicitly in the form of a set of labeled training documents, each of them containing a single labeled field.

For example, if the domain consists of a collection of seminar announcements, we may be interested in the location of the seminar described in a given announcement. Then the training collection should contain the labeled locations. It is of course possible to extract several fields from the same document by using several separately trained models. Each model, however, is designed to extract exactly one field from one document.

The system does its task by modeling the generative process that could generate the document. The HMM model used for this purpose has the following characteristics:

- The observation symbols are the words and other tokens such as numbers.
- The HMM takes an entire document as one observation sequence.
- The HMM contains two classes of states: background states and target states. The background states emit words in which we are not interested, whereas the target states emit words that constitute the information to be extracted.
- The HMM topology is predefined and only a few transitions are allowed between the states.

The hand-built HMM topology is quite simple. One background state exists, which produces all irrelevant words. There are several prefix and suffix states, which are by themselves irrelevant but can provide the context for the target states. There are one or more parallel chains of target states – all of different lengths. And finally, there is an initial state and a final state. The topology has two variable parameters – the size of the context window, which is the number of prefix and suffix states, and the number of parallel paths of target states. Several examples of topologies are shown in Figures VIII.1 and VIII.2.

Training such HMMs does not require using the Baum–Welsh formulas because there is only one way each training document can be generated. Therefore, the maximum likelihood training for each state is conducted simply by counting the number of times each transition or emission occurred in all training sequences and dividing by the total number of times the state was visited.

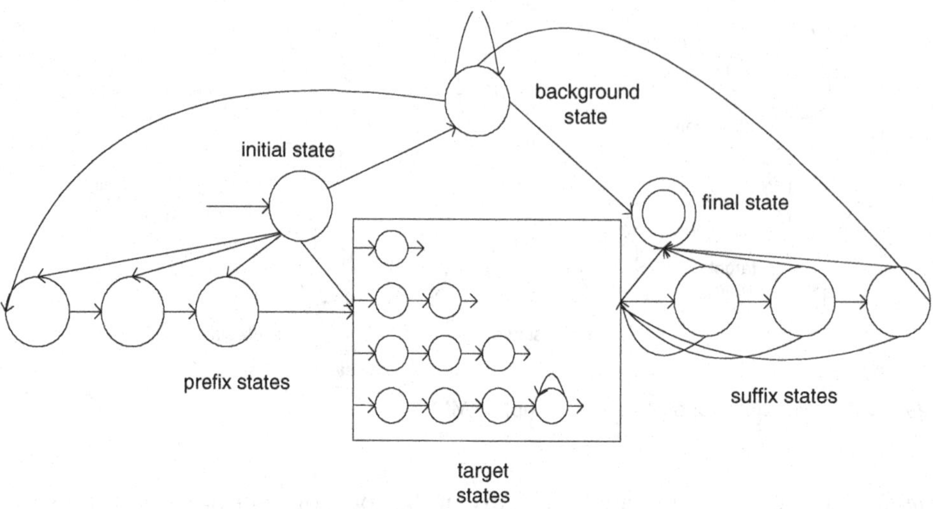

Figure VIII.2. A more general HMM topology.

The data sparseness problem, however, is severe – especially for the more complex topologies with bigger number of states. This problem is solved by utilizing the shrinkage [Crossref -> shrinkage] technique. Several possible shrinkage hierarchies were attempted. The best results were produced by shrinking straight to the simple topology shown in the left of Figure VIII.1. All prefix and suffix states are shrunk together with the background state, and all target states are also shrunk into a single target state.

This simple topology is further shrunk into a single-state HMM. The system also uses a *uniform* level, where the root single-state HMM is further shrunk into a single-state HMM with all emission probabilities equal to each other. This uniform level does the job of smoothing the probabilities by allowing previously nonencountered tokens to have a small nonzero probability. The interpolation weights for different levels were calculated by expectation maximization, using held-out data.

The system achieved some modest success in the task of extracting *speaker, location*, and *time* fields from the seminar announcements, achieving respectively 71-, 84- and 99-percent F1-measure in the best configuration, which included the window size of four as well as four parallel target paths of different sizes.

VIII.1.2 Learning HMM Structure from Data

The next work (Freitag and McCallum 2000) by the same authors explores the idea of automatically learning better HMM topologies. The HMM model works in the same way as the model described in the previous section. However, the HMM structure is not predefined and thus can be more complex. In particular, it is no longer true that every document can be generated by exactly one sequence of states. Therefore, Baum–Welsh formulas, adjusted for label constraints, are used for HMM parameter estimation.

The optimal HMM structure for a given task is built by hill climbing in the space of all possible structures. The initial simplest structure is shown in Figure VIII.3.

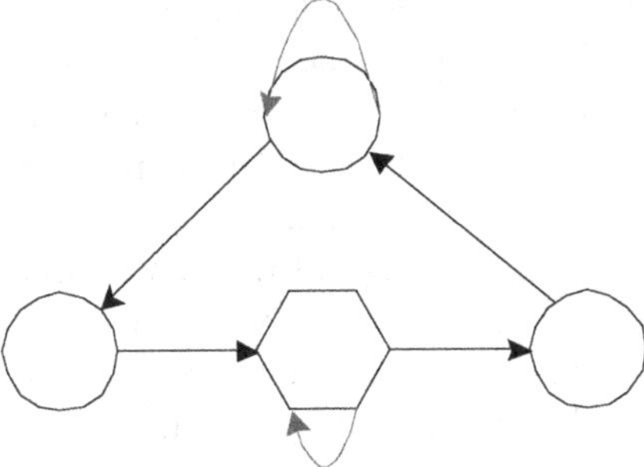

Figure VIII.3. Initial HMM topology.

At each step, each step of the following set of operations is applied to the current model:

- ***Lengthen a prefix***. A single state is added to the end of a prefix. The penultimate state now undergoes transition only to the new state; the new state changes to any target states to which the penultimate state previously changed.
- ***Split a prefix***. A duplicate is made of some prefix. Transitions are duplicated so that the first and last states of the new prefix have the same connectivity to the rest of the network as the old prefix.
- ***Lengthen a suffix***. The dual of the prefix-lengthening operation.
- ***Split a suffix***. Identical to the prefix-splitting operation except that it is applied to a suffix.
- ***Lengthen a target string***. Similar to the prefix lengthening operation, except that all target states, in contrast to prefix and suffix states, have self-transitions. The single target state in the simple model in Figure VIII.1 is a target string of length one.
- ***Split a target string***. Identical to the prefix-splitting operation except that it is applied to a target string.
- ***Add a background state***. Add a new background state to the model, with the same connectivity, with respect to the nonbackground states, as all other background states: the new state has outgoing transitions only to prefix states and incoming transitions only from suffix states.

The model performing best on a separate validation set is selected for the next iteration. After 25 iterations, the best-performing (scored by three-fold cross-validation) model is selected from the set of all intermediate models as the final model.

The experiments show that the models learned in this way usually outperform the simple hand-made models described in the previous section. For instance, in the domain of seminar announcements, the learned model achieves 77- and 87.5-percent F1-measure for the tasks of extracting *speaker* and *location* fields, respectively.

VIII.1.3 Nymble: An HMM with Context-Dependent Probabilities

A different approach was taken by BBN (Bikel et al. 1997) in the named entity extraction system *Nymble* (later called IdentiFinder). Instead of utilizing complex

HMM structures to model the complexity of the problem, Nymble uses a simple, fully connected (*ergodic*) HMM with a single-state-per-target concept and a single state for the background. However, the emission and transition probabilities of the states are not permanently fixed but depend on the context. The system achieved a very good accuracy, outperforming the handcoded rule-based systems.

Nymble contains a handcrafted tokenizer, which splits the text into sentences and the sentences into tokens. Nymble represents tokens as pairs <*w*,*f*>, where *w* is the lowercase version of the token and *f* is the token feature – a number from 1 to 14 according to the first matching description of the token in the following list:

1. digit number (01)
2. digit number (1996)
3. alphanumeric string (A34–24)
4. digits and dashes (12–16–02)
5. digits and slashes (12/16/02)
6. digits and comma (1,000)
7. digits and period (2.34)
8. any other number (100)
9. all capital letters (CLF)
10. capital letter and a period (M.)
11. first word of a sentence (The)
12. initial letter of the word is capitalized (Albert)
13. word in lower case (country)
14. all other words and tokens (;)

The features of the tokens are choosen in such a way as to maximize the similarities in the usage of tokens having the same feature. The Nymble model is designed to exploit those similarities. Note that the list of features depends on the problem domain and on the language. The list of features for different problems, different languages, or both, would be significantly different.

The named entity extraction task, as in MUC evaluation (Chinchor et al. 1994: MUC), is to identify all named locations, named persons, named organizations, dates, times, monetary amounts, and percentages in text. The task can be formulated as a classification problem: given a body of text, to label every word with one of the name class tags such as Person, Organization, Location, Date, Time, Money, Percent, or Not-A-Name.

Nymble utilizes an HMM model, which contains a state per each name class. There are two additional states for the beginning and the end of sentence. The HMM is fully connected (ergodic), and thus there is a nonzero probability of transition from any state to any other state. The HMM topology of Nymble is shown in Figure VIII.4.

Unlike the classical formulation, however, the transition and emission probabilities of the states in Nymble HMM depend on their context. The probability of emitting a first token in a name class is conditioned on the previous name class. The probability of emitting any other token inside a name class is conditioned on the previous token, and the probability of transition to a new name class is conditioned on the last word in the previous name class.

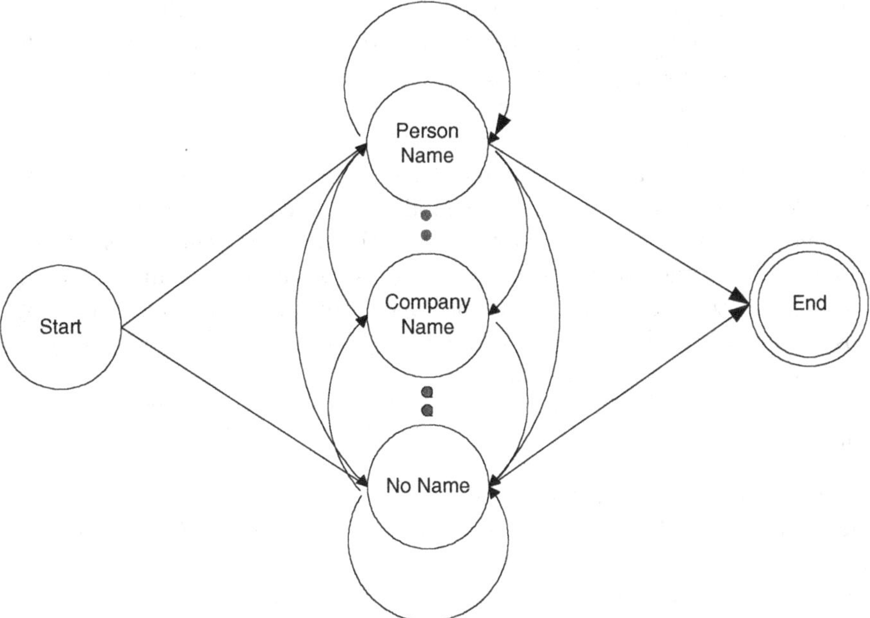

Figure VIII.4. Nymble HMM topology.

Formally, such a model can be described as a classical HMM by substituting |V| new states for each nameclass state, where V is the vocabulary of the system. Each new state will emit the token it corresponds to with the probability one, and the fixed transition probabilities between the states would then be conditioned as required. The nonstandard formulation, however, allows enormously more efficient processing, cleaner formulation of the back-off models below, and the possibility of improving the system by conditioning the probabilities on additional context clues.

As described earlier, there are three different classes of probabilities that the model must be able to estimate:

- The probability $P(<w, f> \mid \text{NC}, \text{NC}^{-1})$ of generating the first token in a name class (NC) conditioned on the previous name class,
- The probability $P(<w,f> \mid \text{NC}, <w^{-1},f^{-1}>)$ of generating the subsequent tokens inside a name class with each token conditioned on the previous one, and
- The probability $P(\text{NC} \mid \text{NC}^{-1}, w^{-1})$ of transition to a new name class conditioned on the previous word.

The model is trained by maximum likelihood. There is no need for Baum–Welsh reestimation because for each sentence there is only one way it can be generated. Thus, the probabilities above are calculated using events/sample-size. For instance,

$$P(< w,\ f > \mid \text{NC}, \text{NC}^{-1}) = c(< w,\ f >, \text{NC}, \text{NC}^{-1})/c(\text{NC}, \text{NC}^{-1}),$$

where the $c(\dots)$ represents the number of occurrences of a particular event in the training data.

The training data sparseness problem manifests itself here especially as the probabilities are conditioned on context. There are two separate cases: tokens that do not appear in the training data (the unknown tokens) and other events for which the training data are insufficiently representative.

We deal with unknown token $<w, f>$ robustly by substituting for it a pair <_UNK_, *f*> having the same feature and a new _UNK_ word. Statistics for the unknown tokens are gathered in a separate model built specifically for dealing with them. The model is trained in the following way: The whole training set is divided into two halves. Then the tokens in the first half that do not appear in the second and the tokens in the second half that do not appear in the first are substituted by the _UNK_ tokens. The unknown words model is trained on the resulting dataset. In this way, all of the training data participate.

For dealing with the general data sparseness problem, several layers of backoff are employed:

- The probability of generating the first word in a name class $P(<w,f> \mid \mathrm{NC}, \mathrm{NC}^{-1})$ is interpolated with $P(<w, f> \mid \mathrm{NC}$ <any>$)$ and further with $P(<w, f> \mid \mathrm{NC})$, with $P(w \mid \mathrm{NC}) \cdot P(f \mid \mathrm{NC})$, and with $|\mathrm{V}|^{-1}|\mathrm{F}|^{-1}$.
- The probability of generating subsequent tokens $P(<w, f> \mid \mathrm{NC}, <w^{-1}, f^{-1}>)$ is interpolated with $P(<w, f> \mid \mathrm{NC})$, with $P(w \mid \mathrm{NC}) \cdot P(f \mid \mathrm{NC})$, and with $|\mathrm{V}|^{-1}|\mathrm{F}|^{-1}$.
- The transition probability $P(\mathrm{NC} \mid \mathrm{NC}^{-1}, w^{-1})$ is interpolated with $P(\mathrm{NC} \mid \mathrm{NC}^{-1})$, with $P(\mathrm{NC})$, and with 1/(number of name classes).

The weights for each back-off model are computed on the fly, using the following formula:

$$\lambda = \left(1 - \frac{c(Y)}{bc(Y)}\right) \frac{1}{1 + \frac{\#(Y)}{bc(Y)}},$$

where $c(Y)$ the count of event Y according to the full model, $bc(Y)$ is the count of event Y according to the backoff model, and $\#(Y)$ is the number of unique outcomes of Y. This λ has two desirable properties. If the full model and the backoff have similar levels of support for an event Y, then the λ will be close to zero and the full model will be used.

The number of unique outcomes is a crude measure of uniformity, or uncertainty, of the model. The more uncertainty the model has, the lower is the confidence in the backoff model, the lower λ is then used.

The experimental evaluation of the Nymble system showed that, given sufficient training, it performs comparably to the best hand-crafted systems (94.9% versus 96.4% F1-measure) for the mixed-case English *Wall Street Journal* documents and significantly outperforms them for the more difficult all-uppercase and speech-form (93.6% and 90.7% versus 89% and 74%, respectively).

VIII.2 USING MEMM FOR INFORMATION EXTRACTION

Very recently the conditional models trained using the maximal entropy approach received much attention. The reason for preferring them over the more traditional generative models lies in their ability to make use of arbitrary features of the observations, possibly overlapping and interdependent, in a consistent and mathematically clean way.

The MEMM is one formalism developed in McCallum et al. (2000) that allows the power of the ME approach to be used. They tested their implementation of MEMMs on the problem of labeling the lines in a long multipart FAQ file according to their function as a *head*, a *question*, an *answer*, and a *tail*.

The problem is especially well suited for a conditional model because such a model can consider each line a single observation unit described by its features. In contrast, a generative model like HMM would have to generate the whole line (i.e., to estimate its probability), which is clearly infeasible.

The 24 binary features (trigger constraint functions) used for classifying lines in the particular problem are shown below:

begins-with-number	contains-question-mark
begins-with-ordinal	contains-question-word
begins-with-punctuation	ends-with-question-mark
begins-with-question-word	first-alpha-is-capitalized
begins-with-subject	indented
blank	indented-1-to-4
contains-alphanum	indented-5-to-10
contains-bracketed-number	more-than-one-third-space
contains-http	only-punctuation
contains-non-space	prev-is-blank
contains-number	prev-begins-with-ordinal
contains-pipe	shorter-than-30

As can be seen, the features of a line do not define the line completely, nor are they independent.

The MEMM was compared with three other learners:

- Stateless ME classifier, which used the 24 features to classify each line separately.
- Traditional, fully connected HMM with four states emitting individual tokens. Similar four-state HMM emitting individual features.
- Each line was converted to a sequence of features before training and testing.

It was found that MEMM performed best of all four, and Feature HMM was second but had significantly worse performance. The other two models functioned poorly.

VIII.3 APPLICATIONS OF CRFs TO TEXTUAL ANALYSIS

VIII.3.1 POS-Tagging with Conditional Random Fields

CRFs were developed in Lafferty et al. (2001) as a conditional ME–based version of HMM, which does not suffer from label bias problems. Lafferty et al. applied the CRF formalism to POS tagging in Penn treebank style and compared its performance with that of HMM and MEMM.

In the first set of experiments, the two types of features were introduced – *tag–word* pairs, and *tag–tag* pairs corresponding to HMM observation and transition features. The results are consistent with the expectations: HMM outperforms MEMM as a consequence of the label bias problem, whereas CRF and HMM perform similarly with CRF slightly better overall but slightly worse for out-of-vocabulary words.

In the second set of experiments, a set of simple morphological features was added: whether a word begins with a digit or uppercase letter, whether it contains a hyphen, and whether it ends in one of the following suffixes: -ing -ogy -ed -s -ly -ion -tion -ity -ies. Here the results also confirm the expectations: Both CRF and MEMM benefit significantly from the use of these features – especially for out-of-vocabulary words.

VIII.3.2 Shallow Parsing with Conditional Random Fields

Shallow parsing is another sequence labeling problem. The task is to identify the nonrecursive cores of various types of phrases. The paradigmatic shallow parsing problem is *NP chunking*, finding the nonrecursive cores of noun phrases, the *base NPs*. Sha and Pereira (2003) adapt CRFs to this problem and show that it beats all known single-model NP chunkers, performing at the level of the best known chunker – voting arrangement of 24 forward- and backward-looking SVM classifiers.

The input to an NP chunker consists of a sentence labeled with POS tags. The chunker's task is to further label each word indicating whether the word is (O)utside the chunk, (B)egins a chunk, or (C)ontinues a chunk.

The chunking CRF in Sha and Pereira (2003) has a second-order Markov dependency between chunk tags. This is encoded by making the labels of CRF pairs of consecutive chunk tags. That is, the label at position i is $y_i = c_{i-1}c_i$ where c_i is the chunk tag of word i, one of O, B, or C. Because B must be used to start a chunk, the label OC is impossible. In addition, successive labels are constrained. These contraints on the model topology are enforced by giving appropriate features a weight of $-\infty$, forcing all the forbidden labelings to have zero probability.

The features of the chunker CRF are represented as

$$f(\boldsymbol{x}, \boldsymbol{y}, i) = g(\boldsymbol{x}, i)h(y_i, y_{i+1}),$$

where $g(x, i)$ is a predicate on the input sequence and position, and $h(y_i\ y_{i+1})$ is a predicate on pairs of labels. The possibilities for the predicates are as follows:

g(x, i)	true	
	w_i=w	
	w_{i-1}=w	w_{i+1}=w
	w_{i-2}=w	w_{i+2}=w
	(w_i=w) and (w_{i-1}=w′)	(w_i=w) and (w_{i+1}=w′)
	t_i=t	
	t_{i-1}=t	t_{i+1}=t
	t_{i-2}=t	t_{i+2}=t
	(t_i=t) and (t_{i-1}=t′)	(t_i=t) and (t_{i+1}=t′)
	(t_{i-1}=t) and (t_{i-2}=t′)	(t_{i+1}=t) and (t_{i+2}=t′)
	(t_i=t) and (t_{i-1}=t′) and (t_{i-2}=t″)	
	(t_i=t) and (t_{i-1}=t′) and (t_{i+1}=t″)	
	(t_i=t) and (t_{i+1}=t′) and (t_{i+2}=t″)	
h(y_i, y_{i+1})	y_i=y	
	(y_i=y) and (y_{i+1}=y′)	
	c(y_i)=c.	

The w_i, t_i, y_i mean, respectively, the word, the POS tag, and the label at position i; $c(y_i)$ means the chunk tag, and thus $c(\text{OB}) = \text{B}$. The $w, w', t, t', t'', y, y', c$ are specific words, tags, labels, and chunk tags chosen from the vocabulary generated by the training data.

A Gaussian weight prior was used to reduce overfitting, and thus the log-likelihood of the training data was taken as

$$L(\boldsymbol{\lambda}) = \Sigma_k[\boldsymbol{\lambda} \cdot \mathbf{F}(\mathbf{x}^{(k)}, \mathbf{y}^{(k)}) - \log Z_{\boldsymbol{\lambda}}(\mathbf{x}^{(k)})] - ||\boldsymbol{\lambda}||^2/2\sigma^2.$$

The experimental evaluation demonstrates the state-of-the-art performance of the CRF chunk tagger. Interestingly, the GIS training method was shown to perform less well than some other general-purpose convex optimization algorithms – especially when many correlated features are involved. The convergence rate of GIS turns out to be much slower.

VIII.4 TEG: USING SCFG RULES FOR HYBRID STATISTICAL–KNOWLEDGE-BASED IE

Another approach has been described that employs a hybrid statistical and knowledge-based information extraction model able to extract entities and relations at the sentence level. The model attempts to retain and improve the high accuracy levels of knowledge-based systems while drastically reducing the amount of manual labor by relying on statistics drawn from a training corpus. The implementation of the model, called trainable extraction grammar (TEG), can be adapted to any IE domain by writing a suitable set of rules in a SCFG-based extraction language and training them using an annotated corpus.

The system does not contain any purely linguistic components such as a POS tagger or parser. We demonstrate the performance of the system on several named entity extraction and relation extraction tasks. The experiments show that our hybrid approach outperforms both purely statistical and purely knowledge-based systems and require orders-of-magnitude less manual rule writing and smaller amounts of training data. The improvement in accuracy is slight for named entity extraction tasks and more pronounced for relation extraction.

By devoting some attention to the details of TEG, we can provide a concrete sense of how hybrid-type systems can be employed for text mining preprocessing operations.

VIII.4.1 Introduction to a Hybrid System

The knowledge engineering (mostly rule-based) systems traditionally were the top performers in most IE benchmarks such as MUC (Chinchor, Hirschman, and Lewis 1994), ACE (ACE 2004), and the KDD CUP (Yeh and Hirschman 2002). Recently, though, the machine learning systems became state of the art – especially for simpler tagging problems such as named entity recognition (Bikel, Schwartz, and Weischedel 1999) or field extraction (McCallum et al. 2000).

Still, the knowledge engineering approach retains some of its advantages. It is focused around manually writing patterns to extract the entities and relations. The patterns are naturally accessible to human understanding and can be improved in a controllable way, but improving the results of a pure machine learning system would require providing it with additional training data. However, the impact of adding more data soon becomes infinitesimal, whereas the cost of manually annotating the data grows linearly.

TEG is a hybrid entities and relations extraction system, which combines the power of knowledge-based and statistical machine learning approaches. The system is based on SCFGs. The rules for the extraction grammar are written manually, and the probabilities are trained from an annotated corpus. The powerful disambiguation ability of PCFGs allows the knowledge engineer to write very simple and naive rules while retaining their power, thus greatly reducing the required labor.

In addition, the size of the needed training data is considerably smaller than that of the training data needed for a pure machine learning system (for achieving comparable accuracy results). Furthermore, the tasks of rule writing and corpus annotation can be balanced against each other.

VIII.4.2 TEG: Bridging the Gap between Statistical and Rule-Based IE Systems

Although the formalisms based on probabilistic finite-state automata are quite successful for entity extraction, they have shortcomings that make them harder to use for the more difficult task of extracting relationships.

One problem is that a finite-state automaton model is flat, and so its natural task is assignment of a tag (state label) to each token in a sequence. This is suitable for the tasks in which the tagged sequences do not nest and there are no explicit relations between the sequences. Part-of-speech tagging and entity extraction tasks belong to this category, and indeed the HMM-based POS taggers and entity extractors are state of the art.

Extracting relationships is different because the tagged sequences can and must nest and there are relations between them, which must be explicitly recognized. Although it is possible to use nested automata to cope with this problem, we felt that using a more general context-free grammar formalism would allow for greater generality and extendibility without incurring any significant performance loss.

VIII.4.3 Syntax of a TEG Rulebook

A TEG rulebook consists of declarations and rules. Rules basically follow the classical grammar rule syntax with a special construction for assigning concept attributes. Notation shortcuts like [ ] and | can be used for easier writing. The nonterminals referred by the rules must be declared before usage. Some of them can be declared as *output concepts*, which are the entities, events, and facts that the system is designed to extract. Additionally, two classes of terminal symbols also require declaration: *termlists* and *ngrams*.

A termlist is a collection of terms from a single semantic category written either explicitly or loaded from external source. Examples of termlists are countries, cities, states, genes, proteins, people's first names, and job titles. Some linguistic concepts such as lists of propositions can also be considered termlists. Theoretically, a termlist is equivalent to a nonterminal symbol that has a rule for every term.

An ngram is a more complex construction. When used in a rule, it can expand to any single token. The probability of generating a given token, however, is not fixed in the rules but learned from the training dataset and may be conditioned on one or more previous tokens. Thus, using ngrams is one of the ways the probabilities of TEG rules can be context-dependent. The exact semantics of ngrams is explained in the next section.

Let us see a simple meaningful example of a TEG grammar:

```
output concept Acquisition(Acquirer, Acquired);
ngram AdjunctWord;
nonterminal Adjunct;
Adjunct:- AdjunctWord Adjunct | AdjunctWord;
termlist AcquireTerm = acquired bought (has acquired) (has bought);
Acquisition :- Company → Acquirer [","Adjunct ","]
AcquireTerm
Company → Acquired;
```

The first line defines a target relation **Acquisition**, which has two attributes, **Acquirer** and **Acquired**. Then an ngram **AdjunctWord** is defined followed by a nonterminal **Adjunct**, which has two rules separated by "|" that together define **Adjunct** as a sequence of one or more **AdjunctWord**-s. Then a termlist **AcquireTerm** is defined containing the main acquisition verb phrase. Finally, the single rule for the **Acquisition** concept is defined as a **Company** followed by optional **Adjunct** delimited by commas that are followed by **AcquireTerm** and a second **Company**. The first **Company** is the **Acquirer** attribute of the output frame and the second is the **Acquired** attribute.

The final rule requires the existence of a defined **Company** concept. The following set of definitions identifies the concept in a manner emulating the behavior of an HMM entity extractor:

```
output concept Company();
ngram CompanyFirstWord;
ngram CompanyWord;
ngram CompanyLastWord;
nonterminal CompanyNext;
Company:- CompanyFirstWord CompanyNext |
CompanyFirstWord;
CompanyNext:- CompanyWord CompanyNext |
CompanyLastWord;
```

Finally, in order to produce a complete grammar, we need a starting symbol and the special nonterminal that would match the strings that do not belong to any of the output concepts:

```
start Text;
nonterminal None;
ngram NoneWord;
None:- NoneWord None | ;
Text:- None Text | Company Text | Acquisition Text;
```

These 20 lines of code are able to find a fair number of Acquisitions accurately after very modest training. Note that the grammar is extremely ambiguous. An ngram can match any token, and so **Company**, **None**, and **Adjunct** are able to match any string. Yet, using the learned probabilities, TEG is usually able to find the correct interpretation.

VIII.4.4 TEG Training

Currently there are three different classes of trainable parameters in a TEG rulebook: the probabilities of rules of nonterminals, the probabilities of different expansions of ngrams, and the probabilities of terms in a wordclass. All those probabilities are smoothed maximum likelihood estimates calculated directly from the frequencies of the corresponding elements in the training dataset.

For example, suppose we have the following simple TEG grammar that finds simple person names:

```
nonterm start Text;
concept Person;
ngram NGFirstName;
ngram NGLastName;
ngram NGNone;
termlist TLHonorific = Mr Mrs Miss Ms Dr;
(1) Person :- TLHonorific NGLastName;
(2) Person :- NGFirstName NGLastName;
(3) Text :- NGNone Text;
(4) Text :- Person Text;
(5) Text :-;
```

By default, the initial untrained frequencies of all elements are assumed to be 1. They can be changed using "<count>" syntax, an example of which is shown below. The numbers in parentheses on the left side are not part of the rules and are used only for reference. Let us train this rulebook on the training set containing one sentence:

```
Yesterday, <person> Dr Simmons, </person> the distinguished scientist, pre-
sented the discovery.
```

The difference is in the expansion of the **Person** nonterminal. Both **Person** rules can produce the output instance; therefore, there is an ambiguity. This is done in two steps. First, the sentence is parsed using the untrained rulebook but with the constraints specified by the annotations. In our case the constraints are satisfied by two different parses that are shown in Figure VIII.5 (the numbers below the nonterminals refer to the rules used to expand them):

The ambiguity arises because both **TLHonorific** and **NGFirstName** can generate the token "Dr." In this case the ambiguity is resolved in favor of the **TLHonorific** interpretation because in the untrained rulebook we have

---

P (Dr | TLHonorific) = 1/5
(choice of one term among five equiprobable ones),
P (Dr | NGFirstName) ≈ 1/N, where *N* is the number
of all known words (untrained ngram behavior).

After the training, the frequencies of the different elements are updated, which produces the following trained rulebook (only lines that were changed are shown). Note the "<Count>" syntax:

```
termlist TLHonorific = Mr Mrs Miss Ms <2> Dr;
Person :- <2>TLHonorific NGLastName;
Text :- <11>NGNone Text;
Text :- <2>Person Text;
Text :- <2>;
```

Additionally, the training will generate a separate file containing the statistics for the ngrams. It is similar but more complex because the bigram frequencies, token feature frequencies, and unknown word frequencies are taken into consideration. In order to understand the details of ngrams training it is necessary to go over the details of their internal working.

An ngram always generates a single token. Any ngram can generate any token, but naturally the probability of generating one depends on the ngram, on the token, and on the immediate preceding context of the token. This probability is calculated at the runtime using the following statistics:

Freq(*) = total number of times the ngram was encountered in the training set.

Freq(*W*), *Freq*(*F*), *Freq*(*T*) = number of times the ngram was matched to the word *W*, the feature *F*, and the token *T*, respectively. Note that a token *T* is a pair consisting of a word *W*(*T*) and its feature *F*(*T*).

Freq($T \mid T_2$) = number of times token *T* was matched to the ngram in the training set and the preceding token was T_2.

Freq($* \mid T_2$) = number of times the ngram was encountered after the token T_2.

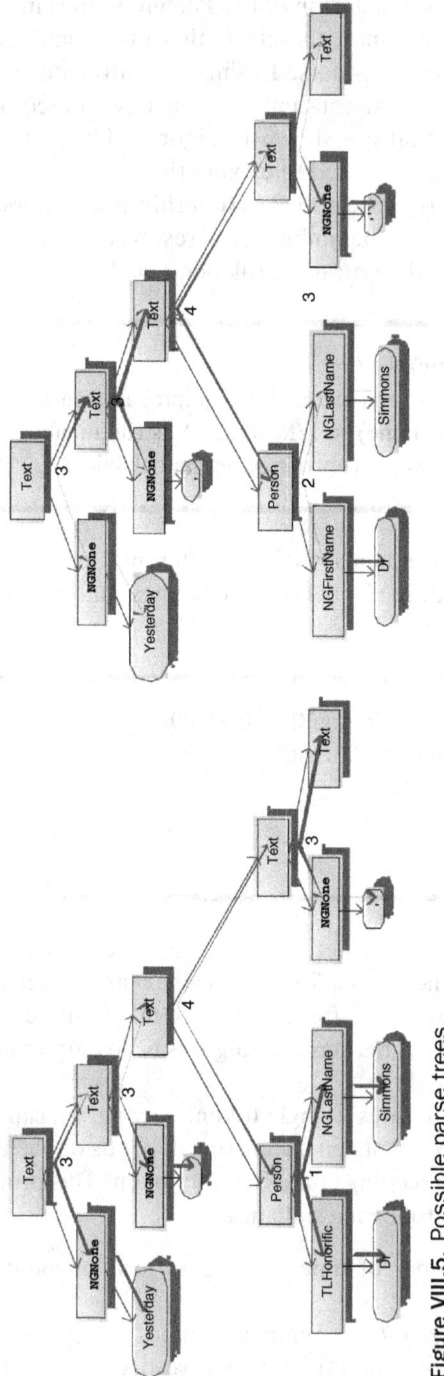

Figure VIII.5. Possible parse trees.

Thus, on the assumption all those statistics are gathered, the probability of the ngram's generating a token T given that the preceding token is T_2 is estimated as

$$\begin{aligned} P(T|T_2) = {} & 1/2 \cdot Freq(T|T_2)/Freq(^*|T_2) \\ & + 1/4 \cdot Freq(T)/Freq(^*) \\ & + 1/4 \cdot Freq(W) \cdot Freq(F)/Freq(^*)^2. \end{aligned}$$

This formula linearly interpolates between the three models: the bigram model, the backoff unigram model, and the further backoff word+feature unigram model. The interpolation factor was chosen to be 1/2, which is a natural choice. The experiments have shown, however, that varying the λ's in reasonable ranges does not significantly influence the performance.

Finally, matters are made somewhat more complicated by the *unknown* tokens. That a token was never encountered during the training gives by itself an important clue to the token's nature. In order to be able to use this clue, the separate "unknown" model is trained. The training set for it is created by dividing the available training data into two halves and treating one-half of the tokens, which are not present in the other half, as special "unknown" tokens. The model trained in this way is used whenever an unknown token is encountered during runtime.

VIII.4.5 Additional features

There are several additional features that improve the system and help to customize it for other domains. First, the probabilities of different rules of a nonterminal need not be fixed but may depend on their context. Currently, the rules for a specific nonterminal can be conditioned on the previous token in a way similar to the dependencey of ngram probabilities on the previous token. Other conditioning is of course possible – even to the extent of using maximal entropy for combining several conditioning events.

Second, an external tokenizer, token feature generator, or both can be substituted for the regular one. It is even possible to use several feature generators simultaneously (different ngrams may use different token feature sets). This is useful for languages other than English as well as for special domains. For instance, in order to extract the names of chemical compounds or complex gene names it may be necessary to provide a feature set based on morphological features. In addition, an external part-of-speech tagger or shallow parser may be used as a feature generator.

For real-life IE tasks it is often necessary to extract very rare target concepts. This is especially true for relations. Although there could be thousands of Persons or Organizations in a dataset, the number of Acquisitions could well be less than 50. The ngrams participating in the rules for such concepts will surely be undertrained. In order to alleviate this problem, the *shrinkage* technique can be used. An infrequent specific ngram can be set to *shrink* to another more common and more general ngram. Then the probability of generating a token by the ngram is interpolated with the corresponding probability for the more common "parent" ngram. A similar technique was used with a great success for HMM, and we found it very useful for TEG as well.

VIII.4.6 Example of Real Rules

This section demonstrates a fragment of the true rules written for the extraction of the PersonAffiliation relation from a real industry corpus. The fragment shows a usage of the advanced features of the system and gives another glimpse of the flavor of rule writing in TEG.

The PersonAffiliation relation contains three attributes – name of the person, name of the organization, and position of the person in the organization. It is declared as follows:

concept output PersonAffiliation(Name, Position, Org);

Most often, this relation is encountered in the text in the form "Mr. Name, Position of Org" or "Org Position Ms. Name." Almost any order of the components is possible with commas and prepositions inserted as necessary. Also, it is common for Name, Position, or both to be conjunctions of pairs of corresponding entities: "Mr. Name1 and Ms. Name2, the Position1 and Position2 of Org," or "Org's Position1 and Position2, Ms. Name." In order to catch those complexities, and for general simplification of the rules, we use several auxiliary nonterms: **Names**, which catches one or two Names; **Positions**, which catches one or two Positions; and **Orgs**, which catches Organizations and Locations. These can also be involved in PersonAffiliation as in "Bush, president of US":

nonterms Names, Positions, Orgs;
Names :- PERSON->Name | PERSON->Name "and" PERSON->Name;
Positions :- POSITION->Position | POSITION->Position "and" POSITION-> Position;
Orgs :- ORGANIZATION->Org | LOCATION->Org;

We also use auxiliary nonterms that catch pairs of attributes:

PosName, and **PosOrg**:
nonterms PosName, PosOrg;
PosName :- Positions Names | PosName "and" PosName;
wordclass wcPreposition = "at" "in" "of" "for" "with";
wordclass wcPossessive = ("' " "s") "' ";
PosOrg :- Positions wcPreposition Orgs;
PosOrg :- Orgs [wcPossessive] Positions;

Finally, the PersonAffiliation rules are as follows:

PersonAffiliation :- Orgs [wcPossessive] PosName;
PersonAffiliation :- PosName wcPreposition Orgs;
PersonAffiliation :- PosOrg [","] Names;
PersonAffiliation :- Names "," PosOrg;
PersonAffiliation :- Names "is" "a" PosOrg;

The rules above catch about 50 percent of all PersonAffiliation instances in the texts. Other instances depart from the form above in several respects. Thus, in order to improve the accuracy, additional rules need to be written. First, the Organization name is often entered into a sentence as a part of a descriptive noun phrase as in "Ms. Name is a Position of the industry leader Org." To catch this in a general way, we define an **OrgNP** nonterm, which uses an external POS tagger:

```
ngram ngOrgNoun featureset ExtPoS restriction Noun;
ngram ngOrgAdj featureset ExtPoS restriction Adj;
ngram ngNum featureset ExtPoS restriction Number;
ngram ngProper featureset ExtPoS restriction ProperName;
ngram ngDet featureset ExtPoS restriction Det;
ngram ngPrep featureset ExtPoS restriction Prep;

nonterm OrgNounList;
OrgNounList :- ngOrgNoun [OrgNounList];
nonterms OrgAdjWord, OrgAdjList;
OrgAdjWord :- ngOrgAdj | ngNum | ngProper;
OrgAdjList :- OrgAdjWord [OrgAdjList];
nonterm OrgNP;
OrgNP :- [ngDet] [OrgAdjList] OrgNounList;
OrgNP :- OrgNP ngPrep OrgNP;
OrgNP :- OrgNP "and" OrgNP;
```

The external POS tagger provides an alternative token feature set, which can be used by ngrams via the ngram *featureset* declaration. The *restriction* clause in the ngram declaration specifies that the tokens matched by the ngram must belong to the specified feature. Altogether, the set of rules above defines an **OrgNP** nonterm in a way similar to the to the definition of a noun phrase by a syntax-parsing grammar. To use the nonterm in the rules, we simply modify the **Orgs** nonterm:

```
Orgs :- [OrgNP] ORGANIZATION->Org | LOCATION->Org;
```

Note that, although OrgNP is internally defined very generally (it is able to match any noun phrase whatsoever), the way it is used is very restricted. During training, the ngrams of OrgNP learn the distributions of words for this particular use, and, during the run, the probability that OrgNP will generate a true organization-related noun phrase is much greater than for any other noun phrase in text.

Finally, we demonstrate the use of ngram shrinkage. There are PersonAffiliation instances in which some irrelevant sentence fragments separate the attributes. For example, "'ORG bla bla bla', said the company's Position Mr. Name." In order to catch the "bla bla bla" part we can use the **None** nonterm, which generates all irrelevant fragments in the text. Alternatively, we can create a separate ngram and a nonterm for the specific use of catching irrelevant fragments inside PersonAffiliation. Both these solutions have their disadvantages. The None nonterm is too general and does not catch the specifics of the particular case. A specific nonterm, on the other hand, is very much undertrained. The solution is to use a specific nonterm but to shrink its ngram to None:

```
nonterm BlaBla;
ngram ngBlaBla -> ngNone;
BlaBla :- ngBlaBla [BlaBla];
PersonAffiliation :- Orgs BlaBla PosName;
```

The rules described above catch 70 percent of all PersonAffiliation instances, which is already a good result for relationship extraction from a real corpus. The process of writing rules, moreover, can be continued to further improve the accuracy.

	HMM			Emulation using TEG			Manual Rules			Full TEG system		
	Recall	Prec	F1	Recall	Prec	F1	Recall	Prec	F1	Recall	Prec	F1
Person	86.91	85.1	**86.01**	86.31	86.83	**86.57**	81.32	93.75	**87.53**	93.75	90.78	**92.24**
Organization	87.94	89.8	**88.84**	85.94	89.53	**87.7**	82.74	93.36	**88.05**	89.49	90.9	**90.19**
Location	86.12	87.2	**86.66**	83.93	90.12	**86.91**	91.46	89.53	**90.49**	87.05	94.42	**90.58**

Figure VIII.6. Accuracy results for MUC-7.

VIII.4.7 Experimental Evaluation of TEG

The TEG techniques were evaluated using two corpora: MUC-7 and ACE-2. The results show the potential of utilizing hybrid approaches for text mining preprocessing.

The MUC-7 Corpus Evaluation – Comparison with HMM-based NER

The MUC-7 named-entity recognition (NER) corpus consists of a set of news articles related to aircraft accidents, containing about 200 thousand words with the named entities manually categorized into three basic categories: PERSON, ORGANIZATION, and LOCATION. Some other entities are also tagged such as dates, times, and monetary units, but they did not take part in our evaluation.

The corpus does not contain tagged relationships, and thus it was used to evaluate the difference in the performance between the four entity extractors: the regular HMM, its emulation using TEG, a set of handcrafted rules written in DIAL, and a full TEG system, which consists of the HMM emulation augmented by a small set of handcrafted rules (about 50 lines of code added).

The results of the experiments are summarized in Figure VIII.6: The small accuracy difference between the regular HMM and its emulation is due to slight differences in probability conditioning methods. It is evident that the handcrafted rules performed better than the HMM-based extractors but were inferior to the performance of the TEG extractor. Significantly, the handcrafted rules achieved the best precision; however, their recall was far worse.

The HMM named-entity recognition results published in Bikel et al. (1997) are somewhat higher than we were able to produce using our version of an HMM entity extractor. We hypothesize that the reason for the difference is the use of additional training data in the Nymble experiments. The paper (Bikel et al. 1997) mentions using approximately 750K words of training data, whereas we had only 200K. Regardless of the reasons for the difference, the experiment clearly shows that the addition of a small number of handcrafted rules can further improve the results of a purely automatic HMM-based named-entity extraction.

ACE-2 Evaluation: Extracting Relationships

The ACE-2 was a follow-up to ACE-1 and included tagged relationships in addition to tagged entities. The ACE-2 annotations are more complex than those supported by the current version of our system. Most significantly, the annotations resolve all anaphoric references, which is outside the scope of the current implementation. Therefore, it was necessary to remove annotations containing anaphoric references. This was done automatically using a simple Perl script.

	Full TEG system (with 7 ROLE rules)		
	Recall	Prec	F
Role	83.44	77.30	**80.25**
Person	89.82	81.68	**85.56**
Organization	59.49	71.06	**64.76**
GPE	88.83	84.94	**86.84**

	HMM entity extractor			Markovian SCFG		
	Recall	Prec	F	Recall	Prec	F
Role				67.55	69.86	**68.69**
Person	85.54	83.22	**84.37**	89.19	80.19	**84.45**
Organization	52.62	64.735	**58.05**	53.57	67.46	**59.71**
GPE	85.54	83.22	**84.37**	86.74	84.96	**85.84**

Figure VIII.7. Accuracy results for ACE-2.

For evaluating relationship extraction we choose the ROLE relation (ACE 2002). The original ACE-2 annotations make finer distinctions between the different kinds of ROLE, but for the current evaluation we felt it sufficient just to recognize the basic relationships and find their attributes.

The results of this evaluation are shown in Figure VIII.7. For comparison we also show the performance of the HMM entity extractor on the entities in the same dataset.

As expected, the accuracy of a purely Markovian SCFG without additional rules is rather mediocre. However, by adding a small number of handcrafted rules (altogether about 100 lines of code), accuracy was raised considerably (by 15% in F1). The performances of the three systems on the named entities differ very little because they are essentially the same system. The slight improvement of the full TEG system is due to better handling of the entities that take part in ROLEs.

In Figure VIII.8 we can see how the accuracy of the TEG system changes as a function of the amount of available training data. There are three graphs in the figure: a graph that represents the accuracy of the grammar with no specific ROLE rules, a graph that represents the accuracy of the grammar with four ROLE rules, and finally a graph that represents the accuracy of the grammar with seven ROLE rules.

Analysis of the graphs reveals that, to achieve about 70-percent accuracy the system needs about 125K of training data when using all of the specific ROLE rules, whereas 250k of training data are needed when no specific rules are present. Thus, adding a small set of simple rules may save 50 percent of the training data requirements.

The seven ROLE rules used by the third TEG are shown below. The rules use nonterminals and wordclasses, which are defined in the rest of the grammar. The whole grammar, which has a length of about 200 lines, is too long to be included here.

```
1. ROLE :- [Position_Before] ORGANIZATION->ROLE_2
   Position ["in" GPE] [","] PERSON→ROLE_1;
2. ROLE :- GPE→ROLE_2 Position [","]
   PERSON→ROLE_1;
3. ROLE :-PERSON→ROLE_1 "of" GPE→ROLE_2;
```

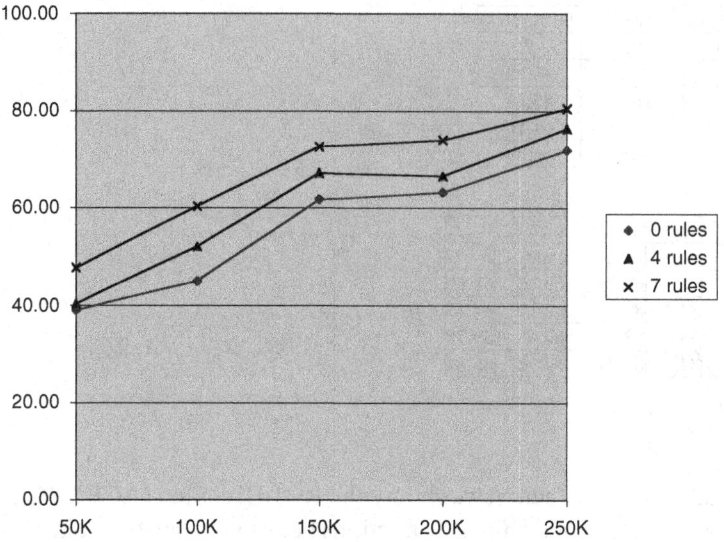

Figure VIII.8. Accuracy (F1) of the TEG system (with different grammars) as a function of the size of the training corpus (ACE-2).

4. ROLE :- ORGANIZATION→ROLE_2 "'" "s" [Position] PERSON→ROLE_1;
5. ROLE :- GPE→ROLE_2 [Position] PERSON→ROLE_1;
6. ROLE :- <5> GPE->ROLE_2 "'" "s"" ORGANIZATION→ROLE_1;

ROLE :- PERSON→ROLE_1 "," Position WCPreposition ORGANIZATION→ROLE_2;

VIII.5 BOOTSTRAPPING

VIII.5.1 Introduction to Bootstrapping: The AutoSlog-TS Approach

One of the main problems of the machine learning–based systems is that they rely on annotated corpora. A *bootstrapping* approach to IE takes a middle ground between the knowledge engineering and machine learning approaches. The main idea behind this approach is that the user provides some initial bias either by supplying a small initial lexicon or a small number of rules for inducing the initial examples. The bootstrapping approach attempts to circumvent the need for an annotated corpus, which can be very expensive and time consuming to produce.

One of the first approaches to bootstrapping was developed by Ellen Riloff and implemented in the *AutoSlog-TS* system (Riloff 1996a). Based on the original *AutoSlog*system developed previously by Riloff (Riloff 1993a), AutoSlog-TS uses a set of documents split into two bins: interesting documents and noninteresting documents. In contrast, the original AutoSlog required all relevant noun phrases within the training corpus to be tagged and, hence, put a much bigger load on the task of the training corpus construction. *Palka* (Kim and Moldovan 1995) was another system similar to AutoSlog, but it required a much heavier tagging in the training corpus:

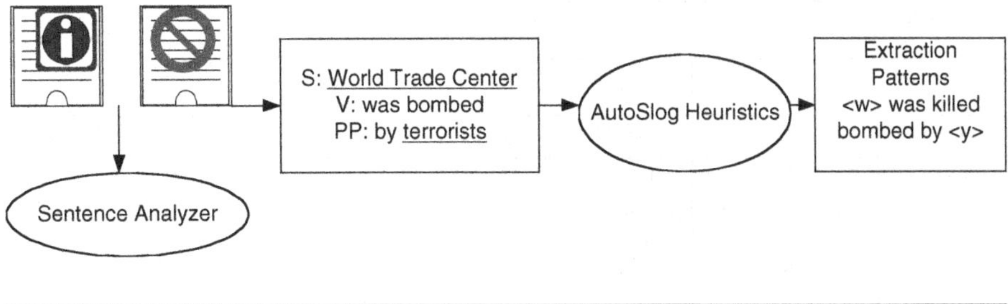

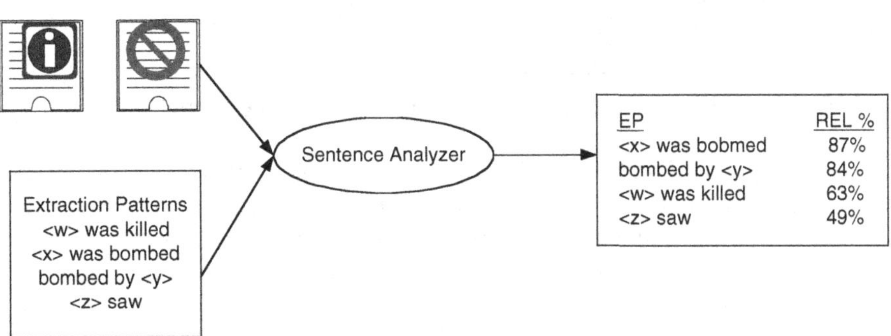

Figure VIII.9. Flow of the AutoSlog-TS system.

Each frame had to be fully tagged, and an ontology had to be provided along with the related lexicons.

AutoSlog-TS starts by using a parser that analyzes the sentences, determines clause boundaries, and marks subjects, verbs, direct objects, and prepositional phrases of each clause. It then uses a set of extraction pattern templates and generates an extraction pattern for each noun phrase in the corpus. The extraction patterns are graded by using the two bins of documents provided by the user. Extraction patterns that appear mostly in the bin of the important documents are ranked higher. An example of the flow of the AutoSlog-TS system is shown in Figure VIII.9.

The main steps within AutoSlog-TS can be broken down as follows:

1. The user provides two sets of documents, interesting (I) and noninteresting (N).
2. Shallow Parsing is performed for all the documents, and, on the basis of the predefined templates all patterns that match one of the templates are extracted (EP).
3. For each extraction pattern in EP, we compute the relevance of the pattern:

$$Rel(Pat) = \Pr(D \in I | Pat \in D) = \frac{\#(I, Pat)}{\#(I \bigcup N)},$$

   where #(I, Pat) is the number of documents in the document collection I that contain pattern P.
4. We compute the importance of each extraction pattern in EP according to the following formula and rank them in a decreased order:

$$Imp(Pat) = Rel(Pat) \log_2(\#(D, Pat)).$$

5. The system presents the top-ranked rules to the user for evaluation.

<subj> exploded	Murder of <np>	Assassination of <np>
<subj> was killed	<subj> was kidnapped	Attack on <np>
<subj> was injured	Exploded in <np>	Death of <np>
<subj> took place	Caused <dobj>	Claimed <dobj>
<subj> was wounded	<subj> occurred	<subj> was loctated
Took place on <np>	Responsibility for <np>	Occurred on <np>
Was wounded in <np>	Destroyed <dobj>	<subj> was murdered
One of <np>	<subj> kidnapped	Exploded on <np>

Figure VIII.10. Table of the top 24 extraction patterns in the AutoSlog-TS evaluation.

The system was evaluated on MUC-4 documents. A total of 1,500 MUC-4 documents were used, and 50 percent of them were relevant according to the user. The system generated 32,345 patterns and after patterns supported only by one document were discarded, 11,225 patterns were left. The top 24 extraction patterns are shown in Figure VIII.10.

The user reviewed the patterns and labeled the ones she wanted to use for actual extraction. So, for instance, "<subj> was killed" was selected for inclusion in the extraction process, and <subj> was replaced by <victim>. It took the user 85 minutes to review the top 1,970 patterns.

Certainly this approach shows much promise in building new extraction systems quickly because very little manual effort is needed in terms of rule writing and corpus annotation. The primary drawback is that a fairly strong parser needs to be used for analyzing the candidate sentences.

VIII.5.2 Mutual Bootstrapping

Riloff and Jones (Riloff and Jones 1999) took this idea of bootstrapping even further by suggesting *mutual bootstrapping*. Here the starting point is a small lexicon of entities (seed) that share the same semantic category.

In a way similar to AutoSlog-TS, the corpus is processed and all possible extraction patterns are generated along with the noun phrases that are extracted by them. The main purpose of this approach is to extend the initial lexicon and to learn accurate extraction patterns that can extract instances for the lexicon.

Initialization

- $N =$ total number of extraction patterns
- $\mathrm{EP}_i =$ one extraction pattern $(i = 1..N)$
- EPData = a list of pairs (EP_i, Noun Phrases generated by the EP_i)
- SemLex = the list of seed words (the initial lexicon)
- EPlist = {}

Loop

1. Score all extraction patterns in EPData : Find for each EP_i how many items from SemLex it can generate.

www location	www company	terrorism location
offices in <x>	owned by <x>	living in <x>
facilities in <x>	<x> employed	traveled to <x>
operations in <x>	<x> is distributor	become in <x>
operates in <x>	<x> positioning	Sought in <x>
seminars in <x>	motivated <x>	presidents of <x>
activities in <x>	sold to <x>	parts of <x>
consulting in <x>	Devoted to <x>	To enter <x>
outlets in <x>	<x> thrive	ministers of <x>
customers in <x>	Message to <x>	part in <x>
distributors in <x>	<x> request information	taken in <x>
services in <x>	<x> has positions	returned to <x>
expanded into <x>	offices of <x>	process in <x>

Figure VIII.11. Table of extraction patterns from mutual bootstrapping.

2. Best_EP = highest scoring extraction pattern (extracted the highest number of items from SemLex)
3. Add Best_EP to EPList
4. Add Best_EP's extractions to SemLex
5. Goto 1

The top 12 extraction patterns in each of 3 problems (locations mentioned in company home pages, company names mentioned in company home pages, and locations mentioned in terrorist-related documents) are shown in Figure VIII.11.

VIII.5.3 Metabootstrapping

One of the main problems encountered with mutual bootstrapping is that once a word is added to the lexicon that does not belong to the semantic category, a domino effect can be created, allowing incorrect extraction patterns to receive high scores and thus adding many more incorrect entries to the lexicon. To prevent this problem, Riloff and Jones suggest using another method called *metabootstrapping*, which allows finer grain control over the instances that are added to the lexicon.

In metabootstrapping, only the top five instances that are extracted by using the best extraction pattern are retained and added to the permanent semantic lexicons. All other instances are discarded. The instances are scored by counting, for each instance, how many extraction patterns can extract it.

Formally, the score of instance I_j is computed as follows:

$$score(I_j) = \sum_{k=1}^{N_j} 1 + (.01 * \text{Imp}(\text{Pattern}_k)),$$

where N_j is the number of extraction patterns that generated I_j.

After the new instances are added to the permanent semantic lexicon, the mutual bootstrapping starts from scratch. A schematic view of the flow of the metabootstrapping process is presented in Figure VIII.12.

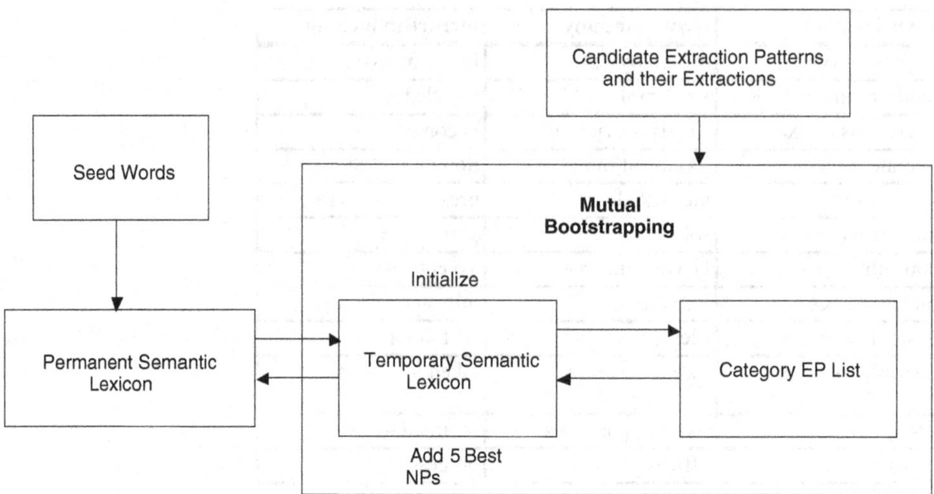

Figure VIII.12. Flow diagram of metabootstrapping.

Evaluation of the Metabootstrapping Algorithm

Two datasets were used: one of 4,160 company Web pages, and one of 1,500 articles taken from the MUC-4 corpus. Three semantic categories were extracted from the Web pages (locations, company names, and titles of people), and two semantic categories were extracted from the terror-related articles (locations and weapons). The metabootstrapping algorithm was run for 50 iterations. During each iteration, the mutual bootstrapping was run until it produced 10 patterns that extracted at least one new instance that could be added to the lexicon.

In Figure VIII.13, one can see how the accuracy of the semantic lexicon changes after each number of iterations. The easiest category is Web location, and the most difficult categories are weapon and Web title (titles of people mentioned on the Web page).

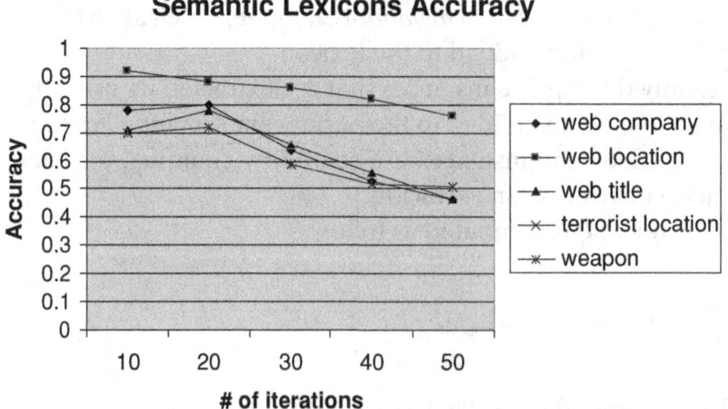

Figure VIII.13. Accuracy of the semantic lexicons as a function of the number of mutual bootstrapping iterations.

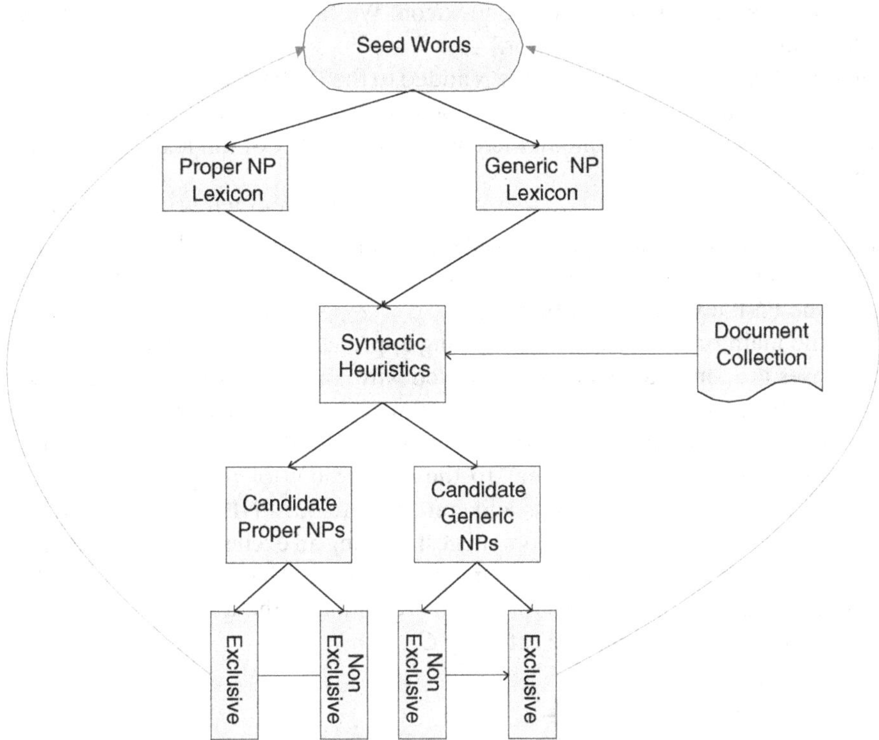

Figure VIII.14. Heuristic-based bootstrapping.

VIII.5.4 Using Strong Syntactic Heuristics

Phillips and Riloff (Phillips and Riloff 2002) took a different approach to building semantic lexicons. They learned two lexicons; one contained proper noun phrases (PNP) and the other generic noun phrases (GN). The lexicons were acquired by using a set of *syntactic heuristics*. In particular, they used three types of patterns. The architecture of the heuristic-based bootstrapping is shown in Figure VIII.14.

The first type included appositives such as "the president, George Bush," or "Mary Smith, the analyst." The second type consisted of IS-A clauses, which are NP followed by "to be" VP followed by NP. An example of an IS-A clause is "Bill Gates, the chairman of Microsoft." The last type comprised compound nouns that have the form GN + PNP. An example of such a construct is "the senator John Kerry."

A mutual property of all three types is that they establish a relationship between at least one GN and one PNP. The bootstrapping algorithm will infer relationships between an element that is already in one of the lexicons and an element that is not yet in any of the lexicons. These relations enable the algorithm each time to extend either the PNP lexicon or the GN lexicon. The algorithm alternates between learning a new GN based on the PNP lexicon and learning a new PNP based on the GN lexicon.

As an example, if one is trying to extend the people lexicons and we have in our PNP person lexicon the name "John Kerry" and the sentence "senator John Kerry" is encountered, one would learn that "senator" is a generic noun that stands for a person; it will be added to the GN person lexicon. We can now learn new names of people that come after the GN "senator."

Normally, when a proper noun phrase is added to the PNP lexicon, the full phrase is used, whereas typically a generic noun phrase is added to the GN lexicon when just the head noun is used. This is done to increase the generality of the lexicon without sacrificing accuracy.

Take, for instance, the generic noun phrase "financial analyst." It is enough just to add analyst to the GN lexicon, and no harm will result. On the other hand, consider the proper noun phrase "Santa Barbara." Clearly, we can not add just Santa or just Barbara to the PNP lexicon of locations.

One of the main problems of bootstrapping approaches in general is that some generic phrases are ambiguous and can be used with a variety of semantic classes. An example is the generic noun "leader." This noun can designate either a company (which is a leader in its area) or a person (in the political domain or in the financial–corporate domain). If we add "leader" to the GN lexicon of people, in the next iteration it will add many corporations and contaminate our PNP people lexicon.

To alleviate this problem, the authors suggested using an exclusivity measure that is attached to each of the noun phrases. Only noun phrases that have an exclusivity measure exceeding some predefined threshold are added to the lexicon.

Given a phrase *P* and a semantic category *C*,

$$Exclusivity(P, C) = \frac{\#(P, C)}{\#(P, \neg C)},$$

where $\#(P, C)$ is the number of sentences in which *P* is collocated with at least one member of *C*, and $\#(P,\ C)$ is the number of sentences in which *P* is collocated with at least one member of all the semantic classes other than *C*. A typical exclusivity threshold is 5.

VIII.5.4.1 Evaluation of the Strong Syntactic Heuristics

This approach was tested on 2,500 *Wall Street Journal* articles (People and Organizations) and on a set of 1,350 press releases from the pharmacology domain (People, Organizations, and Products). The heuristics that added the highest number of entries to the PNP semantic lexicons were the compounds heuristics, whereas the appositives heuristics added the highest number of entries to the GN lexicons. The accuracy for the *Wall Street Journal* articles was between 80 percent and 99 percent for the PNP lexicons and between 30 and 95 percent for the GN lexicons. The accuracy results dropped when tested against the pharmaceutical press releases (77–95% for the PNP and 9–91% for the GN).

VIII.5.4.2 Using Cotraining

Blum and Mitchell (Blum and Mitchell 1998) introduced the notion of cotraining – a learning technique that tries to learn from a variety of views and sources simultaneously. Clearly, because there are three heuristics for learning the semantic lexicons, cotraining can be used after each boot-strapping cycle. All three lexicons will be joined after each step, and will a richer lexicon will result for each of them. A simple filtering mechanism can be used to eliminate entries with low support.

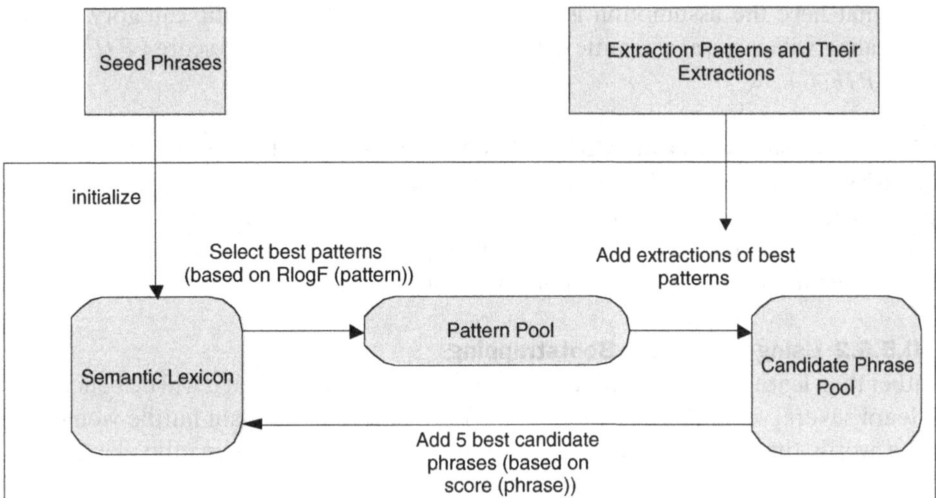

Figure VIII.15. The Basilisk algorithm.

It is common to add just entries supported by at least three sentences to the combined lexicon. Using the cotraining method results in a much more rapid learning of the lexicons (between 20 and 250% more entries were acquired) without much loss in accuracy.

VIII.5.5 The Basilisk Algorithm

Following in the footsteps of Riloff and Jones, Thelen and Riloff (Thelen and Riloff 2002) suggested a similar algorithm called Basilisk (Bootstrapping Approach to SemantIc Lexicon Induction using Semantic Knowledge). Differing from the metabootstrapping approach that uses a two-level loop (with mutual bootstrapping in the inner loop), Basilisk uses just a one-level loop and hence is more efficient. It solves the accuracy problem of the mutual bootstrapping by utilizing a weighted combination of extraction patterns. In particular, the approach utilizes $20 + i$ (where i is the index of the bootstrapping loop) extraction patterns as the pattern pool. The general architecture of Basilisk is shown in Figure VIII.15.

RlogF(pattern) was defined when we discussed the AutoSlog system. Score of phrase PH is defined as average log of the number of valid extraction patterns (for the given semantic category). The rationale is that a pattern is more trusted if it extracts a higher number of valid members of the semantic category. The log of the number of extractions is used so that a small number of extraction patterns having a particularly high number of valid extraction will not affect the average too drastically.

Formally,

- $\#(PH_i)$ is the number of extraction patterns that extract phrase PH_i.
- F_j = the number of valid extractions that were extracted by pattern P_j.

$$score(PH_i) = \frac{\sum_{j=1}^{\#(PH_i)} \log_2(F_j + 1)}{\#(PH_i)} \qquad (1.1)$$

Note that here the assumption is that we have just one semantic category. If we are dealing with several semantic categories, then we will change score (PH_i) to be score(PH_i, C).

VIII.5.5.1 Evaluation of Basilisk on Single-Category Bootstrapping

Basilisk was compared against metabootstrapping on 1,700 MUC-4 documents. In the specific experiment performed by Thelen, just single nouns were extracted in both systems. Basilisk outperformed metabootstrapping in all six categories (building, event, human, location, time, weapon) by a considerable margin.

VIII.5.5.2 Using Multiclass Bootstrapping

Rather than learning one semantic category at a time, it seems that it will be beneficial to learn several semantic classes simultaneously. Clearly, the main hurdle would be those words that are polysemic and could belong to several semantic classes. To alleviate this problem we make the common assumption of "one sense per domain," and so our task is to find a conflict resolution strategy that can decide to which category each polysemic word should belong. The conflict resolution strategy used by Thelen preferred the semantic category assigned in a former iteration of the boot-strapping algorithm to any given phrase, and if two categories are suggested during the same iteration the category for which the phrase got the higher score is selected.

Another change that was able to boost the results and distinguish between the competing categories is to use mscore(PH_i, C_a), as defined below, rather than score(PH_i, C_a), as in equation (1.1).

$$mscore(PH_i, C_a) = score(PH_i, C_a) - \max_{b \neq a}(score(PH_i, C_b)) \quad (1.2)$$

This definition will prefer phrases or words that are highly associated with one category, whereas they are very loosely (if at all) associated with any of the other categories.

VIII.5.5.3 Evaluation of the Multiclass Bootstrapping

The performance of Basilisk improved when using the conflict resolution with the mscore function. The improvement was more notable on the categories BUILDING, WEAPON, and LOCATION. When the same strategy was applied to the metabootstrapping, the improvement was much more dramatic (up to 300% improvement in precision).

In Figure VIII.16 we can see the precision of the Basilisk system on the various semantic categories after 800 entries were added to each of the lexicons. The recall for these categories was between 40 and 60 percent.

VIII.5.6 Bootstrapping by Using Term Categorization

Another method for the semiautomatic generation of thematic lexicons by means of term categorization is presented in Lavelli, Magnini, and Sebastiani (2002). They view the generation of such lexicons as an iterative process of learning previously

Semantic Category	Number of Correct Entries	Precision
Building	109	13.6%
Event	266	26.6%
Human	681	85.1%
Location	509	63.6%
Time	43	5.4%
Weapon	88	11.0%

Figure VIII.16. Precision of the multicategory bootstrapping system Basilisk.

unknown associations between terms and themes. The process is iterative and generates for each theme a sequence of lexicons that are bootstrapped from an initial lexicon. The terms that appear in the documents are represented as vectors in a space of documents and then are labeled with themes by using classic categorization techniques. Specifically, the authors used the AdaBoost algorithm. The intermediate lexicons generated by the AdaBoost algorithm are cleaned, and the process restarts by using the cleaned lexicon as the new positive set of terms. The authors used subsets of the Reuters RCVI Collection as the document corpus and some of WordNetDomains's synsets as the semantic lexicons (split into training and test). The results for various sizes of corpora show that quite an impressive precision (around 75%) was obtained, and the recall was around 5–12 percent. Clearly, because there is no inherent connection between the corpus selected and the semantic lexicons, we can not expect a much higher recall.

VIII.5.7 Summary

The bootstrapping approach is very useful for building semantic lexicons for a variety of categories. The approach is suitable mostly for semiautomatic processes because the precision and recall we can obtain are far from perfect. Bootstrapping is beneficial as a tool to be used in tandem with other machine learning or rule-based approaches to information extraction.

VIII.6 FURTHER READING

Section VIII.1

More information on the use of HMM for text processing can be found in the following papers: Kupiec (1992); Leek (1997); Seymore, McCallum, and Rosenfeld (1999); McCallum, Freitag, and Pereira (2000); and Sigletos, Paliouras, and Karkaletsis (2002).

Section VIII.2

Applications of MEMM for information extraction are described in the following papers: Borthwick (1999), Charniak (2000), and McCallum et al. (2000).

Section VIII.3

Applications of CRF for text processing are described in Lafferty et al. (2001) and Sha and Pereira (2003).

Section VIII.4

TEG is described in Rosenfeld et al. (2004).

Section VIII.5

More details on bootstrapping for information extraction can be found in the following papers: Riloff (1993a), Riloff (1996a), Riloff and Jones (1999), Lavelli et al. (2002), Phillips and Riloff (2002), and Thelen and Riloff (2002).

IX

Presentation-Layer Considerations for Browsing and Query Refinement

Human-centered knowledge discovery places great emphasis on the presentation layer of systems used for data mining. All text mining systems built around a human-centric knowledge discovery paradigm must offer a user robust browsing capabilities as well as abilities to display dense and difficult-to-format patterns of textual data in ways that foster interactive exploration.

A robust text mining system should offer a user control over the shaping of queries by making search parameterization available through both high-level, easy-to-use GUI-based controls and direct, low-level, and relatively unrestricted query language access. Moreover, text mining systems need to offer a user administrative tools to create, modify, and maintain concept hierarchies, concept clusters, and entity profile information.

Text mining systems also rely, to an extraordinary degree, on advanced visualization tools. More on the full gamut of visualization approaches – from the relatively mundane to the highly exotic – relevant for text mining can be found in Chapter X.

IX.1 BROWSING

Browsing is a term open to broad interpretation. With respect to text mining systems, however, it usually refers to the general front-end framework through which an enduser searches, queries, displays, and interacts with embedded or middle-tier knowledge-discovery algorithms.

The software that implements this framework is called a *browser*. Beyond their ability to allow a user to (a) manipulate the various knowledge discovery algorithms they may operate and (b) explore the resulting patterns, most browsers also generally support functionality to link to some portion of the full text of documents underlying the patterns that these knowledge discovery algorithms may return.

Usually, browsers in text mining operate as a user interface to specialized query languages that allow parameterized operation of different pattern search algorithms, though this functionality is now almost always commanded through a graphical user interface (GUI) in real-world text mining applications. This means that, practically,

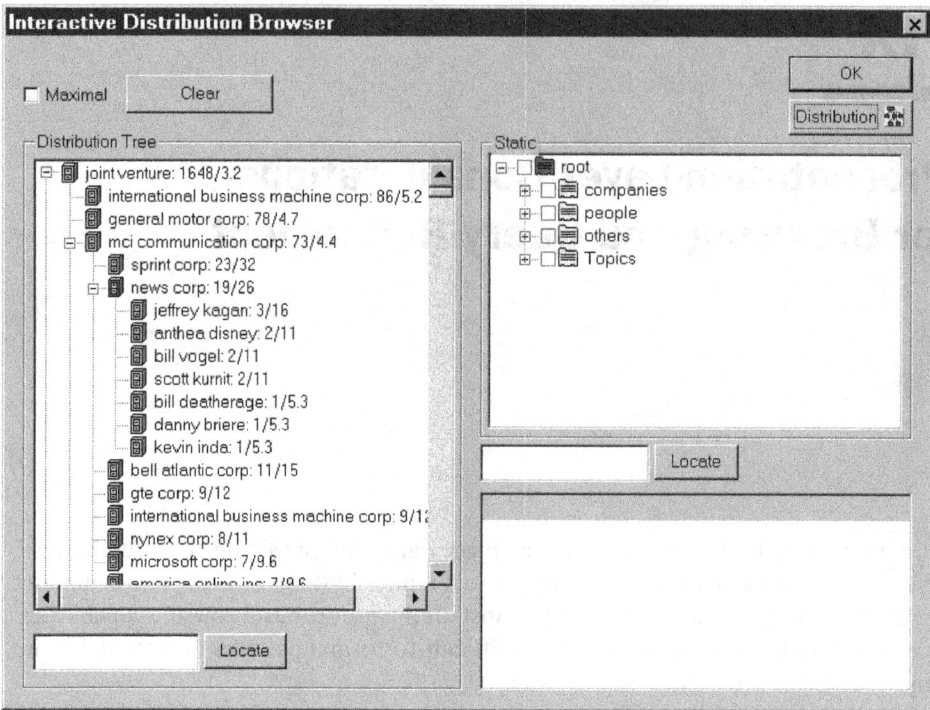

Figure IX.1. Example of an interactive browser for distributions. (From Feldman, Fresko, Hirsh, et al. 1998.)

many discovery operations are "kicked off" by a query for a particular type of pattern through a browser interface, which runs a query argument that executes a search algorithm. Answers are returned via a large number of possible display modalities in the GUI, ranging from simple lists and tables to navigable nodal trees to complex graphs generated by extremely sophisticated data visualization tools.

Once a query is parameterized and run, browsers allow for the exploration of the potentially interesting or relevant patterns generated by search operations. On a basic level, the search algorithms of the core mining operations layer have to process search spaces of instances for a selected pattern type.

This search, however, is structured in relation to certain specified search constraints, and appropriate refinement strategies and pruning techniques are chosen. Such constraints and pruning approaches can be partly or fully specified through a browser interface, though the logic of such refinement techniques may, from a system architecture perspective, reside in as a separate set of services that may be invoked by both presentation-layer and search algorithm components.

All patterns can be studied in the context of a conditioning concept set or context free (i.e., for the general domain of the whole collection). Conditioning a search task therefore means selecting a set of concepts that is used to restrict an analysis task (e.g., a restriction to documents dealing with *USA* and *economic issues* or *IBM* and *hard drive components*). For example, Figure IX.1 shows a simple distribution browser that allows a user to search for specific distributions while looking at a concept hierarchy to provide some order and context to the task.

Many text mining systems provide a heterogeneous set of browsing tools customized to the specific needs of different types of "entities" addressed by the system. Most text mining systems increase the opportunities for user interactivity by offering the user the ability to browse, by means of visual tools, such entities as documents, concept distributions, frequent sets, associations, trends, clusters of documents, and so on. Moreover, it is not uncommon for text mining systems to offer multiple methods for browsing the same entity type (e.g., graphs, lists, and hierarchical trees for documents; maps and hierarchical trees for concept names, etc.).

Although all knowledge discovery operations are susceptible to overabundance problems with respect to patterns, it is typical for text mining systems, in particular, to generate immense numbers of patterns. For almost any document collection of more than a few thousand documents, huge numbers of concept distributions, relations between distributions, frequent concept sets, undirected relations between frequent concept sets, and association rules can be identified.

Therefore, a fundamental requirement for any text mining system's browsing interface is the ability to robustly support the querying of the vast implicit set of patterns available in a given document collection. Practically, however, text mining systems often cope best – and allow users to cope best – with the challenges of pattern overabundance by offering sophisticated refinement tools available while browsing that allow the shaping, constraining, pruning, and filtering of result-set data. Another extremely critical point in managing pattern overabundance is ensuring that the user of a text mining system has an adequate capability for inputting and manipulating what has been referred to as the *measures of interestingness* of patterns in the system.

IX.1.1 Displaying and Browsing Distributions

Traditional document retrieval systems allow a user to ask for all documents containing certain concepts – UK and USA, for example – but then present the entire set of matching documents with little information about the collection's internal structure other than perhaps sorting them by relevance score (which is a shallow measure computed from the frequency and position of concepts in the document) or chronological order.

In contrast, browsing distributions in a text mining system can enable a user to investigate the contents of a document set by sorting it according to the child distribution of any node in a concept hierarchy such as topics, countries, companies, and so on. Once the documents are analyzed in this fashion and the distribution is displayed, a user could, for instance, access the specific documents of each subgroup (see Figure IX.2).

One way to generate a distribution is to provide two Boolean expressions. The first expression could define the selection condition for the documents. The second expression would define the distribution to be computed on the set of chosen documents.

For instance, the user can specify as the selection criteria the expression "*USA* and *UK*" and only documents containing both concepts will be selected for further processing. The distribution expression can be "*topics*," in which case, a set of rules that correlated between *USA* and *UK* and any of the concepts defined under the

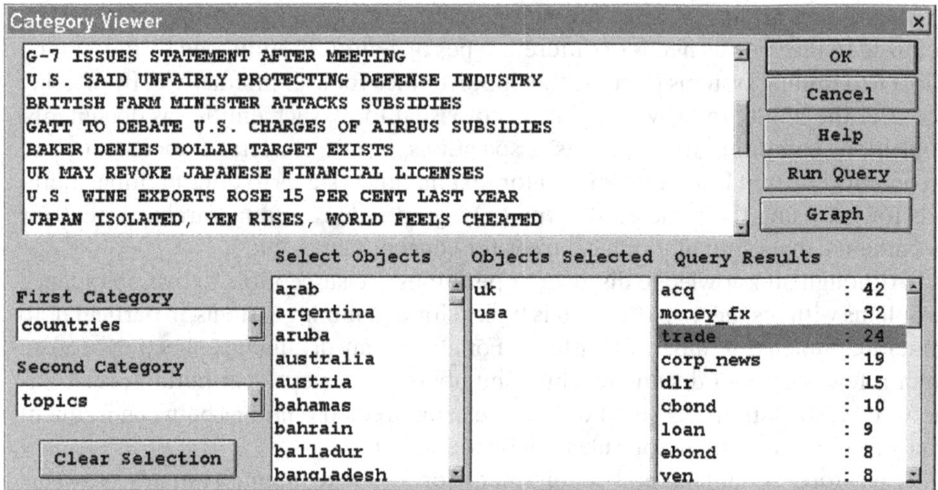

Figure IX.2. Topic (concept) distribution browser from the KDT system selecting for USA and UK. (From Feldman, Dagan, and Hirsh 1998. Reprinted with permission of Springer Science and Business Media.)

node "*topics*" in the taxonomy will be obtained. The results could be shown in a hierarchical way based on the structure of the taxonomy underneath "*topics*."

One can see, for instance, an association rule such as

$$USA, UK \Rightarrow acq \; 42/19.09\%.$$

This rule means that in 19.09 percent of the documents in which both *USA* and *UK* are mentioned, the topic acquisition is mentioned too, which amounts to 42 documents. The user could then click on that rule to obtain the list of 42 documents supporting this rule.

A second association rule could be

$$USA, UK \Rightarrow currency \; 39/17.73\%.$$

In this example, let us assume that *currency* is an internal node and not a concept found in the documents. The meaning of the rule, therefore, is that, in 17.73 percent of the documents in which both *USA* and *UK* are mentioned, at least one of the topics underneath the node "*currency*" in the taxonomy is mentioned too, which amounts to 39 documents.

The user could then expand that rule and get a list of more specialized rules, where the right-hand side (RHS) of each of them would be a child of the node "*currency*." In this case, one would find *UK* and *USA* to be highly associated with *money_fx* (foreign exchange), *dlr* (US Dollar), and *yen*.

IX.1.2 Displaying and Exploring Associations

Even when data from a document collection are moderately sized, association-finding methods will often generate substantial numbers of results. Therefore, association-discovery tools in text mining must assist a user in identifying the useful results out of all those the system generates.

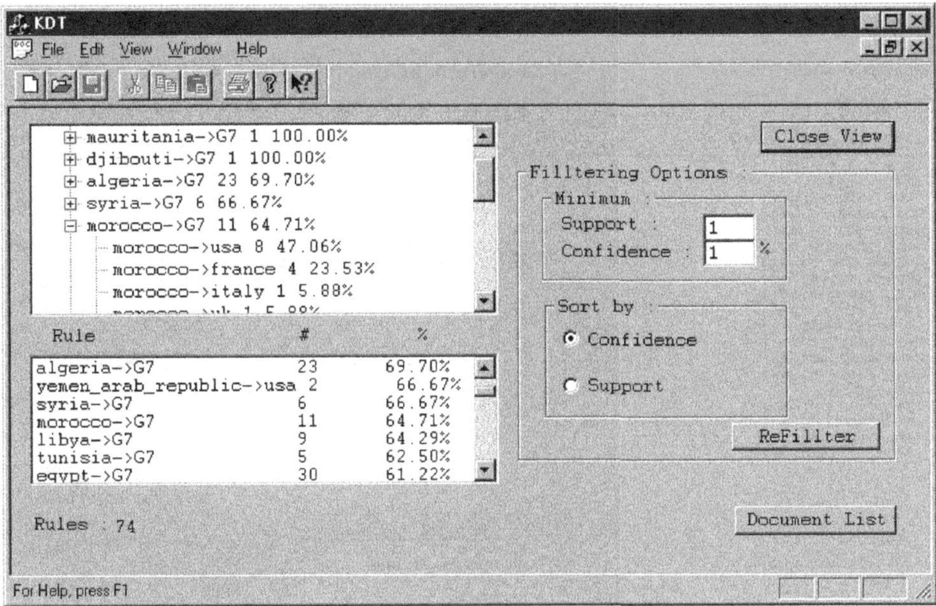

Figure IX.3. An example of an advanced tool for browsing and filtering associations. (From Feldman, Kloesgen, Ben-Yehuda, et al. 1997.)

One method for doing this is to support association browsing by clustering associations with identical left-hand sides (LHSs). Then, these clusters can be displayed in decreasing order of the generality of their LHS.

Associations that have more general LHSs will be listed before more specific associations. The top-level nodes in the hierarchical tree are sorted in decreasing order of the number of documents that support all associations in which they appear.

Some text mining systems include fully featured, association-specific browsing tools (see Figures IX.3 and IX.4) geared toward providing users with an easy way for finding associations and then filtering and sorting them in different orders.

This type of browser tool can support the specification of simple constraints on the presented associations. The user can select a set of concepts from the set of all possible concepts appearing in the associations and then choose the logical test to be performed on the associations.

In even a simple version of this type of tool, the user can see either all associations containing either of these concepts (or), all of these concepts (and), or that the concepts of the association are included in the list of selected concepts (subset). He or she could then also select one of the internal nodes in the taxonomy, and the list of concepts under this node would be used in the filtering.

For instance, if one set the support threshold at 10, and the confidence threshold at 10 percent, an overwhelming number of associations would result. Clearly, no user could digest this amount of information.

An association browser tool, however, would allow the user to choose to view only those associations that might contain, for instance, both the concepts *USA* and *acq* (a shorthand concept label for "company acquisition"). This would allow him or her to see what countries are associated with *USA* with regard to acquisition along with all the statistical parameters related to each association.

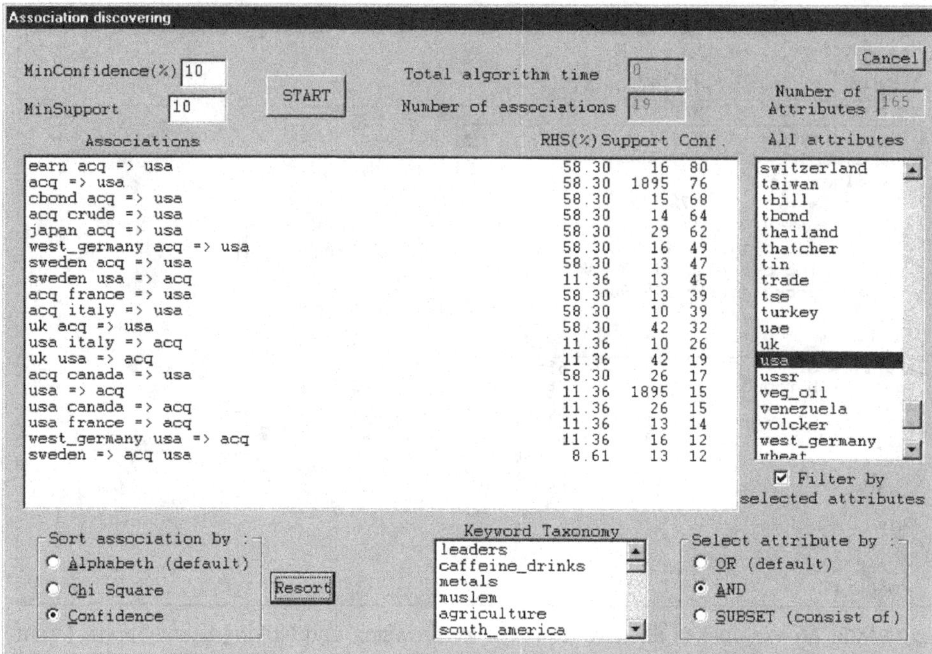

Figure IX.4. An example of another GUI tool for displaying and browsing associations. (From Feldman, Kloesgen, Ben-Yehuda, et al. 1997.)

The utility afforded by even relatively simple techniques, such as sorting, and browsers can provide a user with several sorting options for associations. Two options are rather obvious: sorting the associations in alphabetical order, and sorting the associations in decreased order of their confidence. A third ordering scheme is based on the chi-square value of the association. In a way, this approach attempts to measure how different the probability of seeing the RHS of the association is given that one saw its LHS from the probability of seeing the RHS in the whole population.

IX.1.3 Navigation and Exploration by Means of Concept Hierarchies

Concept hierarchies and taxonomies can play many different roles in text mining systems. However, it is important not to overlook the usefulness of various hierarchical representations in navigation and user exploration.

Often, it is visually easier to traverse a comprehensive tree-structure of nodes relating to all the concepts relevant to an entire document collection or an individual pattern query result set than to scroll down a long, alphabetically sorted list of concept labels. Indeed, sometimes the knowledge inherent in the hierarchical structuring of concepts can serve as an aid to the interactive or free-form exploration of concept relationships, or both – a critical adjunct to uncovering hidden but interesting knowledge.

A concept hierarchy or taxonomy can also enable the user of a text mining system to specify mining tasks concisely. For instance, when beginning the process of generating association rules, the user, rather than looking for all possible rules, can specify interest only in the relationships of companies in the context of business alliances.

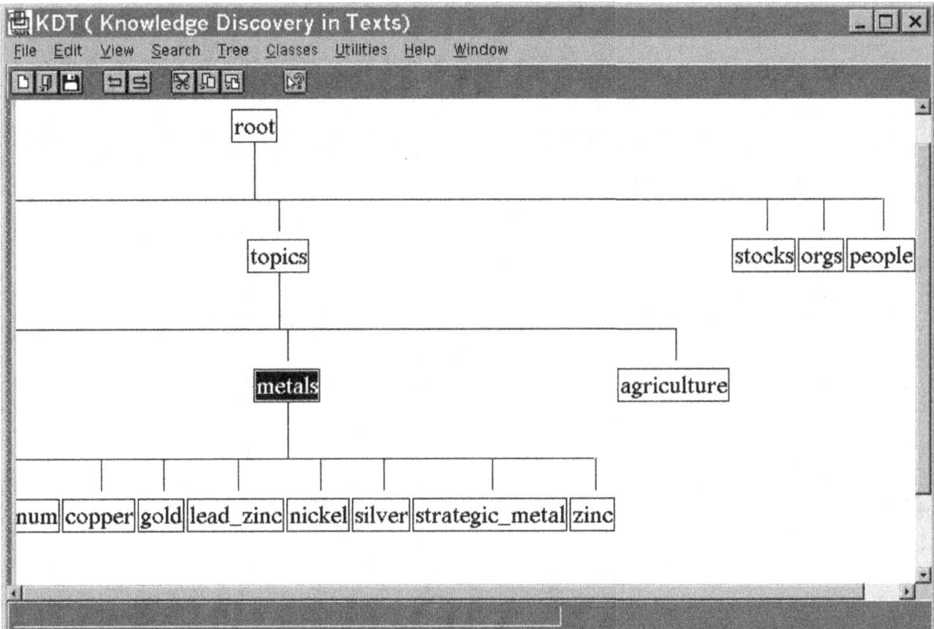

Figure IX.5. A simple graphical interface for creating, exploring, and manipulating a Taxonomy. (From Feldman, Dagan, and Hirsh 1998. Reprinted with permission of Springer Science and Business Media.)

To support this, the text mining system could display a concept hierarchy with two nodes marked "business alliances" and "companies," for instance. The first node would contain terms related to business alliances such as "joint venture," "strategic alliance," "combined initiative," and so on, whereas the second node would be the parent of all company names in the system (which could be the result of human effort specifying such a higher level term, but in many text mining systems a set of rules is employed with knowledge extracted from Internet-based or other commercial directories to generate company names).

In this example, the user could perform a comprehensive search with a few clicks on two nodes of a hierarchical tree. The user would thus avoid the kind of desultory, arbitrary, and incomplete "hunting and pecking" that might occur if he or she had to manually input from memory – or even choose from a pick list – various relevant words relating to business alliances and companies from memory to create his or her query. A very simple graphical display of a concept hierarchy for browsing can be seen in Figure IX.5.

In addition, concept hierarchies can be an important mechanism for supporting the administration and maintenance of user-defined information in a document collection. For instance, entity profile maintenance and user-specified concept or document clustering can often be facilitated by means of the quick navigational opportunities afforded by tree-based hierarchical structures.

IX.1.4 Concept Hierarchy and Taxonomy Editors

Maintaining concept hierarchies and taxonomies is an important but difficult task for users of the text mining systems that leverage them. Therefore, presentation-layer

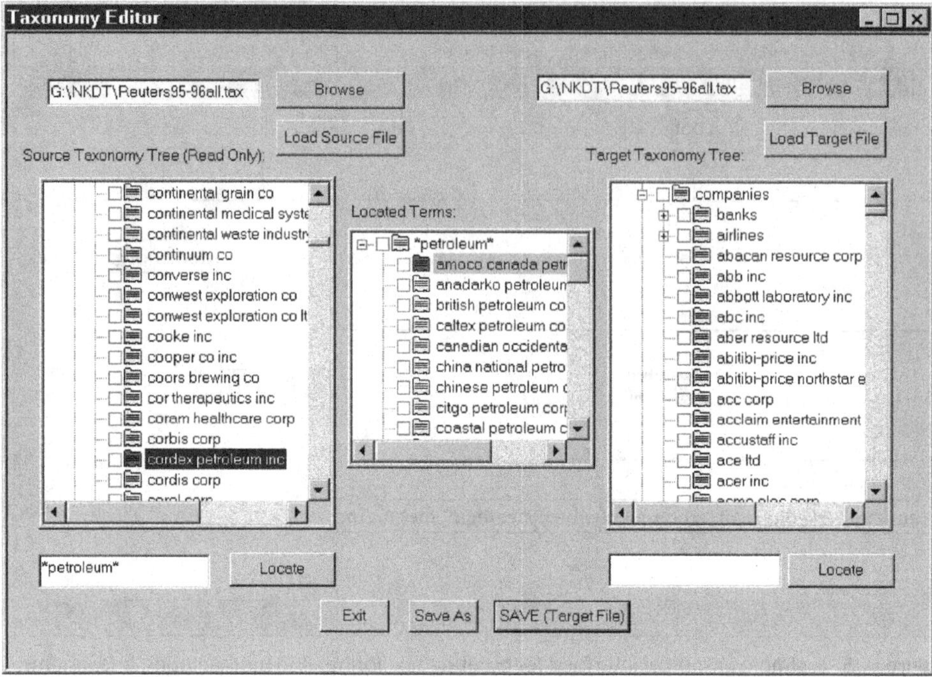

Figure IX.6. User interface for a taxonomy editor showing views of source and target taxonomy trees. (From Feldman, Fresko, Hirsh, et al. 1998.)

tools that allow for easier and more comprehensive administration serve an important role in increasing the usability and effectiveness of the text mining process.

Concept hierarchy editing tools build on many of the same features a user needs to employ a concept hierarchy as a navigational tool. The user must be able to search and locate specific concepts as well as hypernyms and hyponyms; fuzzy search capability is an important adjunct to allowing a user to scrub a hierarchy properly when making major category changes. An example of a graphical hierarchy editing tool appears in Figure IX.6.

Moreover, an important feature in such an editor can be the ability to view the existing *source* concept hierarchy in read-only mode and to edit a *target* concept hierarchy at the same time. This can help a user avoid making time-consuming errors or creating inconsistencies when editing complex tree-structures or making wholesale modifications.

IX.1.5 Clustering Tools to Aid Data Exploration

Although several methods for creating smaller subset-type selections of documents from a text mining system's main document collection have already been discussed, there are numerous situations in which a user may want to organize groups of documents into *clusters* according to more complex, arbitrary, or personal criteria.

For instance, a user of a text mining system aimed at scientific papers on cancer research may want to cluster papers according to the biomedical subdiscipline

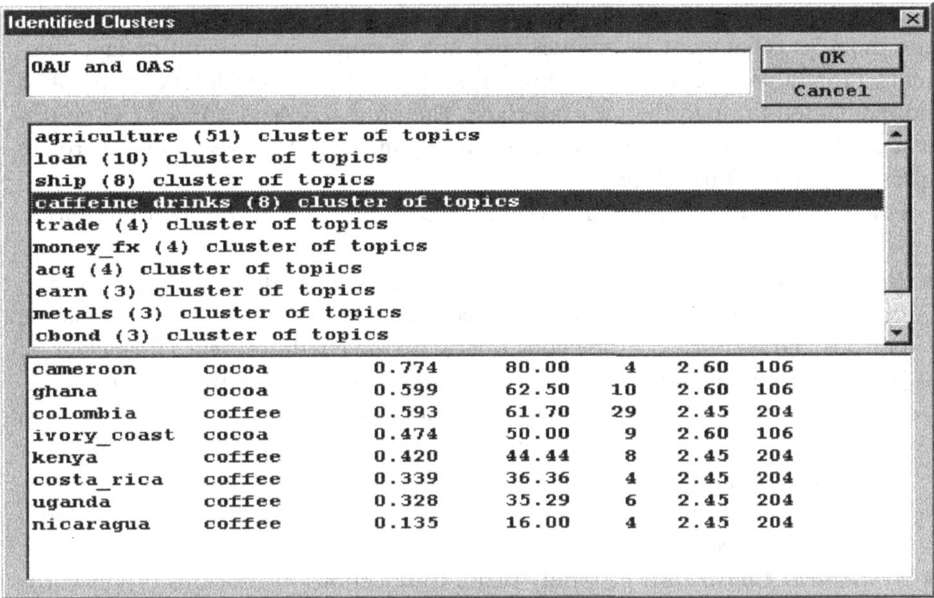

Figure IX.7. Clustering associations using a category hierarchy. (From Feldman, Dagan, and Hirsh 1998. Reprinted with permission of Springer Science and Business Media.)

(e.g., immunology, microbiology, virology, molecular biology, human genetics, etc.) of each paper's lead author. Similarly, a user of a document collection composed of news feeds might want to leverage his or her text mining system's concept hierarchy to cluster patterns involving individual countries under labels representing larger, intercountry groupings (see Figure IX.7).

Clustering operations can involve both automatic and manual processes. Unlike classic taxonomies, groupings of clusters do not need to be strictly hierarchical in structure; individual text mining systems may adopt more or less flexible approaches to such groupings. For this reason, it is generally a requirement that a text mining system offer robust and easy interfaces for a user to view, scrub, and maintain cluster information. Moreover, because both document collections and users' needs can change over time, it is especially important for text mining clustering capabilities to allow flexible reorientation of clusters as a system evolves and matures.

Some text mining systems perform the majority of their manual or unsupervised clustering during preprocessing operations. In these cases, it is still often important to provide users with administrative capability to tweak clusters over the lifetime of a text mining application's use.

IX.2 ACCESSING CONSTRAINTS AND SIMPLE SPECIFICATION FILTERS AT THE PRESENTATION LAYER

Given the immense number of prospective potential patterns that they might identify, text mining systems generally provide support for some level of user-specifiable constraints. These constraints can be employed to restrict the search to returning particular patterns, to limit the number of patterns presented, to offer options for specifying the interestingness of results, or to accomplish all of these objectives.

From a system architecture perspective, the logic of such constraints should be seen more as refinement techniques, and not so much as presentation-layer elements. From a user perspective, however, such constraints and filters are invoked and modulated through the user interface. Therefore, constraint types can be discussed in relation to other elements that can be employed to shape queries through a presentation-layer interface.

Four common types of constraints are typical to text mining browser interfaces:

- ***Background Constraints*** refer to the knowledge of the domain that is given in the form of binary relations between concepts. For example, rules associating persons and countries can be constrained by the condition that an association between a person and a country excludes the nationality of that person. Background constraints typically require a set of predicates to be created relating to certain types of concepts (e.g., entities) in the text mining system's document collection. Binary predicates can allow one input argument and one output argument. Such predicates are usually extracted from some expert or "gold standard" knowledge source.
- ***Syntactical Constraints*** generally relate to selections of concepts or keywords that will be included in a query. More specifically, they can refer to the components of the patterns, for example, to the left- or right-hand side of a rule or the number of items in the components.
- ***Quality Constraints*** most often refer to support and confidence thresholds that can be adjusted by a user before performing a search. However, quality constraints can also include more advanced, customized statistical measures to provide qualities for patterns. An association rule, for instance, can be additionally specified by the significance of a statistical test, or a distribution of a concept group can be evaluated with respect to a reference distribution. These qualities are then used in constraints when searching for significant patterns.
- ***Redundancy Constraints*** have been described as metarules that determine when a pattern is suppressed by another pattern. For example, a redundancy rule could be used to suppress all association rules with a more special left-hand side than another association rule and a confidence score that is not higher than that of the other more general rule.

Constraints are important elements in allowing a user to efficiently browse patterns that are potentially either incrementally or dramatically more relevant to his or her search requirements and exploration inclinations. Moreover, they can be essential to ensuring the basic usability of text mining systems accessing medium or large document collections.

IX.3 ACCESSING THE UNDERLYING QUERY LANGUAGE

Although graphical interfaces make text mining search and browsing operations easier to conduct for users, some search and browsing activities are facilitated if users have direct access to the text mining system's underlying *query language* with well-defined semantics. Many advanced text mining systems, therefore – in addition to

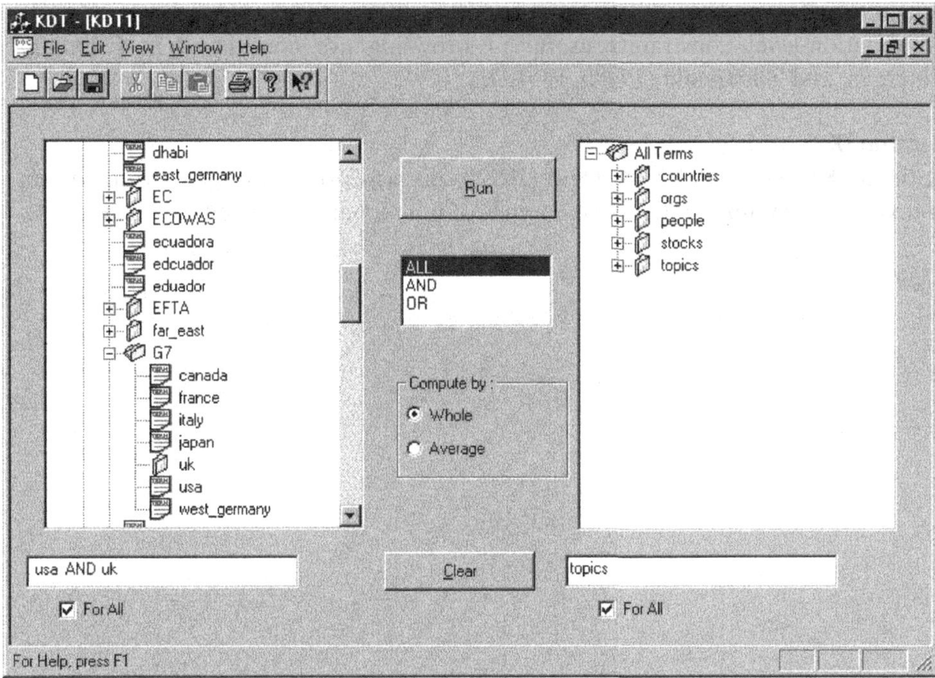

Figure IX.8. Defining a distribution query through a simple GUI in the KDT system. (From Feldman, Kloesgen, Ben-Yehuda, et al. 1997.)

offering pick lists of prespecified query types and common constraint parameters – support direct user access to a query command interpreter for explicit query composition.

Clearly, it is the query language itself that allows a user to search the vast implicit set of patterns available in a given document collection. However, the user environment for displaying, selecting, running, editing, and saving queries should not be given short shrift in the design of a text mining system. Figure IX.8 shows one example of a graphical query construction tool. Regardless of the specific combination of graphical and character-based elements employed, the easier it is for a user to specify his or her query – and understand exactly what that query is meant to return – the more usable and powerful a text mining system becomes.

A more comprehensive discussion of text mining query languages can be found in Section II.3.

IX.4 CITATIONS AND NOTES

Section IX.1

Many of the ideas in Section IX.1 represent an expansion and updating of ideas introduced in Feldman, Kloesgen, Ben-Yehuda, et al. (1997). Methods for display of associations are treated partially in Feldman and Hirsh (1997). Navigation by concept hierarchies is treated in Feldman, Kloesgen, Ben-Yehuda, et al. (1997); and Feldman, Fresko, Hirsh, et al. (1998). Taxonomy editing tools are briefly discussed in Feldman, Fresko, Hirsh, et al. (1998).

Section IX.2

Presentation-level constraints useful in browsing are considered in Feldman, Kloesgen, and Zilberstein (1997a, 1997b).

Section IX.3

Feldman, Kloesgen, and Zilberstein (1997b) discusses the value of providing users of text mining systems with multiple types of functionality to specify a query.

Visualization Approaches

X.1 INTRODUCTION

Human-centric text mining emphasizes the centrality of user interactivity to the knowledge discovery process. As a consequence, text mining systems need to provide users with a range of tools for interacting with data. For a wide array of tasks, these tools often rely on very simple graphical approaches such as pick lists, drop-down boxes, and radio boxes that have become typical in many generic software applications to support query construction and the basic browsing of potentially interesting patterns.

In large document collections, however, problems of pattern and feature over-abundance have led the designers of text mining systems to move toward the creation of more sophisticated visualization approaches to facilitate user interactivity. Indeed, in document collections of even relatively modest size, tens of thousands of identified concepts and thousands of interesting associations can make browsing with simple visual mechanisms such as pick lists all but unworkable. More sophisticated visualization approaches incorporate graphical tools that rely on advances in many different areas of computer and behavioral science research to promote easier and more intensive and iterative exploration of patterns in textual data.

Many of the more mundane activities that allow a user of a text mining system to engage in rudimentary data exploration are supported by a graphic user interface that serves as the type of basic viewer or *browser* discussed in Chapter IX. A typical basic browsing interface can be seen in Figure X.1.

This type of basic browsing often combines a limited number of query-building functions with an already refined or constrained view of a subset of the textual data in the document collection. In addition, sometimes a basic browsing interface supplements its more character-oriented display elements by supporting the simplified execution of subroutines to draw static graphs of query results.

Text mining visualization approaches, on the other hand, generally emphasize a set of purposes different from those that underpin basic browsing interfaces. Although both basic browsers and visualization tools aim at making interaction with data possible, visualization tools typically result in more sophisticated graphical

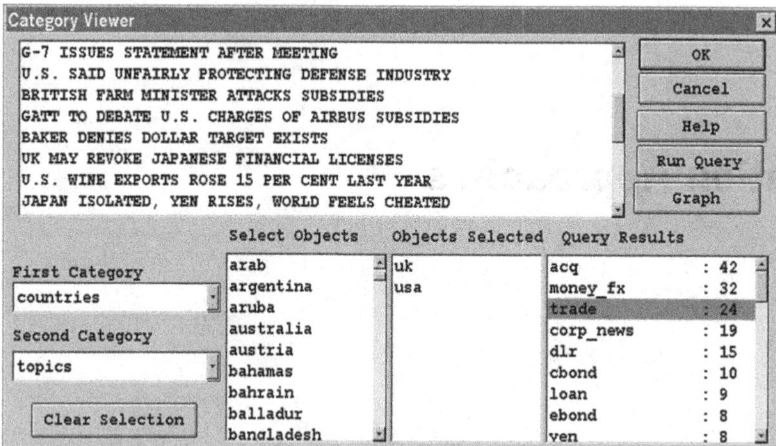

Figure X.1. Basic category browsing in a text mining system. (From Feldman, Kloesgen, Ben-Yehuda, et al. 1997.)

interfaces that attempt to stimulate and exploit the visual capacities of users to identify patterns.

For instance, an interactive circle graph – a common visualization tool in text mining systems – might be tailored specifically to allow cancer researchers to explore an entire corpus of medical research literature broadly in a single graph (see background graph in Figure X.2). By having concepts extracted from the literature represented as nodes on the periphery of the circle and associations between concepts identified by linking lines of various thicknesses that bisect the circle, a researcher could very quickly navigate high-level concepts and then zero-in on relationships emanating from more granular concepts – all while gaining at least a generalized sense of the totality of relationships within the corpus.

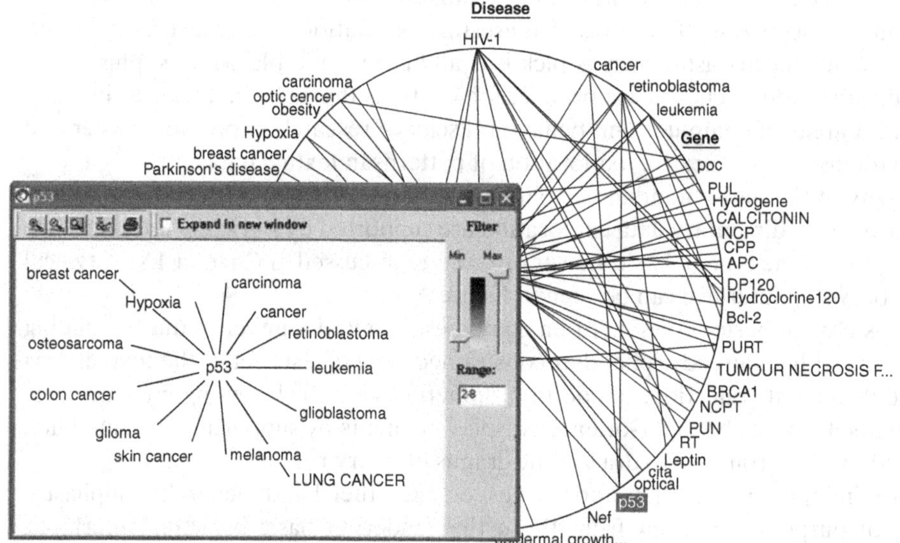

Figure X.2. Circle graph–based category connection map of medical literature relating to AIDS with inset of graphically driven refinement filter. (From Feldman, Regev, et al. 2003.)

This type of visualization tool enables a researcher to appraise, handle, and navigate large amounts of data quickly and with relative ease. Moreover, "control elements" – such as refinement filters or other constraint controls – can be embedded into the overall operations of the visualization interface being executed by as little as a mouse click on a highlighted concept label (see inset in Figure X.2).

Certainly, some kinds of refinement constraints lend themselves to being set quite adequately by character-driven menus or pull-down boxes. By facilitating context-sensitive and graphical refinement of query results, however, more sophisticated visual presentation tools can add to the speed and intuitive ease with which a user can shape knowledge-discovery activities.

Critical advantages that individual visualization approaches can have over character-oriented browsing formats in presenting patterns in data include the following:

- ***Concision:*** the capability of showing large amounts of different types of data all at once;
- ***Relativity and Proximity:*** the ability to easily show clusters, relative sizes of groupings, similarity and dissimilarity of groupings, and outliers among the data in query results;
- ***Focus with Context:*** the ability to interact with some highlighted feature while also being able to see the highlighted feature situated in some of its relational context;
- ***Zoomability:*** the ability to move from micro to macro quickly and easily in one big step or in increments;
- ***"Right Brain" Stimulation:*** the ability to invite user interaction with textual data that is driven not only by premeditated and deliberate search intentions but also as a result of intuitive, reactive, or spatially oriented cognitive processes for identifying interesting patterns.

On the other hand, adding an overabundance of complex graphical features to a visualization interface does not necessarily make the interface more appropriate to its search tasks. Overly complex visualization tools can overdetermine or even inhibit exploration of textual data – particularly if designers of text mining systems lose sight of the main advantages that graphic presentation elements have over more prosaic form- or table-based browser formats.

The evolution from simple, primarily character-based browsers to more powerful and more specialized visualization interfaces has helped transform the orientation of text mining systems. Text mining systems have moved from a focus on the premeditated search for *suspected* patterns to a broader capability that also includes more free-form and unguided exploration of textual data for implicit, obscure, and *unsuspected* patterns.

X.1.1 Citations and Notes

A seminal discussion of human-centered knowledge discovery can be found in Brachman and Anand (1996). Grinstein (1996) also offers a relevant treatment of related topics.

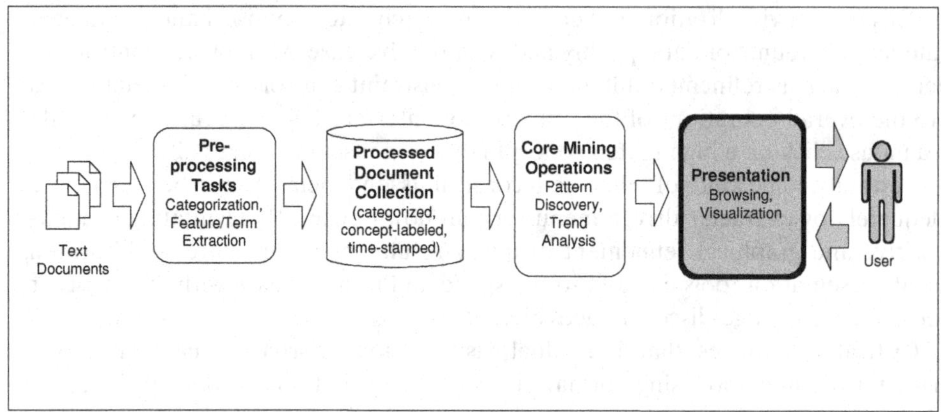

Figure X.3. High-level functional architecture of a text mining system showing position of visualization.

General overviews of information visualization can be found in Tufte (1983), Tufte (1990), Cleveland (1994), Shneiderman (1997), and Spence (2001). Useful works on information visualization techniques in information retrieval and the visual presentation of query results include Rao et al. (1992), Spoerri (1999), Ahlberg and Schneiderman (1994), Masui et al. (1995), Hearst (1999), Lagus (2000b), and Hearst (2003). Important early treatments of information navigation and exploration approaches include Goldstein and Roth (1994), Ahlberg and Wistrand (1995), and Jerding and Stasko (1995).

There really is not yet a comprehensive treatment of visualization techniques specific to text mining. However, several works – including Feldman, Kloesgen, Ben-Yehuda, et al. (1997); Feldman, Kloesgen, and Zilberstein (1997a); Landau et al. (1998); Aumann et al. (1999); Lagus et al. (1999); Wong, Whitney, and Thomas (1999); Lagus (2000a); and Wong et al. (2000) – provide relevant discussions of a limited number of specific visual techniques and their application to text mining activities.

X.2 ARCHITECTURAL CONSIDERATIONS

In the high-level functional architecture of a text mining system illustrated in Figure X.3, visualization tools are among those system elements situated closest to the user. Visualization tools are mechanisms that serve to facilitate human interactivity with a text mining system. These tools are layered on top of – and are dependent upon – the existence of a processed document collection and the various algorithms that make up a text mining system's core mining capabilities.

The increased emphasis on adding more sophisticated and varied visualization tools to text mining systems has had several implications for these systems' architectural design. Although older text mining systems often had rigidly integrated visualization tools built into their user interface (UI) front ends, newer text mining systems emphasize modularity and abstraction between their front-end (i.e., presentation layer) and middle-tier (i.e., core discovery and query execution elements) architectures.

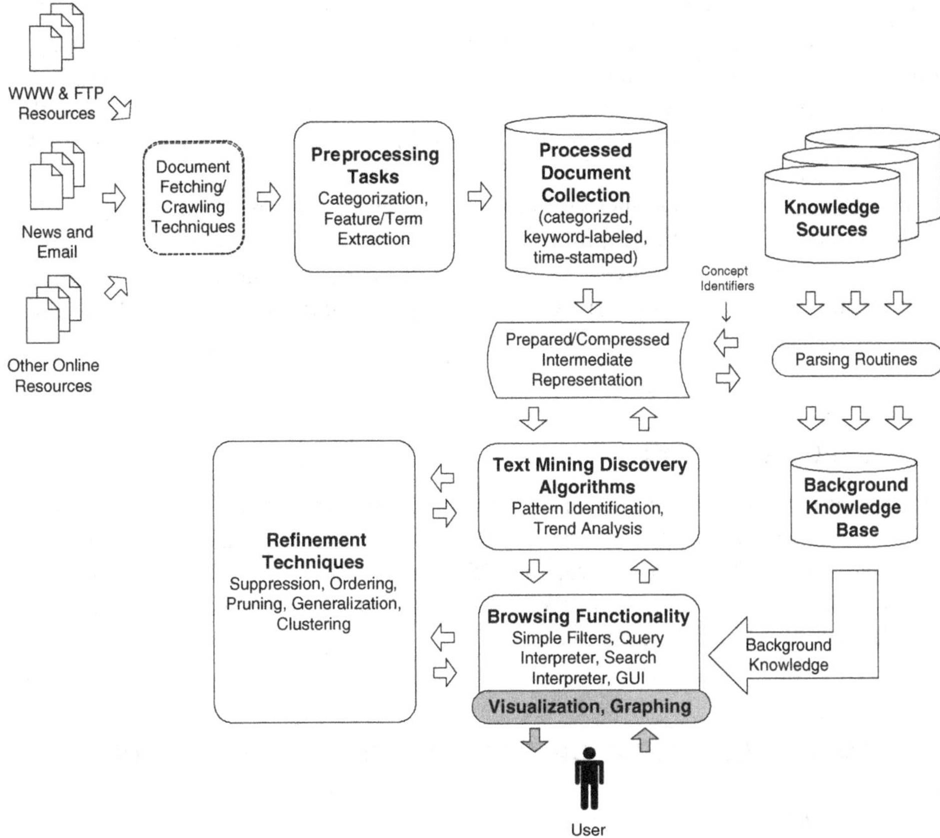

Figure X.4. Situating visualization within text mining system architecture.

Indeed, there are several good reasons for architects of text mining systems to abstract the front and middle tiers of their software platforms. First, visualization tools and knowledge discovery algorithms tend to be modified and upgraded on an ever more iterative basis. A "decoupled" or "loosely coupled" front end and middle tier in text mining system – abstracted from each other by an intermediary connection layer based on a formal and well-defined software interface – allow much better for such unsynchronized development of different elements of the text mining system. Figure X.4 illustrates the general position of visualization components in a text mining system's architecture.

Second, text mining systems are moving from having a few limited visualization and graphing tools to supporting whole suites of different kinds of presentation layer utilities. This is both a reflection of the movement toward facilitating greater user interactivity through more customized (even personalized) UIs and the proliferation of more mature, sophisticated, and specialized visualization tools. With many more types of different visualization approaches now available, architects of text mining systems are probably well advised to keep their options open; instead of scrapping a whole text mining system when its UI has become hopelessly outdated, developers can leverage a more loosely coupled front end and middle-tier architecture to continue to add additional visualization components.

Finally, from a practical perspective, the wider availability of RDF and XML-oriented protocols makes such loose coupling of front ends and middle tiers much more feasible. This fact is underscored by the current availability of a whole spate of specialized and very powerful commercial off-the-shelf visualization software with defined interfaces or feed formats that support various RDF or XML data interchange approaches.

Visualization tools have increasingly played a crucial, even transformative role in current state-of-the-art text mining systems. As with data mining systems, sophisticated visualization tools have become more critical components of text mining applications because of their utility in facilitating the exploration for hidden and subtle patterns in data.

X.2.1 Citations and Notes

For obvious reasons, the architectural discussion in this section is highly generalized. The architectural descriptions have been informed by the visualization elements found in the KDT (Feldman and Dagan 1995), Explora (Kloesgen 1995b), Document Explorer (Feldman, Kloesgen, and Zilberstein 1997a), and TextVis (Landau et al. 1998) knowledge discovery systems.

X.3 COMMON VISUALIZATION APPROACHES FOR TEXT MINING

X.3.1 Overview

A substantial and mature literature already exists relating to the use of visualization tools in a wide range of generic and specific computer science applications. The aim of the next few sections is to illustrate how a select number of commonly seen visualization approaches have been put to good use supplementing text mining functionality.

The potential number of combinations of visual techniques that can be applied to problems in unstructured data is probably limitless. With such a wide array of possible visual techniques, coupled with the subjective nature of assessing the efficacy of visualization approaches across different types of knowledge-discovery problem sets and user groups, it would be problematic to attempt to rate, to any precise degree, the success of a specific visual approach or set of approaches. Nevertheless, several visual approaches have suggested themselves more informally as useful enhancements to knowledge discovery operations involving textual data. These include simple concept graphs, histograms, line graphs, circle graphs, self-organizing maps, and so-called context + focus approaches – like the hyperbolic tree – as well as various derivative and hybrid forms of these main approaches.

Thus, perhaps it should be stated clearly that the intention here is not so much to be *prescriptive* – detailing the circumstances when a particular visualization approach is decidedly more appropriate, more powerful, or more effective than another for a given task – as *descriptive*, or describing how a particular tool has typically been employed to supplement text mining systems.

X.3.2 Simple Concept Graphs

Even rather bare-bones visualization tools such as *simple concept graphs* provide an efficient exploration tool for getting familiar with a document collection. The two main benefits of these types of visualizations are their abilities to *organize* the exploration of textual data and to *facilitate interactivity* – that is, the user can click on each node or edge and get the documents supporting them or can initiate various other operations on the graphs. There is a relationship between these two benefits as well: offering user-friendly organization approaches can do much to promote increased user interactivity with textual data.

This latter type of exploration can be further supported by linking several graphs. Thus, the relevance of selected aspects of one graph can be efficiently studied in the context of another graph. Simple concept graphs have been used, with many variations, in several real-world text mining systems.

Simple Concept Set Graphs

One of the most basic and universally useful visualization tools in text mining is the simple "root and branches" hierarchical tree structure. Figure X.5 shows a classic visualization for a concept taxonomy in a document collection. The root and leaf vertices (nodes) of such a visualization are concept identifiers (i.e., name labels for concepts). The special layout of the presentation elements allows a user to traverse the hierarchical relationships in the taxonomy easily either to identify sought-after concepts or to search more loosely for unexpected concepts that appear linked to other interesting concepts in the hierarchy.

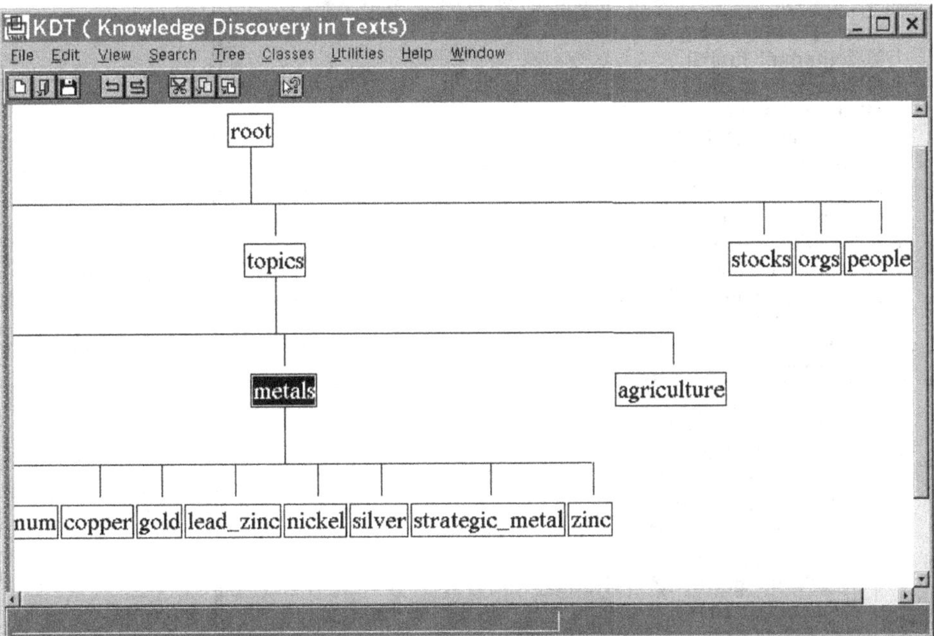

Figure X.5. Interactive graph used to illustrate a concept taxonomy as a hierarchical tree structure. (From Feldman, Dagan, and Hirsh 1998. Reprinted with permission of Springer Science and Business Media.)

This kind of visualization tool can also easily be made to allow a user to click on a node concept and either move to the underlying documents containing the concept or to connect to information about sets or distributions of documents containing the concept within the document collection. This latter type of information – the answer set to a rather routine type of query in many text mining systems – can be demonstrated by means of a concept set graph.

Formally, a *concept set graph* refers to a visual display of a subset of concept sets with respect to their partial ordering. Perhaps the most common and straightforward way to display concept sets graphically is also by means of a simple hierarchical tree structure.

Figure X.5 shows a set graph for frequent sets arranged in a tree structure. The user can operate on this graph by selecting nodes, opening and closing nodes, or defining new search tasks with respect to these nodes, for instance, to expand the tree.

The first level in Figure X.5 relates to country concepts sorted by a simple quality measure (support of the frequent set). The node "USA" (support: 12,814 documents) is expanded by person concepts. Further expansions relate to economical topic concepts (e.g., expansion of the node "James Baker": 124 documents, 0%) and country concepts.

Of course, a hybrid form could be made between the "root and branches"–type visual display format shown in Figure X.5 and the simple concept set graph illustrated in Figure X.6. For some applications, having the percentage support displayed within a concept node on the root and branches visualization might prove more useful to

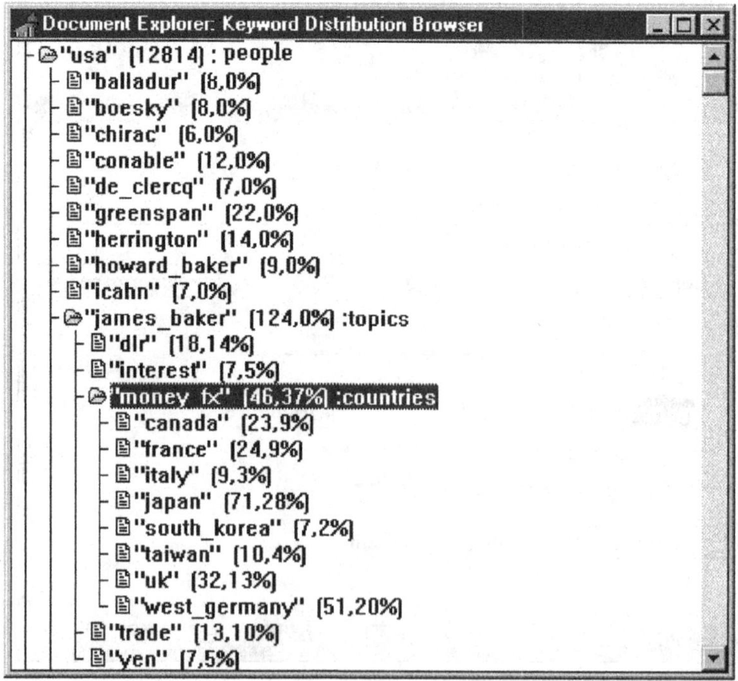

Figure X.6. A hierarchical concept set graph. (From Feldman, Kloesgen, and Zilberstein 1997b.)

navigation and exploration than the "long indented list" appearance of the vertical tree structure in Figure X.6. This form would be a directed graph, the edges of which (usually depicted with directional arrow heads) indicate the hierarchical relationship between nodes at the graph vertices.

Although a hierarchical concept graph may represent a very basic approach to visualizing sets of concepts, it can be also used as the entry point for jumping to more complex visualizations or graphically driven refinement controls. For instance, by clicking on a concept identifier, a user may be able to navigate to another graph that shows associations containing the highlighted concept, or a graphic box could be triggered by clicking on a concept allowing the user to adjust the quality measure that drove the original query.

Another related, commonly used visualization approach applicable to simple concept sets is the organization of set members into a DAG. Formally, a DAG can be described as a directed graph that has no path and that begins and ends at the same vertex. Practically, it might be viewed as a hierarchical form in which child nodes can have more than one parent node.

DAGs can be useful in describing more complex containership relations than those represented by a strict hierarchical form, in that the DAG represents a generalization of a tree structure in which a given subtree can be shared by different parts of the tree. For instance, a DAG is often used to illustrate the somewhat more complex relations between concepts in an ontology that models a real-world relationship set in which "higher level" concepts often have multiple, common directed relationships with "lower level" concepts in the graph. Described in a different way, DAGs permit lower level containers to be "contained" within more than one higher level container at the same time.

A very simple DAG is shown in Figure X.7. Traditional, rigidly directed hierarchical representations might be both much less obvious and less efficient in showing that four separate concepts have a similar or possibly analogous relationship to a fifth concept (e.g., the relationship that the concepts *motor vehicles*, *cars*, *trucks*, and *power tillers* have with the concept *engines*). Because of their ability to illustrate more complex relationships, DAGs are very frequently leveraged as the basis for moderately sophisticated relationship maps in text mining applications.

A more complex and well-known application of a DAG to an ontology can be seen in Zhou and Cui's (Zhou and Cui 2004) visual representations of the Gene Ontology (GO) database. Zhou and Cui created a DAG to visually model a small subset of the GO ontology, focusing only on the root node and three child nodes. When using a DAG to show biological function for 23 query genes, the DAG still ended up having 10 levels and more than 101 nodes.

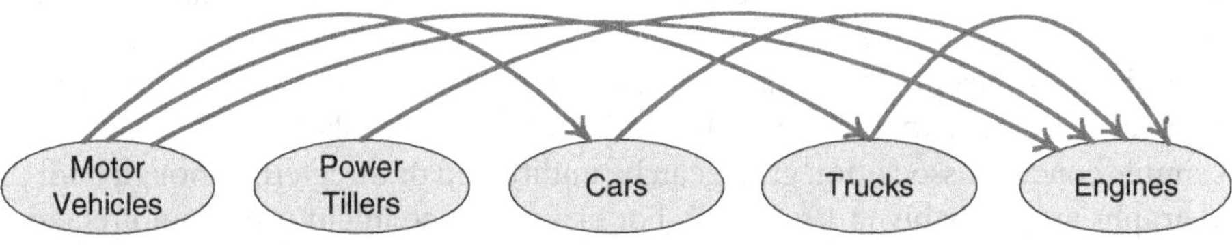

Figure X.7. A simple DAG modeling a taxonomy that includes multiple parent concepts for a single-child concept.

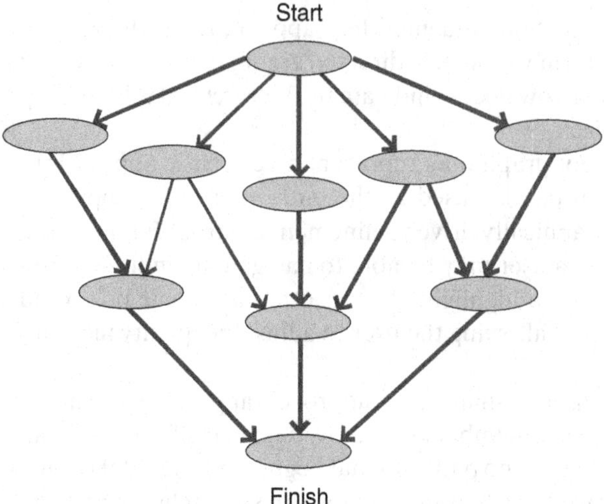

Figure X.8. Visualization of a generic DAG-based activity network.

Visualization techniques based on DAGs have proven very useful for visually modeling complex set-oriented or container-type relationships, such as those found among concepts in the GO ontology, in a relatively straightforward and understandable way. However, Zhou and Cui find DAGs to be limited when illustrating more granular or functional relationship information (such as one finds when exploring concept associations) or when the number of concepts in play becomes large. In these cases, other types of visualization techniques, such as circular graphs or network models, can sometimes provide greater expressive capabilities.

Beyond their use in modeling concept hierarchies, DAGs can also be employed as the basis for modeling *activity networks*. An activity network is a visual structure in which each vertex represents a task to be completed or a choice to be made and the directed edges refer to subsequent tasks or choices. See Figure X.8.

Such networks provide the foundation for more advanced types of text mining knowledge discovery operations. DAG-based activity networks, for instance, form the basis for some of the more popular types of visualizations used in *critical path analysis* – often an important approach in knowledge-discovery operations aimed at link detection.

Simple Concept Association Graphs

Simple concept association graphs focus on representing associations. A simple association graph consists of *singleton vertex* and *multivertex graphs* in which the edges can connect to a set of several concepts. Typically, a simple association graph connects concepts of a selected category. At each vertex of a simple association graph, there is only one concept. Two concepts are connected by an edge if their similarity with respect to a similarity function is larger than a given threshold.

A simple concept association graph can be undirected or directed, although undirected graphs are probably more typical. For example, one might use an undirected graph to model associations visually between generic concepts in a document collection generated from corporate finance documentation. On the other hand, if one

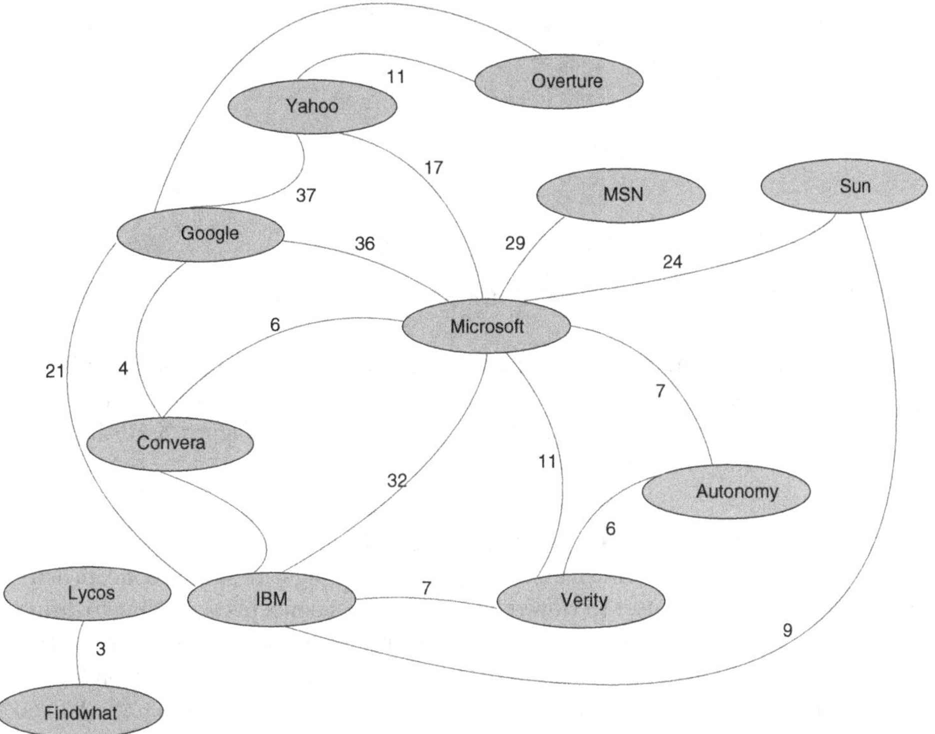

Figure X.9. Concept association graph: single vertex, single category (software companies in the context of search engine software).

were seeking to produce a tool to visualize associations between proteins in a corpus of proteomics research literature, one might want to employ a directed graph with directed edges (as denoted by directional arrowheads) between concept nodes. This type of directed graph would be useful in visually indicating not just general association relationships but also the patterns of one protein's acting upon another.

Figure X.9 shows a concept association graph for the *company* category in the context of *search engine software* and a simple similarity function based on the number of documents in which the companies co-occur. The figure allows a user to quickly infer conclusions about data that might be possible only after a much more careful investigation if that user were forced to make his or her way through large lists or tables of textual and statistical data. Such inferences might include the following:

- Microsft, Google, and IBM are the most connected companies;
- Lycos and Findwhat are the only members of a separate component of the graph;
- MSN is connected only to Microsoft, and so on.

Another type of simple concept association graph can present the associations between different categories such as companies and software topics. The singleton vertex version of this graph is arranged like a map on which different positions of circles are used to include the concepts of categories, and edges (between companies and software topics) present the associations. Often, these singleton vertex graphs

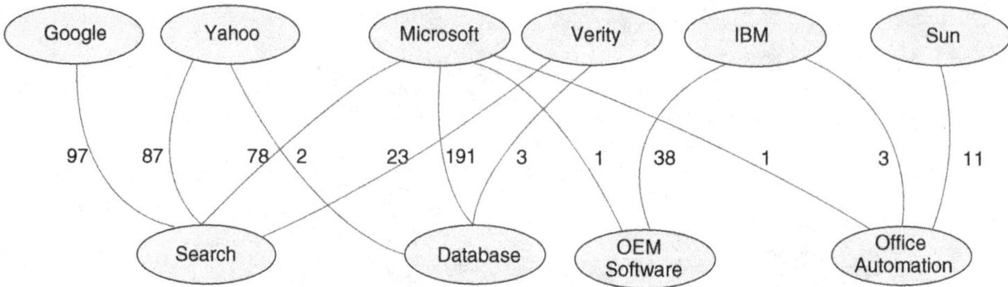

Figure X.10. Concept association graph: single vertex, several categories.

are designed as bipartite graphs displaying two categories of concepts by splitting one category to the top of the graph and another category to the bottom with edges representing connections linking individual pairs of vertices. Figure X.10 shows an example of this kind of concept association graph.

Similarity Functions for Simple Concept Association Graphs

Similarity functions often form an essential part of working with simple concept association graphs, allowing a user to view relations between concepts according to differing weighting measures. Association rules involving sets (or concepts) A and B that have been described in detail in Chapter II are often introduced into a graph format in an undirected way and specified by a support and a confidence threshold. A fixed confidence threshold is often not very reasonable because it is independent of the support from the RHS of the rule. As a result, an association should have a significantly higher confidence than the share of the RHS in the whole context to be considered as interesting. Significance is measured by a statistical test (e.g., t-test or chi-square).

With this addition, the relation given by an association rule is undirected. An association between two sets A and B in the direction $A \Rightarrow B$ implies also the association $B \Rightarrow A$. This equivalence can be explained by the fact that the construct of a statistically significant association is different from implication (which might be suggested by the notation $A \Rightarrow B$). It can easily be derived that if B is overproportionally represented in A, then A is also overproportionally represented in B.

As an example of differences of similarity functions, one can compare the undirected connection graphs given by statistically significant association rules with the graphs based on the cosine function. The latter relies on the cosine of two vectors and is efficiently applied for continuous, ordinal, and also binary attributes. In case of documents and concept sets, a binary vector is associated to a concept set with the vector elements corresponding to documents. An element holds the value 1 if all the concepts of the set appear in the document. Table X.1 (Feldman, Kloesgen, and Zilberstein 1997b), which offers a quick summary of some common similarity functions, shows that the cosine similarity function in this binary case reduces to the fraction built by the support of the union of the two concept sets and the geometrical mean of the support of the two sets.

A connection between two sets of concepts is related to a threshold for the cosine similarity (e.g., 10%). This means that the two concept sets are connected if the support of the document subset that holds all the concepts of both sets is larger than 10 percent of the geometrical mean of the support values of the two concept sets.

Table X.1. *Some Commonly Used Similarity Functions for Two Concept Sets A, B (a = support(A), b = support(B), d = support(A,B))*

Function	Similarity	Characteristic
Support threshold	$d > d_0$ (step function)	evaluates only d, independent from $a - d$, $b - d$
Cosine	$s = d/\sqrt{a \cdot b}$	Low weight of $a - d$, $b - d$
Arithmetical mean	$s = 2d/(a + b)$	middle point between cosine and Tanimoto
Tanimoto	$s = d/(a + b - d)$	high weight of $a - d$, $b - d$
Information measure	weighted documents	only applicable if weights are reasonable
Statistical test	threshold statist. quality	typically for larger samples and covers

The threshold holds a property of monotony: If it is increased, some connections existing for a lower threshold disappear, but no new connections are established. This property is used as one technique to tune the complexity of a simple concept graph.

One can derive a significance measure (factor f) for this situation in which tuning is required in the following way.

Let f be the following factor:

$$f = Ns(A, B)/s(A)s(B).$$

Given the support s for the two concept sets A resp. B and N the number of documents in the collection (or a subcollection given by a selected context), we can calculate the factor. In the case of the independence of the two concept sets, f would be expected around the value 1. Thus, f is larger than 1 for a statistically significant association rule.

The cosine similarity of concept sets A and B can now be calculated as

$$S(A, B) = f \cdot \sqrt{q(A) \cdot q(B)};$$

that is, as the geometrical mean of the relative supports of A and B ($q(A) = s(A)/N$) multiplied by the factor f, thus combining a measure for the relative support of the two sets (geometrical mean) with a significance measure (factor f).

The cosine similarity therefore favors connections between concept sets with a large support (which need not necessarily hold a significant overlapping) and includes connections for concept sets with a small support only if the rule significance is high. This means that the user should select the cosine similarity option if there is a preference for connections between concept sets with a larger support.

On the other side, the statistically based association rule connection should be preferred if the degree of coincidence of the concepts has a higher weight for the analysis. Similar criteria for selecting an appropriate similarity function from Table X.1 can be derived for the other options.

Equivalence Classes, Partial Orderings, Redundancy Filters

Very many pairs of subsets can be built from a given category of concepts, (e.g., all pairs of country subsets for the set of all countries). Each of these pairs is a possible association between subsets of concepts. Even if the threshold of the similarity function is increased, the resulting graph can have too complex a structure. We now define several equivalence relations to build equivalence classes of associations. Only a representative association from each class will then be included in the keyword graph in the default case.

A first equivalence is called *cover equivalence*. Two associations are cover-equivalent iff they have the same cover. For example (Iran, Iraq) => (Kuwait, USA) is equivalent to (Iran, Iraq, Kuwait) => USA because they both have the same cover (Iran, Iraq, Kuwait, USA). The association with the highest similarity is selected as the representative from a cover equivalence class.

Context equivalence is a next equivalence relation. Two associations are context-equivalent iff they are identical up to a different context. That means that two associations are identical when those concepts that appear on both sides are eliminated from each association. For example, (Iran, Iraq) => (Iran, USA) is equivalent to (Kuwait, Iraq) => (Kuwait, USA). The first association establishes a connection between Iraq and USA in the context of Iran, whereas the second association is related to the context of Kuwait. The context-free associations are selected as the representatives from this equivalence class (e.g., Iraq => USA).

The next definition relates to a partial ordering of associations, not an equivalence relation. An association A1 is stronger than an association A2 if the cover of A1 is a subset of the cover of A2. As special cases of this ordering, the right- and left-hand sides are treated separately.

Selecting the representative of an equivalence class or the strongest associations can be applied as a basic redundancy filter. Additionally, criteria can refine these filters (for instance, for the context-equivalence, a context-conditioned association can be selected in addition to the context-free association iff the similarity of the context-conditioned association is much higher with respect to a significance criterion).

There is a duality between frequent sets of concepts and associations. For a given set of frequent concepts, the implied set of all associations between frequent concepts of the set can be introduced. On the other hand, for a given set of associations, the set of all frequent concepts appearing as left- or right-hand sides in the associations can be implied.

In the application area of document collections, users are mainly interested in frequent concept sets when concentrating on basic retrieval or browsing. These frequent concepts are considered as retrieval queries that are discovered by the system to be interesting.

When attempting to gain some knowledge of the domain represented by a document collection, users are often drawn to interacting with association rules, shaping the various measures and refinement filters to explore the nature of the concept relations in the domain. In the simple concept graphs, the concept sets are therefore included as active nodes (activating a query to the collection when selected by the user). Complementary and intersection sets (e.g., related to the cover of an association) can also appear as active nodes.

Typical Interactive Operations Using Simple Concept Graphs

One of the key drivers for employing visualization tools is to promote end user interactivity. Concept graphs derive much of their value from facilitating interactive operations. A user can initiate these operations by manipulating elements in the graphs that execute certain types of system activities.

Some interactive operations relating the concept graphs have already been discussed – or at least suggested – in the previous sections. However, a more systematic review of several types of these operations provides useful insights into kinds of secondary functionality that can be supplemented by simple concept graph visualization approaches.

Browsing-Support Operations

Browsing-support operations enable access to the underlying document collections from the concept set visual interface. Essentially, a concept set corresponds to a query that can be forwarded to the collection retrieving those documents (or their titles as a first summary information), which include all the concepts of the set.

Therefore, each concept set appearing in a graph can be activated for browsing purposes. Moreover, derived sets based on set operations (e.g., difference and intersection) can be activated for retrieval.

Search Operations

Search operations define new search tasks related to nodes or associations selected in the graph. A graph presents the results of a (former) search task and thus puts together sets of concepts or sets of associations. In a GUI, the user can specify the search constraints: syntactical, background, quality, and redundancy constraints.

The former search is now to be refined by a selection of reference sets or associations in the result graph. Some of the search constraints may be modified in the GUI for the scheduled refined search.

In refinement operations, the user can, for example, increase the number of elements that are allowed in a concept set. For instance, selected concept sets in Figure X.6 or selected associations in Figure X.9 can be expanded by modifying restrictions on the maximum number of elements in concept sets.

Link Operations

Link operations combine several concept graphs. Elements in one graph are selected and corresponding elements are highlighted in the second graph. Three types of linked graphs can be distinguished: links between set graphs, between association graphs, and between set and association graphs.

When linking two set graphs, one or several sets are selected in one graph and corresponding sets are highlighted in the second graph. A correspondence for sets can rely, for instance, on the intersections of a selected set with the sets in the other graph. Then all those sets that have a high overlap with a selected set in the first graph are highlighted in the second graph.

When selected elements in a set graph are linked with an association graph, associations in the second graph that have a high overlap with a selected set are highlighted. For instance, in a company graph, all country nodes that have a high intersection with a selected topic in an economical topic graph can be highlighted.

Thus, linkage of graphs relies on the construct of a *correspondence* between two set or association patterns. For example, a correspondence between two sets can be defined by a criterion referring to their intersection, a correspondence between a set and an association by a specialization condition for the more special association constructed by adding the set to the original association, and a correspondence between two associations by a specialization condition for an association constructed by combining the two associations.

Presentation Operations

A first interaction class relates to diverse *presentation options* for the graphs. It includes a number of operations essential to the customization, personalization, calibration, and administration of presentation-layer elements, including

- sorting (e.g., different aspects of quality measures)
- expanding or collapsing
- filtering or finding
- zooming or unzooming nodes, edges, or graph regions.

Although all these presentation-layer operations can have important effects on facilitating usability – and as a result – increased user interaction, some can in certain situations have a very substantial impact on the overall power of systems visualization tools.

Zoom operations, in particular, can add significant capabilities to otherwise very simple concept graphs. For instance, by allowing a user to zoom automatically to a predetermined focal point in a graph (e.g., some concept set or association that falls within a particular refinement constraint), one can add at least something reminiscent of the type of functionality found in much more sophisticated fisheye and self-ordering map (SOM) visualizations.

Drawbacks of Simple Concept Graphs

A few disadvantages of simple concept graphs should be mentioned. First, the functionality and usability of simple concept graphs often become more awkward and limited with high levels of dimensionality in the data driving the models. Hierarchies with vast numbers of nodes and overabundant multiple-parent-noded relationships can be difficult to render graphically in a form that is legible – let alone actionable – by the user of a text mining system; moreover, undirected concept association graphs can become just as intractable for use with large node counts.

In addition, although the streamlined nature of simple concept graphs has its benefits, there are some built-in limitations to interactivity in the very structure of the graph formats. Clearly, tree diagrams can have "hotspots" that allow linking to other graphs, and the type of linked circle node graphs that constitute most simple concept-association graphs can be made to support pruning and other types of refinement operations. However, both forms of simple concept graphs are still relatively rigid formats that are more useful in smaller plots with limited numbers of nodes that can be visually traversed to understand patterns.

As a result, simple concept graphs are far less flexible in supporting the exploration of complex relationships than some other types of visualization approaches. Indeed, other approaches, such as some three-dimensional paradigms and visual methodologies involving greater emphasis of context + focus functionality have been

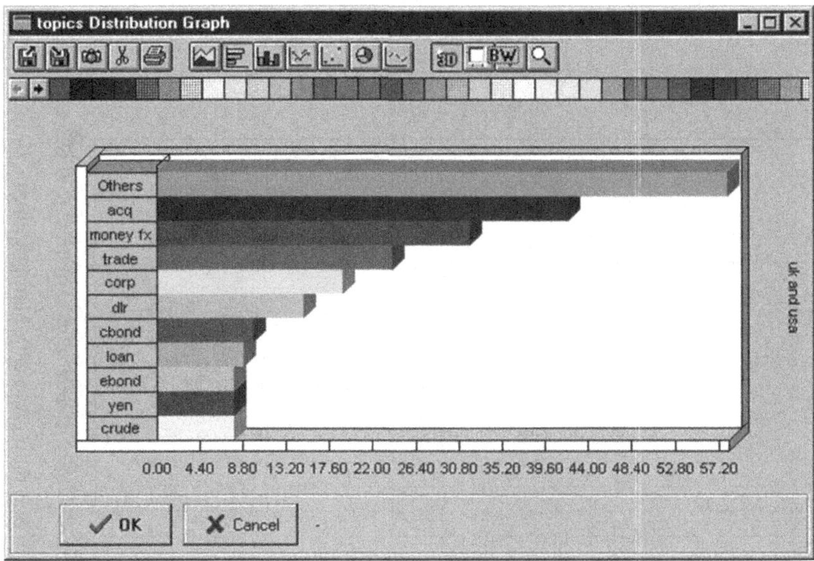

Figure X.11. Early text mining visualization implementation based on a histogram (topic distribution graph from the KDT system ca. 1998). (From Feldman, Kloesgen, and Zilberstein 1997b.)

specifically designed to offer greater flexibility in navigation and exploration of query results than have data with more abundant or complex patterns.

X.3.3 Histograms

In addition to basic "bread and butter" approaches like simple concept graphs, early text mining systems often relied on classic graphing formats such as *histograms*, or bar charts, to provide visualization capabilities. Although architects of text mining systems have shown an increasing willingness to integrate more exotic and complex interactive graphic tools into their systems, histograms still have their uses in exploring patterns in textual data. A very simple histogramatic representation can be seen in Figure X.11.

Histograms still have their uses in text mining systems today and seem particularly well-suited to the display of query results relating to distributions and proportions. However, although two-dimensional (2-D) bar charts themselves have changed little over the last several years, the overall presentation framework in which these bar charts are displayed has become substantially more refined.

Histogrammatic representations are often situated in GUIs with split screens, which also simultaneously display corresponding lists or tables of concept distribution and proportion information of the type described in Chapter II. Histograms are useful in presentation of data related to distributions and proportions because they allow easy comparison of different individual concepts or sets across a wider range of other concepts or sets found within a document collection or subcollection. See Figure X.12. This is not, however, to say that histograms are only useful in displaying results for distribution- or proportion-type queries; for instance, associations can

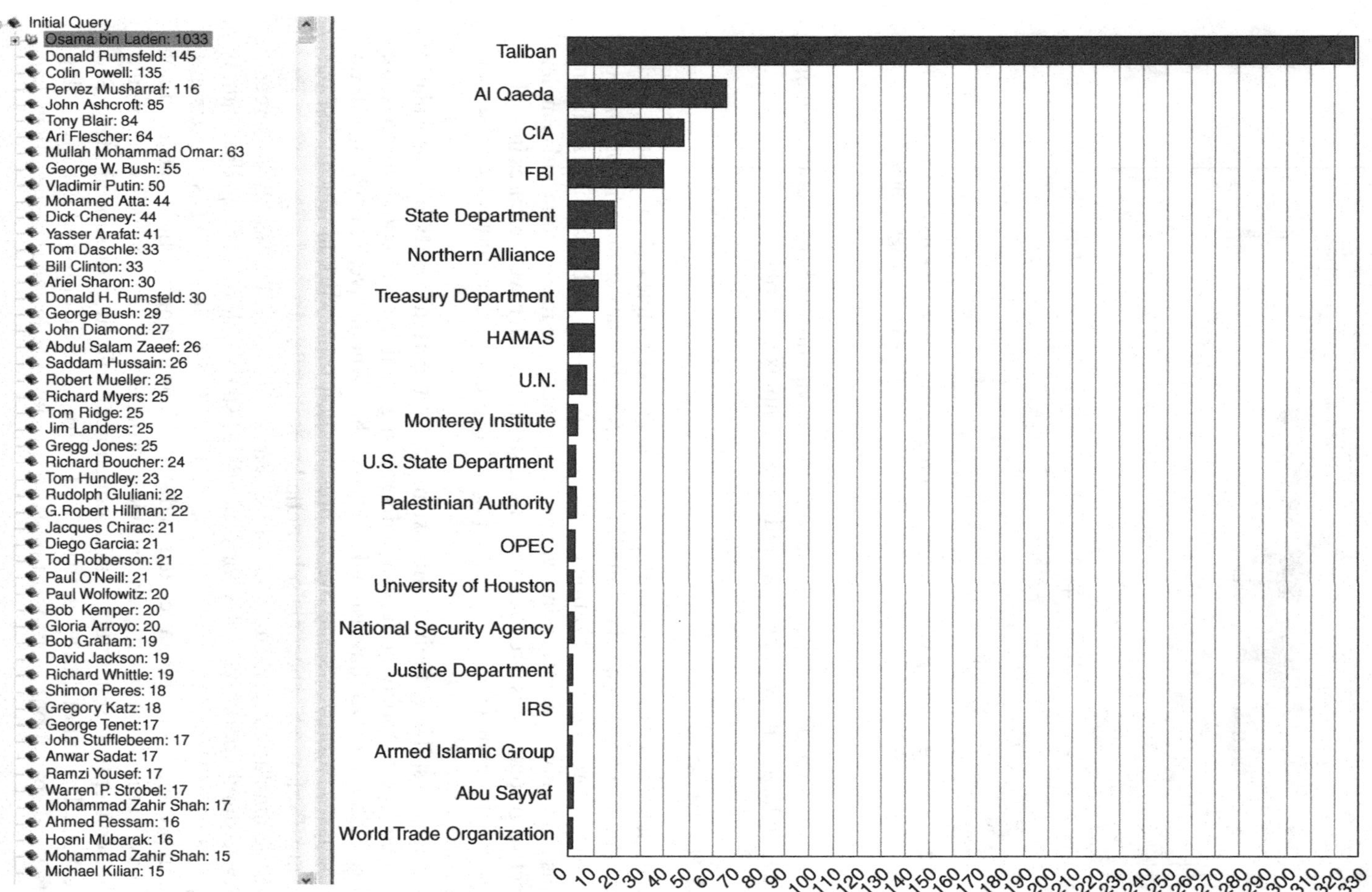

Figure X.12. GUI's left pane shows results of concept distribution query in list form and right pane with histogrammatic representation of this same distribution.

also be compared according to various measures and plotted in stacks. It is true, however, that histograms are more commonly employed to display distribution- and proportion-related results.

Users can thus very easily sort or traverse these lists of concepts (typically along with details pertaining to some measure of quality) while quickly scanning the bar charts for visual cues that suggest relative comparisons of distribution or proportion information, outliers, concepts closer to the average distribution, and so on.

Indeed, histograms now tend to be more interactive inasmuch as users are able to manipulate refinement constraints. The incorporation of pop-ups or separate windows allow filters to be adjusted by means of sliders, dials, buttons, or pull-down boxes to give users a more "real-time" feel for how constraint changes affect query results.

Radical fluctuations in the height of individual bars on a chart are visually much more immediately noticeable to a user than the changes in numerical values in long lists or table grids. Still, smaller differences between bars are harder to discern. Thus, histograms can sometimes be more useful for examining outliers and baseline values among charted items. They are less useful for helping a user visually distinguish between more minute differences in the relative values of individually graphed items.

X.3.4 Line Graphs

Like histograms, line graphs may not at first seem to be the most advanced of visualization approaches for text mining applications. However, these graphs have many advantages. Many academic and commercial text mining systems have at one time or other employed line graphs to support knowledge discovery operations.

Line graphs represent what might be described as "cheap and cheerful" visualization solutions for text mining. They are "cheap" because they combine the virtues of relatively low system overhead and development expense in that there are many widely available free or low-cost line graphing software libraries that can be leveraged to create specific competent presentation elements. They are "cheerful" because many of these mature, prebuilt libraries have been specifically developed to be embedded into a wide range of software applications. As a result, integration and customization of the libraries are often relatively straightforward.

These advantages make line graphs a good choice for developing uncomplicated graphs during the prototyping and early-release stages of text mining systems. The ease of implementing such graphs is helpful because it permits very quick feedback to system developers and users about the performance of text mining algorithms.

Beyond their use as prototyping tools, line graphs have been employed to provide visualizations for numerous tasks relating to a wide array of text mining operations. Two types of visualization approaches relying on line graphs are particularly common.

The first approach involves comparisons across a range of items. By using one axis of the graph to show some measure and the other to itemize elements for comparison, line graphs have been applied to three common analysis techniques:

- Comparisons of the results of different sets of queries,
- Comparisons of a set of common queries run against different document subsets, and

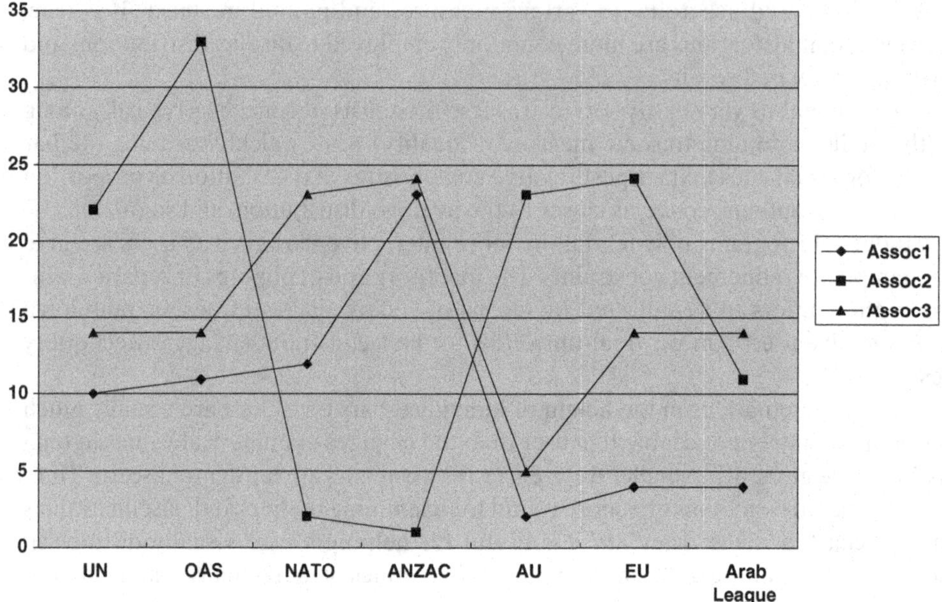

Figure X.13. Line graph showing number of associations for three sets of queries.

- Comparisons of the numbers of concepts that appear under different constraint or quality-measure conditions.

Figure X.13 illustrates the first of these three common techniques in which a line graph displays a comparison of the number of associations for two sets of queries. Note the use of the two axes and the plotting of two distinct lines with different symbols (squares and diamonds) identifying data points.

The second and arguably most prevalent current use of line graphs in text mining is that of graphs displaying trends or quantities over time. Line charts provide a very easily understood graphical treatment for periodicity-oriented analytics with the vertical axis showing quantity levels and the horizontal axis identifying time periods. See Figure X.14.

Line graphs can also be used in hybrids of these two approaches. Using multiline graphs, one can compare various types common to text mining tasks in the context of the time dimension. See example in Figure X.15.

Such applications of line graphs benefit from their concision, for a large amount of information can be displayed simultaneously with clarity. Line graphs, however, may not be the most appropriate visualization modality when a text mining analytical task calls for inviting more immediate interactivity from a user.

X.3.5 Circle Graphs

A circle graph is a visualization approach that can be used to accommodate a large amount of information in a two-dimensional format. It has been referred to as an "at-a-glance" visualization approach because no navigation is required to provide a complete and extremely concise visualization for potentially large volumes of data.

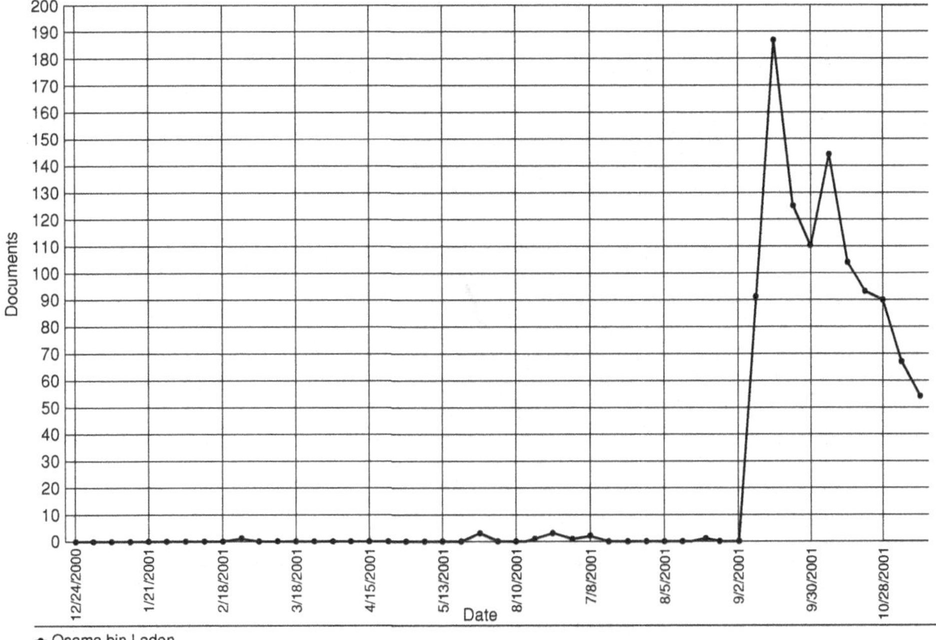

Figure X.14. Line graph showing number of documents containing the entity *Osama bin Laden* over time.

A circle graph is especially useful in visualizing patterns of association rules, though it is also very adaptable to displaying category information (Aumann, Feldman, et al. 1999). The format has been popularized by the widely used commercial data mining visualization tool *NetMap* (Duffet and Vernik 1997). Figure X.16 shows a basic circle graph.

Essentially, a circle graph is, as the name suggests, a circular graph around the circumference of which are mapped items. Relations between these items are represented by edges that connect the items across the interior area of the circle.

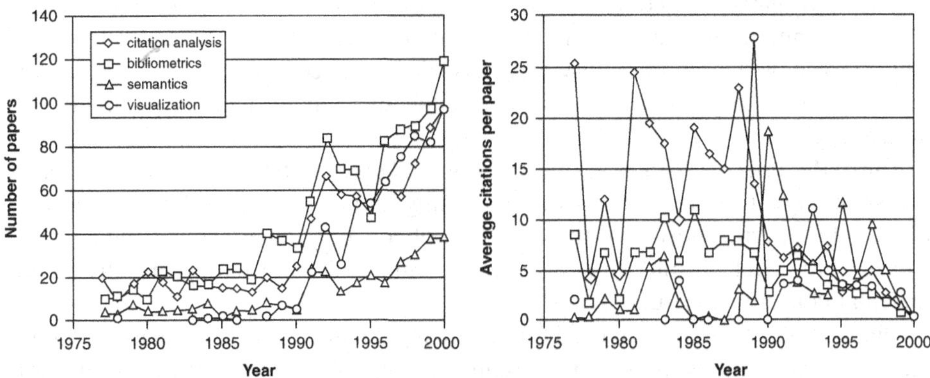

Figure X.15. Two examples of multiline graphs comparing trend lines of quantities over time. (From Borner et al. 2003. Reprinted with permission.)

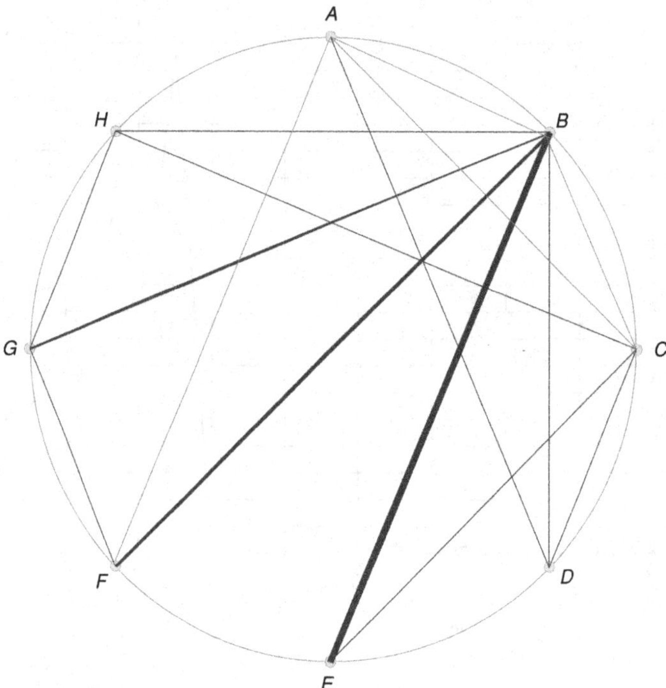

Figure X.16. Circle graph.

Style elements, such as the color and thickness of the connecting lines, can be used to correspond to particular types of information about the connection. In addition, color gradients in the connecting lines can be used to show the direction of a relationship.

Circle graphs excel at modeling association rules that appear in the answer sets to queries (see Figure X.17). It is common for individual concepts to appear as points around the rim of the circle in association-oriented circle graphs. And their association with another concept is demonstrated by a connecting edge.

Several additional visual enhancements are common in association-oriented circle graphs to enable users to have a richer graphic model of underlying textual data. First, it is common for connecting lines to use color gradients (e.g., going from yellow to blue) to show the directionality of an association. Second, a single distinct color (e.g., bright red) might also be used for a connecting line to denote a bidirectional association.

Third, the relative thickness of connecting edges may be used to suggest some corresponding information about values relating to the association. Finally, the size, color, and font type chosen for the depiction of concept names around the circumference of the circle graph can be used to communicate information visually about particular concepts in a query result set.

One method that has been used for enhancing the interactivity of an association-oriented circle graph is to make the graph's peripheral concept names and interior connecting lines "click-sensitive" jumping points to other information. A user could click or mouse-over a concept name and obtain additional ontological information

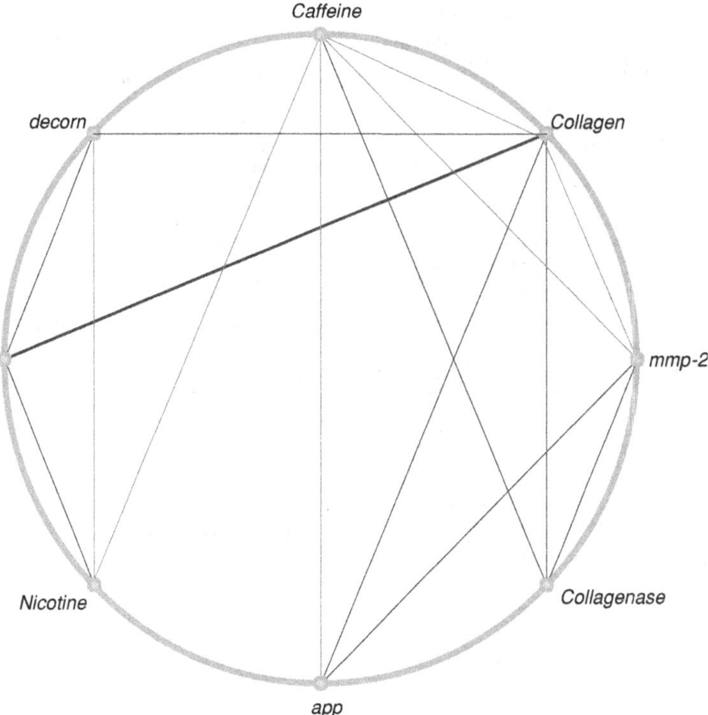

Figure X.17. Association-oriented circle graph.

relating to the concept, or, by clicking on a linking edge, a user could see the highlighted association's position in a list of associations ranked according to some quality measure.

Although circle graphs are particularly well-suited to modeling large volumes of association data, it is important to recognize that this visualization approach – like most others – can still have its effectiveness impaired by too many concepts or associations. Therefore, with circle graphs, it is often advisable to offer users easy access to controls over refinement constraints. This allows users to calibrate a circle graph's own visual feature dimensionality quickly to a level most suitable to a given search task and a particular user's subjective ability to process the visual information in the graph.

Category-Connecting Maps

Circle graphs often serve as the basis for *category-connecting maps*, another visualization tool useful in text mining. Beyond the basic taxonomical view afforded by a more traditional information retrieval-type category map, a category-connecting map builds on an association-oriented circle graph by including the additional dimension of category context for the concepts in the graph.

Category-connecting maps generally show associations between concepts in several categories – all within a particular context. For instance, Figure X.18 shows a category-connecting map with associations between individuals in the category *People* and entities in the category *Organization* – all within the context of *Terrorism*.

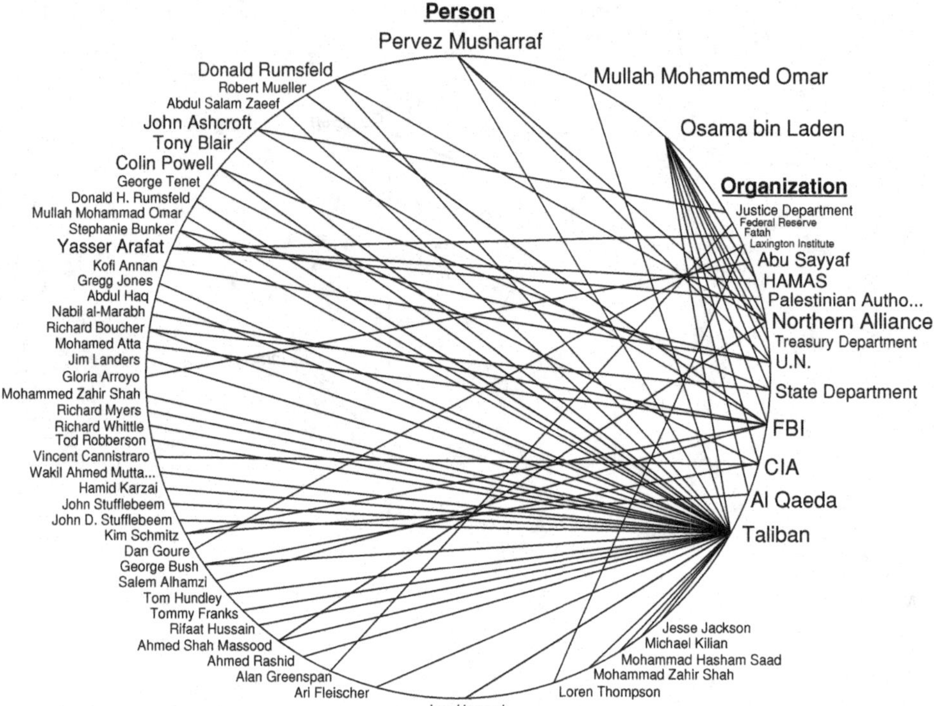

Figure X.18. Category-connecting map of associations in the context of person and organization.

In creating category-connecting maps, special attention is typically paid to the formatting of graphical and text elements on the periphery of the circle. In Figure X.18, concepts are plotted around the periphery of the circle in a way that concentrates concepts within each category together. Such concentration of concepts on the periphery of the circle can leverage preprocessed hierarchical ordering of concepts within broader "contexts" to speed rendering. However, context concepts and categories for category-connecting maps can also be generated on the fly by various algorithmic techniques ranging from the leveraging of association rules to more specialized approaches like those discussed in Chapter II relating to the generation of context graphs.

Concepts within a given category will typically have their concept labeling all formatted in the same color or font type to reinforce the visual layout technique of showing concepts within categories, and this color or font type will contrast with those used for other categories displayed in the graph. Finally, higher level category labels are often displayed to the center and outside of the "cluster" of their concepts (e.g., the category names *Person* and *Organization* are underlined and offset from the circle in Figure X.18).

Multiple Circle Graph and Combination Graph Approaches

Often, text mining applications that employ circle graphs have graphical interfaces supporting the generation and display of more than one complete circle graph at a time. One reason for this is that, because of a circle graph's strength in showing a large amount of data about a given query set at a glance, multiple circle graphs displayed together can have tremendous value in helping establish explicit or implicit comparisons between different query results.

This advantage might be leveraged in a text mining set through the plotting of two or more circle graphs on screen at the same time, each having different refinement constraint values. Another example of this approach is category-connecting maps run against the same document collection and same main category groupings but with different contexts. Each of these examples would allow a user to make side-by-side assessments of differences and similarities in the graphing patterns of multiple graphs. Figure X.19 illustrates the use of multiple circle graphs in a single visualization.

Another technique that relies on showing multiple circle graphs on screen at the same time results from trying to emphasize or isolate "subgraphs," or to do both, from within a circle graph. For instance, because circle graphs can be used to model so much data all at once, some more subtle relationships can become de-emphasized and obscured by the general clutter of the graph. By allowing a user to click on several items that are part of a main circle graph, a text mining system can offer subgraphs that display only the relationships between these items. Being able to see such subgraphs discretely while viewing the main circle graph as a whole can lead to new forms and levels of user interactivity.

Similarly, circle graphs can benefit from side-by-side comparisons with other graphs. For instance, instead of limiting a text mining system's graphing options to circle graphs and their subgraphs, one could also use simple concept association graphs to graph highlighted relationships shown within an association-oriented circle graph or concept-connecting map.

X.3.6 Self-Organizing Map (SOM) Approaches

Text mining visualization has benefited from contributions made by research into how artificial neural networks can aid information visualization. Perhaps one of the most important of these contributions is the paradigm of self-organizing maps, or SOMS, introduced by Kohonen in 1982 and first applied in 1991 to problems in information visualization in Lin, Soergel, and Marchionini (1991).

SOMs are generated by algorithms that, during a learning phase, attempt to iteratively adjust weighting vectors derived from the relationships found in a high-dimensional statistical data input file into various forms of two-dimensional output maps. Because of this approach, SOMs have advantages in treating and organizing data sets that are extremely large in volume and connecting relationships.

WEBSOM

One of the most widely known and used applications of SOMs to textual data is WEBSOM. WEBSOM uses an adapted version of Kohonen's original SOM algorithm to organize large amounts of data into visualizations that applications designers refer to as "document maps," which are essentially graphical models similar to topographical maps (see Figure X.20).

Shading on the map face displays concentrations of textual data around or near a particular keyword or concept; lighter areas show less concentration. Hence, the

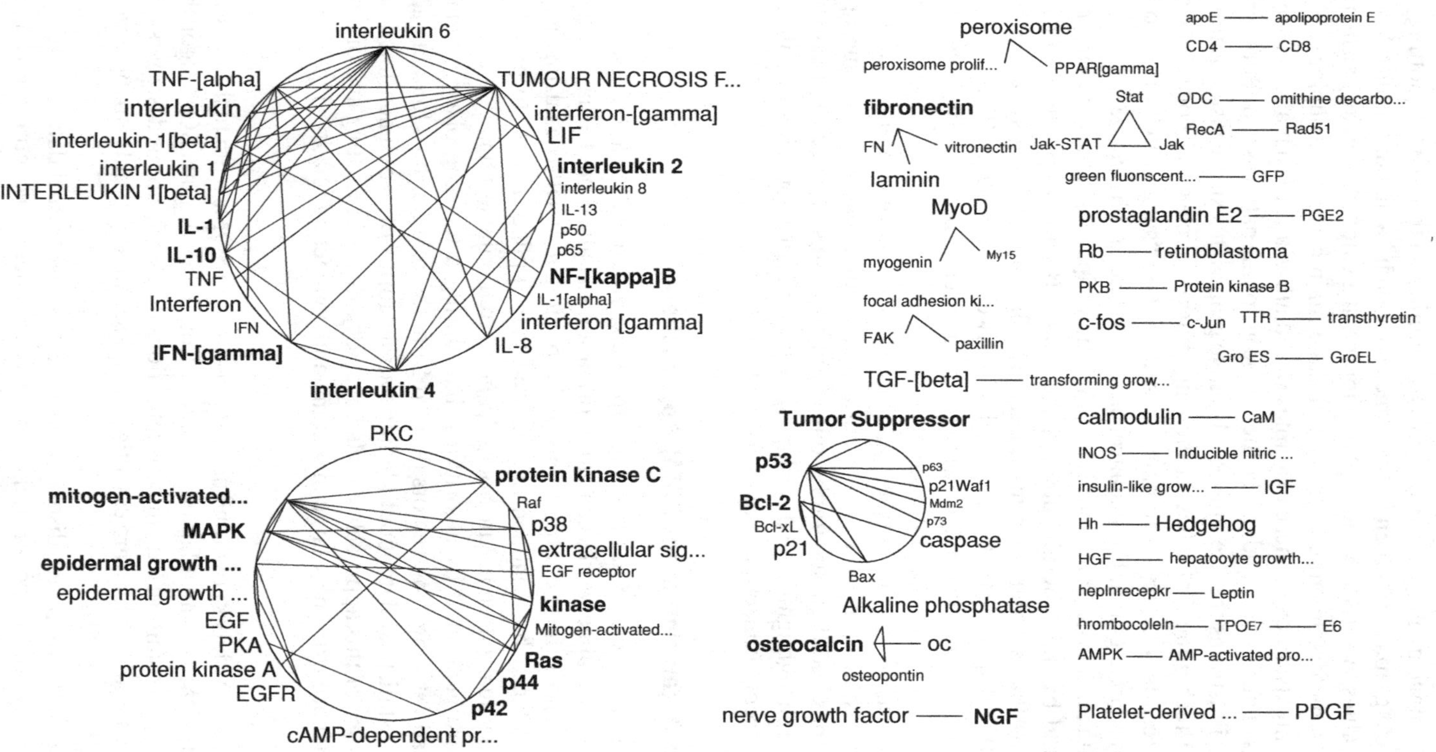

Figure X.19. Side-by-side circle graphs with subgraphs. (From Feldman, Regev, et al. 2003.)

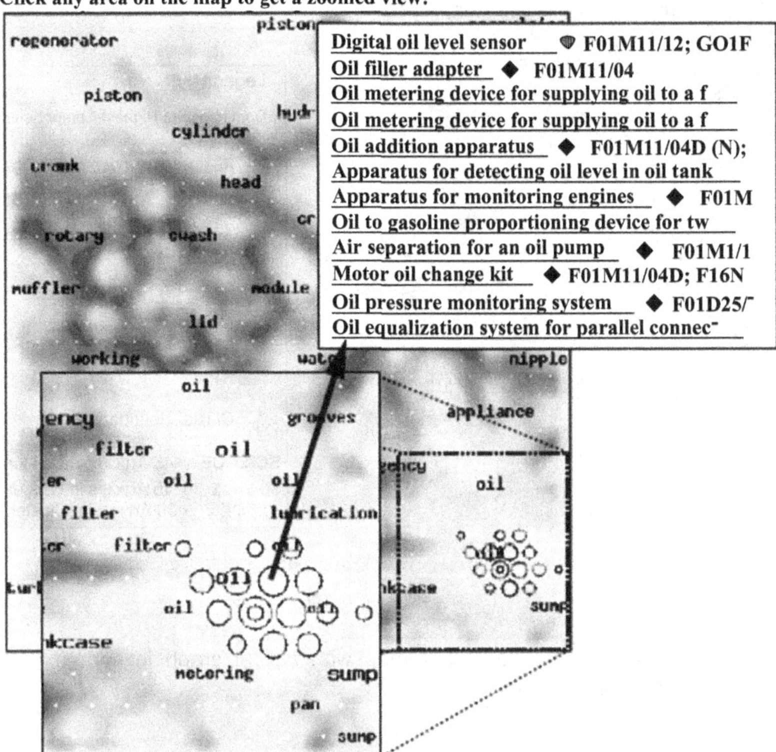

Figure X.20. WEBSOM – during queries, users are guided by a document map via visual cues in a GUI that supports both interactive zooming and browsing support functions. (From Lagus et al. 1999. Reprinted with permission of Springer Science and Business Media.)

graphical approach represented by WEBSOM is particularly suited to text mining analytics involving some element of reference to a category. However, the system has proven flexible enough to be applied to other tasks as well. Moreover, although WEBSOM may initially have been geared more toward solving problems in information retrieval for high-dimensionality document collections, academic attention has been devoted specifically to its uses as a toolkit for building text mining interfaces. A basic WEBSOM document map can be seen in Figure X.21.

One of the strongest advantages of WEBSOM – and similar SOM-based systems that it has inspired – has been a proven ability to handle large amounts of data. WEBSOM has built a document map to address more than one million documents, and its automatic algorithm for building document maps is reportedly able to complete a visualization for a small-to-modest document collection (approximately 10,000 documents) in less than a few hours.

Another advantage of WEBSOM is the robustness of the interface's functionality. WEBSOM is a fully zoomable interface that enables sections of a full document map to be repeatedly zoomed at various levels of magnification. The document map GUI is also very interactive in that clicking on a highlighted concept identifier or a section of the document map will bring up lists of corresponding documents, statistical information about the documents, or both typically in a pop-up or separate window.

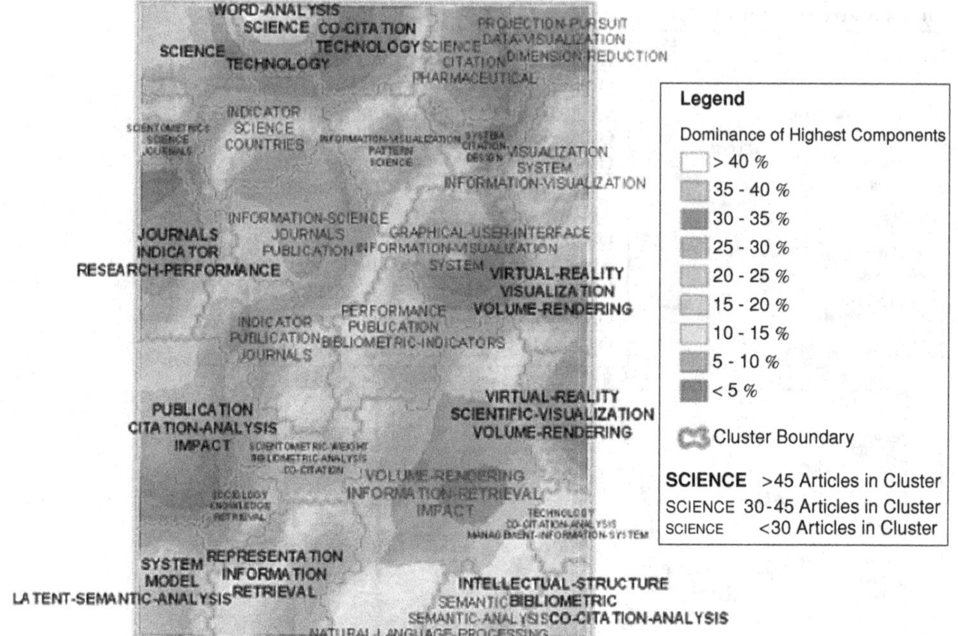

Figure X.21. WebSOM-like cartographic document map with typical graph legend. (From Borner et al. 2003. Reprinted with permission.)

SOM Algorithm

Honkela (1997) has summarized the SOM algorithm along the following lines:

- Assume an input dataset of concepts is configured as a table, with the intended output being the mapping of these data onto an array of nodes. The set of input data is described by a vector $X(t) \in R^n$, where t is the index of the input data. In terms of output, each node i in the map contains a model vector $m_i(t) \in R^n$; this model vector has the same number of elements as the input vector $X(t)$.
- The SOM algorithm is stochastic and performs a regression process. Therefore, the initial values of the elements of the model vector, $m_i(t)$, may be selected at random.
- Input data are mapped into a location in the output array, the $m_i(t)$ of which "matches" best with $x(t)$ in some metric. The SOM algorithm creates an ordered mapping by repeating the following tasks:
  - An input vector $x(t)$ is compared with all the model vectors $m_i(t)$; the best-matching element (node) on the map (i.e., the node where the model vector is most similar to the input vector according to some metric) is discerned. The best-matching node on the output map is sometimes referred to as the "winner."
  - The model vectors of the winner and a number of its neighboring nodes (sometimes called "neighbors") in the array are changed toward the input vector according to a customized learning process in which, for each data element input vector $x(t)$, the winner and its neighbors are changed closer to $x(t)$ in the input data space. During the learning process, individual changes may

actually be contradictory, but the overall outcome in the process results in having ordered values for $m_i(t)$ gradually appear across the array.

- Adaptation of the model vectors in the learning process takes place according to the following equations:

$$m_i(t+1) = m_i(t) + \alpha(t)[(t) - m_i(t)] \text{ for each } i \in N_c(t);$$
$$\text{otherwise, } m_i(t+1) = m_i(t),$$

where t is the discrete-time index of the variables, the factor $\alpha(t) \in [0, 1]$ is a scalar that defines the relative size of the learning step, and $N_c(t)$ describes the neighborhood around the winner node in the map array. Typically, at the beginning of the learning process, the radius of the neighborhood can be quite large, but it is made to consolidate during learning.

One suggested method for examining the quality of the output map that results from the running the SOM algorithm is to calculate the average quantization error over the input data, which is defined as $E\{\|X - m_c(X)\|\}$, where c indicates the best-matching unit (sometimes referred to as the BMU) for x. After training, for each input sample vector, the BMU in the map is searched for, and the average of the individual quantization errors is returned.

Several deficiencies, however, have been identified in WEBSOM's approach. Some have pointed out that WEBSOM's algorithm lacks both a cost function and any sophisticated neighborhood parameters to ensure consistent ordering. From a practical standpoint some have commented that a user can get "lost" in the interface and its many zoomable layers. In addition, the generalized metaphor of the topographical map is not a precise enough aid in displaying patterns to support all text mining pattern-identification functions.

X.3.7 Hyperbolic Trees

Initially developed at the Xerox Palo Alto Research Center (PARC), *hyperbolic trees* were among the first *focus and context* approaches introduced to facilitate visualization of large amounts of data. Relying on a creative interpretation of Poincaré's model of the hyperbolic non-Euclidean plane, the approach gives more display area to a part of a hierarchy (the focus area) while still situating it within the entire – though visually somewhat de-emphasized – context of the hierarchy. A widely known commercial toolkit for building hyperbolic tree visualization interfaces is marketed by Inxight Software under the name *StarTree Studio* (see Figure X.22).

Hyperbolic tree visualizations excel at analysis tasks in which it is useful for an analyst to see both detail and context at the same time. This is especially true in situations in which an analyst needs to traverse very complex hierarchically arranged data or hierarchies that have very large amounts of nodes.

Other more common methods for navigating a large hierarchy of information include viewing one page or "screen" of data at a time, zooming, or panning. However all of these methods can be disorienting and even distracting during intensive visual data analysis. A hyperbolic tree visualization allows an analyst always to keep perspective on the many attached relationships of a highlighted feature.

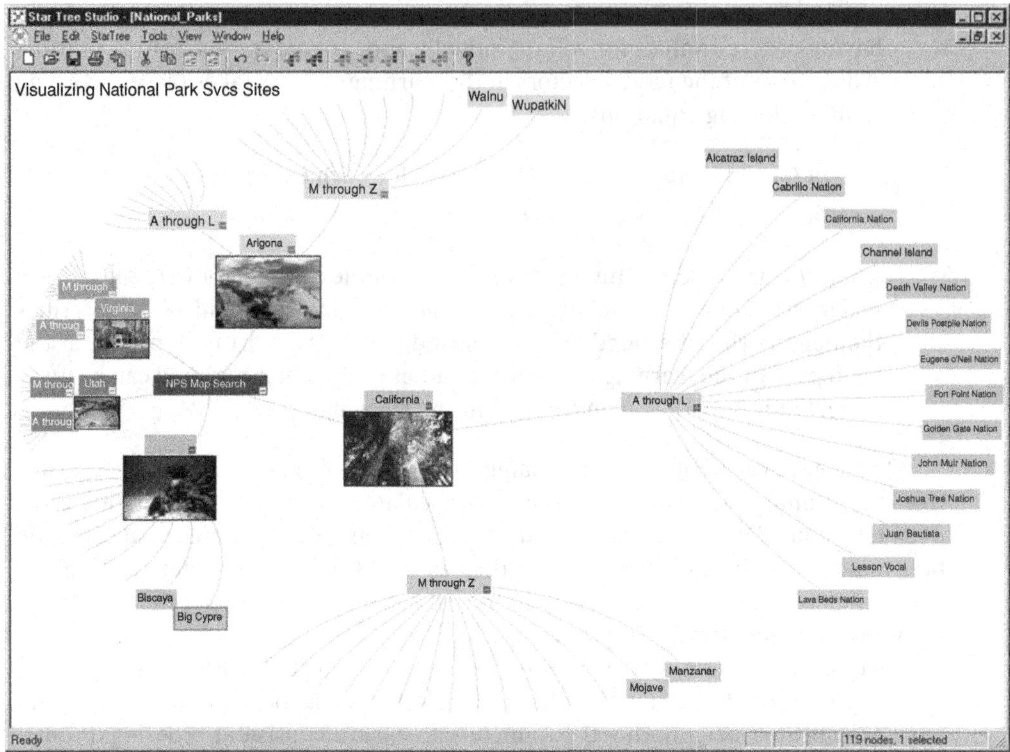

Figure X.22. Hyperbolic tree for visualizing National Park Service sites. (From Inxight StarTree Studio. Copyright Inxight Software.)

Hyperbolic tree visualization tools have from their inception been designed to be highly dynamic aids for textual data exploration. Initially, a hyperbolic tree diagram displays a tree with its root at the center of a circular space. The diagram can be smoothly manipulated to bring other nodes into focus. The main properties that support the capabilities of the hyperbolic tree are that

- elements of the diagram diminish in size as they move outward, and
- there is an exponential growth in the number of potential components.

Effectively, these two properties might be described as a form of fisheye distortion and the ability to uniformly embed an exponentially growing structure. Together, they allow the hyperbolic tree visualization tool to leverage Poincaré mapping of the non-Euclidean plane to explore very large hierarchies in a visualization frame relatively limited in size.

The hyperbolic tree's peculiar functionality does more than simply allow a user to interact with a larger number of hierarchical nodes than other more traditional methods or to view a highlighted feature with reference to a richer amount of its context. It also very much encourages hands-on interaction from a user with a hierarchical dataset. Figure X.23 shows another example of a hyperbolic tree.

By enabling a user to stretch and pull a complex hierarchy around a focused-on item with a mouse and then skip to another node with a mouse click and view the rest of its hierarchy context at various angles, a hyperbolic tree diagram promotes dynamic, visualization-based browsing of underlying data. Instead of being

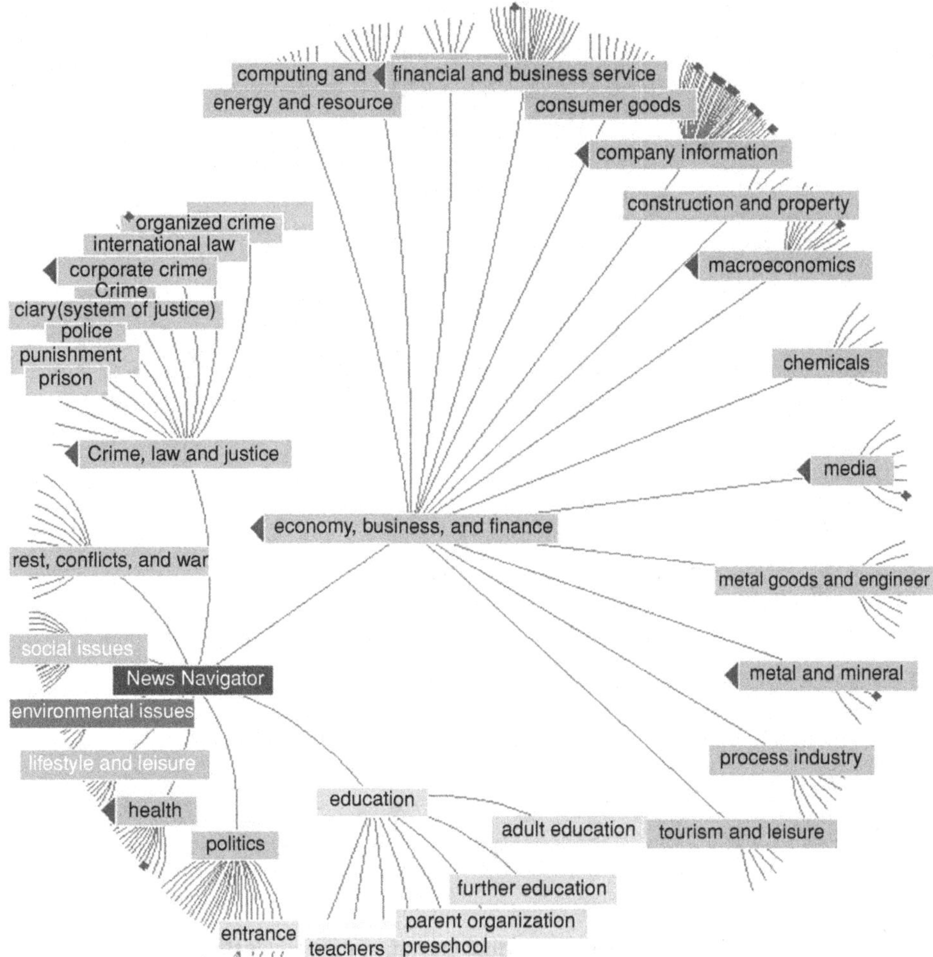

Figure X.23. Hyperbolic tree visualization of a document collection composed of news articles. (Courtesy of Inxight Software.)

semipassive viewers and inputters of query data, users become fully engaged participants in pattern exploration.

X.3.8 Three-Dimensional (3-D) Effects

Many text mining systems have attempted to leverage three-dimensional (3-D) effects in creating more effective or flexible visualization models of the complex relationships that exist within the textual data of a document collection. 3-D visualizations offer the hope that, by increasing the apparent spatial dimensionality available for creating graphic models of representations such as those produced by more complex, second-generation, multiple-lattice SOMs, users may be able to examine and interact with models that make fewer compromises than are required by traditional (2-D) hierarchical or node-and-edge representations.

Moreover, higher powered 3-D rendering algorithms and wider availability of sophisticated workstation graphics cards create the conditions for making such 3-D visualizations more practical for use in text mining systems than ever before. In

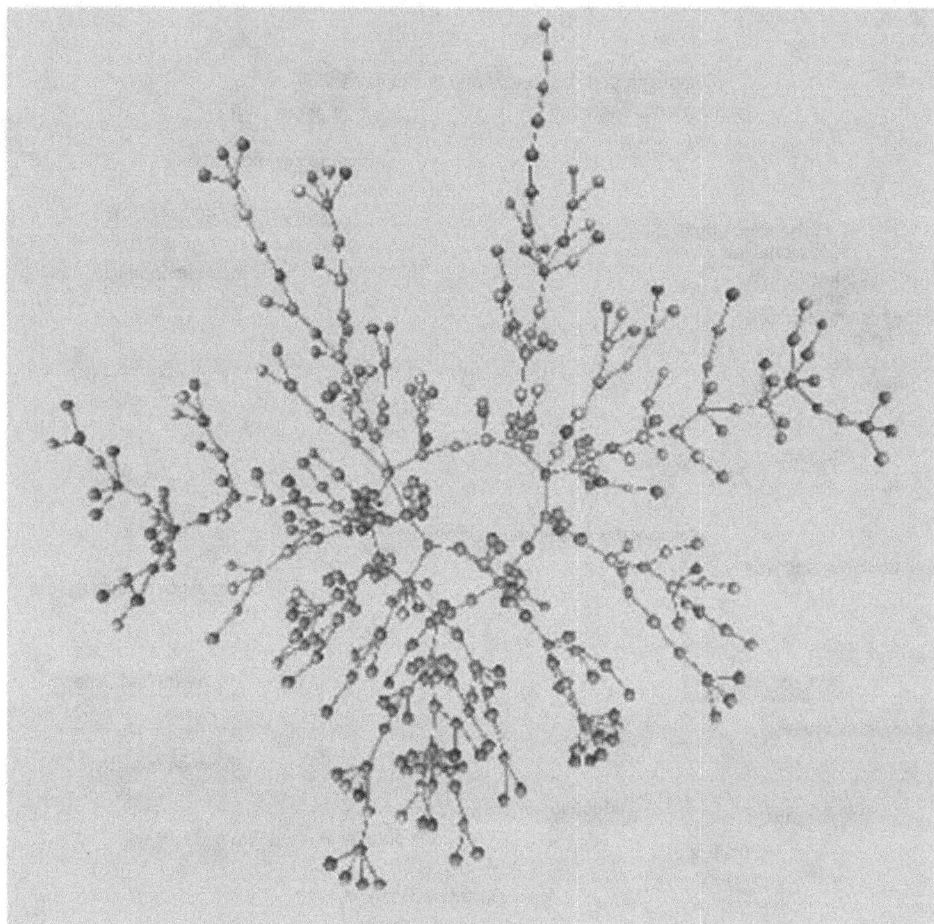

Figure X.24. A 3-D overview of a scientific author cocitation map suggesting a diverse, unconcentrated domain. (From Borner et al. 2003.)

addition, to supplement navigation in a non-2-D environment, many relatively lightweight VR rendering and exploration environments are available now that can easily be embedded into front-end interfaces. An example of a 3-D network map can be seen in Figure X.24.

Despite all of the potential opportunities offered by 3-D treatments of models for information visualization, these models also introduce several new challenges and problems. Two significant problems for using 3-D visualization approaches in text mining are occlusion and effective depth cueing (see example in Figure X.25). Both of these problems are exacerbated in situations in which presentation of high-dimensional data is required. Unfortunately, such situations are precisely those in which text mining applications will be likely to incorporate 3-D visualization tools.

Moreover, 3-D visualizations do not generally simplify the process of navigating and exploring textual data presentations. Often, some level of specialized navigational operations must be learned by the user of a 3-D projection or VR-based visualization. This can become something of a barrier to inspiring intuitional

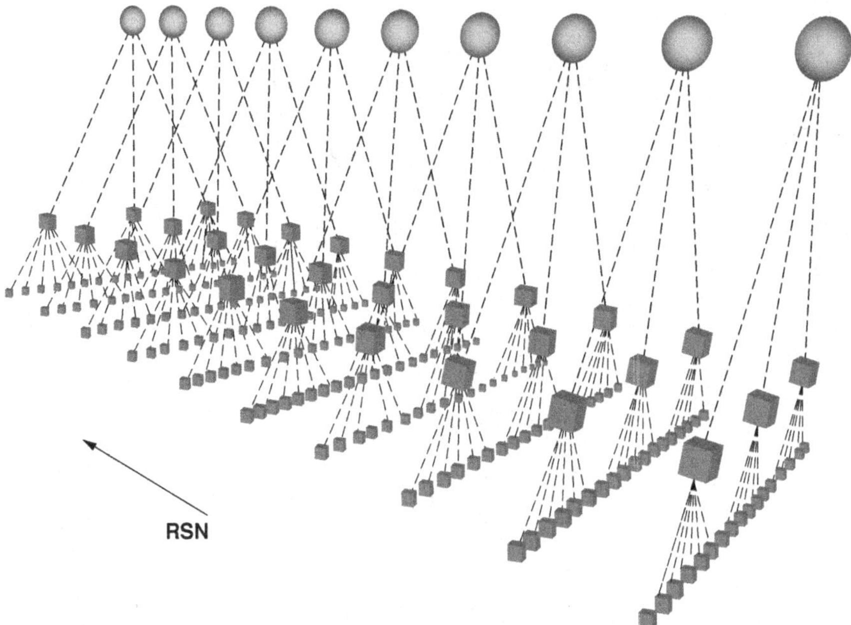

Figure X.25. Presentation from a visualization suggested by Gall et al. (1999). Visualization represents hierarchies over time. However, challenges of element occlusion occur at lower levels of the various hierarchies. Such a presentation may also not be understood intuitively by users. (From Graham 2001. Reprinted with permission, © 2001 IEEE.)

navigation of a data presentation. Increased complexity in navigation is generally inversely proportional to stimulating high levels of iterative user interaction.

There is no doubt that the verdict will be out for some time on the impact of 3-D treatments on text mining visualization. Certainly, there will be a great deal of continued research and experimentation in an effort to make 3-D approaches more practically useful. Currently, the disadvantages of 3-D approaches outweigh the proposed advantages; 3-D visualization may never be very useful in comprehending nonspatial information like that encountered in text mining.

In the short term, designers of text mining systems should carefully evaluate the practical benefits and drawbacks inherent in the potential inclusion of a 3-D visualization tool in their applications before being carried away by the theoretical advantages of such new graphical tools.

X.3.9 Hybrid Tools

In the discussion of circle graphs in Section X.3.5, it was noted that sometimes combinations of identical multiple graphs or different types of multiple graphs have a special role in providing analytical information about the results from a text mining query's answer set. Designers of visualization tools often come up with presentation techniques that might be seen as hybrid forms incorporating components of different visualization formats into a coherent, new form. Three creative examples of hybrid visualization approaches can be seen in Figures X.26, X.27, and X.28.

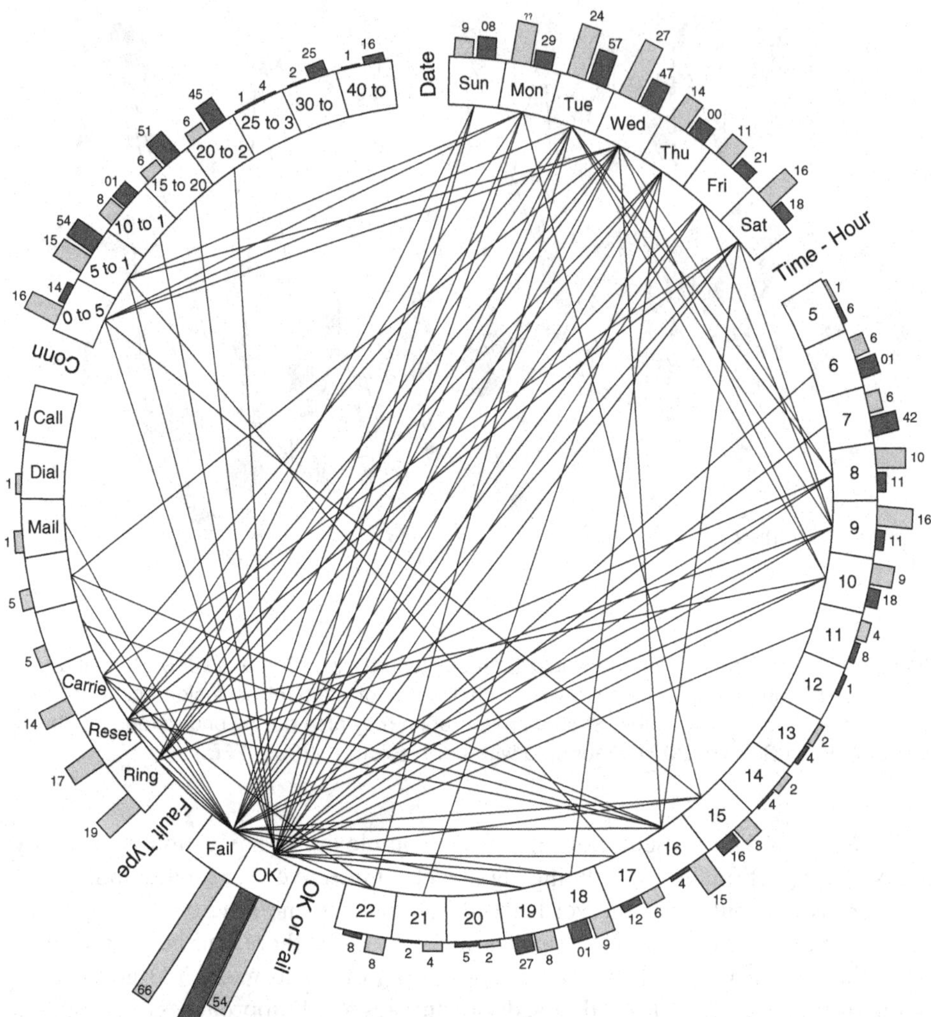

Figure X.26. Daisy chart combining aspects of a circle graph and complex comparative histogram. (Reprinted with permission from James Miller.)

One critical driver for the innovation of such forms is the desire to achieve more presentation concision. By supplementing currently well-known graphical formats with additional new elements, one might at least theoretically be able to increase dramatically the amount of information communicated by the graphical tool.

One of the possible pitfalls in creating such hybrid forms is overcomplication; ideally, users should be able to understand the major "messages" communicated by a presentation approach without too much potential for confusion. Another potential pitfall is decreased visual clarity of a graph; because text mining visualizations so often involve overabundance in patterns, more complex visualizations can also result in greater presentation "clutter" issues.

Because most designers of text mining systems actually implement visualization approaches initially developed by information visualization specialists, these considerations should be weighed when evaluating the possible graphical tool alternatives

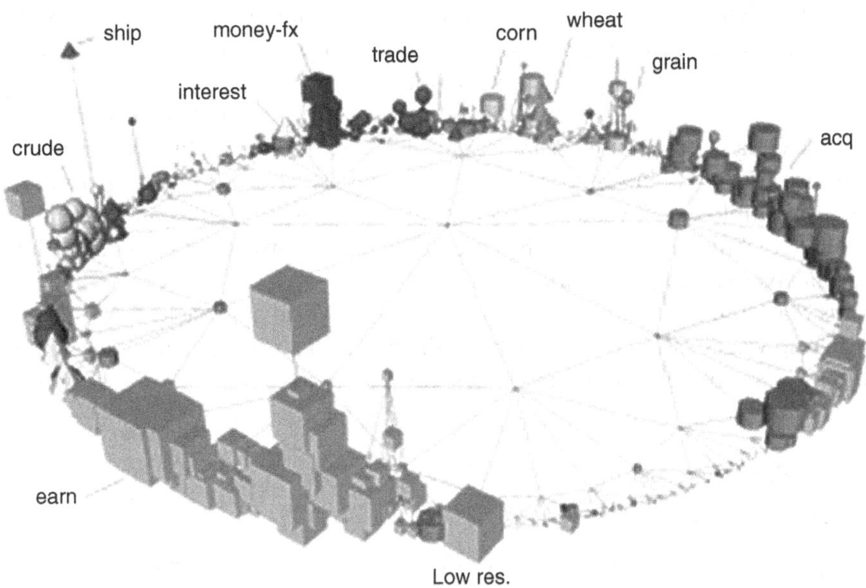

Figure X.27. View of an HSOM or hyperbolic self-organizaing map that projects 3-D elements on a triangularly tesselated hyperbolic tree grid. (From Ontrup and Ritter 2001a. Reprinted with permission of The MIT Press.)

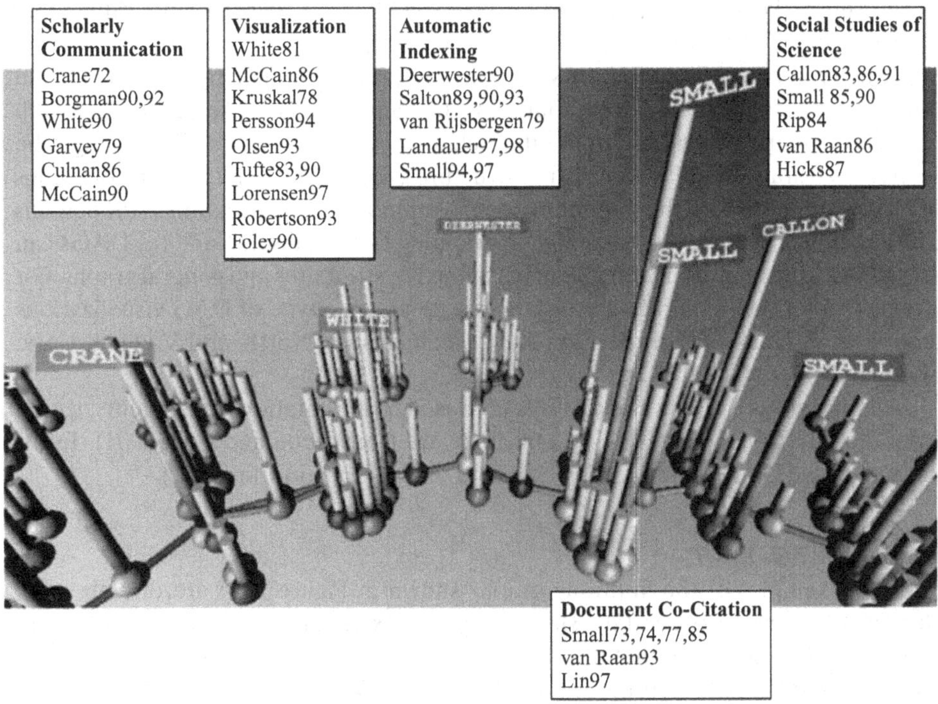

Figure X.28. Specialized network diagram that includes elements of nodes and links graphs and histogrammatic presentation with 3-D effects and character-based tables. From the Arist Co-Citation Project. (From Borner et al. 2003. Reprinted with permission.)

for a given text mining application. Designers of text mining systems need to be able to consider several commercial or freeware visualization alternatives from the perspective of their text mining system's intended functionality.

Above all, these system designers need to be careful to avoid the temptation of having "a visualization solution in search of a text mining problem." Creating the conditions for maximum interaction from a user depends on ensuring a more seamless, compatible fit between a visualization approach's strengths and the algorithmic search techniques that form the core of the text mining situation a particular presentation layer is meant to support.

For this reason, it sometimes does pay to look for hybrid approaches. A special-purpose hybrid visualization form may meet the needs of a very specific text mining application in ways better than more generic forms.

X.3.10 Citations and Notes

Sections X.3.1–X.3.3

The Document Explorer application is described in Feldman, Kloesgen, and Zilberstein (1997a) and Feldman, Fresko, Hirsh, et al. (1998) and summarized in Section VI.5.1.

Discussions of relevant hierarchical visualization approaches can be found in Karrer and Scacchi (1990); Johnson and Shneiderman (1991); Robertson, Mackinlay, and Card (1991); and Hearst and Karadi (1997). *Simple concept graphs* are an updating of the simple keyword graphs introduced in Feldman, Kloesgen, and Zilberstein (1997a).

A good general discussion of some of the considerations employing DAGs in information visualization can be found in Melancon and Herman (2000), in which the authors make several useful points, including the following: (a) DAGs might be seen as a natural generalization of tree structures, (b) aesthetically pleasing drawings of DAGs are those with the minimum possible number of edge crossings (though this can sometimes be difficult to manage in graphing large datasets), and (c) DAGs can serve as a a kind of intermediary form between tree structures and general graphs. For a review of a DAG-generating program that creates the type of DAG visualizations described and illustrated in Section X.3.2, see Gansner, North, and Vo (1988). See also Gansner et al. (1993).

All references to Zhou and Cui's DAG-based representations of elements of data from the GO Consortium's Gene Ontology are from Zhou and Cui (2004). Information on the Gene Ontology can be found in GO Consortium (2001).

Sections X.3.4–X.3.7

The two examples of the multiline graphs shown in Figure X.15 are directly from Borner, Chen, and Boyack (2003). At least one examination of 2-D histograms in text mining has suggested that they are not especially useful at displaying some basic types of query results relating to association rules (Wong et al. 2000).

Aumann et al. (1999) provides an early treatment of circle graphs in text-oriented knowledge discovery. Rainsford and Roddick (2000) underscores the comprehensive "at-a-glance" property that circle graphs have in concisely showing an entire representation of relationships in large amounts of data. The NetMap circle graph information visualization tool is described in Duffet and Vernik (1997). Information about commercial Netmap products is available at <www.netmap.com>.

Important background reference materials on SOMs include Kohonen (1981), Kohonen (1982), Lin et al. (1991), Lin (1992), Kohonen (1995), Kohonen (1997), Lin (1997), Kohonen (1998), and Lagus (2000b). Background reference materials on WEBSOM include Honkela et al. (1997); Honkela, Lagus, and Kaski (1998); Lagus (1998); and Lagus et al. (1999). The SOM algorithm described in Section VI.3.6. has been summarized from Honkela (1997).

Beyond WEBSOM, many systems and computer science research projects have incorporated SOM-style visualizations. Some representatives of the wide influence of SOM-style interfaces can be seen in Merkl (1998), Borner et al. (2003), and Yang, Chen, and Hong (2003).

Hyperbolic trees are introduced and discussed in Lamping and Rao (1994); Lamping, Rao, and Pirolli (1995); and Munzner and Burchard (1995). StarTree Studio is a product of Inxight Software; additional product information can be found at <www.inxight.com>. All images from StarTree Studio are the property of Inxight Software. The hyperbolic tree representation of the Internet comes from Munzner and Burchard (1995). Another interactive "focus + context" approach, the Table Lens, is discussed in Rao and Card (1994).

Section X.3.8–X.3.9

Borner et al. (2003) provides a brief but practical review of some 3-D approaches used in visualizing knowledge domains that would also be applicable to text mining activities Koike (1993) is another useful source. The effects of such things as potential drawbacks as occlusion and effective depth cueing in 3-D visualizations are discussed in Rokita (1996) and Hubona, Shirah, and Fout (1997).

The visualization in Figure X.25 appears as a reference in Graham (2001) that originally appeared in Gall et al. (1999). Graham (2001) points out that there is growing consensus that 3-D visualizations are not that useful in comprehending non-spatial information, whereas Cockburn (2004) seems to suggest the opposite view.

The Daisy Chart displayed in Figure X.26 is a visualization copyrighted by James Miller of Daisy Analysis (<www.daisy.co.uk>). The daisy chart also appears in Westphal and Bergeron (1998).

Figure X.27 illustrates one application of the hyperbolic self-organizing map or HSOM. The HSOM is discussed in Ontrup and Ritter (2001a, 2000b).

The hybrid 3-D network diagram illustrated in Figure X.28 comes from Borner et al. (2003).

X.4 VISUALIZATION TECHNIQUES IN LINK ANALYSIS

Although the discipline of link analysis encompasses many activities, several specific tasks are frequently addressed by a few specialized visualization approaches. In particular, these tasks include

- analysis of a single known concept for the relatedness to, or degrees of separation from, other concepts, and
- the identification and exploration of networks or pathways that link two (or more) concepts.

Although various generic text mining activities generally involve, as a primary exploratory approach, the investigation of query result sets in a browser supplemented by visualization techniques, current, state-of-the-art link analysis methods almost always depend on the visualization approach as a central operation. The exploration of pathways and patterns of connectedness is substantially enhanced by visualizations that allow tracking of complex concept relationships within large networks of concepts.

Chapter XI focuses on essential link analysis concepts such as paths, cycles, and types of centrality and also offers a detailed, running example involving the construction of a model of a social network appropriate to link analysis activities in the form of a spring graph. Although spring graphs are certainly one of the more common graphing forms used in link analysis, many visualization techniques have been applied in this quickly evolving discipline. This section surveys some visualization approaches that have been adapted to support link analysis.

X.4.1 Practical Approaches Using Generic Visualization Tools

Developers of graphical interfaces to aid in link detection and analysis often slightly modify more generic visualization formats to orient these graphic approaches more toward link detection activities. In particular, simple concept graphs, circle graphs, and hyperbolic trees have been applied to and, in some cases, modified for the support of link detection tasks. Even histograms and line graphs have been put into service for link analytics.

For example, a common simple concept association graph could be used to show *persons* associated with *organizations* within the context of some other concept. Such a graph could be oriented toward link detection activities by centering the graph on a single known person and allowing the outwardly radiating edges and vertices to constitute a relationship map.

In a sense, this type of manipulation of the simple concept association graph creates at least an informal *focus* for the graph. Ease of following the relationships in the map can be enhanced by stylistic devices: person nodes and labels and concept nodes and labels could be drawn in contrasting colors, edge thickness could be determined by the number of documents in which an association between two linked concepts occurs, and so on.

Figure X.29 shows the results of a query for all *person* concepts with associations to *organization* concepts within the context of the concept *terrorism* within a given document collection. After a simple concept association graph was generated from the results of the query, a single person concept, Osama bin Laden, was highlighted and drawn to form a central "hub" for the diagram. All person concepts were identified in a darker typeface, whereas all organization concepts were denoted by a lighter typeface.

An analyst can traverse relationships (associations) emanating from Osama bin Laden in a quick and orderly fashion. The methodology also has the advantages of being relatively quick to implement and, often, requiring only some customization of the more standard visualization approaches found bundled with most text mining-type applications.

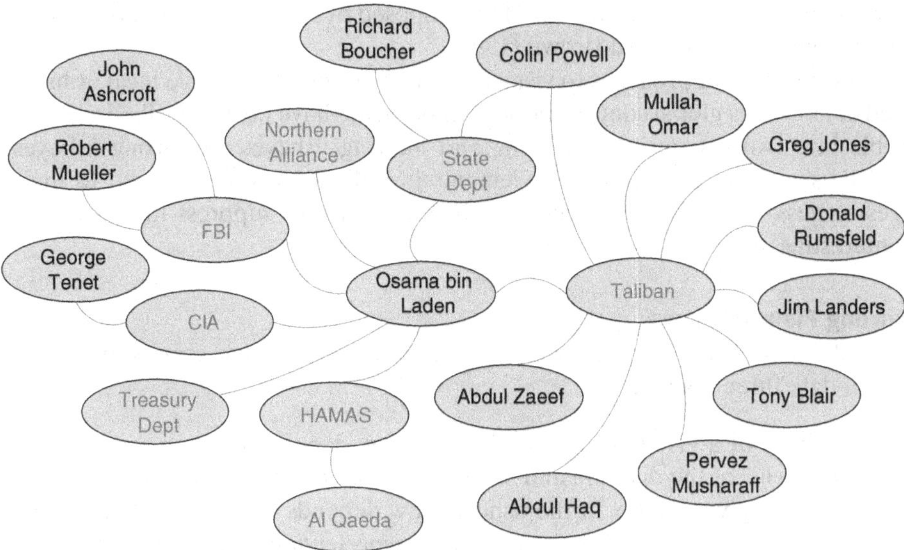

Figure X.29. Graphing results to a search query for all *Person* concepts with associations to organization concepts within the context of the concept terrorism with the concept *Osama bin Laden* as central vertex.

Of course, there are some notable limitations to this approach. First, there are a rather limited number of nodes radiating out from a central "hub" node that a user can take in at any one time. This limitation can be offset somewhat by zooming and panning capabilities.

Second, there is no sophisticated or automatic weighting methodology for emphasizing stronger or more interesting associations by some sort of visual proximity cue within a confined and manageable visualization space. This is a particularly limiting factor in the case of very large node-and-edge graphs. Certainly, one can easily increase line density between nodes or prune nodes from the graph altogether based on some quality measures.

In graphs in which very large numbers of nodes and associations are present, there is significant risk that these two limitations will prevent the user from maintaining his or her focus on the central node (because of the need to pan, page down, or zoom to a very large graph) and receiving much information about the comparative relatedness of nodes to the central focus node by means of strong spatial or proximic visual cues. Other types of specialized visualization formats do relatively better jobs in addressing these limitations.

X.4.2 "Fisheye" Diagrams

Fisheye diagrams show a distorted, lenslike view of a graph to highlight ostended "focal point" detail while maintaining relatively easy viewing of its broader, more global visual context. The term "fisheye" derives from the diagram's analogy to the super-wide-angle or fisheye lens used in photography (fisheye lenses magnify the image at the focal point while de-emphasizing, but still showing, images at the periphery). Fisheye views of data were first proposed by Furnas in 1981 and substantially enhanced by Sarkar and Brown (1992).

The best fisheye approaches to visualizing data attempt to balance local or highlighted detail with a global context. Fisheye approaches have been described as being divisible into two categories: distorting and filtering fisheyes. Distorting fisheyes adjust the size of various graphical elements in a diagram to correspond to their interestingness, whereas filtering fisheyes de-emphasize or suppress the display of less interesting data.

Distorting Fisheye Views

Fisheye diagrams have vertices and edges, like node-and-edge graphs, but must accommodate three main ideas:

- The position of a given vertex in a fisheye view depends on its *position in the "normal view"* of the diagram and *its distance from the fisheye view's focus.*
- The size of a given vertex in the fisheye view depends on its *distance from the focus*, its *size in the normal view*, and *a value representing the relative importance of this vertex in the global structure.*
- The amount of detail in a vertex depends on its size in the fisheye view.

Sarkar and Brown (1992) formalized these concepts in the following way:

1. The position of vertex v in the fisheye view is a function of its position in normal coordinates and the position of focus f:

   $$P_{\text{feye}}(v, f) = F_1(P_{\text{norm}}(v), P_{\text{norm}}(f)).$$

2. The size of the vertex in the fisheye view is a function of its size and position in normal coordinates, the position of the focus, and its *a priori importance*, or *API*, which is a measure of the relative importance of the vertex in the global structure:

   $$S_{\text{feye}}(v, f) = F_2(S_{\text{norm}}(v), P_{\text{norm}}(v), P_{\text{norm}}(f), API(v)).$$

3. The amount of detail to be shown for a vertex depends on the size of a vertex in the fisheye view and the maximum detail that can be displayed:

   $$DTL_{\text{feye}}(v, f) = F_3(S_{\text{feye}}(v), DTL_{\text{max}}(v)).$$

4. The visual worth of a vertex depends on the distance between the vertex and the focus in normal coordinates and on the vertex's API:

   $$VW(v, f) = F_4(P_{norm}(v), P_{norm}(f), API(v)).$$

Fisheye diagrams represent a good fit with the visualization requirements of many link analysis tasks. By applying a fisheye treatment to vertices of a graph that are interesting to a user, he or she can scan, without visual interruption or panning, among many contextual relationships, as shown in the diagrammatic elements presented in the periphery of the graph. Figure X.30 shows some fisheye treatments of a SOM.

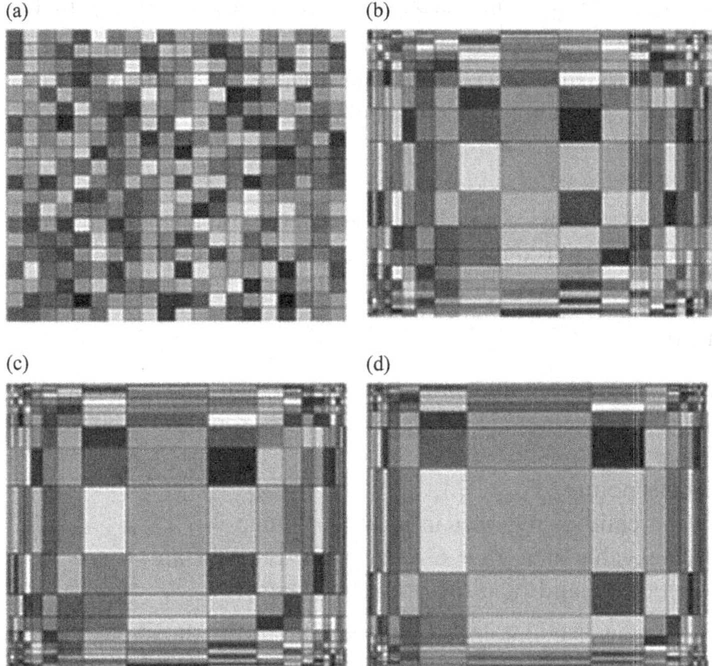

Figure X.30. Fisheye treatments of a SOM mapped onto a 20 × 20 grid with various distortion values; this type of display is commonly used in maps of concepts within categories. (From Yang, Chen, and Hong 2003. Reprinted with permission from Elsevier.)

Filtering Fisheye Views

Filtering fisheye approaches, such as *fractal approaches*, focus on the control of information in the creation of display layouts. Such approaches attempt, through approximation, to create simpler abstractions of complex structures by filtering the amount of information displayed in a way corresponding to some system- or user-defined threshold. Examples of filtering view approaches are found in Figure X.31.

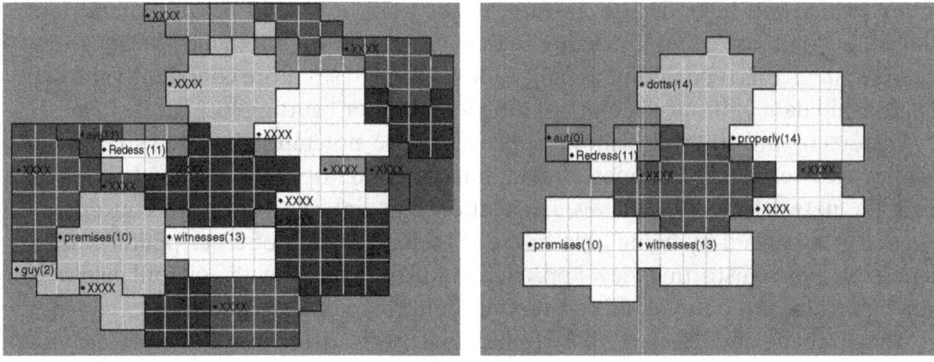

Figure X.31. Filtering view approaches (fractal view) applied to the same category map at different threshold settings. (From Yang, Chen, and Hong 2003. Reprinted with permission from Elsevier.)

Yang, Chen, and Hong (2003) has summarized an approach to creating a fractal view of a category map:

- The fractal dimension of a structure D is the similarity dimension of a structure, which is controlled by a scale factor and a branching factor,

  $$D = -\log_{r_x} N_x,$$

  where r_x represents the scale factor and N_x represents the branching factor.
- Solving the fractal requirement requires that the relation between the number of branches and the scale factor at each node of the structure shown below exist:

  $$\log_{r_x} N_x = \text{constant}.$$

- Formalizing the fractal views entails taking the focus point into account and regarding it as root. Fractal values are propagated to other nodes based on the following formulation:
  - Fractal value of focus point $= F_{\text{focus}} = 1$.
  - Fractal values of the child of region x in a category map $= F_{\text{child of } x} = r_x F_x$, where F_x is the fractal value of x, $r_x = C \times N_x^{-1/D}$, C is a constant, $0 \leq C \leq 1$, D is the fractal dimension, and N_x is the branching factor.

Control in this type of view is maintained by the setting of the threshold values. Regions of the category map with fractal values below the threshold disappear or become diminished.

Applications to Link Detection and General Effectiveness of Fisheye Approaches

Both distorting and filtering fisheye approaches are particularly useful to link detection operations aimed at performing degree-of-relatedness or degree-of-separation analyses. By being able to maintain a focal point on vertices representing known data, users substantially enhance their ability to identify and explore connections with vertices on the diminished but still viewable periphery of the graph.

Moreover, the ability – supported by many fisheye-type interfaces – to move an item that is on the periphery to the focal point quickly through direct manipulation of graph elements while not completely losing sight of the earlier focused-upon vertex (which will have moved, in turn, to the periphery) can be quite important. Indeed, beyond just generally acting to encourage greater interaction with the text mining system, this type of functionality allows users to sift more confidently through relationship data without a feeling of disorientation or "getting lost."

Distorting and filtering fisheye approaches are not mutually exclusive. When dealing with very large volumes of data, link detection operations aimed at discovering the network of truly *interesting* relationships linked to a known concept can be greatly enhanced by being able both (a) to see as much of a peripheral context as possible (via a distorting view approach) and (b) to winnow the overall display of data by means of the threshold setting (via a filtering view algorithm).

Yang, Chen, and Hong (2003) found that both distorting and filtering view approaches were substantially more effective (speed measure) in helping users discover information versus having no visualization tool at all. Yang et al. also found that users achieved faster discovery results employing filtering view approaches versus distorting view approaches but found that visualizations incorporating both

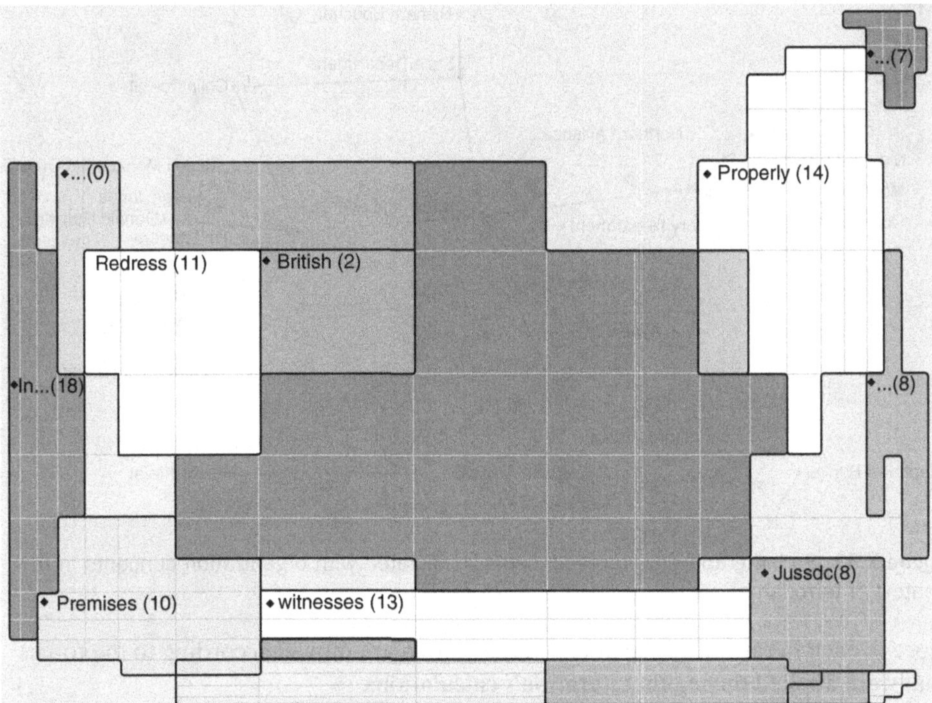

Figure X.32. Visualization of a category map relying on both distorting view and filtering view techniques. (From Yang, Chen, and Hong 2003. Reprinted with permission from Elsevier.)

distorting view and filtering view functionality were the most effective at increasing the speed of discovering useful data. An example of a visualization incorporating both distorting view and filtering view approaches can be seen in Figure X.32.

X.4.3 Spring-Embedded Network Graphs

Link analysis activities benefit from visualization approaches that offer quick spatial and layout cues to the relative proximity that certain relations between concepts possess. *Spring embedding* is a graph generation technique first described by Eades (and later refined in significant ways by both Kamada and Kawai and Fruchterman and Rheingold) that distributes nodes in a two-dimensional plane with some level of separation while attempting to keep connected nodes closer together relative to some form of weighting scheme. Spring graphs are a common form in many academic and commercial text mining applications with an orientation toward link detection such as ClearForest's *ClearResearch* (see Figure X.33) and Paul Mutton's *PieSpy* social network visualization software (Mutton 2004) (see Figure X.34).

In generating a *spring-embedded network graph*, or *spring graph*, we regard each node as a kind of "charged particle" within a graph model that simulates a closed-force system. This formulation creates a repulsive force between every pair of nodes in the system. Each edge in the graph, on the other hand, is modeled as a spring that applies an attractive force between the pair of nodes it links.

Ultimately, the full spring graph is drawn in iterations that calculate the totality of repulsive and attractive forces acting on nodes within the closed system. At the

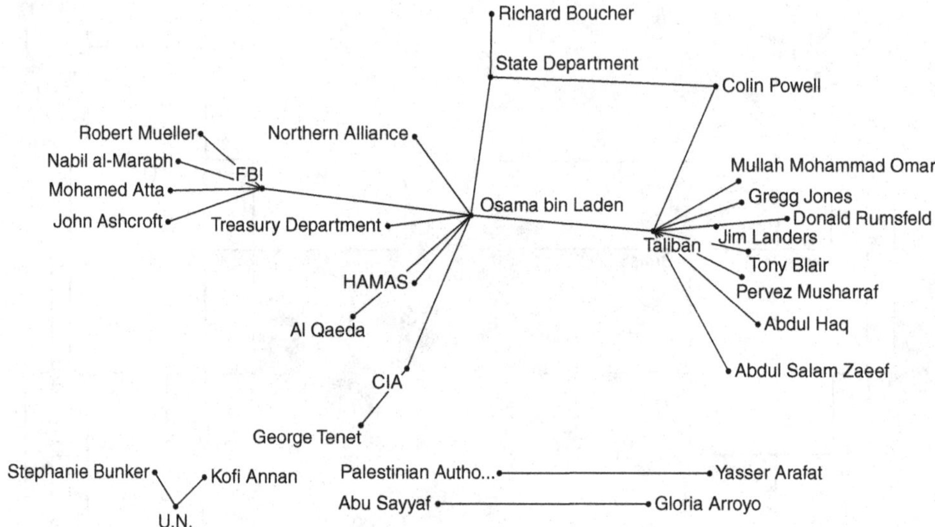

Figure X.33. Spring graph of person concepts associated with organization concepts in the context of terrorism.

close of each iteration, all the nodes in the system are moved according to the forces that were applied during that iteration's calculations.

Typically, in most practical situations, the creation of spring graphs occurs in a multistage process. Running a spring-embedder algorithm is only one stage in

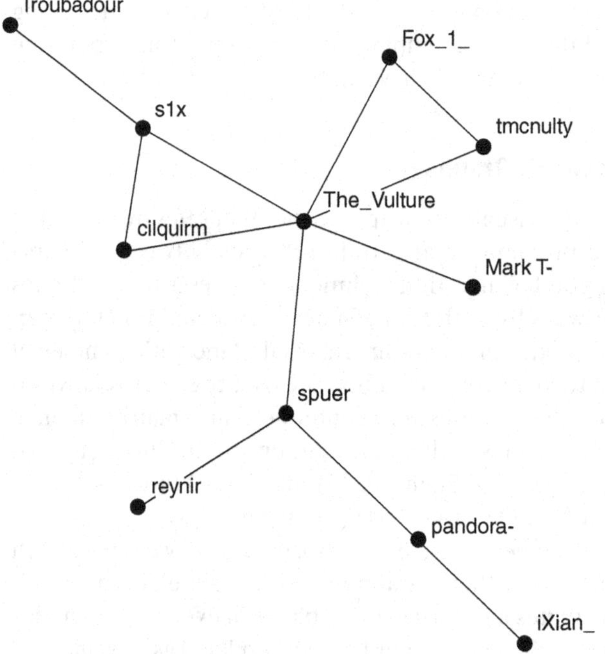

Figure X.34. Simple social network of Internet Relay Chart (IRC) users depicted in a spring graph by the PieSpy social network visualization application. (From Mutton 2004. Reprinted with permission, © 2001 IEEE.)

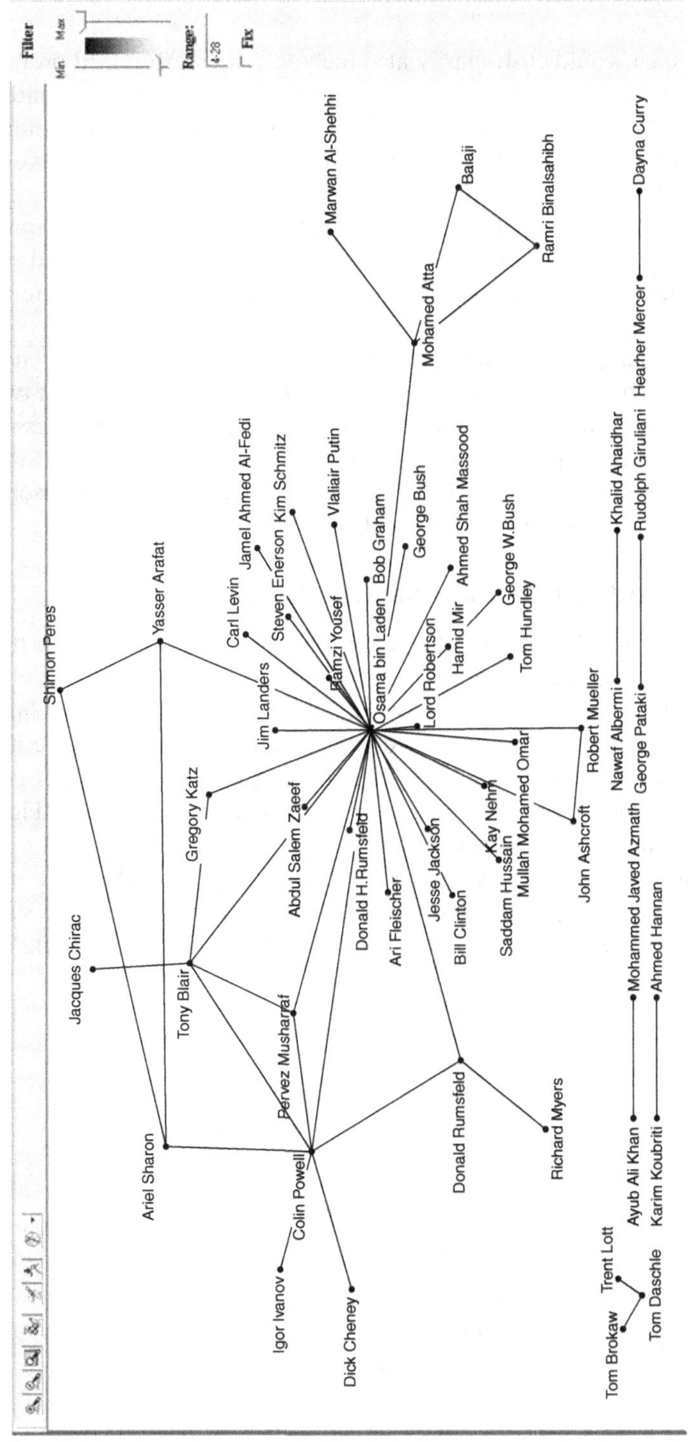

Figure X.35. GUI with visualization of disconnected spring graph showing person co-occurrence patterns.

this process, which would customarily also include some customized preprocessing routines to reduce complexity and heuristics to help establish clusters and perform other processes to promote faster generation of spring graphs in real-time graph-rendering situations. A full example of the construction of a social network spring graph can be found in Chapter XI.

Spring graphs can range in size from a handful of nodes to the hundreds of thousands. Spring graphs whose nodes are all linked by edges are called *connected spring graphs*; those in which discrete networks of nodes appear are referred to as *disconnected spring graphs* (see Figure X.35).

Link detection applications leverage spring graphs to provide visual cues in network maps in which edge length corresponds to the actual relatedness of two nodes. These visual cues allow a user to visually trace out degrees of relatedness and separation quickly, making pattern exploration more effective. Moreover, the spring graphs' ability to model extremely large networks makes them doubly useful in link detection activities involving very large data collections.

X.4.4 Critical Path and Pathway Analysis Graphs

Link analysis can also be visualized through directed graphs that show the linked events or paths of interrelated actions. *Critical path diagrams* are typically based on a graphical model called an activity network, which is a form of DAG. Unlike most DAGs, in which emphasis is usually placed on the vertices of the graph, critical path diagrams equally emphasize the nodes – which typically represent either entities or events – and the edges – which can represent tasks, actions, or decisions. Figure X.36 shows a rudimentary critical path diagram.

In such diagrams, a *critical path* is a chain of specific nodes and edges – or entities events, and the tasks or actions that connect them – that demonstrate some level of interestingness. As in Figure X.36, the patterns formed by such chains of nodes

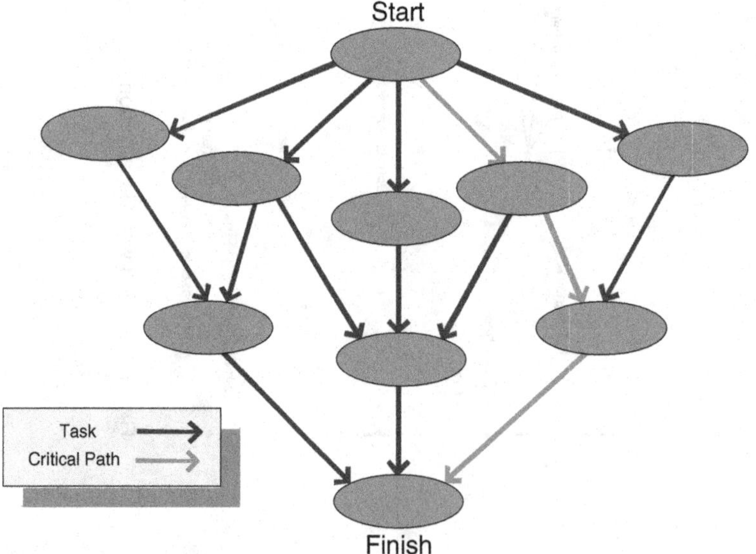

Figure X.36. Critical path diagram.

and edges can be highlighted by stylistic elements in the visualization process (e.g., a different color for edges that link nodes in this chain, etc.). Frequently, though not always, these critical paths will have an identifiable start and finish and thus constitute a directed subgraph that is part of a wider activity network.

Critical path graphs are a staple part of link detection activities aimed at investigations of criminal activities. In crime analysis visualization graphs, nodes may represent both entities (persons, places, items) and events (crimes, pretrial proceedings, trials). Also, a timeline may be introduced to frame actions that occur over time.

Visualizations that support critical path analysis share similarities with the graphic approaches used in pathways analysis for genomics and proteomics research, though there are also some differences. Link detection systems emphasize the search for chains or pathways of interactions between proteins, drugs, and diseases in directed graphs. Edges in these directed graphs are often highlighted in color coding to identify a pathway – but this color coding of edges is also used to specify different types of interactions.

X.4.5 Citations and Notes

Sections X.4–X.4.3

Fisheye views were introduced by G. Furnas; probably the best early description is in Furnas (1986). Subsequently, Sarkar and Brown (1992) added useful upgrades to fisheye views of data and abstracted the general algorithmic approach used to generate fisheye views. The algorithmic formulation for fisheye views comes from Sarkar and Brown (1992). Yang, Chen, and Hong (2003) provides a good treatment of distorting and filtering approaches taken with fisheye views; Noik (1996) also contains a useful discussion.

Figures X.30, X.31, and X.32, as well as the generalized approach to creating a fractal view of a category map discussed in Section VI.4.2, have been summarized from Yang, Chen, and Hong (2003). Yang et al. apply various fisheye approaches to a category map generated using a Kohonen-style SOM. Koike (1995) offers very useful background on the use of fractal approaches as filtering-view techniques.

Sections X.4.4–X.4.5

Spring-embedded network graphs were introduced in Eades (1984) and refined in several subsequent papers – perhaps most notably, Kamada and Kawai (1989) and Fruchterman and Reingold (1991). More on ClearForest's ClearResearch product can be found at <www.clearforest.com>. Further discussion of PieSpy can be found in Mutton and Rodgers (2002) and Mutton (2004).

Mutton and Golbeck (2003) suggests the formulation of a spring graph as a closed-force system in which every node is a "charged particle." The spring graph in Figure X.34 comes from Mutton (2004).

X.5 REAL-WORLD EXAMPLE: THE DOCUMENT EXPLORER SYSTEM

Initially developed in 1997, Document Explorer is a full-featured text mining system that searches for patterns in document collections. Such a collection represents an application domain, and the primary goal of the system is to derive patterns that provide knowledge about this domain. The derived patterns can be used as the basis for further browsing and exploration of the collection.

Document Explorer searches for patterns that capture relations between concepts in the domain. The patterns that have been verified as interesting are structured and presented in a visual user interface allowing the user to operate on the results, to refine and redirect mining queries, or to access the associated documents. Like many general text mining systems, Document Explorer focuses on the three most common pattern types (e.g., frequent sets, associations, distributions); however, it also supports exploration of textual data by means of keyword graphs.

Perhaps most notably for a real-world system of its time frame, Document Explorer provides a well-rounded suite of complementary browsing and visualization tools to facilitate interactive user exploration of its document collection. Examination of Document Explorer with this in mind can provide useful insights into how a practical text mining system leverages presentation-layer tools.

The Document Explorer system contains three main modules. A diagram of the overall Document Explorer system architecture is shown in Figure X.37. The first module is the backbone of the system and includes the KDTL query front end (see Section II.3), into which the user can enter his or her queries for patterns; the interpreter, which parses a query and translates it into function calls in the lower levels; and the data mining and the data management layer. These two layers are responsible for the actual execution of the user's query. The data mining layer contains all the search and pruning strategies that can be applied for mining patterns. The main patterns offered in the system are frequent concept sets, associations, and distributions.

The embedded search algorithms control the search for specific pattern instances within the target database. This level also includes the refinement methods that filter redundant information and cluster closely related information. The data management layer is responsible for all access to the actual data stored in the target database. This layer isolates the target database from the rest of the system.

The second module performs source preprocessing and categorization functions. This module includes the set of source converters and the text categorization software. It is responsible for converting the information fetched from each of the available sources into a canonical format for tagging each document with the predefined categories, and for extracting all multiword terms from the documents. In this preprocessing component, the system extracts all the information that will subsequently be used by the data mining methods.

The target database is represented as a compressed data structure. Besides the target database, the text mining methods in Document Explorer exploit a knowledge base on the application domain. The terms of this domain are arranged in a DAG and belong to several hierarchically arranged categories. In the Reuters newswire collection used in this example, the main categories correspond to countries, economic topics, persons, and so on. Each category (e.g., economic topics) has, for example, subcategories such as currencies and main economic indicators. Relations between these categories give further background knowledge. The knowledge base for the Reuters collection includes relations between pairs of countries (such as countries with land boundaries), between countries and persons, countries and commodities, and so on. These relations can be defined by the user or transformed by special

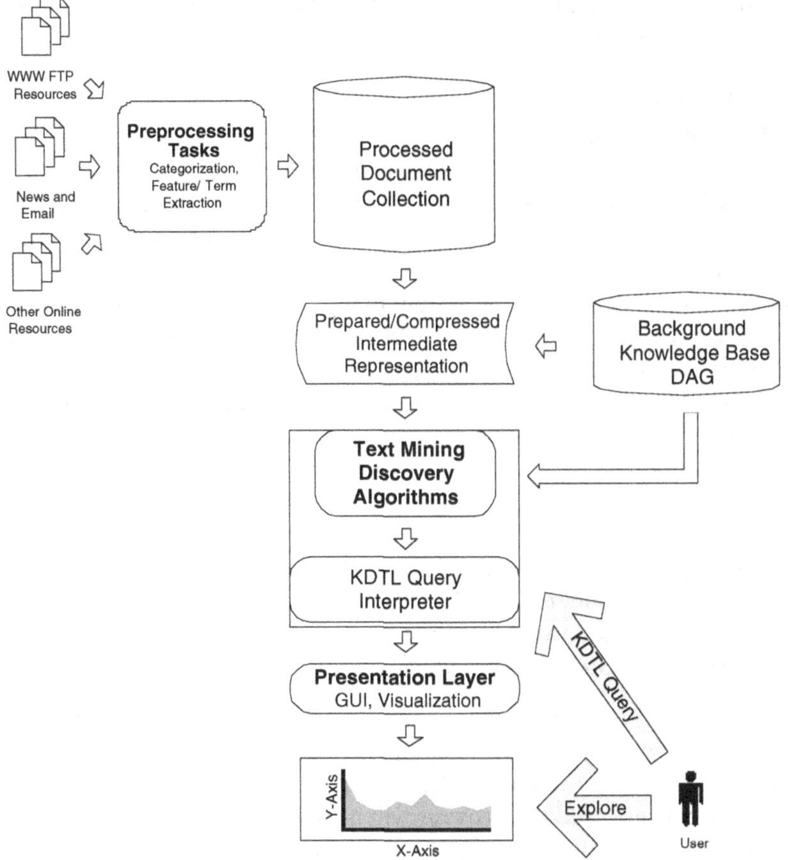

Figure X.37. Architecture of the Document Explorer system.

utilities from generally available sources such as the CIA World Fact Book or companies' home pages.

Finally, the third module performs presentation-layer functions and is responsible for providing an attractive set of GUI-based text mining tools and graph-based visualization techniques that give the user a much easier access to the system. Simple concept graphs are a special interactive visualization technique to present data mining results. Simple concept graphs extend the notion of association rules to relations between keywords and phrases occurring in different documents. The focus of the following functional descriptions is on this presentation layer module.

X.5.1 Presentation-Layer Elements

Visual Administrative Tools: Term Hierarchy Editor

To make full use of Document Explorer's knowledge discovery tools, the documents' annotations are grouped into categories of related terms (e.g. country names, machine parts, etc.) and placed in a hierarchical structure. The *Term-Hierarchy* editor, included in Document Explorer, provides a graphical tool for easy construction and manipulation of such hierarchies. Document Explorer also comes with a predefined term hierarchy for common topics.

The Knowledge Discovery Toolkit

Document Explorer places extensive visualization and browsing tools at the user's disposal for viewing the results of the discovery process. The user is provided with dynamic browsers, which allow dynamic drill-down and roll-up in order to focus on the relevant results. Any part of the discovery process can either be applied to the entire collection or to any subsets of the collection.

Throughout the mining operation, the system maintains the links to the original documents. Thus, at any stage in the discovery process, the user can always access the actual documents that contributed to the discovered pattern.

Document Explorer tools can be grouped into four main categories: Browsers, Profile Analysis, Clustering, and Pattern Discovery. In addition, the system provides novel visualization techniques.

Browsers

The Document Explorer discovery process starts at the browsing level. Browsing is guided by the actual data at hand, not by fixed, rigid structures.

Document Explorer provides two dynamic, content-based browsers: *distribution browser*, and the *interactive distribution browser.*

- ***Distribution Browser.*** The distribution browser presents the user with the frequency of all terms (concepts) in the collections grouped by category and allows the collection to be browsed based on these frequencies. In addition, the user can specify a *base* concept, and the browser will present him or her with the distribution of all other concepts with respect to the base concept. With this tool, the user can immediately find the most relevant term related to whatever he or she is interested in. For example, given a collection of news articles, the user may immediately learn that the main business of Philip Morris is tobacco, or that Wang Yeping is strongly affiliated with China (she is the President's wife). This information is obtained before even reading a single document. At any time, the user may drill down and access the actual documents of interest.
- ***Interactive Distribution Browser.*** The interactive distribution browser provides the user with a flexible, interactive browsing facility, allowing him or her to navigate through the data while being guided by the data itself (see Figure X.38). This browser allows the user to zoom in and out on sets of concepts in the collection and obtain online information on the distribution of these concepts within the collection and their relation to other concepts. At any time, the user may drill down and access any document of interest by first clicking on a term in the interactive distribution browser's distribution tree GUI, hitting a button to locate all documents containing the term, and then choosing from a list of titles for these documents to access the full text of the document.

Visualization Tools

Document Explorer is equipped with a suite of visualization tools. These aid the user in gaining a quick understanding of the main features of the collection. The

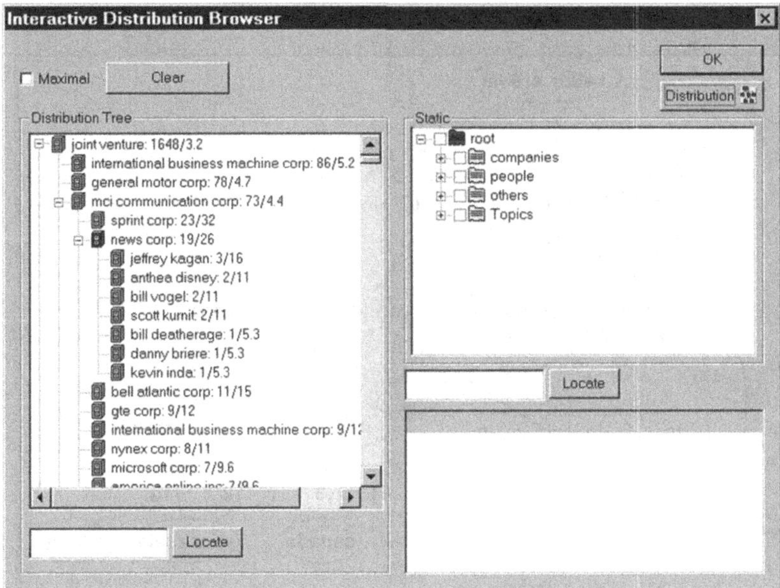

Figure X.38. The GUI for Document Explorer's interactive distribution browser. (From Feldman, Kloesgen, and Zilberstein 1997b.)

visualization tools afford a graphical representation of the connection between terms (concepts) in the collection. The graphical representations provide the user with a high-level, bird's-eye summary of the collection. Three of Document Explorer's main visualization tools – *simple concept graphs, trend graphs*, and *category connection maps* – are described here.

- ***Simple Concept Graphs.*** As described in Section IV.3.1, a simple concept graph in Document Explorer consists of a typical set of graph vertices and edges representing concepts and the affinities between them. A simple concept graph in Document Explorer is generally defined with respect to a *context*, which determines the context in which the similarity of keywords is of interest. Figure X.39 shows a simple concept graph for the "country" category in the context of "crude oil," while Figure X.40 illustates a simple concept association graph with multiple categories but only one vertex.

  In Document Explorer, simple concept graphs can either be defined for the entire collection, or for subsets of the collection, and for arbitrarily complex contexts (see Figure X.41). The system provides the user with an interactive tool for defining and refining the graphs.
- ***Trend Graphs.*** Trend graphs (see Section II.1.5) provide a graphical representation of the *evolution* of the collection. The user is presented with a dynamic picture whose changes reflect the changes in the collection.

  The user can focus on any slice in time and obtain the state of the information at the given time. The user can also define the granularity at which the information is analyzed and presented.
- ***Category Connection Maps.*** This visualization tool enables the user to view the connections between several different categories in relation to a given context.

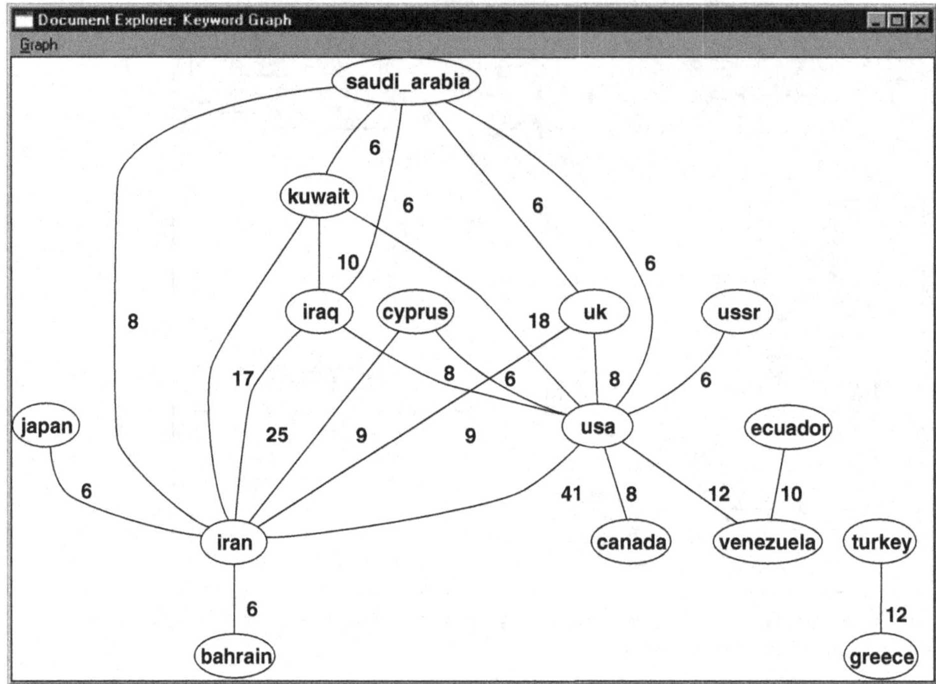

Figure X.39. A Document Explorer simple concept graph – "Countries" in the context of "Crude Oil." (From Feldman, Kloesgen, and Zilberstein 1997b.)

Figure X.42 presents the connections between the categories: *people*, *brokerage houses*, and *computer companies* within the context of *mergers*. (Some similar sample implementations of the circle graph as category connection map are described in Section XII.2.2.)

X.5.2 Citations and Notes

For a comprehensive overview of Document Explorer, see Feldman, Kloesgen, and Zilberstein (1997a, 1997b). The original Document Explorer development team included Ronen Feldman, Yonatan Aumann, David Landau, Orly Lipshtat, Amir Zilberstien, and Moshe Fresko.

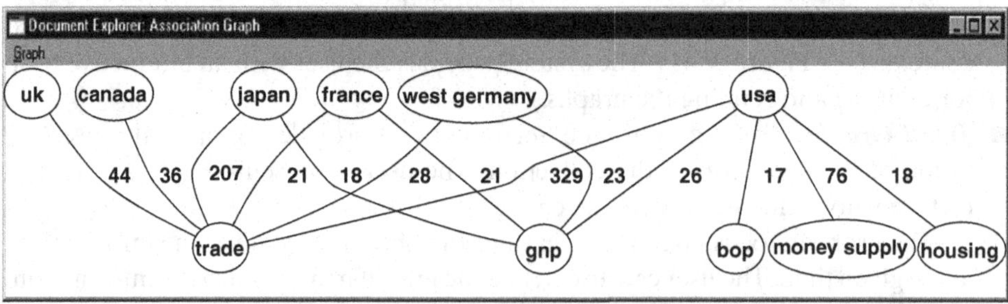

Figure X.40. Simple concept association graph from Document Explorer – many categories but one vertex. (From Feldman, Kloesgen, and Zilberstein 1997b.)

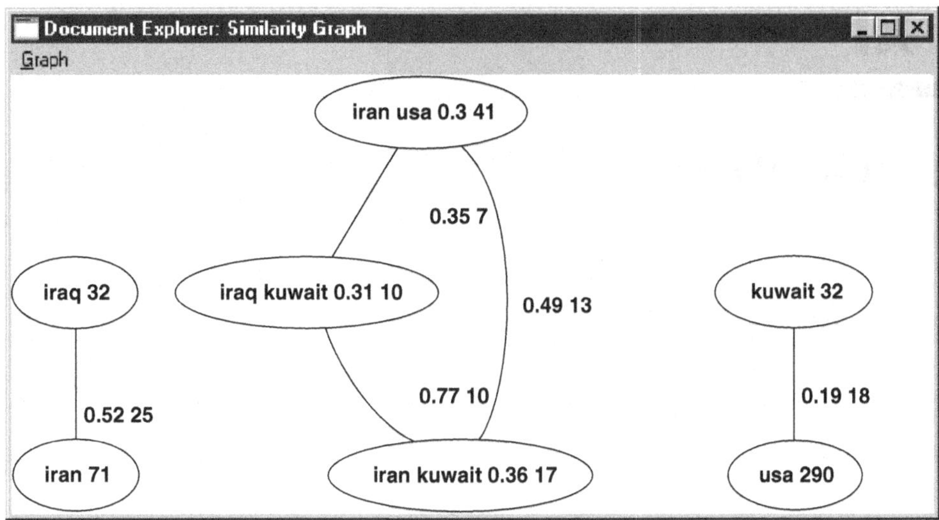

Figure X.41. Simple concept graph from Document Explorer – interesting concept sets and their associations context: crude oil; categories: countries. (From Feldman, Kloesgen, and Zilberstein 1997b.)

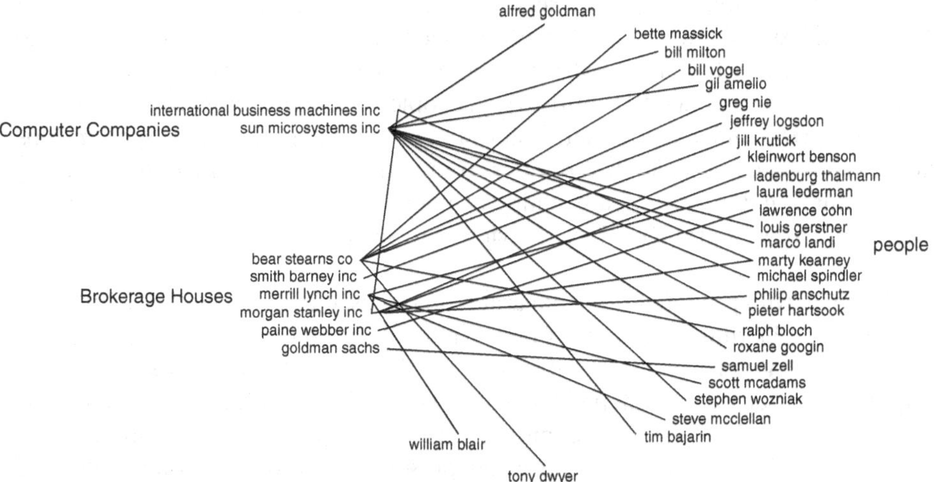

Figure X.42. Category map for "People," "Brokerage Houses," and "Computer Companies" with respect to "Mergers." (From Feldman, Fresko, Hirsh, et al. 1998.)

Link Analysis

Based on the outcome of the preprocessing stage, we can establish links between entities either by using co-occurrence information (within some lexical unit such as a document, paragraph, or sentence) or by using the semantic relationships between the entities as extracted by the information extraction module (such as family relations, employment relationship, mutual service in the army, etc.). This chapter describes the link analysis techniques that can be applied to results of the preprocessing stage (information extraction, term extraction, and text categorization).

A social network is a set of entities (e.g., people, companies, organizations, universities, countries) and a set of relationships between them (e.g., family relationships, various types of communication, business transactions, social interactions, hierarchy relationships, and shared memberships of people in organizations). Visualizing a social network as a graph enables the viewer to see patterns that were not evident before.

We begin with preliminaries from graph theory used throughout the chapter. We next describe the running example of the 9/11 hijacker's network followed by a brief description of graph layout algorithms. After the concepts of paths and cycles in graphs are presented, the chapter proceeds with a discussion of the notion of centrality and the various ways of computing it. Various algorithms for partitioning and clustering nodes inside the network are then presented followed by a brief description of finding specific patterns in networks. The chapter concludes with a presentation of three low-cost software packages for performing link analysis.

XI.1 PRELIMINARIES

We model the set of entities and relationships as a graph, and most of the operations performed on those sets are modeled as operations on graphs. The following notation is used throughout the chapter:

Let $V = \{V_1, V_2, V_3, \ldots V_n\}$ be a set of entities extracted from the documents.

A *binary relation* R over V is a subset of $V \times V$.

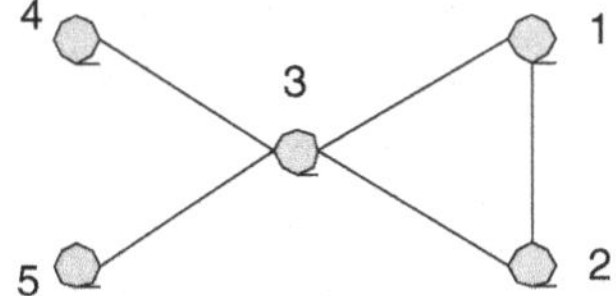

Figure XI.1. A simple undirected network with $V = \{1, 2, 3, 4, 5\}$, $R_1 = \{(1, 2), (1, 3), (2, 3), (3, 4), (3, 5)\}$ and $N = (V, R_1)$.

We use the prefix notation for relations – that is, if X and Y are related by relation R_1, then it will be denoted by $R_1(X, Y)$.

Examples of such binary relations are friendship, marriage, school mates, army mates, and so on.

A *network* N is a tuple $(V, R_1, R_2, R_3 \ldots R_m)$, where R_i $(1 \leq i \leq m)$ is a binary relation over V.

A visual representation of N is shown in Figure XI.1.

We can also describe a binary relation R using a binary matrix M, where $M_{ij} = 1$ if $R(V_i, V_j)$, and 0 otherwise. For example, the matrix that represents the relation R

$$\begin{pmatrix} 0 & 1 & 1 & 0 & 0 \\ 1 & 0 & 1 & 0 & 0 \\ 1 & 1 & 0 & 1 & 1 \\ 0 & 0 & 1 & 0 & 0 \\ 0 & 0 & 1 & 0 & 0 \end{pmatrix}$$

shown in Figure XI.1 is as follows:

Each row in the matrix corresponds to the connection vector of one of the vertices. The ith row $(M_{i1}, \ldots, M_{in})$ corresponds to the connection vector of the ith vertex.

The set of edges connecting all vertices in the undirected graph is denoted by E, and $|E|$ is the number of edges in the graph. If the graph is directed, then the lines that connect the vertices are called arcs. Our focus is mostly on undirected networks and hence also on undirected graphs, and so we use vertices and edges. The network can also have weights or values attached to each of its edges. The weight function denoted $W: E \to R$ (the real numbers) is attaching a real value to each edge. If there are no values for any of the edges, then $\forall e \in E, W(e) = 1$.

If the relations R are not symmetric, then $G = (V, E)$ is a directed graph:

A sequence of vertices $(v_1, v_2, \ldots, v_k)$ in G is called a ***walk*** if $(v_i, v_{i+1}) \in E; i = 1 \ldots k - 1$.

A sequence of vertices $(v_1, v_2, \ldots, v_k)$ in G is called a ***chain*** if $((v_i, v_{i+1}) \in E || (v_{i+1}, v_i) \in E) i = 1 \ldots k - 1$.

In a walk, we care about the direction of the edge, whereas in a chain we do not.

A ***path*** is a walk in which no vertices, except maybe the initial and terminal ones, are repeated.

A walk is ***simple*** if all its edges are different.

A ***cycle*** is a simple path of at least three vertices, where $v_1 = v_k$.

The length of the path $(v_1, v_2, \ldots, v_k)$ is $k-1$.

A special type of network is a ***two-mode network***. This network contains two types of vertices, and there are edges that connect the two sets of vertices. A classic example would be a set of people and a set of events as vertices with edges connecting a person vertex to an event vertex if the person participated in the event.

If there are no self-loops in the network (i.e., a vertex can not connect to itself), then the maximal number of edges in an undirected network with n vertex is $n(n-1)/2$. Such network, in which each vertex is connected to every other vertex, is also called a ***clique***. If the number of edges is roughly the same as the number of vertices, we say that the network is ***sparse***, whereas if the network is close to being a clique we say that it is ***dense***.

We can quantify the density level of a given undirected network by using the following formula:

ND (Network Density) $= \frac{|E|}{\frac{n(n-1)}{2}} = \frac{2|E|}{n(n-1)}$
Clearly $0 \leq \text{ND} \leq 1$.
Similarly, ND for a directed network would be $\frac{|E|}{n(n-1)}$
For example ND for the network of Figure XI.1 is $\frac{2 \cdot 5}{5 \cdot 4} = 0.5$.

XI.1.1 Running Example: 9/11 Hijackers

We have collected information about the 19 9/11 hijackers from the following sources:

1. Names of the 19 hijackers, and the flights they boarded were taken from the FBI site <http://www.fbi.gov/pressrel/pressrel01/091401hj.htm> (see Table XI.1).
2. Prior connections between the hijackers are based on information collected from the *Washington Post* site given below. If there was a connection between $n \geq 2$ people, it was converted to $C(n, 2)$ symmetric binary relations between each pair of people. <http://www.washingtonpost.com/wp-srv/nation/graphics/attack/investigation_24.html.>

The undirected graph of binary relations between the hijackers is shown in Figure XI.2. The graph was drawn using Pajek dedicated freeware link analysis software (Batagelj and Mrvar 2003). More details on Pajek are presented in Section XI.7.1.

The 19 hijackers boarded 4 flights, and in Table XI.1 we can see the names of the hijackers who boarded each flight. The flight information is used when we discuss the various clustering schemes of the hijackers.

XI.2 AUTOMATIC LAYOUT OF NETWORKS

To display large networks on the screen, we need to use automatic layout algorithms. These algorithms display the graphs in an aesthetic way without any user intervention.

The most commonly used aesthetic objectives are to expose symmetries and to make the drawing as compact as possible or, alternatively, to fill the space available for

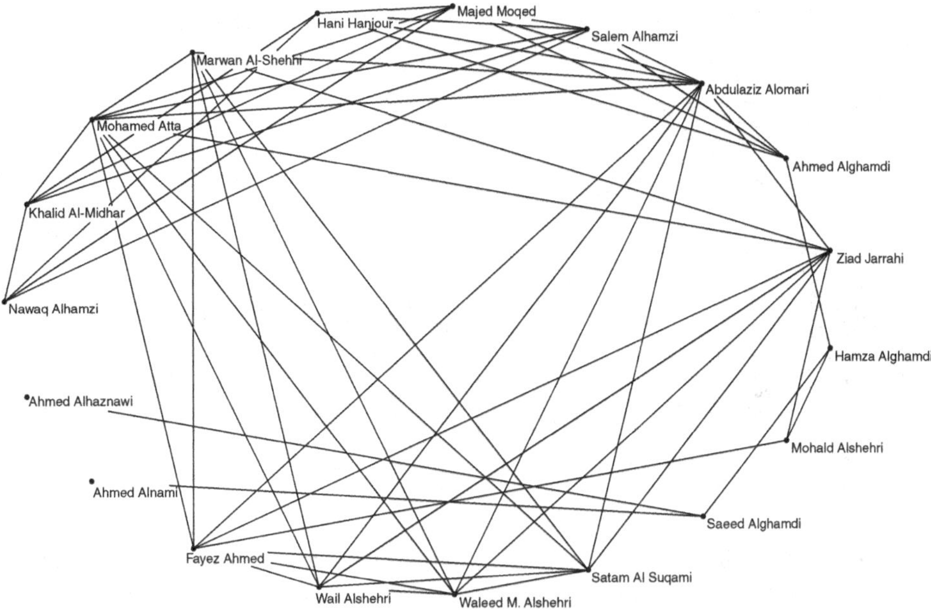

Figure XI.2. Connections between the 9/11 hijackers.

the drawing. Many of the "higher level" aesthetic criteria are implicit consequences of the

- minimized number of edge crossings,
- evenly distributed edge length,
- evenly distributed vertex positions on the graph area,
- sufficiently large vertex-edge distances, and
- sufficiently large angular resolution between edges.

XI.2.1 Force-Directed Graph Layout Algorithms

Force-directed or spring-based algorithms are among the most common automatic network layout strategies. These algorithms treat the collection of vertices and edges as a system of forces and the layout as an "equilibrium state" of the system. The edges between vertices are represented as an attractive force (each edge is simulated by

Table XI.1. The 19 Hijackers Ordered by Flights

Flight 77: Pentagon	Flight 11: WTC 1	Flight 175: WTC 2	Flight 93: PA
Khalid Al-Midhar	Satam Al Suqami	Marwan Al-Shehhi	Saeed Alghamdi
Majed Moqed	Waleed M. Alshehri	Fayez Ahmed	Ahmed Alhaznawi
Nawaq Alhamzi	Wail Alshehri	Ahmed Alghamdi	Ahmed Alnami
Salem Alhamzi	Mohamed Atta	Hamza Alghamdi	Ziad Jarrahi
Hani Hanjour	Abdulaziz Alomari	Mohald Alshehri	

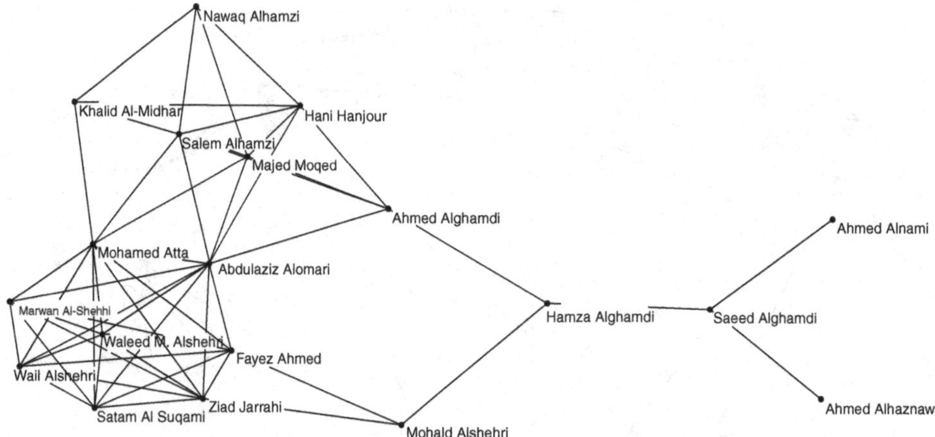

Figure XI.3. KK layout of the hijackers' graph.

a spring that pulls the vertices together), whereas distinct vertices are pushed apart by some constraint to help prevent them from being drawn at the same point. The method seeks equilibrium of these contradicting constraints. The first such algorithm was introduced by Eades (Eades 1984). Following Eades, two additional layout algorithms were introduced by Kamada and Kawai (KK) (Kamada and Kawai 1989) and Fruchterman and Reingold (FR) (Fruchterman and Reingold 1991).

Kamada and Kawai's (KK) Method

Utilizing Hooke's law, Kamada and Kawai modeled a graph as a system of springs. Every two vertices are connected by a spring whose rest length is proportional to the graph-theoretic distance between its two endpoints. Each spring's stiffness is inversely proportional to the square of its rest length. The optimization algorithm used by the KK method tries to minimize the total energy of the system and achieves faster convergence by calculating the derivatives of the force equations. One of the main benefits of the KK method is that it can be used for drawing weighted graphs if the edge lengths are proportional to their weights. The KK method proceeds by moving a single vertex at a time, choosing the "most promising" vertex – that is, the one with the maximum gradient value.

In Figure XI.3 we can see the graph shown in Figure XI.2 drawn by using the KK layout. Unlike the circular drawing of Figure XI.2 in which it is hard to see who the leaders of the groups are, we can see here that the main leaders are Mohamed Atta, Abdulaziz Alomari, and Hamza Alghamdi.

Fruchterman–Reingold (FR) Method

This method utilizes a simple heuristic approach to force-directed layout that works surprisingly well in practice. The underlying physical model roughly corresponds to electrostatic attraction in which the attractive force between connected vertices is balanced by a repulsive force between all vertices. The basic idea is just to calculate the attractive and repulsive forces at each vertex independently and to update all vertices iteratively. As in simulated annealing, the maximum displacement of each

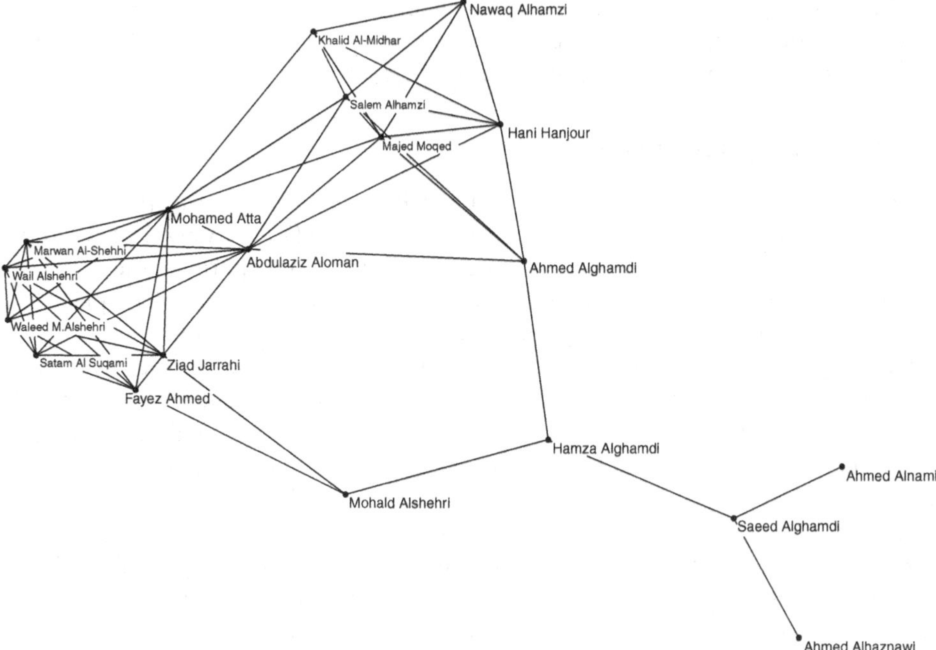

Figure XI.4. FR layout of the hijackers' graph.

vertex in any iteration is limited by a constant that is slightly decreased with each iteration. In Figure XI.4 we can see the graph shown in Figure XI.2 drawn by using the FR layout.

For both KK and FR, the relations between vertices must be expressed as distances between the vertices. For both algorithms we need to build a "dissimilarity" matrix. In the KK algorithm this matrix is constructed from geodesic distances between vertices, whereas in the FR algorithm the matrix is constructed directly from adjacencies between the vertices. Spring-based methods are very successful with small-sized graphs of up to around 100 vertices.

Simulated annealing has also been successfully applied to the layout of general undirected graphs (Davidson and Harel 1996).

Although force-directed methods are quite useful in automatically exposing most of the symmetries of the given graphs, they share several disadvantages:

- They are computationally expensive, and hence minimizing the energy function when dealing with large graphs is computationally prohibitive.
- Because all methods rely on heuristics, there is no guarantee that the "best" layout will be found.
- The methods behave as black boxes, and thus it is almost impossible to integrate additional constraints on the layout (such as fixing the positions of certain vertices or specifying the relative ordering of the vertices)
- Even when the graphs are planar it is quite possible that we will obtain edge crossings.

- The methods try to optimize just the placement of vertices and edges while ignoring the exact shape of the vertices or the possibility the vertices have labels (and hence the labels, vertices, or both may overlap each other).

XI.2.2 Drawing Large Graphs

A fast algorithm for drawing general graphs with straight edges was proposed by Harel and Koren based on the work of Hadany and Harel (Hadany and Harel 2001). Their algorithm works by producing a sequence of improved approximations of the final layout. Each approximation allows vertices to deviate from their final place by an extent limited by a decreasing constant r. As a result, the layout can be computed using increasingly coarse representations of the graph in which closely drawn vertices are collapsed into a single vertex. Each layout in the sequence is generated very rapidly by performing a local beautification on the previously generated layout. The main idea of Hadany and Harel's work is to consider a series of abstractions of the graph called coarse graphs in which the combinatorial structure is significantly simplified but important topological features are well preserved. The energy minimization is divided between these coarse graphs in such a way that globally related properties are optimized on coarser graphs, whereas locally related properties are optimized on finer graphs. As a result, the energy minimization process considers only small neighborhoods at once, yielding a quick running time.

XI.3 PATHS AND CYCLES IN GRAPHS

Given two vertices in a directed graph, we can compute the shortest path between them. The diameter of a graph is defined as the length of the longest shortest path between any two vertices in the graph. Albert et al. (Albert, Jeong, and Barabasi 1999) found that, when the Web contained around 8×108 documents, the average shortest path between any 2 pages was 19. The interpretation of the shortest path in this case is the smallest number of URL links that must be followed to navigate from one Web page to the other.

There are many kinds of paths between entities that can be traced in a dataset. In the Kevin Bacon game, for example, a player takes any actor and finds a path between the actor and Kevin Bacon that has less than six edges. For instance, Kevin Costner links to Kevin Bacon by using one direct link: Both were in *JFK*. Julia Louis-Dreyfus of TV's *Seinfeld*, however, needs two links to make a path: Julia Louis-Dreyfus was in *Christmas Vacation* (1989) with Keith MacKechnie. Keith MacKechnie was in *We Married Margo* (2000) with Kevin Bacon. You can play the game by using the following URL: <http://www.cs.virginia.edu/oracle>.

A similar idea is also used in the mathematical society and is called the Erdös number of a researcher. Paul Erdös (1913–1996) wrote hundreds of mathematical research papers in many different areas – many in collaboration with others. There is a link between any two mathematicians if they coauthored a paper. Paul Erdös is the root of the mathematical research network, and his Erdös number is 0. Erdös's coauthors have Erdös number 1. People other than Erdös who have written a joint paper with someone with Erdös number 1 but not with Erdös have Erdös number 2, and so on.

In Figure XI.5 we can see the split of the hijackers into five levels according to their distance from Mohammed Atta. The size of the little circle associated with each hijacker manifests the proximity of the hijacker to Atta; the larger the circle, the shorter the geodesic (the shortest path between two vertices in the graph) between the hijacker and Atta. There are ten hijackers who have a geodesic of size 1, four hijackers who have a geodesic of size 2, one hijacker who has a geodesic of size 3, one hijacker who has a geodesic of size 4, and finally two hijackers who have a geodesic of size 5. A much better visualization of the different degree levels can be seen in Figure XI.6. The diagram was produced by using Pajek's drawing module and selecting Layers | in *y* direction. The various levels are coded by the distance from the nodes with the highest degree. Connections are shown just between entities of different levels.

XI.4 CENTRALITY

The notion of centrality enables us to identify the main and most powerful actors within a social network. Those actors should get special attention when monitoring the behavior of the network.

Centrality is a structural attribute of vertices in a network; it has nothing to do with the features of the actual objects represented by the vertices of the network (i.e., if it is a network of people, their nationality, title, or any physical feature). When dealing with directed networks we use the term *prestige*. There are two types of prestige; the one defined on outgoing arcs is called *influence*, whereas the one defined on incoming arcs is called *support*. Because most of our networks are based on co-occurrence of entities in the same lexical unit, we will confine our attention to undirected networks and use the term centrality. The different measures of centrality we will present can be adapted easily for directed networks and measure influence or support.

Five major definitions are used for centrality: degree centrality, closeness centrality, betweeness centrality, eigenvector centrality, and power centrality. We discuss these in the next several sections.

XI.4.1 Degree Centrality

If the graph is undirected, then the degree of a vertex $v \in V$ is the number of other vertices that are directly connected to it.

Definition: $\text{degree}(v) = |\{(v1, v2) \in E \mid v1 = v \textit{ or } v2 = v\}|$

If the graph is directed, then we can talk about in-degree or out-degree. An edge $(v1, v2) \in E$ in the directed graph is leading from vertex $v1$ to $v2$.

$\text{In-degree}(v) = |\{(v1, v) \in E\}|$

$\text{Out-degree}(v) = |\{(v, v2) \in E\}|$

If the graph represents a social network, then clearly people who have more connections to other people can be more influential and can utilize more of the resources of the network as a whole. Such people are often mediators and dealmakers in exchanges among others and are able to benefit from this brokerage.

When dealing with undirected connections, people differ from one another only in how many connections they have. In contrast, when the connections are directed,

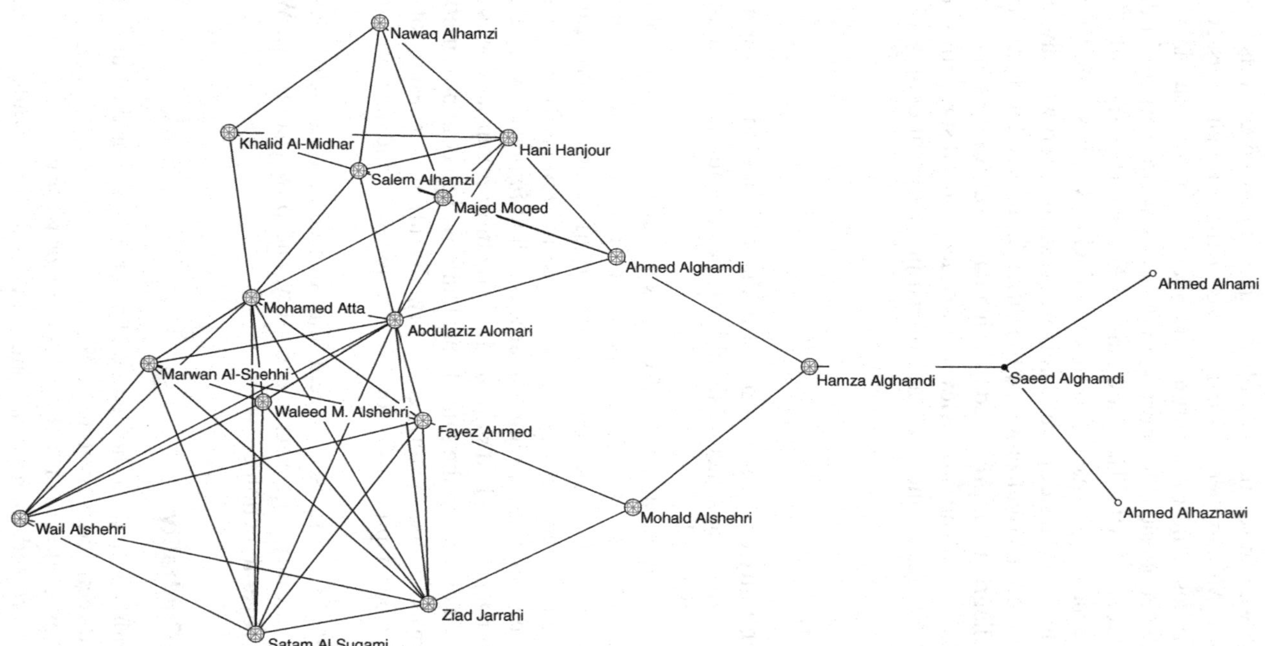

Figure XI.5. Computing the shortest distance between Atta and all other 18 hijackers.

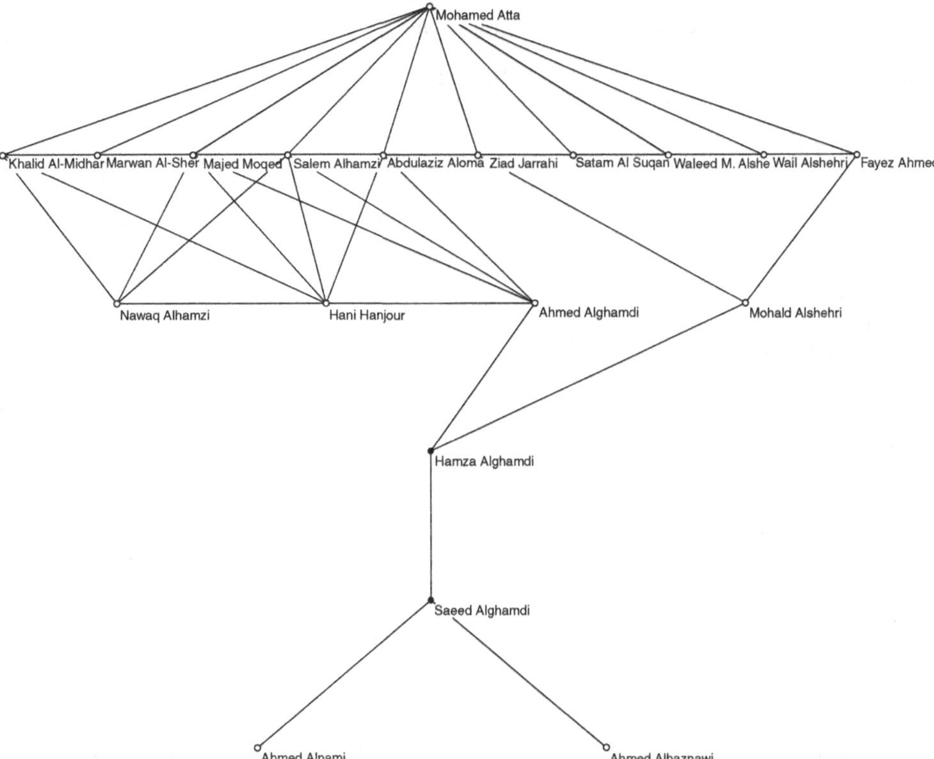

Figure XI.6. Layered display of the geodesic distance between Atta and the other hijackers.

it is important to distinguish centrality based on in-degree from centrality based on out-degree. If a person has a high in-degree, we say that this person is *prominent* and has high *prestige*. Many people seek direct connections to him or her, indicating that persons's importance. People who have high out-degree are people who are able to interact with many others and possibly spread their ideas. Such people are said to be *influential*. In Table XI.2, we can see the hijackers sorted in decreasing order of their (undirected) degree measures. We can see that Mohamed Atta and Abdulaziz Alomari have the highest degree.

XI.4.2 Closeness Centrality

Degree centrality measures might be criticized because they take into account only the direct connections that an entity has rather than indirect connections to all other entities. One entity might be directly connected to a large number of entities that might be rather isolated from the network. Such an entity is central only in a local neighborhood of the network.

To solve the shortcomings of the degree measure, we can utilize the closeness centrality. This measure is based on the calculation of the geodesic distance between the entity and all other entities in the network. We can either use directed or undirected geodesic distances between the entities. In our current example, we have decided to look at undirected connections. The sum of these geodesic distances for each entity

Table XI.2. All Degree Measures of the Hijackers

Name	Degree
Mohamed Atta	11
Abdulaziz Alomari	11
Ziad Jarrahi	9
Fayez Ahmed	8
Waleed M. Alshehri	7
Wail Alshehri	7
Satam Al Suqami	7
Salem Alhamzi	7
Marwan Al-Shehhi	7
Majed Moqed	7
Khalid Al-Midhar	6
Hani Hanjour	6
Nawaq Alhamzi	5
Ahmed Alghamdi	5
Saeed Alghamdi	3
Mohald Alshehri	3
Hamza Alghamdi	3
Ahmed Alnami	1
Ahmed Alhaznawi	1

is the "farness" of the entity from all other entities. We can convert this into a measure of closeness centrality by taking its reciprocal. We can normalize the closeness measure by dividing it by the closeness measure of the most central entity.

Formally, let $d(v_1, v_2)$ = the minimal distance between v_1 and v_2 – that is, the minimal number of vertices we need to pass on the way from v_1 to v_2.

The closeness centrality of vertex v_i is defined as $C_i = \frac{|V|-1}{\sum_{j \neq i} d(v_i, v_j)}$. This is the reciprocal of the average geodesic distance between v_i and any other vertex in the network. In Table XI.3, we can see the hijackers sorted in decreasing order of their closeness.

XI.4.3 Betweeness Centrality

Betweeness centrality measures the effectiveness in which a vertex connects the various parts of the network. Entities that are on many geodesic paths between other pairs of entities are more powerful because they control the flow of information between the pairs. That is, the more other entities depend on a certain entity to make connections, the more power this entity has. If, however, two entities are connected by more than one geodesic path and a given entity is not on all of them, it loses some power. If we add up, for each entity, the proportion of times this entity is "between" other entities for transmission of information, we obtain the betweeness centrality of that entity. We can normalize this measure by dividing it by the maximum possible betweeness that an entity could have had (which is the number of possible pairs of entities for which the entity is on every geodesic between them $= \frac{(|V|-1)(|V|-2)}{2}$).

Table XI.3. Closeness Measures of the Hijackers

Name	Closeness
Abdulaziz Alomari	0.6
Ahmed Alghamdi	0.5454545
Ziad Jarrahi	0.5294118
Fayez Ahmed	0.5294118
Mohamed Atta	0.5142857
Majed Moqed	0.5142857
Salem Alhamzi	0.5142857
Hani Hanjour	0.5
Marwan Al Shehhi	0.4615385
Satam Al Suqami	0.4615385
Waleed M. Alshehri	0.4615385
Wail Alshehri	0.4615385
Hamza Alghamdi	0.45
Khalid Al Midhar	0.4390244
Mohald Alshehri	0.4390244
Nawaq Alhamzi	0.3673469
Saeed Alghamdi	0.3396226
Ahmed Alnami	0.2571429
Ahmed Alhaznawi	0.2571429

Formally,
g_{jk} = the number of geodetic paths that connect v_j with v_k;
$g_{jk}(v_i)$ = the number of geodetic paths that connect v_j with v_k and pass via v_i.

$$B_i = \sum_{j<k} \frac{g_{jk}(v_i)}{g_{jk}}$$

$$NB_i = \frac{2B_i}{(|V|-1)(|V|-2)}$$

In Table XI.4, we can see the hijackers sorted in decreasing order of their between measures.

XI.4.4 Eigenvector Centrality

The main idea behind eigenvector centrality is that entities receiving many communications from other well-connected entities will be better and more valuable sources of information and hence be considered central. The eigenvector centrality scores correspond to the values of the principal eigenvector of the adjacency matrix M.

Formally, the vector $\mathbf{v}$ satisfies the equation $\lambda\mathbf{v} = M\mathbf{v}$, where λ is the corresponding eigenvalue and M is the adjacency matrix.

The score of each vertex is proportional to the sum of the centralities of neighboring vertices. Intuitively, vertices with high eigenvector centrality scores are connected to many other vertices with high scores, which are, in turn, connected to many other vertices, and this continues recursively. Clearly, the highest score will be obtained

Table XI.4. Betweeness Measures of the Hijackers

Name	Betweeness (B_i)
Hamza Alghamdi	0.3059446
Saeed Alghamdi	0.2156863
Ahmed Alghamdi	0.210084
Abdulaziz Alomari	0.1848669
Mohald Alshehri	0.1350763
Mohamed Atta	0.1224783
Ziad Jarrahi	0.0807656
Fayez Ahmed	0.0686275
Majed Moqed	0.0483901
Salem Alhamzi	0.0483901
Hani Hanjour	0.0317955
Khalid Al-Midhar	0.0184832
Nawaq Alhamzi	0
Marwan Al-Shehhi	0
Satam Al Suqami	0
Waleed M. Alshehri	0
Wail Alshehri	0
Ahmed Alnami	0
Ahmed Alhaznawi	0

by vertices that are members of large cliques or large p-cliques. In Table XI.5 we can see that the members of the big clique (with eight members) are those that got the highest scores. Atta and Al-Shehhi got much higher scores than all the other hijackers mainly because the connection between them is so strong. They were also the pilots of the planes going into WTC1 and WTC2 and are believed to have been the leaders of the hijackers.

XI.4.5 Power Centrality

Power centrality was introduced by Bonacich. Given an adjacency matrix M, the power centrality of vertex i (denoted c_i) is given by

$$c_i = \sum_{j \neq i} M_{ij}(\alpha + \beta \cdot c_j),$$

where α is used to normalize the score (the normalization parameter is automatically selected so that the sum of squares of the vertices's centralities is equal to the number of vertices in the network) and β is an attenuation factor that controls the effect that the power centralities of the neighboring vertices should have on the power centrality of the vertex.

As in the eigenvector centrality, the power centrality of each vertex is determined by the centrality of the vertices it is connected to. By specifying positive or negative values to β, the user can control whether a vertex's being connected to powerful vertices should have a positive effect on its score or a negative effect. The rationale for specifying a positive β is that, if you are connected to powerful colleagues it makes you more powerful. On the other hand, the rationale for a negative β is

Table XI.5. Eigenvector Centrality Scores of the Hijackers

Name	E1
Mohamed Atta	0.518
Marwan Al-Shehhi	0.489
Abdulaziz Alomari	0.296
Ziad Jarrahi	0.246
Fayez Ahmed	0.246
Satam Al Suqami	0.241
Waleed M. Alshehri	0.241
Wail Alshehri	0.241
Salem Alhamzi	0.179
Majed Moqed	0.165
Hani Hanjour	0.151
Khalid Al-Midhar	0.114
Ahmed Alghamdi	0.085
Nawaq Alhamzi	0.064
Mohald Alshehri	0.054
Hamza Alghamdi	0.015
Saeed Alghamdi	0.002
Ahmed Alnami	0
Ahmed Alhaznawi	0

that powerful colleagues have many connections and hence are not controlled by you, whereas isolated colleagues have no other sources of information and hence are largely controlled by you. In Table XI.6, we can see the hijackers sorted in decreasing order of their power measure.

XI.4.6 Network Centralization

In addition to the individual vertex centralization measures, we can assign a number between 0 and 1 that will signal the whole network's level of centralization. The network centralization measures are computed based on the centralization values of the network's vertices; hence, we will have for each type of individual centralization measure an associated network centralization measure. A network structured like a circle will have a network centralization value of 0 (because all vertices have the same centralization value), whereas a network structured like a star will have a network centralization value of 1. We now provide some of the formulas for the different network centralization measures.

Degree

$$Degree^*(V) = \mathrm{Max}_{v \in V} Degree(v)$$

$$\mathrm{NET}_{\mathrm{Degree}} = \frac{\sum_{v \in V} Degree^*(V) - Degree(v)}{(n-1) * (n-2)}$$

Table XI.6. Power Centrality for the Hijackers Graph

	Power : $\beta = 0.99$	Power : $\beta = -0.99$
Mohamed Atta	2.254	2.214
Marwan Al-Shehhi	2.121	0.969
Abdulaziz Alomari	1.296	1.494
Ziad Jarrahi	1.07	1.087
Fayez Ahmed	1.07	1.087
Satam Al Suqami	1.047	0.861
Waleed M. Alshehri	1.047	0.861
Wail Alshehri	1.047	0.861
Salem Alhamzi	0.795	1.153
Majed Moqed	0.73	1.029
Hani Hanjour	0.673	1.334
Khalid Al-Midhar	0.503	0.596
Ahmed Alghamdi	0.38	0.672
Nawaq Alhamzi	0.288	0.574
Mohald Alshehri	0.236	0.467
Hamza Alghamdi	0.07	0.566
Saeed Alghamdi	0.012	0.656
Ahmed Alnami	0.003	0.183
Ahmed Alhaznawi	0.003	0.183

Clearly, if we have a circle, all vertices have a degree of 2; hence, $\text{NET}_{\text{Degree}} = 0$. If we have a star of n nodes (one node in the middle), then that node will have a degree of $n-1$, and all other nodes will have a degree of 1; hence,

$$\text{NET}_{\text{Degree}} = \frac{\sum_{v \in V \setminus v^*} (n-1) - 1}{(n-1)(n-2)} = \frac{(n-1)(n-2)}{(n-1)(n-2)} = 1.$$

For the hijackers' graph, $\text{NET}_{\text{Degree}} = 0.31$

Betweenness

$$NB^*(V) = \text{Max}_{v \in V} NB(v)$$

$$\text{NET}_{\text{Bet}} = \frac{\sum_{v \in V} NB^*(V) - NB(v)}{(n-1)}$$

For the hijackers' network, $\text{NET}_{\text{Bet}} = 0.24$

XI.4.7 Summary Diagram

Figure XI.7 presents a summary diagram of the different centrality measures as they are applied to the hijacker's network. We marked by solid arrows the hijackers who got the highest value for the various centrality measures and by dashed arrows

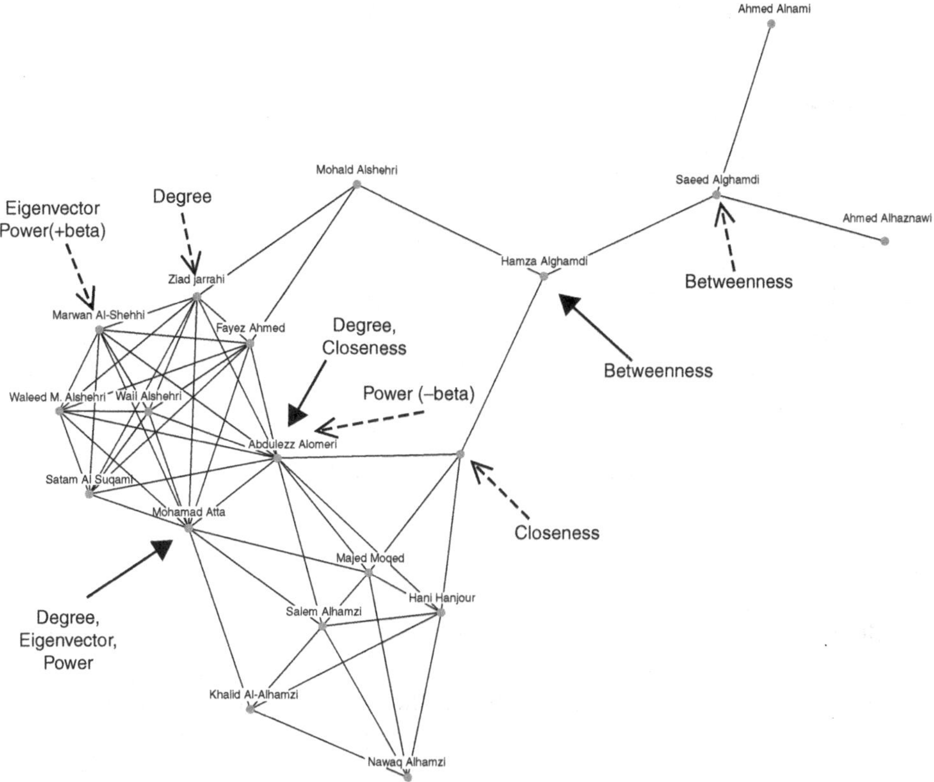

Figure XI.7. Summary diagram of centrality measures (solid arrows point to highest value; dashed arrows point to second largest (done using Netminer (Cyram 2004)).

the runners-up. We can see for instance that Atta has the highest value for degree centrality, eigenvector centrality, and power centrality, whereas Alomari has the highest value for degree centrality (tied with Atta) and closeness centrality and is the runner-up for power centrality (with a negative beta).

On the basis of our experience the most important centrality measures are power and eigenvector (which are typically in agreement). Closeness and, even more so, betweeness centrality signal the people who are crucial in securing fast communication between the different parts of the network.

XI.5 PARTITIONING OF NETWORKS

Often we obtain networks that contain hundreds and even thousands of vertices. To analyze the network effectively it is crucial to partition it into smaller subgraphs.

We present three methods below for taking a network and partitioning it into clusters. The first method is based on core computation, the second on classic graph algorithms for finding strong and weak components and biconnected components, and the third on block modeling.

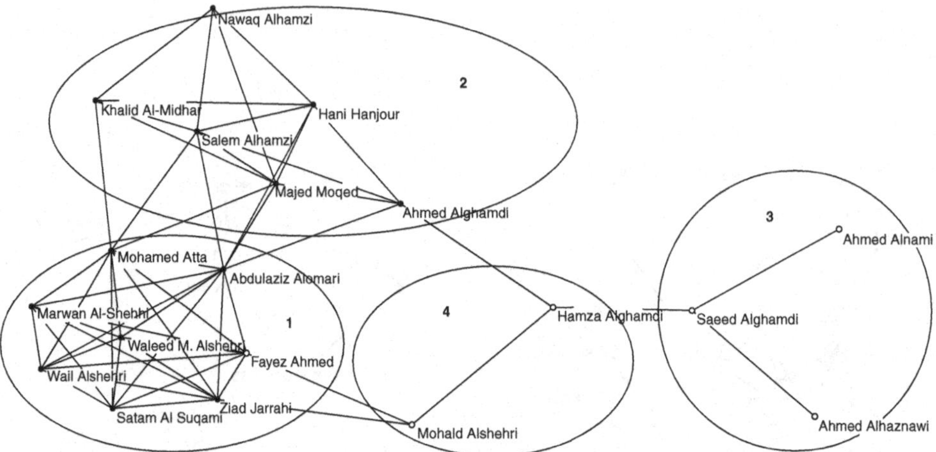

Figure XI.8. Core partitioning of the hijackers' graph.

XI.5.1 Cores

Definition: Let $G = (V, E)$ be a graph. A subgraph $S = (W, E\,|\,W)$ induced by the vertex set W is a *k-core* or a *core* of order k iff $\forall n \in W : \deg_S(n) \geq k$ and S is a maximal with respect to this property. The *main core* is the core of highest order. The *core number* of vertex n is the highest order of a core that contains this vertex.

Algorithm for finding the main core

Given a graph $G = (V, E)$, delete all vertices n and edges attached to them such that $\deg_S(n) < k$ and repeat until no vertices or edges can be deleted. The subgraph that remains after the iterative deletion is a core of order k. If an empty graph results, we know that no core of order k exists. We can perform a simple log $|V|$ search for the order of the main core. After the main core is discovered, we can remove these vertices and the associated edges from the graph and search again for the next core in the reduced graph. The process will terminate when an empty graph is reached. In Figure XI.8, we can see the cores that were discovered in the hijacker's graph. When a core was discovered, it was deleted from the graph and the search for the biggest core in the remaining graph started again.

We can see that four cores were found. The main core contains eight nodes and is of order seven (each vertex is connected to all other seven vertices), the second largest core has six vertices in it and an order of 3, the third core has three vertices and an order of 1, and the fourth one has two vertices and an order of 1.

We then used the shrinking option of Pajek (Operations | Shrink Network | Partition) to obtain a schematic view of the network based on the core partition. Each core is reduced to the name of its first member. For instance, the first member in the core marked 1 is Mohammed Atta, and hence the core is reduced to him. If there is at least one edge between the vertices of any two cores, then we will have an edge between the associated vertices in the reduced graph. The reduced graph,

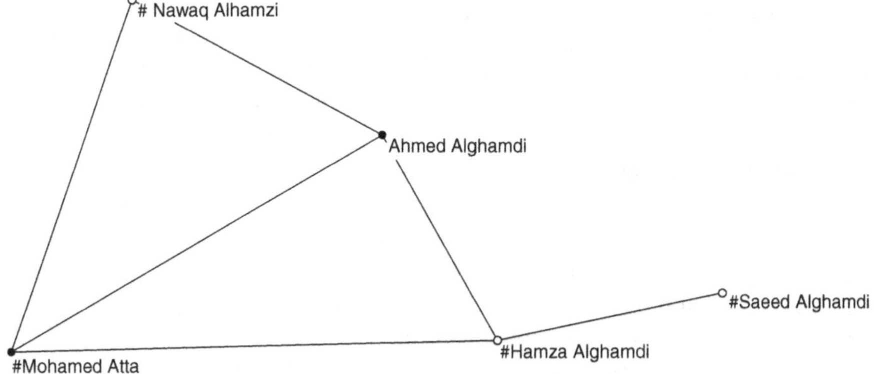

Figure XI.9. Shrinking the hijackers' graphs based on the core partition.

which is based on the shrinking of the core partitioning, is shown in Figure XI.9. A layered display of the cores is shown in Figure XI.10.

Alternatively, we can use a layered display of the network to see the different cores and the relations between them better. Each core is shown in a different y-level. This representation mainly enables us to focus on the intraconnections between the cores.

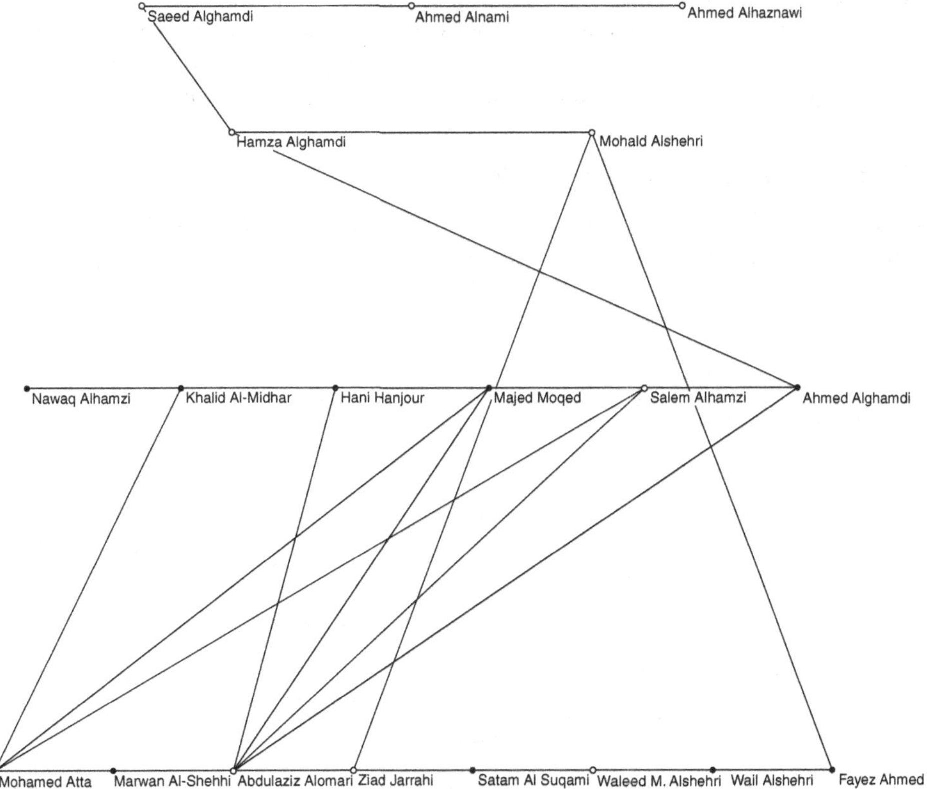

Figure XI.10. Layered display of the cores.

XI.5.2 Classic Graph Analysis Algorithms

Another way of partitioning a network is to use classic graph algorithms such as weak and strong component analysis and identification of bidirectional components.

Strong and Weak Components

Whether the network is directed or undirected is crucial to the component analysis of the network. A subset of vertices is called a strongly connected component if there is at least one walk from any vertex to any other vertex in the subset. A subset of vertices is called a weakly connected component if there exists at least one chain from any vertex to any other vertex in the subset.

A subset of vertices is called a biconnected component if there exist at least two chains from any vertex to any other vertex in the subset, where the chains share no common vertex.

Biconnected Components and Articulation Points

A vertex d of the network is an articulation point of the network if there exist two additional vertices b and c so that every chain between b and c also includes d. It follows that vertex d is an articulation point if the removal of d from the network disconnects it. A network is termed biconnected if, for every triple of vertices d, b, and c, there is a chain between b and c that does not include d. This means that a biconnected network remain connected even after any vertex from it is removed. There are no articulation points in a biconnected network. Articulation points expose weaknesses of networks, and elimination of articulation points will cause the network to be fragmented. The articulation points of the hijackers' graph are shown in Figure XI.11.

XI.5.3 Equivalence between Entities

Given a network of entities, we are often interested in measuring the similarity between the entities based on their interaction with other entities in the network. This

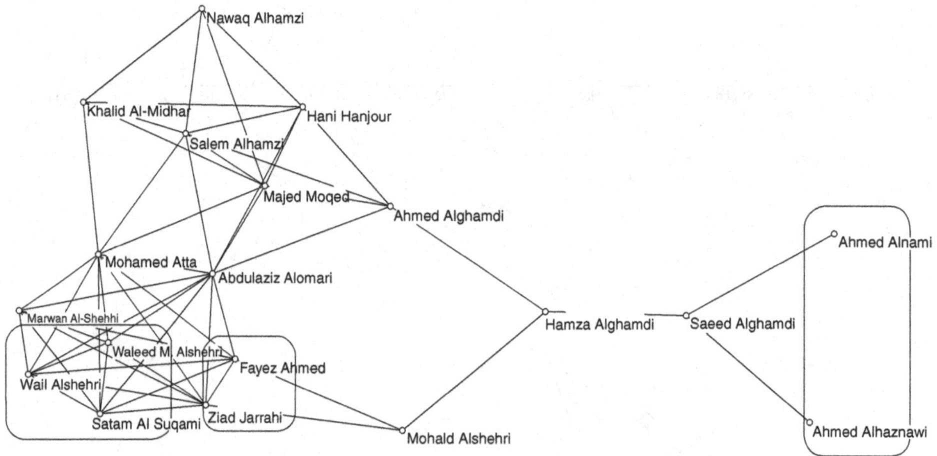

Figure XI.11. Articulation points of the hijackers' network (the number above the arrow signals the number of components that will result after removing the articulation point).

section formalizes this notion of similarity between entities and provides examples of how to find similar entities and how to use the similarity measure to cluster the entities.

Structural Equivalence

Two entities are said to be exactly structurally equivalent if they have the same relationships to all other entities. If A is "structurally equivalent" to B, then these two entities are "substitutable." Typically, we will not be able to find entities that are exactly structurally equivalent; hence, we are interested in calculating the degree of structural equivalence between entities. This measure of distance makes it possible to perform hierarchical clustering of the entities in our network.

We present two formal definitions for structural equivalence. Both are based on the connection vectors of each of the entities. The first definition is based on the Euclidian distance between the connection vectors and other on the number of exact matches between the elements of the vectors.

$$\mathrm{EDis}(V_i, V_j) = \sqrt{\sum_k (M_{ik} - M_{jk})^2}$$

$$\mathrm{Match}(V_i, V_j) = \frac{\sum_{k=1}^{n} \mathrm{eq}(M_{ik}, M_{jk})}{n}, \quad \text{where} \quad \mathrm{eq}(a, b) = \begin{cases} 1 & a = b \\ 0 & \text{otherwise} \end{cases}$$

Regular Equivalence

Two entities are said to be regularly equivalent if they have an identical profile of connections with other entities that are also regularly equivalent. In order to establish regular equivalence, we need to classify the entities into semantic sets such that each set contains entities with a common role. An example would be the sets of surgeons, nurses, and anesthesiologists. Let us assume that each surgeon is related to a set of three nurses and one anesthesiologist. We say that two such surgeons are regularly equivalent (and so are the nurses and the anesthesiologist) – that is, they perform the same function in the network.

Entities that are "structurally equivalent" are also "regularly equivalent." However, entities that are "regularly equivalent" do not have to be "structurally equivalent." It is much easier to examine if two entities are structurally equivalent because there is a simple algorithm for finding EDis and Match. It is much harder to establish if two entities are regularly equivalent because we need to create a taxonomy of semantic categories on top of the entities. In Figure XI.12 we can see two pairs of people and one triplet that are structurally equivalent. In Table XI.7 we can see the EDis computed for each pair of entities. Entities that are structurally equivalent will have an EDis of 0. For instance, Waleed M. Alshehri and Wail Alshehri are structurally equivalent, and hence their EDis is 0. Based on this table, we were able to use a hierarchical clustering algorithm (via the UCINET software package; see Section XI.7.2) and generate the dendogram shown in Figure XI.13. People who are very close in the dendogram are similar structurally (i.e, they have low EDis), whereas people who are far away in the dendogram are different structurally.

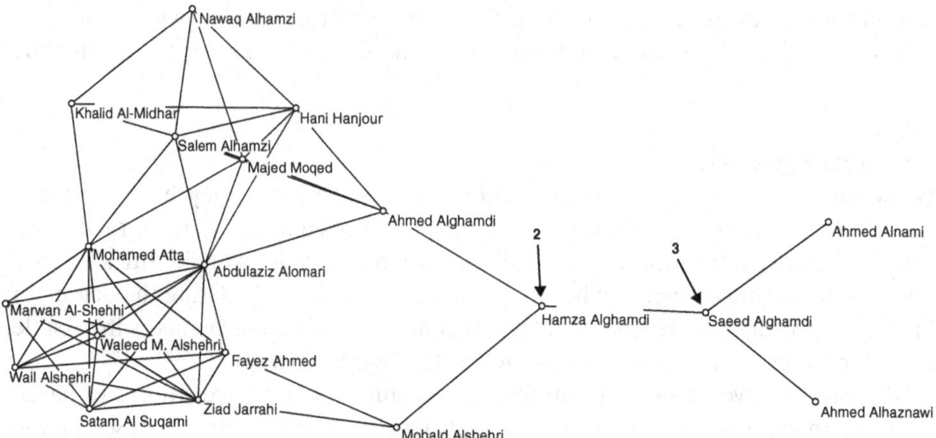

Figure XI.12. Structural equivalences in the hijackers' graph.

XI.5.4 Block Modeling

Block modeling is an analysis technique for finding clusters of vertices that behave in a similar way. Block modeling is based on the notions of structural and regular equivalence between vertices and as such is far more sensitive to the interconnections between vertices than the standard clustering techniques introduced before. Block modeling was introduced by Borgatti and Everett (1993). The technique is fairly general and can use a variety of equivalence relations between the vertices. The

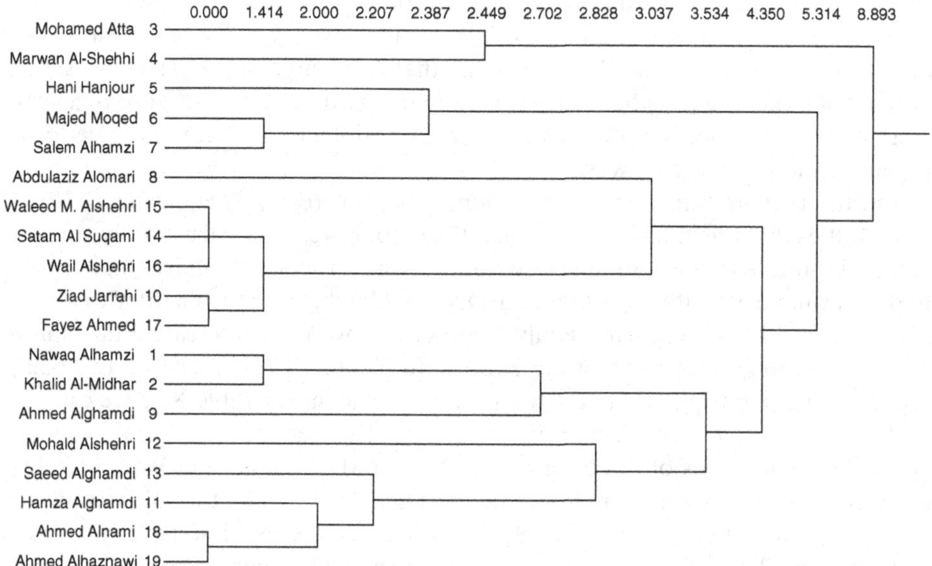

Figure XI.13. Clustering-based structural equivalence between the hijackers (we can see that {15,14,16} as well as {10,17} and {18,19} are structural equivalence classes).

Table XI.7. Euclidian Distance (Edis) between Each Pair of Entities

	1	2	3	4	5	6	7	8	9	10	11	12	13	14	15	16	17	18	19
1 Nawaq Alhamzi	0.0	1.4	9.3	9.6	3.7	2.8	3.7	4.2	2.4	4.9	3.7	3.7	3.7	4.7	4.7	4.7	4.9	3.2	3.2
2 Khalid Al-Midhar	1.4	0.0	9.4	8.4	4.0	2.4	3.5	4.0	2.8	4.7	4.0	4.0	4.0	4.5	4.5	4.5	4.7	3.5	3.5
3 Mohamed Atta	9.3	9.4	0.0	2.4	9.8	9.7	10.2	7.5	9.4	7.6	9.8	9.4	9.8	7.5	7.5	7.5	7.6	9.6	9.6
4 Marwan Al-Shehhi	9.6	8.4	2.4	0.0	10.7	8.7	9.3	7.6	9.5	7.2	9.5	9.1	9.5	7.1	7.1	7.1	7.2	9.3	9.3
5 Hani Hanjour	3.7	4.0	9.8	10.7	0.0	3.2	2.0	5.3	4.0	6.8	6.0	6.3	6.3	6.6	6.6	6.6	6.8	6.0	6.0
6 Majed Moqed	2.8	2.4	9.7	8.7	3.2	0.0	1.4	4.2	3.2	5.3	4.7	5.1	5.1	5.1	5.1	5.1	5.3	4.7	4.7
7 Salem Alhamzi	3.7	3.5	10.2	9.3	2.0	1.4	0.0	4.9	4.0	6.2	5.7	6.0	6.0	6.0	6.0	6.0	6.2	5.7	5.7
8 Abdulaziz Alomari	4.2	4.0	7.5	7.6	5.3	4.2	4.9	0.0	4.0	3.2	4.9	4.5	5.3	2.8	2.8	2.8	3.2	4.9	4.9
9 Ahmed Alghamdi	2.4	2.8	9.4	9.5	4.0	3.2	4.0	4.0	0.0	4.7	3.5	3.5	3.5	4.5	4.5	4.5	4.7	3.5	3.5
10 Ziad Jarrahi	4.9	4.7	7.6	7.2	6.8	5.3	6.2	3.2	4.7	0.0	4.2	3.7	4.7	1.4	1.4	1.4	0.0	4.2	4.2
11 Hamza Alghamdi	3.7	4.0	9.8	9.5	6.0	4.7	5.7	4.9	3.5	4.2	0.0	2.8	2.8	4.5	4.5	4.5	4.2	2.0	2.0
12 Mohald Alshehri	3.7	4.0	9.4	9.1	6.3	5.1	6.0	4.5	3.5	3.7	2.8	0.0	2.8	3.5	3.5	3.5	3.7	2.8	2.8
13 Saeed Alghamdi	3.7	4.0	9.8	9.5	6.3	5.1	6.0	5.3	3.5	4.7	2.8	2.8	0.0	4.5	4.5	4.5	4.7	2.0	2.0
14 Satam Al Suqami	4.7	4.5	7.5	7.1	6.6	5.1	6.0	2.8	4.5	1.4	4.5	3.5	4.5	0.0	0.0	0.0	1.4	4.0	4.0
15 Waleed M. Alshehri	4.7	4.5	7.5	7.1	6.6	5.1	6.0	2.8	4.5	1.4	4.5	3.5	4.5	0.0	0.0	0.0	1.4	4.0	4.0
16 Wail Alshehri	4.7	4.5	7.5	7.1	6.6	5.1	6.0	2.8	4.5	1.4	4.5	3.5	4.5	0.0	0.0	0.0	1.4	4.0	4.0
17 Fayez Ahmed	4.9	4.7	7.6	7.2	6.8	5.3	6.2	3.2	4.7	0.0	4.2	3.7	4.7	1.4	1.4	1.4	0.0	4.2	4.2
18 Ahmed Alnami	3.2	3.5	9.6	9.3	6.0	4.7	5.7	4.9	3.5	4.2	2.0	2.8	2.0	4.0	4.0	4.0	4.2	0.0	0.0
19 Ahmed Alhaznawi	3.2	3.5	9.6	9.3	6.0	4.7	5.7	4.9	3.5	4.2	2.0	2.8	2.0	4.0	4.0	4.0	4.2	0.0	0.0

general block modeling problem is composed of two subproblems:

1. Performing clustering of the vertices; each cluster serves as a block.
2. Calculating the links (and their associated value) between the blocks.

Formal Notations

Given two clusters C_1 and C_2, $L(C_1, C_2)$ is the set of edges that connect vertices in C_1 to vertices in C_2. Formally, $L(C_1, C_2) = \{(x, y)|(x, y) \in E, x \in C_1, y \in C_2\}$.

Because there are many ways to partition our vertices into clusters, we will introduce an optimization criterion that will help pick the optimal clustering scheme.

Before defining the problem formally, we will introduce a few predicates on the connections between two clusters. Visualizations of some of these predicates are shown in Figure XI.14

Predicate name	Formula and Acronym	Explanation
Null	$Null(C_1, C_2) \equiv \forall x \in C_1, \forall y \in C_2, (x, y) \notin E$	No connection at all between the clusters
Com (Complete)	$Com(C_1, C_2) \equiv \forall x \in C_1, \forall y (y \neq x) \in C_2, (x, y) \in E$	Full connection between the clusters
Row Regular	$Rreg(C_1, C_2) \equiv \forall x \in C_1, \exists y \in C_2, (x, y) \in E$	Each vertex in the first cluster is connected to at least one vertex in the second cluster.
Column Regular	$Creg(C_1, C_2) \equiv \forall y \in C_2, \exists x \in C_1, (x, y) \in E$	Each vertex in the second cluster is connected to at least one vertex in the first cluster.
Regular	$Reg(C_1, C_2) \equiv Rreg(C_1, C_2) \wedge Creg(C_1, C_2)$	All vertices in both clusters must have at least one vertex in the other cluster to which they are connected.
Row Dominant	$Rdom(C_1, C_2) \equiv \exists x \in C_1, \forall y (y \neq x) \in C_2, (x, y) \in E$	There is at least one vertex in the first cluster that is connected to all the vertices in the second cluster.
Column Dominant	$Cdom(C_1, C_2) \equiv \exists y \in C_2, \forall x (x \neq y) \in C_1, (x, y) \in E$	There is at least one vertex in the second cluster that is connected to all the vertices in the first cluster.
Row Functional	$Rfun(C_1, C_2) \equiv \forall y \in C_2, \exists$ single $x \in C_1, (x, y) \in E$	All vertices in the second cluster are connected to exactly one vertex in the first cluster.
Column Functional	$Cfun(C_1, C_2) \equiv \forall x \in C_1, \exists$ single $y \in C_2, (x, y) \in E$	All vertices in the first cluster are connected to exactly one vertex in the second cluster.

Formally, a block model of graph $G = (V, E)$ is a tuple $M = (U, K, T, Q, \pi, \alpha)$, where

- U is the set of clusters that we get by partitioning V.
- K is the set of connections between elements of U, $K \subseteq U \times U$.

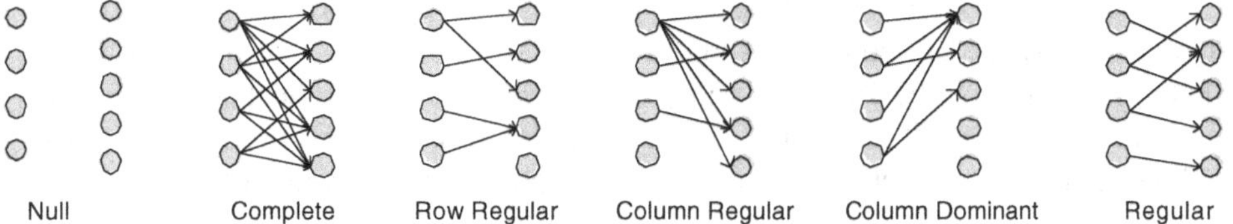

Figure XI.14. Visualization of some of the predicates on the connections between clusters.

- T is a set of predicates that describe the connections between the clusters.
- π is a mapping function between the cluster's connections and the predicates – $\pi : K \to T \backslash \{Null\}$.
- Q is a set of averaging rules enabling us to compute the strength of the connection between any two clusters.
- α is a mapping function from the connection between the clusters to the averaging rules – $\alpha : K \to Q$

Averaging rules (Q)

Listed below are a few options for giving a value to a connection between two clusters C_1 and C_2 based on the weights assigned to edges in $L(C_1,C_2)$.

$$Ave(C_1, C_2) = \frac{\sum_{e \in L(C_1,C_2)} w(e)}{|L(C_1, C_2)|}$$

$$Max(C_1, C_2) = \max_{e \in L(C_1,C_2)} w(e)$$

$$Med(C_1, C_2) = \text{median}_{e \in L(C_1,C_2)} w(e)$$

$$Ave - row(C_1, C_2) = \frac{\sum_{e \in L(C_1,C_2)} w(e)}{|C_1|}$$

$$Ave - col(C_1, C_2) = \frac{\sum_{e \in L(C_1,C_2)} w(e)}{|C_2|}$$

Finding the Best Block Model

We can define a quality measure for any clustering and on the basis of that measure seek the clustering that will yield the ultimate block model of the network. First, we compute the quality of any clustering of the vertices.

We start with a fundamental problem. Given two clusters C_1 and C_2 and a predicate $t \in T$, how can we find the deviation of $L(C_1, C_2)$ that satisfies t? This deviation will be denoted by $\delta(C_1, C_2, t)$. The approach here is to measure the number of 1's missing in the matrix $C_1 \times C_2$ from a perfect matrix that satisfies t. Clearly, $\delta(C_1, C_2, t) = 0$ iff $t(C_1, C_2)$ is true.

For example, if the matrix that represents $L(C_1, C_2)$ is

$$\begin{matrix} 1 & 0 & 1 & 1 \\ 0 & 1 & 1 & 0 \\ 1 & 1 & 1 & 1 \\ 1 & 1 & 0 & 1, \end{matrix}$$

then, because there are four 0's in the matrix, $\delta(C_1, C_2, \text{Com}) = 4$.

If we assign some weight to each predicate t, we can introduce the notion of error with respect to two clusters and a predicate $\varepsilon(C_1, C_2, t) = w(t) \cdot \delta(C_1, C_2, t)$. This notion can now be extended to the error over a set of predicates. We seek the minimal error from all individual errors on the members of the predicate set. This will also determine which predicate should selected to be the value of $\pi(C_1, C_2)$.

$$\varepsilon(C_1, C_2, T) = \min_{t \in T} \; \varepsilon(C_1, C_2, t)$$

$$\pi(C_1, C_2, T) = \arg\min_{t \in T} \; \varepsilon(C_1, C_2, t)$$

Now that the error for a pair of clusters has been defined, we can define the total error for the complete clustering. Basically, it will be the sum of the errors on all pairs of clusters as expressed by

$$P(U, T) = \sum_{C_1 \in U, C_2 \in U} \varepsilon(C_1, C_2, T).$$

If, for a given U, $P(U, T) = 0$, we can say that U is a perfect block model of the graph $G = (V, E)$ with respect to T. In most cases, it will not be possible to find a perfect block model; hence, we will try to find the clustering U' that minimizes the total error over all possible clustering of V.

If $T = \{\text{Null}, \text{Com}\}$ we are seeking a structural block model (Lorrain and White 1971), and if $T = \{\text{Null}, \text{Reg}\}$ we are seeking a regular block model (White and Reitz 1983).

Block Modeling of the Hijacker Network

We present two experiments with the hijacker network. In both experiments we seek a structural block model. The objective of the first experiment is to obtain four blocks (mainly because there were four flights). Using Pajek to do the modeling, we obtain the following connection matrix between the blocks (shown in Figure XI.15):

Final predicate matrix for the block modeling of Figure XI.15

	1	**2**	**3**	**4**
1	Com	–	–	–
2	null	com	–	–
3	Com	com	null	–
4	null	null	null	Null

We can see that only four almost complete connections were identified (after removing the symmetric entries). Two of them are the clique of cluster 2 and the almost clique of cluster 1. In addition, we have almost a complete connection between clusters 1 and 3 and between clusters 2 and 3. All other connections between clusters are closer to satisfying the null predicate than they are to satisfying the com predicate.

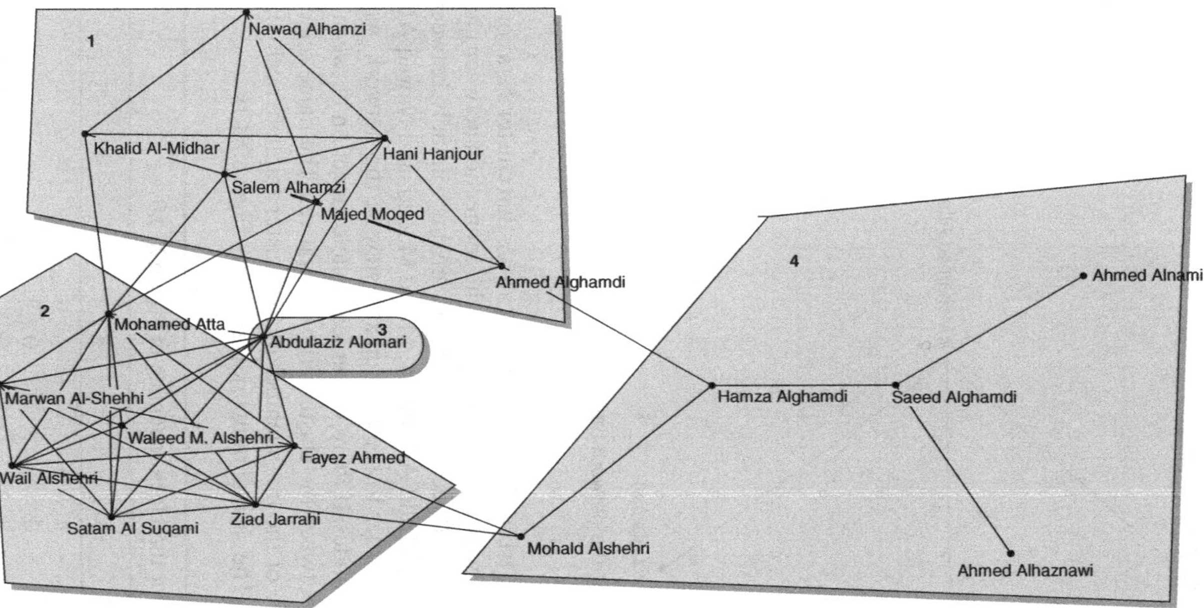

Figure XI.15. Block modeling with four blocks.

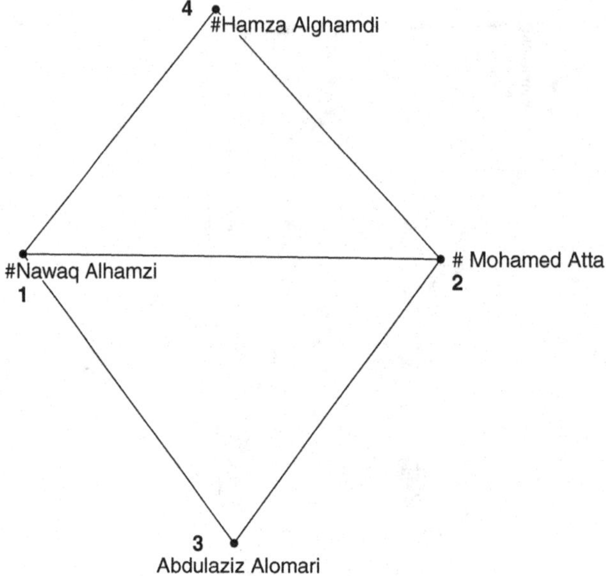

Figure XI.16. Shrinking the network based on the 4 blocks of 15.

The final error matrix is shown below; we can see that cluster 2 is a complete clique because its error is 0, whereas we can see that the connection between clusters 3 and 1 is not complete because three connections are missing – namely, between Abdulaziz Alomari and any of {Khalid Al-Midhar, Majed Moqed, and Nawaq Alhamzi}. The total error is 16. In order to see a schematic view of the network, we shrank the clusters into single nodes. If there was at least one connection between the clusters, we will see a line between the cluster's representatives. The name selected for each cluster is the name of the first member of the cluster (alphabetically based on last name, first name). The shrunk network is shown in Figure XI.16.

Final error matrix for the block modeling of Figure XI.16

	1	**2**	**3**	**4**
1	4	–	–	–
2	3	0	–	–
3	2	0	0	–
4	1	2	0	4

The objective of the second experiment is to see how the clustering and associated error cost changes when we set a higher number of target clusters. We run the block modeling of Pajek again specifying that we want to obtain six blocks or clusters. In this case the total error dropped to 9. The six blocks are shown in Figure XI.14 and then we show the predicate matrix of the block modeling and the final error matrix. We can see that five of the six blocks are close to a complete block (clique), whereas there are only three connections between the blocks.

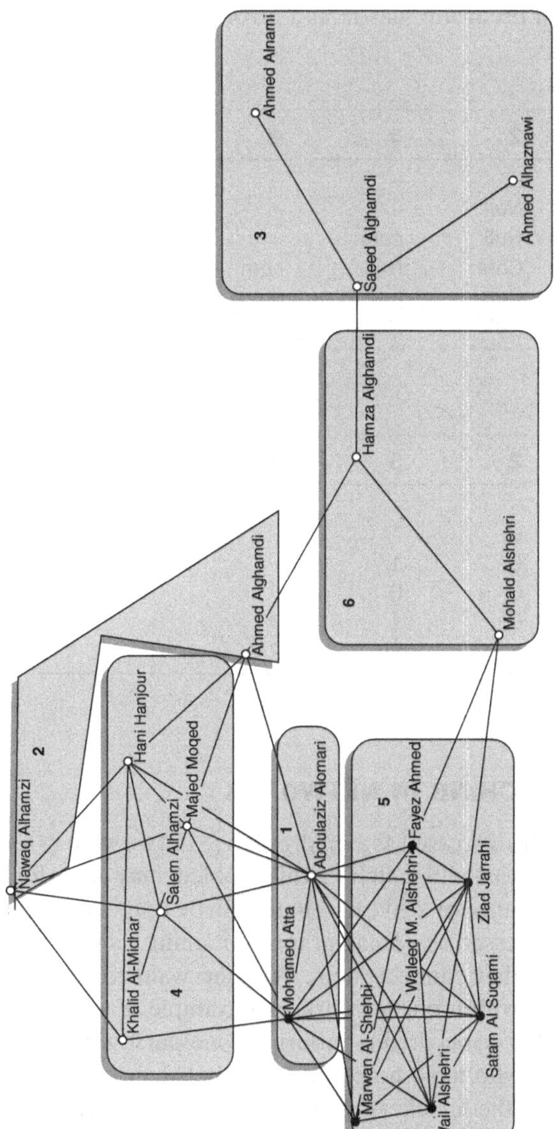

Figure XI.17. Block modeling with six blocks.

Here are the final predicate matrix and error matrix for the block modeling of Figure XI.17

	1	2	3	4	5	6
1	com	–	–	–	–	–
2	null	Null	–	–	–	–
3	null	Null	com	–	–	–
4	com	Com	Null	com	–	–
5	com	Null	Null	null	Com	–
6	null	Null	Null	null	Null	Com

	1	2	3	4	5	6
1	0	–	–	–	–	–
2	0	0	–	–	–	–
3	1	0	1	–	–	–
4	0	0	0	0	–	–
5	2	0	1	0	0	–
6	0	1	1	2	0	0

XI.6 PATTERN MATCHING IN NETWORKS

Often we have a pattern expressed as a small graph P and we want to see if it is possible to find a subgraph of G that will match P. This problem may arise, for instance, when we want to see if an instance of a given scenario can be found in a large network. The scenario would be expressed as a small graph containing a small number of vertices with specific relations that connect them. We then want to see if instances of the scenario can be found within our network. An example of such a pattern is shown in Figure XI.18. We have specified a pattern of one person who is connected *only* to three other people who have no connections between themselves. We can find three subgraphs within the hijackers' graph that contain a vertex connected to only three other vertices (marked 1, 2, and 3 in the figure); however, only 1 and 2 fully match the pattern. Subgraph 3 does not match the pattern because Fayez Ahmed and Ziad Jarrahi are connected. The naïve algorithm for finding exact matches of the pattern is based on simple backtracking – that is, if a mismatch is found the algorithm backtracks to the most recent junction in the graph visited before the failure. We can also search for approximate matches using techniques such as edit distances to find subgraphs that are similar to the pattern at hand. One of the most common patterns to be searched in a graph is some form of a directed graph that involves three vertices and some arcs connecting the vertices. This form of pattern is called a triad, and there are 16 different types of triads. One of them is the empty triad, in which there are no arcs at all, and another one is the full triad in which six arcs connect every possible pair of vertices in the triad.

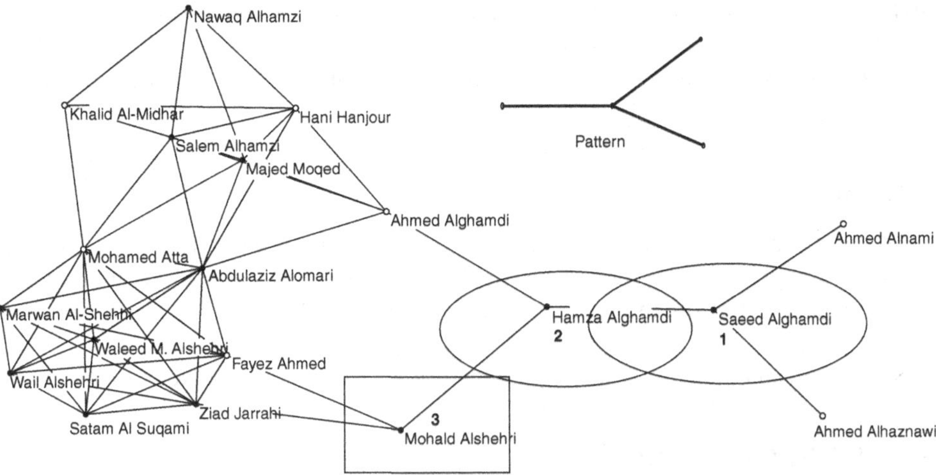

Figure XI.18. Pattern matching in the hijackers' graph.

XI.7 SOFTWARE PACKAGES FOR LINK ANALYSIS

There are several packages for performing link analysis in networks. Some are fairly expensive and hence are probably out of reach for the causal user. We describe here three packages that are either totally free or relatively inexpensive.

XI.7.1 Pajek

Pajek is a freeware developed by the University of Ljubljana that can handle networks containing hundreds of thousands of vertices. Pajek expects to get the input networks in a proprietary format, which includes the list of vertices and then lists of arcs (directed) and edges (undirected) between the vertices. There are programs that enable converting a simple set of binary connections to the Pajek (.net) format. Pajek supports a very large number of operations on networks, including centrality computations, path finding, component analysis, clustering, block modeling, and many other operations. In addition it includes a built-in drawing module that incorporates most the layout algorithms described in this chapter.

Pajek can be downloaded from
<http://vlado.fmf.uni-lj.si/pub/networks/pajek/>.
The converters can be downloaded from

<http://vlado.fmf.uni-lj.si/pub/networks/pajek/howto/text2pajek.htm> and
<http://vlado.fmf.uni-lj.si/pub/networks/pajek/howto/excel2Pajek.htm>.

XI.7.2 UCINET

UCINET is a fairly robust network analysis package. It is not free, but even for nonacademics it costs less than 300 dollars. It covers all the operations described in this chapter, including centrality measures (with a larger variety of options than

Pajek), clustering, path finding, and component analysis. UCINET can export and import Pajek files. Netdraw is the visualization package of UCINET.

UCINET and Netdraw can be downloaded from <http://www.analytictech.com/download_products.htm>.

XI.7.3 NetMiner

NetMiner is the most comprehensive package of the three, but it is also the most expensive. The professional version costs a little less than 1,000 dollars for commercial use. The package offers all the operations included in UCINET and Pajek and is fairly intuitive to use.

NetMiner can be downloaded from <http://www.netminer.com/NetMiner>.

XI.8 CITATIONS AND NOTES

Section XI.1

For a great introduction to graph algorithms, please refer to Aho, Hopcroft, and Ullman (1983). For in-depth coverage of the area of social network analysis, see Wasserman and Faust (1994) and Scott (2000).

Section XI.2

Force-based graph drawing algorithms are described in Kamada and Kawai (1989) and Fruchterman and Reingold (1991). Algorithms for drawing large graphs are addressed in Davidson and Harel (1996), Harel and Koren (2000), and Hadany and Harel (2001).

Section XI.4

The degree centrality was introduced in Freeman (1979). The betweenness centrality measure is due to Freeman (1977, 1979). The closeness centrality measure was introduced in Sabidussi (1966). The power centrality is due to Bonacich (1987). The eigenvector centrality originates from Bonacich (1972). Good descriptions of basic graph algorithms can be found in Aho et al. (1983). Cores have been introduced in Seidman (1983).

Section XI.5

The notions of structural equivalence and regular equivalence were introduced in Lorrain and White (1971) and further expanded in Batagalj, Doreian, and Ferligoi (1992) and Borgatti and Everett (1993). Block modeling was introduced in Borgatti and Everett (1992) and Hummon and Carley (1993). The implementation of block modeling in Pajek is described in Batagelj (1997) and De Nooy, Mrvar, and Batageli (2004).

Section XI.6

The notion of edit distance between graphs as vehicles for finding patterns in graphs is described in Zhang, Wang, and Shasha (1995). Finding approximate matches in undirected graphs is discussed in Wang et al. (2002).

XII

Text Mining Applications

Many text mining systems introduced in the late 1990s were developed by computer scientists as part of academic "pure research" projects aimed at exploring the capabilities and performance of the various technical components making up these systems. Most current text mining systems, however – whether developed by academic researchers, commercial software developers, or in-house corporate programmers – are built to focus on specialized applications that answer questions peculiar to a given problem space or industry need. Obviously, such specialized text mining systems are especially well suited to solving problems in academic or commercial activities in which large volumes of textual data must be analyzed in making decisions.

Three areas of analytical inquiry have proven particularly fertile ground for text mining applications. In various areas of *corporate finance*, bankers, analysts, and consultants have begun leveraging text mining capabilities to sift through vast amounts of textual data with the aims of creating usable forms of business intelligence, noting trends, identifying correlations, and researching references to specific transactions, corporate entities, or persons. In *patent research*, specialists across industry verticals at some of the world's largest companies and professional services firms apply text mining approaches to investigating patent development strategies and finding ways to exploit existing corporate patent assets better. In *life sciences*, researchers are exploring enormous collections of biomedical research reports to identify complex patterns of interactivities between proteins.

This chapter discusses prototypical text mining solutions adapted for use in each of these three problem spaces. Corporate intelligence and protein interaction analysis applications are useful as examples of software platforms widely applicable to various problems within very specific industry verticals. On the other hand, a patent research application is an example of a single, narrowly focused text mining application that can be used by specialists in corporations across a wide array of different industry verticals such as manufacturing, biotechnology, semiconductors, pharmaceuticals, materials sciences, chemicals, and other industries as well as patent professionals in law firms, consultancies, engineering companies, and even some government agencies.

The discussions of applications in this chapter intentionally emphasize those elements of a text mining system that have the greatest impact on user activities, although some broader architectural and functional points will at least be peripherally considered. This emphasis is chosen partly because many text mining applications, by their very nature, build on generic text mining components (e.g., preprocessing routines, search algorithms) and create application specificity by means of customizing search refinement and user-interface elements in ways that are more oriented toward specialized user activities with particular problem space emphases. This approach also serves to permit discussion of how some example text mining applications tend to "look and feel" in the real world to users.

This chapter first discusses some general considerations before exploring in detail a business intelligence application aimed at addressing corporate finance questions. Discovery and exploration of biological pathways information and patent search are more briefly treated.

XII.1 GENERAL CONSIDERATIONS

The three text mining applications examined in this chapter exhibit a fair amount of commonality in terms of basic architecture and functionality – especially with respect to the preprocessing operations and core text mining query capabilities on which they depend. However, the systems differ markedly in their implementations of background knowledge, their preset queries, and their visualization functionality as well as specifics of the content they address.

XII.1.1 Background Knowledge

Background knowledge, preset queries, and visualization capabilities are the areas in which custom text mining applications are most commonly oriented toward the particularities of a specific problem space. A discussion of general considerations germane to these three areas is useful in considering how text mining applications are crafted – especially when they are crafted from – or "on top of" – components derived from more generic text mining systems.

XII.1.2 Generalized Background Knowledge versus Specialized Background Knowledge

As has already been discussed in Chapter II, background knowledge can play many different useful roles in the architecture of text mining systems. However, beyond the question of *how* background knowledge is architecturally integrated into a system, questions of *what* constitutes the content of the background knowledge most often relate to the nature of that system's application.

Indeed, many text mining applications rely on both generalized and specialized background knowledge. As the name implies, generalized background knowledge derives from general-information source materials that are broadly useful within a single language. Generalized background knowledge tends to involve background knowledge from very broadly applicable knowledge domains.

Generalized background knowledge frequently comes in the form of taxonomies, lexicons, and whole ontologies derived from widely useful knowledge sources. Such sources can be as formalized as the WordNet ontology or as informal as simpler taxonomies or lexicons based on general-use knowledge sources such as commercial dictionaries, encyclopedias, fact books, or thesauri. The rise of various aids to ontology creation and translation, including the DARPA Agent Markup Language (DAML) and Ontology Web Language (OWL), has increased the availability and number of such generalized background knowledge sources.

Specialized background knowledge originates from knowledge sources that relate more specifically to a particular problem area or sphere of activity. Such knowledge need not come from overly complex ontological source materials.

For instance, many text mining applications aimed at solving problems in the life sciences make use of partial or whole listings of terms and term relationships from the National Library of Medicine's controlled vocabulary, MeSH, to create taxonomies or refinement constraints useful and consistent with document collections populated by MEDLINE/PubMed documents. However, text mining applications can also incorporate more comprehensive background knowledge by integrating elements of various public domain or commercial formal ontologies; examples of such sources include the GO Consortium's ontologies and ontologies developed by companies such as Reed Elsevier or BioWisdom.

Even the most general-purpose text mining applications can usually benefit from generalized background knowledge, but text mining applications aimed at niche activities in particular benefit from the inclusion of specialized background knowledge. Text mining applications may implement both types of background knowledge or may meet application needs modestly with information from only one type of background knowledge source. Some text mining applications implement specialized background knowledge from diverse multiple domains. For instance, a text mining application aimed at investigating patents in the automotive industry might benefit from specialized background knowledge related to patent-specific activities as well as topics in the automotive industry. Figure XII.1 illustrates how a taxonomy of corporate information can help provide context and structure to the browsing of distributions. Figure XII.2 shows how an interactive visualization graph can be made more relevant to an industry specialist by leverage background knowledge in the form of a controlled vocabulary.

Designers of text mining systems need to carefully weigh the real benefits of including various types of background in their applications. Including too much background knowledge can have negative impacts on system performance, maintenance, and usability. Using multiple sources of background knowledge in any text mining application can increase the likelihood of introducing inconsistencies in terms of how data are categorized or defined and, as a consequence, increase the maintenance work required to make the background knowledge consistent. Also, larger amounts of background knowledge – even if internally consistent – can make using a text mining application more cumbersome for the user.

For instance, an application oriented toward exploring a collection of proteomics research documents might have available a listing of the chemical terms pertinent to proteomics as elements of a query or refinement constraint. If, However, one were to include a comprehensive, controlled vocabulary of terms useful across all of the various academic disciplines concerned with chemical compounds in this proteomics-oriented application's background knowledgebase, users might be forced to navigate much larger hierarchical trees of less relevant concepts when choosing entities for

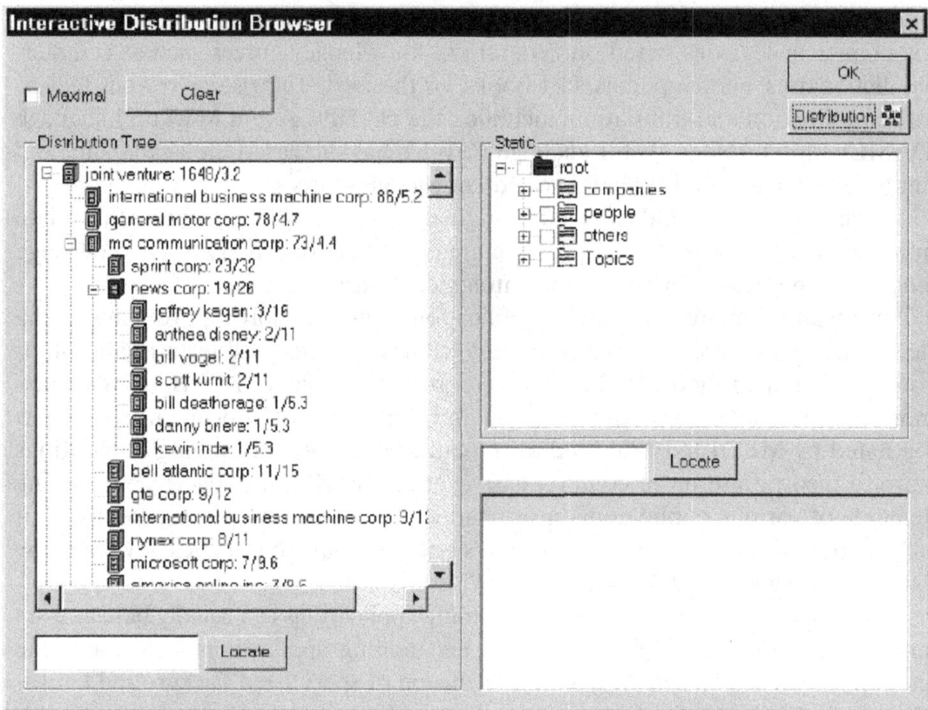

Figure XII.1. A distribution browser that makes use of a taxonomy based on specialized background knowledge. (From Feldman, Fresko, Hirsh, et al. 1998.)

queries. Similarly, these users might encounter endlessly scrolling pull-down boxes when attempting to create refinement conditions. Both of these circumstances would limit the intuitiveness and speed of knowledge discovery activities for users interested only in topics pertinent to proteomics research.

Finally, inclusion of larger specialized background knowledge data, in particular, can lead to much more labor-intensive and difficult data pruning requirements over time. Complex background knowledge maintenance requirements may also introduce additional overhead in terms of application GUI screens devoted to optimizing maintenance activities. As a result, there is significant incentive for designers to adopt a "best overall bang for the buck" approach to employing background knowledge in their applications.

XII.1.3 Leveraging Preset Queries and Constraints in Generalized Browsing Interfaces

In addition to leveraging the power of specialized background knowledge, a text mining system can gain a great deal of de facto domain customization by offering users lists of prespecified queries and search refinement constraints meaningful to the problem space they are interested in investigating. With respect to queries, preset or "canned" query lists commonly make use of two simple approaches to providing helpful queries to speed along knowledge discovery in a given application domain.

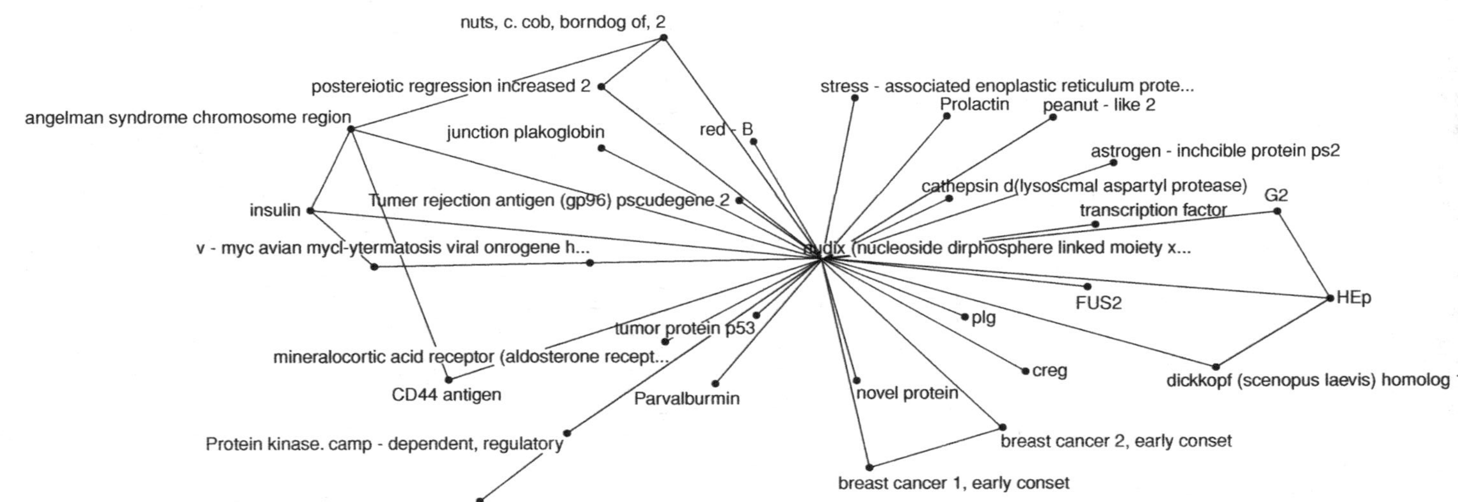

Figure XII.2. Spring graph of concepts (informed by the MeSH-controlled vocabulary). (From Feldman, Fresko, Hirsh, et al. 1998.)

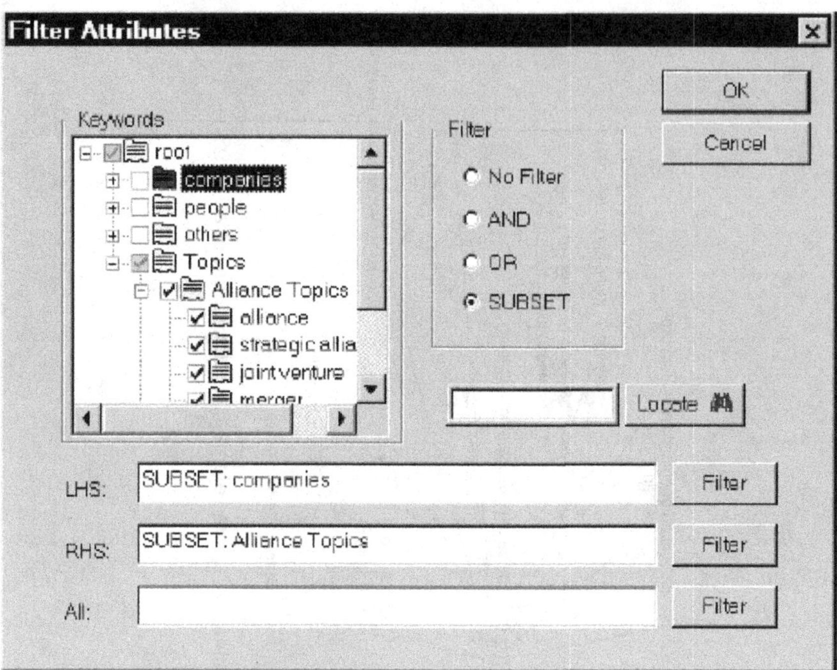

Figure XII.3. A constraint filter interface for exploring association rules that leverages corporate M&A background knowledge.

First, the types of queries typical to a given domain can be made available in a custom GUI. For instance, if it is frequently true that knowledge workers in proteomics are looking for associations between proteins, a text mining application aimed at proteomics researchers could use an association-oriented query construction GUI as the default query interface. This query construction interface can be supplemented to enable rapid creation of association rule-type queries with a pick list of prespecified queries to allow quick interrogation of the problem space.

Second, text mining applications often make use of such "canned query" pick lists to help create templates with which to populate new queries similar to those common for the domain. Query templates can be enhanced with pull-downs to help support filling in various entities and parameters in the query to speed along query construction.

Often, grouping and labeling of preset queries can greatly improve the ease of query construction and execution. Compared with generic query construction interfaces like those illustrated in Section II.5, which provide great flexibility but force a user to think through each choice of constraint parameters and query variables (such as entities or events), well-organized and identified picklists of queries appropriate for a problem space trade flexibility for speed and ease of use during query construction.

With regard to query constraints, specialized background knowledge can be used not only to help create a consistent, domain-specific nomenclature for concepts found among documents in a document collection and useful taxonomies in which to place concepts but also to facilitate the use of postquery refinement constraints relevant to the applications aims (see Figure XII.3). For instance, instead of having all concepts from a domain within the refinement lists, "pruned" lists of taxonomical groupings or entities useful as parameters can be used to populate pulldowns of constraints that are meaningful to specialists.

Designers of text mining applications can also preset variables appropriate to the text mining application's realistic universe of potentially useful constraints. Doing so provides "assisted" constraint creation more relevant to the problem space addressed by the application.

XII.1.4 Specialized Visualization Approaches

As mentioned in Section X.1, visualization approaches demonstrate strengths and weaknesses with respect to graphing different types of data. This is a key consideration in determining the types of visualization approaches useful for a given text mining application. Providing circle graphs to investment bankers interested in tracking trends in corporate events over time might not stimulate much exploration of these trends by users, whereas providing for the quick generation of histograms of corporate names mentioned in articles for a given period might prove very useful to this same group of investment bankers when tracking corporate activity and press coverage.

One important consideration for developers of text mining applications when considering the best use of visualization methodologies is the integration of specialized background knowledge in the generation of graphs. Just as specialized background knowledge can be used to inform domain-specific constraints, specialized background knowledge can also be used to help format the information presented in graphs to make them more relevant to the problem space they model.

For instance, in assigning colors to the elements of a visualization, a text mining application can offer a GUI a palette of colors associated with concept names derived from a specialized background knowledge lexicon. Alternatively, a visualization GUI itself can contain a slider widget that allows constraint filters to switch between values that come from prespecified thresholds relevant to the text mining application's problem space.

XII.1.5 Citations and Notes

Some general introductory materials useful to gaining perspective on text mining applications include Hearst (1999); Nasukawa and Nagano (2001); and Varadarajan, Kasravi, and Feldman (2002).

Information resources on the DARPA DAML program can be found at <www.daml.org>. Resources on MeSH and UMLS are available from the United States National Library of Medicine Medical Subject Headings Web site <http://www.nlm.nih.gov/mesh/meshhome.html.>

XII.2 CORPORATE FINANCE: MINING INDUSTRY LITERATURE FOR BUSINESS INTELLIGENCE

Text mining approaches lend themselves to many of the business intelligence tasks performed in corporate finance. Text mining tools are particularly well suited to automating, augmenting, and transforming business intelligence activities more traditionally accomplished by means of labor-intensive, manual reviews of industry literature for patterns of information. These manual reviews typically entail sifting through vast amounts of textual data relating to companies, corporate executives, products, financial transactions, and industry trends.

In the past, such reviews of industry literature have been performed by large cadres of analysts in investment banks, corporate development departments, management consultancies, research think tanks, and other organizations that now face continuing pressure to streamline operational costs while increasing the comprehensiveness and quality of their analytical work. Employing text mining applications customized for use in business intelligence tasks can dramatically improve the speed, exhaustiveness, and quality of such reviews. As a result, business intelligence systems based on text mining methodologies are fast becoming a critical part of many corporate analysts' professional tool chests.

This section describes a system we will call *Industry Analyzer* – a simple example of a business intelligence application based on many of the technical approaches discussed throughout this book. The example is purposely meant to be a simple one, using only a small data collection, very simple background knowledge support, and no link detection functionality, with an emphasis on a high-level, user-oriented view of the application.

Specifically, Industry Analyzer is an application developed to allow banking analysts – as well as their peers in corporate development and M&A groups – to explore industry information about companies, people, products, and events (transactions, corporate actions, financial reporting announcements) in a given industry vertical. The implementation example has been configured to support knowledge discovery in news stories about the life sciences business sector.

The life sciences business sector – which includes a number of constituent industries such as pharmaceuticals, biotechnology, health care provisioning, and so on – is a complex sector for small industry groups to follow given the thousands of companies developing and selling tens of thousands of major products to hundreds of millions of people in the United States alone. Business analysts of the life sciences sector need to sift through vast numbers of references in news stories quickly to find information relevant to their concerns: how well a company or a product is doing, what a company's strategic partners or competitors are, which companies have announced corporate actions, what products company managers are pushing in interviews, which companies' products are getting the most coverage, and so on. Some analysts seek information suggesting potential merger or acquisition pairings, for much investment banking business comes from being an advisor on such transactions. Others look for smaller life sciences companies that show signs of one day going public, whereas still others seek news that might indicate a company may be open to divesting itself of a product or division and entering either an asset sale or structuring a spin-out.

Industry Analyzer assists in allowing industry analysts to comb large amounts of trade information in their daily work more effectively. In a straightforward way, it facilitates the creation of simple searches and, perhaps most importantly, supports visualizations that help analysts better digest and interact with information collected from numerous individual, industry-specific news stories.

The implementation example of Industry Analyzer presented here has a narrow focus on biomedical companies involved in cancer research and treatment. This is

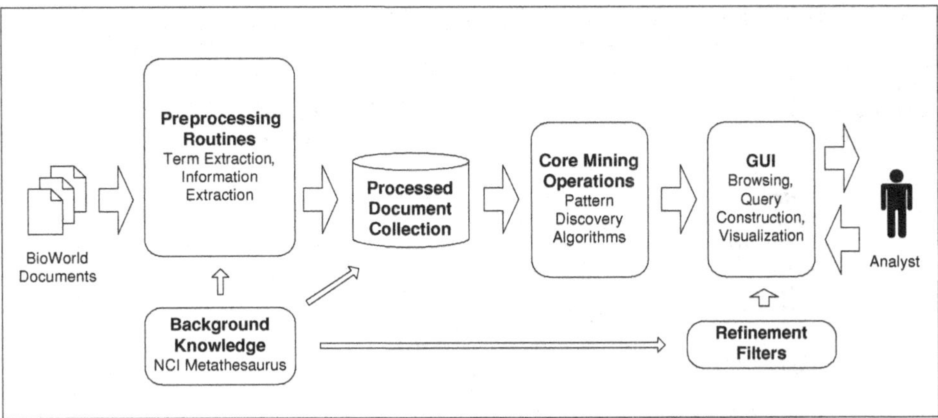

Figure XII.4. Industry Analyzer functional architecture.

not inconsistent with the types of implementations encountered in reasonable, real-world scenarios, for banking analysts typically specialize in exploring information related to particular niches within an overall industry vertical.

XII.2.1 Industry Analyzer: Basic Architecture and Functionality

Industry Analyzer follows the rough architectural outline for a text mining system illustrated in Section II.2. Because it is not a complex system, it exhibits a relatively simple functional architecture (see Figure XII.4).

Other than its content, background knowledge sources, and some of its presentation layer elements, the Industry Analyzer is built around quite generic preprocessing and core mining components of the type discussed at length in Chapters II, III, IV, V, VI, VII, and VIII. The application can be described in terms of the main components that make up its functional architecture.

Data and Background Knowledge Sources

The raw data source for Industry Analyzer's document collection is a group of 124 news articles from *BioWorld*, an industry publication that reports news relating to M&A activities in the life sciences business sector. The articles had a particular focus on biotech and pharmaceutical companies and their products.

The articles were collected from a period stretching from 11 October 2004 to 17 November 2004. The following is a typical text example from these *BioWorld* articles:

> Biogen Idec Inc. ended its third quarter with $543 million in revenues, slightly lower than analyst estimates, as it nears the one-year anniversary of a merger that made it the world's largest biotech company.
>
> The Cambridge, Mass.-based company reported non-GAAP earnings per share of 37 cents and net income of $132 million, compared with 35 cents and $123 million for the quarter last year. Analysts consensus estimate for the quarter was 35 cents.

Industry Analyzer utilizes a very simple specialized background knowledge implementation primarily consisting of taxonomies of drug names, genes, and

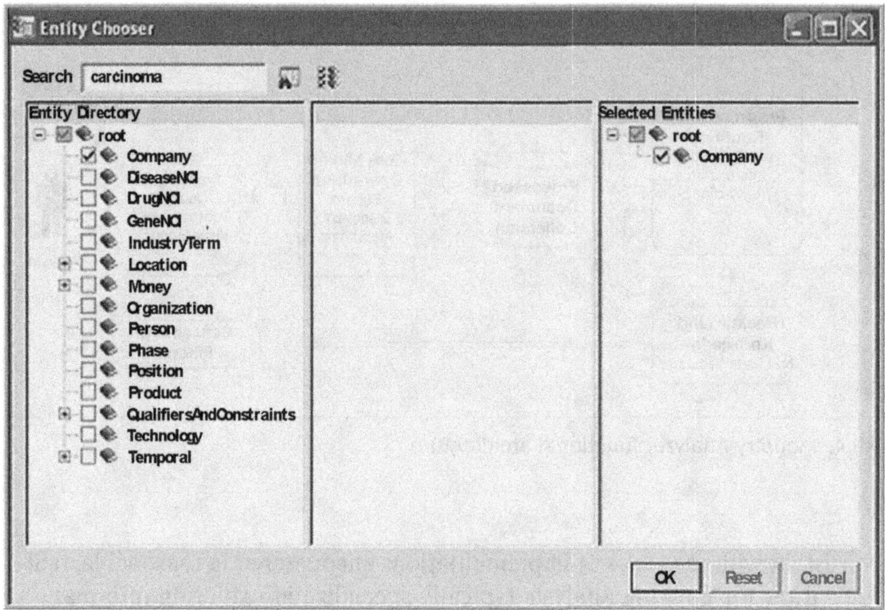

Figure XII.5. The taxonomy used by Industry Analyzer supplemented by background knowledge. (Courtesy of the ClearForest Corporation.)

diseases taken from the National Cancer Institute's NCI Thesaurus, which is in part based on the National Library of Medicine's Unified Medical Language System (UMLS) Metathesaurus. The taxonomies can be leveraged with little modification from the NCI Thesaurus's formalized hierarchical nomenclature and positioned within an overarching taxonomy of entities to support all of Industry Analyzer's functional requirements.

The NCI Thesaurus is a generally useful background knowledge source for building text mining application taxonomies, for although it probably cannot be described as a full-blown ontology it nevertheless includes true IS_A-type hierarchies. These hierarchies detail semantic relationships among drugs, genes, diseases, chemicals, organisms, anatomy, and proteins for thousands of defined domain concepts.

The implementation of Industry Analyzer presented in this example also includes some less formal background knowledge for corporate organizations, locations, and industry concepts culled from various online sources. An example of an Industry Analyzer GUI for choosing entities based on a hierarchy informed by background knowledge can be seen in Figure XII.5.

Preprocessing Operations

Industry Analyzer uses a simple regimen of preprocessing operations to prepare the application's processed document collection. The *BioWorld* documents are first subjected to a series of term-extraction methodologies like those described in Section III.4. This involves the labeling of each document (i.e., *BioWorld* article) with a set of terms extracted from the document.

Biogen Idec Inc. ended its third **quarter** with **$543 million** in **revenues**, slightly lower than **analyst estimates**, as it nears the one-year anniversary of a **merger** that made it the world's largest **biotech company**.

The **Cambridge, Mass.**-based **company** reported non-GAAP **earnings per share** of **37 cents** and **net income** of **$132 million**, compared with **35 cents** and **$123 million** for the **quarter** last year. Analysts **consensus estimate** for the **quarter** was **35 cents**.

Figure XII.6. Example of output from Industry Analyzer's term extraction process. (Courtesy of *BioWorld*.)

Initially, standard linguistic processing routines are run against each document, performing various tokenization, POS-tagging, and lemmatization operations with the aid of an external lexicon and a limited amount of manually tagged data for training. Then, lists of term candidates are generated for each document, after which filtering routines are run to create a final list of terms with which to tag each document. In addition, a date stamp is added to each document based on the publication date of the article.

Industry Analyzer's term extraction processes actually save the output and all the tags generated by the preprocessing routines in an XML-based, tagged file format. A highly simplified version of the output from the term extraction process can be seen in Figure XII.6.

Feature extraction at the term level is important for an application like Industry Analyzer because word-level or even more granular feature-level extraction would miss or misinterpret many of the multiword terms-of-art used in both corporate finance and the life sciences. A simple example can be seen in Figure XII.6 in which the term *Biogen Idec Inc.* has been extracted. Because Biogen and Idec were both individual company names before a merger that created Biogen Idec Inc., identifying Biogen Idec Inc. as a single entity is important information that marks this article's content as referring to a time after the two companies merged to become the world's largest biotechnology company. Similarly, terms like *net income, consensus estimate,* and *earning per share* all have very specific meanings to corporate finance analysts that are highly relevant to knowledge discovery activities relating to corporate events.

Term-level extraction also better integrates with concept-level categorization of documents, which appends concept names descriptive of a particular document that may not actually appear as terms in that document. For instance, in the fragment illustrated in Figure XII.6, concept tags such as *midcap, earnings report, publicly held* (versus *privately held*), or *company-neutral* (as opposed to *company-positive* or *company-negative*) might also be automatically or manually added to the postprocessed document to provide useful supplementary information to the entity-related data revealed by the term extraction process so as to enhance the quality of subsequent information extraction–oriented processing.

After completing the term extraction processes, Industry Analyzer subjects documents to a rule-based information extraction process based on a simplified version of the DIAL language described in Appendix A. By taking advantage of sets of formal financial and biomedical rule bases, Industry Analyzer is able to identify not only repeated instances of patterns involving entities but to construct basic "facts" (e.g., *Biogen Idec is the world's largest biotech company, AlphaCo and BetaCo are strategic*

```
FStrategicAllianceCCM(C1, C2) :-
Company(Comp1) OptCompanyDetails "and" skip(Company(x), SkipFail,
10) Company(Comp2)
OptCompanyDetails skip(WCStrategicAllianceVerbs, SkipFailComp, 20)
WCStrategicPartnershipVerbs skip(WCStrategicAlliance,
SkipFail, 20) WCStrategicAlliance
verify(WholeNotInPredicate(Comp1, @PersonName))
verify(WholeNotInPredicate(Comp2, @PersonName))
@% @!
{ C1 = Comp1; C2 = Comp2} ;
```

Figure XII.7. IE rule for identifying a strategic partnership between two companies. (Courtesy of the ClearForest Corporation.)

alliance partners, or *third quarter net income for Acme Biotech was $22 million*) and "events" (e.g., *the Glaxo and Smith Kline merger, the filing of BetaCo's Chapter 11 bankruptcy*, or *the Theravance IPO*) involving entities derived from these patterns. An example of a DIAL-like rule can be found in Figure XII.7.

This rule is one of several possible ones for identifying strategic alliances between companies (within a rule-based language syntax like that of the DIAL language). Note that the rule also includes a few constraints for discarding any potential pairings between a company and a person as a strategic alliance.

After rule-based information extraction has been completed, a queryable processed document collection is created that not only contains entity-related information but also information related to a large number of identified "facts" and "events." A formal list of the types of facts and events identified within this document collection is also stored and made available to support fact- or event-based querying by Industry Analyzer's core mining operations.

Core Mining Operations and Refinement Constraints

Industry Analyzer supports a reasonably broad range of common text mining query types like those discussed in Chapter II. It supports queries to produce various distribution and proportion results as well as the ability to generate and display information relating to frequent sets and associations found within its document collection. Industry Analyzer can also support the construction and execution of maximal association queries.

As a general rule, with most current corporate finance–oriented text mining applications, there is little need for exotic query types. What is more important for the vast majority of corporate finance users is

(a) a rich and flexible set of entities, fact types, and event types with which to shape queries, and
(b) a relatively easy way to generate and display results that lead to iterative exploration of the data stored in the document collection.

For instance, queries, regardless of the kind of result set display chosen by the user, should be easily constructible on the basis of combinations of entity, fact, and event information for corporate finance users. To support this, Industry Analyzer offers GUI-driven query generation with prepopulated pick lists and pull-downs of entities, fact types, and event types for all of its main forms of queries. Figure XII.8 shows how a query can be generated in industry Analyzer.

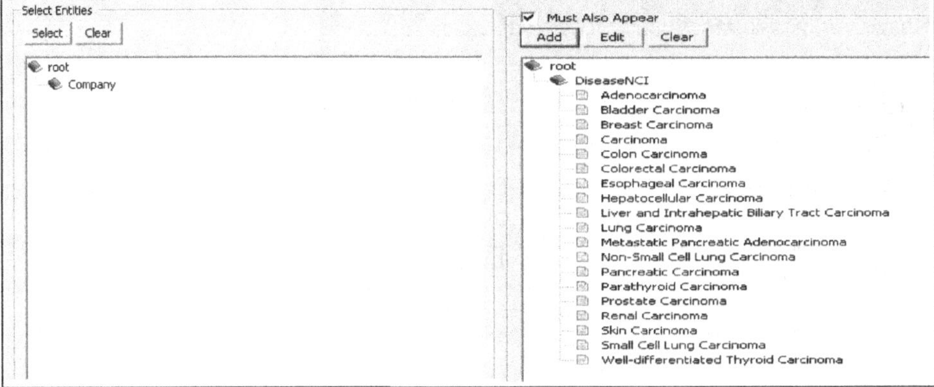

Figure XII.8. Generating a query of the type "entity within the context of" in Industry Analyzer. (Courtesy of the ClearForest Corporation.)

In addition to these ease-of-use features, Industry Analyzer has the capability of offering a user a menu of common queries. The prototype described here contains preset, distribution-type queries for querying a company name supplied by the user in the context of *merger, acquisition*, and *strategic alliance*. It also contains a list of preconfigured association-type queries for a given company name and *product*, other *company*, and *person*. These extremely easy-to-execute queries allow even less technically literate analysts or infrequent users of the Industry Analyzer system to derive some value from it. On the other hand, more experienced users can leverage such preconfigured queries as a quick way to create a broad "jump-start" query that can then be shaped through refinement, browsing, and further query-based search.

Refinement constraints carefully customized to the needs of corporate finance professionals can also do much to achieve the goal of making knowledge-discovery query operations intuitive, useful, and iterative. Industry Analyzer supports a wide range of background, syntactical, quality-threshold, and redundancy constraints.

Presentation Layer – GUI and Visualization Tools

Industry Analyzer approached the design of its GUI and its choice of visualization approaches with the understanding that industry analysts are savvy computer users but that they are not typically programmers. As a result, Industry Analyzer's GUI can be seen to be more of a dashboard or workbench through which nearly all functionality is available via graphical menus and pop-ups – and, consequently, with less emphasis on giving the analysts direct, script-level access to the underlying query language (or to any of the preprocessing routines such as the rule bases for Information Extraction, etc.).

A very important part of creating a custom application for a particular audience of users is ensuring that presentation-layer elements speak to the specific knowledge discovery needs of that audience. Much of this can be accomplished by having all knowledge discovery search and display elements "make sense" in terms of the nomenclature and taxonomical groupings relevant to the audience – that is, by simply exposing the domain-relevant entity, fact, and event information derived both by background knowledge sources and by preprocessing extraction routines.

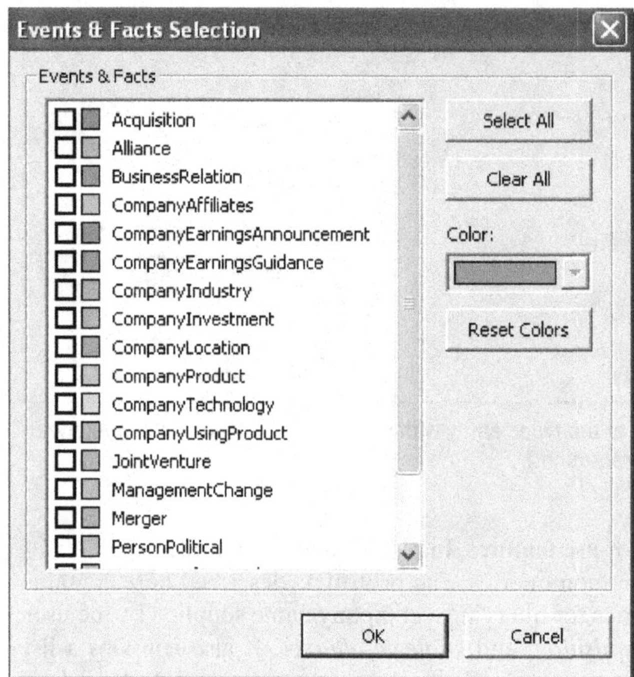

Figure XII.9. GUI-enabled pick list for selecting facts and events for a visualization. (Courtesy of the ClearForest Corporation.)

Industry Analyzer attempts to accomplish this last objective through its reliance on consistent display of an entity hierarchy for queries including entity names in their search parameters. The system reinforces this main GUI-enabled search construction paradigm through an additional emphasis on supporting the construction of fact- and event-oriented searches via consistent pull-down and pop-up listings of event and fact types. The application also attempts to use these same pick-lists for formatting visualizations in an effort to acclimate users further to a familiar listing of these event and fact types (see Figure XII.9).

In terms of display and visualization of search results, Industry Analyzer defaults to returning search results in a simple table view display. See the example in Figure XII.10.

Industry Analyzer also supports a range of more sophisticated visual graphing and mapping options for displaying query results, including the following:

- ***Histograms*** for visualizing absolute occurrence number counts, counts in context, and distribution-type queries;
- ***Simple concept graphs*** for clearly displaying relationship information between entities, facts, or events; and
- ***Circle graphs*** for visualizing associations, associations within context and organized according to some taxonomical ordering, and large-scale relationship maps with large numbers of constituent points.

Such visualizations can be executed either from a dedicated pop-up GUI after a query is run or directly from the table view display for a partial or full set of query

150 Rows in Query Result

Company	Person	Documents
Prometheus Laboratories Inc.	Michael Allen	2
Prometheus Laboratories Inc.	Toni Wayne	2
Trubion Pharmaceuticals Inc.	Judith Woods	2
Varian Medical Systems Inc.	Chris Hanna	1
Vasomedical Inc.	Thomas Glover	1
VaxInnate Corp.	David Jackson	1
VaxInnate Corp.	Janet Smart	1
Vicuron Pharmaceuticals Inc.	Alan Dunton	1
Vivus Inc.	Timothy Morris	1
Xenomics Inc.	Thomas Adams	1
XenoPort Inc.	William Rieflin	1
Y's Therapeutics Co. Ltd.	John Wulf	1
Zyomyx Inc.	Peter Wagner	1
Zyomyx Inc.	Robert Monaghan	1
Questcor Pharmaceuticals Inc.	Albert Hansen	1
R2 Technology Inc.	Terance Kinninger	1
Response Biomedical Corp.	Michael Groves	1
Resverlogix Corp.	Ravindra Jahagirdar	1
Saegis Pharmaceuticals Inc.	Jack Anthony	1
Salix Pharmaceuticals Ltd.	David Taylor	1
Savient Pharmaceuticals Inc.	Jeremy Hayward-Surry	1
Scios Inc.	George Schreiner	1
Serono International SA	Stuart Grant	1
Skye Pharma plc	Alan Bray	1
Spectrum Pharmaceuticals Inc.	Kolli Prasad	1
Spectrum Pharmaceuticals Inc.	Paul Vilk	1
Stem Cells Inc.	Judi Lum	1
Synta Pharmaceuticals Corp.	William Reardon	1
Theratechnologies Inc.	Luc Tanguay	1
Theratechnologies Inc.	Yves Rosconi	1

Figure XII.10. Table view of connections between persons and companies in the context of management changes. (Courtesy of the ClearForest Corporation.)

results. For example, a user could interactively decide to generate a circle graph visualization after choosing the first two companies from the query results displayed in the Table View illustrated in Figure XII.10. The resulting circle graph can be seen in Figure XII.11.

Finally, from any of the result-set displays, a user can interactively navigate through point-and-click actions to either a summarized or full, annotated version of the actual document text underlying the query results. This allows a corporate analyst to move quickly from high-level entity, fact, and event views that consider

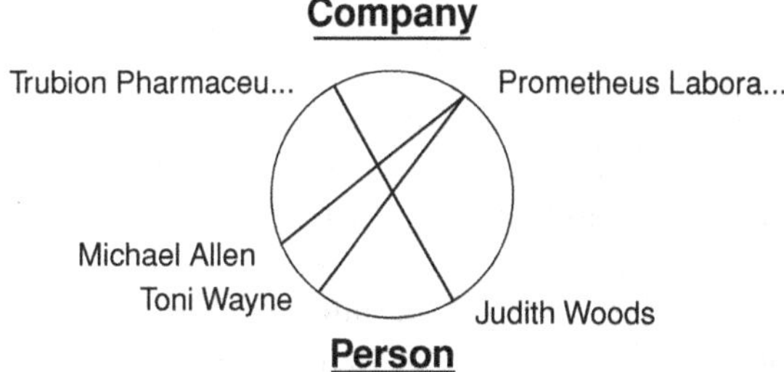

Figure XII.11. Circle graph showing connections between people and companies in the context of management change. (Courtesy of the ClearForest Corporation.)

information based on all or part of a corpus of documents to more specific information included in a particular article.

XII.2.2 Application Usage Scenarios

Corporate finance professionals in banks and corporate M&A groups often have overriding themes for the research that they do. We can examine how a few of these might be translated into typical interactions with Industry Analyzer's knowledge discovery capabilities.

Examining the Biotech Industry Trade Press for Information on Merger Activity

Much of the time of corporate finance analysts at investment banks and in the corporate development organizations of companies is spent tracking potential and actual merger activity. Knowing about specific potential mergers can allow corporate finance professionals to get involved with the participants in those transactions before a deal is completed, or better advise existing clients about the prospective ramifications of a transaction on the overall market in a timely fashion. Having a full and current sense of completed mergers in an industry vertical is critical to understanding the competitive landscape within that vertical; this type of knowledge is a necessary component to client advisory in a competitive corporate environment in which all public corporations – and most private – are potential merger targets.

Trends in merger activity can also directly affect many specific areas of a corporate analyst's work. For instance, if there is a sudden up-tick in trade journal reports of merger activity, an overall industry consolidation may be taking place. If mergers are all clustered around a common set of product types, merger activity may suggest a hot area for new products because the activity may reflect pent-up customer demand or failures among some big companies' in-house R&D efforts on these products. Conversely, a leveling off of valuations paid in cash and stock for the smaller of the merged entities may suggest some cooling or maturation of the markets that might indicate less favorable short- or midterm trends.

To explore merger activity with Industry Analyzer, an analyst might initiate a broad search for all "merger" events among biotech companies available in the document collection to see if any look interesting and worthy of further, more detailed investigation. In Industry Analyzer, this can be done simply through a series of graphical menus, starting with a pick list of events and facts available for search selection (see Figure XII.12). A subsequent pop-up menu offers the ability for a user to add constraints to the query.

In our example, the user chooses not to add any constraints to his or her query because of the modest number of articles in the document collection. After the user clicks the OK button to initiate the query, the default table view brings back formatted results for the query results (see Figure XII.13).

At this stage, the analyst decides that he or she is quite interested in looking at a reference to the Biogen–Idec merger. The analyst can then simply highlight the desired event and click on it to "jump" either to a summarized version of the relevant article or an annotated view of the full text of the article containing the

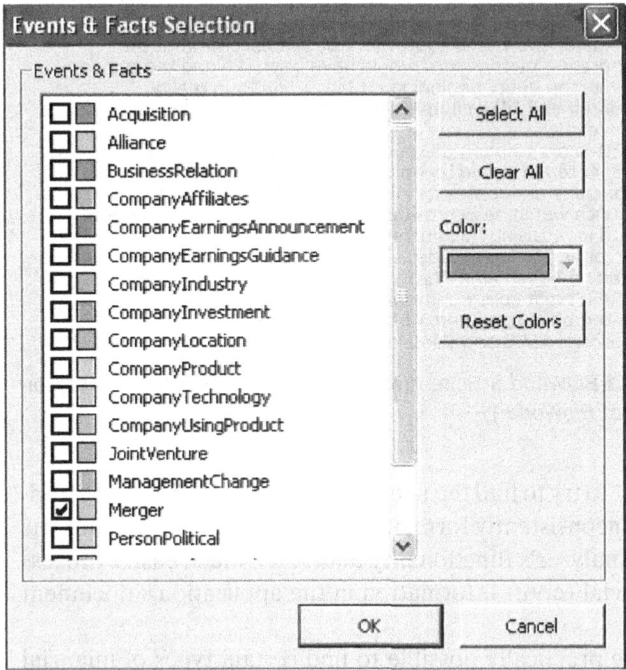

Figure XII.12. Initiating a query for all merger events in the document collection. (Courtesy of the ClearForest Corporation.)

highlighted merger reference. Figure XII.14 shows what the analyst would encounter upon choosing the full, annotated view of the article text.

When moving from the table view entry to the annotated full text of the article, the analyst is taken to the point in the article containing the reference. A consistent color-coding coding methodology for identifying event and fact types can be used throughout Industry Analyzer. This color-key approach can be used to identify event and fact occurrences visually by type in document text; it can also be used in a way that is carried over consistently into graph-type visualizations. In both cases, the user may choose which color-key scheme works best for his or her purposes.

Exploring Corporate Earnings Announcements

Corporate finance analysts also expend a great deal of effort finding financial reports on companies that they do not typically follow. Unfortunately, although public company financial announcements are widely available, it is often very

Acquisition Merger

Company	Company
Enhance Biotech Inc.	U.S. Ardent
Biogen Inc.	Idec Pharmaceuticals Inc
Biogen Idec Inc.	Idec Pharmaceuticals Inc
Amgen Inc.	Immunex Corp

Figure XII.13. Table view of all reported mergers between biotech companies in the document collection. (Courtesy of the ClearForest Corporation.)

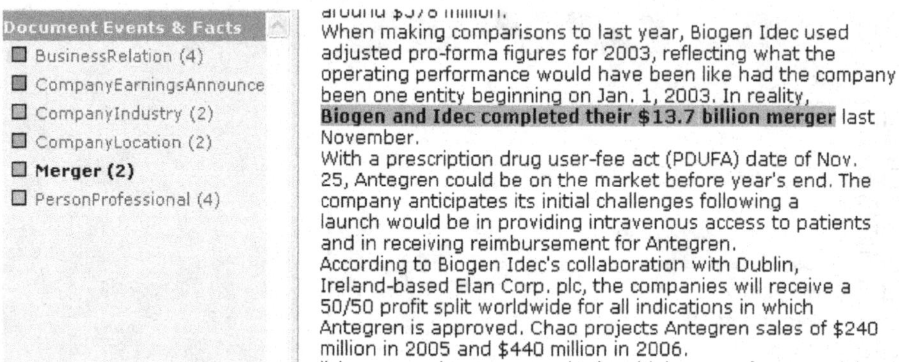

Document Events & Facts
BusinessRelation (4)
CompanyEarningsAnnounce
CompanyIndustry (2)
CompanyLocation (2)
Merger (2)
PersonProfessional (4)
When making comparisons to last year, Biogen Idec used adjusted pro-forma figures for 2003, reflecting what the operating performance would have been like had the company been one entity beginning on Jan. 1, 2003. In reality, Biogen and Idec completed their $13.7 billion merger last November.
With a prescription drug user-fee act (PDUFA) date of Nov. 25, Antegren could be on the market before year's end. The company anticipates its initial challenges following a launch would be in providing intravenous access to patients and in receiving reimbursement for Antegren.
According to Biogen Idec's collaboration with Dublin, Ireland-based Elan Corp. plc, the companies will receive a 50/50 profit split worldwide for all indications in which Antegren is approved. Chao projects Antegren sales of $240 million in 2005 and $440 million in 2006.

Figure XII.14. A merger event in a *BioWorld* article. (Image courtesy of the ClearForest Corporation. Text in image courtesy of *BioWorld*.)

time-consuming for the analyst to try to find the needed financial information by wading through large numbers of inconsistently formatted financial reporting documents and press releases. Industry Analyzer's functionality makes it a much easier process to investigate corporate financial report information in the application's document collection.

Indeed, it may not even be practically possible to find certain types of financial reporting information without an application like Industry Analyzer. Suppose an analyst vaguely remembers hearing that a biotech company reported net income in the $130–140 million range for the third quarter of 2004. This analyst, however, does not remember or never learned the name of the company. In this type of situation – which represents one potential variation on very common scenario in which an analyst has only partial bits of tantalizing information about a company but not its name – the analyst could spend days sifting through voluminous financial reports issued by larger biotech and pharmaceutical companies before happening upon the right one.

The analyst might further want to know if more than one company met the criteria for the period. Hunting and pecking through financial reports and online databases even for a few days might not bring a sense of resolution for this search because so many traditional corporate information resources are (a) published in various types of financial reporting documents and are (b), in general, rigidly organized around explicit knowledge of a company name one is interested in investigating.

The first step in Industry Analyzer would be to execute a query on the event type called *Company Earnings Announcement*. The analyst could find this by simply scrolling the main pick list of fact and event types in Industry Analyzer's main search menu (see Figure XII.15).

Unlike the earlier simple search for all companies reporting mergers in the document article collections, this query also relies on some adjustment of constraint filters to help pinpoint potentially useful answers to the analyst's query. As can be seen in Figure XII.15, after selecting *Company Earnings Announcement* as the main event for his or her query, the analyst is given an opportunity to choose certain types of constraints. In the current example, the constraint filters are set to allow viewing of several attributes that have been extracted and identified as relating to *Company Earnings Announcement*–type events. The table view of the result set from this query can be seen in Figure XII.16.

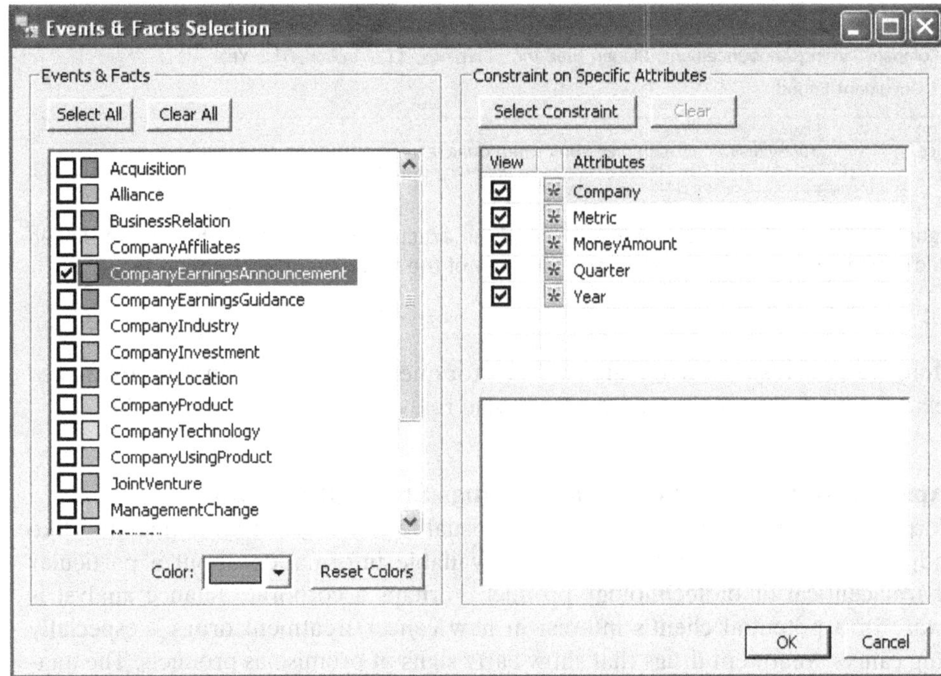

Figure XII.15. Constructing a query around company earnings announcement events. (Courtesy of the ClearForest Corporation.)

Scanning the columns of the table view would show that Biogen Idec meets the criteria being sought by the analyst. The analyst can then highlight the appropriate table row, click, and choose to see a summary of the text in the article containing the original reference (see Figure XII.17).

Of course, the quality of search results for this type of information within a text mining application like Industry Analyzer will depend on the comprehensiveness of the data in the documents of the document collection and the sophistication of the various information extraction rule bases used during preprocessing to identify events and link relevant attributes properly to these events. However, querying for partially known corporate information against the vast amounts of text documents in which it is buried can be made vastly more practical with Industry Analyzer.

CompanyEarningsAnnouncement

Company	Metric	MoneyAmount	Quarter	Year
Biogen Idec Inc.	Earning Per-Share	37 cents		This Year
Biogen Idec Inc.	Earnings	$132 million		This Year
Biogen Idec Inc.	Earnings	35 cents - $123 million		Last Year
Genzyme Corp.	Revenues	$281.7 million		This Year
Stem Cells Inc.	Net Loss Per-Share	8 cents		This Year
Stem Cells Inc.	Net Loss Per-Share	7 cents		Last Year
Chiron Corp.	Per-Share	26 cents		This Year
MedImmune Inc.	Net Loss	$65 million		This Year
MedImmune Inc.	Net Loss Per-Share	26 cents		This Year
MedImmune Inc.	Earning Per-Share	7 cents		Last Year
Advancis Pharmaceutical Corp.	Net Loss	$8.5 million	second quarter	2004
Advancis Pharmaceutical Corp.	Net Loss	$29.1 million	third quarter	2003
Advancis Pharmaceutical Corp.	Net Loss	37 cents	third quarter	Last Year
Advancis Pharmaceutical Corp.	Earning Per-Share	$20.19	third quarter	Last Year
Advancis Pharmaceutical Corp.	Net Loss Per-Share	$15.65	third-quarter	Last Year
CuraGen Corp.			third- quarter	

Figure XII.16. Table view of company earnings reports. (Courtesy of the ClearForest Corporation.)

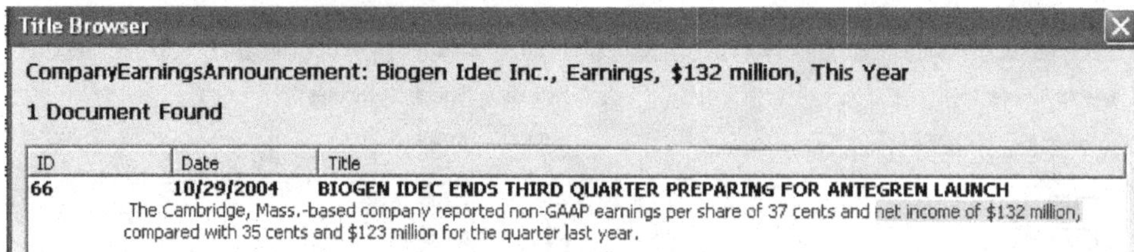

Figure XII.17. Browsing the summary view of the article containing the reference to Biogen Idec's third-quarter 2004 net income. (Courtesy of the ClearForest Corporation.)

Moreover, the result sets that are returned for queries encourage analysts to browse related data that may also be interesting and relevant to their overall mission.

Exploring Available Information about Drugs Still in Clinical Trials

Corporate analysts can also turn to the visualization tools of an application like Industry Analyzer to help explore the available information about a particular pharmaceutical or biotechnology product. Perhaps a corporate finance analyst is aware of a potential client's interest in new cancer treatment drugs – especially lung cancer treatment drugs that show early signs of promise as products. The analyst may have only a general awareness of this market niche. He or she may thus want to leverage Industry Analyzer's visualization tools more directly to ferret out potentially interesting information from the articles in the applications document collection.

As a first step, the analyst may want to generate a query whose result set could be used to create a visualization of all connections (associations) between drugs and particular diseases in the *BioWorld* articles to get a quick sense of the drugs that might be related to cancer treatment within the overall universe of drugs mentioned in the trade press. An example of the result set visualization can be seen in Figure XII.18. After viewing the circle graph visualization that identifies all the relationships, the analyst might note the relationships between *lung carcinoma* and the anticancer drugs *Erlotinib* and *Cisplatin*.

Note that by simply highlighting any node along the circumference of the circle graph, a user can also highlight the edges representing connections with various other associated nodes in the figure. For instance, as illustrated in Figure XII.18, if the user highlighted the disease *Rheumatoid Arthritis*, the four drugs with which this disease is associated in the underlying document collection would be identified. This type of visualization functionality would allow the user to bounce quickly among diseases and drugs and to browse their various relationships at a high level.

After looking at this broad view of drug-disease relationships, the analyst might want to start focusing on cancer-related drugs and execute a distribution-type query showing all occurrences of drug names in *BioWorld* articles given a context of carcinoma and a proximity constraint of "within the same sentence." This would give the analyst a list of the most prominent anticancer drugs (i.e, those most frequently mentioned over a given period of time in the trade press). The analyst would then be able to generate a result set in a histogram like the type shown in Figure XII.19.

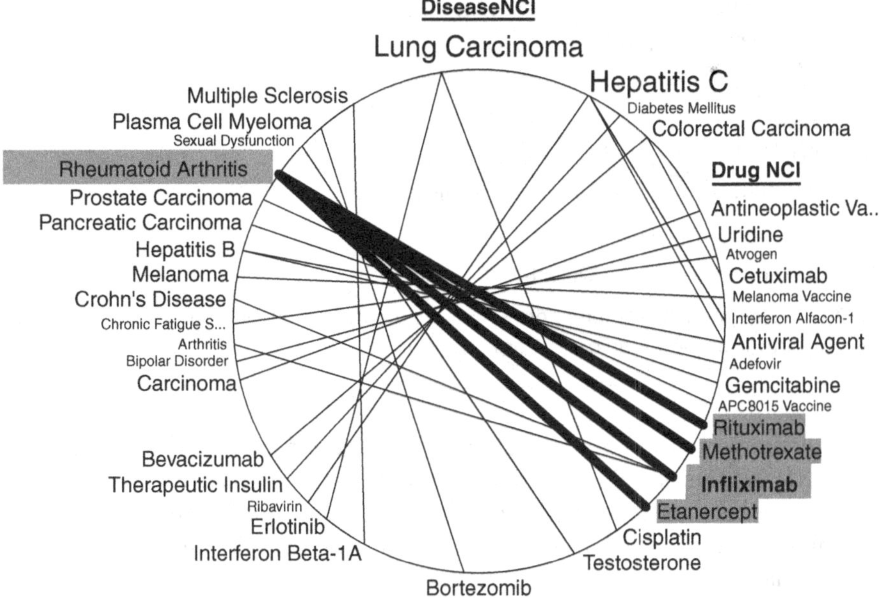

Figure XII.18. Circle graph showing connections between drugs and diseases. (Courtesy of the ClearForest Corporation.)

Exploring this graph might lead the analyst to the question: What are the cross-relationships, if any, between these drugs? Again, the analyst could generate a circle-graph relationship map, this time showing connections between drugs in the context of carcinoma (Figure XII.20).

Seeing Cisplatin in each of the last two graphs, the analyst might be interested in generating a query on Cisplatin and related companies within the context of

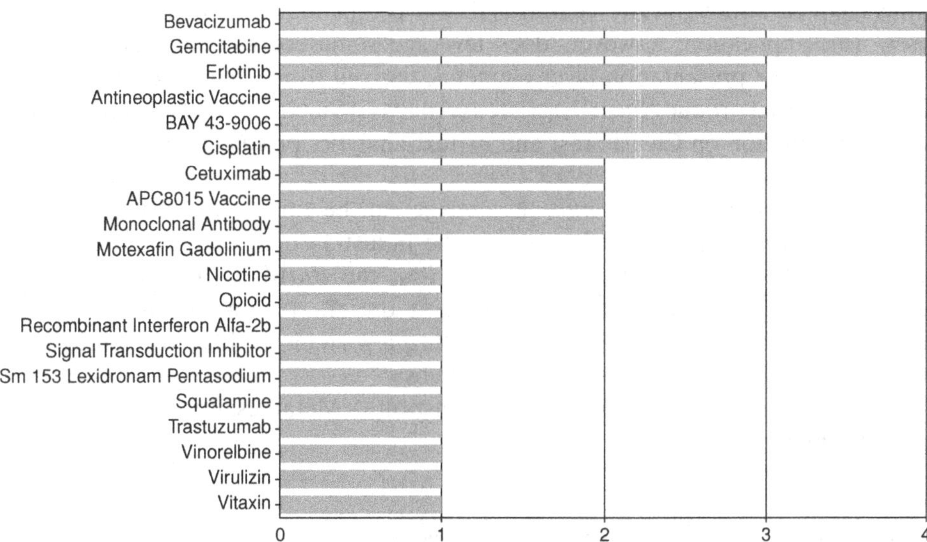

Figure XII.19. Histogram showing occurrences of drug names in *BioWorld* (context of carcinoma, in the same sentence). (Courtesy of the ClearForest Corporation.)

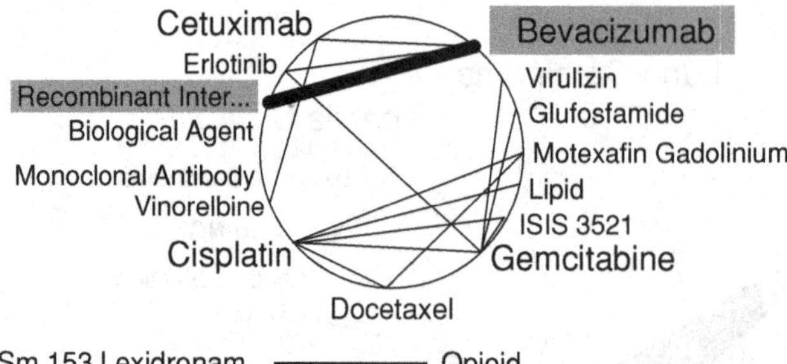

Figure XII.20. Circle graph of relations between drugs (context of carcinoma, within the same sentence). (Courtesy of the ClearForest Corporation.)

carcinoma. A simple concept graph could be generated for the results of this query (see Figure XII.21). Thicker lines between concepts in this graph are weighted to a potentially more meaningful connection according to some quality measure.

The analyst could then discover more by clicking on the edge linking Cisplatin and Isis Pharmaceuticals to jump to a summary of the article containing the two concepts. See Figure XII.22.

The summary of the article can then be read quickly for business news related to the two drugs. From this Title Browser interface, the user can also jump to the full text of the article.

XII.2.3 Citations and Notes

Some resources on text mining applications for finance include Spenke and Beilken (1999), IntertekGroup (2002), and Kloptchenko et al. (2002).

Industry Analyzer is not a commercial product, and the implementation described in this chapter, although fully operational, was completed for demonstration purposes. This application, however, does leverage some commercial technologies, particularly in its presentation-layer elements, derived from ClearForest Corporation's commercial product ClearForest Text Analytics Suite. All rights belong to the owner. Information on ClearForest and its text analytics products can be found at <www.clearforest.com>.

The Thomson *BioWorld Online* homepage can be found at <www.bioworld.com>. Textual content for articles used in the Industry Analyzer examples comes from *BioWorld*. All rights to the content from the *BioWorld* articles used for the examples in this section are held by their owners. A comprehensive listing of *BioWorld* publications can be found at <http://www.bioworld.com/servlet/com.accumedia.web.Dispatcher?next=bioWorldPubs>.

A public version of the National Cancer Institute's Metathesaurus is available at <http://ncimeta.nci.nih.gov.>

Pharmacyclics Inc. ——— Cisplatin ▬▬▬ Isis Pharmaceutic...

Figure XII.21. Simple concept graph of cisplatin and related companies within the context of carcinoma. (Courtesy of the ClearForest Corporation.)

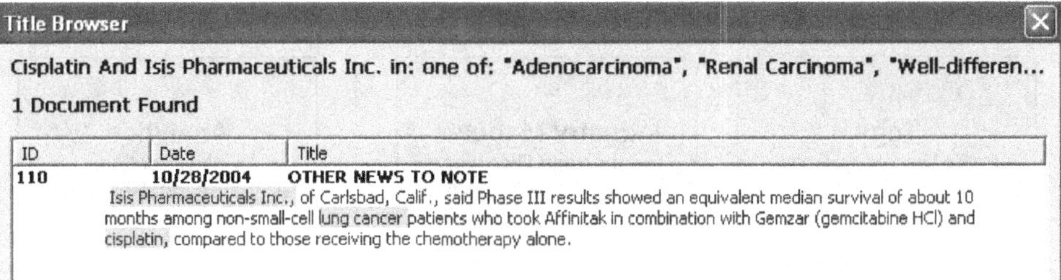
Title Browser

Cisplatin And Isis Pharmaceuticals Inc. in: one of: "Adenocarcinoma", "Renal Carcinoma", "Well-differen...

1 Document Found

ID	Date	Title
110	10/28/2004	OTHER NEWS TO NOTE

Isis Pharmaceuticals Inc., of Carlsbad, Calif., said Phase III results showed an equivalent median survival of about 10 months among non-small-cell lung cancer patients who took Affinitak in combination with Gemzar (gemcitabine HCl) and cisplatin, compared to those receiving the chemotherapy alone.

Figure XII.22. Annotated view of the summary of the article containing both Cisplatin and Isis Pharmaceuticals within the context of carcinoma. (Courtesy of the ClearForest Corporation.)

XII.3 A "HORIZONTAL" TEXT MINING APPLICATION: PATENT ANALYSIS SOLUTION LEVERAGING A COMMERCIAL TEXT ANALYTICS PLATFORM

Patent research and analysis have become the business foci of a growing number of professionals charged with helping organizations understand how best to leverage intellectual property – and avoid problems created by other organizations' intellectual property rights – in their business activities. Patent research encompasses a wide range of at least partially related activities involving the investigation of the registration, ownership rights, and usage, of patents. A common denominator among almost all of these activities, however, is the need to collect, organize, and analyze large amounts of highly detailed and technical text-based documents.

Patent analysis solutions might be called "horizontal" applications because, although they have a narrow functional focus on patent-related documents, patent analysis has wide applicability to many different businesses. Professionals in both public and private companies across many different industries – not to mention the intellectual property (IP) departments of many law firms and consultancies – have responsibility for providing input into corporate patent strategies. Such input needs to take into account not just the potentially "harvestable" IP that a particular company may have but also all of the published indications of IP rights that other companies may already possess.

Patent strategy, however, is not just about the particulars of what is patented (both in-house or within the larger market) but also relates to which individuals and companies are creating patents (and for what technologies), which companies are licensing patents (and for what technologies), and the relationships between these various market participants. Patent research should yield more than good defensive information about IP; it should also yield new business opportunities by identifying new development partners, likely licensers or licensees, or wider market trends about particular types of patents.

This section describes a patent analysis application called *Patent Researcher*. One of the interesting aspects of presenting this application is how it can leverage the functionality of a more generic commercial text mining platform derived primarily from components marketed by ClearForest Corporation.

Patent Researcher processes patent-related documents – primarily granted U.S. patents – to enable a patent manager to mine information related to patented technologies, patent claims, original patent inventors, original patent owners, and patent assignees by means of queries and interactive visualization tools.

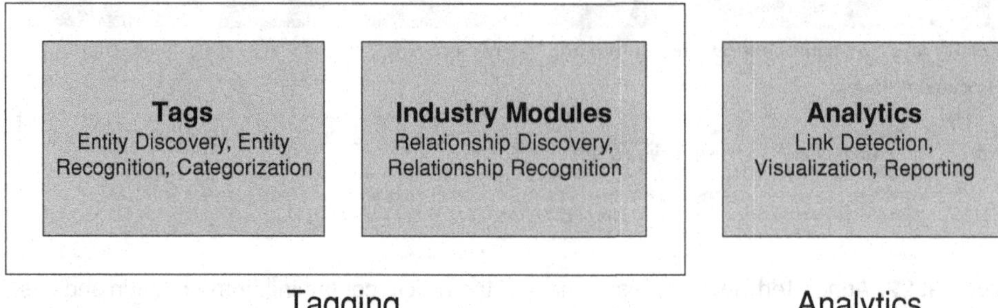

Figure XII.23. ClearForest Corporation's approach to describing the high-level architecture of the ClearForest text analytics suite.

The implementation of the Patent Researcher application discussed in the following sections has been configured to handle typical patent analysis activities. A sample corpus of patent documents related to commercial defibrillator device technologies is used as a raw data source. This illustrative implementation reflects the types of application settings and usage one might encounter among patent professionals in corporate intellectual property departments, attorneys at patent-oriented law firms, or patent engineers at specialist engineering consultancies.

XII.3.1 Patent Researcher: Basic Architecture and Functionality

Patent Researcher relies on ClearForest Corporation's suite of text mining software components and, as a result, shares the general architecture of these components. ClearForest's Text Analytics Suite follows a general pattern not too unlike that described in the Section I.2, though the company's high-level description of it has perhaps been made simple for the commercial market. See Figure XII.23.

Effectively, ClearForest's platform follows in a generalized way most of the architectural principles presented in Section I.2 and in Section XII.2.1 of this chapter's discussion of Industry Analyzer. On a slightly more granular level, the functional architecture for Patent Researcher is described in Figure XII.24.

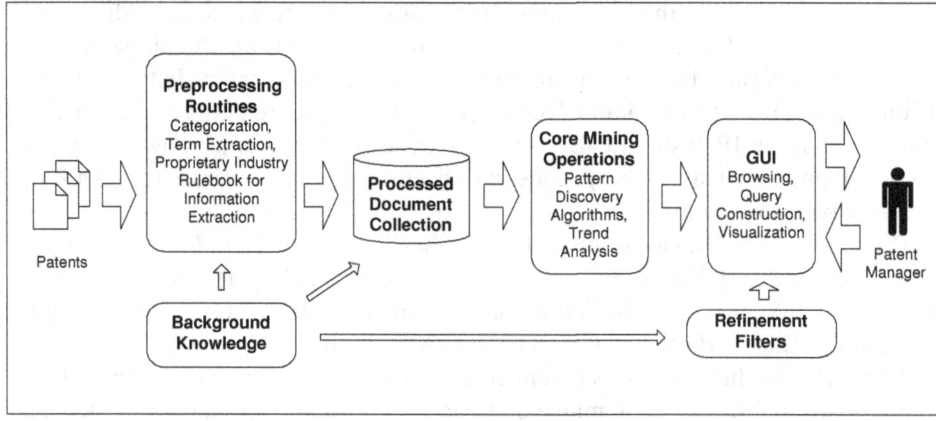

Figure XII.24. Patent Researcher's functional architecture.

Although quite similar to the overall architecture described for the Industry Analyzer application illustrated in Section XII.2.1, Patent Researcher's architecture evinces a few distinct differences and leverages several advantages provided by the commercial ClearForest Text Analytics Suite platform. The most notable of these are discussed in the following sections.

Data and Background Knowledge Sources

The raw data for the Patent Researcher application consists of 411 granted U.S. patents for external defibrillator devices. A "quick search" for the key term "external defibrillator" was executed at the U.S. Patent and Trademark Office Web site to find 411 patents for the period from 1 January 1976 to 1 January 2004. These full-text, semistructured (HTML-formatted) documents constitute the target corpus for preprocessing operations.

Patent Researcher has the capacity to integrate various external thesauri, taxonomies, and ontological dictionaries. These knowledge sources are particularly valuable when document collections need to include trade journals, news articles, or internal corporate documents in which there is an increased need to infer meaning or relationship information about extracted concepts.

However, even in implementations of patent analysis text mining applications – like the one discussed here – that make use of formal granted-patent documents as their exclusive source of document data, background knowledge sources can be particularly helpful in preprocessing extraction activities for entities, facts, and events involving technical terminology, company names (often as patent assignees), and legal language. The Patent Researcher implementation described here uses only three simple knowledge sources: a lexicon of English words; a simple, manually created dictionary of important legal and patent terms; and a simple dictionary of corporate names.

Preprocessing Operations

Patent Researcher's preprocessing operations have similarities with those discussed for the Industry Analyzer application. Both rely on term extraction and information extraction techniques to create a processed document collection that identifies entities, facts, and events. In addition, both use very similar rule-based languages (Patent Researcher uses a robust commercial version of the DIAL language).

One significant additional approach of Patent Researcher, however, is its implementation of categorization routines to automatically create a taxonomy for use in the application. Making use of the semistructured nature of patent documents (U.S. patent grants – especially after 1976 – generally follow a standardized U.S. Patent and Trademark Office format), automatic taxonomy generation typically yields a very useful taxonomy for organizing patent registrations and claim details, assignees, inventors, examiners, relevant corporate information, technical terms, as well as high-level categories for various aspects of patented items' functionality, usage, related patents, and so on. A typical taxonomy displayed by Patent Researcher's Taxonomy Chooser interface is shown in Figure XII.25; the figure illustrates the hierarchical positioning and a partial listing of relevant invention terms.

Patent Researcher implements a productionized version of a Ripper-like machine-learning algorithm (for more description on this algorithm, see Chapter III).

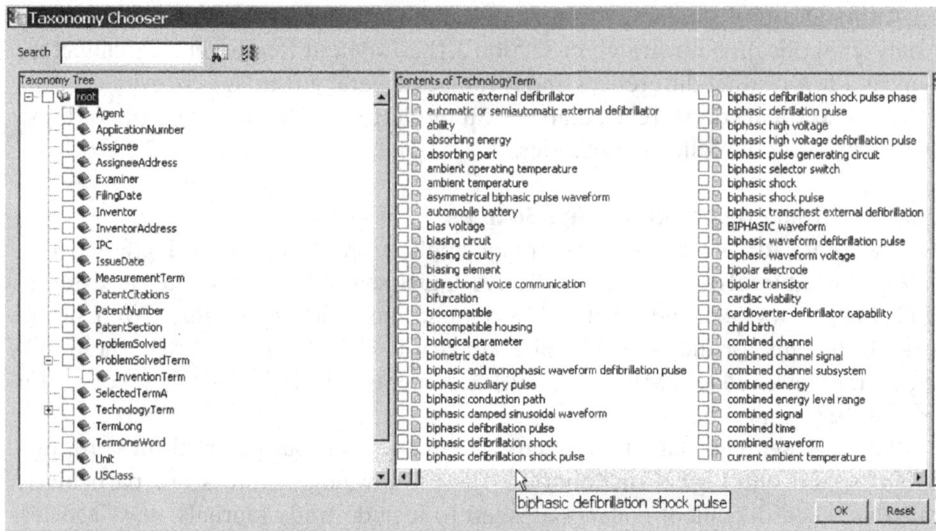

Figure XII.25. Viewing the taxonomy created by means of automatic categorization in Patent Researcher. (Courtesy of the ClearForest Corporation and Joseph F. Murphy.)

The Ripper algorithm has proven useful across a wide range of categorization situations. In the case of patent information, the semistructured nature of much of the textual data would allow many categorization algorithms to perform relatively well, but the Ripper-like algorithm's capacity for building constructing classifiers that allow what might be described as the "context" of a term impact – whether or not that term affects a classification – can be beneficial for categorizing large numbers of technical terms used in patent documents.

Categorization is especially useful in patent analysis, for many very typical searches performed by patent professionals can benefit from using category information – particularly when using a category label, which may not be a term found within an individual patent document's native set of extracted terms, as a part of a query's context. For instance, patent investigators often use various intra-, inter-, and cross-category searches to determine the answers to numerous questions about potential patent overlap or infringement, competitive landscape situations among patent assignees and licensees, areas of potential synergy between assignees holding intellectual property in similar or complementary business areas, and patterns of development of new patents across niche business industries.

Core Mining Operations and Refinement Constraints

Patent Researcher is able to leverage the capabilities of the extremely large range of query types afforded by the commercial platform on which it is built. This means that the application provides a full range of distribution, proportion, frequent set, and association queries (including maximal association queries).

Although patent managers certainly benefit from flexible exploration of patterns in the data of patent document corpora, Patent Researcher offers several preconfigured query formats that are used very often during patent analysis activities. These include the following:

- Frequency distribution of assignees with patents in the current collection;
- Distribution of patents representing a particular technology over time; and
- Assignees that appear together on the same patent (indicates joint venture, joint development, partnership, or other corporate relationship).

Indeed, with respect to the second of these preconfigured queries, a particularly notable difference from the capabilities offered to users of Industry Analyzer is Patent Researcher's ability to generate simple but extremely useful trend analysis results for patent professionals interested in diverse types of trend and time-series information. Granted patents have consistent descriptions for various important dates (date of initial application, patent issue date, etc.). These dates are extracted during preprocessing operations and made available to a wide range of distribution queries that can chart various micro- and macrotrends over time.

Patent Researcher supports more narrowly focused knowledge discovery operations such as allowing a patent manager to create a query yielding a result set describing the distribution of patents over time for a particular company. The application also has the ability to compare this distribution against the distribution of patents issued for a competing company over the same period.

To allow examination of wider trends, Patent Researcher supports queries that would permit a user to request all patents issued for several different broad areas of technology over some period. This type of search might reveal what areas of intellectual property are hot, which are growing cold, and which have dried up, based – all in relation to other areas of intellectual property – on patterns of patent application and issuance.

Patent Researcher supports a wide assortment of constraints on nearly all of its query types, including typical background, syntactical, quality-threshold, and redundancy constraints. The application also supports time-based constraints on many queries, allowing variation on trend analysis queries and flexibility in comparing distributions over different time-based divisions of the document collection.

Presentation Layer – GUI and Visualization Tools

Patent Researchers offers patent professionals an extremely rich selection of graphical browsing and visualization tools. Queries are all performed from GUI screens that make it possible for users to populate search input variables from either pull-downs or pop-up hierarchies of entities, facts, events, and categories appropriate as input to the query. Almost all queries in the system – including preconfigured queries – support various constraints that can be chosen from scroll-bars or pull-downs.

Users can browse hierarchies of categories, entities, facts; and events. From many of the hierarchy browser screens, patent professionals can pull up various GUI-type query screens and use highlighted elements of a hierarchy to populate queries – that is, users can easily move from browsing the hierarchies to executing queries based on information discovered while browsing.

In addition, users can pull up full or partial listings of all patents in Patent Researcher's document collection and browse these listings by patent title. From this Title Browser, patent professionals can shape the ordering of patents within the browser by a several parameters, including date, category, and assignee. By clicking on any title in the title browser, a user can be brought to either an annotated view

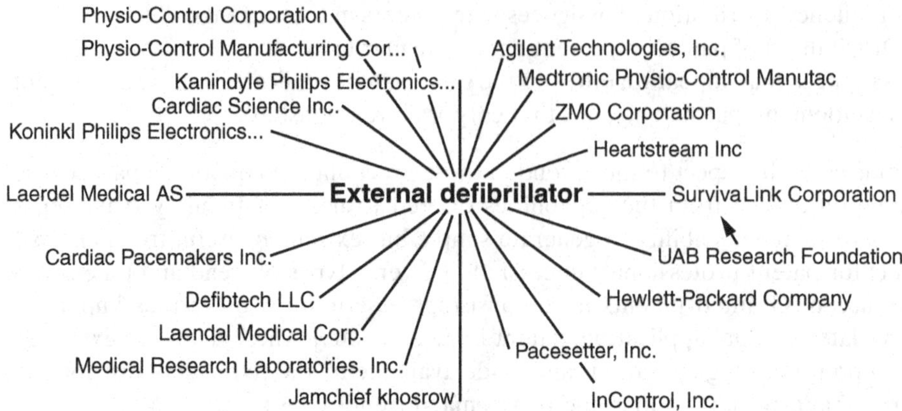

Figure XII.26. A Patent Researcher spring graph of concepts associated with the concept "external defibrillator." (Courtesy of the ClearForest Corporation and Joseph F. Murphy.)

of the full text of the associated patent document or a URL link to the actual patent document on the U.S. Patent and Trademark Office Web site.

Upon executing a formal query, a user of Patent Manager will receive the answer set in a default table-view format. Even trend data in the result sets from trend analysis queries are available in a table view.

From this table view, a patent professional can perform a few functions. First, he or she can generate a visualization of the data in a result set. Second, the user can access a pop-up query screen and reexecute the query with different input variables or constraints. Third, the user can click on a row in the table view to move to a pop-up of the Title Browser with a listing of relevant patents, from which he or she can navigate to the full text of a patent. Finally, a comma-delimited file of the data displayed in the table view can be downloaded.

In addition to basic histograms, circle graphs (as relation or association graphs), and simple concept graphs common to text mining applications (and seen in Industry Analyzer), Patent Researcher also supports the following visualization types: circle graphs (as category graphs), line- and histogram-based trend graphs, spring graphs, and multigraph and hybrid circle graph visualizations. Figure XII.26 shows an example of a Patent Researcher spring graph.

All visualizations implement a consistent point-and-click paradigm that allows a user to highlight any point in a graph and click to navigate to actual patents related to the highlighted entity, fact, event, or category. Typically, when a highlighted node in a visualization is clicked, the Title Browser pop-up is initiated. From this pop-up, a user can either elect, as usual, to click on a particular patent title and go to an annotated version of the patent text in Patent Researcher's document collection or click on the URL for the live version of the appropriate patent on the U.S. Patent and Tradmark Office's official Web site.

XII.3.2 Application Usage Scenarios

Patent Researcher has several common usage scenarios. A brief review of a few of these from the perspective of the patent professional can be useful for understanding

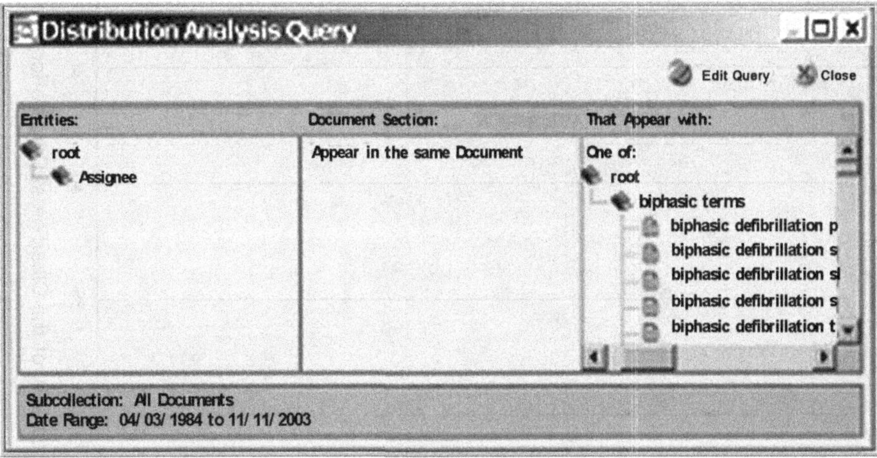

Figure XII.27. Distribution analysis query screen. (Courtesy of the ClearForest Corporation and Joseph F. Murphy.)

how text mining techniques can be leveraged to provide solutions to real-world business problems involving the management of intellectual property.

Looking at the Frequency Distributions among Patents in the Document Collection

Among the most basic and common tasks that patent professionals perform is the review of large numbers of patents to discern the frequency of patent activities among companies with respect to a given area of technology or business focus. Patent Research makes such a review a simple and easy process for patents in its collection.

In a typical scenario, a patent manager might be interested in exploring the distribution of patents among assignees in the field of external defibrillators. First, he or she would execute a distribution analysis query for all assignees with relevant patents (see Figure XII.27).

After executing the query, the user would receive a table view of all assignees ordered according to the number of patents they had been issued in the document collection. From this screen, a quick histogram graphically demonstrating the distribution pattern could be generated. The resulting graph is shown in Figure XII.28.

This graph shows that *SurvivaLink, InControl,* and *Heartstream* are the top three assignees for external defibrillator patents in the document collection with *Medtronic* and *Agilent Technologies* rounding out the top five. Patent Researcher's visualizations are highly interactive, and thus by clicking on either one of the assignee names on the left side of the graph or one of the histogram bars on the right, a user is given a choice of editing his or her original query and generating a refreshed graph for the new search results or of seeing a Title Browser listing of all patents connected to the assignee chosen.

Let us say our user clicks on the fourth-place assignee, Medtronic, and chooses to see a Title Browser listing Medtronic's patents. A Title Browser in a pop-up like the one illustrated in Figure XII.29 will then appear.

After navigating through the list of patents, the user could *select all* and see a listing that includes a few descriptive sentences extracted from each patent as an aid to browsing. The user could also click on a patent and go either to an annotated

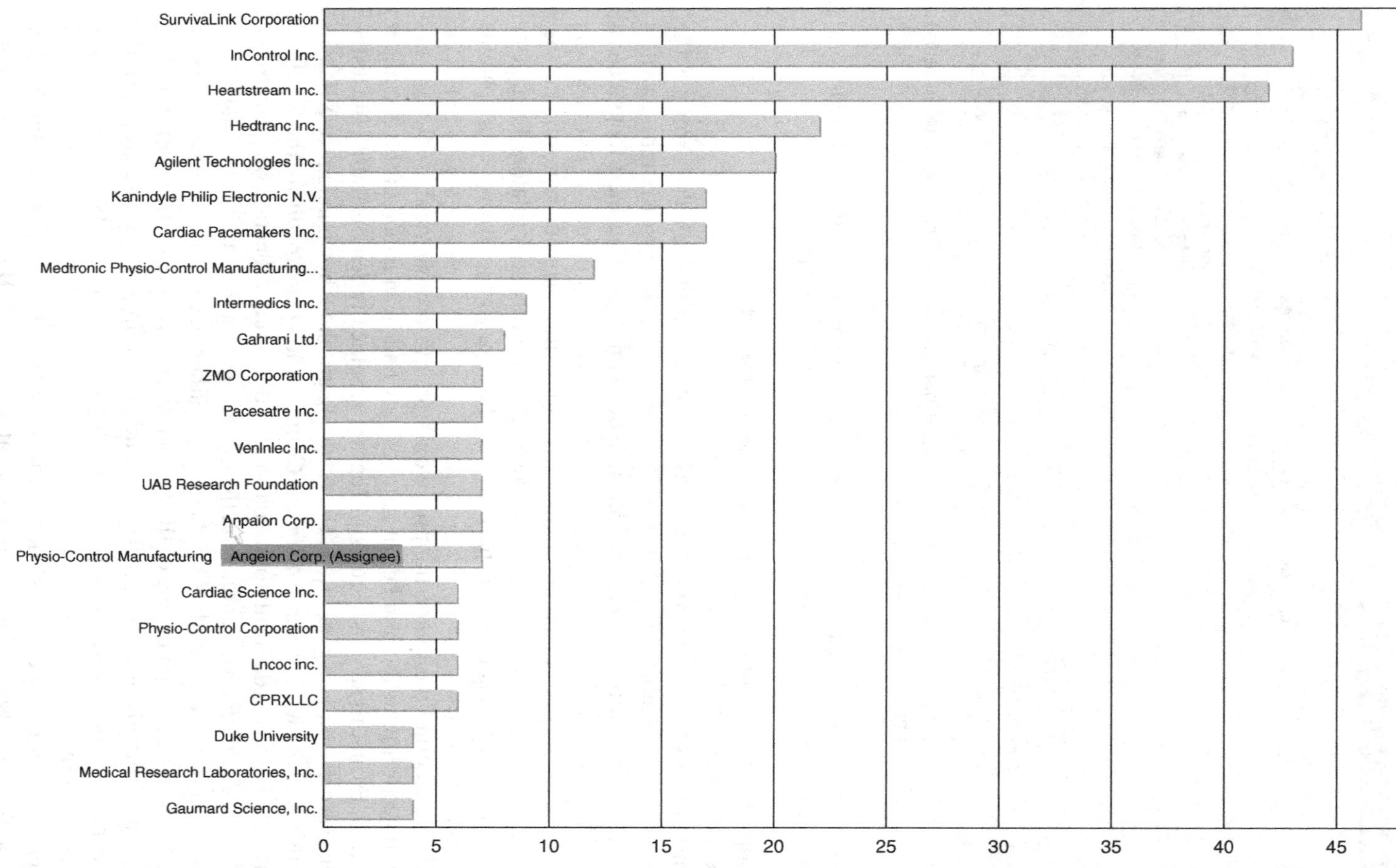

Figure XII.28. Histogram of results from distribution query for issued patents by assignee. (Courtesy of the ClearForest Corporation and Joseph F. Murphy.)

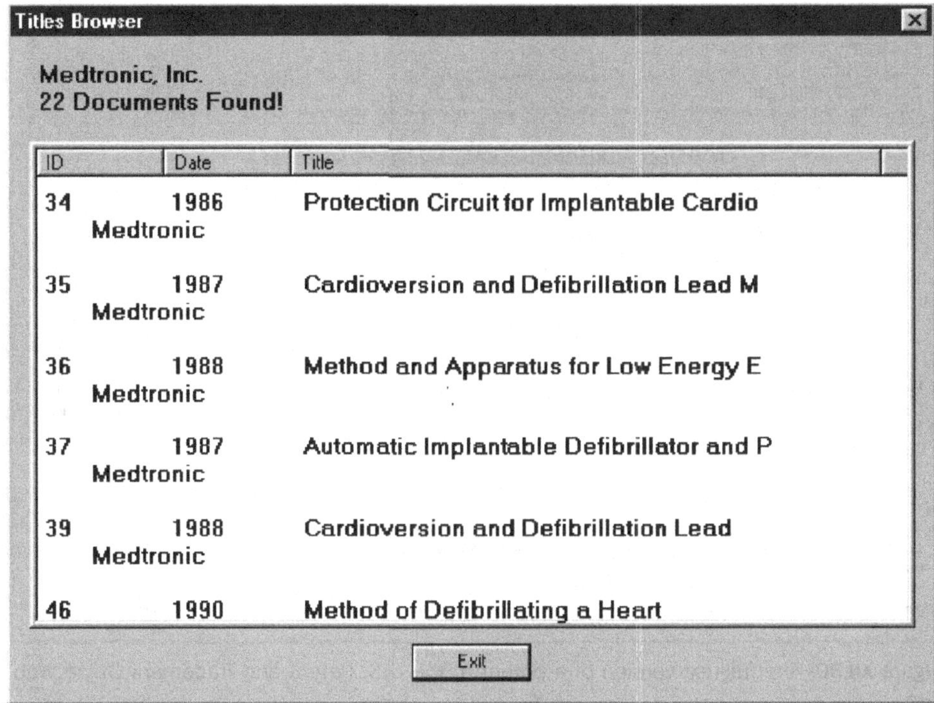

Figure XII.29. Patent Researcher's title browser showing a listing of relevant patents. (Courtesy of the ClearForest Corporation and Joseph F. Murphy.)

full-text version of the patent in the document collection or to the URL for the official patent text at the U.S. Patent and Trademark Office Web site (see Figure XII.30).

Exploring Trends in Issued Patents

Another usage scenario commonly encountered in patent analysis activities is exploring how patterns of patent issuance (or application) for particular technologies evolve. Understanding such trends can be critical to deciding whether a company should develop its own technology, patent its own technology, or attempt to license another company's technology. These trends can also show whether the number of new patents is rising, plateauing, or falling, indicating the current strength of interest in innovation for a particular technology area.

A patent manager might interpret a steadily increasing, multiyear trend in patents related to a technology that his or her client company is developing as encouraging because it shows a growing interest in related business areas. Conversely, a precipitous recent fall in the number of issued patents for a technology that comes on the heels of a sudden spike might indicate some sort of problem; perhaps a small number of patents have dominated the business area, or the underlying business demand for this technology area has cooled or even disappeared. Often, in answering these questions, it is useful to be able to compare trend lines for several different related events within the same visualization. Patent Researcher provides such trend analysis capabilities.

A sample patent analysis problem might involve a patent manager's wanting to see the trends for two different defibrillator technologies – "biphasic" and "auto external

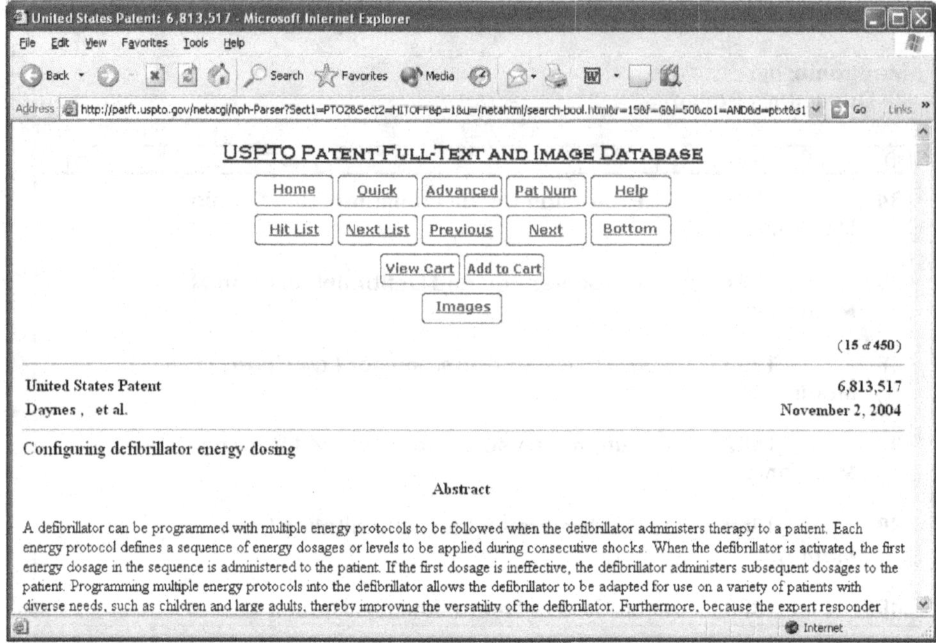

Figure XII.30. The full-text version of a patent at the U.S. Patent and Trademark Office Web site.

defibrillation" devices – from 1984 to the present. Further, the patent manager might want to compare these two trends against a trend line showing all the defibrillator patents issued to a single company, Medtronic, over the same period. Because patent documents provide very clear date-related information for several events – perhaps most notably patent application and patent issuance – preprocessing operations can comprehensively tag a document collection with the type of date-related information that allows analysis of trend information across documents – and generally facts and events as well – in the collection.

In this case, the user would first go to the trend analysis query screen and set up the simple parameter of this search. The result set would initially be provided in a table view with rows representing one of the search concepts (auto external defibrillation, biphasic, Medtronic) and columns representing quarters. Columns could be set in increments as granular as one day or as broad as one year. The user could then elect to view the data as a line-based trend graph (see Figure XII.31).

The user can set the graph to show a version of the table view at the bottom of the trend graph and examine the two views at the same time. The user can also scroll left or right to see the full extent of the timeline or call up his or her query screen again to change any of the parameters of the original search. Lines in the graph can be shown in different colors defined in a key at the bottom left part of the screen.

For clarity of visualization, Patent Researcher can bundle related terms together under a single label. In the example shown within Figure XII.32, the second and third searched-for concepts (biphasic and Medtronic) are groupings of concepts under one label. This capability is generally important in text mining applications but is

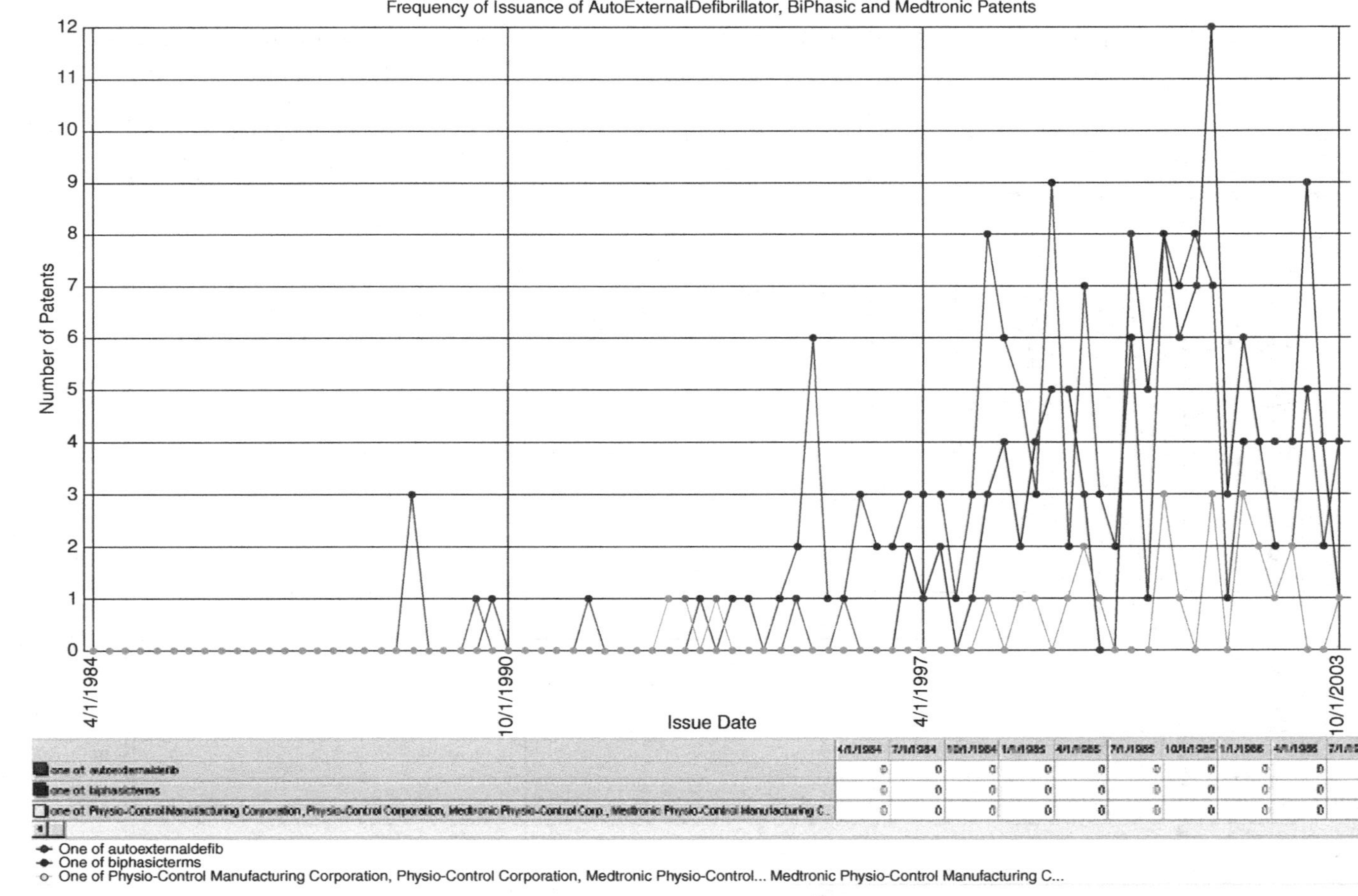

Figure XII.31. Line-based trend graph. (Courtesy of the ClearForest Corporation and Joseph F. Murphy.)

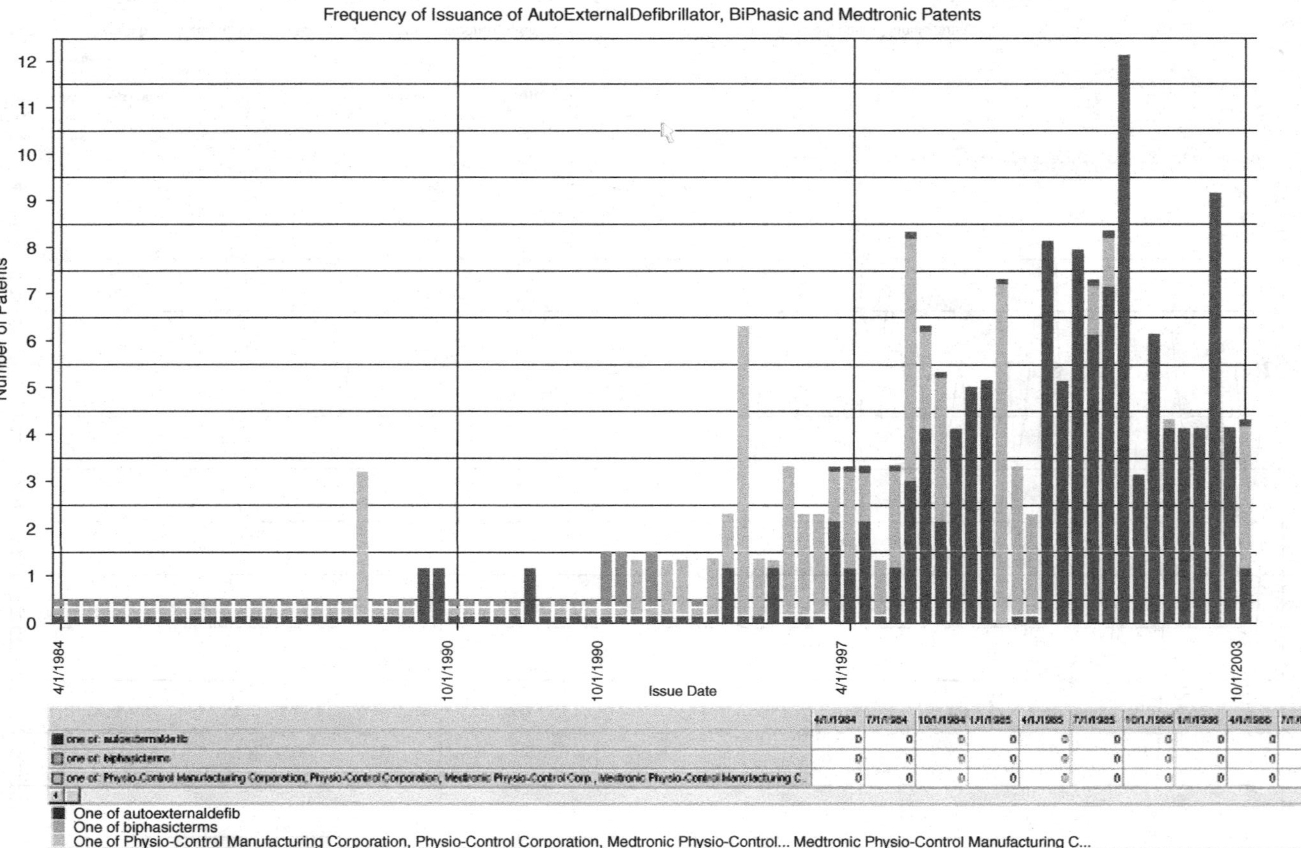

Figure XII.32. Histogram-based trend graph. (Courtesy of the ClearForest Corporation and Joseph F. Murphy.)

particularly so in applications like Patent Researcher, in which many technical terms and corporate entity names may actually refer to the same real-world entity (or be more useful grouped together on an ad hoc basis because the terms belong to some logical set interesting to the user).

Of course, a patent manager may also want to look at the same trend data in a way that shows the cumulative number of patents for all search-on entities while also making it visually clear what rough percentage each entity makes up of this cumulative number. For this, the patent manager could choose to generate a histogram-based trend graph. Figure XII.32 shows an example of this type of graph.

In Figure XII.32, a portion of the table view of the concept-occurrence data is still viewable at the bottom of the screen. Patent Researcher allows a patent manager to move back and forth between the two trend graph visualization types or to generate each in a separate window to permit visual comparisons.

XII.3.3 Citations and Notes

Patent Researcher is not a commercial product. However, it has been partly based on feedback provided by ClearForest Corporation on real-world, commercial uses of the company's Text Analytics Suite product by patent professionals.

Ideas and input for the usage scenarios come from the work of patent attorney Joseph Murphy using the ClearForest Text Analytics Suite product. Joseph Murphy's Web site can be found at <www.joemurphy.com>.

XII.4 LIFE SCIENCES RESEARCH: MINING BIOLOGICAL PATHWAY INFORMATION WITH GENEWAYS

GeneWays, Columbia University's ambitious application for processing and mining text-based documents for knowledge relating to molecular pathways presents a contrast to Industry Analyzer and Patent Researcher. Whereas Industry Analyzer and Patent Researcher have architectures that exhibit a relatively balanced emphasis on preprocessing, core mining algorithms, and presentation-layer elements (with a somewhat less aggressive emphasis on background knowledge and refinement techniques), GeneWays emphasizes complex preprocessing and background knowledge components with significantly less focus – at least up to the present – on query algorithm, presentation-layer, and refinement elements. These differences derive from several difficult challenges that arise in processing life sciences research documents containing molecular pathways information.

The GeneWays application is an attempt to build a comprehensive knowledge discovery platform using several processes for high-quality extraction of knowledge from research papers relating to the interaction of proteins, genes, and messenger (mRNA). GeneWays' RNA core mission is the construction – or reconstruction – of molecular interaction networks from research documents, and the eventual aim is to include information on all known molecular pathways useful to biomedical researchers. As a first step, the application is focused on molecular interactions related to signal-transduction pathways.

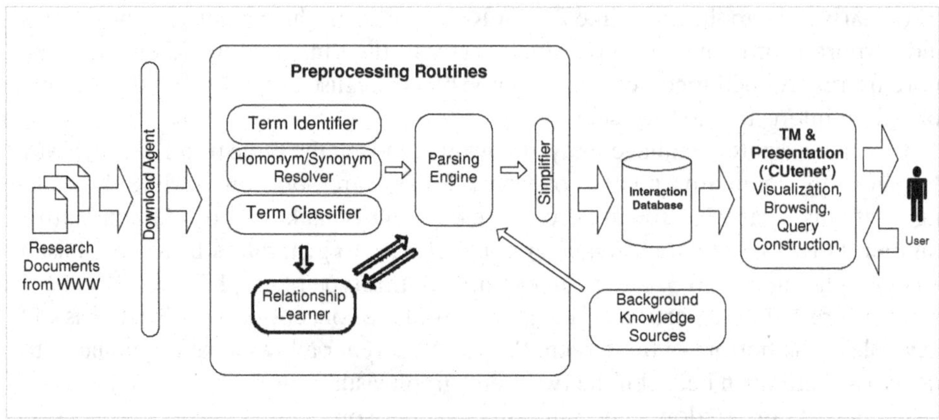

Figure XII.33. GeneWays' functional architecture.

XII.4.1 GeneWays: Basic Architecture and Functionality

From published sources, GeneWays seems to follow along the lines of the same rough architecture for a text mining system shown in Industry Analyzer and Patent Researcher. However, GeneWays is a complex application, and specialized nuances appear in many elements of this architecture when the system is examined in any detail. A generalized view of this architecture can be seen in Figure XII.33.

Data and Background Knowledge Sources

Raw data for GeneWays comes from English language biomedical research documents on molecular pathways that are downloaded from online World Wide Web resources; these documents are saved first in HTML and then converted into a basic XML format. After GeneWays' extensive array of preprocessing operations are run against this still semiraw data, processed data are stored in an interaction database that combines entity information with relationship information to allow users to interact complex network-type models of molecular-level protein interactions.

GeneWays uses several aids to providing background knowledge to inform its various operations – particularly preprocessing operations. The GenBank database is used to furnish expert knowledge for protein extraction activites at the term level in the Term Identifier; GenBank is supplemented by information from the Swiss-Prot database for further tagging activities in GeneWays' Parsing Engine GENIES (GENomics Information Extraction System), which performs a few additional tagging roles and acts as the GeneWays' information extraction utility. In addition, GENIES has the ability to make use of external lexicons and formal grammars appropriate to life sciences applications.

Preprocessing Operations

Textual data containing molecular pathways information have been described as "noisy data" because it is not a straightforward or simple task to identify entities or interaction-type relationships reliably from scientific literature. GeneWays' preprocessing operations represent one of the most advanced attempts to extract

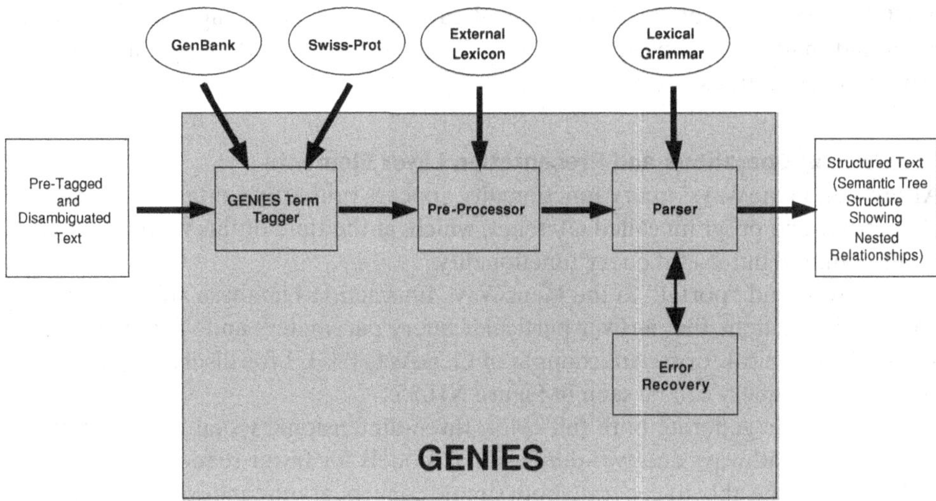

Figure XII.34. GENIES information extraction subsystem.

information and allow scientists to explore high-quality models of protein interaction networks based on natural language processing techniques.

After biomedical literature has been culled from various Web sources, it is sorted and converted into a basic, tagged XML-like format. GeneWays' first major preprocessing operation is the Term Identifier module, which extracts biologically significant concepts in the text of documents, such as the names of proteins, genes, processes, molecules, and diseases. After an initial set of such concepts has been identified, GeneWays runs the results through its Synonym/Homonym Resolver, which attempts to resolve the meaning of a particular entity by assigning a single "canonical" name to each concept's multiple aliases. The Term Classifier acts as a series of disambiguation operations are next run against these results of the Synonym/Homonym Resolver in an effort to resolve any sense ambiguities.

After these three preprocessing operations have been run, GENIES begins its processing tasks. GENIES combines several processing activities in its operations; a generalized architecture can be seen in Figure XII.34.

The GENIES system is based on the MedLEE medical NLP system and incorporates both rules and external knowledge sources in its sophisticated term-tagging. It also extracts information to output semantic trees – essentially, a machine-readable format identifying nested relationships with normalized forms of verbs (e.g., *bind, binding*, and *binder*).

The final preprocessing step for GeneWays is to take the nested relationship information output by GENIES and run a Simplifier process. This Simplifier converts nested relationships into a collection of more useful binary statements of the form "interleukin-2 activates interleukin-2 receptor," which is a formal statement that includes two entities with an action verb. These statements are then saved directly into GeneWays' Interaction Database.

One final component of the preprocessing operations of GeneWays is the system's Relationship Learner module. This takes the output of the Term Identification/Synonym-Homonym/Term Classifier processes and identifies new semantic patterns that can be examined by system developers and later incorporated into GENIES. However, the Relationship Learner is only run during system improvement and maintenance periods and thus is not a normal part of production data processing operations.

Core Mining Operations and Presentation Layer Elements

At present, GeneWays' query functionality appears primarily contained in a standalone front-end program called CUtenet, which, at the time of this writing, appears to offer limited but useful query functionality.

The front-end "portal" to the GeneWays Interaction Database allows a user to retrieve interactions that answer particular query parameters and view these interactions in graphical form. An example of GeneWays' GUI for displaying results of an interaction query can be seen in Figure XII.35.

CUtenet can generate both full-color, three-dimensional visual representations of molecular pathways and two-dimensional models for faster rendering. The front end appears to be able to generate both simple concept graphs and complex network representations (see Figure XII.36). By interacting with the visualization (i.e., by clicking on edges connecting entities), a user can jump to the underlying binary statement and either build new queries around that statement or jump to the actual online full-text version of the article(s) from which the interaction came (this assumes that the user has an appropriate password for the journals or online sources hosting the online article).

CUtenet also supports a fair amount of additional functionality. For instance, users can save images in various formats ranging from VRML to BMP, JPEG, PNG, and Postscript. Users can edit the layout and content of molecular map images. More importantly, they can actually edit the original pathway data in text format. CUtenet also supports an interface to allow a user to upload a single article into GeneWays for processing and storage of its molecular pathway information in the GeneWays Interaction Database; at the end of processing, the user can see a visual model of the molecular interaction in the article that he or he has input to the system.

XII.4.2 Implementation and Typical Usage

The GeneWays implementation hosted at Columbia University has extracted molecular pathways information related to signal transduction from more than 150,000 articles. The Interaction Database has been described as containing several hundred unique binary molecular pathways statements.

Rzhetzky, Iossifov, et al. (2004) describes a typical user interaction with the application. If a user is interested in exploring interactions involving the protein *collagen*, he or she would enter the a query into CUtenet for all statements (binary formal statements each describing a formal protein-to-protein interaction) in the Interaction Database involving the concept collagen. The query would return a listing of all 1,355 interactions in the database involving collagen.

The user can then choose to use GeneWays' primary practical refinement filter based on a simple threshold parameter. This threshold filter allows a user to filter out all interaction statements that do not appear at least a certain number of times in unique sentences within the articles from which the Interaction Database was created.

Database Geneways 4.0

ActionTable

Action	Known since	Instance count	Article count	Journal count
ppar (geneorprotein) --attach--> insulin (geneorprotein)	23 Dec 1999	12	11	6
ppar (geneorprotein) --promote--> insulin (geneorprotein)	8 Dec 1998	11	9	5
ppar (geneorprotein) --activate--> insulin (geneorprotein)	1 Oct 1997	15	15	6
insulin (geneorprotein) --activate--> ppar (geneorprotein)	1 Jun 1996	24	15	8

Action's Details

Action

ppar (geneorprotein) --attach--> insulin (geneorprotein)

Article CURROPINLIPIDOL_11_4_429 (MedLine)

- Dominant negative mutations in human ppar associated with severe insulin resistance, diabetes mellitus and hypertension.

Article MOLCELLBIOL_20_14_5343 (MedLine) (FullText)

- Dominant negative mutations in human ppar associated with severe insulin resistance, diabetes mellitus, and hypertension.

Article NATURE_414_6865_788 (MedLine) (FullText)

- Dominant negative mutations in human ppar associated with severe insulin resistance, diabetes mellitus and hypertension.

Article NATURE_409_6818_307 (MedLine) (FullText)

- Dominant negative mutations in human ppar associated with severe insulin resistance, diabetes mellitus, and hypertension.

Article NATURE_405_6788_857 (MedLine) (FullText)

- Dominant negative mutations in human ppar associated with severe insulin resistance, diabetes mellitus and hypertension

Internet

Figure XII.35. CUtenet's "action table" – A query-results GUI for interaction information found in articles. (Courtesy of Andrei Rzhetsky.)

If the user set the threshold requirement to request only interactions that appeared in the database at least 15 times from different unique sentences, the query would bring back a result set of 12 interactions. The user could then use CUtenet to generate a visualization like the one seen in Figure XII.37.

By clicking on a given edge in the graph the user can see the specific interaction statement contained in the Interaction Database. Clicking a second time shows the exact sentence in the specific article from which this interaction was originally extracted.

This is the primary query type supported by the system. However, by changing the input entity being searched for among statements and manipulating the simple threshold filter, a user can navigate through the entire molecular interaction model represented by the ontology-like Interaction Database.

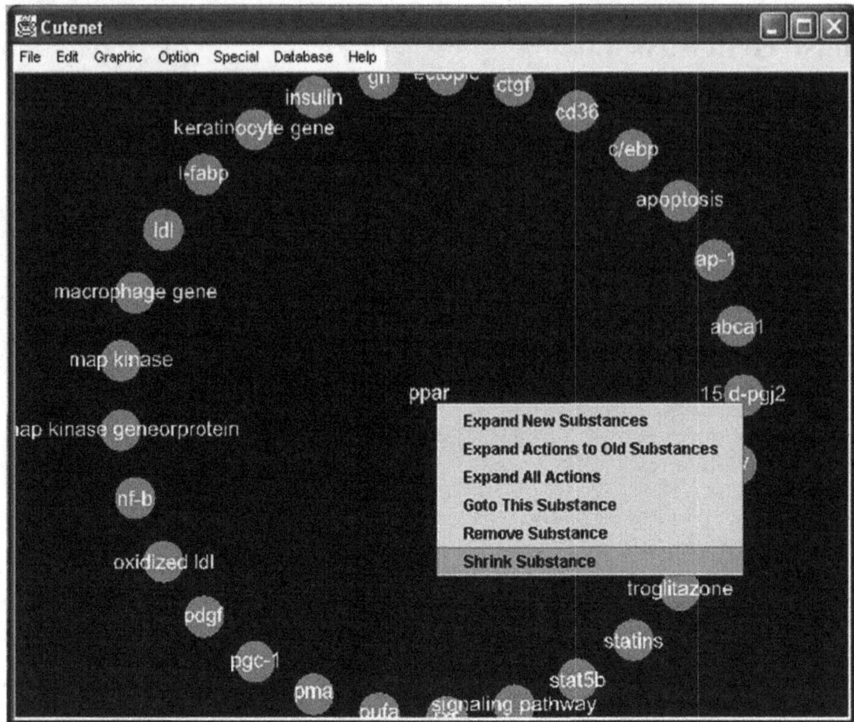

Figure XII.36. A CUtenet dimensional visualization showing the PPAR protein's interactions with other proteins. (Courtesy of Andrei Rzhetsky.)

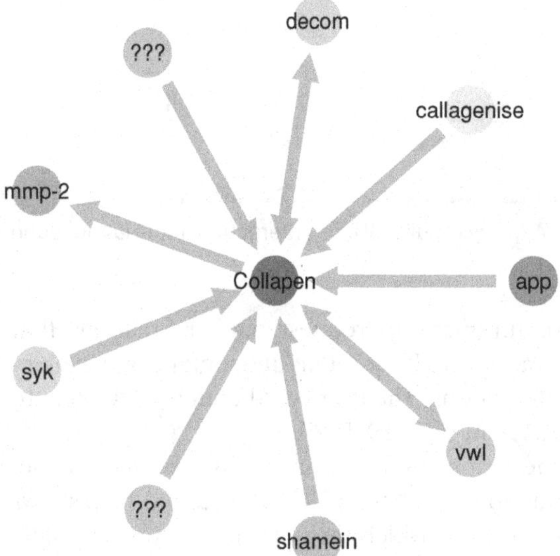

Figure XII.37. Interactions involving Collagen that appear in at least 15 independent sentences. (From Rzhetsky, Iossifov, et al. 2004.)

XII.4.3 Citations and Notes

General articles relevant to text mining for exploring molecular pathways include Fukuda et al. (1998); Craven and Kumlien (1999); Rindflesch, Hunter, and Aronson (1999); Salamonsen et al. (1999); Rindflesch et al. (2000); Stapley and Benoit (2000); Dickerson et al. (2003); Pustejovsky et al. (2002); Caldon (2003); Yao et al. (2004); and Zhou and Cui (2004).

GeneWays is a system in continuing development. Articles describing elements of the GeneWays project include Koike and Rzhetsky (2000); Krauthammer et al. (2000); Rzhetsky et al. (2000); Hatzivassiloglou, Duboue, and Rzhetsky (2001); and Rzhetsky et al. (2004). Examples in this section are taken from Rzhetsky et al. (2004), as is Figure XII.35. The generalized architectural views presented in Figures XII.32 and XII.33 are derived in particular from Rzhetsky et al. (2000), Hatzivassiloglou et al. (2001), and Rzhetsky et al. (2004). Information on the National Center for Biotechnology Information's (NCBI) Genbank database can be found at <http://www.ncbi.nlm.nih.gov/Genbank/>. A good description of the Swiss-Prot database is contained in Bairoch and Apweiler (2000).

APPENDIX A

DIAL: A Dedicated Information Extraction Language for Text Mining

A.1 WHAT IS THE DIAL LANGUAGE?

This appendix provides an example of a dedicated information extraction language called DIAL (declarative information analysis language). The purpose of the appendix is to show the general structure of the language and offer some code examples that will demonstrate how it can be used to extract concepts and relationships; hence, we will not cover all aspects and details of the language.

The DIAL language is a dedicated information extraction language enabling the user to define **concepts** whose instances are found in a text body by the DIAL engine. A DIAL concept is a logical entity, which can represent a noun (such as a person, place, or institution), an event (such as a business merger between two companies or the election of a president), or any other entity for which a text pattern can be defined. Instances of concepts are found when the DIAL engine succeeds in matching a concept pattern to part of the text it is processing. Concepts may have **attributes**, which are properties belonging to the concept whose values are found in the text of the concept instance. For instance, a "Date" concept might have numeric day, month, and year attributes and a string attribute for the day of the week.

A DIAL concept declaration defines the concept's name, attributes, and optionally some additional code common to all instances of the concept. Each concept may have several **rules**, each of which corresponds to a different text pattern and each of which finds an instance of the same concept. Because each pattern is different, each rule will have separate code for handling that specific pattern.

A **text pattern** is a sequence of text elements such as string constants, parts of speech (nouns, verbs, adjectives, etc.), and scanner elements (such as a capital word or a number) as well as other concepts and elements.

The following is a simple example of patterns for finding instances of "Person":

```
concept Person{
attributes:
string      Title;
string      FirstName;
string      MiddleName;
string      LastName;
};
rule Person {
pattern:
  "mr."->title Capital->first Capital->last;
actions:
    Add(Title<-title,FirstName<-first, LastName<-last);
};
rule Person {
pattern:
  "dr."->title Capital->first Capital->last;
actions:
  Add(Title<-title,FirstName<-first, LastName<-last);
};
rule Person {
pattern:
  Capital->first MiddleNameConcept->mid Capital->last;
actions:
  Add(FirstName<-first, MiddleName<-mid, LastName<-last);
};
```

In this example, the concept "Person" has three different rules (with the same name as the concept), each of which has a different text pattern. Each rule finds an instance of "Person." Note that not all patterns fill all attributes of "Person." For instance, in the first rule, there is no value for the "MiddleName" attribute, whereas in the last rule there is no value for the "Title" attribute.

A.2 INFORMATION EXTRACTION IN THE DIAL ENVIRONMENT

There are many types and methods of information extraction. In the DIAL language, text patterns are defined, and an automated search for these patterns is executed. When a match for a pattern is found, the text matching the pattern is marked as an instance of the particular pattern's concept.

A DIAL **module** is a collection of concepts and their rules contained in one or more DIAL code files but defined by a single DIAL module file. Concepts grouped in the same module will usually have some common characteristic. For instance, there might be a module for finding different types of financial entities that contains the concepts of those entities and any utility concepts they rely on. Grouping DIAL code into different modules makes it easier to understand and maintain each

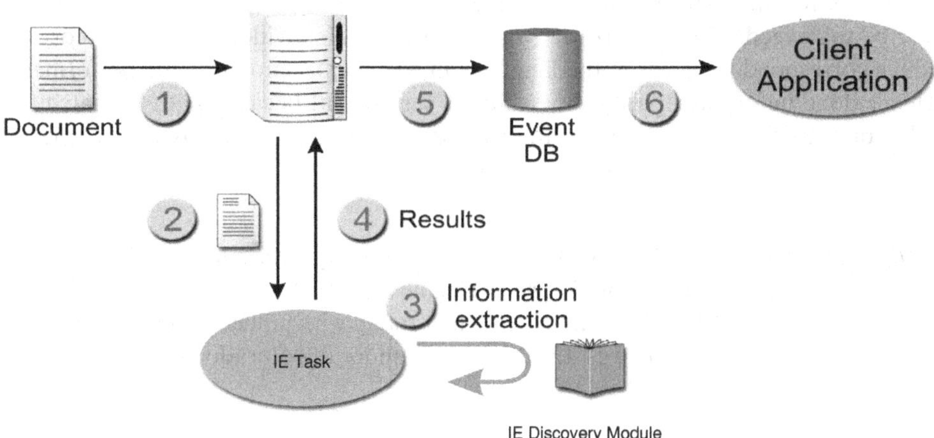

Figure A.1. IE task as run by the extraction server.

module, allows a single module to be changed and recompiled without having to recompile any other modules, and enables reuse of the module in several Discovery Modules.

A DIAL **Discovery Module** is a collection of several DIAL modules and plug-ins, all of which are run on all text documents in order to perform a complete information extraction process. The DIAL language's rules are developed in a dedicated development environment called ClearLab. This is a GUI application that enables editing and compiling of DIAL rules as well as running the information extraction process using these rules. One can then examine the results of the information extraction process and modify the rules where necessary. This is similar to the debugging process for any programming language.

Once a DIAL Discovery Module has been developed, it can be used by a tagging server that has several components for text processing, including categorization, pattern-based extraction, topological extraction, and so on. The component that performs information extraction based on a DIAL Discovery Module is called **IE Task**. Figure A.1 describes the operation of the IE Task in the tagging server environment.

1. A document is sent to the Extraction Server for processing.
2. The Extraction Server then sends the document to the IE task for information extraction.
3. The IE task applies an IE Discovery Module, as defined for it by the Extraction server, to the document.
4. Information extraction results are returned from the IE task to the Extraction server.
5. The results are written to the Event database.
6. The results may then be accessed by a client application – for example, either a graphical application such as any Text Analytics application or a user-supplied application.

A.3 TEXT TOKENIZATION

Before performing pattern matching on a text, the DIAL engine requires that the text be **tokenized**. This is a process whereby the text is divided into units, most of which correspond to words in the language in which extraction is being performed. This is done before any pattern matching is carried out because pattern matching relies on the existence of tokens in the Shared Memory (SM). Here is an example of how the standard DIAL tokenizer operates on text:

Untokenized text:	"The CEO of U.S. Motors met today with James A. Smith, the founder of Colorado Engines."
Tokenized text:	"the ceo of u.s. motors met today with james a. smith 0 1 2 3 4 5 6 7 8 9 10 11 12 13 14, the founder of colorado engines." 15 16 17 18 19 20 21

Note that tokenized text omits capitalization and that punctuation and other nonalphanumeric characters are also tokens. Token numbering is zero based.

When instances of concepts are found, they are stored with their offsets and lengths (in tokens) in relation to the entire text body being processed. For example, if our text body were the tokenized sentence above, we would store two instances of companies: "U.S. Motors" at token offset 3, with a length of 5 tokens, and "Colorado Engines" with a token offset of 19 and a length of 2 tokens.

The standard DIAL English tokenizer, provided with all DIAL products, also determines which **scanner properties** apply to each token. Scanner properties are attributes of a single token's characters such as **Capital** (begins with a capital letter), **Number** (expresses a numeric value), **Alpha** (contains only alphabet characters), and so on.

A.4 CONCEPT AND RULE STRUCTURE

This section presents a brief outline of the concept and rule structure of the DIAL code. The details of each code section, its use and various options, are omitted to keep the description simple.

The DIAL code consists mostly of concept and rule **code blocks**. In a concept code block, we define the name and attributes of the concept as well as some operations and settings that we wish to be common to all instances of the concept.

A concept may have one or more rule code blocks with the same name as the concept. These are the concept's rules. A concept's rules determine what patterns to search for when trying to find an instance of the concept and how to add an instance of the concept and with which attribute values.

Both concept and rule blocks have **sections** with different names, each serving a certain purpose. Sections are headed by the section name followed by a colon.

The following table summarizes the different sections and their associated concept or rule code blocks:

Code Block	Section	Description	Mandatory
Concept	Attributes	Defines the names and types of concept attributes. These are usually filled with values from the concept instance's matching text.	No
Concept	Guards	Similar to rule constraints, concept guards are logical conditions on the concept attributes' values that must be met. If they are not, the instance is discarded.	No
Concept	Actions	Code operations to perform after finding a concept instance. Concept actions are performed only if all the concept's guard conditions are true or if the concept has no guards.	No
Concept	Internal	A section for defining internal concepts. These are concepts that can be used only within the scope of the concept in which they are defined and any inheriting concepts.	No
Concept	Function	A section for defining add-on (Perl) functions that can be used only in the scope of the concept in which they are defined and any inheriting concepts.	No
Concept	Context	Defines the text units in which to search for the concept instances. Usually this section will not appear, and then the concept will be searched for within the module's context.	No
Concept	Dependencies	Permits definition of an explicit dependency of one concept on another.	No
Rule	Pattern	Defines the text pattern to match when searching for a concept instance.	Yes
Rule	Constraints	Defines logical conditions to apply to values extracted from the pattern match. If these conditions are not met for a specific match, the actions block of the rule will not be performed on that match.	No
Rule	Action	Code operations to perform after finding a pattern match. Among other things, this is where concept instances are added. Rule actions are performed only if all the rule's constraints are met or if the rule has no constraints.	Yes

A.4.1 Context

When the DIAL engine searches for concept instances, it does so within a certain **context**. The most commonly used context is a **sentence**, for most concept instances are contained within a single sentence. A "Sentence" concept is defined, and instances of this concept are found and inserted into the SM via a standard DIAL plug-in. If a concept is searched for within the context of a "Sentence," each sentence instance is searched separately for the concept instances. This means that an instance's entire token range must be within a single "Sentence" and cannot overlap with two or more "Sentences."

The section for defining the **module context** is located in the module file. The module context is the default context for all concepts in that module.

Any context (both module context and concept context) may be a single concept name or a combination of concept names and logical operators (AND, OR, NOT).

Most concepts use the module context. If a concept's context section is missing or empty, that concept will use the module context. However, it is possible to override the module context for a specific concept and set it to be any concept required. For instance, a user might wish to search not within sentences but within the entire document or within each two or three consecutive sentences. Another example might be to apply certain concepts only to the document's title (on the assumption that the title has a recognizable format) or to identify tables of numbers within a document and apply certain concepts only to them. Some examples are shown in the following code samples:

```
concept TableColumnTotal{
context:
  NumberTable; //NumberTable is the name of a defined concept
...};
concept TitlePerson {
context:
  Title;// Title is the name of a concept
...};
concept CompanyPersonnel {
context:
NOT ContactSection; //avoid searching the contact section of a document for
                    //company personnel
...}
concept DocumentSubjects {
context:
  Title OR FirstParagraph; //search only the title and first paragraph of
                           //each document for its subjects
...};
concept TitleSubjects {
context:
  Title AND DocumentSubjects; //look only at document subjects found
                              //in the title
...};
```

A.5 PATTERN MATCHING

Patterns are at the core of pattern-based extraction logic. The first operation to be performed on a rule is an attempt to match its pattern. Only if the pattern is matched is the rest of the rule code applied.

A **text pattern** is a formal and general definition of what an instance of the concept looks like. A pattern is a sequence of **pattern elements** (which define types of text elements) with or without **pattern operators**. Pattern operators mostly denote something about the number of times the elements should appear or a relationship between pattern elements. For a text to match a pattern, it must match each of the pattern elements in the order in which they appear in the pattern.

For example, the pattern Number "-" Number "-" Number "-" Number would be matched by the text: "1-800-973-5651."

On the one hand, a pattern should be general enough to match many instances of a concept. On the other, if a pattern is too general, it might match text that is not really an instance of the concept.

Consider the following examples of patterns for Person:

The pattern
"Mr. John Smith"

will certainly correctly identify all people referred to as "Mr. John Smith" but nothing else. This pattern is too specific.

The pattern
"Capital Capital"

will probably match many names of people but will also match such texts as "General Motors," "Information Extraction," and "Buenos Aires." This pattern is too general.

The pattern
"Mr. Capital Capital"

however, is a good example of a general pattern that will catch many of the required instances without mistakenly matching texts that are not names of people. It can be further enhanced as

"Mr. Capital Capital? Capital",

where the Capital? element stands for an optional middle name. However, this pattern will match only male people whose title happens to be "Mr." Additional rules would still be needed if this pattern were used.

Clearly, pattern writing may require a great deal of fine-tuning and iterative improvement to ensure that all the required instances are found.

A.6 PATTERN ELEMENTS

A pattern element is a type of textual entity that may appear in a pattern. The patterns are the core elements that allow defining a pattern. A variety of options are provided to describe pattern elements, including exact string constants (e.g., "George Bush"); wordclasses (i.e., predefined lists of words or phrases); other concept names, regular expressions, scanner properties (e.g., AllCaps, digits, etc.); and wild cards.

A pattern element is a type of textual entity that may appear in a pattern.

The pattern elements are as follows:

- *String Constants*
- *Wordclass Names*
- *Thesaurus Names*
- *Concept Names*
- *Character-Level Regular Expressions*
- *Character Classes*
- *Scanner Properties*
- *Token Elements*

A.6.1 String Constants

String constants are elements consisting of characters surrounded by double quotation marks (" ").

Note that a single string constant may contain several tokens. String constants in patterns are tokenized automatically, using the tokenizer defined in the module, which is also used on the text at runtime. This means that when the engine searches for a string constant, it will ignore letter case and token spacing, as shown in the example below.

When a pattern is being matched, string comparison between string constants in the pattern and the text being matched is case insensitive. This means that, when letters are compared, upper- or lowercase versions of the same character are considered identical as follows:

Example:

Pattern	Text Matching the Pattern
"U.S.A."	"U.S.A." "u.s.a." "U.S.A."

A.6.2 Wordclass Names

Wordclass names are alphanumeric strings that have previously been declared as wordclasses in one of the DIAL source files – either in the same module in which the wordclass is referred to or in an imported module, which exports the wordclass. A wordclass is a collection of words or phrases that have some common characteristic. By convention, wordclass names start with "wc."

Wordclass contents may be loaded dynamically from a file. The dynamic load option is useful for wordclasses that tend to change frequently – for example, a wordclass that contains names of companies. A wordclass that is not loaded dynamically requires recompilation of its module if it is changed, but a dynamically loaded wordclass does not.

Wordclass members are tokenized automatically so that the text is matched against their tokenized versions.

A wordclass member may be one of the following:

- A single all-letter token.
- Any string surrounded by quotes.

Example:

```
wordclass wcPersonTitle = "mr." "mrs." miss "dr." president king queen con-
gressman "prime minister";
```

Pattern	Text Matching the Pattern
WCPersonTitle	"Mr." "mr." "Miss"

A.6.3 Thesaurus Names

Thesaurus names are alphanumeric strings that have previously been declared as thesaurus objects in one of the DIAL source files – either in the same module in which the thesaurus is referred to or in an imported module that exports the wordclass.

A thesaurus is like a collection of several wordclasses. Within each class, the members are either synonyms of each other or serve some similar semantic purpose, as in wordclasses. Thesaurus members are tokenized automatically, and thus the text is matched against their tokenized versions.

The thesaurus **head** members have a special status. Within a thesaurus class, the first member is called the "head" and is used as the identifier of the class; it may also be used to normalize instances of the class to a single display value (canonization). Thesauri may also be extended dynamically – that is, new classes and members of classes may be added to a thesaurus at run time. Thesaurus contents may be loaded dynamically from a file.

Example:

```
thesaurus thNationalities =
        {American "U.S." "U.S.A." " United States" }
        {British English "U.K." "United Kingdom" };
```

Pattern	Text Matching the Pattern
thNationalities	"American" "u.s.a." "English"

A.6.4 Concept Names

Concept names are case-sensitive alphanumeric strings that have been declared as concepts. The concepts used in concept patterns must either have already been declared in the current module or public concepts from one of its imported modules; otherwise, the current module will not compile.

The ability of one concept to refer to another concept in its pattern enables the user to create very complex patterns in a concise and modular fashion. It also makes it possible to refer to concepts in modules developed by someone else without having to be aware of their code.

Example:
Suppose that you have defined the following concepts:

- **Person** – a concept for finding people.
- **Position** – a concept for finding professional positions, such as "CEO," "general manager," "team leader," "vice president," and so on.
- **Company** – a concept for finding names of companies.

One could then write the following simple pattern for finding a person's position in a company:

Pattern	Text Matching the Pattern
Person "is employed as" "a"? Position "at" Company	"James White is employed as a senior programmer at Software Inc." "Harvey Banes is employed as vice president at MegaStorage"

A.6.5 Character-Level Regular Expressions

Character-level regular expressions are used relatively rarely in most Discovery Modules. They are used only when it is necessary to have control over the pattern at the character level. Most pattern elements can be matched only on whole units of tokens. Character-level regular expressions and character classes can find matches that contain parts of tokens.

Character-level regular expressions have standard Perl-compliant syntax but must be surrounded by 'regexp(" ")' within the pattern. Here are some examples of metacharacters used in character-level regular expressions:

Pattern	Texts matching the pattern
regexp(".")	"a", "?", "*"
regexp("Mc[A-Z][a-z]+")	"McDonald", "McReady"
regexp("h2o(co4)?[hoc0–9]*")	"h2oco4", "h2och4o"

A.6.6 Character Classes

It is possible to define character classes, which are sets of character-level regular expressions. Character classes may appear as pattern items.

Example:

```
charclass ccScotchIrishLastname = {"Mc[A-Z][a-z]+",
"Mac[A-Z][a"z]+",
"O'[A-Z][a-z]+", ...};
```

Pattern	Text Matching the Pattern
ccScotchIrishLastname	"McPhee" "McPhee" "O'Leary"

A.6.7 Scanner Properties

Scanner properties are attributes of a single token's characters such as Capital (begins with a capital letter), Number (expresses a numeric value), Alpha (contains only alphabet characters), and so on.

A.6.8 Token Elements

The Token pattern element is used as a placeholder for any token. It is used when defining a pattern in which there may be one or more tokens whose value is unimportant.

Example:

Pattern	Text Matching the Pattern
"He said: '"Token+"' and she said"	He said: 'What time is it?' and she said He said: 'Miss Barker, please move my three-o'-clock meeting to 4:30' and she said

A.7 RULE CONSTRAINTS

Sometimes, when writing a rule pattern, we find that the definition of the pattern is not precise enough on its own and that additional conditions on the pattern, which cannot be expressed by pattern elements and operators, must be added. **Constraints** are conditions on pattern variables. All the constraints must have a "true" value, or the actions section will not be performed – that is, the match will be disqualified even though the pattern has been found.

A constraint may be composed of a single Boolean clause, the negation of such a clause (in the format NOT(...) or !(...)), or several clauses with "AND" and "OR" operators between them.

The following is a simple example:

Suppose we want a rule for a sequence of capital words of any length except 5. The condition "any length except 5" cannot be expressed in a single pattern. It can be expressed in a constraint, however, as follows:

```
...
pattern:
  Capital+;
constraints:
  this_match.TokenCount() != 5;
...
```

A.7.1 Comparison Constraints

The preceding example illustrates a comparison constraint. Comparison operators in DIAL4 are as follows:

==, !=, <, <=, >, >=

All comparison operators may be applied to numeric values. Only "==" (equal to) and "!=" (not equal to) may be applied to string and phrase values. No comparison operators may be applied to concept and list values.

Comparison operators may be used in "if" clauses as well as in constraints.

A.7.2 Boolean Constraints

If a constraint clause is a numeric value (e.g., "var.IsEmpty()" or "varNumber"), it will be considered false if the value is zero and true otherwise.

A.8 CONCEPT GUARDS

Guards may be applied to concept attributes when a rule attempts to add a concept instance to the SM. Only if all guard conditions are met will the instance be added and the actions section of the concept performed.

All of the rule constraint syntax applies to concept guards as well. The difference between them is that rule constraints are applied to pattern variables, whereas concept guards are applied to concept attribute values.

Guards enable the concept to ensure conditions on its attribute values in a central location without having to add these conditions to each rule of the concept.

Example:

```
concept Date {
attributes:
   number nDay;
   number nMonth;
   number nYear;
guards:
   (nDay >= 1) AND (nDay <= 31);
   (nMonth >= 1) AND (nMonth <=12);
   (nYear > 0);
};
```

Actions are blocks of code operations to be performed after a pattern match, in the case of rule actions, or after adding a concept instance, in the case of concept actions. Concept actions are not mandatory and in most cases will not be used at all. Rule actions, however, are always used: If a rule has no actions, it will not add an instance to the SM even if it matches the text properly and therefore will have no effect on the Discovery Module output. The most important action a rule performs is to add a concept instance with its appropriate attribute values. It may also perform other actions.

All actions are performed with or on variables. Rule actions may use pattern variables, local variables, and global variables. Concept actions may use attribute variables, local variables, and global variables.

A.9 COMPLETE DIAL EXAMPLES

A.9.1 Extracting People Names Based on Title/Position

In the following code fragment we define two concepts. The first concept is PersonNameStruct, which simply looks for some variation of First Name, Middle Name, and Last Name. This concept is rather naïve because it does not enforce any constraints, and as a result the precision of extracting people names using the rules associated with this concept would be rather poor. The second concept is Person. This concept has the same pattern as the PersonNameStruct concept with the addition of some constraints. The constraints (which are explained in the code) considerably increase the precision of the concept.

```
wordclass wcPosition = adviser minister spokesman
                       president (vice president)
                       general
                       (gen.);
/* note that wordclass members are tokenized and entries containing multiple
tokens should be enclosed within () */
```

```
concept PersonNameStruct{          //we define this concept to
                                   //allow  the code reuse
attributes:
   string FirstName;
   string MiddleName;
   string LastName;
 };
wordclass wcNamePrefix = ben abu abed von al;
/* common prefixes of family names */
rule PersonNameStruct {
pattern:
   Capital -> first (Capital "."?)? -> middle
      ((wcNamePrefix "-"?)? Capital) ->last;
/* the pattern looks for 3 elements, where the 2nd element
(middle name) is optional, and the 3rd element may have an  optional
prefix */
actions:
   Add(FirstName <- first.Text(), MiddleName <-
      middle.Text (), LastName <- last.Text( ));
*/ add an instance of PersonNameStruct to the Shared Memory */
 };
rule Person {
pattern:
   Capital -> first (MiddleName -> middle)?
      ((wcNamePrefix "-"?)? Capital) ->last;
constraints:
   (first IS_IN wcFirstNames) OR !(middle.IsEmpty())
   OR (first {1 }AFTER wcPosition);
   !(first.FirstToken() IS_IN wcPosition);
/* The constraints filter out erroneous instances:
Either first needs to be in the lexicon of first names, or that middle is not
empty (since it is  optional) or that the token preceding first was a position
In addition, we make sure that the first token of first is not part of know
position */
actions:
   Add(FirstName <- first.Text(), MiddleName <- middle.Text(),LastName <-
last.Text());
/* add an instance of Person to the Shared Memory */
 };
```

If there are several rules to a concept, then the order between rules is important. The first rule will be applied before the second rule, and if it succeeds, it will block the pattern's range such that no other rules can be applied to this text fragment.

A.9.2 Extracting Lists of People Names Based on a Preceding Verb

We want to extract a list of people and feed them into a list variable called pList. The pattern is looking for one of a predefined set of verbs followed by "are" or "were" and then a list of people names separated by commas. The code extracts the list of people and then iterates over the list to create a new instance of Person in the shared memory for each member of the list.

```
concept PersonsList{};
  wordclass wcCriminalIndicatingVerbs =
    charged blamed arrested;
  wordclass wcPluralBe = are were;
  rule PersonsList {
  pattern:
    wcCriminalIndicatingVerbs wcPluralBe
    (PersonNameStruct->> pList ","?)+ "and"
    PersonNameStruct ->> pList;
/* we are looking for a criminal verb followed by are or were, and then a list
of people (separated by commas). plist will hold the list of people by using
the->> (append to list operator)*/
  actions:
    iterate (pList) begin
      currPerson = pList.CurrentItem();
      Add(Person, currPerson,
      FirstName <- currPerson.FirstName,
      LastName <- currPerson.LastName);
    End
/*
       };
```

A.9.3 Using a Thesaurus to Extract Location Names

In this example we look for country names in the text. If the country appears in the thesaurus it will be replaced by the canonic entry; otherwise, it will remain unchanged. The constraint makes sure that the entry contains a capital letter.

```
thesaurus thsCountries;
rule Location {
    pattern:
    wcCountries-> the_country;
  constraints:
  the_country CONTAINS Capital;
    actions:
    canonic_country = thsCountries.GetHead(the_country);
```

```
        if(canonic_country.IsEmpty())
          Add(Location,this_match,"country",
            the_country.Text());
        else
          Add(Location,this_match,"country",
            canonic_country);
};
```

A.9.4 Creating a Thesaurus of Local People Names

In this example we augment the definition of the person concept with the ability to add the name of the person to a local thesaurus. The thesaurus will contain all names of people in the document and then can be used for anaphora resolution (as in cases in which just the last name appears in the text after the full name of that person was mentioned earlier).

In the action part of the rule we check if the person was added already to the thesaurus. If the petson's name was still not added, a new entry is created with the full name as the leader (the canonic form) and three additional variations (first name and last name, last name alone, and first name alone).

```
thesaurus thLocalPersons;
concept Person {
attributes:
  string FullName;
  string FirstName;
  string MiddleName;
  string LastName;
actions:
  if
  (thLocalPersons.GetHead(FullName).IsEmpty())
  begin
    thLocalPersons.AddSynonym(FullName.Text(), FullName);
    thLocalPersons.AddSynonym(FullName.Text(), FirstName + LastName);
    thLocalPersons.AddSynonym(FullName.Text(), LastName);
    thLocalPersons.AddSynonym(FullName.Text(), FirstName);
  end
  FullName = FullName.Text();
};
```

A.9.5 A Simplified Anaphora Resolution Rule for Resolving a Person's Pronoun

In this example we illustrate a sample anaphora resolution rule. The rule will be activated if we encounter a pronoun (Pron) whose type is person. We then look if there is a person name in the previous sentence. If there is a person in the previous sentence, we resolve the pronoun to point to that person. Note that this is just one simple rule in the overall anaphora resolution solution.

```
concept PersonAnaphora {
attributes:
   string FullName;
 };
rule PersonAnaphora {
pattern:
   Pron -> p;
constraints:
   p.type == "person";
actions:
   prevSentence = this_match.Previous(Sentence);
   prevPerson = prevSentence.Next(Person);
   if (!prevPerson.IsEmpty())
Add(prevPerson.FullName);
 };
```

A.9.6 Anaphoric Family Relation

In the following example we show a DIAL rule for extracting a simple pattern of anaphoric FamilyRelation as in the following extract from a Pakistani newspaper (October 2002):

PML(Q)'s provincial leader ***Amanullah Khan*** *is contesting election from NA-17 Abbottabad-1 while* ***his nephew Inayatullah Khan Jadoon*** *is contesting from PF-45 under PML(N) ticket*

```
public concept FamilyRelation {
attributes:
   string Person;
   string FamilyRelation;
   string Person_Relative;
 };
wordclass wcThirdPersonPossessPronoun = "his" "her";
wordclass wcFamilyRelation = "father" "mother" "son" ...
"nephew";
rule FamilyRelation {
pattern:
PersonAnaphora->pron        //his
   wcFamilyRelation->relation //nephew
   wcComma? // optional comma
   PersonOrPersonDetails -> relative;
```

```
    //Inayatullah Khan
  //Jadoon
  constraints:
    //pron is a relevant pronoun
    pron IS_A wcThirdPersonPossessPronoun;
    //make sure that the antecedent (here: "Amanullah Khan") isn't empty
    ! pron.Antecedent.IsEmpty();
    //person is never a relative of himself !
    pron.Antecedent! = relative.Person;
  actions:
    Add(Person<-pron.Antecedent,FamilyRelation<-
      Relation, Person_Relative<-relative.Person);
  };
```

The meaning of the rule above is as follows:

- Extract a FamilyRelation instance if the following sequence was matched: A pronoun resolved as PersonAnaphora (in earlier module) followed by a family relation noun, followed by an optional comma, and then an instance of PersonOrPersonDetails (a Person name or a noun phrase or an appositive clause with person name as head).
- Subject to the constraints:

  1. The pronoun is a third person possessive pronoun ("his" or "her").
  2. A resolved person (for the pronoun) was found (i.e., it is not empty).
  3. The resolved person (to which the pronoun relates is not equal to the person identified within the pattern ("relative").

- Add one instance of FamilyRelation. The first attribute (Person) should be the pronoun refers to (pron.Antecedent). The second attribute should be the relation word (in the example above: "nephew"). The third attribute, Person_Relative, should be the person found within the pattern itself (relative – here Inayatullah Khan Jadoon).

A.9.7 Meeting between People

We will demonstrate the implementation of a simple rule for the PersonMeeting concept, which stands for a meeting between two people.

Consider the following extract from a publication of IRNA (official Iranian News Agency), October 2002:

> *During his three-day stay in Iran, the Qatari official is to meet Interior minister Mousavi Lari, Majlis Speaker Mehdi Karroubi and First Vice-President Mohammad Reza Aref.*

We first present the concept's prototype:

```
public concept PersonMeeting {
attributes:
  string Person1;
  string Person2;
  string PersonDescription1;
  string PersonDescription2;
  string Organization;
  string MeetingStatus;
  string Date;
};
```

Person1, Person2, PersonDescription1, PersonDescription2 and Organization are the participants in the meeting. We extract a different instance for every pair of people that met. This means that in the preceding example we extract one instance for the meeting of "the Qatari official" with "Mousavi Lari," one instance for his meeting with "Mehdi Karroubi," and one instance for his meeting with "Mohammad Reza Aref."

If the first party of the meeting is a name of a person (such as "Mousavi Lari"), then the Person1 attribute is filled. The same is true for Person2 (regarding the second party). Similarly, in cases in which we do not have a specific name but rather a description such as "the Qatari official," then PersonDescription1 (or PersonDescription2) is filled.

The Organization attribute is filled in the case of a meeting (or a speech given) between a person and an organization.

MeetingStatus may be "announced" (actual meeting has taken place) or "planned" (future).

Date is the meeting date (if available).

The following rule implements the concept:

```
wordclass wcCommaAnd = "and" "," ",and";
rule PersonMeeting {
pattern:
LONGEST(
  PersonDescription->the_nominal
  //"the Qatari official"
  ExtendedVGForMeeting->meeting_phrase
  //verb group: "is to meet"
(PersonOrPersonDetails->> meeting_list wcCommaAnd){0,3}
  //"Interior minister Mousavi Lari, Majlis
  // Speaker Mehdi Karroubi"
  ///last item: "First Vice-President Mohammad Reza Aref"
  PersonOrPersonDetails->> meeting_list
```

```
);
actions:
  iterate(meeting_list)
    //Iterate on the items of the list
    //meeting_list
  begin
    //Create a separate instance for each
    //instance
    Add(PersonMeeting,
      meeting_list.CurrentItem(),
      PersonDescription1<-
        the_nominal.PersonDescription,
      Person1<-meeting_
      list.CurrentItem().Person.Text(),
    // the status of the meeting: "announced" or
    // (as here): "planned" (Found according to
    //the tense of the verb used)
    MeetingStatus<-meeting_phrase.Status
);
  end
  };
```

This rule demonstrates the usage of lists in DIAL. The "->>" operator concatenates all the items to one list (here – first up to three elements in the beginning of the list and then the last item: "First Vice-President Mohammad Reza Aref." Note that only the item itself is concatenated to the list, not the delimiters between the items (wcCommaAnd). The actions part of the rule demonstrates again the DIAL operator "iterate." This operator allows going through each item of the list and performing, for each item, the required actions – in this case adding for each of the persons a separate instance of the PersonCommunications concept. Note that the person from the list is inserted to Person1, whereas PersonDescription1 is fixed for all items – the PersonDescription from the beginning of the pattern (Here: "the Qatari official").

Bibliography

Abney, S. (1996). *Partial Parsing via Finite-State Cascades.* In Proceedings of Workshop on Robust Parsing, 8th European Summer School in Logic, Language, and Information. Prague, Czech Republic: 8–15.

ACE (2004). *Annotation Guidelines for Entity Detection and Tracking (EDT).* http://www.ldc.upenn.edu/Projects/ACE/.

Adam, C. K., Ng, H. T., and Chieu, H. L. (2002). *Bayesian Online Classifiers for Text Classification and Filtering.* In Proceedings of SIGIR-02, 25th ACM International Conference on Research and Development in Information Retrieval. Tampere, Finland, ACM Press, New York: 97–104.

Adams, T. L., Dullea, J., Barrett, T. M., and Grubin, H. (2001). "Technology Issues Regarding the Evolution to a Semantic Web." *ISAS-SCI* **1**: 316–322.

Aggarwal, C. C., Gates, S. C., and Yu, P. S. (1999). *On the Merits of Building Categorization Systems by Supervised Clustering.* In Proceedings of EDBT-00, 7th International Conference on Extending Database Technology. Konstanz, Germany, ACM Press, New York: 352–356.

Agrawal, R., Bayardo, R. J., and Srikant, R. (2000). *Athena: Mining-based Interactive Management of Text Databases.* In Proceedings of EDBT-00, 7th International Conference on Extending Database Technulogy. Konstanz, Germany, Springer-Verlag, Heidelberg: 365–379.

Agrawal, R., Imielinski, T., and Swami, A. (1993). *Mining Association Rules between Sets of Items in Large Databases.* In Proceedings of the ACM SIGMOD Conference on Management of Data. Washington, DC, ACM Press, New York: 207–216.

Agrawal, R., and Srikant, R. (1994). *Fast Algorithms for Mining Association Rules.* In Proceedings of the 20th International Conference on Very Large Databases (VLDB-94). Santiago, Chile, Morgan Kaufmann Publishers, San Francisco: 487–499.

Agrawal, R., and Srikant, R. (1995). *Mining Sequential Patterns.* In Proceedings of the 11th International Conference on Data Engineering. Taipei, Taiwan, IEEE Press, Los Alamitos, CA: 3–14.

Agrawal, R., and Srikant, R. (2001). *On Integrating Catalogs.* In Proceedings of WWW-01, 10th International Conference on the World Wide Web. Hong Kong, ACM Press, New York: 603–612.

Ahlberg, C., and Schneiderman, B. (1994). *Visual Information Seeking: Tight Coupling of Dynamic Query Filters with Starfield Displays.* In Proceedings of the International Conference on Computer-Human Interaction. Boston, ACM Press, New York: 313–317.

Ahlberg, C., and Wistrand, E. (1995). *IVEE: An Information Visualization and Exploration Environment.* In Proceedings of Information Visualization '95 Symposium. Atlanta, GA, IEEE, Los Alamitos, CA: 66–73.

Aho, A., Hopcroft, J., and Ullman, J. (1983). *Data Structures and Algorithms.* Reading, MA, Addison-Wesley.

Ahonen-Myka, H. (1999). *Finding All Frequent Maximal Sets in Text.* In Proceedings of the 16th International Conference on Machine Learning, ICML-99 Workshop on Machine Learning in Text Data Analysis. Ljubljana, AAAI Press, Menlo Park, CA: 1–9.

Ahonen, H., Heinonen, O., Klemettinen, M., and Verkamo, A. (1997a). *Applying Data Mining Techniques in Text Analysis.* Helsinki, Department of Computer Science, University of Helsinki.

Ahonen, H., Heinonen, O., Klemettinen, M., and Verkamo, A. (1997b). *Mining in the Phrasal Frontier.* In Proceedings of Principles of Knowledge Discovery in Databases Conference. Trondheim, Norway, Springer-Verlag, London.

Aitken, J. S. (2002). *Learning Information Extraction Rules: An Inductive Logic Programming Approach.* In Proceedings of the 15th European Conference on Artificial Intelligence. Lyon, France, IOS Press, Amsterdam.

Aizawa, A. (2000). *The Feature Quantity: An Information-Theoretic Perspective of TFIDF-like Measures.* In Proceedings of SIGIR-00, 23rd ACM International Conference on Research and Development in Information Retrieval. Athens, ACM Press, New York: 104–111.

Aizawa, A. (2001). *Linguistic Techniques to Improve the Performance of Automatic Text Categorization.* In Proceedings of NLPRS-01, 6th Natural Language Processing Pacific Rim Symposium. Tokyo, NLPRS, Tokyo: 307–314.

Al-Kofahi, K., Tyrrell, A., Vachher, A., Travers, T., and Jackson, P. (2001). *Combining Multiple Classifiers for Text Categorization.* In Proceedings of CIKM-01, 10th ACM International Conference on Information and Knowledge Management. Atlanta, ACM Press, New York: 97–104.

Albert, R., Jeong, H., and Barabasi, A.-L. (1999). "Diameter of the World-Wide Web." *Nature* **401**: 130–131.

Alias, F., Iriondo, I., and Barnola, P. (2003). *Multi-Domain Text Classification for Unit Selection Text-to-Speech Synthesis.* In Proceedings of ICPhS-03, 15th International Congress on Phonetic Sciences. Barcelona.

Allen, J. (1995). *Natural Language Understanding.* Redwood City, CA, Benjamin Cummings.

Amati, G., and Crestani, F. (1999). "Probabilistic Learning for Selective Dissemination of Information." *Information Processing and Management* **35**(5): 633–654.

Amati, G., Crestani, F., and Ubaldini, F. (1997). *A Learning System for Selective Dissemination of Information.* In Proceedings of IJCAI-97, 15th International Joint Conference on Artificial Intelligence. M. E. Pollack, ed. Nagoya, Japan, Morgan Kaufmann Publishers, San Francisco: 764–769.

Amati, G., Crestani, F., Ubaldini, F., and Nardis, S. D. (1997). *Probabilistic Learning for Information Filtering.* In Proceedings of RIAO-97, 1st International Conference "Recherche d'Information Assistée par Ordinateur." Montreal: 513–530.

Amati, G., D'Aloisi, D., Giannini, V., and Ubaldini, F. (1996). *An Integrated System for Filtering News and Managing Distributed Data.* In Proceedings of PAKM-96, 1st International Conference on Practical Aspects of Knowledge Management. Basel, Switzerland, Springer-Verlag, London.

Amati, G., D'Aloisi, D., Giannini, V., and Ubaldini, F. (1997). "A Framework for Filtering News and Managing Distributed Data." *Journal of Universal Computer Science* **3**(8): 1007–1021.

Amir, A., Aumann, Y., Feldman, R., and Fresko, M. (2003). "Maximal Association Rules: A Tool for Mining Associations in Text." *Journal of Intelligent Information Systems* **25**(3): 333–345.

Amir, A., Aumann, Y., Feldman, R., and Katz, O. (1997). *Efficient Algorithm for Association Generation*. Department of Computer Science, Bar-Ilan University.

Anand, S. S., Bell, D. A., and Hughes, J. G. (1995). *The Role of Domain Knowledge in Data Mining*. In Proceedings of ACM CIKM'95. Baltimore, ACM Press, New York: 37–43.

Anand, T., and Kahn, G. (1993). *Opportunity Explorer: Navigating Large Databases Using Knowledge Discovery Templates*. In Proceedings of the 1993 Workshop on Knowledge Discovery in Databases. Washington, DC, AAAI Press, Menlo Park, CA: 45–51.

Androutsopoulos, I., Koutsias, J., Chandrinos, K. V., and Spyropoulos, C. D. (2000). *An Experimental Comparison of Naive Bayesian and Keyword-Based Anti-Spam Filtering with Personal E-mail Messages*. In Proceedings of SIGIR-00, 23rd ACM International Conference on Research and Development in Information Retrieval. Athens, ACM Press, New York: 160–167.

Aone, C., and Bennett, S. (1995). *Evaluating Automated and Manual Acquisition of Anaphora Resolution Strategies*. In Proceedings of Meeting of the Association for Computational Linguistics. Cambridge, MA, Association for Computational Linguistics, Morristown, NJ: 122–129.

Appelt, D., Hobbs, J., Bear, J., Israel, D., Kameyama, M., Kehler, A., Martin, D., Meyers, K., and Tyson, M. (1993). *SRI International FASTUS System: MUC-6 Test Results and Analysis*. In Proceedings of 16th MUC. Columbia, MD, Association for Computational Linguistics, Morristown, NJ: 237–248.

Appelt, D., Hobbs, J., Bear, J., Israel, D., Kameyama, M., and Tyson, M. (1993). *FASTUS: A Finite-State Processor for Information Extraction from Real-World Text*. In Proceedings of the 13th International Conference on Artificial Intelligence (IJCAI). Chambery, France, Morgan Kaufmann Publishers, San Mateo, CA: 1172–1178.

Appiani, E., Cesarini, F., Colla, A., Diligenti, M., Gori, M., Marinai, S., and Soda, G. (2001). "Automatic Document Classification and Indexing in High-Volume Applications." *International Journal on Document Analysis and Recognition* **4**(2): 69–83.

Apte, C., Damerau, F., and Weiss, S. (1994a). *Towards Language Independent Automated Learning of Text Categorization Models*. In Proceedings of ACM-SIGIR Conference on Information Retrieval. Dublin, Springer-Verlag, New York: 23–30.

Apte, C., Damerau, F. J., and Weiss, S. M. (1994b). "Automated Learning of Decision Rules for Text Categorization." *ACM Transactions on Information Systems* **12**(3): 233–251.

Apte, C., Damerau, F. J., and Weiss, S. M. (1994c). *Towards Language-Independent Automated Learning of Text Categorization Models*. In Proceedings of SIGIR-94, 17th ACM International Conference on Research and Development in Information Retrieval. Dublin, Springer-Verlag, Heidelberg: 23–30.

Arning, A., Agrawal, R., and Raghavan, P. (1996). *A Linear Method for Deviation Detection in Large Databases*. In Proceedings of the 2nd International Conference on Knowledge Discovery in Databases and Data Mining. Portland, OR, AAAI Press, Menlo Park, CA: 164–169.

Ashish, N., and Knoblock, C. A. (1997). *Semi-Automatic Wrapper Generation for Internet Information Sources*. In the Proceedings of the 2nd IFCIS International Conference on Cooperative Information Systems. Charleston, SC, IEEE Press, Los Alamitos, CA: 160–169.

Attardi, G., Gulli, A., and Sebastiani, F. (1999). *Automatic Web Page Categorization by Link and Context Analysis*. In Proceedings of THAI-99, 1st European Symposium on Telematics, Hypermedia and Artificial Intelligence. Varese, Italy: 105–119.

Attardi, G., Marco, S. D., and Salvi, D. (1998). "Categorization by Context." *Journal of Universal Computer Science* **4**(9): 719–736.

Aumann, Y., Feldman, R., Yehuda, Y., Landau, D., Liphstat, O., and Schler, Y. (1999). *Circle Graphs: New Visualization Tools for Text-Mining*. In Proceedings of the 3rd European Conference on Principles and Practice of Knowledge Discovery in Databases, (PKDD-99). Prague, Czech Republic, Springer-Verlag, London: 277–282.

Avancini, H., Lavelli, A., Magnini, B., Sebastiani, F., and Zanoli, R. (2003). *Expanding Domain-Specific Lexicons by Term Categorization*. In Proceedings of SAC-03, 18th ACM Symposium on Applied Computing. Melbourne, FL, ACM Press, New York: 793–797.

Azzam, S., Humphreys, K., and Gaizauskas, R. (1998). *Evaluating a Focus-Based Approach to Anaphora Resolution*. In Proceedings of the 36th Annual Meeting of the Association for Computational Linguistics and 17th International Conference on Computational Linguistics. Quebec, Morgan Kaufmann Publishers, San Francisco: 74–78.

Backer, F. B., and Hubert, L. G. (1976). "A Graphtheoretic Approach to Goodness-of-Fit in Complete-Link Hierarchical Clustering." *Journal of the American Statistical Association* **71**: 870–878.

Baeza-Yates, R., and Ribeira-Neto, B. (1999). *Modern Information Retrieval*. New York, ACM Press.

Bagga, A., and Biermann, A. W. (2000). *A Methodology for Cross-Document Coreference*. In Proceedings of the 5th Joint Conference on Information Sciences (JCIS 2000). Atlantic City, NJ: 207–210.

Bairoch, A., and Apweiler, R. (2000). "The Swiss-Prot Protein Synthesis Database and Its Supplement TrEMBL in 2000." *Nucleic Acids Research* **28**: 45–48.

Baker, L. D., and McCallum, A. K. (1998). *Distributional Clustering of Words for Text Classification*. In Proceedings of SIGIR-98, 21st ACM International Conference on Research and Development in Information Retrieval. Melbourne, Australia, ACM Press, New York: 96–103.

Baldwin, B. (1995). *CogNIAC: A Discourse Processing Engine*. Ph.D. thesis, Department of Computer and Information Sciences, University of Pennsylvania.

Baluja, S., Mittal, V. O., and Sukthankar, R. (2000). "Applying Machine Learning for High-Performance Named-Entity Extraction." *Computational Intelligence* **16**(4): 586–596.

Bao, Y., Aoyama, S., Du, X., Yamada, K., and Ishii, N. (2001). *A Rough Set-Based Hybrid Method to Text Categorization*. In Proceedings of WISE-01, 2nd International Conference on Web Information Systems Engineering. Kyoto, Japan, IEEE Computer Society Press, Los Alamitos, CA: 254–261.

Bapst, F., and Ingold, R. (1998). "Using Typography in Document Image Analysis." *Lecture Notes in Computer Science* **1375**: 240–260.

Barbu, C., and Mitkov, R. (2001). *Evaluation Tool for Rule-Based Anaphora Resolution Methods*. In Proceedings of Meeting of the Association for Computational Linguistics. Toulouse, France, Morgan Kaufmann Publishers, San Mateo, CA: 34–41.

Basili, R., and Moschitti, A. (2001). *A Robust Model for Intelligent Text Classification*. In Proceedings of ICTAI-01, 13th IEEE International Conference on Tools with Artificial Intelligence. Dallas, IEEE Computer Society Press, Los Alamitos, CA: 265–272.

Basili, R., Moschitti, A., and Pazienza, M. T. (2000). *Language-Sensitive Text Classification*. In Proceedings of RIAO-00, 6th International Conference "Recherche d'Information Assistée par Ordinateur." Paris: 331–343.

Basili, R., Moschitti, A., and Pazienza, M. T. (2001a). *An Hybrid Approach to Optimize Feature Selection Process in Text Classification*. In Proceedings of AI*IA-01, 7th Congress of the Italian Association for Artificial Intelligence. F. Esposito, ed. Bari, Italy, Springer-Verlag, Heidelberg: 320–325.

Basili, R., Moschitti, A., and Pazienza, M. T. (2001b). *NLP-Driven IR: Evaluating Performances over a Text Classification Task*. In Proceedings of IJCAI-01, 17th International Joint Conference on Artificial Intelligence. B. Nebel, ed. Seattle, IJCAI, Menlo Park, CA: 1286–1291.

Basu, S., Mooney, R., Pasupuleti, K., and Ghosh, J. (2001). *Evaluating the Novelty of Text-Mined Rules Using Lexical Knowledge*. In Proceedings of the 7th International Conference on Knowledge Discovery and Data Mining (KDD-01). San Francisco, CA, ACM Press, New York: 233–239.

Batagelj, V. (1997). "Notes on Blockmodeling." *Social Networks* **19**: 143–155.

Batagalj, V., Doreian, P., and Ferligoj, A. (1992). "An Optimization Approach to Regular Equivalence." *Social Networks* **14**: 121–135.

Batagelj, V., Ferligoj, A., and Doreian, P. (1999). "Generalized Blockmodeling." *Informatica* **23**: 501–506.

Batagelj, V., and Mrvar, A. (2003). *Pajek – Analysis and Visualization of Large Networks.* Graph Drawing Software. Springer-Verlag, Berlin.

Batagelj, V., Mrvar, A., and Zaversnik, M. (1999). *Partitioning Approach to Visualization of Large Networks.* Graph Drawing '99. Castle Stirin, Czech Republic.

Batagelj, V., and Zaversnik, M. (2001). *Cores Decomposition of Networks.* Presented at Recent Trends in Graph Theory, Algebraic Combinatorics, and Graph Algorithms. Bled, Slovenia. http://vlado.fmf.uni-lj.si/pub/networks/doc/cores/pCores.pdf.

Bayer, T., Kressel, U., Mogg-Schneider, H., and Renz, I. (1998). "Categorizing Paper documents. A Generic System for Domain and Language-Independent Text Categorization." *Computer Vision and Image Understanding* **70**(3): 299–306.

Becker, B. (1998). *Visualizing Decision Table Classifiers.* In Proceedings of IEEE Information Visualization (InfoVis '98). North Carolina, IEEE Computer Society Press, Washington, DC: 102–105.

Beeferman, D., Berger, A., and Lafferty, J. D. (1999). "Statistical Models for Text Segmentation." *Machine Learning* **34**(1–3): 177–210.

Beil, F., and Ester, M. (2002). *Frequent Term-Based Text Clustering.* In Proceedings of the 8th International Conference on Knowledge Discovery and Data Mining (KDD) 2002. Edmonton, Canada, ACM Press, New York: 436–442.

Bekkerman, R., El-Yaniv, R., Tishby, N., and Winter, Y. (2001). *On Feature Distributional Clustering for Text Categorization.* In Proceedings of SIGIR-01, 24th ACM International Conference on Research and Development in Information Retrieval. New Orleans, ACM Press, New York: 146–153.

Bel, N., Koster, C. H., and Villegas, M. (2003). *Cross-Lingual Text Categorization.* In Proceedings of ECDL-03, 7th European Conference on Research and Advanced Technology for Digital Libraries. Trodheim, Norway, Springer-Verlag, Heidelberg: 126–139.

Benkhalifa, M., Bensaid, A., and Mouradi, A. (1999). *Text Categorization Using the Semi-Supervised Fuzzy C-means Algorithm.* In Proceedings of NAFIPS-99, 18th International Conference of the North American Fuzzy Information Processing Society. New York, IEEE Press, New York: 561–565.

Benkhalifa, M., Mouradi, A., and Bouyakhf, H. (2001a). "Integrating External Knowledge to Supplement Training Data in Semi-Supervised Learning for Text Categorization." *Information Retrieval* **4**(2): 91–113.

Benkhalifa, M., Mouradi, A., and Bouyakhf, H. (2001b). "Integrating WordNet Knowledge to Supplement Training Data in Semi-Supervised Agglomerative Hierarchical Clustering for Text Categorization." *International Journal of Intelligent Systems* **16**(8): 929–947.

Bennett, P. N. (2003). *Using Asymmetric Distributions to Improve Text Classifier Probability Estimates.* In Proceedings of SIGIR-03, 26th ACM International Conference on Research and Development in Information Retrieval. Toronto, ACM Press, New York: 111–118.

Bennett, P. N., Dumais, S. T., and Horvitz, E. (2002). *Probabilistic Combination of Text Classifiers Using Reliability Indicators: Models and Results.* In Proceedings of SIGIR-02, 25th ACM International Conference on Research and Development in Information Retrieval. Tampere, Finland, ACM Press, New York: 207–214.

Berendt, B., Hotho, A., and Stumme, G. (2002). *Towards Semantic Web Mining.* In Proceedings of the International Semantic Web Conference (ISWC02). Sardinia, Italy, Springer, Berlin/Heidelberg: 264–278.

Berners-Lee, T., Hendler, J., and Lassila, O. (2001). "The Semantic Web." *Scientific American*, May 2001. http://www.scientificamerican.com/2001/0501issue/0501berners-lee.html.

Berry, M. (1992). "Large-Scale Sparse Singular Value Computations." *International Journal of Supercomputer Applications.* **6**(1): 13–49.

Bettini, C., Wang, X., and Jojodia, S. (1996). *Testing Complex Temporal Relationships Involving Multiple Granularities and Its Application to Data Mining.* In Proceedings of the 15th ACM SIGACT-SIGMOD-SIGART Symposium on Principles of Database Systems (PODS-96). Montreal, Canada, ACM Press, New York: 68–78.

Biebricher, P., Fuhr, N., Knorz, G., Lustig, G., and Schwantner, M. (1988). *The Automatic Indexing System AIR/PHYS. From Research to Application.* In Proceedings of SIGIR-88, 11th ACM International Conference on Research and Development in Information Retrieval. Y. Chiaramella, ed. Grenoble, France, ACM Press, New York: 333–342.

Bigi, B. (2003). *Using Kullback–Leibler Distance for Text Categorization.* In Proceedings of ECIR-03, 25th European Conference on Information Retrieval. F. Sebastiani, ed. Pisa, Italy, Springer-Verlag, Berlin/Heidelberg: 305–319.

Bikel, D. M., Miller, S., Schwartz, R., and Weischedel, R. (1997). Nymble: *A High-Performance Learning Name-Finder.* In Proceedings of ANLP-97. Washington, DC, Morgan Kaufmann Publishers, San Francisco: 194–201.

Bikel, D. M., Schwartz, R. L., and Weischedel, R. M. (1999). "An Algorithm that Learns What's in a Name." *Machine Learning* **34**(1–3): 211–231.

Blake, C., and Pratt, W. (2001). *Better Rules, Fewer Features: A Semantic Approach to Selecting Features from Text.* In Proceedings of the 2001 IEEE International Conference on Data Mining. San Jose, CA, IEEE Computer Society Press, New York: 59–66.

Blanchard, J., Guillet, F., and Briand, H. (2003). *Exploratory Visualization for Association Rule Rummaging.* In Proceedings of the 4th International Workshop on Multimedia Data Mining MDM/KDD2003. Washington, DC, ACM Press, New York: 107–114.

Blei, D. M., Ng, A. Y., and Jordan, M. I. (2003). "Latent Dirichlet Allocation." *Journal of Machine Learning Research* **3**: 993–1022.

Bloedorn, E., and Michalski, R. S. (1998). "Data-Driven Constructive Induction." *IEEE Intelligent Systems* **13**(2): 30–37.

Blosseville, M. J., Hebrail, G., Montell, M. G., and Penot, N. (1992). *Automatic Document Classification: Natural Langage Processing and Expert System Techniques Used Together.* In Proceedings of SIGIR-92, 15th ACM International Conference on Research and Development in Information Retrieval. Copenhagen, ACM Press, New York: 51–57.

Blum, A., and Mitchell, T. M. (1998). *Combining Labeled and Unlabeled Data with Co-Training. COLT.* Madison, WI, ACM Press, New York: 92–100.

Bod, R., and Kaplan, R. (1998). *A Probabilistic Corpus-Driven Model for Lexical-Functional Analysis.* In Proceedings of the 36th Annual Meeting of the Association for Computational Linguistics and 17th International Conference on Computational Linguistics. Montreal, Morgan Kaufmann Publishers, San Francisco: 145–151.

Bonacich, P. (1972). "Factoring and Weighting Approaches to Status Scores and Clique Identification." *Journal of Mathematical Sociology* **2**: 113–120.

Bonacich, P. (1987). "Power and Centrality: A Family of Measures." *American Journal of Sociology* **92**: 1170–1182.

Bonnema, R., Bod, R., and Scha, R. (1997). *A DOP Model for Semantic Interpretation.* In Proceedings of the 35th Annual Meeting of the Association for Computational Linguistics and 8th Conference of the European Chapter of the Association for Computational Linguistics. Somerset, NJ, Morgan Kaufmann Publishers, San Francisco: 159–167.

Borgatti, S. P., and Everett, M. G. (1992). "Notions of Positions in Social Network Analysis." In *Sociological Methodology*, P. V. Marsden, ed. San Francisco, Jossey Bass: 1–35.

Borgatti, S. P., and Everett, M. G. (1993). "Two Algorithms for Computing Regular Equivalence." *Social Networks* **15**: 361–376.

Borgatti, S. P., Everett, M. G., and Freeman, L. C. (2002). *Ucinet 6 for Windows*, Cambridge, MA, Harvard: Analytic Technologies. http://www.analytictech.com.

Borko, H., and Bernick, M. (1963). "Automatic Document Classification." *Journal of the Association for Computing Machinery* **10**(2): 151–161.

Borko, H., and Bernick, M. (1964). "Automatic Document Classification. Part II: Additional Experiments." *Journal of the Association for Computing Machinery* **11**(2): 138–151.

Borner, K., Chen, C., and Boyack, K. (2003). "Visualizing Knowledge Domains." *Annual Review of Information Science and Technology* **37**: 179–255.

Borthwick, A. (1999). *A Maximum Entropy Approach for Named Entity Recognition.* Computer Science Department, New York University.

Brachman, R., and Anand, T. (1996). In "The Process of Knowledge Discovery in Databases: A Human Centered Approach." *Advances in Knowledge Discovery and Data Mining.* U. M. Fayyad, G. Piatetsky-Shapiro, P. Smyth, and R. Uthurusamy, eds. Menlo Park, CA, AAAI Press and MIT Press: 37–58.

Brachman, R., Selfridge, P., Terveen, L., Altman, B., Borgida, A., Halper, F., Kirk, T., Lazar, A., McGuinness, D., and Resnick, L. (1993). "Integrated Support for Data Archeology." *International Journal of Intelligent and Cooperative Information Systems.* **2**(2): 159–185.

Bradley, P. S., Fayyad, U., and Reina, C. (1998). *Scaling Clustering Algorithms to Large Databases.* In Proceedings of the Knowledge Discovery and Data Mining Conference (KDD '98). New York, AAAI Press, Menlo Park, CA: 9–15.

Brank, J., Grobelnik, M., Milic-Frayling, N., and Mladenic, D. (2002). *Feature Selection Using Support Vector Machines.* In Proceedings of the 3rd International Conference on Data Mining Methods and Databases for Engineering, Finance, and Other Fields. Bologna, Italy.

Brill, E. (1992). *A Simple Rule-Based Part of Speech Tagger.* In Proceedings of the 3rd Annual Conference on Applied Natural Language Processing. Trento, Italy, Morgan Kaufmann Publishers, San Francisco: 152–155.

Brill, E. (1995). "Transformation-Based Error-Driven Learning and Natural Language Processing: A Case Study in Part-of-Speech Tagging." *Computational Linguistics* **21**(4): 543–565.

Brin, S. (1998). *Extracting Patterns and Relations from the World Wide Web.* In Proceedings of WebDB Workshop, EDBT '98. Valencia, Spain, Springer, Berlin: 172–183.

Brown, R. D. (1999). *Adding Linguistic Knowledge to a Lexical Example-Based Translation System.* In Proceedings of the 8th International Conference on Theoretical and Methodological Issues in Machine Translation (TMI-99). Chester, UK: 22–32.

Bruckner, T. (1997). *The Text Categorization System TEKLIS at TREC-6.* In Proceedings of TREC-6, 6th Text Retrieval Conference. Gaithersburg, MD, National Institute of Standards and Technology, Gaithersburg, MD: 619–621.

Cai, L., and Hofmann, T. (2003). *Text Categorization by Boosting Automatically Extracted Concepts.* In Proceedings of SIGIR-03, 26th ACM International Conference on Research and Development in Information Retrieval. Toronto, ACM Press, New York: 182–189.

Caldon, P. (2003). *Using Text Classification to Predict the Gene Knockout Behaviour of* S. Cerevisiae. In Proceedings of APBC-03, 1st Asia-Pacific Bioinformatics Conference. Y.-P. P. Chen, ed. Adelaide, Australia, Australian Computer Society: 211–214.

Califf, M. E., and Mooney, R. J. (1998). *Relational Learning of Pattern-Match Rules for Information Extraction.* In Working Notes of AAAI Spring Symposium on Applying Machine Learning to Discourse Processing. Menlo Park, CA, AAAI Press, Palo Alto, CA: 6–11.

Carbonell, J., Cohen, W. W., and Yang, Y. (2000). "Guest Editors' Introduction to the Special Issue on Machine Learning and Information Retrieval." *Machine Learning* **39**(2/3): 99–101.

Card, S., MacKinlay, J., and Shneiderman, B. (1998). *Readings in Information Visualization: Using Vision to Think.* San Francisco, Morgan Kaufmann Publishers.

Cardie, C. (1994). *Domain Specific Knowledge Acquisition for Conceptual Sentence Analysis.* Department of Computer Science, University of Massachusetts, Amherst, MA.

Cardie, C. (1995). "Embedded Machine Learning Systems for Natural Language Processing: A General Framework." In *Connectionist, Statistical and Symbolic Approaches to Learning for Natural Language Processing.* S. Wermter, E. Riloff, and G. Scheler, eds. Berlin, Springer: 315–328.

Cardie, C. (1997). "Empirical Methods in Information Extraction." *AI Magazine* **18**(4): 65–80.

Cardie, C. (1999). "Integrating Case-Based Learning and Cognitive Biases for Machine Learning of Natural Language." *JETAI* **11**(3): 297–337.

Cardie, C., and Howe, N. (1997). *Improving Minority Class Prediction Using Case-Specific Feature Weights*. In Proceedings of 14th International Conference on Machine Learning. Nashville, TN, Morgan Kaufmann Publishers, San Francisco: 57–65.

Cardoso-Cachopo, A., and Oliveira, A. L. (2003). *An Empirical Comparison of Text Categorization Methods*. In Proceedings of SPIRE-03, 10th International Symposium on String Processing and Information Retrieval. Manaus, Brazil, Springer-Verlag, Heidelberg: 183–196.

Carlis, J., and Konstan, J. (1998). *Interactive Visualization of Serial Periodic Data*. In Proceedings of the 11th Annual Symposium on User Interface Software and Technology (UIST '98). San Francisco, ACM Press, New York: 29–38.

Caropreso, M. F., Matwin, S., and Sebastiani, F. (2001). "A Learner-Independent Evaluation of the Usefulness of Statistical Phrases for Automated Text Categorization." In *Text Databases and Document Management: Theory and Practice*. A. G. Chin, ed. Hershey, PA, Idea Group Publishing: 78–102.

Carpineto, C., and Romano, G. (1996). "Information Retrieval through Hybrid Navigation of Lattice Representations." *International Journal of Human-Computer Studies* **45**(5): 553–578.

Carreras, X., and Marquez, L. (2001). *Boosting Trees for Anti-Spam Email Filtering*. In Proceedings of RANLP-01, 4th International Conference on Recent Advances in Natural Language Processing. Tzigov Chark, Bulgaria.

Carroll, G., and Charniak, E. (1992). *Two Experiments on Learning Probabilistic Dependency Grammars from Corpora*. Technical Report CS-92-16.

Cattoni, R., Coianiz, T., Messelodi, S., and Modena, C. (1998). *Geometric Layout Analysis Techniques for Document Image Understanding: A Review*. Technical Report. Trento, Italy, ITC-IRST I-38050.

Cavnar, W. B., and Trenkle, J. M. (1994). *N-Gram-Based Text Categorization*. In Proceedings of SDAIR-94, 3rd Annual Symposium on Document Analysis and Information Retrieval. Las Vegas, UNLV Publications/Reprographics, Las Vegas: 161–175.

Ceci, M., and Malerba, D. (2003). *Hierarchical Classification of HTML Documents with WebClassII*. In Proceedings of ECIR-03, 25th European Conference on Information Retrieval. F. Sebastiani, ed. Pisa, Italy, Springer-Verlag, Berlin: 57–72.

Cerny, B. A., Okseniuk, A., and Lawrence, J. D. (1983). *A Fuzzy Measure of Agreement between Machine and Manual Assignment of Documents to Subject Categories*. In Proceedings of ASIS-83, 46th Annual Meeting of the American Society for Information Science. Washington, DC, American Society for Information Science, Washington, DC: 265.

Chai, K. M., Ng, H. T., and Chieu, H. L. (2002). *Bayesian Online Classifiers for Text Classification and Filtering*. In Proceedings of SIGIR-02, 25th ACM International Conference on Research and Development in Information Retrieval. Tampere, FI, ACM Press, New York: 97–104.

Chakrabarti, S., Dom, B. E., Agrawal, R., and Raghavan, P. (1997). *Using Taxonomy, Discriminants, and Signatures for Navigating in Text Databases*. In Proceedings of VLDB-97, 23rd International Conference on Very Large Data Bases. Athens, Morgan Kaufmann Publishers, San Francisco: 446–455.

Chakrabarti, S., Dom, B. E., Agrawal, R., and Raghavan, P. (1998). "Scalable Feature Selection, Classification and Signature Generation for Organizing Large Text Databases into Hierarchical Topic Taxonomies." *Journal of Very Large Data Bases* **7**(3): 163–178.

Chakrabarti, S., Dom, B. E., and Indyk, P. (1998). *Enhanced Hypertext Categorization Using Hyperlinks*. In Proceedings of SIGMOD-98, ACM International Conference on Management of Data. Seattle, ACM Press, New York: 307–318.

Chakrabarti, S., Dom, B. E., Kumar, S. R., Raghavan, P., Rajagopalan, S., Tomkins, A., Gibson, D., and Kleinberg, J. (1999). "Mining the Web's Link Structure." *IEEE Computer* **32**(8): 60–67.

Chakrabarti, S., Roy, S., and Soundalgekar, M. (2002). *Fast and Accurate Text Classification via Multiple Linear Discriminant Projections.* In Proceedings of VLDB-02, 28th International Conference on Very Large Data Bases. Hong Kong: 658–669.

Chalmers, M., and Chitson, P. (1992). *Bead: Exploration in Information Visualization.* In Proceedings of the 15th Annual ACM/SIGIR Conference. Copenhagen, ACM Press, New York: 330–337.

Chandrinos, K. V., Androutsopoulos, I., Paliouras, G., and Spyropoulos, C. D. (2000). *Automatic Web Rating: Filtering Obscene Content on the Web.* In Proceedings of ECDL-00, 4th European Conference on Research and Advanced Technology for Digital Libraries. Lisbon, Springer-Verlag, Heidelberg: 403–406.

Chang, S.-J., and Rice, R. (1993). "Browsing: A Multidimensional Framework." *Annual Review of Information Science and Technology* **28**: 231–276.

Charniak, E. (1993). *Statistical Language Learning.* Cambridge, MA, MIT Press.

Charniak, E. (2000). *A Maximum-Entropy-Inspired Parser.* In Proceedings of the Meeting of the North American Association for Computational Linguistics. Seattle, ACM Press, New York: 132–139.

Chen, C. (2002). "Visualization of Knowledge Structures." In *Handbook of Software Engineering and Knowledge Engineering.* S. K. Chang, ed. River Edge, NJ, World Scientific Publishing Co.: 201–238.

Chen, C., and Paul, R. (2001). "Visualizing a Knowledge Domain's Intellectual Structure." *Computer* **34**(3): 65–71.

Chen, C. C., Chen, M. C., and Sun, Y. (2001). *PVA: A Self-Adaptive Personal View Agent.* In Proceedings of KDD-01, 7th ACM SIGKDD International Conferece on Knowledge Discovery and Data Mining. San Francisco, ACM Press, New York: 257–262.

Chen, C. C., Chen, M. C., and Sun, Y. (2002). "PVA: A Self-Adaptive Personal View Agent." *Journal of Intelligent Information Systems* **18**(2/3): 173–194.

Chen, H., and Dumais, S. T. (2000). *Bringing Order to the Web: Automatically Categorizing Search Results.* In Proceedings of CHI-00, ACM International Conference on Human Factors in Computing Systems. The Hague, ACM Press, New York: 145–152.

Chen, H., and Ho, T. K. (2000). *Evaluation of Decision Forests on Text Categorization.* In Proceedings of the 7th SPIE Conference on Document Recognition and Retrieval. San Jose, CA, SPIE – The International Society for Optical Engineering, Bellingham, WA: 191–199.

Chenevoy, Y., and Bela'id, A. (1991). *Hypothesis Management for Structured Document Recognition.* In Proceedings of the 1st International Conference on Document Analysis and Recognition (ICDAR'91). St.-Malo, France: 121–129.

Cheng, C.-H., Tang, J., Wai-Chee, A., and King, I. (2001). *Hierarchical Classification of Documents with Error Control.* In Proceedings of PAKDD-01, 5th Pacific-Asia Conferenece on Knowledge Discovery and Data Mining. Hong Kong, Springer-Verlag, Heidelberg: 433–443.

Cheung, D. W., Han, J., Ng, V. T., and Wong, C. Y. (1996). *Maintenance of Discovered Association Rules in Large Databases: An Incremental Updating Technique.* In Proceedings of the 12th ICDE, New Orleans, IEEE Computer Society Press, Los Alamitos, CA: 106–114.

Cheung, D. W., Lee, S. D., and Kao, B. (1997). *A General Incremental Technique for Maintaining Discovered Association Rules.* In Proceedings of the International Conference on Database Systems for Advanced Applications (DASFAA). Melbourne, Australia: 185–194.

Chinchor, N., Hirschman, L., and Lewis, D. (1994). "Evaluating Message Understanding Systems: An Analysis of the Third Message Understanding Conference (MUC-3)." *Computational Linguistics* **3**(19): 409–449.

Chouchoulas, A., and Shen, Q. (2001). "Rough Set-Aided Keyword Reduction for Text Categorization." *Applied Artificial Intelligence* **15**(9): 843–873.

Chuang, W. T., Tiyyagura, A., Yang, J., and Giuffrida, G. (2000). *A Fast Algorithm for Hierarchical Text Classification.* In Proceedings of DaWaK-00, 2nd International Conference on Data Warehousing and Knowledge Discovery. London, Springer-Verlag, Heidelberg: 409–418.

Ciravegna, F. (2001). *Adaptive Information Extraction from Text by Rule Induction and Generalization.* In Proceedings of the 17th IJCAI. Seattle, Morgan Kaufmann Publishers, San Francisco: 1251–1256.

Ciravegna, F., Lavelli, A., Mana, N., Matiasek, J., Gilardoni, L., Mazza, S., Black, W. J., and Rinaldi, F. (1999). *FACILE: Classifying Texts Integrating Pattern Matching and Information Extraction.* In Proceedings of IJCAI-99, 16th International Joint Conference on Artificial Intelligence. T. Dean, ed. Stockholm, Morgan Kaufmann Publishers, San Francisco: 890–895.

Clack, C., Farringdon, J., Lidwell, P., and Yu, T. (1997). *Autonomous Document Classification for Business.* In Proceedings of the 1st International Conference on Autonomous Agents. W. L. Johnson, ed. Marina Del Rey, CA, ACM Press, New York: 201–208.

Cleveland, W. S. (1994). *The Elements of Graphing Data.* Summit, NJ, Hobart Press.

Clifton, C., and Cooley, R. (1999). *TopCat: Data Mining for Topic Identification in a Text Corpus.* In Proceedings of the 3rd European Conference on Principles of Knowledge Discovery and Data Mining. Prague, Springer, Berlin: 174–183.

Cockburn, A. (2004). *Revisiting 2D vs 3D Implications on Spatial Memory.* In Proceedings of the 5th Conference on Australasian User Interface, Volume 28. Dunedin, New Zealand, Australian Computer Society, Inc.: 25–31.

Cohen, W., and Singer, Y. (1996). *Context-Sensitive Learning Methods for Text Categorization.* In Proceedings of SIGIR-96, 19th ACM. International Conference on Research and Development in Information Retrieval. H.-P Frei, D. Harman, P. Schauble and R. Wilkinson, eds. Zurick, Switzerland, ACM Press, New York, 307–315.

Cohen, W. W. (1992). *Compiling Prior Knowledge into an Explicit Bias.* In Proceedings of the 9th International Workshop on Machine Learning. D. Sleeman and P. Edwards, eds. Morgan Kaufmann Publishers, San Francisco: 102–110.

Cohen, W. W. (1995a). "Learning to Classify English Text with ILP Methods." In *Advances in Inductive Logic Programming.* L. D. Raedt, ed. Amsterdam, IOS Press: 124–143.

Cohen, W. W. (1995b). *Text Categorization and Relational Learning.* In Proceedings of ICML-95, 12th International Conference on Machine Learning. Lake Tahoe, NV, Morgan Kaufmann Publishers, San Francisco: 124–132.

Cohen, W. W., and Hirsh, H. (1998). *Joins that Generalize: Text Classification Using Whirl.* In Proceedings of KDD-98, 4th International Conference on Knowledge Discovery and Data Mining. New York, AAAI Press, Menlo Park, CA: 169–173.

Cohen, W. W., and Singer, Y. (1996). *Context-Sensitive Learning Methods for Text Categorization.* In Proceedings of SIGIR-96, 19th ACM International Conference on Research and Development in Information Retrieval. Zurich, ACM Press, New York: 307–315.

Cohen, W. W., and Singer, Y. (1999). "Context-Sensitive Learning Methods for Text Categorization." *ACM Transactions on Information Systems* **17**(2): 141–173.

Collins, M. (1997). *Three Generative, Lexicalized Models for Statistical Parsing.* In Proceedings of the 35th Annual Meeting of the Association for Computational Linguistics. Madrid, ACM Press, New York: 16–23.

Collins, M., and Miller, S. (1998). *Semantic Tagging Using a Probabilistic Context Free Grammar.* In Proceedings of the 6th Workshop on Very Large Corpora. Montreal, Morgan Kaufmann Publishers, San Francisco: 38–48.

Cooper, J. (1997). *What Is Lexical Navigation*? IBM Thomas J. Watson Research Center. http://www.research.ibm.com/people/j/jwcnmr/LexNav/lexical_navigation.htm.

Cover, T. M., and Thomas, J. A. (1991). *Elements of Information Theory.* New York, John Wiley and Sons.

Cowie, J., and Lehnert, W. (1996). "Information Extraction." *Communications of the Association of Computing Machinery* **39**(1): 80–91.

Crammer, K., and Singer, Y. (2002). *A New Family of Online Algorithms for Category Ranking.* In Proceedings of SIGIR-02, 25th ACM International Conference on Research and Development in Information Retrieval. Tampere, Finland, ACM Press, New York: 151–158.

Craven, M., DiPasquo, D., Freitag, D., McCallum, A. K., Mitchell, T. M., Nigam, K., and Slattery, S. (1998). *Learning to Extract Symbolic Knowledge from the World Wide Web.* In Proceedings of AAAI-98, 15th Conference of the American Association for Artificial Intelligence. Madison, WI, AAAI Press, Menlo Park, CA: 509–516.

Craven, M., DiPasquo, D., Freitag, D., McCallum, A. K., Mitchell, T. M., Nigam, K., and Slattery, S. (2000). "Learning to Construct Knowledge Bases from the World Wide Web." *Artificial Intelligence* **118**(1/2): 69–113.

Craven, M., and Kumlien, J. (1999). *Constructing Biological Knowledge-Bases by Extracting Information from Text Sources.* In Proceedings of the 7th International Conference on Intelligent Systems for Molecular Biology (ISMB-99). Heidelberg, AAAI Press, Menlo Park, CA: 77–86.

Craven, M., and Slattery, S. (2001). "Relational Learning with Statistical Predicate Invention: Better Models for Hypertext." *Machine Learning* **43**(1/2): 97–119.

Creecy, R. M., Masand, B. M., Smith, S. J., and Waltz, D. L. (1992). "Trading MIPS and Memory for Knowledge Engineering: Classifying Census Returns on the Connection Machine." *Communications of the ACM* **35**(8): 48–63.

Cristianini, N., Shawe-Taylor, J., and Lodhi, H. (2001). *Latent Semantic Kernels.* In Proceedings of ICML-01, 18th International Conference on Machine Learning. Williams College, MA, Morgan Kaufmann Publishers, San Francisco: 66–73.

Cristianini, N., Shawe-Taylor, J., and Lodhi, H. (2002). "Latent Semantic Kernels." *Journal of Intelligent Information Systems* **18**(2/3): 127–152.

Cutting, C., Karger, D., and Pedersen, J. O. (1993). *Constant Interaction-Time Scatter/Gather Browsing of Very Large Document Collections.* In Proceedings of ACM–SIGIR Conference on Research and Development in Information Retrieval. Pittsburgh, ACM Press, New York: 126–134.

Cutting, D. R., Karger, D. R., Pedersen, J. O., and Tukey, J. W. (1992). *Scatter/Gather: A Cluster-Based Approach to Browsing Large* Document Collections. In Proceedings of the 15th Annual International ACM–SIGIR Conference on Research and Development in Information Retrieval. Copenhagen, ACM Press, New York: 318–329.

Cyram Company, Ltd. (2004). NetMiner Webpage http://www.netminer.com.

D'Alessio, S., Murray, K., Schiaffino, R., and Kershenbaum, A. (1998). *Category Levels in Hierarchical Text Categorization.* In Proceedings of EMNLP-98, 3rd Conference on Empirical Methods in Natural Language Processing. Granada, Spain, Association for Computational Linguistics, Morristown, NJ.

D'Alessio, S., Murray, K., Schiaffino, R., and Kershenbaum, A. (2000). *The Effect of Using Hierarchical Classifiers in Text Categorization.* In Proceedings of RIAO-00, 6th International Conference "Recherche d'Information Assistée par Ordinateur." Paris: 302–313.

Daelemans, W., Buchholz, S., and Veenstra, J. (1999). *Memory-Based Shallow Parsing.* In Proceedings of CoNLL. Bergen, Norway, Association for Computational Linguistics, Somerset, NJ: 53–60.

Dagan, I., Feldman, R., and Hirsh, H. (1996). *Keyword-Based Browsing and Analysis of Large Document Sets.* In Proceedings of SDAIR-96, 5th Annual Symposium on Document Analysis and Information Retrieval. Las Vegas, UNLV Publications/Reprographics, Las Vegas: 191–207.

Dagan, I., Karov, Y., and Roth, D. (1997). *Mistake-Driven Learning in Text Categorization.* In Proceedings of EMNLP-97, 2nd Conference on Empirical Methods in Natural Language Processing. Providence, RI, Association for Computational Linguistics, Morristown, NJ: 55–63.

Dagan, I., Pereira, F., and Lee, L. (1994). *Similarity-Based Estimation of Word Cooccurrence Probabilities.* In Proceedings. of the Annual Meeting of the Association for Computational

Linguistics. Las Cruces, NM, Association for Computational Linguistics, Morristown, NJ: 272–278.

Damashek, M. (1995). "Gauging Similarity with N-Grams: Language-Independent Categorization of Text." *Science* **267**(5199): 843–848.

Dasigi, V., Mann, R. C., and Protopopescu, V. A. (2001). "Information Fusion for Text Classification: An Experimental Comparison." *Pattern Recognition* **34**(12): 2413–2425.

Davidson, G. S., Hendrickson, B., Johnson, D. K., Meyers, C. E., and Wylie, B. N. (1999). "Knowledge Mining with VxInxight: Discovery through Interaction." *Journal of Intelligent Information Systems* **11**(3): 259–285.

Davidson, R., and Harel, D. (1996). "Drawing Graphs Nicely Using Simulated Annealing." *ACM Transactions on Graphics* **15**(4): 301–331.

de Buenaga Rodriguez, M., Gomez Hidalgo, J. M., and Diaz-Agudo, B. (2000). *Using WordNet to Complement Training Information in Text Categorization. Recent Advances in Natural Language Processing II*. Amsterdam, J. Benjamins: 189.

De Nooy, W., Mrvar, A., and Batagelj, V. (2004). *Exploratory Social Network Analysis with Pajek*. New York, Cambridge University Press.

De Sitter, A., and Daelemans, W. (2003). *Information Extraction via Double Classification*. International Workshop on Adaptive Text Extraction and Mining. Catvat-Dubroknik, Croatia, Springer, Berlin: 66–73.

Debole, F., and Sebastiani, F. (2003). *Supervised Term Weighting for Automated Text Categorization*. In Proceedings of SAC-03, 18th ACM Symposium on Applied Computing. Melbourne, FL, ACM Press, New York: 784–788.

Decker, S., Melnik, S., Harmelen, F. V., Fensel, D., Klein, M. C. A., Broekstra, J., Erdmann, M., and Horrocks, I. (2000). "The Semantic Web: The Roles of XML and RDF." *IEEE Internet Computing* **4**(5): 63–74.

Deerwester, S., Dumais, S. T., Furnas, G. W., Landauer, T. K., and Harshman, R. (1990). "Indexing by Latent Semantic Analysis." *Journal of the American Society of Information Science* **41**(6): 391–407.

Denoyer, L., and Gallinari, P. (2003). *A Belief Networks–Based Generative Model for Structured Documents. An Application to the XML Categorization*. In Proceedings of MLDM-03, 3rd International Conference on Machine Learning and Data Mining in Pattern Recognition. Leipzig, Springer-Verlag, Heidelberg: 328–342.

Denoyer, L., Zaragoza, H., and Gallinari, P. (2001). *HMM-Based Passage Models for Document Classification and Ranking*. In Proceedings of ECIR-01, 23rd European Colloquium on Information Retrieval Research. Darmstadt, Germany, Springer, Berlin: 126–135.

Dermatas, E., and Kokkinakis, G. (1995). "Automatic Stochastic Tagging of Natural Language Texts." *Computational Linguistics* **21**(2): 137–163.

Dhillon, I., Mallela, S., and Kumar, R. (2002). *Enhanced Word Clustering for Hierarchical Text Classification*. In Proceedings of KDD-02, 8th ACM International Conference on Knowledge Discovery and Data Mining. Edmonton, Canada, ACM Press, New York: 191–200.

Di-Nunzio, G., and Micarelli, A. (2003). *Does a New Simple Gaussian Weighting Approach Perform Well in Text Categorization*? In Proceedings of IJCAI-03, 18th International Joint Conference on Artificial Intelligence. Acapulco, Morgan Kaufmann Publishers, San Francisco: 581–586.

Diao, Y., Lu, H., and Wu, D. (2000). *A Comparative Study of Classification-Based Personal E-mail Filtering*. In Proceedings of PAKDD-00, 4th Pacific-Asia Conference on Knowledge Discovery and Data Mining. Kyoto, Japan, Springer-Verlag, Heidelberg: 408–419.

Dickerson, J., Berleant, D., Cox, Z., Qi, W., and Syrkin Wurtele, E. (2003). *Creating and Modeling Metabolic and Regulatory Networks Using Text Mining and Fuzzy Expert Systems*. In Proceedings of Computational Biology and Genome Informatics Conference. World Scientific Publishing, Hackensack, NJ: 207–238.

Diederich, J., Kindermann, J., Leopold, E., and Paass, G. (2003). "Authorship Attribution with Support Vector Machines." *Applied Intelligence* **19**(1/2): 109–123.

Ding, Y., Fensel, D., Klein, M. C. A., and Omelayenko, B. (2002). "The Semantic Web: Yet Another Hip?" *DKE* **41**(2–3): 205–227.

Dixon, M. (1997). "An Overview of Document Mining Technology." Unpublished manuscript.

Doan, A., Madhavan, J., Domingos, P., and Halevy, A. Y. (2002). "Learning to Map between Ontologies on the Semantic Web." In Proceedings of WWW'02, 11th International Conference on World Wide Web. Honolulu, ACM Press, New York: 662–673.

Domingos, P. (1999). "The Role of Occam's Razor in Knowledge Discovery." *Data Mining and Knowledge Discovery* **3**(1999): 409–425.

Domingos, P., and Pazzani, M. (1997). "On the Optimality of the Simple Bayesian Classifier under Zero-One Loss." *Machine Learning* **29**: 103–130.

Dorre, J., Gerstl, P., and Seiffert, R. (1999). *Text Mining: Finding Nuggets in Mountains of Textual Data*. In Proceedings of KDD-99, 5th ACM International Conference on Knowledge Discovery and Data Mining. San Diego, ACM Press, New York: 398–401.

Dou, D., McDermott, D., and Qi, P. (2003). *Ontology Translation on the Semantic Web*. In Proceedings of the International Conference on Ontologies, Databases and Applications of Semantics. Catania (Sicily), Italy, Springer, Berlin: 952–969.

Doyle, L. B. (1965). "Is Automatic Classification a Reasonable Application of Statistical Analysis of Text?" *Journal of the ACM* **12**(4): 473–489.

Drucker, H., Vapnik, V., and Wu, D. (1999). "Support Vector Machines for Spam Categorization." *IEEE Transactions on Neural Networks* **10**(5): 1048–1054.

Duffet, P. L., and Vernik, R. J. (1997). *Software System Visualisation: Netmap Investigations*. Technical Report, DSTO-TR-0558, Defense Science and Technology Organization, Government of Australia.

Dumais, S. T., and Chen, H. (2000). *Hierarchical Classification of Web Content*. In Proceedings of SIGIR-00, 23rd ACM International Conference on Research and Development in Information Retrieval. Athens, ACM Press, New York: 256–263.

Dumais, S. T., Platt, J., Heckerman, D., and Sahami, M. (1998). *Inductive Learning Algorithms and Representations for Text Categorization*. In Proceedings of 7th International Conference on Information and Knowledge Management. Bethesda, MD, ACM Press, New York: 148–155.

Dzbor, M., Domingue, J., and Motta, E. (2004). *Magpie: Supporting Browsing and Navigation on the Semantic Web*. In Proceedings of International Conference on Intelligent User Interfaces (IUI04), Madeira, Funchal, Portugal, ACM Press, New York: 191–197.

Eades, P. (1984). "A Heuristic for Graph Drawing." *Congressus Numerantium* **44**: 149–160.

El-Yaniv, R., and Souroujon, O. (2001). *Iterative Double Clustering for Unsupervised and Semi-Supervised Learning*. In Proceedings of ECML-01, 12th European Conference on Machine Learning. Freiburg, Germany, Springer-Verlag, Heidelberg: 121–132.

Elworthy, D. (1994). *Does Baum–Welch Re-estimation Help Taggers*? In Proceedings of the 4th Conference on Applied Natural Language Processing. Stuttgart, Germany, Morgan Kaufmann Publishers, San Francisco: 53–58.

Escudero, G., Màrquez, L., and Rigau, G. (2000). *Boosting Applied to Word Sense Disambiguation*. In Proceedings of ECML-00, 11th European Conference on Machine Learning. Barcelona, Springer-Verlag, Heidelberg: 129–141.

Esteban, A. D., Rodriguez, M. D. B., Lopez, L. A. U., and Vega, M. G. (1998). *Integrating Linguistic Resources in a Uniform Way for Text Classification Tasks*. In Proceedings of LREC-98, 1st International Conference on Language Resources and Evaluation. Grenada, Spain: 1197–1204.

Etemad, K., Doermann, D. S., and Chellappa, R. (1997). "Multiscale Segmentation of Unstructured Document Pages Using Soft Decision Integration." *IEEE Transactions on Pattern Analysis and Machine Intelligence* **19**(1): 92–96.

Etzioni, O., Cafarella, M., Downey, D., Kok, S., Popescu, A., Shaked, T., Soderland, S., Weld, D., and Yates, A. (2004). *Web-Scale Information Extraction in KnowItAll.* In Proceedings of WWW-04, 13th International World Wide Web Conference. New York, ACM Press, New York: 100–110.

Etzioni, O., Cafarella, M., Downey, D., Popescu, A., T. Shaked, Soderland, S., Weld, D., and Yates, A. (2004). *Methods for Domain-Independent Information Extraction from the Web: An Experimental Comparison.* In Proceedings of the 19th National Conference on Artificial Intelligence.

Ezawa, K., and Norton, S. (1995). *Knowledge Discovery in Telecommunication Services Data Using Bayesian Network Models.* In Proceedings of the First International Conference on Knowledge Discovery (KDD-95). Montreal, AAAI Press, Menlo Park, CA: 100–105.

Fall, C. J., Torcsvari, A., Benzineb, K., and Karetka, G. (2003). "Automated Categorization in the International Patent Classification." *SIGIR Forum* **37**(1): 10–25.

Fangmeyer, H., and Lustig, G. (1968). *The EURATOM Automatic Indexing Project.* In Proceedings of the IFIP Congress (Booklet J). Edinburgh, North Holland Publishing Company, Amsterdam: 66–70.

Fangmeyer, H., and Lustig, G. (1970). *Experiments with the CETIS Automated Indexing System.* In Proceedings of the Symposium on the Handling of Nuclear Information, International Atomic Energy Agency: 557–567.

Fayyad, U., Grinstein, G., and Wierse, A., Eds. (2001). *Information Visualization in Data Mining and Knowledge Discovery.* San Francisco, Morgan Kaufmann Publishers.

Fayyad, U., Piatetsky-Shapiro, G., and Smyth, P. (1996). "From Data Mining to Knowledge Discovery in Databases." In *Advances in Knowledge Discovery and Data Mining.* U. Fayyad, G. Piatetsky-Shapiro, P. Smyth, and R. Uthuruswamy, eds. Cambridge, MA, AAAI/MIT Press: 1–36.

Fayyad, U., Piatetsky-Shapiro, G., Smyth, P., and Uthuruswamy, R., eds. (1996). *Advances in Knowledge Discovery and Data Mining.* Cambridge, MA, AAAI/MIT Press.

Fayyad, U. M., Reina, C. A., and Bradley, P. S. (1998). *Initialization of Iterative Refinement Clustering Algorithms.* Technical Report MSR-TR-98-38, Jet Proplusion Laboratories.

Feldman, R. (1993). *Probabilistic Revision of Logical Domain Theories.* Ph.D. thesis, Department of Computer Science, Cornell University.

Feldman, R. (1996). *The KDT System – Using Prolog for KDD.* In Proceedings of 4th Conference of Practical Applications of Prolog. London: 91–110.

Feldman, R. (1998). *Practical Text Mining.* In Proceedings of the 2nd European Symposium on Principles of Data Mining and Knowledge Discovery. London: 478.

Feldman, R. (2002). "Text Mining." In *Handbook of Data Mining and Knowledge Discovery.* W. Kloesgen and J. Zytkow, eds. New York, Oxford University Press.

Feldman, R., Amir, A., Aumann, Y., and Zilberstein, A. (1996). *Incremental Algorithms for Association Generation.* In Proceedings of the First Pacific Conference on Knowledge Discovery. Singapore.

Feldman, R., Aumann, Y., Amir, A., Zilberstein, A., and Kloesgen, W. (1997). *Maximal Association Rules: A New Tool for Keyword Co-occurrences in Document Collections.* In Proceedings of 3rd International Conference on Knowledge Discovery and Data Mining. Newport Beach, CA, AAAI Press, Menlo Park, CA: 167–170.

Feldman, R., Aumann, Y., Finkelstein-Landau, M., Hurvitz, E., Regev, Y., and Yaroshevich, A. (2002). *A Comparative Study of Information Extraction Strategies.* In Proceedings of the 3rd International Conference on Intelligent Text Processing and Computational Linguistics. Mexico City, Springer, New York: 349–359.

Feldman, R., Aumann, Y., Zilberstein, A., and Ben-Yehuda, Y. (1997). *Trend Graphs: Visualizing the Evolution of Concept Relationships in Large Document Collections.* In Proceedings of the 2nd European Symposium of Principles of Data Mining and Knowledge Discovery. Nantes, France, Springer, Berlin: 38–46.

Feldman, R., and Dagan, I. (1995). *Knowledge Discovery in Textual Databases (KDT)*. In Proceedings of the 1st International Conference on Knowledge Discovery and Data Mining. Montreal, Canada, AAAI Press, Menlo Park, CA: 112–117.

Feldman, R., Dagan, I., and Hirsh, H. (1998). "Mining Text Using Keyword Distributions." *Journal of Intelligent Information Systems* **10**(3): 281–300.

Feldman, R., Dagan, I., and Kloesgen, W. (1996a). *Efficient Algorithms for Mining and Manipulating Associations in Texts.* In Proceedings of the 13th European Meeting on Cybernetics and Systems Research. Vienna, Austria: 949–954.

Feldman, R., Dagan, I., and Kloesgen, W. (1996b). *KDD Tools for Mining Associations in Textual Databases*. In Proceedings of the 9th International Symposium on Methodologies for Intelligent Systems. Zakopane, Poland: 96–107.

Feldman, R., Fresko, M., Hirsh, H., Aumann, Y., Liphstat, O., Schler, Y., and Rajman, M. (1998). *Knowledge Management: A Text Mining Approach.* In Proceedings of the 2nd International Conference on Practical Aspects of Knowledge Management (PAKM98). Basel, Switzerland.

Feldman, R., Fresko, M., Kinar, Y., Lindell, Y., Liphstar, O., Rajman, M., Schler, Y., and Zamir, O. (1998). *Text Mining at the Term Level.* In Proceedings of the 2nd European Symposium on Principles of Data Mining and Knowledge Discovery. Nantes, France, Springer, Berlin: 65–73.

Feldman, R., and Hirsh, H. (1996a). "Exploiting Background Information in Knowledge Discovery from Text." *Journal of Intelligent Information Systems* **9**(1): 83–97.

Feldman, R., and Hirsh, H. (1996b). *Mining Associations in Text in the Presence of Background Knowledge*. In Proceedings of the 2nd International Conference on Knowledge Discovery from Databases. Portland, OR, AAAI Press, Menlo Park, CA: 343–346.

Feldman, R., and Hirsh, H. (1997). "Finding Associations in Collections of Text." In *Machine Learning and Data Mining: Methods and Applications.* R. S. Michalski, I. Bratko, and M. Kubat, eds. New York, John Wiley and Sons: 223–240.

Feldman, R., Kloesgen, W., Ben-Yehuda, Y., Kedar, G., and Reznikov, V. (1997). *Pattern Based Browsing in Document Collections.* In Proceedings of the 1st European Symposium of Principles of Data Mining and Knowledge Discovery. Trondheim, Norway, Springer, Berlin: 112–122.

Feldman, R., Kloesgen, W., and Zilberstein, A. (1997a). *Document Explorer: Discovering Knowledge in Document Collections*. In Proceedings of the 10th International Symposium on Methodologies for International Systems. Trondheim, Norway, Springer, Berlin: 137–146.

Feldman, R., Kloesgen, W., and Zilberstein, A. (1997b). *Visualization Techniques to Explore Data Mining Results for Document Collections.* In Proceedings of the 3rd International Conference on Knowledge Discovery and Data Mining. Newport Beach, CA, AAAI Press, Menlo Park, CA: 16–23.

Feldman, R., Regev, Y., Hurvitz, E., and Landau-Finkelstein, M. (2003). "Mining the Biomedical Literature Using Semantic Analysis and Natural Language Processing Techniques." *Biosilico* **1** (2): 69–72.

Fellbaum, C. D., ed. (1998). *WordNet: An Electronic Lexical Database*. Cambridge, MA, MIT Press.

Fensel, D., Angele, J., Decker, S., Erdmann, M., Schnurr, H.-P., Staab, S., Studer, R., and Witt, A. (1999). "On2broker: Semantic-Based Access to Information Sources at the WWW." *WebNet* **1**: 366–371.

Ferilli, S., Fanizzi, N., and Semeraro, G. (2001). *Learning Logic Models for Automated Text Categorization.* In Proceedings of AI*IA-01, 7th Congress of the Italian Association for Artificial Intelligence. F. Esposito, ed. Bari, Italy, Springer-Verlag, Heidelberg: 81–86.

Ferrndez, A., Palomar, M., and Moreno, L. (1998). *Anaphor Resolution in Unrestricted Texts with Partial Parsing.* In Proceedings of the 36th Annual Meeting of the Association for Computational Linguistics. Montreal, Morgan Kaufmann Publishers, San Francisco: 385–391.

Field, B. J. (1975). "Towards Automatic Indexing: Automatic Assignment of Controlled-Language Indexing and Classification from Free Indexing." *Journal of Documentation* **31**(4): 246–265.

Finch, S. (1994). *Exploiting Sophisticated Representations for Document Retrieval.* In Proceedings of the 4th Conference on Applied Natural Language Processing. Stuttgart, Germany, Morgan Kaufmann Publishers, San Francisco: 65–71.

Finn, A., Kushmerick, N., and Smyth, B. (2002). *Genre Classification and Domain Transfer for Information Filtering.* In Proceedings of ECIR-02, 24th European Colloquium on Information Retrieval Research. Glasgow, Springer-Verlag, Heidelberg: 353–362.

Fisher, D., Soderland, S., McCarthy, J., Feng, F., and Lehnert, W. (1995). *Description of the UMass System as Used for MUC-6.* In Proceedings of the 6th Message Understanding Conference (MUC-6). Columbia, MD, Morgan Kaufmann Publishers, San Francisco: 127–140.

Fisher, M., and Everson, R. (2003). *When Are Links Useful? Experiments in Text Classification.* In Proceedings of ECIR-03, 25th European Conference on Information Retrieval. F. Sebastiani, ed. Pisa, Italy, Springer-Verlag, Berlin: 41–56.

Forsyth, R. S. (1999). "New Directions in Text Categorization." In *Causal Models and Intelligent Data Management.* A. Gammerman, ed. Heidelberg, Springer-Verlag: 151–185.

Frank, E., Chui, C., and Witten, I. H. (2000). *Text Categorization Using Compression Models.* In Proceedings of DCC-00, IEEE Data Compression Conference. Snowbird, UT, IEEE Computer Society Press, Los Alamitos, CA: 200–209.

Frank, E., Paynter, G. W., Witten, I. H., Gutwin, C., and Neville-Manning, C. G. (1999). *Domain-Specific Keyphrase Extraction.* In Proceedings of the 16th International Joint Conference on Artificial Intelligence. Stockholm, Morgan Kaufmann Publishers, San Francisco: 668–673.

Frasconi, P., Soda, G., and Vullo, A. (2001). *Text Categorization for Multi-page Documents: A Hybrid Naive Bayes HMM Approach.* In Proceedings of JCDL, 1st ACM-IEEE Joint Conference on Digital Libraries. Roanoke, VA, IEEE Computer Society Press, Los Alamitos, CA: 11–20.

Frasconi, P., Soda, G., and Vullo, A. (2002). "Text Categorization for Multi-page Documents: A Hybrid Naive Bayes HMM Approach." *Journal of Intelligent Information Systems* **18**(2/3): 195–217.

Frawley, W. J., Piatetsky-Shapiro, G., and Matheus, C. J. (1991). "Knowledge Discovery in Databases: An Overview." In *Knowledge Discovery in Databases.* G. Piatetsky-Shapiro and W. J. Frawley, eds. Cambridge, MA, MIT Press: 1–27.

Freeman, L. C. (1977). "A Set of Measures of Centrality Based on Betweenness." *Sociometry* **40**: 35–41.

Freeman, L. C. (1979). "Centrality in Social Networks: Conceptual Clarification." *Social Networks* **1**: 215–239.

Freitag, D. (1997). *Using Grammatical Inference to Improve Precision in Information Extraction.* In Proceedings of the Workshop on Grammatical Inference, Automata Induction, and Language Acquisition (ICML '97). Nashville, TN, Morgan Kaufmann Publishers, San Mateo, CA.

Freitag, D. (1998a). *Information Extraction from HTML: Application of a General Machine Learning Approach.* In Proceedings of the 15th National Conference on Artificial Intelligence. Madison, WI, AAAI Press, Menlo Park, CA: 517–523.

Freitag, D. (1998b). *Machine Learning for Information Extraction in Informal Domains.* Ph.D. thesis, Computer Science Department, Carnegie Mellon University.

Freitag, D., and Kushmerick, N. (2000). *Boosted Wrapper Induction.* In Proceedings of AAAI 2000. Austin, TX, AAAI Press, Menlo Park, CA: 577–583.

Freitag, D., and McCallum, A. (2000). *Information Extraction with HMM Structures Learned by Stochastic Optimization.* In Proceedings of the 17th National Conference on Artificial Intelligence. Austin, TX, AAAI Press, Menlo Park, CA: 584–589.

Freitag, D., and McCallum, A. L. (1999). *Information Extraction with HMMs and Shrinkage.* In Papers from the AAAI-99 Workshop on Machine Learning for Information Extraction: 31–36.

Freund, J., and Walpole, R. (1990). *Estadística Matemática con Aplicaciones.* Prentice Hall.

Frommholz, I. (2001). *Categorizing Web Documents in Hierarchical Catalogues.* In Proceedings of ECIR-01, 23rd European Colloquium on Information Retrieval Research. Darmstadt, Germany: 18–20.

Fruchterman, T., and Reingold, E. (1991). "Graph Drawing by Force-Directed Placement." *Software – Practice and Experience* **21**(11): 1129–1164.

Fuhr, N. (1985). *A Probabilistic Model of Dictionary-Based Automatic Indexing.* In Proceedings of RIAO-85, 1st International Conference "Recherche d'Information Assistee par Ordinateur." Grenoble, France: 207–216.

Fuhr, N., Hartmann, S., Knorz, G., Lustig, G., Schwantner, M., and Tzeras, K. (1991). *AIR/X – A Rule-Based Multistage Indexing System for Large Subject Fields.* In Proceedings of RIAO-91, 3rd International Conference "Recherche d'Information Assistée par Ordinateur." A. Lichnerowicz, ed. Barcelona, Elsevier Science Publishers, Amsterdam: 606–623.

Fuhr, N., and Knorz, G. (1984). *Retrieval Test Evaluation of a Rule-Based Automated Indexing (AIR/PHYS).* In Proceedings of SIGIR-84, 7th ACM International Conference on Research and Development in Information Retrieval. C. J. v. Rijsbergen, ed. Cambridge, UK, Cambridge University Press, Cambridge: 391–408.

Fuhr, N., and Pfeifer, U. (1991). *Combining Model-Oriented and Description-Oriented Approaches for Probabilistic Indexing.* In Proceedings of SIGIR-91, 14th ACM International Conference on Research and Development in Information Retrieval. Chicago, ACM Press, New York: 46–56.

Fuhr, N., and Pfeifer, U. (1994). "Probabilistic Information Retrieval as Combination of Abstraction Inductive Learning and Probabilistic Assumptions." *ACM Transactions on Information Systems* **12**(1): 92–115.

Fukuda, K., Tamura, A., Tsunoda, T., and Takagi, T. (1998). *Toward Information Extraction: Identifying Protein Names.* In Proceedings of the Pacific Symposium on Biocumputing. Maui, Hawaii, World Scientific Publishing Company, Hackensack, NJ: 707–718.

Fung, G. P. C., Yu, J. X., and Lu, H. (2002). *Discriminative Category Matching: Efficient Text Classification for Huge Document Collections.* In Proceedings of ICDM-02, 2nd IEEE International Conference on Data Mining. Maebashi City, Japan, IEEE Computer Society Press, Los Alamitos, 187–194.

Furnas, G. (1981). "The FISHEYE View: A New Look at Structured Files." Bell Laboratories Technical Report, reproduced in *Reading in Information Visualization: Using Vision to Think.* S. K. Card, J. D. Mackinlay, and B. Schneiderman, eds. San Francisco, Morgan Kaufmann Publishers: 312–330.

Furnas, G. (1986). *Generalized Fisheye Views.* In Proceedings of the ACM SIGCHI Conference on Human Factors in Computing Systems. ACM Press, New York: 16–23.

Furnkranz, J. (1999). *Exploiting Structural Information for Text Classification on the WWW.* In Proceedings of IDA-99, 3rd Symposium on Intelligent Data Analysis. Amsterdam, Springer-Verlag, Heidelberg: 487–497.

Furnkranz, J. (2002). "Hyperlink Ensembles: A Case Study in Hypertext Classification." *Information Fusion* **3**(4): 299–312.

Gaizauskas, R., and Humphreys, K. (1997). "Using a Semantic Network for Information Extraction." *Natural Language Engineering* **3**(2): 147–196.

Galavotti, L., Sebastiani, F., and Simi, M. (2000). *Experiments on the Use of Feature Selection and Negative Evidence in Automated Text Categorization.* In Proceedings of ECDL-00, 4th European Conference on Research and Advanced Technology for Digital Libraries. Lisbon, Springer-Verlag, Heidelberg: 59–68.

Gale, W. A., Church, K. W., and Yarowsky, D. (1993). "A Method for Disambiguating Word Senses in a Large Corpus." *Computers and the Humanities* **26**(5): 415–439.

Gall, H., Jazayeri, M., and Riva, C. (1999). *Visualizing Software Release Histories: The Use of Color and Third Dimension.* In Proceedings of the International Conference on Software Maintenance (ICSM '99). Oxford, UK, IEEE Computer Society Press, Los Alamitos, CA: 99.

Gansner, E., Koutsofias, E., North, S., and Vo, K. (1993). "A Technique for Drawing Directed Graphs." *IEEE Transactions on Software Engineering* **19**(3): 214–230.

Gansner, E., North, S., and Vo, K. (1988). "DAG – A Program that Draws Directed Graphs." *Software Practice and Experience* **18**(11): 1047–1062.

Ganter, B., and Wille, R. (1999). *Formal Concept Analysis: Mathematical Foundations.* Berlin, Springer-Verlag.

Gao, S., Wu, W., Lee, C.-H., and Chua, T.-S. (2003). *A Maximal Figure-of-Merit Learning Approach to Text Categorization.* In Proceedings of SIGIR-03, 26th ACM International Conference on Research and Development in Information Retrieval. Toronto, ACM Press, New York: 174–181.

Gaussier, E., Goutte, C., Popat, K., and Chen, F. (2002). *A Hierarchical Model for Clustering and Categorising Documents.* In Proceedings of ECIR-02, 24th European Colloquium on Information Retrieval Research. Glasgow, Springer-Verlag, Heidelberg: 229–247.

Gelbukh, A., ed. (2002). *Computational Linguistics and Intelligent Text Processing.* In Proceedings of 3rd International Conference, CICLing 2001. Mexico City, Springer-Verlag, Berlin and New York.

The Gene Ontology (GO) Consortium. (2000). "Gene Ontology: Tool for the Unification of Biology." *Nature Genetics* **25**: 25–29.

The Gene Ontology (GO) Consortium. (2001). "Creating the Gene Ontology Resource: Design and Implementation." *Genome Research* **11**: 1425–1433.

Gentili, G. L., Marinilli, M., Micarelli, A., and Sciarrone, F. (2001). "Text Categorization in an Intelligent Agent for Filtering Information on the Web." *International Journal of Pattern Recognition and Artificial Intelligence* **15**(3): 527–549.

Geutner, P., Bodenhausen, U., and Waibel, A. (1993). *Flexibility through Incremental Learning: Neural Networks for Text Categorization.* In Proceedings of WCNN-93, World Congress on Neural Networks. Portland, OR, Lawrence Erlbaum Associates, Hillsdale, NJ: 24–27.

Ghani, R. (2000). *Using Error-Correcting Codes for Text Classification.* In Proceedings of ICML-00, 17th International Conference on Machine Learning. P. Langley, ed. Stanford, CA, Morgan Kaufmann Publishers, San Francisco: 303–310.

Ghani, R. (2001). *Combining Labeled and Unlabeled Data for Text Classification with a Large Number of Categories.* In Proceedings of the IEEE International Conference on Data Mining. San Jose, CA, IEEE Computer Society Press, Los Alamitos, CA: 597–598.

Ghani, R. (2002). *Combining Labeled and Unlabeled Data for MultiClass Text Categorization.* In Proceedings of ICML-02, 19th International Conference on Machine Learning. Sydney, Australia, Morgan Kaufmann Publishers, San Francisco: 187–194.

Ghani, R., Slattery, S., and Yang, Y. (2001). *Hypertext Categorization Using Hyperlink Patterns and Meta Data.* In Proceedings of ICML-01, 18th International Conference on Machine Learning. Williams College, Morgan Kaufmann Publishers, San Francisco: 178–185.

Giorgetti, D., and Sebastiani, F. (2003a). "Automating Survey Coding by Multiclass Text Categorization Techniques." *Journal of the American Society for Information Science and Technology* **54**(12): 1269–1277.

Giorgetti, D., and Sebastiani, F. (2003b). *Multiclass Text Categorization for Automated Survey Coding.* In Proceedings of SAC-03, 18th ACM Symposium on Applied Computing. Melbourne, Australia, ACM Press, New York: 798–802.

Giorgio, M. D. N., and Micarelli, A. (2003). *Does a New Simple Gaussian Weighting Approach Perform Well in Text Categorization?* In Proceedings of IJCAI-03, 18th International Joint Conference on Artificial Intelligence. Acapulco, Morgan Kaufmann Publishers, San Francisco: 581–586.

Glover, E. J., Tsioutsiouliklis, K., Lawrence, S., Pennock, D. M., and Flake, G. W. (2002). *Using Web Structure for Classifying and Describing Web Pages.* In Proceedings of WWW-02,

International Conference on the World Wide Web. Honolulu, ACM Press, New York: 562–569.

Goldberg, J. L. (1995). *CDM: An Approach to Learning in Text Categorization.* In Proceedings of ICTAI-95, 7th International Conference on Tools with Artificial Intelligence. Herndon, VA, IEEE Computer Society Press, Los Alamitos, CA: 258–265.

Goldberg, J. L. (1996). "CDM: An Approach to Learning in Text Categorization." *International Journal on Artificial Intelligence Tools* **5**(1/2): 229–253.

Goldstein, J., and Roth, S. (1994). *Using Aggregation and Dynamic Queries for Exploring Large Data Sets.* In Proceedings of Human Factors in Computing Systems CHI '94 Conference. Boston, ACM, New York: 23–29.

Goldszmidt, M., and Sahami, M. (1998). *Probabilistic Approach to Full-Text Document Clustering.* Technical Report ITAD-433-MS-98-044, SRI International.

Gomez-Hidalgo, J. M. (2002). *Evaluating Cost-Sensitive Unsolicited Bulk Email Categorization.* In Proceedings of SAC-02, 17th ACM Symposium on Applied Computing. Madrid, ACM Press, New York: 615–620.

Gomez-Hidalgo, J. M., Rodriguez, J. M. D. B., Lopez, L. A. U., Valdivia, M. T. M., and Vega, M. G. (2002). *Integrating Lexical Knowledge in Learning-Based Text Categorization.* In Proceedings of JADT-02, 6th International Conference on the Statistical Analysis of Textual Data. St.-Malo, France.

Goodman, M. (1990). *Prism: A Case-Based Telex Classifier.* In Proceedings of IAAI-90, 2nd Conference on Innovative Applications of Artificial Intelligence. Boston, AAAI Press, Menlo Park, CA: 25–37.

Gotlieb, C. C., and Kumar, S. (1968). "Semantic Clustering of Index Terms." *Journal of the ACM* **15**(4): 493–513.

Govert, N., Lalmas, M., and Fuhr, N. (1999). *A Probabilistic Description-Oriented Approach for Categorising Web Documents.* In Proceedings of CIKM-99, 8th ACM International Conference on Information and Knowledge Management. Kansas City, MO, ACM Press, New York: 475–482.

Graham, M. (2001). *Visualising Multiple Overlapping Classification Hierarchies.* Ph.D. diss., Napier University.

Gray, W. A., and Harley, A. J. (1971). "Computer-Assisted Indexing." *Information Storage and Retrieval* **7**(4): 167–174.

Greene, B. B., and Rubin, G. M. (1971). *Automatic Grammatical Tagging of English.* Technical Report. Providence, RI, Brown University.

Grieser, G., Jantke, K. P., Lange, S., and Thomas, B. (2000). *A Unifying Approach to HTML Wrapper Representation and Learning. Discovery Science.* In Proceedings of 3rd International Conference, DS 2000. Kyoto, Japan, Springer-Verlag, Berlin: 50–64.

Grinstein, G. (1996). *Harnessing the Human in Knowledge Discovery.* In Proceedings of the 2nd ACM SIGKDD International Conference on Knowledge Discovery and Data Mining. Portland, OR, AAAI Press, CA: 384–385.

Grishman, R. (1996). "The Role of Syntax in Information Extraction." In *Advances in Text Processing: Tipster Program Phase II.* San Francisco, Morgan Kaufmann Publishers.

Grishman, R. (1997). "Information Extraction: Techniques and Challenges." In Materials of Information Extraction International Summar School – SCIE '97. Springer, Berlin: 10–27.

Gruber, T. R. (1993). "A Translation Approach to Portable Ontologies." *Knowledge Acquisition* **5**: 199–220.

Guthrie, L., Guthrie, J. A., and Leistensnider, J. (1999). "Document Classification and Routing." In *Natural Language Information Retrieval.* T. Strzalkowski, ed. Dordrecht, Kluwer Academic Publishers: 289–310.

Guthrie, L., Walker, E., and Guthrie, J. A. (1994). *Document Classification by Machine: Theory and Practice.* In Proceedings of COLING-94, 15th International Conference on Computational Linguistics. Kyoto, Japan, Morgan Kaufmann Publishers, San Francisco: 1059–1063.

Hadany, R., and Harel, D. (2001). "A Multi-Scale Method for Drawing Graphs Nicely." *Discrete Applied Mathematics* **113**: 3–21.

Hadjarian, A., Bala, J., and Pachowicz, P. (2001). *Text Categorization through Multistrategy Learning and Visualization.* In Proceedings of CICLING-01, 2nd International Conference on Computational Linguistics and Intelligent Text Processing. A. Gelbukh, ed. Mexico City, Springer-Verlag, Heidelberg: 423–436.

Hahn, U., and Schnattinger, K. (1997). *Knowledge Mining from Textual Sources.* In Proceedings of the 6th International Conference on Information and Knowledge Management. Las Vegas, ACM, New York: 83–90.

Hamill, K. A., and Zamora, A. (1978). *An Automatic Document Classification System Using Pattern Recognition Techniques.* In Proceedings of ASIS-78, 41st Annual Meeting of the American Society for Information Science. E. H. Brenner, ed. New York, American Society for Information Science, Washington, DC: 152–155.

Hamill, K. A., and Zamora, A. (1980). "The Use of Titles for Automatic Document Classification." *Journal of the American Society for Information Science* **33**(6): 396–402.

Han, E.-H., Karypis, G., and Kumar, V. (2001). *Text Categorization Using Weight-Adjusted k-Nearest Neighbor Classification.* In Proceedings of PAKDD-01, 5th Pacific-Asia Conferenece on Knowledge Discovery and Data Mining. Hong Kong, Springer-Verlag, Heidelberg: 53–65.

Han, J., and Fu, Y. (1995). *Discovery of Multiple-Level Association Rules from Large Databases.* In Proceedings of the 1995 International Conference on Very Large Data Bases (VLDB'95). Zurich, Morgan Kaufmann Publishers, San Francisco: 420–431.

Hanauer, D. (1996). "Integration of Phonetic and Graphic Features in Poetic Text Categorization Judgements." *Poetics* **23**(5): 363–380.

Hao, M., Dayal, U., Hsu, M., Sprenger, T., and Gross, M. (2001). *Visualization of Directed Associations in E-commerce Transaction Data.* In Proceedings of Data Visualization (EG and IEEE's VisSym '01). Ascona, Switzerland, Springer, Berlin: 185–192.

Haralick, R. M. (1994). *Document Image Understanding: Geometric and Logical Layout.* In Proceedings of CVPR94, IEEE Computer Society Conference on Computer Vision and Pattern Recognition. Seattle, IEEE Computer Society Press, Los Alamitos, CA: 385–390.

Hardt, D., and Romero, M. (2002). *Ellipsis and the Structure of Discourse.* In Proceedings of Sinn und Bedeutung VI, Osnabrück, Germany, Institute for Cognitive Science, University of Osnabrück: 85–98.

Harel, D., and Koren, Y. (2000). *A Fast Multi-Scale Method for Drawing Large Graphs.* In Proceedings of the 8th International Symposium on Graph Drawing. Willamsburg, VA, Springer-Verlag, Heidelberg: 282–285.

Hatzivassiloglou, V., Duboue, P. A., and Rzhetsky, A. (2001). "Disambiguating Proteins, Genes, and RNA in Text: A Machine Learning Approach." *Bioinformatics* **17**(Suppl 1): S97–106.

Havre, S., Hetzler, B., and Nowell, L. (1999). *ThemeRiver(TM): In Search of Trends, Patterns and Relationships.* In Proceedings of IEEE Symposium on Information Visualization (InfoVis 1999). San Francisco, IEEE Press, New York: 115–123.

Hayes, P. (1992). "Intelligent High-Volume Processing Using Shallow, Domain-Specific Techniques." In *Text-Based Intelligent Systems: Current Research and Practice in Information Extraction and Retrieval.* P. S. Jacobs, ed. Hillsdale, NJ, Lawrence Earlbaum: 227–242.

Hayes, P. J., Andersen, P. M., Nirenburg, I. B., and Schmandt, L. M. (1990). *Tcs: A Shell for Content-Based Text Categorization.* In Proceedings of CAIA-90, 6th IEEE Conference on Artificial Intelligence Applications. Santa Barbara, CA, IEEE Computer Society Press, Los Alamitos, CA: 320–326.

Hayes, P. J., Knecht, L. E., and Cellio, M. J. (1988). *A News Story Categorization System.* In Proceedings of ANLP-88, 2nd Conference on Applied Natural Language Processing. Austin, JX, Association for Computational Linguistics, Morristown, NJ: 9–17.

Hayes, P. J., and Weinstein, S. P. (1990). *Construe/Tis: A System for Content-Based Indexing of a Database of News Stories.* In Proceedings of IAAI-90, 2nd Conference on Innovative Applications of Artificial Intelligence. Boston, AAAI Press, Menlo Park, CA: 49–66.

He, J., Tan, A.-H., and Tan, C.-L. (2003). "On Machine Learning Methods for Chinese Document Categorization." *Applied Intelligence* **18**(3): 311–322.

Heaps, H. S. (1973). "A Theory of Relevance for Automatic Document Classification." *Information and Control* **22**(3): 268–278.

Hearst, M. (1992). *Automatic Acquisition of Hyponyms From Large Text Corpora.* In Proceedings of the 14th International Conference on Computational Linguistics. Nantes, France, Association for Computational Linguistics, Morristown, NJ: 539–545.

Hearst, M. (1995). *TileBars: Visualization of Term Distribution Information in Full-Text Information Access.* In Proceedings of the ACM SIGCHI Conference on Human Factors in Computing Systems, Denver, CO, ACM, New York: 59–66.

Hearst, M. (1999a). *Untangling Text Mining.* In Proceedings of the 37th Annual Meeting of the Association of Computational Linguistics. College Park, MD, Association of Computational Linguistics, Morristown, NJ: 3–10.

Hearst, M. (1999b). "User Interfaces and Visualization." In *Modern Information Retrieval.* R. Baeza-Yates and B. Ribeira-Neto, eds. Boston, Addison-Wesley Longman Publishing Company: 257–323.

Hearst, M. (2003). *Information Visualization: Principles, Promise and Pragmatics Tutorial Notes.* In Proceedings of CHI 03. Fort Lauderdale, FL.

Hearst, M., and Hirsh, H. (1996). *Machine Learning in Information Access.* Papers from the 1996 AAAI Spring Symposium. Stanford, CA, AAAI Press, Menlo Park, CA.

Hearst, M., and Karadi, C. (1997). *Cat-a-Cone: An Interactive Interface for Specifying Searches and Viewing Retrieval Results Using a Large Category Hierarchy.* In Proceedings of the 20th Annual International ACM/SIGIR Conference. Philadelphia, ACM Press, New York: 246–255.

Hearst, M. A. (1991). *Noun Homograph Disambiguation Using Local Context in Large Corpora.* In Proceedings of the 7th Annual Conference of the University of Waterloo Centre for the *New Oxford English Dictionary.* Oxford, UK: 1–22.

Hearst, M. A., Karger, D. R., and Pedersen, J. O. (1995). *Scatter/Gather as a Tool for the Navigation of Retrieval Results.* Working Notes, AAAI Fall Symposium on AI Applications in Knowledge Navigation. Cambridge, MA, AAAI Press, Menlo Park, CA: 65–71.

Hearst, M. A., and Pedersen, J. O. (1996). *Reexamining the Cluster Hypothesis: Scatter/Gather on Retrieval Results.* In Proceedings of ACM SIGIR '96. Zurich, ACM Press, New York: 76–84.

Hersh, W., Buckley, C., Leone, T. J., and Hickman, D. (1994). *OHSUMED: An Interactive Retrieval Evaluation and New Large Text Collection for Research.* In Proceedings of SIGIR-94, 17th ACM International Conference on Research and Development in Information Retrieval. Dublin, Springer-Verlag, Heidelberg: 192–201.

Hetzler, B., Harris, W. M., Havre, S., and Whitney, P. (1998). *Visualizing the Full Spectrum of Document Relationships.* In Proceedings of the 5th International Society for Knowledge Organization (ISKO) Conference. Lille, France, Ergon-Verlog, Würzburg, Germany: 168–175.

Hetzler, B., Whitney, P., Martucci, L., and Thomas, J. (1998). *Multi-Faceted Insight through Interoperable Visual Information Analysis Paradigms.* In Proceedings of Information Visualization '98. Research Triangle Park, NC, IEEE Computer Society Press, Los Alamitos, CA: 137–144.

Hill, D. P., Blake, J. A., Richardson, J. E., and Ringwald, M. (2002). "Extension and Integration of the Gene Ontology (GO): Combining GO Vocabularies with External Vocabularies." *Genome Research* **12**: 1982–1991.

Hindle, D. (1989). *Acquiring Disambiguation Rules from Text.* In Proceedings of 27th Annual Meeting of the Association for Computational Linguistics. Vancouver, Association for Computational Linguistics, Morristown, NJ: 118–125.

Hirschman, L., Park, J. C., Tsujii, J., Wong, L., and Wu, C. H. (2002). "Accomplishments and Challenges in Literature Data Mining for Biology." *Bioinformatics Review* **18**(12): 1553–1551.

Hoashi, K., Matsumoto, K., Inoue, N., and Hashimoto, K. (2000). *Document Filtering Methods Using Non-Relevant Information Profile.* In Proceedings of SIGIR-00, 23rd ACM International Conference on Research and Development in Information Retrieval. Athens, ACM Press, New York: 176–183.

Hobbs, J. (1986). "Resolving Pronoun References." In *Readings in Natural Language Processing.* B. J. Grosz, K. S. Jones and B. L. Webber, eds. Los Altos, CA, Morgan Kaufmann Publishers: 339–352.

Hobbs, J., Douglas, R., Appelt, E., Bear, J., Israel, D., Kameyama, M., Stickel, M., and Tyson, M. (1996). "FASTUS: A Cascaded Finite-State Transducer for Extracting Information from Natural-Language Text." In *Finite State Devices for Natural Language Processing.* E. Roche, and Y. Schabes, eds. Cambridge, MA, MIT Press: 383–406.

Hobbs, J. R. (1993). *FASTUS: A System for Extracting Information from Text.* In Proceedings of DARPA Workshop on Human Language Technology. Princeton, NJ, Morgan Kaufmann Publishers, San Mateo, CA: 133–137.

Hobbs, J. R., Appelt, D. E., Bear, J., Tyson, M., and Magerman, D. (1991). *The TACITUS System: The MUC-3 Experience.* Menlo Park, CA, SRI.

Hoch, R. (1994). *Using IR Techniques for Text Classification in Document Analysis.* In Proceedings of SIGIR-94, 17th ACM International Conference on Research and Development in Information Retrieval. Dublin, Springer-Verlag, Heidelberg: 31–40.

Honkela, T. (1997). *Self-Organizing Maps in Natural Language Processing.* Neural Networks Research Centre. Helsinki, Helsinki University of Technology.

Honkela, T., Kaski, S., Kohonen, T., and Lagus, K. (1998). "Self-Organizing Maps of Very Large Document Collections: Justification for the WEBSOM Method." In *Classification, Data Analysis and Data Highways.* I. Balderjahn, R. Mathar and M. Schader, eds. Berlin, Springer-Verlag: 245–252.

Honkela, T., Kaski, S., Lagus, K., and Kohonen, T. (1997). *WEBSOM – Self-Organizing Maps of Document Collections.* In Proceedings of WSOM '97, Workshop on Self-Organizing Maps. Espoo, Finland, Helsinki University of Technology. Helsinki: 310–315.

Honkela, T., Lagus, K., and Kaski, S. (1998). "Self-Organizing Maps of Large Document Collections." In *Visual Explorations in Finance with Self-Organizing Maps.* G. Deboeck and T. Kohonen, eds. London, Springer: 168–178.

Hornbaek, K., Bederson, B., and Plaisant, C. (2002). "Navigation Patterns and Usability of Zoomable User Interfaces With and Without an Overview." *ACM Transactions on Computer–Human Interaction* **9**(4): 362–389.

Hotho, A., Maedche, A., Staab, S., and Zacharias, V. (2002). "On Knowledgeable Supervised Text Mining." In *Text Mining: Theoretical Aspects and Applications.* J. Franke, G. Nakhaeizadeh, and I. Renz, eds. Heidelberg, Physica-Verlag (Springer): 131– 152.

Hotho, A., Staab, S., and Maedche, A. (2001). *Ontology-Based Text Clustering.* In Proceedings of the IJCAI-2001 Workshop Text Learning: Beyond Supervision. Seattle.

Hotho, A., Staab, S., and Stumme, G. (2003). *Text Clustering Based on Background Knowledge.* Institute of Applied Informatics and Formal Descriptive Methods, University of Karlsruhe, Germany: 1–35.

Hoyle, W. G. (1973). "Automatic Indexing and Generation of Classification by Algorithm." *Information Storage and Retrieval* **9**(4): 233–242.

Hsu, W.-L., and Lang, S.-D. (1999). *Classification Algorithms for NETNEWS Articles.* In Proceedings of CIKM-99, 8th ACM International Conference on Information and Knowledge Management. Kansas City, MO, ACM Press, New York: 114–121.

Hsu, W.-L., and Lang, S.-D. (1999). *Feature Reduction and Database Maintenance in NETNEWS Classification.* In Proceedings of IDEAS-99, 1999 International Database Engineering and Applications Symposium. Montreal, IEEE Computer Society Press, Los Alamitos, CA: 137–144.

Huang, S., Ward, M., and Rudensteiner, E. (2003). *Exploration of Dimensionality Reduction for Text Visualization.* Worcester, MA, Worcester Polytechnic Institute.

Hubona, G. S., Shirah, G., and Fout, D. (1997). "The Effects of Motion and Stereopsis on Three-Dimensional Visualization." *International Journal of Human Computer Studies* **47**(5): 609–627.

Huffman, S. (1995). *Acquaintance: Language-Independent Document Categorization by N-Grams*. In Proceedings of TREC-4, 4th Text Retrieval Conference. Gaithersburg, MD, National Institute of Standards and Technology, Gaithersburg, MD: 359–371.

Huffman, S., and Damashek, M. (1994). *Acquaintance: A Novel Vector-Space N-Gram Technique for Document Categorization*. In Proceedings of TREC-3, 3rd Text Retrieval Conference, D. K. Harman, ed. Gaithersburg, MD, National Institute of Standards and Technology, Gaithersburg, MD: 305–310.

Huffman, S. B. (1995). "Learning Information Extraction Patterns from Examples." In *Connectionist, Statistical, and Symbolic Approaches to Learning for Natural Language Processing*. S. Wermter, E. Riloff, and G. Scheler, eds. London, Springer-Verlag: 246–260.

Hull, D. (1996). "Stemming Algorithms – A Case Study for Detailed Evaluation." *Journal of the American Society for Information Science* **47**(1): 70–84.

Hull, D. A. (1994). *Improving Text Retrieval for the Routing Problem Using Latent Semantic Indexing*. In Proceedings of SIGIR-94, 17th ACM International Conference on Research and Development in Information Retrieval. Dublin, Springer-Verlag, Heidelberg: 282–289.

Hull, D. A. (1998). *The TREC-7 Filtering Track: Description and Analysis*. In Proceedings of TREC-7, 7th Text Retrieval Conference. Gaithersburg, MD, National Institute of Standards and Technology, Gaithersburg, MD: 33–56.

Hull, D. A., Pedersen, J. O., and Schutze, H. (1996). *Method Combination for Document Filtering*. In Proceedings of SIGIR-96, 19th ACM International Conference on Research and Development in Information Retrieval. H.-P. Frei, D. Harman, P. Schable, and R. Wilkinson, eds. Zurich, ACM Press, New York: 279–288.

Hummon, M. P., and Carley, K. (1993). "Social Networks as Normal Science." *Social Networks* **14**: 71–106.

Humphreys, K., Gaizauskas, R., and Azzam, S. (1997). *Event Coreference for Information Extraction*. In Proceedings of the Workshop on Operational Factors in Practical, Robust, Anaphora Resolution for Unrestricted Texts. Madrid, Spain, Association for Computational Linguistics, Morristown, NJ: 75–81.

Igarashi, T., and Hinckley, K. (2000). *Speed-Dependent Automatic Zooming for Browsing Large Documents*. In Proceedings of the 11th Annual Symposium on User Interface Software and Technology (UIST '00). San Diego, CA, ACM Press, New York: 139–148.

IntertekGroup (2002). *Leveraging Unstructured Data in Investment Management*. http://www.taborcommunications.com/dsstar/02/0604/104317.html.

Ipeirotis, P. G., Gravano, L., and Sahami, M. (2001). *Probe, Count, and Classify: Categorizing Hidden Web Databases*. In Proceedings of SIGMOD-01, ACM International Conference on Management of Data. W. G. Aref, ed. Santa Barbara, CA, ACM Press, New York: 67–78.

Ittner, D. J., Lewis, D. D., and Ahn, D. D. (1995). *Text Categorization of Low Quality Images*. In Proceedings of SDAIR-95, 4th Annual Symposium on Document Analysis and Information Retrieval. Las Vegas, NV, ISRI, University of Nevada, Las Vegas, NV: 301–315.

Iwayama, M., and Tokunaga, T. (1994). *A Probabilistic Model for Text Categorization: Based on a Single Random Variable with Multiple Values*. In Proceedings of ANLP-94, 4th Conference on Applied Natural Language Processing. Stuttgart, Germany, Association for Computational Linguistics, Morristown, NJ: 162–167.

Iwayama, M., and Tokunaga, T. (1995a). *Cluster-Based Text Categorization: A Comparison of Category Search Strategies*. In Proceedings of SIGIR-95, 18th ACM International Conference on Research and Development in Information Retrieval. E. A. Fox, P. Ingwersen, and R. Fidel, eds. Seattle, ACM Press, New York: 273–281.

Iwayama, M., and Tokunaga, T. (1995b). *Hierarchical Bayesian Clustering for Automatic Text Classification*. In Proceedings of IJCAI-95, 14th International Joint Conference on Artificial

Intelligence. C. E. Mellish, ed. Montreal, Morgan Kaufmann Publishers, San Francisco: 1322–1327.

Iwazume, M., Takeda, H., and Nishida, T. (1996). *Ontology-Based Information Gathering and Text Categorization from the Internet*. In Proceedings of IEA/AIE-96, 9th International Conference in Industrial and Engineering Applications of Artificial Intelligence and Expert Systems. T. Tanaka, S. Ohsuga, and M. Ali, eds. Fukuoka, Japan: 305–314.

Iyer, R. D., Lewis, D. D., Schapire, R. E., Singer, Y., and Singhal, A. (2000). *Boosting for Document Routing*. In Proceedings of CIKM-00, 9th ACM International Conference on Information and Knowledge Management. A. Agah, J. Callan, and E. Rundensteiner, eds. McLean, VA, ACM Press, New York: 70–77.

Jacobs, P. S. (1992). *Joining Statistics with NLP for Text Categorization*. In Proceedings of ANLP-92, 3rd Conference on Applied Natural Language Processing. M. Bates and O. Stock, eds. Trento, Italy, Association for Computational Linguistics, Morristown, NJ: 178–185.

Jacobs, P. S. (1993). "Using Statistical Methods to Improve Knowledge-Based News Categorization." *IEEE Expert* **8**(2): 13–23.

Jain, A., and Dubes, R. (1988). *Algorithms for Clustering Data*. Englewood Cliffs, NJ, Prentice Hall.

Jain, A. K., and Chellappa, R., eds. (1993). *Markov Random Fields: Theory and Application*. Boston, Academic Press.

Jain, A. K., Murty, M. N., and Flynn, P. J. (1999). "Data Clustering: A Review." *ACM Computing Surveys* **31**(3): 264–323.

Jensen, J. R. (1996). *Introductory Digital Image Processing – A Remote Sensing Perspective*. Englewood Cliffs, NJ, Prentice Hall.

Jerding, D., and Stasko, J. (1995). *The Information Mural: A Technique for Displaying and Navigating Large Information Spaces*. In Proceedings of Information Visualization '95 Symposium. Atlanta, IEEE Computer Society, Washington, DC: 43.

Jo, T. C. (1999a). "News Article Classification Based on Categorical Points from Keywords in Backdata." In *Computational Intelligence for Modelling, Control and Automation*. M. Mohammadian, ed. Amsterdam, IOS Press: 211–214.

Jo, T. C. (1999b). "News Articles Classification Based on Representative Keywords of Categories." In *Computational Intelligence for Modelling, Control and Automation*. M. Mohammadian, ed. Amsterdam, IOS Press: 194–198.

Jo, T. C. (1999c). *Text Categorization with the Concept of Fuzzy Set of Informative Keywords*. In Proceedings of FUZZ-IEEE '99, IEEE International Conference on Fuzzy Systems. Seoul, KR, IEEE Computer Society Press, Los Alamitos, CA: 609–614.

Joachims, T. (1997). *A Probabilistic Analysis of the Rocchio Algorithm with TFIDF for Text Categorization*. In Proceedings of ICML-97, 14th International Conference on Machine Learning. D. H. Fisher, ed. Nashville, TN, Morgan Kaufmann Publishers, San Francisco: 143–151.

Joachims, T. (1998). *Text Categorization with Support Vector Machines: Learning with Many Relevant Features*. In Proceedings of ECML-98, 10th European Conference on Machine Learning. C. Nedellec and C. Rouveirol, eds. Chemnitz, Germany, Springer-Verlag, Heidelberg: 137–142.

Joachims, T. (1999). *Transductive Inference for Text Classification Using Support Vector Machines*. In Proceedings of ICML-99, 16th International Conference on Machine Learning. I. Bratko and S. Dzeroski, eds. Bled, Morgan Kaufmann Publishers, San Francisco: 200–209.

Joachims, T. (2000). *Estimating the Generalization Performance of a SVM Efficiently*. In Proceedings of ICML-00, 17th International Conference on Machine Learning. P. Langley, ed. Stanford, CA, Morgan Kaufmann Publishers, San Francisco: 431–438.

Joachims, T. (2001). *A Statistical Learning Model of Text Classification with Support Vector Machines*. In Proceedings of SIGIR-01, 24th ACM International Conference on Research and Development in Information Retrieval. W. B. Croft, D. J. Harper, D. H. Kraft, and J. Zobel, eds. New Orleans, ACM Press, New York: 128–136.

Joachims, T. (2002). *Learning to Classify Text Using Support Vector Machines*. Dordrecht, Kluwer Academic Publishers.

Joachims, T., Cristianini, N., and Shawe-Taylor, J. (2001). *Composite Kernels for Hypertext Categorisation*. In Proceedings of ICML-01, 18th International Conference on Machine Learning. C. Brodley and A. Danyluk, eds. Williams College, MA, Morgan Kaufmann Publishers, San Francisco: 250–257.

Joachims, T., Freitag, D., and Mitchell, T. M. (1997). *WebWatcher: A Tour Guide for the Word Wide Web*. In Proceedings of IJCAI-97, 15th International Joint Conference on Artificial Intelligence. M. E. Pollack, ed. Nagoya, Japan, Morgan Kaufmann Publishers, San Francisco: 770–775.

Joachims, T., and Sebastiani, F. (2002). "Guest Editors' Introduction to the Special Issue on Automated Text Categorization." *Journal of Intelligent Information Systems* **18**(2/3): 103–105.

Johnson, B., and Shneiderman, B. (1991). "Treemaps: A Space-Filling Approach to the Visualization of Hierarchical Information." In Proceedings of IEEE Visualization '91 Conference. G. Nielson and L. Rosenblum, eds. San Diego, CA, IEEE Computer Society Press, Los Alamitos, CA: 284–291.

Juan, A., and Vidal, E. (2002). "On the Use of Bernoulli Mixture Models for Text Classification." *Pattern Recognition* **35**(12): 2705–2710.

Junker, M., and Abecker, A. (1997). *Exploiting Thesaurus Knowledge in Rule Induction for Text Classification*. In Proceedings of RANLP-97, 2nd International Conference on Recent Advances in Natural Language Processing. Tzigov Chark, Bulgaria: 202–207.

Junker, M., and Dengel, A. (2001). *Preventing Overfitting in Learning Text Patterns for Document Categorization*. In Proceedings of ICAPR-01, 2nd International Conference on Advances in Pattern Recognition. S. Singh, N. A. Murshed, and W. G. Kropatsch, eds. Rio de Janeiro, Springer-Verlag, Heidelberg: 137–146.

Junker, M., and Hoch, R. (1998). "An Experimental Evaluation of OCR Text Representations for Learning Document Classifiers." *International Journal on Document Analysis and Recognition* **1**(2): 116–122.

Junker, M., Sintek, M., and Rinck, M. (2000). *Learning for Text Categorization and Information Extraction with ILP*. In Proceedings of the 1st Workshop on Learning Language in Logic. Bled, Slovenia, Springer-Verlag, Heidelberg: 247–258.

Kaban, A., and Girolami, M. (2002). "A Dynamic Probabilistic Model to Visualise Topic Evolution in Text Streams." *Journal of Intelligent Information Systems* **18**(2/3): 107–125.

Kamada, T., and Kawai, S. (1989). "An Algorithm for Drawing General Undirected Graphs." *Information Processing Letters* **31**: 7–15.

Kar, G., and White, L. J. (1978). "A Distance Measure for Automated Document Classification by Sequential Analysis." *Information Processing and Management* **14**(2): 57–69.

Karrer, A., and Scacchi, W. (1990). *Requirements for an Extensible Object-Oriented Tree/Graph Editor*. In Proceedings of ACM SIGGRAPH Symposium on User Interface Software and Technology. Snowbird, UT, ACM Press, New York: 84–91.

Karypis, G., and Han, E.-H. (2000). *Fast Supervised Dimensionality Reduction Algorithm with Applications to Document Categorization and Retrieval*. In Proceedings of CIKM-00, 9th ACM International Conference on Information and Knowledge Management. A. Agah, J. Callan, and E. Rundensteiner, eds. McLean, VA, ACM Press, New York: 12–19.

Kaski, S. (1997). *Data Exploration Using Self-Organizing Maps*. Tech thesis, Helsinki University of Technology.

Kaski, S., Honkela, T., Lagus, K., and Kohonen, T. (1998). "WEBSOM-Self-Organizing Maps of Document Collections." *Neurocomputing* **21**: 101–117.

Kaski, S., Lagus, K., Honkela, T., and Kohonen, T. (1998). "Statistical Aspects of the WEBSOM System in Organizing Document Collections." *Computing Science and Statistics* **29**: 281–290.

Kawatani, T. (2002). *Topic Difference Factor Extraction between Two Document Sets and Its Application to Text Categorization.* In Proceedings of SIGIR-02, 25th ACM International Conference on Research and Development in Information Retrieval. K. Jarvelin, M. Beaulieu, R. Baeza-Yates, and S. H. Myaeng, eds. Tampere, Finland, ACM Press, New York: 137–144.

Kehagias, A., Petridis, V., Kaburlasos, V. G., and Fragkou, P. (2003). "A Comparison of Word- and Sense-Based Text Categorization Using Several Classification Algorithms." *Journal of Intelligent Information Systems* **21**(3): 227–247.

Kehler, A. (1997). *Probabilistic Coreference in Information Extraction.* In Proceedings of the 2nd Conference on Empirical Methods in Natural Language Processing. C. Cardie and R. Weischedel, eds. Providence, RI, Association for Computational Linguistics, Somerset, NJ: 163–173.

Keim, D. (2002). "Information Visualization and Visual Data Mining." *IEEE Transactions on Visualization and Computer Graphics* **8**(1): 1–8.

Keller, B. (1992). *A Logic for Representing Grammatical Knowledge.* In Proceedings of European Conference on Artificial Intelligence. Vienna, Austria, John Wiley and Sons, New York: 538–542.

Kennedy, C., and Boguraev, B. (1997). *Anaphora for Everyone: Pronominal Anaphora Resolution Without a Parser.* In Proceedings of the 16th International Conference on Computational Linguistics. J. Tsujii, ed. Copenhagen, Denmark, Association for Computationsl Linguistics, Morristown, NJ: 113–118.

Keogh, E., and Smyth, P. (1997). *A Probabilistic Approach to Fast Pattern Matching in Time Series Databases.* In Proceedings of the 3rd International Conference on Knowledge Discovery and Data Mining (KDD'97). D. Heckerman, H. Mannila, D. Pregibon, and R. Uthurusamy, eds. Newport Beach, CA, AAAI Press, Menlo Park, CA: 24–30.

Kessler, B., Nunberg, G., and Schutze, H. (1997). *Automatic Detection of Text Genre.* In Proceedings of ACL-97, 35th Annual Meeting of the Association for Computational Linguistics. P. R. Cohen and W. Wahlster, eds. Madrid, Morgan Kaufmann Publishers, San Francisco: 32–38.

Khmelev, D. V., and Teahan, W. J. (2003). *A Repetition Based Measure for Verification of Text Collections and for Text Categorization.* In Proceedings of SIGIR-03, 26th ACM International Conference on Research and Development in Information Retrieval. C. Clarke, G. Cormack, J. Callan, D. Hawking, and A. Smeaton, eds. Toronto, ACM Press, New York: 104–110.

Kim, H. (2002). "Predicting How Ontologies for the Semantic Web Will Evolve." *CACM* **45**(2): 48–54.

Kim, J.-T., and Moldovan, D. I. (1995). "Acquisition of Linguistic Patterns for Knowledge-Based Information Extraction." *TKDE* **7**(5): 713–724.

Kim, Y.-H., Hahn, S.-Y., and Zhang, B.-T. (2000). *Text Filtering by Boosting Naive Bayes Classifiers.* In Proceedings of SIGIR-00, 23rd ACM International Conference on Research and Development in Information Retrieval. N. J. Belkin, P. Ingwersen, and M. K. Leong, eds. Athens, ACM Press, New York: 168–75.

Kindermann, J., Paass, G., and Leopold, E. (2001). *Error Correcting Codes with Optimized Kullback–Leibler Distances for Text Categorization.* In Proceedings of ECML-01, 12th European Conference on Machine Learning. L. de Raedt and A. Siebes, eds. Freiburg, Germany, Springer-Verlag, Heidelberg: 266–275.

Kindermann, R., and Snell, J. L. (1980). *Markov Random Fields and Their Applications.* Providence, RI, American Mathematical Society.

Klas, C.-P., and Fuhr, N. (2000). *A New Effective Approach for Categorizing Web Documents.* In Proceedings of BCSIRSG-00, 22nd Annual Colloquium of the British Computer Society Information Retrieval Specialist Group. Cambridge, UK, BCS, Swinden, UK.

Klebanov, B., and Wiemer-Hastings, P. M. (2002). *Using LSA for Pronominal Anaphora Resolution.* In Proceedings of the 3rd International Conference on Computational Linguistics and Intelligent Text Processing. A. F. Gelbukh, ed. Mexico City, Springer, Berlin: 197–199.

Klingbiel, P. H. (1973a). "Machine-Aided Indexing of Technical Literature." *Information Storage and Retrieval* **9**(2): 79–84.

Klingbiel, P. H. (1973b). "A Technique for Machine-Aided Indexing." *Information Storage and Retrieval* **9**(9): 477–494.

Klinkenberg, R., and Joachims, T. (2000). *Detecting Concept Drift with Support Vector Machines*. In Proceedings of ICML-00, 17th International Conference on Machine Learning. P. Langley, ed. Stanford, CA, Morgan Kaufmann Publishers, San Francisco: 487–494.

Kloesgen, W. (1992). "Problems for Knowledge Discovery in Databases and Their Treatment in the Statistics Interpreter EXPLORA." *International Journal for Intelligent Systems* **7**(7): 649–673.

Kloesgen, W. (1995a). "Efficient Discovery of Interesting Statements in Databases." *Journal of Intelligent Information Systems* **4**: 53–69.

Kloesgen, W. (1995b). "EXPLORA: A Multipattern and Multistrategy Discovery Assistant." In *Advances in Knowledge Discovery and Data Mining*. U. Fayyad, G. Piatetsky-Shapiro, and R. Smyth, eds. Cambridge, MA, MIT Press: 249–271.

Kloesgen, W., and Zytkow, J., eds. (2002). *Handbook of Data Mining and Knowledge Discovery*. Oxford, UK, Oxford University Press.

Kloptchenko, A., Eklund, T., Back, B., Karlson, J., Vanharanta, H., and Visa, A. (2002). "Combining Data and Text Mining Techniques for Analyzing Financial Reports." *International Journal of Intelligent Systems in Accounting, Finance, and Management* **12**(1): 29–41.

Knorr, E., Ng, R., and Tucatov, V. (2000). "Distance Based Outliers: Algorithims and Applications." *The VLDB Journal* **8**(3): 237–253.

Knorz, G. (1982). *A Decision Theory Approach to Optimal Automated Indexing*. In Proceedings of SIGIR-82, 5th ACM International Conference on Research and Development in Information Retrieval. G. Salton and H.-J. Schneider, eds. Berlin, Springer-Verlag, Heidelberg: 174–193.

Ko, Y., Park, J., and Seo, J. (2002). *Automatic Text Categorization Using the Importance of Sentences*. In Proceedings of COLING-02, 19th International Conference on Computational Linguistics. Taipei, Taiwan, Association for Computational Linguistics, Morristown NJ/Morgan Kaufmann Publishers, San Francisco, CA: 1–7.

Ko, Y., and Seo, J. (2000). *Automatic Text Categorization by Unsupervised Learning*. In Proceedings of COLING-00, 18th International Conference on Computational Linguistics. Saarbrücken, Germany, Association for Computational Linguistics, Morristown, NJ: 453–459.

Ko, Y., and Seo, J. (2002). *Text Categorization Using Feature Projections*. In Proceedings of COLING-02, 19th International Conference on Computational Linguistics. Taipei, Taiwan, Association for Computational Linguistics, Morristown, NJ/Morgan Kauffman Publishers, San Francisco, CA: 453–459.

Kobsa, A. (2001). *An Empirical Comparison of Three Commercial Information Visualization Systems*. In Proceedings of Infovis 2001, IEEE Symposium on Information Visualization. San Diego, CA, IEEE Computer Society Press, Washington, DC: 123.

Koehn, P. (2002). *Combining Multiclass Maximum Entropy Text Classifiers with Neural Network Voting*. In Proceedings of PorTAL-02, 3rd International Conference on Advances in Natural Language Processing. Faro, Portugal, Springer, Berlin: 125–132.

Kohlhase, M. (2000). "Model Generation for Discourse Representation Theory." In Proceedings of the 14th European Conference on Artificial Intelligence. W. Horn, ed. Berlin, IOS Press, Amsterdam: 441–445.

Kohonen, T. (1981). *Automatic Formation of Topological Maps of Patterns in a Self-Organizing System*. In Proceedings of 2SCIA, 2nd Scandinavian Conference on Image Analysis. E. Uja and O. Simula, eds. Helsinki, Finland, Suomen Hahmontunnistustutkimuksen Seura r.y.: 214–220.

Kohonen, T. (1982). "Analysis of Simple Self-Organizing Process." *Biological Cybernetics* **44**(2): 135–140.

Kohonen, T. (1995). *Self-Organizing Maps*. Berlin, Springer-Verlag.

Kohonen, T. (1997). *Exploration of Very Large Databases by Self-Organizing Maps*. In Proceedings of ICNN '97, International Conference on Neural Networks. Houston, TX, IEEE Service Center Press, Piscataway, NJ: 1–6.

Kohonen, T. (1998). *Self-Organization of Very Large Document Collections: State of the Art*. In Proceedings of ICANN98, 8th International Conference on Artificial Neural Networks. M. Niklasson and T. Zienkke, eds. Skövde, Sweden, Springer-Verlag, London: 65–74.

Kohonen, T., Kaski, S., Lagus, K., and Honkela, T. (1996). *Very Large Two-Level SOM for the Browsing of Newsgroups*. In Proceedings of ICANN96, International Conference on Artificial Neural Networks. Bochum, Germany, Springer-Verlag, Berlin: 269–274.

Kohonen, T., Kaski, S., Lagus, K., Salojarvi, J., Honkela, T., Paatero, V., and Saarela, A. (1999). "Self-Organization of a Massive Text Document Collection." In *Kohonen Maps*. E. Oja and S. Kaski, eds. Amsterdam, Elsevier: 171–182.

Koike, H. (1993). "The Role of Another Spatial Dimension in Software Visualization." *ACM Transactions on Information Systems* **11**(3): 266–286.

Koike, H. (1995). "Fractal Views: A Fractal-Based Method for Controlling Information Display." *ACM Transactions on Information Systems* **13**(3): 305–323.

Koike, T., and Rzhetsky, A. (2000). "A Graphic Editor for Analyzing Signal-Transduction Pathways." *Gene* **259**: 235–244.

Kolcz, A., Prabakarmurthi, V., and Kalita, J. K. (2001). *String Match and Text Extraction: Summarization as Feature Selection for Text Categorization*. In Proceedings of CIKM-01, 10th ACM International Conference on Information and Knowledge Management. W. Paques, L. Liu, and D. Grossman, eds. Atlanta, ACM Press, New York: 365–370.

Koller, D., and Sahami, M. (1997). *Hierarchically Classifying Documents Using Very Few Words*. In Proceedings of ICML-97, 14th International Conference on Machine Learning. D. H. Fisher, ed. Nashville, TN, Morgan Kaufmann Publishers, San Francisco: 170–178.

Kongovi, M., Guzman, J. C., and Dasigi, V. (2002). *Text Categorization: An Experiment Using Phrases*. In Proceedings of ECIR-02, 24th European Colloquium on Information Retrieval Research. F. Cresteni, M. Girotami, and C. J. v. Rijsbergen, eds. Glasgow, Springer-Verlag, Heidelberg: 213–228.

Kopanis, I., Avouris, N. M., and Daskalaki, S. (2002). *The Role of Knowledge Mining in a Large Scale Data Mining Project*. In Proceedings of Methods and Applications of Artificial Intelligence, 2nd Hellenic Conference on AI. I. P. Vlahavas and C. Spyropoulos, eds. Thessaloniki, Greece, Springer-Verlag, Berlin: 288–299.

Koppel, M., Argamon, S., and Shimoni, A. R. (2002). "Automatically Categorizing Written Texts by Author Gender." *Literary and Linguistic Computing* **17**(4): 401–412.

Kosmynin, A., and Davidson, I. (1996). *Using Background Contextual Knowledge for Document Representation*. In Proceedings of PODP-96, 3rd International Workshop on Principles of Document Processing. C. Nicholas and D. Wood, eds. Palo Alto, CA, Springer-Verlag, Heidelberg: 123–133.

Koster, C. H., and Seutter, M. (2003). *Taming Wild Phrases*. In Proceedings of ECIR-03, 25th European Conference on Information Retrieval. F. Sebastiani, ed. Pisa, Italy, Springer-Verlag, Heidelberg: 161–176.

Krauthammer, M., Rzhetsky, A., Morozov, P., and Friedman, C. (2000). "Using BLAST for Identifying Gene and Protein Names in Journal Articles." *Gene* **259**: 245–252.

Krier, M., and Zacc, F. (2002). "Automatic Categorization Applications at the European Patent Office." *World Patent Information* **24**: 187–196.

Krishnapuram, R., Chitrapura, K., and Joshi, S. (2003). *Classification of Text Documents Based on Minimum System Entropy*. In Proceedings of ICML-03, 20th International Conference on Machine Learning. Washington, DC, Morgan Kaufmann Publishers, San Francisco: 384–391.

Kupiec, J. (1992). "Robust Part-of-Speech Tagging Using a Hidden Markov model." *Computer Speech and Language* **6**: 225–243.

Kushmerick, N. (1997). *Wrapper Induction for Information Extraction.* Ph.D. thesis, Department of Computer Science and Engineering, University of Washington.

Kushmerick, N. (2000). "Wrapper Induction: Efficiency and Expressiveness." *Artificial Intelligence* **118**(1–2): 15–68.

Kushmerick, N. (2002). *Finite-State Approaches to Web Information Extraction.* In Proceedings of the 3rd Summer Convention on Information Extraction in the Web Era: Natural Language Communication for Knowledge Acquisition and Intelligent Information Agents. M. Pazienza, ed. Rome, Springer-Verlag, Berlin: 77–91.

Kushmerick, N., Johnston, E., and McGuinness, S. (2001). *Information Extraction by Text Classification.* In Proceedings of IJCAI-01 Workshop on Adaptive Text Extraction and Mining. Seattle, Morgan Kaufmann Publishers, San Francisco.

Kushmerick, N., Weld, D. S., and Doorenbos, R. B. (1997). *Wrapper Induction for Information Extraction.* In Proceedings of the 15th International Joint Conference on Artificial Intelligence (IJCAI). Nagoya, Japan, Morgan Kaufmann Publishers, San Francisco: 729–735.

Kwok, J. T. (1998). *Automated Text Categorization Using Support Vector Machine.* In Proceedings of ICONIP '98, 5th International Conference on Neural Information Processing. Kitakyushu, Japan: 347–351.

Kwon, O.-W., Jung, S.-H., Lee, J.-H., and Lee, G. (1999). *Evaluation of Category Features and Text Structural Information on a Text Categorization Using Memory-Based Reasoning.* In Proceedings of ICCPOL-99, 18th International Conference on Computer Processing of Oriental Languages. Tokushima, Japan: 153–158.

Kwon, O.-W., and Lee, J.-H. (2003). "Text Categorization Based on *k*-nearest Neighbor Approach for Web Site Classification." *Information Processing and Management* **39**(1): 25–44.

Labrou, Y., and Finin, T. (1999). *Yahoo! as an Ontology: Using Yahoo! Categories to Describe documents.* In Proceedings of CIKM-99, 8th ACM International Conference on Information and Knowledge Management. Kansas City, MO, ACM Press, New York: 180–187.

Lafferty, J., McCallum, A., and Pereira, F. (2001). *Conditional Random Fields: Probabilistic Models for Segmenting and Labeling Sequence Data.* In Proceedings of 18th International Conference on Machine Learning. Williamstown, MA, Morgan Kaufmann Publisher, San Francisco: 282–289.

Lager, T. (1998). *Logic for Part-of-Speech Tagging and Shallow Parsing.* In Proceedings of NODALIDA '98. Copenhagen, Denmark, Center for Sprogteknologi, Univio Copenhagen, Copenhagen.

Lagus, K. (1998). *Generalizability of the WEBSOM Method to Document Collections of Various Types.* In Proceedings of 6th European Congress on Intelligent Techniques and Soft Computing (EUFIT'98). Aachen, Germany, Verlag Mainz, Mainz: 210–215.

Lagus, K. (2000a). *Text Mining with the WEBSOM.* D. Sc. (Tech) thesis, Department of Computer Science and Engineering, Helsinki University of Technology.

Lagus, K. (2000b). *Text Retrieval Using Self-Organized Document Maps.* Technical Report A61, Laboratory of Computer and Information Science, Helsinki University of Technology.

Lagus, K., Honkela, T., Kaski, S., and Kohonen, T. (1999). "WEBSOM for Textual Data Mining." *Artificial Intelligence Review* **13**(5/6): 345–364.

Lai, K.-Y., and Lam, W. (2001). *Meta-Learning Models for Automatic Textual Document Categorization.* In Proceedings of PAKDD-01, 5th Pacific-Asia Conference on Knowledge Discovery and Data Mining. D. Cheung, Q. Li, and G. Williams, eds. Hong Kong, Springer Verlag, Heidelberg: 78–89.

Lai, Y.-S., and Wu, C.-H. (2002). "COLUMN: Meaningful Term Extraction and Discriminative Term Selection in Text Categorization via Unknown-Word Methodology." *ACM Transactions on Asian Language Information Processing* **1**(1): 34–64.

Lam, S. L., and Lee, D. L. (1999). *Feature Reduction for Neural Network Based Text Categorization.* In Proceedings of DASFAA-99, 6th IEEE International Conference on Database

Advanced Systems for Advanced Application. A. L. Chen and F. H. Lochovsky, eds. Hsinchu, Taiwan, IEEE Computer Society Press, Los Alamitos, CA: 195–202.

Lam, W., and Ho, C. Y. (1998). *Using a Generalized Instance Set for Automatic Text Categorization.* In Proceedings of SIGIR-98, 21st ACM International Conference on Research and Development in Information Retrieval. W. B. Croft, A. Moffat, C. J. van Rijsergen, R. Wilkinson, and J. Zobel, eds. Melbourne, Australia, ACM Press, New York: 81–89.

Lam, W., and Lai, K.-Y. (2001). *A Meta-Learning Approach for Text Categorization.* In Proceedings of SIGIR-01, 24th ACM International Conference on Research and Development in Information Retrieval. W. B. Croft, D. J. Harper, D. H. Kraft, and J. Zobel, eds. New Orleans, ACM Press, New York: 303–309.

Lam, W., Low, K. F., and Ho, C. Y. (1997). *Using a Bayesian Network Induction Approach for Text Categorization.* In Proceedings of IJCAI-97, 15th International Joint Conference on Artificial Intelligence. M. E. Pollack, ed. Nagoya, Japan, Morgan Kaufmann Publishers, San Francisco: 745–750.

Lam, W., Ruiz, M. E., and Srinivasan, P. (1999). "Automatic Text Categorization and Its Applications to Text Retrieval." *IEEE Transactions on Knowledge and Data Engineering* **11**(6): 865–879.

Lamping, J., and Rao, R. (1994). *Laying Out and Visualizing Large Trees Using a Hyperbolic Space.* In Proceedings of the ACM UIST (UIST '94). P. Szekely, ed. Marina Del Rey, CA, ACM Press, New York: 13–14.

Lamping, L., Rao, R., and Pirolli, P. (1995). *A Focus-Context Technique Based on Hyperbolic Geometry for Visualizing Large Hierarchies.* In Proceedings of the ACM SIGCHI Conference on Human Factors in Computer Systems. I. Katz, R. Mack, L. Marks, M. B. Rosson, and J. Nielsen, eds. Denver, CO, ACM Press, New York: 401–408.

Landau, D., Feldman, R., Aumann, Y., Fresko, M., Lindell, Y., Liphstat, O., and Zamir, O. (1998). *TextVis: An Integrated Visual Environment for Text Mining.* In Proceedings of the 2nd European Symposium on Principles of Data Mining and Knowledge Discovery (PKDD98). Nantes, France, Springer-Verlag, Heidelberg: 56–64.

Landauer, T. K., Foltz, P. W., and Laham, D. (1998). "Introduction to Latent Semantic Analysis." *Discourse Processes* **25**: 259–284.

Lang, K. (1995). *NewsWeeder: Learning to Filter Netnews.* In Proceedings of ICML-95, 12th International Conference on Machine Learning. A. Prieditis and S. J. Russell, eds. Lake Tahoe, NV, Morgan Kaufmann Publishers, San Francisco: 331–339.

Lanquillon, C. (2000). *Learning from Labeled and Unlabeled Documents: A Comparative Study on Semi-Supervised Text Classification.* In Proceedings of PKDD-00, 4th European Conference on Principles of Data Mining and Knowledge Discovery. D. A. Zighed, H. J. Komorowsky and J. M. Zytkow, eds. Lyon, France, Springer-Verlag, Heidelberg: 490–497.

Lappin, S., and Leass, H. J. (1994). "An Algorithm for Pronominal Anaphora Resolution." *Computational Linguistics* **20**(4): 535–561.

Larkey, L. S. (1998). *Automatic Essay Grading Using Text Categorization Techniques.* In Proceedings of SIGIR-98, 21st ACM International Conference on Research and Development in Information Retrieval. W. B. Croft, A. Moffat, C. J. v. Rijsbergen, R. Wilkinson, and J. Zobel, eds. Melbourne, Australia, ACM Press, New York: 90–95.

Larkey, L. S. (1999). *A Patent Search and Classification System.* In Proceedings of DL-99, 4th ACM Conference on Digital Libraries. E. A. Fox and N. Rowejeds, eds. Berkeley, CA, ACM Press, New York: 179–187.

Larkey, L. S., and Croft, W. B. (1996). *Combining Classifiers in Text Categorization.* In Proceedings of SIGIR-96, 19th ACM International Conference on Research and Development in Information Retrieval. H. P. Frei, D. Harmon, P. Schaubie, and R. Wilkinson, eds. Zurich, ACM Press, New York: 289–297.

Lavelli, A., Califf, M. E., Ciravegna, F., Freitag, D., Giuliano, C., Kushmerick, N., and Romano, L. (2004). *A Critical Survey of the Methodology for IE Evaluation.* In Proceedings of the 4th

International Conference on Language Resources and Evaluation. Lisbon, ELRA, Paris: 1655–1658.

Lavelli, A., Magnini, B., and Sebastiani, F. (2002). *Building Thematic Lexical Resources by Bootstrapping and Machine Learning*. In Proceedings of the LREC 2002 Workshop on Linguistic Knowledge Acquisition and Representation: Bootstrapping Annotated Language Data. Las Palmas, Canary Islands, ELRA, Paris: 53–62.

Lee, K. H., Kay, J., Kang, B. H., and Rosebrock, U. (2002). *A Comparative Study on Statistical Machine Learning Algorithms and Thresholding Strategies for Automatic Text Categorization*. In Proceedings of PRICAI-02, 7th Pacific Rim International Conference on Artificial Intelligence. Milshizuka and A. Sattar, eds. Tokyo, Springer-Verlag, Heidelberg: 444–453.

Lee, M. D. (2002). *Fast Text Classification Using Sequential Sampling Processes*. In Proceedings of the 14th Australian Joint Conference on Artificial Intelligence. M. Stumptner, D. Corbett and M. J. Brooks, eds. Adelaide, Australia, Springer-Verlag, Heidelberg: 309–320.

Lee, Y.-B., and Myaeng, S. H. (2002). *Text Genre Classification with Genre-Revealing and Subject-Revealing Features*. In Proceedings of SIGIR-02, 25th ACM International Conference on Research and Development in Information Retrieval. M. Beavliev, E. Beazz-Yakes, S. Myaeng, and K. Jarvelin, eds. Tampere, Finland, ACM Press, New York: 145–150.

Leek, T. R. (1997). *Information Extraction Using Hidden Markov Models*. Master's thesis, Computer Science Department, University of California San Diego.

Lehnert, W., Soderland, S., Aronow, D., Feng, F., and Shmueli, A. (1994). "Inductive Text Classification for Medical Applications." *Journal of Experimental and Theoretical Artificial Intelligence* **7**(1): 49–80.

Lent, B., Agrawal, R., and Srikant, R. (1997). *Discovering Trends in Text Databases*. In Proceedings of the 3rd Annual Conference on Knowledge Discovery and Data Mining (KDD-97) D. Heckerman, H. Mannila, D. Pregibon, and R. Uthrysamy, eds. Newport Beach, CA, AAAI Press, Menlo Park, CA: 227–230.

Leopold, E., and Kindermann, J. (2002). "Text Categorization with Support Vector Machines: How to Represent Texts in Input Space?" *Machine Learning* **46**(1/3): 423–444.

Lesk, M. (1997). *Practical Digital Libraries: Books, Bytes and Bucks*. San Francisco, Morgan Kaufmann Publishers.

Leung, C.-H., and Kan, W.-K. (1997). "A Statistical Learning Approach to Automatic Indexing of Controlled Index Terms." *Journal of the American Society for Information Science* **48**(1): 55–67.

Leung, Y. K., and Apperley, M. D. (1994). "A Review and Taxonomy of Distortion-Oriented Presentation Techniques." *ACM Transactions on Computer–Human Interaction* **1**(2): 126–160.

Lewin, I., Becket, R., Boye, J., Carter, D., Rayner, M., and Wir'en, M. (1999). *Language Processing for Spoken Dialogue Systems: Is Shallow Parsing Enough?* Technical Report CRC-074, SRI, Cambridge, MA: 107–110.

Lewis, D., and Catlett, J. (1994). *Heterogeneous Uncertainty Sampling for Supervised Learning*. In Proceedings of the 11th International Conference on Machine Learning. New Brunswick, NJ, Morgan Kaufmann Publishers, San Francisco: 148–156.

Lewis, D. D. (1991). *Data Extraction as Text Categorization: An Experiment with the MUC-3 Corpus*. In Proceedings of MUC-3, 3rd Message Understanding Conference. San Diego, CA, Morgan Kaufmann Publishers, San Francisco: 245–255.

Lewis, D. D. (1992a). *An Evaluation of Phrasal and Clustered Representations on a Text Categorization task*. In Proceedings of SIGIR-92, 15th ACM International Conference on Research and Development in Information Retrieval. N. Belkin, P. Ingwersen, and A. M. Pejtersen, eds. Copenhagen, ACM Press, New York: 37–50.

Lewis, D. D. (1992b). *Representation and Learning in Information Retrieval.* Ph.D. thesis, Department of Computer Science, University of Massachusetts.

Lewis, D. D. (1995a). *Evaluating and Optmizing Autonomous Text Classification Systems.* In Proceedings of SIGIR-95, 18th ACM International Conference on Research and Development in Information Retrieval. E. A. Fox, P. Ingwersen, and R. Fidel, eds. Seattle, ACM Press, New York: 246–254.

Lewis, D. D. (1995b). "A Sequential Algorithm for Training Text Classifiers: Corrigendum and Additional Data." *SIGIR Forum* **29**(2): 13–19.

Lewis, D. D. (1995c). *The TREC-4 Filtering Track: Description and Analysis.* In Proceedings of TREC-4, 4th Text Retrieval Conference. D. K. Warmon, and E. M. Voorhees, eds. Gaithersburg, MD, National Institute of Standards and Technology, Gaithersburg, MD: 165–180.

Lewis, D. D. (1997). "Reuters-21578 Text Categorization Test Collection. Distribution 1.0." AT&T Labs-Research, http://www.research.att.com/lewis.

Lewis, D. D. (1998). *Naive (Bayes) at Forty: The Independence Assumption in Information Retrieval.* In Proceedings of ECML-98, 10th European Conference on Machine Learning. C. N'edellec and C. Rouveirol, eds. Chemnitz, Germany, Springer-Verlag, Heidelberg: 4–15.

Lewis, D. D. (2000). *Machine Learning for Text Categorization: Background and Characteristics.* In Proceedings of the 21st Annual National Online Meeting. M. E. Williams, ed. New York, Information Today, Medford, OR: 221–226.

Lewis, D. D., and Gale, W. A. (1994). *A Sequential Algorithm for Training Text Classifiers.* In Proceedings of SIGIR-94, 17th ACM International Conference on Research and Development in Information Retrieval. W. B. Croft and C. J. v. Rijsbergen, eds. Dublin, Springer-Verlag, Heidelberg: 3–12.

Lewis, D. D., and Hayes, P. J. (1994). "Guest Editors' Introduction to the Special Issue on Text Categorization." *ACM Transactions on Information Systems* **12**(3): 231.

Lewis, D. D., Li, F., Rose, T., and Yang, Y. (2003). "Reuters Corpus Volume I as a Text Categorization Test Collection." *Journal of Machine Learning Research* **5**: 361–391.

Lewis, D. D., and Ringuette, M. (1994). *A Comparison of Two Learning Algorithms for Text Categorization.* In Proceedings of SDAIR-94, 3rd Annual Symposium on Document Analysis and Information Retrieval. Las Vegas, NV, IRSI, University of Nevada, Las Vegas: 81–93.

Lewis, D. D., Schapire, R. E., Callan, J. P., and Papka, R. (1996). *Training Algorithms for Linear Text Classifiers.* In Proceedings of SIGIR-96, 19th ACM International Conference on Research and Development in Information Retrieval. Zurich, ACM Press, New York: 298–306.

Lewis, D. D., Stern, D. L., and Singhal, A. (1999). *Attics: A Software Platform for On-line Text Classification.* In Proceedings of SIGIR-99, 22nd ACM International Conference on Research and Development in Information Retrieval. M. A. Wearst, F. Gey, and R. Tong, eds. Berkeley, CA, ACM Press, New York: 267–268.

Li, C., Wen, J.-R., and Li, H. (2003). *Text Classification Using Stochastic Keyword Generation.* In Proceedings of ICML-03, 20th International Conference on Machine Learning. Washington, DC, Morgan Kaufmann Publishers, San Francisco: 469–471.

Li, F., and Yang, Y. (2003). *A Loss Function Analysis for Classification Methods in Text Categorization.* In Proceedings of ICML-03, 20th International Conference on Machine Learning. Washington, DC, Morgan Kaufmann Publishers, San Francisco: 472–479.

Li, H., and Yamanishi, K. (1997). *Document Classification Using a Finite Mixture Model.* In Proceedings of ACL-97, 35th Annual Meeting of the Association for Computational Linguistics. P. Cohen and W. Wahlster, eds. Madrid, Morgan Kaufmann Publishers, San Francisco: 39–47.

Li, H., and Yamanishi, K. (1999). *Text Classification Using ESC-Based Stochastic Decision Lists.* In Proceedings of CIKM-99, 8th ACM International Conference on Information and Knowledge Management. Kansas City, MO, ACM Press, New York: 122–130.

Li, H., and Yamanishi, K. (2002). "Text Classification Using ESC-based Stochastic Decision Lists." *Information Processing and Management* **38**(3): 343–361.

Li, W., Lee, B., Krausz, F., and Sahin, K. (1991). *Text Classification by a Neural Network*. In Proceedings of the 23rd Annual Summer Computer Simulation Conference. D. Pace, ed. Baltimore, Society for Computer Simulation, San Diego, CA: 313–318.

Li, X., and Roth, D. (2002). *Learning Question Classifiers*. In Proceedings of COLING-02, 19th International Conference on Computational Linguistics. Taipei, Taiwan, Morgan Kaufmann Publishers, San Francisco: 556–562.

Li, Y. H., and Jain, A. K. (1998). "Classification of Text Documents." *The Computer Journal* **41**(8): 537–546.

Liang, J., Phillips, I., Ha, J., and Haralick, R. (1996). *Document Zone Classification Using the Sizes of Connected Components*. In Proceedings of Document Recognition III. San Jose, CA, SPIE, Bellingham, WA: 150–157.

Liang, J., Phillips, I., and Haralick, R. (1997). *Performance Evaluation of Document Layout Analysis on the UW Data Set*. In Proceedings of Document Recognition IV. San Jose, CA, SPIE, Bellingham, WA: 149–160.

Liao, Y., and Vemuri, V. R. (2002). *Using Text Categorization Techniques for Intrusion Detection*. In Proceedings of the 11th USENIX Security Symposium. D. Boneh, ed. San Francisco: 51–59.

Liddy, E. D., Paik, W., and Yu, E. S. (1994). "Text Categorization for Multiple Users Based on Semantic Features from a Machine-Readable Dictionary." *ACM Transactions on Information Systems* **12**(3): 278–295.

Liere, R., and Tadepalli, P. (1997). *Active Learning with Committees for Text Categorization*. In Proceedings of AAAI-97, 14th Conference of the American Association for Artificial Intelligence. Providence, RI, AAAI Press, Menlo Park, CA: 591–596.

Liere, R., and Tadepalli, P. (1998). *Active Learning with Committees: Preliminary Results in Comparing Winnow and Perceptron in Text Categorization*. In Proceedings of CONALD-98, 1st Conference on Automated Learning and Discovery. Pittsburgh, PA, AAAI Press, Menlo Park, CA.

Lim, J. H. (1999). *Learnable Visual Keywords for Image Classification*. In Proceedings of DL-99, 4th ACM Conference on Digital Libraries. E. A. Fox and N. Rowe, eds. Berkeley, CA, ACM Press, New York: 139–145.

Lima, L. R. D., Laender, A. H., and Ribeiro-Neto, B. A. (1998). A Hierarchical Approach to the Automatic Categorization of Medical Documents. In Proceedings of CIKM-98, 7th ACM International Conference on Information and Knowledge Management. G. Gardarin, G. J. French, N. Pissinou, K. Makki, and L. Bouganim, eds. Bethesda, MD, ACM Press, New York: 132–139.

Lin, D. (1995). "A Dependency-based Method for Evaluating Broad-Coverage Parsers." *Natural Language Engineering* **4**(2): 97–114.

Lin, X. (1992). *Visualization for the Document Space*. In Proceedings of Visualization '92. Los Alamitos, CA, Center for Computer Legal Research, Pace University/IEEE Computer Society Press, Piscataway, NJ: 274–281.

Lin, X. (1997). "Map Displays for Information Retrieval." *Journal of the American Society for Information Science* **48**: 40–54.

Lin, X., Soergel, D., and Marchionini, G. (1991). *A Self-Organizing Semantic Map for Information Retrieval*. In Proceedings of 14th Annual International ACM/SIGIR Conference on Research & Development in Information Retrieval. Chicago, ACM Press, New York: 262–269.

Litman, D. J., and Passonneau, R. J. (1995). *Combining Multiple Knowledge Sources for Discourse Segmentation*. In Proceedings of the 33rd Annual Meeting of the Association for Computational Linguistics. Cambridge, MA, Association for Computational Linguistics, Morristown, NJ: 108–115.

Liu, H., Selker, T., and Lieberman, H. (2003). *Visualizing the Affective Structure of a Text Document.* In Proceedings of the Conference on Human Factors in Computing Systems (CHI 2003). Fort Lauderdale, FL, ACM Press, New York: 740–741.

Liu, X., and Croft, W. B. (2003). "Statistical Language Modeling for Information Retrieval." *Annual Review of Information Science and Technology* **39**.

Liu, Y., Carbonell, J., and Jin, R. (2003). *A New Pairwise Ensemble Approach for Text Classification.* In Proceedings of ECML-03, 14th European Conference on Machine Learning. N. Lavrac, D. Gamberger, L. Todorovski, and H. Blockeel, eds. Cavtat-Dubrovnik, Croatia, Springer-Verlag, Heidelberg: 277–288.

Liu, Y., Yang, Y., and Carbonell, J. (2002). *Boosting to Correct the Inductive Bias for Text Classification.* In Proceedings of CIKM-02, 11th ACM International Conference on Information and Knowledge Management. McLean, VA, ACM Press, New York: 348–355.

Lodhi, H., Saunders, C., Shawe-Taylor, J., Cristianini, N., and Watkins, C. (2002). "Text Classification Using String Kernels." *Journal of Machine Learning Research* **2**: 419–444.

Lodhi, H., Shawe-Taylor, J., Cristianini, N., and Watkins, C. J. (2001). "Discrete Kernels for Text Categorisation." In *Advances in Neural Information Processing Systems.* T. K. Leen, T. Ditterich, and V. Tresp, eds. Cambridge, MA, MIT Press: 563–569.

Lombardo, V. (1991). *Parsing Dependency Grammars.* In Proceedings of the 2nd Congress of the Italian Association for Artificial Intelligence on Trends in Artificial Intelligence. E. Ardizzone, S. Gaglio, and F. Sorbello, eds. Springer-Verlag, London: 291–300.

Lorrain, F., and White, H. C. (1971). "Structural Equivalence of Individuals in Social Networks." *Journal of Mathematical Sociology* **1**: 49–80.

Lu, S. Y., and Fu, K. S. (1978). "A Sentence-to-Sentence Clustering Procedure for Pattern Analysis." *IEEE Translations on Systems, Man and Cybernetics.* **8**: 381–389.

Di., Nunzio, G. M., and Micarelli, A. (2003). *Does a New Simple Gaussian Weighting Approach Perform Well in Text Categorization?* In Proceedings of IJCAI-03, 18th International Joint Conference on Artificial Intelligence. Acapulco, Morgan Kaufmann Publishers, San Francisco: 581–586.

Macskassy, S. A., Hirsh, H., Banerjee, A., and Dayanik, A. A. (2001).*Using Text Classifiers for Numerical Classification.* In Proceedings of IJCAI-01, 17th International Joint Conference on Artificial Intelligence. B. Nebel, ed. Seattle, Morgan Kaufmann Publishers, San Francisco: 885–890.

Macskassy, S. A., Hirsh, H., Banerjee, A., and Dayanik, A. A. (2003). "Converting Numerical Classification into Text Classification." *Artificial Intelligence* **143**(1): 51–77.

Maderlechner, G., Suda, P., and Bruckner, T. (1997). "Classification of Documents by Form and Content." *Pattern Recognition Letters* **18**(11/13): 1225–1231.

Maedche, A., and Staab, S. (2001). "Learning Ontologies for the Semantic Web." *IEEE Intelligent Systems* **16**(2), Special Issue on the Semantic Web.

Maltese, G., and Mancini, F. (1991). *A Technique to Automatically Assign Parts-of-Speech to Words Taking into Account Word-Ending Information through a Probabilistic Model.* In Proceedings of Eurospeech 1991. Genoa, Italy, Genovalle Institute fuer Kommunikations Forschung und Phonetick, Bonn, Germany: 753–756.

Manevitz, L. M., and Yousef, M. (2001). "One-Class SVMs for Document Classification." *Journal of Machine Learning Research* **2**: 139–154.

Mannila, H., and Toivonen, H. (1996). *On an Algorithm for Finding All Interesting Sentences.* In Proceedings of the 13th European Meeting on Cybernetics and Systems Research. R. Trappl, ed. Vienna, Austria, University of Helsinki, Department of Computer Science: 973–978.

Mannila, H., Toivonen, H., and Verkamo, A. (1994). *Efficient Algorithms for Discovering Association Rules.* In Proceedings of Knowledge Discovery in Databases, AAAI Workshop (KDD'94). U. M. Eayyad and R. Uthurusamy, eds. Seattle, AAAI Press, Menlo Park, CA: 181–192.

Mannila, H., Toivonen, H., and Verkamo, A. (1995). *Discovering Frequent Episodes in Sequences*. In Proceedings of the 1st International Conference of Knowledge Discovery and Data Mining. Montreal, AAAI Press, Menlo Park, CA: 210–215.

Mannila, H., Toivonen, H., and Verkamo, A. (1997). "Discovery of Frequent Episodes in Event Sequences." *Data Mining and Knowledge Discovery* **1**(3): 259–289.

Manning, C., and Schutze, H. (1999). *Foundations of Statistical Natural Language Processing*. Cambridge, MA, MIT Press.

Marchionini, G. (1995). *Information Seeking in Electronic Environments*. Cambridge, UK, Cambridge University Press.

Marcus, M. P., Santorini, B., and Marcinkiewicz, M. A. (1994). "Building a Large Annotated Corpus of English: The Penn Treebank." *Computational Linguistics* **19**(2): 313–330.

Maron, M. E. (1961). "Automatic Indexing: An Experimental Inquiry." *Journal of the Association for Computing Machinery* **8**(3): 404–417.

Martin, P. (1995). *Using the WordNet Concept Catalog and a Relation Hierarchy for Knowledge Acquisition*. In Proceedings of Peirce'95, 4th International Workshop on Peirce. E. Ellis and R. Levinson, eds. Santa Cruz, CA, University of Maryland, MD: 36–47.

Masand, B. (1994). Optimising Confidence of Text Classification by Evolution of Symbolic Expressions. In *Advances in Genetic Programming*. K. E. Kinnear, ed. Cambridge, MA, MIT Press: 459–476.

Masand, B., Linoff, G., and Waltz, D. (1992). *Classifying News Stories Using Memory-Based Reasoning*. In Proceedings of SIGIR-92, 15th ACM International Conference on Research and Development in Information Retrieval. N. Belkin, P. Ingwersen, and A. M. Pejtersen, eds. Copenhagen, Denmark, ACM Press, New York: 59–65.

Masui, T., Minakuchi, M., Borden, G., and Kashiwagi, K. (1995). *Multiple-View Approach for Smooth Information Retrieval*. In Proceedings of the ACM Symposium on User Interface Software and Technology (UIST'95). G. Robertson, ed. Pittsburgh, ACM Press, New York: 199–206.

Matsuda, K., and Fukushima, T. (1999). *Task-Oriented World Wide Web Retrieval by Document-Type Classification*.In Proceedings of CIKM-99, 8th ACM International Conference on Information and Knowledge Management. S. Gruch, ed. Kansas City, MO, ACM Press, New York: 109–113.

McCallum, A., Freitag, D., and Pereira, F. (2000). *Maximum Entropy Markov Models for Information Extraction and Segmentation*. In Proceedings of the 17th International Conference on Machine Learning. Stanford University, Palo Alto, CA, Morgan Kaufmann Publishers, San Francisco: 591–598.

McCallum, A., and Jensen, D. (2003). *A Note on the Unification of Information Extraction and Data Mining Using Conditional-Probability, Relational Models*. In Proceedings of IJCAI03 Workshop on Learning Statistical Models from Relational Data. D. Jensen and L. Getoo, eds. Acapulco, Mexico, published electronically by IJCAI and AAAI: 79–87.

McCallum, A. K., and Nigam, K. (1998). *Employing EM in Pool-Based Active Learning for Text Classification*. In Proceedings of ICML-98, 15th International Conference on Machine Learning. J. W. Shavlik, ed. Madison, WI, Morgan Kaufmann Publishers, San Francisco: 350–358.

McCallum, A. K., Rosenfeld, R., Mitchell, T. M., and Ng, A. Y. (1998). *Improving Text Classification by Shrinkage in a Hierarchy of Classes*. In Proceedings of ICML-98, 15th International Conference on Machine Learning. J. W. Shavlik, ed. Madison, WI, Morgan Kaufmann Publishers, San Francisco: 359–367.

McCarthy, J. F., and Lehnert, W. G. (1995). *Using Decision Trees for Coreference Resolution*. In Proceedings of the 14th International Joint Conference on Artificial Intelligence (IJCAI-95). C. Mellish, ed. Montreal, Morgan Kaufmann Publishers, San Francisco: 1050–1055.

Melancon, G., and Herman, I. (2000). *DAG Drawing from an Information Visualization Perspective.* In Proceedings of Data Visualization '00, Amsterdam, Springer-Verlag, Heidelberg: 3–12.

Meretakis, D., Fragoudis, D., Lu, H., and Likothanassis, S. (2000). *Scalable Association-Based Text Classification.* In Proceedings of CIKM-00, 9th ACM International Conference on Information and Knowledge Management. A. Agoh, J. Callan, S. Gauch, and E. Rundensteiner, eds. McLean, VA, ACM Press, New York: 373–374.

Merialdo, B. (1994). "Tagging English text with a Probabilistic Model." *Computational Linguistics* **20**(2): 155–172.

Merkl, D. (1998). "Text Classification with Self-Organizing Maps: Some Lessons Learned." *Neurocomputing* **21**(1/3): 61–77.

Miller, D., Schwartz, R., Weischedel, R., and Stone, R. (1999). *Named Entity Extraction from Broadcast News.* In Proceedings of DARPA Broadcast News Workshop. Herndon, VA, Morgan Kaufmann Publishers, San Francisco: 37–40.

Miller, N., Wong, P. C., Brewster, M., and Foote, H. (1998). *TOPIC ISLANDS(TM): A Wavelet-Based Text Visualization System.* In Proceedings of IEEE Visualization '98. Research Triangle Park, NC, ACM Press, New York: 189–196.

Mitkov, R. (1998). *Robust Pronoun Resolution with Limited Knowledge.* In Proceedings of the 39th Annual Meeting on Association for Computational Linguistics. Montreal, Canada, Association for Computational Linguistics, Morristown, NJ: 869–875.

Mladenic, D. (1998a). *Feature Subset Selection in Text Learning.* In Proceedings of ECML-98, 10th European Conference on Machine Learning. C. Nedellec and C. Rouveirol, eds. Chemnitz, Germany, Springer-Verlag, London: 95–100.

Mladenic, D. (1998b). *Machine Learning on Non-homogeneous, Distributed Text Data.* Ph.D. thesis, J. Stefan Institute, University of Ljubljana.

Mladenic, D. (1998c). *Turning Yahoo! into an Automatic Web Page Classifier.* In Proceedings of ECAI-98, 13th European Conference on Artificial Intelligence. H. Prade, ed. Brighton, UK, John Wiley and Sons, Chichester, UK: 473–474.

Mladenic, D. (1999). "Text Learning and Related Intelligent Agents: A Survey." *IEEE Intelligent Systems* **14**(4): 44–54.

Mladenic, D., and Grobelnik, M. (1998). *Word Sequences as Features in Text-Learning.* In Proceedings of ERK-98, 7th Electrotechnical and Computer Science Conference. Ljubljana, Slovenia: 145–148.

Mladenic, D., and Grobelnik, M. (1999). *Feature Selection for Unbalanced Class Distribution and Naive Bayes.* In Proceedings of ICML-99, 16th International Conference on Machine Learning. I. Bratko and S. Dzeroski, eds. Bled, Slovenia, Morgan Kaufmann Publishers, San Francisco: 258–267.

Mladenic, D., and Grobelnik, M. (2003). "Feature Selection on Hierarchy of Web Documents." *Decision Support Systems* **35**(1): 45–87.

Mock, K. (1998). *A Comparison of Three Document Clustering Algorithms: TreeCluster, Word Intersection GQF, and Word Intersection Hierarchical Agglomerative Clustering.* Technical Report, Intel Architecture Labs.

Moens, M.-F., and Dumortier, J. (2000). "Text Categorization: The Assignment of Subject Descriptors to Magazine Articles." *Information Processing and Management* **36**(6): 841–861.

Montes-y-Gomez, M., Gelbukh, A., and Lopez-Lopez, A. (2001a). *Discovering Association Rules in Semi-Structured Data Sets.* In Proceedings of the Workshop on Knowledge Discovery from Distributed, Dynamic, Heterogeneous, Autonomous Data and Knowledge Source at 17th International Joint Conference on Artificial Intelligence (IJCAI'2001). Seattle, AAAI Press, Menlo Park, CA: 26–31.

Montes-y-Gomez, M., Gelbukh, A., and Lopez-Lopez, A. (2001b). "Mining the News: Trends, Associations and Deviations." *Computaĉión y Sistemas* **5**(1): 14–25.

Mooney, R. J., and Roy, L. (2000). *Content-Based Book Recommending Using Learning for Text Categorization*. Proceedings of DL-00, 5th ACM Conference on Digital Libraries. San Antonio, TX, ACM Press, New York: 195–204.

Moschitti, A. (2003). *A Study on Optimal Parameter Tuning for Rocchio Text Classifier*. In Proceedings of ECIR-03, 25th European Conference on Information Retrieval. F. Sebastiani, ed. Pisa, Italy, Springer-Verlag, Heidelberg: 420–435.

Mostafa, J., and Lam, W. (2000). "Automatic Classification Using Supervised Learning in a Medical Document Filtering Application." *Information Processing and Management* **36**(3): 415–444.

Moulinier, I. (1997). *Feature Selection: A Useful Preprocessing Step*. In Proceedings of BCSIRSG-97, 19th Annual Colloquium of the British Computer Society Information Retrieval Specialist Group. J. Furner and D. Harper, eds. Aberdeen, UK, Springer-Verlag, Heidelberg, Germany: 1–11.

Moulinier, I., and Ganascia, J.-G. (1996). "Applying an Existing Machine Learning Algorithm to Text Categorization." In *Connectionist, Statistical, and Symbolic Approaches to Learning for Natural Language Processing*. S. Wermter, E. Riloff, and G. Scheler, eds. Heidelberg, Springer-Verlag: 343–354.

Moulinier, I., Raskinis, G., and Ganascia, J.-G. (1996). *Text Categorization: A Symbolic Approach*. In Proceedings of SDAIR-96, 5th Annual Symposium on Document Analysis and Information Retrieval. Las Vegas, NV, ISRI, University of Nevada, Las Vegas: 87–99.

Munoz, M., Punyakanok, V., Roth, D., and Zimak, D. (1999). *A Learning Approach to Shallow Parsing*. Technical Report 2087, University of Illinois at Urbana-Champaign: 18.

Munzner, T., and Burchard, P. (1995). *Visualizing the Structure of the World Wide Web in 3D Hyperbolic Space*. In Proceedings of VRML '95. San Diego, CA, ACM Press, New York: 33–38.

Mutton, P. (2004). "Inferring and Visualizing Social Networks on Internet Relay Chat." *Journal of WSCG* **12**(1–3).

Mutton, P., and Golbeck, J. (2003). *Visualization of Semantic Metadata and Ontologies*. In Proceedings of Information Visualization 2003 (IV03). London, UK, IEEE Computer Society Press, Washington, DC: 300.

Mutton, P., and Rodgers, P. (2002). *Spring Embedder Preprocessing for WWW Visualization*. In Proceedings of 6th International Conference on Information Visualization. London, IEEE Computer Society Press, Washington, DC: 744–749.

Myers, K., Kearns, M., Singh, S., and Walker, M. A. (2000). *A Boosting Approach to Topic Spotting on Subdialogues*. In Proceedings of ICML-00, 17th International Conference on Machine Learning. P. Langley, ed. Stanford, CA, Morgan Kaufmann Publishers, San Francisco: 655–662.

Nahm, U., and Mooney, R. (2000). *A Mutually Beneficial Integration of Data Mining and Information Extraction*. In Proceedings of the 17th Conference of Artificial Intelligence, AAAI-2000. Austin, TX, AAAI Press, Menlo Park, CA: 627-632.

Nahm, U., and Mooney, R. (2001). *Mining Soft Matching Rules from Text Data*. In Proceedings of the 7th International Joint Conference on Artificial Intelligence. Seattle, WA, Morgan Kaufmann Publishers, San Francisco: 978–992.

Nahm, U. Y., and Mooney, R. J. (2002). *Text Mining with Information Extraction*. In Proceedings of the AAAI 2002 Spring Symposium on Mining Answers from Texts and Knowledge Bases. S. Harabagio and V. Chaudhri, eds. Palo Alto, CA, AAAI Press, Menlo Park, CA: 60–68.

Nardiello, P., Sebastiani F., and Sperduti, A. (2003). *Discretizing Continuous Attributes in AdaBoost for Text Categorization*. In Proceedings of ECIR-03, 25th European Conference on Information Retrieval. F. Sebastiani, ed. Pisa, Italy, Springer-Verlag, Heidelberg: 320–334.

Nasukawa, T., and Nagano, T. (2001). "Text Analysis and Knowledge Mining System." *IBM Systems Journal* **40**(4): 967–984.

Neuhaus, P., and Broker, N. (1997). *The Complexity of Recognition of Linguistically Adequate Dependency Grammars.* In Proceedings of the 35th Annual Meeting of the Association for Computational Linguistics and 8th Conference of the European Chapter of the Association for Computational Linguistics. P. R. Cohen and W. Wahlster, eds. Somerset, NJ, Association for Computational Linguistics: 337–343.

Ng, G. K.-C. (2000). *Interactive Visualisation Techniques for Ontology Development.* Ph.D. thesis, Department of Computer Science, University of Manchester.

Ng, H. T., Goh, W. B., and Low, K. L. (1997). *Feature Selection, Perceptron Learning, and a Usability Case Study for Text Categorization.* In Proceedings of SIGIR-97, 20th ACM International Conference on Research and Development in Information Retrieval. N. J. Belkin, A. Narasimhalu, W. Hersh, and P. Willett, eds. Philadelphia, ACM Press, New York: 67–73.

Ng, V., and Cardie, C. (2002). *Improving Machine Learning Approaches to Coreference Resolution.* In Proceedings of the 40th Annual Meeting of the Association for Computational Linguistics. Philadelphia, Association for Computational Linguistics, Morristown, NJ: 104–111.

Ng, V., and Cardie, C. (2003). *Bootstrapping Coreference Classifiers with Multiple Machine Learning Algorithms.* In Proceedings of the 2003 Conference on Empirical Methods in Natural Language Processing (EMNLP-2003), Sappora, Japan, Association for Computational Linguistics, Morristown, NJ: 113–120.

Nigam, K. (2001). *Using Unlabeled Data to Improve Text Classification.* Ph.D. thesis, Computer Science Department, Carnegie Mellon University.

Nigam, K., and Ghani, R. (2000). *Analyzing the Applicability and Effectiveness of Co-training.* In Proceedings of CIKM-00, 9th ACM International Conference on Information and Knowledge Management. A. Agah, J. Callan, S. Gauch, and E. Rundensteiner, eds. McLean, VA, ACM Press, New York: 86–93.

Nigam, K., McCallum, A. K., Thrun, S., and Mitchell, T. M. (1998). *Learning to Classify Text from Labeled and Unlabeled Documents.* In Proceedings of AAAI-98, 15th Conference of the American Association for Artificial Intelligence. Madison, WI, AAAI Press, Menlo Park, CA: 792–799.

Nigam, K., McCallum, A. K., Thrun, S., and Mitchell, T. M. (2000). "Text Classification from Labeled and Unlabeled Documents Using EM." *Machine Learning* **39**(2/3): 103–134.

Niyogi, D. (1995). *A Knowledge-Based Approach to Deriving Logical Structure from Document Images.* Doctoral dissertation, State University of New York, Buffalo.

Niyogi, D., and Srihari, S. (1996). *Using Domain Knowledge to Derive the Logical Structure of Documents.* In Proceedings of Document Recognition III. SPIE, Bellingham, WA: 114–125.

Noik, E. (1996). *Dynamic Fisheye Views: Combining Dynamic Queries and Mapping with Database View Definition.* Ph.D. thesis, Graduate Department of Computer Science, University of Toronto.

Nong, Y., ed. (2003). *The Handbook of Data Mining.* Boston, Lawrence Erlbaum Associates.

Oh, H.-J., Myaeng, S. H., and Lee, M.-H. (2000). *A Practical Hypertext Categorization Method Using Links and Incrementally Available Class Information.* In Proceedings of SIGIR-00, 23rd ACM International Conference on Research and Development in Information Retrieval. N. Belkin, P. Ingwersen, and M.-K. Leong, eds. Athens, ACM Press, New York: 264–271.

Ontrup, J., and Ritter, H. (2001a). *Hyperbolic Self-Organizing Maps for Semantic Navigation.* In Proceedings of NIPS 2001. T. Dietterich, S. Becker, and Z. Chahramani, eds. Vancouver, MIT Press, Cambridge, MA: 1417–1424.

Ontrup, J., and Ritter, H. (2001b). *Text Categorization and Semantic Browsing with Self-Organizing Maps on Non-Euclidean Spaces.* In Proceedings of PKDD-01, 5th European

Conference on Principles and Practice of Knowledge Discovery in Databases. Freiburg, Germany, Springer-Verlag, Heidelberg: 338–349.

Paijmans, H. (1999). "Text Categorization as an Information Retrieval Task." *The South African Computer Journal.* 31: 4–15.

Paliouras, G., Karkaletsis, V., and Spyropoulos, C. D. (1999). *Learning Rules for Large Vocabulary Word Sense Disambiguation.* In Proceedings of IJCAI-99, 16th International Joint Conference on Artificial Intelligence. T. Dean, ed. Stockholm, Morgan Kaufmann Publishers, San Francisco: 674–679.

Pang, B., Lee, L., and Vaithyanathan, S. (2002). *Thumbs Up? Sentiment Classification Using Machine Learning Techniques.* In Proceedings of EMNLP-02, 7th Conference on Empirical Methods in Natural Language Processing. Philadelphia, Association for Computational Linguistics, Morristown, NJ: 79–86.

Patel-Schneider, P., and Simeon, J. (2002). *Building the Semantic Web on XML.* In Proceedings of the 1st International Semantic Web Conference (ISWC). I. Horrocks and J. Hendler, eds. Sardinia, Italy, Springer-Verlag, Heidelberg, Germany: 147–161.

Pattison, T., Vernik, R., Goodburn, D., and Phillips, M. (2001). *Rapid Assembly and Deployment of Domain Visualisation Solutions.* In Proceedings of Australian Symposium on Information Visualization, ACM International Conference. Sydney, Australian Computer Society, Darlinghurst, Australia: 19–26.

Pedersen, T., and Bruce, R. (1997). *Unsupervised Text Mining.* Dallas, TX, Department of Computer Science and Engineering, Southern Methodist University.

Peng, F., and Schuurmans, D. (2003). *Combining Naive Bayes n-gram and Language Models for Text Classification.* In Proceedings of ECIR-03, 25th European Conference on Information Retrieval. F. Sebastiani, ed. Pisa, Italy, Springer-Verlag, Heidelberg: 335–350.

Peng, F., Schuurmans, D., and Wang, S. (2003). *Language and Task Independent Text Categorization with Simple Language Models.* In Proceedings of HLT-03, 3rd Human Language Technology Conference. Edmonton, CA, ACL Press, Morgan Kaufmann Publishers, San Francisco: 110–117.

Petasis, G., Cucchiarelli, A., Velardi, P., Paliouras, G., Karkaletsis, V., and Spyropoulos, C. D. (2000). *Automatic Adaptation of Proper Noun Dictionaries through Cooperation of Machine Learning and Probabilistic Methods.* In Proceedings of SIGIR-00, 23rd ACM International Conference on Research and Development in Information Retrieval. N. Belkin, Peter Ingwersen, and M.-K. Leong, eds. Athens, ACM Press, New York: 128–135.

Peters, C., and Koster, C. H. (2002). *Uncertainty-Based Noise Reduction and Term Selection in Text Categorization.* In Proceedings of ECIR-02, 24th European Colloquium on Information Retrieval Research. F. Crestani, M. Girolomi, and C. J. v. Rijsbergen, eds. Glasgow, Springer-Verlag, London: 248–267.

Phillips, W., and Riloff, E. (2002). *Exploiting Strong Syntactic Heuristics and Co-Training to Learn Semantic Lexicons.* In Proceedings of the 2002 Conference on Empirical Methods in Natural Language Processing (EMNLP 2002). Philadelphia, Association for Computational Linguistics: 125–132.

Piatetsky-Shapiro, G., and Frawley, W. J., eds. (1991). *Knowledge Discovery in Databases.* Cambridge, MA, MIT Press.

Pierre, J. M. (2002). *Mining Knowledge from Text Collections Using Automatically Generated Metadata.* In Proceedings of the 4th International Conference on Practical Aspects of Knowledge Management (PAKM-02). D. Karagiannis and Reimer, eds. Vienna, Austria, Springer-Verlag, London: 537–548.

Pollard, C., and Sag, I. A. (1994). *Head-Driven Phrase Structure Grammar.* Chicago, University of Chicago Press and CSLI Publications.

Porter, A. (2002). *Text Mining.* Technology Policy and Assessment Center, Georgia Institute of Technology.

Pottenger, W., and Yang, T.-h. (2001). *Detecting Emerging Concepts in Textual Data Mining.* Philadelphia, SIAM.

Punyakanok, V., and Roth, D. (2000). *Shallow Parsing by Inferencing with Classifiers.* In Proceedings of the 4th Conference on Computational Natural Language Learning and of the 2nd Learning Language in Logic Workshop. Lisbon, Association for Computational Linguistics, Somerset, NJ: 107–110.

Pustejovsky, J., Castano, J., Zhang, J., Kotecki, M., and Cochran, B. (2002). *Robust Relational Parsing over Biomedical Literature: Extracting Inhibit Relations.* In Proceedings of the 2002 Pacific Symposium on Biocomputing (PSB-2002). Lihue, Hawaii, World Scientific Press, Hackensack, NJ: 362–373.

Rabiner, L. R. (1986). "An Introduction to Hidden Markov Models." *IEEE ASSP Magazine* **3**(1): 4–16.

Rabiner, L. R. (1990). "A Tutorial on Hidden Markov Models and Selected Applications in Speech Recognition." In *Readings in Speech Recognition.* A. Waibel and K.-F. Lee, eds. Los Altos, CA, Morgan Kaufmann Publishers: 267–296.

Ragas, H., and Koster, C. H. (1998). *Four Text Classification Algorithms Compared on a Dutch Corpus.* In Proceedings of SIGIR-98, 21st ACM International Conference on Research and Development in Information Retrieval. W. B. Croft, A. Moffat, C. J. v. Rijsbergen, R. Wilkinson and J. Zobel, eds. Melbourne,Australia, ACM Press, New York: 369–370.

Rainsford, C., and Roddick, J. (2000). *Visualization of Temporal Interval Association Rules.* In Proceedings of the 2nd International Conference on Intelligent Data Engineering and Automated Learning. Hong Kong, Springer-Verlag, London: 91–96.

Rajman, M., and Besancon, R. (1997a). *A Lattice Based Algorithm for Text Mining.* Technical Report TR-LIA-LN1/97, Swiss Federal Institute of Technology.

Rajman, M., and Besancon, R. (1997b). *Text Mining: Natural Language Techniques and Text Mining Applications.* In Proceedings of the 7th IFIP 2.6 Working Conference on Database Semantics (DS-7). Leysin, Switzerland, Norwell, MA.

Rajman, M., and Besancon, R. (1998). *Text Mining – Knowledge Extraction from Unstructured Textual Data.* In Proceedings of the 6th Conference of the International Federation of Classification Societies. Rome: 473–480.

Rambow, O., and Joshi, A. K. (1994). "A Formal Look at Dependency Grammars and Phrase-Structure Grammars, with Special Consideration of Word-Order Phenomena." In *Current Issues in Meaning-Text Theory.* L. Wanner, ed. London, Pinter.

Rao, R., and Card, S. (1994). *The Table Lens: Merging Graphical and Symbolic Representations in an Interactive Focus + Context Visualization for Tabular Information.* In Proceedings of the International Conference on Computer-Human Interaction '94. Boston, MA, ACM Press, New York: 318–322.

Rao, R., Card, S., Jellinek, H., Mackinlay, J., and Robertson, G. (1992). *The Information Grid: A Framework for Information Retrieval and Retrieval-Centered Applications.* In Proceedings of the 5th Annual Symposium on User Interface Software and Technology (UIST) '92. Monterdy, CA, ACM Press, New York: 23–32.

Raskutti, B., Ferra, H., and Kowalczyk, A. (2001). *Second Order Features for Maximising Text Classification Performance.* In Proceedings of ECML-01, 12th European Conference on Machine Learning. L. D. Raedt and P. A. Flach, eds. Freiburg, Germany, Springer-Verlag, London: 419–430.

Rau, L. F., and Jacobs, P. S. (1991). *Creating Segmented Databases from Free Text for Text Retrieval.* In Proceedings of SIGIR-91, 14th ACM International Conference on Research and Development in Information Retrieval. Chicago, ACM Press, New York: 337–346.

Reape, M. (1989). *A Logical Treatment of Semi-free Word Order and Bounded Discontinuous Constituency.* In Proceedings of the 4th Meeting of the European ACL. Monchester, UK, Association for Computational Linguistics, Morristown, NJ: 103–110.

Rennie, J., and McCallum, A. K. (1999). *Using Reinforcement Learning to Spider the Web Efficiently.* In Proceedings of ICML-99, 16th International Conference on Machine Learning. I. Bratko and S. Dzeroski, eds. Bled, Slovenia, Morgan Kaufmann Publishers, San Francisco: 335–343.

Rennie, J., Shih, L., Teevan, J., and Karger, D. (2003). *Tackling the Poor Assumptions of Naive Bayes Text Classifiers*. In Proceedings of ICML-03, 20th International Conference on Machine Learning. Washington, DC, Morgan Kaufmann Publishers, San Francisco: 616–623.

Reynar, J., and Ratnaparkhi, A. (1997). *A Maximum Entropy Approach to Identifying Sentence Boundaries*. In Proceedings of the 5th Conference on Applied Natural Language Processing. Washington, DC, Morgan Kaufmann Publishers, San Francisco: 16–19.

Ribeiro-Neto, B., Laender, A. H. F., and Lima, L. R. D. (2001). "An Experimental Study in Automatically Categorizing Medical Documents." *Journal of the American Society for Information Science and Technology* **52**(5): 391–401.

Rich, E., and LuperFoy, S. (1988). *An Architecture for Anaphora Resolution.* In ACL Proceedings of the 2nd Conference on Applied Natural Language Processing. Austin, TX, Association for Computational Linguistics, Morristown, NJ: 18–24.

Rijsbergen, C. J. v. (1979). *Information Retrieval*, 2nd ed. London, Butterworths.

Riloff, E. (1993a). *Automatically Constructing a Dictionary for Information Extraction Tasks*. In Proceedings of the 11th National Congress on Artificial Intelligence. Washington, DC, AAAI/MIT Press, Menlo Park, CA: 811–816.

Riloff, E. (1993b). *Using Cases to Represent Context for Text Classification.* In Proceedings of CIKM-93, 2nd International Conference on Information and Knowledge Management. Washington, DC, ACM Press, New York: 105–113.

Riloff, E. (1994). *Information Extraction as a Basis for Portable Text Classification Systems*. Amherst, MA, Department of Computer Science, University of Massachusetts.

Riloff, E. (1995). *Little Words Can Make a Big Difference for Text Classification.* In Proceedings of SIGIR-95, 18th ACM International Conference on Research and Development in Information Retrieval. E. A. Fox, P. Ingwersen, and R. Fidel, eds. Seattle, ACM Press, New York: 130–136.

Riloff, E. (1996a). *Automatically Generating Extraction Patterns from Untagged Text.* In Proceedings of the 13th National Conference on Artificial Intelligence. AAAI/MIT Press, Menlo Park, CA: 1044–1049.

Riloff, E. (1996b). "Using Learned Extraction Patterns for Text Classification." In *Connectionist, Statistical, and Symbolic Approaches to Learning for Natural Language Processing*. S. Wermter, E. Riloff, and G. Scheler, eds. Springer-Verlag, London: 275–289.

Riloff, E., and Jones, R. (1999). *Learning Dictionaries for Information Extraction by Multi-level Boot-Strapping*. In Proceedings of the 16th National Conference on Artificial Intelligence. Orlando, AAAI Press/MIT Press, Menlo Park, CA: 1044–1049.

Riloff, E., and Lehnert, W. (1994). "Information Extraction as a Basis for High-Precision Text Classification." *ACM Transactions on Information Systems,* **12**(3): 296–333.

Riloff, E., and Lehnert, W. (1998). *Classifying Texts Using Relevancy Signatures*. In Proceedings of AAAI-92, 10th Conference of the American Association for Artificial Intelligence. San Jose, CA, AAAI Press, Menlo Park, CA: 329–334.

Riloff, E., and Lorenzen, J. (1999). "Extraction-Based Text Categorization: Generating Domain-Specific Role Relationships." In *Natural Language Information Retrieval.* T. Strzalkowski, ed. Dordrecht, Kluwer Academic Publishers: 167–196.

Riloff, E., and Schmelzenbach, M. (1998). *An Empirical Approach to Conceptual Case Frame Acquisition.* In Proceedings of the 6th Workshop on Very Large Corpora. E. Chemiak, ed. Montreal, Quebec, Association for Computational Linguistics, Morgan Kaufmann Publishers, San Francisco: 49–56.

Riloff, E., and Shoen, J. (1995). *Automatically Acquiring Conceptual Patterns Without an Automated Corpus*. In Proceedings of the 3rd Workshop on Very Large Corpora. Boston, MA, Association for Computational Linguistics, Somerset, NJ: 148–161.

Rindflesch, T. C., Hunter, L., and Aronson, A. R. (1999). *Mining Molecular Binding Terminology from Biomedical Text.* In Proceedings of the '99 AMIA Symposium. Washington, DC, AMIA, Bethesda, MD: 127–131.

Rindflesch, T. C., Tanabe, L., Weinstein, J. N., and Hunter, L. (2000). *EDGAR: Extraction of Drugs, Genes and Relations from the Biomedical Literature.* In Proceedings of the 2000 Pacific Symposium on Biocomputing. Waikiki Beach, Hawaii, World Scientific Press, Hackensack, NJ: 517–528.

Roark, B., and Johnson, M. (1999). *Efficient Probabilistic Top-Down and Left-Corner Parsing.* In Proceedings of the 37th Annual Meeting of the ACL. College Park, MD, Association for Computational Linguistics, Morristown, NJ: 421–428.

Robertson, G., Mackinlay, J., and Card, S. (1991). *Cone Trees: Animated 3D Visualizations of Hierarchical Information.* In Proceedings of the ACM SIGCHI Conference on Human Factors in Computing Systems. New Orleans, ACM Press, New York: 189–194.

Robertson, S. E., and Harding, P. (1984). "Probabilistic Automatic Indexing by Learning from Human Indexers." *Journal of Documentation* **40**(4): 264–270.

Rodriguez, M. D. B., Gomez-Hidalgo, J. M., and Diaz-Agudo, B. (1997). *Using WordNet to Complement Training Information in Text Categorization.* In Proceedings of RANLP-97, 2nd International Conference on Recent Advances in Natural Language Processing. R. Mitkov and N. Nikolov, eds. Tzigov Chark, Bulgaria, John Benjamins, Philadelphia: 353–364.

Rokita, P. (1996). "Generating Depth-of-Field Effects in Virtual Reality Applications." *IEEE Computer Graphics and Applications* **16**(2): 18–21.

Rose, T., Stevenson, M., and Whitehead, M. (2002). *The Reuters Corpus Volume 1 – From Yesterday's News to Tomorrow's Language Resources.* In Proceedings of LREC-02, 3rd International Conference on Language Resources and Evaluation. Las Palmas, Spain, ELRA, Paris: 827–832.

Rosenfeld, B., Feldman, R., Fresko, M., Schler, J., and Aumann, Y. (2004). *TEG: A Hybrid Approach to Information Extraction.* In Proceedings of CIKM 2004. Arlington, VA, ACM Press, New York: 589–596.

Roth, D. (1998). *Learning to Resolve Natural Language Ambiguities: A Unified Approach.* In Proceedings of AAAI-98, 15th Conference of the American Association for Artificial Intelligence. Madison, WI, AAAI Press, Menlo Park, CA: 806–813.

Ruiz, M., and Srinivasan, P. (2002). "Hierarchical Text Classification Using Neural Networks." *Information Retrieval* **5**(1): 87–118.

Ruiz, M. E., and Srinivasan, P. (1997). *Automatic Text Categorization Using Neural Networks.* In Proceedings of the 8th ASIS/SIGCR Workshop on Classification Research. E. Efthimiadis, ed. Washington, DC, American Society for Information Science, Washington, DC: 59–72.

Ruiz, M. E., and Srinivasan, P. (1999a). *Combining Machine Learning and Hierarchical Indexing Structures for Text Categorization.* In Proceedings of the 10th ASIS/SIGCR Workshop on Classification Research. Washington, DC, American Society for Information Science, Washington, DC.

Ruiz, M. E., and Srinivasan, P. (1999b). *Hierarchical Neural Networks for Text Categorization.* In Proceedings of SIGIR-99, 22nd ACM International Conference on Research and Development in Information Retrieval. M. A. Hearst, F. Gey, and R. Tong, eds. Berkeley, CA, ACM Press, New York: 281–282.

Rzhetsky, A., Iossifov, I., Koike, T., Krauthammer, M., Kra, P., Morris, M., Yu, H., Duboue, P. A., Weng, W., Wilbur, J. W., Hatzivassiloglou, V., and Friedman, C. (2004). "GeneWays: A System for Extracting, Analyzing, Visualizing, and Integrating Molecular Pathway Data." *Journal of Biomedical Informatics* **37**: 43–53.

Rzhetsky, A., Koike, T., Kalachikov, S., Gomez, S. M., Krauthammer, M., Kaplan, S. H., Kra, P., Russo, J. J., and Friedman, C. (2000). "A Knowledge Model for Analysis and Simulation of Regulatory Networks." *Bionformatics* **16**: 1120–1128.

Sabidussi, G. (1966). "The Centrality Index of a Graph." *Psychometrika* **31**: 581–603.

Sable, C., and Church, K. (2001). *Using Bins to Empirically Estimate Term Weights for Text Categorization.* In Proceedings of EMNLP-01, 6th Conference on Empirical Methods in Natural Language Processing. Pittsburgh, Association for Computational Linguistics, Morristown, NJ: 58–66.

Sable, C. L., and Hatzivassiloglou, V. (1999). *Text-Based Approaches for the Categorization of Images*. In Proceedings of ECDL-99, 3rd European Conference on Research and Advanced Technology for Digital Libraries. S. Abitebout and A.-M. Vercoustre, eds. Paris, Springer-Verlag, Heidelberg: 19–38.

Sable, C. L., and Hatzivassiloglou, V. (2000). "Text-Based Approaches for Non-topical Image Categorization." *International Journal of Digital Libraries* **3**(3): 261–275.

Sahami, M., ed. (1998). *Learning for Text Categorization*. Papers from the 1998 AAAI Workshop. Madison, WI, AAAI Press, Menlo Park, CA.

Sahami, M., Hearst, M. A., and Saund, E. (1996). *Applying the Multiple Cause Mixture Model to Text Categorization*. In Proceedings of ICML-96, 13th International Conference on Machine Learning. L. Saitta, ed. Bari, Italy, Morgan Kaufmann Publishers, San Francisco: 435–443.

Sahami, M., Yusufali, S., and Baldonado, M. Q. (1998). *SONIA: A Service for Organizing Networked Information Autonomously*. In Proceedings of DL-98, 3rd ACM Conference on Digital Libraries. I. Witten, R. Aksyn, and F. M. Shipman, eds. Pittsburgh, ACM Press, New York: 200–209.

Sakakibara, Y., Misue, K., and Koshiba, T. (1996). "A Machine Learning Approach to Knowledge Acquisitions from Text Databases." *International Journal of Human Computer Interaction* **8**(3): 309–324.

Sakkis, G., Androutsopoulos, I., Paliouras, G., Karkaletsis, V., Spyropoulos, C. D., and Stamatopoulos, P. (2001). *Stacking Classifiers for Anti-Spam Filtering of E-Mail*. In Proceedings of EMNLP-01, 6th Conference on Empirical Methods in Natural Language Processing. Pittsburgh, Association for Computational Linguistics, Morristown, NJ: 44–50.

Sakkis, G., Androutsopoulos, I., Paliouras, G., Karkaletsis, V., Spyropoulos, C. D., and Stamatopoulos, P. (2003). "A Memory-Based Approach to Anti-Spam Filtering for Mailing Lists." *Information Retrieval* **6**(1): 49–73.

Salamonsen, W., Mok, K., Kolatkar, P., and Subbiah, S. (1999). *BioJAKE: A Tool for the Creation, Visualization and Manipulation of Metabolic Pathways*. In Proceedings of the Pacific Symposium on Biocomputing. Hawaii, World Scientific Press, Hackensack NJ: 392–400.

Salton, G. (1989). *Automatic Text Processing*. Reading, MA, Addison-Wesley.

Sanchez, S. N., Triantaphyllou, E., and Kraft, D. (2002). "A Feature Mining Based Approach for the Classification of Text Documents into Disjoint Classes." *Information Processing and Management* **38**(4): 583–604.

Sarkar, M., and Brown, M. (1992). *Graphical Fisheye Views of Graphs*. In Proceedings of the ACM SIGCHI '92 Conference on Human Factors in Computing Systems. Monterey, CA, ACM Press, New York: 83–91.

Sasaki, M., and Kita, K. (1998). *Automatic Text Categorization Based on Hierarchical Rules*. In Proceedings of the 5th International Conference on Soft Computing and Information. Iizuka, Japan, World Scientific, Singapore: 935–938.

Sasaki, M., and Kita, K. (1998). *Rule-Based Text Categorization Using Hierarchical Categories*. In Proceedings of SMC-98, IEEE International Conference on Systems, Man, and Cybernetics. La Jolla, CA, IEEE Computer Society Press, Los Alamitos, CA: 2827–2830.

Schapire, R. E., and Singer, Y. (2000). "BoosTexter: A Boosting-Based System for Text Categorization." *Machine Learning* **39**(2/3): 135–168.

Schapire, R. E., Singer, Y., and Singhal, A. (1998). *Boosting and Rocchio Applied to Text Filtering*. In Proceedings of SIGIR-98, 21st ACM International Conference on Research and Development in Information Retrieval. W. S. Croft, A. Moffat, C. J. v. Rijsbergen, R. Wilkinson, and J. Zobel, eds. Melbourne, Australia, ACM Press, New York: 215–223.

Scheffer, T., and Joachims, T. (1999). *Expected Error Analysis for Model Selection*. In Proceedings of ICML-99, 16th International Conference on Machine Learning. I. Bratko and S. Dzeroski, eds. Bled, Slovenia, Morgan Kaufmann Publishers, San Francisco: 361–370.

Schneider, K.-M. (2003). *A Comparison of Event Models for Naive Bayes Anti-Spam E-Mail Filtering*. In Proceedings of EACL-03, 11th Conference of the European Chapter of the

Association for Computational Linguistics. Budapest, Hungary, Association for Computational Linguistics, Morristown, NJ: 307–314.

Schutze, H. (1993). *Part-of-Speech Induction from Scratch*. In Proceedings of the 31st Annual Meeting of the Association for Computational Linguistics. Columbus, OH, Association for Computational Linguistics, Morristown, NJ: 251–258.

Schutze, H. (1998). "Automatic Word Sense Discrimination." *Computational Linguistics* **24**(1): 97–124.

Schutze, H., Hull, D. A., and Pedersen, J. O. (1995). *A Comparison of Classifiers and Document Representations for the Routing Problem*. In Proceedings of SIGIR-95, 18th ACM International Conference on Research and Development in Information Retrieval. E. A. Fox, P. Ingwersen, and R. Fidel, eds. Seattle, ACM Press, New York: 229–237.

Scott, J. (2000). *Social Network Analysis: A Handbook*. London, Sage Publications.

Scott, S. (1998). *Feature Engineering for a Symbolic Approach to Text Classification*. Master's thesis, Computer Science Department, University of Ottawa.

Scott, S., and Matwin, S. (1999). *Feature Engineering for Text Classification*. In Proceedings of ICML-99, 16th International Conference on Machine Learning. I. Bratko and S. Dzeroski, eds. Bled, Slovenia, Morgan Kaufmann Publishers, San Francisco: 379–388.

Sebastiani, F. (1999). *A Tutorial on Automated Text Categorisation*. In Proceedings of ASAI-99, 1st Argentinian Symposium on Artificial Intelligence. A. Anandi and R. Zunino, eds. Buenos Aires: 7–35.

Sebastiani, F. (2002). "Machine Learning in Automated Text Categorization." *ACM Computing Surveys* **34**(1): 1–47.

Sebastiani, F., Sperduti, A., and Valdambrini, N. (2000). *An Improved Boosting Algorithm and Its Application to Automated Text Categorization*. In Proceedings of CIKM-00, 9th ACM International Conference on Information and Knowledge Management. A. Ayah, J. Callan, and E. Rundensteiner, eds. McLean, VA, ACM Press, New York: 78–85.

Seidman, S. B. (1983). "Network Structure and Minimum Degree." *Social Networks* **5**: 269–287.

Seymore, K., McCallum, A., and Rosenfeld, R. (1999). *Learning Hidden Markov Model Structure for Information Extraction*. In AAAI 99 Workshop on Machine Learning for Information Extraction. Orlando, FL, AAAI Press, Menlo Park, CA: 37–42.

Sha, F., and Pereira, F. (2003). *Shallow Parsing with Conditional Random Fields*. In Technical Report C15 TR MS-C15-02-35, University of Pennsylvania.

Shin, C., Doermann, D., and Rosenfeld, A. (2001). "Classification of Document Pages Using Structure-Based Features." *International Journal on Document Analysis and Recognition* **3**(4): 232–247.

Shneiderman, B. (1996). *The Eyes Have It: A Task by Data Type Taxonomy for Information Visualizations.* In Proceedings of the 1996 IEEE Conference on Visual Languages. Boulder, CO, IEEE Computer Society Press, Washington, DC: 336–343.

Shneiderman, B. (1997). *Designing the User Interface: Strategies for Effective Human–Computer Interaction*. Reading, MA, Addison-Wesley.

Shneiderman, B., Byrd, D., and Croft, W. B. (1998). "Sorting Out Searching: A User Interface Framework for Text Searches." *Communications of the ACM* **41**(4): 95–98.

Sigletos, G., Paliouras, G., and Karkaletsis, V. (2002). *Role Identification from Free Text Using Hidden Markov Models.* In Proceedings of the 2nd Hellenic Conference on AI: Methods and Applications of Artificial Intelligence. I. P. Vlahavas and C. D. Spyropoulos, eds. Thessaloniki, Greece, Springer-Verlag, London: 167–178.

Silberschatz, A., and Tuzhilin, A. (1996). "What Makes Patterns Interesting in Knowledge Discovery Systems." *IEEE Transactions on Knowledge and Data Engineering* **8**(6): 970–974.

Silverstein, C., Brin, S., and Motwani, R. (1999). "Beyond Market Baskets: Generalizing Association Rules to Dependence Rules." *Data Mining and Knowledge Discovery* **2**(1): 39–68.

Siolas, G., and d'Alche-Buc, F. (2000). *Support Vector Machines Based on a Semantic Kernel for Text Categorization*. In Proceedings of IJCNN-00, 11th International Joint Conference on Neural Networks. Como, Italy, IEEE Computer Society Press, Los Alamitos, CA: 205–209.

Skarmeta, A. G., Bensaid, A., and Tazi, N. (2000). "Data Mining for Text Categorization with Semi-supervised Agglomerative Hierarchical Clustering." *International Journal of Intelligent Systems* **15**(7): 633–646.

Slattery, S., and Craven, M. (1998). *Combining Statistical and Relational Methods for Learning in Hypertext Domains*. In Proceedings of ILP-98, 8th International Conference on Inductive Logic Programming. D. Page, ed. Madison, WI, Springer-Verlag, Heidelberg: 38–52.

Slattery, S., and Craven, M. (2000). *Discovering Test Set Regularities in Relational Domains*. In Proceedings of ICML-00, 17th International Conference on Machine Learning. P. Langley, ed. Stanford, CA, Morgan Kaufmann Publishers, San Francisco: 895–902.

Slonim, N., and Tishby, N. (2001). *The Power of Word Clusters for Text Classification*. In Proceedings of ECIR-01, 23rd European Colloquium on Information Retrieval Research. Darmstadt, Germany Academic Press, British Computer Society, London.

Smith, D. (2002). *Detecting and Browsing Events in Unstructured Text*. In Proceedings of the 25th Annual ACM SIGIR Conference. Tampere, Finland, ACM Press, New York: 73–80.

Soderland, S. (1999). "Learning Information Extraction Rules for Semi-Structured and Free Text." *Machine Learning* **34**(1–3): 233–272.

Soderland, S., Etzioni, O., Shaked, T., and Weld, D. S. (2004). *The Use of Web-based Statistics to Validate Information Extraction*. In Proceedings of the AAAI-2004 Workshop on Adaptive Text Extraction and Mining (ATEM-2004). San Jose, CA, AAAI Press, Menlo Park, CA: 21–27.

Soderland, S., Fisher, D., Aseltine, J., and Lehnert, W. (1995). *CRYSTAL: Inducing a Conceptual Dictionary*. In Proceedings of the 14th International Joint Conference on Artificial Intelligence. C. Mellish, ed. Montreal, Canada, Morgan Kaufmann Publishers, San Francisco: 1314–1319.

Soh, J. (1998). *A Theory of Document Object Locator Combination*. Doctoral Dissertation, State University of New York of Buffalo.

Sondag, P.-P. (2001). *The Semantic Web Paving the Way to the Knowledge Society*. In Proceedings of the 27th International Conference on Very Large Databases, (VLDB). Rome, Morgan Kaufmann Publishers, San Francisco: 16.

Soon, W. M., Ng, H. T., and Lim, D. C. Y. (2001). "A Machine Learning Approach to Coreference Resolution in Noun Phrases." *Computational Linguistics* **27**(4): 521–544.

Soucy, P., and Mineau, G. W. (2001a). *A Simple Feature Selection Method for Text Classification*. In Proceedings of IJCAI-01, 17th International Joint Conference on Artificial Intelligence. B. Nebel, ed. Seattle, AAAI Press, Menlo Park, CA: 897–902.

Soucy, P., and Mineau, G. W. (2001b). *A Simple KNN Algorithm for Text Categorization*. In Proceedings of ICDM-01, IEEE International Conference on Data Mining. N. Cerone, T. Y. Lin, and X. Wu, eds. San Jose, CA, IEEE Computer Society Press, Los Alamitos, CA: 647–648.

Soucy, P., and Mineau, G. W. (2003). *Feature Selection Strategies for Text Categorization*. In Proceedings of CSCSI-03, 16th Conference of the Canadian Society for Computational Studies of Intelligence. Y. Xiang and B. Chaib-Draa, eds. Halifax: 505–509.

Spence, B. (2001). *Information Visualization*. Harlow, UK, Addison-Wesley.

Spenke, M., and Beilken, C. (1999). *Visual, Interactive Data Mining with InfoZoom – The Financial Data Set*. In Proceedings of the 3rd European Conference on Principles and Practice of Knowledge Discovery in Databases. Prague, Springer Verlag, Berlin.

Spitz, L., and Maghbouleh, A. (2000). *Text Categorization Using Character Shape Codes*. In Proceedings of the 7th SPIE Conference on Document Recognition and Retrieval. San Jose, CA, SPIE, The International Society for Optical Engineering, Bellingham, WA: 174–181.

Spoerri, A. (1999). "InfoCrystal: A Visual Tool for Information Retrieval." In *Readings in Information Visualization: Using Vision to Think.* S. Card, J. Mackinlay, and B. Shneiderman, eds. San Francisco, Morgan Kaufmann Publishers: 140–147.

Srikant, R., and Agrawal, R. (1995). *Mining Generalized Association Rules.* In Proceedings of the 21st International Conference on Very Large Databases. U. Dayal, P. Gray, and S. Nishio, eds. Zurich, Switzerland, Morgan Kaufmann Publishers, San Francisco, CA: 407–419.

Srikant, R., and Agrawal, R. (1996). *Mining Sequential Patterns: Generalizations and Performance Improvements.* In Proceedings of the 5th Annual Conference on Extending Database Technology. P. Apers, M. Boozeghoub, and G. Gardarin, eds. Avignon, France, Springer-Verlag, Berlin: 3–17.

Stamatatos, E., Fakotakis, N., and Kokkinakis, G. (2000). "Automatic Text Categorization in Terms of Genre and Author." *Computational Linguistics* **26**(4): 471–495.

Stapley, B. J., and Benoit, G. (2000). *Biobibliometrics: Information Retrieval and Visualization from Co-occurrences of Gene Names in Medline Abstracts.* In Proceedings of the Pacific Symposium on Biocomputing. Honolulu, Hawaii, World Scientific Press, Hackensack, NJ: 526–537.

Steinbach, M., Karypis, G., and Kumar, V. (2000). *A Comparison of Document Clustering Techniques.* In Proceedings of the 6th ACM SIGKDD International Conference on Knowledge Discovery and Data Mining. Boston, ACM Press, New York.

Sun, A., and Lim, E.-P. (2001). *Hierarchical Text Classification and Evaluation.* In Proceedings of ICDM-01, IEEE International Conference on Data Mining. N. Cercone, T. Lin, and X. Wu, eds. San Jose, CA, IEEE Computer Society Press, Los Alamitos, CA: 521–528.

Sun, A., Lim, E.-P., and Ng, W.-K. (2003a). "Hierarchical Text Classification Methods and Their Specification." In *Cooperative Internet Computing.* A. T. Chan, S. Chan, H. Y. Leong, and V. T. Y. Ng., eds. Dordrecht, Kluwer Academic Publishers: 236–256.

Sun, A., Lim, E.-P., and Ng, W.-K. (2003b). "Performance Measurement Framework for Hierarchical Text Classification." *Journal of the American Society for Information Science and Technology* **54**(11): 1014–1028.

Sun, A., Naing, M., Lim, E., and Lam, W. (2003). *Using Support Vector Machine for Terrorism Information Extraction.* In Proceedings of the Intelligence and Security Informatics: 1st NSF/NIJ Symposium on Intelligence and Security Informatics. H. Chen, R. Miranda, D. Zeng, C. Demchek, J. Schroeder, and T. Madhusudan, eds. Tucson, AZ, Springer-Verlag, Berlin: 1–12.

Taghva, K., Nartker, T. A., Borsack, J., Lumos, S., Condit, A., and Young, R. (2000). *Evaluating Text Categorization in the Presence of OCR Errors.* In Proceedings of the 8th SPIE Conference on Document Recognition and Retrieval. San Jose, CA, SPIE, The International Society for Optical Engineering, Washington, DC: 68–74.

Taira, H., and Haruno, M. (1999). *Feature Selection in SVM Text Categorization.* In Proceedings of AAAI-99, 16th Conference of the American Association for Artificial Intelligence. Orlando, FL, AAAI Press, Menlo Park, CA: 480–486.

Taira, H., and Haruno, M. (2001). *Text Categorization Using Transductive Boosting.* In Proceedings of ECML-01, 12th European Conference on Machine Learning. L. D. Raedt and P. A. Flach, eds. Freiburg, Germany, Springer-Verlag, Heidelberg: 454–465.

Takamura, H., and Matsumoto, Y. (2001). *Feature Space Restructuring for SVMs with Application to Text Categorization.* In Proceedings of EMNLP-01, 6th Conference on Empirical Methods in Natural Language Processing. Pittsburgh, Association for Computational Linguistics, Morristown, NJ: 51–57.

Tan, A.-H. (2001). *Predictive Self-Organizing Networks for Text Categorization.* In Proceedings of PAKDD-01, 5th Pacific-Asia Conference on Knowledge Discovery and Data Mining. Hong Kong, Springer-Verlag, Heidelberg: 66–77.

Tan, A. (1999). *Text Mining: The State of the Art and the Challenges.* In Proceedings of the PAKDD'99 Workshop on Knowledge Discovery from Advanced Databases (KDAD'99). Beijing: 71–76.

Tan, C.-M., Wang, Y.-F., and Lee, C.-D. (2002). "The Use of Bigrams to Enhance Text Categorization." *Information Processing and Management* **38**(4): 529–546.

Taskar, B., Abbeel, P., and Koller, D. (2002). *Discriminative Probabilistic Models of Relational Data.* In Proceedings of UAI-02, 18th Conference on Uncertainty in Artificial Intelligence. Edmonton, Canada, Morgan Kaufmann Publishers, San Francisco: 485–492.

Taskar, B., Segal, E., and Koller, D. (2001). *Probabilistic Classification and Clustering in Relational Data.* In Proceedings of IJCAI-01, 17th International Joint Conference on Artificial Intelligence. B. Nebel, ed. Seattle, Morgan Kaufmann Publishers, San Francisco: 870–878.

Tauritz, D. R., Kok, J. N., and Sprinkhuizen-Kuyper, I. G. (2000). "Adaptive Information Filtering Using Evolutionary Computation." *Information Sciences* **122**(2/4): 121–140.

Tauritz, D. R., and Sprinkhuizen-Kuyper, I. G. (1999). *Adaptive Information Filtering Algorithms.* In Proceedings of IDA-99, 3rd Symposium on Intelligent Data Analysis. D. J. Wand, J. N. Kok, and M. R. Berthold, eds. Amsterdam, Springer-Verlag, Heidelberg: 513–524.

Teahan, W. J. (2000). *Text Classification and Segmentation Using Minimum Cross-entropy.* In Proceedings of RIAO-00, 6th International Conference "Recherche d'Information Assistée par Ordinateur." Paris: 943–961.

Teytaud, O., and Jalam, R. (2001). *Kernel Based Text Categorization.* In Proceedings of IJCNN-01, 12th International Joint Conference on Neural Networks. Washington, DC, IEEE Computer Society Press, Los Alamitos, CA: 1892–1897.

Theeramunkong, T., and Lertnattee, V. (2002). *Multi-Dimensional Text Classification.* In Proceedings of COLING-02, 19th International Conference on Computational Linguistics. Taipei, Taiwan Association for Computational Linguistics, Morristown, NJ.

Thelen, M., and Riloff, E. (2002). *A Bootstrapping Method for Learning Semantic Lexicons Using Extraction Pattern Contexts.* In Proceedings of the Conference on Empirical Methods in Natural Language Processing (EMNLP 2002). Philadelphia, Association for Computational Linguistics, Morristown, NJ: 214–221.

Thomas, J., Cook, K., Crow, V., Hetzler, B., May, R., McQuerry, D., McVeety, R., Miller, N., Nakamura, G., Nowell, L., Whitney, P., and Wong, P. C. (1999). *Human Computer Interaction with Global Information Spaces: Beyond Data Mining.* In Proceedings of the British Computer Society Conference. Bradford, UK, Springer-Verlag, London.

Thompson, P. (2001). *Automatic Categorization of Case Law.* In Proceedings of ICAIL-01, 8th International Conference on Artificial Intelligence and Law. St. Louis, MO, ACM Press, New York: 70–77.

Toivonen, H., Klemettinen, M., Ronkainen, P., Hatonen, K., and Mannila, H. (1995). *Pruning and Grouping Discovered Association Rules.* In Workshop Notes: Statistics, Machine Learning and Knowledge Discovery in Databases, ECML-95. N. Lavrac and S. Wrobel, eds. Heraclion, Greece, Springer-Verlag, Berlin: 47–52.

Tombros, A., Villa, R., and Rijsbergen, C. J. (2002). "The Effectiveness of Query-Specific Hierarchic Clustering in Information Retrieval." *Information Processing & Management* **38**(4): 559–582.

Tong, R., Winkler, A., and Gage, P. (1992). *Classification Trees for Document Routing: A Report on the TREC Experiment.* In Proceedings of TREC-1, 1st Text Retrieval Conference. D. K. Harman, ed. Gaithersburg, MD, National Institute of Standards and Technology, Gaithersburg, MD: 209–228.

Tong, S., and Koller, D. (2000). *Support Vector Machine Active Learning with Applications to Text Classification.* In Proceedings of ICML-00, 17th International Conference on Machine Learning. P. Langley, ed. Stanford, CA, Morgan Kaufmann Publishers, San Francisco, CA: 999–1006.

Tong, S., and Koller, D. (2001). "Support Vector Machine Active Learning with Applications to Text Classification." *Journal of Machine Learning Research* **2**: 45–66.

Toutanova, K., Chen, F., Popat, K., and Hofmann, T. (2001). *Text Classification in a Hierarchical Mixture Model for Small Training Sets.* In Proceedings of CIKM-01, 10th ACM

International Conference on Information and Knowledge Management. H. Paques, L. Liu, and D. Grossman, eds. Atlanta, ACM Press, New York: 105–113.

Trastour, D., Bartolini, C., and Preist, C. (2003). "Semantic Web Support for the Business-to-Business E-Commerce Pre-Contractual Lifecycle." *Computer Networks* **42**(5): 661–673.

Tufte, E. (1983). *The Visual Display of Quantitative Informaiton.* Chelshire, CT, Graphics Press.

Tufte, E. (1990). *Envisioning Information.* Chelshire, CT, Graphics Press.

Tufte, E. (1997). *Visual Explanations.* Cheshire, CT, Graphics Press.

Turney, P. (1997). *Extraction of Keyphrases from Text: Evaluation of Four Algorithms.* Technical Report ERB 1051, National Research Council of Canada, Institute for Information Technology: 1–27.

Turney, P. D. (2000). "Learning Algorithms for Keyphrase Extraction." *Information Retrieval* **2**(4): 303–336.

Tzeras, K., and Hartmann, S. (1993). *Automatic Indexing Based on Bayesian Inference Networks.* In Proceedings of SIGIR-93, 16th ACM International Conference on Research and Development in Information Retrieval. R. Korfhage, E. M. Rasmussen, and P. Willett, eds. Pittsburgh, ACM Press, New York: 22–34.

Tzoukermann, E., Klavans, J., and Jacquemin, C. (1997). *Effective Use of Natural Language Processing Techniques for Automatic Conflation of Multi-Word Terms: The Role of Derivational Morphology, Part of Speech Tagging, and Shallow Parsing.* In Proceedings of the 20th Annual International ACM SIGIR Conference on Research and Development in Information Retrieval. Philadelphia, ACM Press, New York: 148–155.

Ureña-Lopez, L. A., Buenaga, M., and Gomez, J. M. (2001). "Integrating linguistic resources in TC through WSD." *Computers and the Humanities* **35**(2): 215–230.

Uren, V. S., and Addis, T. R. (2002). "How Weak Categorizers Based upon Different Principles Strengthen Performance." *The Computer Journal* **45**(5): 511–524.

Vapnik, V. (1995). *The Nature of Statistical Learning Theory.* Berlin, Springer-Verlag.

Varadarajan, S., Kasravi, K., and Feldman, R. (2002). *Text-Mining: Application Development Challenges.* In Proceedings of the 22nd SGAI International Conference on Knowledge Based Systems and Applied Artificial Intelligence. Cambridge, UK, Springer-Verlag, Berlin.

Vel, O. Y. D., Anderson, A., Corney, M., and Mohay, G. M. (2001). "Mining Email Content for Author Identification Forensics." *SIGMOD Record* **30**(4): 55–64.

Vert, J.-P. (2001). *Text Categorization Using Adaptive Context Trees.* In Proceedings of CICLING-01, 2nd International Conference on Computational Linguistics and Intelligent Text Processing. A. Gelbukh, ed. Mexico City, Springer-Verlag, Heidelberg: 423–436.

Viechnicki, P. (1998). *A Performance Evaluation of Automatic Survey Classifiers.* In Proceedings of ICGI-98, 4th International Colloquium on Grammatical Inference. V. Honavar and G. Slutzki, eds. Ames, IA, Springer-Verlag, Heidelberg: 244–256.

Vinokourov, A., and Girolami, M. (2001). *Document Classification Employing the Fisher Kernel Derived from Probabilistic Hierarchic Corpus Representations.* In Proceedings of ECIR-01, 23rd European Colloquium on Information Retrieval Research. Darmstadt, Germany, Springer-Verlag, Berlin: 24–40.

Vinokourov, A., and Girolami, M. (2002). "A Probabilistic Framework for the Hierarchic Organisation and Classification of Document Collections." *Journal of Intelligent Information Systems* **18**(2/3): 153–172.

Wang, H., and Son, N. H. (1999). *Text Classification Using Lattice Machine.* In Proceedings of ISMIS-99, 11th International Symposium on Methodologies for Intelligent Systems. A. Skowron and Z. W. Ras, eds. Warsaw, Springer-Verlag, Heidelberg: 235–243.

Wang, J. T. L., Zhang, K., Chang, G., and Shasha, D. (2002). "Finding Approximate Patterns in Undirected Acyclic Graphs." *Pattern Recognition* **35**(2): 473–483.

Wang, K., Zhou, S., and He, Y. (2001). *Hierarchical Classification of Real Life Documents.* In Proceedings of the 1st SIAM International Conference on Data Mining. Chicago, SIAM Press, Philadelphia.

Wang, K., Zhou, S., and Liew, S. C. (1999). *Building Hierarchical Classifiers Using Class Proximity*. In Proceedings of VLDB-99, 25th International Conference on Very Large Data Bases. M. P. Atkinson, M. E. Orlowska, P. Valduriez, S. B. Zdonik, and M. L. Brodie, eds. Edinburgh, Morgan Kaufmann Publishers, San Francisco: 363–374.

Wang, W., Meng, W., and Yu, C. (2000). *Concept Hierarchy Based Text Database Categorization in a Metasearch Engine Environment*. In Proceedings of WISE-00, 1st International Conference on Web Information Systems Engineering. Hong Kong, IEEE Computer Society Press, Los Alamitos, CA: 283–290.

Wang, Y., and Hu, J. (2002). *A Machine Learning Based Approach for Table Detection on the Web*. In Proceedings of the 11th International World Web Conference. Honolulu, HI, ACM Press, New York: 242–250.

Ware, C. (2000). *Information Visualization: Perception for Design*, San Francisco, Morgan Kaufmann Publishers.

Wasserman, S., and Faust, K. (1994). *Social Network Analysis: Methods and Applications*. Cambridge, UK, Cambridge University Press.

Wei, C.-P., and Dong, Y.-X. (2001). *A Mining-based Category Evolution Approach to Managing Online Document Categories*. In Proceedings of HICSS-01, 34th Annual Hawaii International Conference on System Sciences. R. H. Sprague, ed. Maui, HI, IEEE Computer Society Press, Los Alamitos, CA: 7061–7062.

Weigend, A. S., Wiener, E. D., and Pedersen, J. O. (1999). "Exploiting Hierarchy in Text Categorization." *Information Retrieval* **1**(3): 193–216.

Weischedel, R., Meteer, M., Schwartz, R., Ramshaw, L., and Palmucci, J. (1993). "Coping with Ambiguity and Unknown Words through Probabilistic Methods." *Computational Linguistics* **19**(2): 361–382.

Weiss, S. M., Apte, C., Damerau, F. J., Johnson, D. E., Oles, F. J., Goetz, T., and Hampp, T. (1999). "Maximizing Text-Mining Performance." *IEEE Intelligent Systems* **14**(4): 63–69.

Wermter, S. (2000). "Neural Network Agents for Learning Semantic Text Classification." *Information Retrieval* **3**(2): 87–103.

Wermter, S., Arevian, G., and Panchev, C. (1999). *Recurrent Neural Network Learning for Text Routing*. In Proceedings of ICANN-99, 9th International Conference on Artificial Neural Networks. Edinburgh, Institution of Electrical Engineers, London, UK: 898–903.

Wermter, S., and Hung, C. (2002). *Self-Organizing Classification on the Reuters News Corpus*. In Proceedings of COLING-02, the 19th International Conference on Computational Linguistics. Taipei, Morgan Kaufmann Publishers, San Francisco.

Wermter, S., Panchev, C., and Arevian, G. (1999). *Hybrid Neural Plausibility Networks for News Agents*. In Proceedings of AAAI-99, 16th Conference of the American Association for Artificial Intelligence. Orlando, FL, AAAI Press, Menlo Park, CA: 93–98.

Westphal, C., and Bergeron, R. D. (1998). *Data Mining Solutions: Methods and Tools for Solving Real-Word Problems*. New York, John Wiley and Sons.

White, D. R., and Reitz, K. P. (1983). "Graph and Semigroup Homomorphisms on Networks of Relations." *Social Networks* **5**: 193–234.

Wibowo, W., and Williams, H. E. (2002). *Simple and Accurate Feature Selection for Hierarchical Categorisation*. In Proceedings of the 2002 ACM Symposium on Document Engineering. McLean, VA, ACM Press, New York: 111–118.

Wiener, E. D. (1995). *A Neural Network Approach to Topic Spotting in Text*. Boulder, CO, Department of Computer Science, University of Colorado at Boulder.

Wiener, E. D., Pedersen, J. O., and Weigend, A. S. (1995). *A Neural Network Approach to Topic Spotting*. In Proceedings of SDAIR-95, 4th Annual Symposium on Document Analysis and Information Retrieval. Las Vegas, ISRI, University of Nevada, Las Vegas: 317–332.

Wilks, Y. (1997). "Information Extraction as a Core Language Technology." In M. T. Pazienza, ed. Information Extraction: A Multidisciplinary Approach to an Emerging Information Technology. *Lecture Notes in Computer Science* **1229**: 1–9.

Williamson, C., and Schneiderman, B. (1992). *The Dynamic HomeFinder: Evaluating Dynamic Queries in a Real-Estate Information Exploration System.* In Proceedings of the 15th Annual, ACM-SIGIR. N. Belkin, P. Ingwersen, A. Pejtersen, eds. Copenhagen, ACM Press, New York: 338–346.

Wills, G. (1999). "NicheWorks' Interactive Visualization of Very Large Graphs." *Journal of Computational and Graphical Statistics* **8**(2): 190–212.

Wise, J., Thomas, J., Pennock, K., Lantrip, D., Pottier, M., Schur, A., and Crow, V. (1995). *Visualizing the Non-Visual: Spatial Analysis and Interaction with Information from Text Documents.* In Proceedings of IEEE Information Visualization '95. Atlanta, GA, IEEE Computer Society Press, Los Alamitos, CA: 51–58.

Witten, I. H., Bray, Z., Mahoui, M., and Teahan, W. J. (1999). *Text Mining: A New Frontier for Lossless Compression.* In Proceedings of IEEE Data Compression Conference. J. Ai. Storer and M. Cohn, eds. Snowbird, UT, IEEE Computer Society Press, Los Alamitos, CA: 198–207.

Wong, J. W., Kan, W.-K., and Young, G. H. (1996). "Action: Automatic Classification for Full-Text Documents." *SIGIR Forum* **30**(1): 26–41.

Wong, P. C. (1999). "Visual Data Mining – Guest Editor's Introduction." *IEEE Computer Graphics and Applications* **19**(5): 2–12.

Wong, P. C., Cowley, W., Foote, H., Jurrus, E., and Thomas, J. (2000). *Visualizing Sequential Patterns for Text Mining.* In Proceedings of the IEEE Information Visualization Conference (INFOVIS 2000). Salt Lake City, UT, ACM Press, New York: 105–115.

Wong, P. C., Whitney, P., and Thomas, J. (1999). *Visualizing Association Rules for Text Mining.* In Proceedings of IEEE Information Visualization (InfoVis '99). San Francisco, IEEE Computer Society Press, Washington, DC: 120–124.

Xu, Z., Yu, K., Tresp, V., Xu, X., and Wang, J. (2003). *Representative Sampling for Text Classification Using Support Vector Machines.* In Proceedings of ECIR-03, 25th European Conference on Information Retrieval. F. Sebastiani, ed. Pisa, Italy, Springer-Verlag, Berlin: 393–407.

Xue, D., and Sun, M. (2003). *Chinese Text Categorization Based on the Binary Weighting Model with Non-binary Smoothing.* In Proceedings of ECIR-03, 25th European Conference on Information Retrieval. F. Sebastiani, ed. Pisa, Italy, Springer-Verlag, Berlin: 408–419.

Yamazaki, T., and Dagan, I. (1997). *Mistake-Driven Learning with Thesaurus for Text Categorization.* In Proceedings of NLPRS-97, the Natural Language Processing Pacific Rim Symposium. Phuket, Thailand: 369–374.

Yang, C. C., Chen, H., and Hong, K. (2003). "Visualization of Large Category Map for Internet Browsing." *Decision Support Systems* **35**: 89–102.

Yang, H.-C., and Lee, C.-H. (2000a). *Automatic Category Generation for Text Documents by Self-Organizing Maps.* In Proceedings of IJCNN-00, 11th International Joint Conference on Neural Networks, Volume 3. Como, Italy, IEEE Computer Society Press, Los Alamitos, CA, 3581–3586.

Yang, H.-C., and Lee, C.-H. (2000b). *Automatic Category Structure Generation and Categorization of Chinese Text Documents.* In Proceedings of PKDD-00, 4th European Conference on Principles of Data Mining and Knowledge Discovery. D. Zighed, A. Komorowski, and D. Zytkow, eds. Lyon, France, Springer-Verlag, Heidelberg, Germany: 673–678.

Yang, T. (2000). *Detecting Emerging Contextual Concepts in Textual Collections.* M.Sc. thesis, Department of Computer Science, University of Illinois at Urbana-Champaign.

Yang, Y. (1994). *Expert Network: Effective and Efficient Learning from Human Decisions in Text Categorisation and Retrieval.* In Proceedings of SIGIR-94, 17th ACM International Conference on Research and Development in Information Retrieval. W. B. Croft and C. J. v. Rijsbergen, eds. Dublin, Springer-Verlag, Heidelberg: 13–22.

Yang, Y. (1995). *Noise Reduction in a Statistical Approach to Text Categorization.* In Proceedings of SIGIR-95, 18th ACM International Conference on Research and Development in

Information Retrieval. E. A. Fox, P. Ingwersen, and R. Fidel, eds. Seattle, ACM Press, New York: 256–263.

Yang, Y. (1996). *An Evaluation of Statistical Approaches to MEDLINE Indexing.* In Proceedings of AMIA-96, Fall Symposium of the American Medical Informatics Association. J. J. Cimino, ed. Washington, DC, Hanley and Belfus, Philadelphia: 358–362.

Yang, Y. (1999). "An Evaluation of Statistical Approaches to Text Categorization." *Information Retrieval* **1**(1/2): 69–90.

Yang, Y. (2001). *A Study on Thresholding Strategies for Text Categorization.* In Proceedings of SIGIR-01, 24th ACM International Conference on Research and Development in Information Retrieval. W. B. Croft, D. J. Harper, D. H. Kroft, and J. Zobel, eds. New Orleans, ACM Press, New York: 137–145.

Yang, Y., Ault, T., and Pierce, T. (2000). *Combining Multiple Learning Strategies for Effective Cross-Validation.* In Proceedings of ICML-00, 17th International Conference on Machine Learning. P. Langley, ed. Stanford, CA, Morgan Kaufmann Publishers, San Francisco: 1167–1182.

Yang, Y., Ault, T., Pierce, T., and Lattimer, C. W. (2000). *Improving Text Categorization Methods for Event Tracking.* In Proceedings of SIGIR-00, 23rd ACM International Conference on Research and Development in Information Retrieval. N. J. Belkin, P. Ingwersen, and M.-K. Leong, eds. Athens, Greece, ACM Press, New York: 65–72.

Yang, Y., and Chute, C. G. (1993). *An Application of Least Squares Fit Mapping to Text Information Retrieval.* In Proceedings of SIGIR-93, 16th ACM International Conference on Research and Development in Information Retrieval. R. Korthage, E. Rasmussen, and P. Willett, eds. Pittsburgh, ACM Press, New York: 281–290.

Yang, Y., and Chute, C. G. (1994). "An Example-Based Mapping Method for Text Categorization and Retrieval." *ACM Transactions on Information Systems* **12**(3): 252–277.

Yang, Y., and Liu, X. (1999). *A Re-examination of Text Categorization Methods.* In Proceedings of SIGIR-99, 22nd ACM International Conference on Research and Development in Information Retrieval. M. Hearst, F. Gey, and R. Tong, eds. Berkeley, CA, ACM Press, New York: 42–49.

Yang, Y., and Pedersen, J. O. (1997). *A Comparative Study on Feature Selection in Text Categorization.* In Proceedings of ICML-97, 14th International Conference on Machine Learning. D. H. Fisher. Nashville, TN, Morgan Kaufmann Publishers, San Francisco: 412–420.

Yang, Y., Slattery, S., and Ghani, R. (2002). "A Study of Approaches to Hypertext Categorization." *Journal of Intelligent Information Systems* **18**(2/3): 219–241.

Yang, Y., and Wilbur, J. W. (1996a). "An Analysis of Statistical Term Strength and Its Use in the Indexing and Retrieval of Molecular Biology Texts." *Computers in Biology and Medicine* **26**(3): 209–222.

Yang, Y., and Wilbur, J. W. (1996b). "Using Corpus Statistics to Remove Redundant Words in Text Categorization." *Journal of the American Society for Information Science* **47**(5): 357–369.

Yang, Y., Zhang, J., and Kisiel, B. (2003). *A Scalability Analysis of Classifiers in Text Categorization.* In Proceedings of SIGIR-03, 26th ACM International Conference on Research and Development in Information Retrieval. J. Callan, G. Cormack, C. Clarke, D. Hawking, and A. Smeaton, eds. Toronto, ACM Press, New York: 96–103.

Yao, D., Wang, J., Lu, Y., Noble, N., Sun, H., Zhu, X., Lin, N., Payan, D., Li, M., and Qu, K. (2004). *Pathway Finder: Paving the Way Towards Automatic Pathway Extraction.* In Proceedings of the 2nd Asian Bioinformatics Conference. Dunedin, New Zealand, Australian Computer Society, Darlinghurst, Australia: 53–62.

Yavuz, T., and Guvenir, H. A. (1998). *Application of k-nearest Neighbor on Feature Projections Classifier to Text Categorization.* In Proceedings of ISCIS-98, 13th International Symposium on Computer and Information Sciences. U. Gudukbay, T. Dayar, A. Gorsoy, and E. Gelenbe, eds. Ankara, Turkey, IOS Press, Amsterdam: 135–142.

Ye, N. (2003). *The Handbook of Data Mining*. Mahwah, NJ, Lawrence Erlbaum Associates.

Yee, K.-P., Fisher, D., Dhamija, R., and Hearst, M. (2001). *Animated Exploration of Dynamic Graphs with Radial Layout*. In Proceedings of IEEE Symposium on Information Visualization (InfoVis 2001). San Diego, CA, IEEE Computer Society Press, Washington, DC: 43–50.

Yeh, A., and Hirschman, L. (2002). "Background and Overview for KDD Cup 2002 Task 1: Information Extraction from Biomedical Articles." *KDD Explorarions* **4**(2): 87–89.

Yi, J., and Sundaresan, N. (2000). *A Classifier for Semi-Structured Documents*. In Proceedings of KDD-00, 6th ACM International Conference on Knowledge Discovery and Data Mining. Boston, ACM Press, New York: 340–344.

Yoon, S., Henschen, L. J., Park, E., and Makki, S. (1999). *Using Domain Knowledge in Knowledge Discovery*. In Proceedings of the ACM Conference CIKM '99. Kansas City, MO, ACM Press, New York: 243–250.

Yu, E. S., and Liddy, E. D. (1999). *Feature Selection in Text Categorization Using the Baldwin Effect Networks*. In Proceedings of IJCNN-99, 10th International Joint Conference on Neural Networks. Washington, DC, IEEE Computer Society Press, Los Alamitos, CA: 2924–2927.

Yu, K. L., and Lam, W. (1998). *A New On-Line Learning Algorithm for Adaptive Text Filtering*. In Proceedings of CIKM-98, 7th ACM International Conference on Information and Knowledge Management. G. Gardarin, J. French, N. Pissinou, K. Makki, and L. Bouganim, eds. Bethesda, MD, ACM Press, New York: 156–160.

Yumi, J. (2000). *Graphical User Interface and Visualization Techniques for Detection of Emerging Concepts*. M.S. thesis, Department of Computer Science, University of Illinois at Urbana-Champaign.

Zaiane, O. R., and Antonie, M.-L. (2002). *Classifying Text Documents by Associating Terms with Text Categories*. In Proceedings of the 13th Australasian Conference on Database Technologies. Melbourne, Australia, ACM Press, New York: 215–222.

Zamir, O., and Etzioni, O. (1999). "Grouper: A Dynamic Clustering Interface to Web Search Results." *Computer Networks*. **31**(11–16): 1361–1374.

Zaragoza, H., Massih-Reza, A., and Gallinari, P. (1999). *A Dynamic Probability Model for Closed-Query Text Mining Tasks*. Draft submission to KDD '99.

Zelikovitz, S., and Hirsh, H. (2000). *Improving Short Text Classification Using Unlabeled Background Knowledge*. In Proceedings of ICML-00, 17th International Conference on Machine Learning. P. Langley, ed. Stanford, CA, Morgan Kaufmann Publishers, San Francisco: 1183–1190.

Zelikovitz, S., and Hirsh, H. (2001). *Using LSI for Text Classification in the Presence of Background Text*. In Proceedings of CIKM-01, 10th ACM International Conference on Information and Knowledge Management. H. Paques, L. Liu, and D. Grossman, eds. Atlanta, ACM Press, New York: 113–118.

Zhang, D., and Lee, W. S. (2003). *Question Classification Using Support Vector Machines*. In Proceedings of SIGIR-03, 26th ACM International Conference on Research and Development in Information Retrieval. J. Callan, G. Cormack, C. Clarke, D. Hawking, and A. Smeaton, eds. Toronto, ACM Press, New York: 26–32.

Zhang, J., Jin, R., Yang, Y., and Hauptmann, A. (2003). *Modified Logistic Regression: An Approximation to SVM and Its Applications in Large-Scale Text Categorization*. In Proceedings of ICML-03, 20th International Conference on Machine Learning. Washington, DC, Morgan Kaufmann Publishers, San Francisco: 888–895.

Zhang, J., and Yang, Y. (2003). *Robustness of Regularized Linear Classification Methods in Text Categorization*. In Proceedings of SIGIR-03, 26th ACM International Conference on Research and Development in Information Retrieval. J. Collan, G. Cormack, C. Clarke, D. Hawking, and A. Smeaton, eds. Toronto, ACM Press, New York: 190–197.

Zhang, K., Wang, J. T. L., and Shasha, D. (1995). "On the Editing Distance Between Undirected Acyclic Graphs." *International Journal of Foundations of Computer Science* **7**(1): 43–57.

Zhang, T., and Oles, F. J. (2001). "Text Categorization Based on Regularized Linear Classification Methods." *Information Retrieval* **4**(1): 5–31.

Zhao, Y., and Karypis, G. (2002). *Criterion Functions for Document Clustering: Experiments and Analysis*. Technical Report, TR 01–40. Minneapolis, Department of Computer Science, University of Minnesota.

Zhdanova, A. V., and Shishkin, D. V. (2002). *Classification of Email Queries by Topic: Approach Based on Hierarchically Structured Subject Domain*. In Proceedings of IDEAL-02, 3rd International Conference on Intelligent Data Engineering and Automated Learning. H. Yin, N. Allinson, R. Freeman, J. Keane, and S. Hubbard, eds. Manchester, UK, Springer-Verlag, Heidelberg: 99–104.

Zhong, S., and Ghosh, J (2003). "A Comparative Study of Generative Models for Document Clustering." *Knowledge and Information Systems: An International Journal* **8**: 374–384.

Zhou, M., and Cui, Y. (2004). "GeneInfoViz: Constructing and Visualizing Gene Relation Networks." *In Silico Biology* **4**(3): 323–333.

Zhou, S., Fan, Y., Hua, J., Yu, F., and Hu, Y. (2000). *Hierachically Classifying Chinese Web Documents without Dictionary Support and Segmentation Procedure*. In Proceedings of WAIM-00, 1st International Conference on Web-Age Information Management. Shanghai, China, Springer-Verlag, Heidelberg: 215–226.

Zhou, S., and Guan, J. (2002a). *An Approach to Improve Text Classification Efficiency*. In Proceedings of ADBIS-02, 6th East-European Conference on Advances in Databases and Information Systems. Y. M., and P. Navrat, eds. Bratislava, Slovakia, Springer-Verlag, Heidelberg: 65–79.

Zhou, S., and Guan, J. (2002b). *Chinese Documents Classification Based on N-Grams*. In Proceedings of CICLING-02, 3rd International Conference on Computational Linguistics and Intelligent Text Processing. A. F. Gelbukh, ed. Mexico City, Springer-Verlag, Heidelberg: 405–414.

Zhou, S., Ling, T. W., Guan, J., Hu, J., and Zhou, A. (2003). *Fast Text Classification: A Training-Corpus Pruning Based Approach*. In Proceedings of DASFAA-03, 8th IEEE International Conference on Database Advanced Systems for Advanced Application. Kyoto, Japan, IEEE Computer Society Press, Los Alamitos, CA: 127–136.

Index

Printed in the United States
By Bookmasters